PRIVILEGED COMMUNICATIONS
BETWEEN
PHYSICIAN AND PATIENT

PRIVILEGED COMMUNICATIONS BETWEEN PHYSICIAN AND PATIENT

By

CLINTON DeWITT

Professor of Law, Western Reserve University

Cleveland

CHARLES C THOMAS • PUBLISHER

Springfield · Illinois · U.S.A.

CHARLES C THOMAS · PUBLISHER

BANNERSTONE HOUSE

301-327 East Lawrence Avenue, Springfield, Illinois, U.S.A.

Published simultaneously in the British Commonwealth of Nations by

BLACKWELL SCIENTIFIC PUBLICATIONS, LTD., OXFORD, ENGLAND

Published simultaneously in Canada by

THE RYERSON PRESS, TORONTO

Copyright 1958 by CHARLES C THOMAS · PUBLISHER

Library of Congress Catalog Card Number: 58-8418

With THOMAS BOOKS *careful attention is given to all details
of manufacturing and design. It is the Publisher's desire to
present books that are satisfactory as to their physical qualities
and artistic possibilities and appropriate for their particular use.*
THOMAS BOOKS *will be true to those laws of quality that
assure a good name and good will.*

Printed in the United States of America

TO MY WIFE

PREFACE

Various kinds of testimonial privileges exist in practically every jurisdiction. Perhaps none of these presents more serious problems to the trial lawyer and to the trial judge than does the privilege concerning the confidential relationship existing between a physician and his patient. The importance of the physician-patient privilege can scarcely be overestimated because of its effect upon the administration of justice.

It is common knowledge that the vast majority of litigated cases—perhaps ninety per cent or more—are actions to recover the proceeds of life, accident, or health insurance contracts; actions for damages for personal injury, for wrongful death, for malpractice; and testamentary actions. In addition, there are actions for divorce, lunacy proceedings, actions to obtain benefits under Workmen's Compensation Laws, and criminal prosecutions wherein, usually, the charge is abortion, some sexual offense, or homicide. In most of these, the physician-patient privilege is involved, since the physical or mental condition of some person is an important issue in the trial and medical testimony is necessary to ascertain the truth. Yet incredible as it may seem, in many of these cases the surgeon, the physician, or the nurse who attended the afflicted person is not permitted to testify unless the patient consents thereto or, by his conduct, waives the protection of the privilege. Moreover, the privilege generally applies with equal force to the patient's hospital chart and other records.

This treatise is the outgrowth of thirty years of experience in trial and appellate courts, both federal and state. It is my opinion that members of the Bench and Bar have too often misunderstood the paramount purpose of the privilege, with the lamentable result that persons not within its intended scope have been permitted to invoke its protection, and that material and relevant evidence concerning communications and information not within the ban of the statute has been excluded. Furthermore, the doctrine of waiver has often been improperly applied, or overlooked entirely. I have endeavored, therefore, to produce a comprehensive yet practical treatise which will be helpful to the trial lawyer and the trial judge in solving many of the problems that constantly arise from this troublesome and much abused rule of evidence. I hope, too, that medical men and teachers of law will find it beneficial. No textbook dealing exclusively with this testimonial privilege has hitherto been available. Due to the dissimilarity of the statutes which create the privilege and to the disparate attitudes of the courts toward it in general, the great mass of reported cases presents a formidable task to any author who would attempt to write a treatise on this subject. This, however, I have undertaken to do.

An appendix is included wherein appear the existing statutes pertaining to the privilege; and also the appropriate rules which form a part of the Uniform Rules of Evidence. Reference to these, I believe, will readily enable the reader to acquire a better understanding of some of the cases which are discussed in the text and in the notes of this treatise.

I wish gratefully to acknowledge the courtesy of the following copyright owners in permitting me to reprint or to otherwise make use of some portions of their publications: American Law Institute (*The Model Code of Evidence*); American Medical Association (*Principles of Medical Ethics*); Bancroft-Whitney Company (*American Law Reports*); Bobbs-Merrill Company, Inc. (*Herzog's Medical Jurisprudence*); Butterworth & Company Limited (*Halsbury's Laws of England*); Hospital Textbook Company (*Hayt, Hayt and Groeschel's Law of Hospital, Physician and Patient*); Lawyers Co-Operative Publishing Company (*American Law Reports*); Little, Brown & Company (*Wigmore's Treatise on Evidence*); Mathew Bender & Company (*Moore's Federal Practice*); National Conference of Commissioners on Uniform State Laws (*Uniform Rules of Evidence*); W. W. Norton & Company, Inc. (*Guttmacher and Weihofen's Psychiatry and The Law*); West Publishing Company (*McCormick on Evidence*).

I desire particularly to acknowledge my indebtedness to a large number of Law Reviews across the country. In the preparation of this treatise I have been greatly helped by the perusal of many of their leading articles, student notes and case comments pertaining to the physician-patient privilege.

CLINTON DEWITT

School of Law
Western Reserve University
March, 1958

TABLE OF CONTENTS

Chapter V

NATURE OF THE PRIVILEGE

Chapter VI

CONSTRUCTION OF STATUTE

Chapter VII

WHAT LAW GOVERNS

Chapter VIII

MEDICAL PERSONS PROTECTED BY THE PRIVILEGE

Chapter IX

RELATIONSHIP OF PHYSICIAN AND PATIENT

Chapter X

WHAT COMMUNICATIONS AND INFORMATION ARE PRIVILEGED

Chapter XI

MODE OF ATTEMPTED INTRODUCTION IMMATERIAL

Chapter XII

ACTIONS AND PROCEEDINGS IN WHICH PRIVILEGE MAY OR MAY NOT BE INVOKED

Sec.

Chapter XIII

PRE-TRIAL PROCEEDINGS: STATE COURTS

Sec.

Chapter XIV

PRE-TRIAL PROCEEDINGS: FEDERAL COURTS

Sec.

Chapter XV

TRIAL PRACTICE

Chapter XVI

WAIVER OF THE PRIVILEGE

Chapter XVII

WAIVER RESULTING FROM COMMENCEMENT OF CERTAIN ACTIONS AND PROCEEDINGS

Chapter XVIII

WAIVER BY CONDUCT

Privileged Communications Between Physician and Patient

CHAPTER I

The Common Law Doctrine of Testimonial Privilege Applicable to Particular Confidential Relationships

Sec.
1. Introductory
2. Attorney and Client
3. Priest and Penitent
4. Physician and Patient

1. *Introductory*

In ancient times, wholesale exclusion of classes of persons from the opportunity of testifying was the rule. A person might be disqualified to be a witness because of race, color, sex, infancy, condition of servitude, religion, relationship, interest in the outcome of the litigation, mental illness, or conviction of crime.[1] In later years, as the common law developed, much, though not all, of the policy of exclusion was incorporated into the expanding rules of evidence. The courts considered this necessary in order to bar persons believed to be biased, unstable, or untrustworthy from appearing as witnesses in a court of justice. At the beginning of the nineteenth century, most of the rules of exclusion were well established, but with a resulting loss of a vast amount of relevant evidence which might have aided the court, or the jury, in the final determination of the factual matters in dispute; moreover, the policy of exclusion had progressed so far that it had almost reached the realm of absurdity. With the passage of time, however, most of the grounds of absolute incompetency were swept away, the courts laying more emphasis upon the *credibility* of the witness; less upon his *competency*.

---

[1] Barnhart, Theory of Testimonial Competency and Privilege, (1950) 4 Ark. L. Rev. 377; Rowley, The Competency of Witnesses, (1939) 24 Iowa L. Rev. 483.

In England, for nearly four hundred years, compulsion of witnesses to appear and to testify has been the rule. Prior to that time, a person, if he could qualify as a witness, might testify or not as he chose; he could not be compelled to do so. In 1562, by Act of Eliz. c. 9, § 12, provision was made for the service of process out of any court of record requiring the person served to appear and to testify concerning any cause or matter pending in the court, under penalty of ten pounds besides damages to be recovered by the party aggrieved. This was based on the fundamental principle of government that the administration of justice is a mutual benefit to all members of a community, and every competent citizen is under an obligation to further it as a matter of public duty; that the personal sacrifice is a part of the necessary contribution to the welfare of the public.[2]

Shortly after the policy of testimonial compulsion became established in England, the courts occasionally were confronted by witnesses who refused to answer particular questions put to them on the ground that their testimony would necessarily result in the disclosure of confidential communications or information which, for reasons of public policy or personal honor, they ought not to be compelled to reveal. Usually it was claimed by such witnesses that matters of a genuinely confidential character were not the proper subject of inquiry in courts of law; that, to improve the administration of justice, all persons should be encouraged to come forward with their evidence by shielding them as far as possible from compulsory disclosure of matters strictly confidential. On the other hand, it was urged that the courts were duty bound to see that complete justice was done; that to achieve this objective, no barrier should be erected against the discovery of the truth; that, therefore, no witness should have the right to withhold relevant evidence and thus suppress or conceal the truth, or any portion thereof, no matter how harmful to himself or to others its effect might be,[3] provided it did not tend to convict him of a crime, or subject him to a penalty.

---

[2] Blair v. United States, (1918) 250 U. S. 273, 281, 63 Law Ed. 979, 39 S. Ct. 468; *In re* Herrnstein, (1941) 20 Ohio Op. 405, 412; Ealy v. Shetler Ice Cream Co., (1929) 108 W. Va. 184, 187, 150 S. E. 539.

[3] Learned Hand, J., in McMann v. Securities and Exchange Commission, (1937) 87 F.

⟫→

Ultimately, however, the courts became persuaded that the duty of testifying, so onerous at times yet so necessary to the administration of justice, should properly be subject to mitigation in exceptional circumstances. Accordingly, throughout the course of its history, the common law, both in British and American jurisdictions, has conferred ever-increasing privileges of non-disclosure in favor of particular persons who have been lawfully summoned to attend and to give evidence in the courts of justice,[4] privileges which enable them to decline to answer questions which elicit the disclosure of confidential communications and information inimical to the interest of the witness,[5] or of the state, or of society in general. Broadly speaking, the matters affected by the doctrine of privilege may be classified as political, judicial, social, and professional. The more widely-known of these privileges are those which relate to state secrets, political votes, trade secrets, religious beliefs, anti-marital facts, and self-incriminating matters; those which have been extended to persons standing in a confidential relationship such as husband and wife, grand jurors, petit jurors, judges, arbitrators, public officers, and informers who furnish government officials evidence of crime;[6] and that which is granted to attorneys acting in a professional capacity.

In justification of these privileges, it has been said that all of these matters lie in the policy of the state which considers that the injury to such relationships which would result from enforced dis-

←—▨

2d 377, 378, cert. denied, 301 U. S. 684, 81 Law. Ed. 1342, 57 Su. Ct. 785, 109 A. L. R. 1445: "* * * the duty to disclose in a court all information within one's control, testimonially or by the production of documents, is usually paramount over any private interest that may be affected."

[4] As to the basis of privileges, see 8 Wigmore, Evidence, §§ 2192, 2197, 2285.

[5] It does not necessarily follow, however, that because a communication is made in confidence or upon a promise of secrecy, it comes under the protection of privilege. 8 Wigmore, Evidence, § 2286; 5 Jones, Evidence, § 2219. See McMann v. Securities and Exchange Commission, supra, note 3; *In re* Frye, (1951) 155 Ohio St. 345, 98 N. E. 2d 798.

[6] Discussion of the various privileges is outside the scope of this treatise. It may be noted, however, that some of them are now embodied in the statutory law in many jurisdictions.

closure of confidential information acquired therein, would be greater than the loss to justice occasioned by granting the privilege.[7]

2. *Attorney and Client*

The oldest of the privileges for confidential communications is that accorded to the relationship of attorney and client,[1] and it appears to have been unquestioned as far back as the reign of Elizabeth I.[2] Briefly stated, the privilege, derivable from the decisions of the courts of the common law,[3] is that no attorney is permitted, whether during or after the termination of his employment as such, unless with his client's consent, to testify as a witness and disclose

---

[7] This view, however, has not been universally approved; in fact, there has been at times, strong opposition to the whole policy of testimonial privilege.

Purrington, An Abused Privilege, (1906) 6 Col. L. Rev. 388: "Privilege, the exception of a person or class from the common rule, if not an abuse in its inception, is proverbially sure to become one. The less there is of it under a reign of law the better. In its administration of justice the State's purpose—whatever that of litigants may be —is, presumably, to ascertain the truth between the parties and dispense justice on that basis. * * * It seems paradoxical that a system devised for the ascertainment of truth should embody rules expressly framed to conceal it; yet every privilege that allows a witness to stand mute is such a rule." See also, Whipple, The Legal Privilege of Concealing the Truth, (1925) 10 Mass. L. Q. 31.

There is eminent authority for the view that the traditional justifications for various testimonial privileges are inept and fallacious. Morgan, Foreword to the Model Code of Evidence, (1942) pp. 22-30; McCormick, The Scope of Privilege in the Law of Evidence, (1938) 16 Tex. L. Rev. 447.

It is not likely, however, that any of the existing testimonial privileges will be abolished; in fact, the present trend of legislation is in the opposite direction. Within comparative recent years, the legislatures of a number of states have granted the privilege of non-disclosure to newspapermen, press associations, radio broadcasters, stenographers, and public accountants. See, Privileged Communications—Some Recent Developments, (1952) 5 Vanderbilt L. Rev. 590, 601. Wigmore deplored the creation of such privileges. 8 Wigmore, Evidence, § 2286. See also Report of the American Bar Association Committee on Improvement in the Law of Evidence, Vanderbilt, Minimum Standards of Judicial Administration, Appendix A, p. 583 (1949).

Bankers, investment brokers, and social workers also are clamoring for testimonial privileges, but up to this time no legislature has succumbed to their appeals.

[1] The privilege was recognized by the Roman Law although based upon a different policy than that of the common law. Radin, The Privilege of Confidential Communication Between Lawyer and Client, (1928) 16 Calif. L. Rev. 487, 488.

[2] Berd v. Lovelace, (1577) Cary 88; Dennis v. Codrington, (1580) Cary 143; 8 Wigmore, Evidence, § 2290.

[3] It is now embodied in the statutory law of practically every American Jurisdiction.

any communication, oral or documentary, made to him as such attorney, by or on behalf of his client in the course and for the purpose of his employment, whether in reference to any matter as to which a dispute has arisen or otherwise, or to disclose any advice given by him to his client; provided, however, that any such communication is not made or advice given in furtherance of any criminal or fraudulent purpose. The privilege applies not only to the attorney, but also to his secretary or clerical assistant; furthermore, the client himself cannot be compelled to disclose any communication between himself and his attorney, which his attorney could not disclose without his consent.[4]

According to Wigmore, the original theory supporting the exclusion of such evidence "was an objective one, not a subjective one,—a consideration for the oath and the honor of the attorney, rather than the apprehension of his client."[5] This theory was later repudiated and, since the latter part of the eighteenth century, the policy of the privilege has been based on subjective considerations only.[6] It appears to be everywhere conceded that the purpose of the privilege is to encourage the employment of professional advisers by persons in need of their services and to promote absolute freedom of consultation by removing all fear on the part of the client that his attorney may be compelled to disclose in court the communications made to, or the information acquired by, him in the course of his professional employment.[7]

Notwithstanding the almost universal approval by the bench and bar of this ancient privilege, it has been severely criticized at times. Jeremy Bentham was, perhaps, the first to denounce it in

---

[4] For excellent discussion of this privilege, see McCormick, Evidence, §§ 91-100.

[5] 8 Wigmore, Evidence, § 2290.

[6] McCormick, Evidence, § 91; Barnhart, Theory of Testimonial Competency and Privilege, (1950) 4 Ark. L. Rev. 377, 400. See also Spitzer v. Stillings, (1924) 109 Ohio St. 297, 302, 142 N. E. 365.

[7] Wade v. Ridley, (1895) 87 Me. 368, 373, 32 Atl. 975; People v. Shapiro, (1955) 308 N. Y. 453, 459, 126 N. E. 2d 559; Whitney v. Barney, (1864) 30 N. Y. 330, 332; Rochester City Bank v. Suydam, Sage & Co., (1851) 5 How. Pr. (N. Y.) 254; Anderson v. Bank of British Columbia, (1875) L. R. 2 Ch. D. 644, 648; Greenough v. Gaskell, (1833) 1 Myl. & K. 98, 103.

England.[8] In America, Appleton, Chief Justice of the Supreme Court of Maine, was no less vehement in expressing his dislike of it.[9] However, the attorney-client privilege has successfully withstood all criticism,[10] and today practically all of the states have enacted statutes which embody the common law rule.

3. *Priest and Penitent*

Confidential communications made by parishioners and penitents to clergymen and priests were not privileged at common law from disclosure in courts of justice.[1] Occasionally, however, there were judges who were disinclined to deny the privilege if it was claimed.[2] In England, at the present time, the right of a clergyman

---

[8] Portions of his criticism are quoted in 8 Wigmore, Evidence, § 2291.

[9] Appleton, (1860) The Rules of Evidence 170: "The rule of law by which the confidential communications of the client to his attorney are clothed with inviolable and compulsory secrecy, is dishonorable and degrading to the legal profession—injurious to the public, and entirely unnecessary to the client for any proper and legitimate purpose. Were the rule abolished, the relation between the client and the attorney, wherever it existed, would be confined within the bounds of integrity and enlightened public policy, as it should be." See also McCormick, Evidence, § 91; Dumont, (1825) A Treatise on Judicial Evidence 246; Morgan, Suggested Remedy for Obstruction to Expert Testimony by Rules of Evidence, (1943) 10 U. of Chic. L. Rev. 284, 289; Whipple, The Legal Privilege of Concealing the Truth, (1925) 10 Mass. L. Q. 31, 35.

[10] Wigmore believed that the privilege is worth saving, but admitted that it is an obstacle to the discovery of truth. 8 Wigmore, Evidence, § 2291. The Model Code of Evidence, (1942) included it in Rules 209-213, but not without some reluctance on the part of the Reporter. See Foreword, p. 27. The Uniform Rules of Evidence (1953) also recognize it. See Rule 26.

[1] Jessel, M. R., in Wheeler v. Le Marchant, (1881) 17 L. R. Ch. D. 675, 681: "Communications made to a priest in the confessional on matters perhaps considered by the penitent to be more important even than his life or his fortune, are not protected."

Normanshaw v. Normanshaw, (1893) 69 L. T. R. (ns) 468; Anderson v. Bank of British Columbia, (1875) 2 L. R. Ch. D. 644; Russell v. Jackson, (1851) 9 Hare, 386, 390; Greenlaw v. King, (1838) 1 Beavan 137, 145. For discussion of English cases, see Nokes, Professional Privilege, (1950) 66 Law Q. Rev. 88, 94.

See also Cloud, Communications to Spiritual Advisers—Whether Privileged, (1899) 33 Am. L. Rev. 544; Note, (1928) 21 Law. and Bank. 255; 8 Wigmore, Evidence, § 2394.

[2] Best, C. J., in Broad v. Pitt, (1828) 3 C. & P. 518, 519: "The privilege does not apply to clergymen * * * I, for one, will never compel a clergyman to disclose communications, made to him by a prisoner; but if he chooses to disclose them, I shall receive them in evidence." See also Reg. v. Griffin, (1853) 6 Cox, Cr. Cas. 219.

or priest to decline to reveal confidential communications appears to be recognized *by custom* in the courts.[3]

In thirty-one American jurisdictions, the common law rule has been discarded and the privilege is granted by statute.[4] The policy of the statutory privilege has generally been approved, but the courts will strictly construe such statutes.[5]

4. *Physician and Patient*

Contrary to the rule of the Civil Law,[1] confidential communi-

---

[3] The rule of the common law remains unchanged, but there seems to be a tacit agreement between members of the bar that if a clergyman or priest declines to divulge a confidential communication made to him in his capacity as the spiritual adviser of a person, further examination of the witness on that subject will not be pressed. See Professional Secrecy, an address by Lord Dawson of Penn, (April, 1922) The Lancet 619. Moreover, it is not likely that a court will adjudge a member of the clergy guilty of contempt of court who considers it his duty to maintain the sacred trust reposed in him. See comment, The Witness Box, the Confessional and the Consulting Room, (1932) 96 Just. P. 677. In Quebec, the privilege is granted by statute. Quebec Code of Civ. Proc., art. 332.

[4] For example: West's La. Stat. Ann. § 15:477 (1951) : "No clergyman is permitted, without the consent of the person making the communication, to disclose any communication made to him in confidence by one seeking his spiritual advice or consolation, or any information that he may have gotten by reason of such communication."

The privilege is recognized in Rule 29 of the Uniform Rules of Evidence, (1953).

[5] Buuck v. Kruckeberg, (1950) 121 Ind. App. 262, 95 N. E. 2d 304, 22 A. L. R. 2d 1145; Johnson v. Commonwealth, (1949) 310 Ky. 557, 221 S. W. 2d 87; 58 Am. Jur., Witnesses, § 532. See also Hogan, A Modern Problem on the Privilege of the Confessional, (1951) 6 Loyola L. Rev. 1.

For matters to which the privilege extends, see Note, 22 A. L. R. 2d 1152.

[1] Under the Civil Law, communications between a physician and his patient were at all times considered confidential and sacred. Without the consent of the patient, the physician could not disclose at any time, either in court or elsewhere, any information regarding the health or physical condition of the patient which he acquired in his professional capacity. Today, in most European countries, the relationship of physician and patient is completely protected by a cloak of privilege.

See Hammelman, Professional Privilege, (1950) 28 Can. B. Rev. 751, 753-757; Herzog, (1931) Medical Jurisprudence, § 147; Riddell, Law and Ethics of Medical Confidences, (1927) 333 Living Age 320; Lord Dawson of Penn., (April, 1922) The Lancet 619, 620; Purrington, An Abused Privilege, (1906) 6 Col. L. Rev. 388, 394-400; Bach, The Medico-Legal Aspect of Privileged Communications, (1892) 10 Medico-Leg. J. 33, 37; Penal Code of France, art. 378.

See also *In re* Robbins Will, (1950) 105 N. Y. S. 2d 290; Mut. Life Ins. Co. v. Jeannotte-Lamarche, (1935) 59 Que. Q. B. 510.

For an example of how the privilege works in France, see comment, (1922) 80 J. of Am. Med. Ass'n. 1787.

cations between a physician[2] and his patient were not privileged from disclosure at common law.[3] Outside the walls of a court of law, the physician was left to the dictates of his own conscience, the ethics of his profession, or the force of any compact he may have made with the person who confided in him.[4] When summoned to court as a witness, the physician was competent to disclose any information acquired by him, or communicated to him, in the course of his attendance upon, or treatment of, his patient; nor could he refuse to give, nor the patient by objection exclude, such testimony despite the effect such disclosure might have upon the rights, reputation, or feelings of either the patient or the physician.[5] The theory underlying the rule was that disclosure of the whole truth was essential to the proper administration of justice and that the need for it far outweighed any considerations of professional confidence.[6] Notwith-

---

[2] *Unless otherwise indicated,* the word "physician," when used by the author of this treatise, means a physician who is engaged in the general practice of medicine, and also a surgeon who is engaged in the general practice of surgery, each of whom is duly licensed to practice in his respective field. *It does not include* practitioners who are licensed to engage in a limited or specialized practice only.

[3] Countless American decisions confirm this statement, among which are: Mut. Life Ins. Co. v. Owen, (1914) 111 Ark. 554, 164 S. W. 720; People v. Lane, (1894) 101 Cal. 513, 36 Pac. 16; Springer v. Byram, (1894) 137 Ind. 15, 36 N. E. 361, 23 L. R. A. 244; Prader v. Nat'l. Masonic Acc. Ass'n., (1895) 95 Iowa 149, 63 N. W. 601; Campau v. North, (1878) 39 Mich. 606; *In re* Koenig's Estate, (1956) 247 Minn. 580, 78 N. W. 2d 364; Price v. Standard Life & Acc. Ins. Co., (1903) 90 Minn. 264, 95 N. W. 1118; Green v. Terminal R. R., (1908) 211 Mo. 18, 109 S. W. 715; Matter of New York City Council v. Goldwater, (1940) 284 N. Y. 296, 31 N. E. 2d 31, 133 A. L. R. 728; Fuller v. Knights of Pythias, (1901) 129 N. C. 318, 40 S. E. 65; Commonwealth v. Edwards, (1935) 318 Pa. 1, 178 Atl. 20; Munz v. Salt Lake City R. R., (1902) 25 Utah 220, 70 Pac. 852; Estate of Gallun, (1934) 215 Wis. 314, 254 N. W. 542.

[4] See DeWitt, Medical Ethics and the Law: the Conflict Between Dual Allegiances. (1953) 5 Western Res. L. Rev. 5.

[5] Boyle v. Northwestern Mut. Relief Ass'n., (1897) 95 Wis. 312, 70 N. W. 351; Nat'l. Mut. Life Ass'n. v. Godrich, (1909) 10 Comm. L. R. (Australia) 1.

[6] Garrow, B., in Earl of Falmouth v. Moss, (1822) 11 Price 455, 470: "What can be a stronger appeal to the feelings on this question than the sensibly delicate situation in which men of the medical profession are so frequently placed, to whom communications of the most anxious kind must often be made, admitting of not a moment's delay, and frequently by the other sex, having the strongest claims on their confidence and fidelity; and yet, we have seen that, on authority, they are liable to be called on to disclose with bleeding hearts, the painful secrets which have been necessarily entrusted to

⋙→

standing the fact that, since the sixteenth century, the relationship of attorney and client had been sedulously protected by a privilege of non-disclosure, the courts of England resolutely refused to extend a similar privilege to members of the medical profession.[7]

The inception of the common law rule occurred in the trial of the Duchess of Kingston.[8] In the year 1776, that notorious peeress was placed on trial before the House of Lords on a charge of bigamy. It being incumbent on the Crown to offer evidence of her first marriage, the Solicitor-General called as a witness Mr. Caesar Hawkins, an eminent surgeon, who, on different occasions, had attended professionally the Duchess, her husband, and their child. When asked whether the accused had admitted the first marriage, the witness replied: "I do not know how far anything that has come before me, in a confidential trust in my profession, should be disclosed consistent with my professional honour." The Earl of Mansfield, in his office as Lord High Steward at the trial, ruled that the question must be answered, and added:

> I suppose Mr. Hawkins means to demur to the question upon the ground that it came to his knowledge some way from his being employed as a surgeon for one or both of the parties; * * * Mr. Hawkins will understand * * * that a surgeon has

them, and under the most distressing circumstances; but sacred as those communications must ever be held, the ends of truth and justice have been hitherto deemed paramount."

State v. Martin, (1921) 182 N. C. 846, 849, 109 S. E. 74: "At common law no privilege existed as to communications between physician and patient. * * * The public interest in the disclosure of all facts relevant to a litigated issue was deemed to be superior to the policy of recognizing, for the benefit of the patient, the inviolability of confidential communications."

[7] Garner v. Garner, (1920) 36 T. L. R. 196; Wheeler v. Le Marchant, (1881) 17 L. R. Ch. D. 675; Anderson v. Bank of British Columbia, (1875) 2 L. R. Ch. D. 644; Russell v. Jackson, (1851) 9 Hare 387; Greenlaw v. King, (1838) 1 Beav. 137; Greenough v. Gaskell, (1833) 1 M. & K. 99; Broad v. Pitt, (1828) 3 C. & P. 518; Rex. v. Gibbons, (1823) 1 C. & P. 97; Earl of Falmouth v. Moss, (1822) 11 Price 455; Wilson v. Rastall, (1792) 4 Term Rep. 753.

Except in the province of Quebec which has a statutory privilege, the courts of Canada follow the English rule. Brown v. Carter, (1865) 9 L. C. Jur. 163.

See editorial, Medical Practitioners' Communications (Privilege) Bill, (1937) 83 L. J. 320; Nokes, Professional Privilege, (1950) 66 L. Q. Rev. 88.

[8] 20 How. St. Trials 355.

no privilege, where it is a material question, in a civil or a criminal case, to know whether the parties were married, or whether
a child was born, to say that his introduction to the parties was
in the course of his profession, and in that way he came to the
knowledge of it. I take it for granted, that if Mr. Hawkins under-
stands that, it is a satisfaction to him, and a clear justification to
all the world. If a surgeon was voluntarily to reveal these secrets,
to be sure he would be guilty of a breach of honour, and of great
indiscretion; but, to give that information in a court of justice,
which by the law of the land he is bound to do, will never be
imputed to him as any indiscretion whatever.

Thus from the lips of Lord Mansfield came the first formal
announcement of the common law rule. It should be noted, perhaps, that the confidences which the surgeon vainly tried to protect—for it was he, not the Duchess, who objected to the disclosure—
did not relate to any physical fact discoverable by observation or
examination, or to any communication by his patient with reference
to her condition of health; on the contrary, the confidence which he
tried to shield and keep secret was as to a marriage having taken
place, a fact which was quite irrelevant to the health or physical condition of the Duchess. The courts, however, have never considered
this as a limitation of the rule, but have consistently construed and
applied it, sometimes reluctantly,[9] as one which compels the physician, when called as a witness, to disclose all relevant facts of which
he has knowledge whether such facts concern the physical imperfections of the patient, his state of health, or otherwise.[10]

---

[9] Buller, J., in Wilson v. Rastall, (1792) 4 Term Rep. 753, 760: "There are cases, to
which it is much to be lamented that the law of privilege is not extended; those in
which medical persons are obliged to disclose the information which they acquire by
attending in their professional characters."

Brougham, L. C., in Greenough v. Gaskell, (1833) 1 M. & K. 98, 103, expressed a
similar sentiment.

Physicians have sometimes protested the lack of a privilege for their profession.
Tidy, (1844) Legal Medicine 20: "It seems a monstrous thing to require that secrets
affecting the honour of families, and perhaps confided to the medical adviser in a
moment of weakness, should be dragged into the garish light of a law suit."

[10] It was not until 1920, in Garner v. Garner, 36 T. L. R. 196, that the high water mark
was reached in the application of the rule. The plaintiff sued for divorce on the
grounds of adultery and cruelty. The cruelty alleged consisted of the communication

⟫→

The common law is still the law in England,[11] and in most of the jurisdictions of the British Commonwealth of Nations.[12] From time to time, however, in comparative recent years, members of the medical profession in England have strongly urged the passage of a law which would afford the same protection for the medical profession as that enjoyed by the legal profession, but their recommendations have been rejected.[13]

←‑《《

of syphilis by her husband to her. Dr. K. was called as a witness by plaintiff to prove she was suffering from that disease. He declined to testify, protesting that the Venereal Diseases Regulations (a national scheme for dealing with venereal diseases) *absolutely prohibited him* from disclosing any information acquired by him in the course of his duties at a venereal disease clinic. The court ordered him to make the disclosure, and held that the Venereal Disease Regulations could not override the general law of England which requires a physician to disclose the health of the patient whenever that is relevant to the issue before the court. See editorial, (1920) 84 Just. P. 51 and (1920) 64 Sol. L. J. 218. Lord Dawson of Penn discussed a similar case. (April, 1922) The Lancet 619. See also C. v. C. (1946) 1 All E. R. 562.

[11] 22 Halsbury's Laws of England, (2d ed.) Medicine and Pharmacy, § 610: "The relationship between a medical practitioner and his patient does not excuse the former, whatever medical etiquette may require, from the obligation, if called upon, to give evidence in a court of law. He is in the same position as any other person who is not specially privileged in this respect by the law. He may be summoned to give evidence in civil or criminal causes; and is liable to imprisonment if he neglects to attend. He may be asked to disclose on oath information which came to him through his professional relationship with a patient; and, if the question is not inadmissible on other grounds, he may be committed to prison if he refuses to answer."

See editorial, Medical Men and Professional Secrecy, (1915) 79 Just. P. 3.

There is no privilege in Scotland. A. B. v. C. D., (1851) 14 Court of Sess. Cas. (2d series) 177.

[12] The Province of Quebec, the State of Victoria in Australia, and the Commonwealth of New Zealand have discarded the common law rule and have enacted statutes which create a privilege of non-disclosure. See Appendix, herein.

[13] London Times, June 28, 1920: (1920) 64 Sol. J. 612. Meetings have also been held at which members of the legal and medical professions have presented arguments upon the subject of privilege, but no tangible results have so far been achieved. (1922) 153 L. T. 228; (1927) 164 L. T. 10; (1933) 2 So. Afr. L. J. 140 and 159.

Bills have been introduced in Parliament to create a privilege for medical persons but have failed to pass the second reading. (July-Dec., 1927) The Lancet 1161 and 1269; (1937) 83 L. J. 320. The British Admiralty compels naval surgeons to disclose their patients' secrets when testifying before courts martial. (1920) 75 J. of Am. Med. Ass'n. 1438.

In many American jurisdictions, the common law rule remains in full force and effect.[14]

---

[14] Dyer v. State, (1941) 241 Ala. 679, 4 So. 2d 311; Zeiner v. Zeiner, (1935) 120 Conn. 161, 179 Atl. 644; Hollenbacher v. Bryant, (1943) 42 Del. 242, 30 A. 2d 561; Morrison v. Malmquist, (1953) _____ Fla._____ , 62 So. 2d 415; Elliott v. Georgia Power Co., (1938) 58 Ga. App. 151, 197 S. E. 914; approved in Collins v. Howard, (1957) 156 F. Supp. 322 (D. C. of Ga); H. H. Waegner & Co. v. Moock, (1946) 303 Ky. 222, 197 S. W. 2d 254; Boyd v. Wynn, (1941) 286 Ky. 173, 150 S. W. 2d 648; O'Brien v. State, (1915) 126 Md. 270, 94 Atl. 1934; Kramer v. John Hancock Mut. Life Ins. Co., (1957) _____ Mass. _____ , 146 N. E. 2d 357; Gretsky v. Basso, (1955) 136 F. Supp. 640 (D. C. of Mass.); Epstein v. Nat'l. Cas. Co., (1949) 1 N. J. 409, 64 A. 2d 67; Remington v. Rhode Island Co., (1915) 37 R. I. 393, 93 Atl. 33; Banigan v. Banigan, (1914) 26 R. I. 454, 59 Atl. 313; Caddo Groc. & Ice Co. v. Carpenter, (1955) _____ Tex. Civ. App._____ , 285 S. W. 2d 470; Bonewald v. State, (1952) 157 Tex. Crim. 521, 251 S. W. 2d 255; Mohr v. Mohr, (1937) 119 W. Va. 253, 193 S. E. 121. In this state, however, a statutory privilege is available in the court of a Justice of the Peace.

The Uniform Code of Military Justice, 50 U. S. C. (c. 22) § 551-736, provides: "Art. 36. The procedure, including modes of proof * * * may be prescribed by the President by regulations which shall, so far as he deems practicable, apply the principles of law and the rules of evidence generally recognized in the trial of criminal cases in the United States district courts * * *." President Truman's Executive Order #10214, February 8, 1951, prescribed the Manual for Courts Martial, 1951. In the regulation relating to Evidence, paragraph 151c provides:

"c. Certain nonprivileged communications.

(2.) It is the duty of medical officers to attend sick members of the armed forces, * * *. Although the ethics of the medical profession forbid medical officers and civilian physicians to disclose without authority information acquired when acting in a professional capacity, *no privilege attaches to such information or to statements made to them by patients.*" (Italics supplied)

CHAPTER II

The Physician-Patient Privilege Statute

5. *Origin and History*

The first privilege of non-disclosure in Anglo-American jurisprudence applicable to the relationship of physician and patient, was created by the legislature of the State of New York in 1828. For some time prior thereto, distinguished members of the state's Bench and Bar were engaged in a needful and thoroughgoing movement of legal reform and the statutory law of the state was in the process of augmentation and revision. Whatever it was that prompted the revisers to recommend the creation of a testimonial privilege never before recognized in England or America has never been made clear, but admittedly the revisers were influenced to some extent[1] by the comment of Mr. Justice Buller in *Wilson* v. *Rastall*.[2] It seems likely, too, that a compelling, if not paramount, consideration was the desire to give the medical profession the same protection which the legal profession enjoyed.

The original statute[3] which, for many years, served as a pattern for those enacted later in other states and in some foreign countries provided:

No person duly authorized to practice physic or surgery shall be allowed to disclose any information which he may have acquired in attending any patient, in a professional character, and

---

[1] See Report of Revisers, Vol. V, 34; N. Y. Stat. (2d ed. 1836) . Vol. III, 737.

[2] See § 4, note 9, herein.

[3] N. Y. Rev. Stat. 1828 II, 406, Part III, c. VII, art. 8, § 73.

which information was necessary to enable him to prescribe for such patient as a physician, or to do any act for him, as a surgeon.

During the period from 1835 to 1930, a large number of states, political subdivisions, and insular possessions of the United States, enacted statutes which expressly create this testimonial privilege;[4] likewise, several jurisdictions within the British Commonwealth of Nations.[5]

6. Dissimilarity of Modern Statutes

The early statutes were surprisingly similar in style and content.[1] Unfortunately, they were not felicitously drafted; clarity was sacrificed to brevity with the result that their sheer inadequacy produced shocking injustices unforeseen by the lawmakers. Ensuing

---

[4] Alaska, Arizona, Arkansas, California, Canal Zone, Colorado, District of Columbia, Guam, Hawaii, Idaho, Indiana, Iowa, Kansas, Kentucky (limited), Louisiana (limited), Michigan, Minnesota, Mississippi, Missouri, Montana, Nebraska, Nevada, New Mexico (limited), North Carolina (limited), North Dakota, Ohio, Oklahoma, Oregon, Pennsylvania (limited), Philippine Islands (limited), Puerto Rico, South Dakota, Utah, Virgin Islands, Washington, West Virginia (limited), Wisconsin, Wyoming. For the convenience of the reader, the statutes are set forth in the Appendix, herein.

Although the courts have universally held that the privilege can be created by statute only, the Supreme Court of South Carolina appears to have held otherwise. In Next of Kin of Clinton Cole v. Anderson Cotton Mills, (1939) 191 S. C. 458, 4 S. E. 2d 908, it was said: "It has long been established law that communications made to one's doctor are privileged * * *," but the court cited no authority. Moreover, the Workmens' Compensation Law of South Carolina, (1952) S. C. Code § 72-307, provides that information acquired by a physician is not privileged in hearings conducted under that law. This seems to infer that a privilege exists even in the absence of a statute creating one. In Holbert v. Chase, (1952) 12 F. R. D. 171, it was held that the statement of the Supreme Court of South Carolina, even though regarded as dictum, must be accepted by a federal court, sitting in that state, as the law of that state. In a recent case, however, the Supreme Court repudiated the dictum of the Clinton Cole Case and upheld the common law rule. See Peagler v. Atlantic Coast Line R. R., (1958) .... S. C........., 101 S. E. 2d 821.

In a rather unique case, a trial court in Illinois appears to have recognized a patient-psychiatrist privilege based on common law. See comment, (1952) 47 Northwestern U. L. Rev. 384.

[5] Victoria (Australia), Province of Quebec (Canada), New Zealand. See Appendix, herein.

[1] This was probably the result of a desire to match the novel New York statute.

revisions have so altered the original statutes that, except in a few jurisdictions, the modern ones bear little resemblance to them.[2]

Basically, of course, the policy underlying the modern statutes is the same, yet there is a wide disparity in their wordage, content, and limitations.[3] Most of the statutes accord the privilege to licensed physicians only, but a few extend it to professional or registered nurses, or to the physician's stenographer or confidential clerk. In New York, the privilege has been accorded to dentists. In some jurisdictions, the statute expressly provides that it may be invoked in civil actions only; in others, it is applicable in both civil and criminal cases. In Louisiana, it can be claimed in criminal proceedings only. In most of the statutes, the prohibition of disclosure is expressly confined to information which was acquired by the physician in his professional capacity and which was necessary to enable the physician to prescribe for, or treat, the patient. In the District of Columbia, the statute plainly states that it is immaterial whether such information shall have been obtained from the patient, or from his family, or from the person in charge of him. In a few states, the statute excludes evidence disclosing *any* information acquired by the physician while attending the patient. In Kansas, the statute prohibits a physician disclosing any information relating to the patient's condition, injury, or the time, manner or circumstances under which the ailment was incurred. In Pennsylvania and the Philippine Islands, "information," no matter how obtained, is not protected; only "communications" made by the patient to the physician "which shall tend to blacken the character of the patient," are within the purview of the statute. In New Mexico, the privilege is limited "to any real or supposed venereal or loathesome disease," except in cases involving the Workmen's Compensation Law where the scope of the privilege is enlarged. In Kentucky, the privilege is limited to cases which have to do with the subject of Vital Statistics

---

[2] For example: New York's first statute contained only fifty-five words and articles. Subsequent amendments have vastly extended the wording of the privilege. See also the California and Nevada statutes.

[3] It is not our purpose at this point to discuss all of the variances. These will be taken up in detail in subsequent chapters.

In West Virginia, the privilege can be availed of only in cases origi
nating in the court of a Justice of the Peace.

Practically all of the early statutes made no provision whatever
for waiver of the privilege, and some of them are still deficient in
this respect. However, by the process of amendment, the more
modern statutes include multifarious provisions governing the exercise of this valuable right by persons representing the patient or
acting in his stead.

It is interesting to note—and, perhaps, we can take it as an
earnest of better to come—that there is an increasing tendency on
the part of legislators to withhold the right to exercise the privilege
in certain classes of actions or proceedings, civil and criminal. In a
few states, the statute expressly debars the patient, or his representative, from invoking the privilege in actions where he has voluntarily
put in issue the patient's condition of health, the nature and extent
of his injury, or the cause of his death. Furthermore, in some states,
the legislature has authorized the attending physician of the victim
of an illegal abortion to testify in a criminal prosecution of the abor-
tionist. In Minnesota, a physician may be compelled to testify in a
bastardy case as to the probable date of inception of the pregnancy.
In Michigan, in prosecutions for illegal marriage of persons sexually
diseased, any physician who has attended the husband or wife for
gonorrhea or syphilis can be compelled to testify to any facts found
by him from such attendance.

These are but some, certainly not all, of the dissimilarities in
the existing statutes; but these are sufficient, we believe, to show the
necessity of examining carefully the scope and meaning of the particular statute which is involved in any given case.[4]

---

[4] The statutes which grant the testimonial privilege are set forth in the Appendix,
herein. These are believed to be in full force and effect at the time of the publication
of this treatise, but the reader must constantly be on the watch for amendments
thereof.

CHAPTER III

The Model Code of Evidence and the Uniform Rules of Evidence

Sec.
7. The Physician-Patient Privilege

7. *The Physician-Patient Privilege*

Bench and Bar almost universally concede that there is no branch of our jurisprudence which is more in need of reform than the Law of Evidence. All agree that it is high time to revise, perhaps abolish, some of the strict and antiquated rules, especially those which operate to exclude relevant evidence of material facts. In an effort to meet this need, the American Law Institute, in 1942, completed and promulgated the Model Code of Evidence.[1] In each of the earlier tentative drafts and in the final tentative draft, the physician-patient privilege was purposely omitted.[2] When the Code was submitted to the members of the Institute at its annual meeting, considerable discussion was had concerning the wisdom and policy of the privilege,[3] and strong opposition was aroused to the omission of the privilege with the result that the vote of the meeting instructed the Reporter to include one. Accordingly, the privilege was restored and is embodied in Rules 220 to 223.[4] Although The

---

[1] For history, scope, and purpose of the Code, see Ladd, A Modern Code of Evidence, (1942) 27 Iowa L. Rev. 213; Lewis, Introduction, (1942) The Model Code of Evidence, p. vii; Morgan, Foreword, (1942) The Model Code of Evidence, p. 1.

[2] The Reporter, Professor Edmund M. Morgan, the Chief Consultant, John H. Wigmore, and the Advisers were unanimously opposed to such privilege.

[3] For complete report thereof, see Proceedings of American Law Institute, (1942) vol. 19, p. 187, *et seq.*

[4] In addition to these rules The Model Code of Evidence contains four procedural

⟫⟶

Model Code received the approval of many lawyers and scholars, its drastic revision of some of the well-established rules of evidence alienated the vast majority of the legal profession with the result that it failed of adoption by the legislature of any state.[5]

The urge for reform however, did not abate. In 1948, the National Conference of Commissioners on Uniform State Laws decided to enter the field. With the approval of the American Law Institute, the Conference used the Model Code as a basis of study. After four years' work the proposed Uniform Rules of Evidence were drafted and submitted to the Conference.[6] At the 1950 meeting of the Conference, it was voted that the physician-patient privilege should not be recognized. Three years later, however, the Conference—probably to placate the medical profession—reversed its action and agreed, by way of compromise, to include the privilege.[7] It is embodied in Rule 27.[8]

Notwithstanding their decision to include a physician-patient privilege, it is manifest that the sponsors of the Model Code of Evidence and of the Uniform Rules of Evidence considered such a privilege highly undesirable and mischief-making. Rule 27 of the

---

Rules which relate to personal privileges generally, including, of course, the physician-patient privilege. See Rules 231 to 234.

[5] The Model Code has been cited on many occasions, usually as a supporting authority. (1949) N. Y. U. School of Law Annual Survey of American Law 977, Note. 5.

[6] For history, scope, and purpose of the Uniform Rules of Evidence, see A Symposium on the Uniform Rules of Evidence and Illinois Evidence Law, (1954) 49 Nw. U. L. Rev. 481; McCormick, Some High Lights of the Uniform Evidence Rules, (1955) 33 Tex. L. Rev. 559; Jacobs, The Uniform Rules of Evidence, (1956) 10 Rutgers L. Rev. 485; McCormick, Law and the Future: Evidence, (1956) 51 Nw. U. L. Rev. 218; Chadbourn, The "Uniform Rules" and the California Law of Evidence, (1954) 2 U. C. L. A. L. Rev. 1; Gard, Panel on Uniform Rules of Evidence, (1953) 8 Ark. L. Rev. 44; Nokes, American Uniform Rules of Evidence, (1955) 4 Int'l. and Comp. L. Q. 48.

The Uniform Rules of Evidence were approved by the Conference and the American Bar Association in 1953; and by the American Law Institute in 1954.

[7] Professor McCormick has pointed out that the privilege is printed in brackets, the inference being that it is optional with the States which adopt the Uniform Rules to include or omit this privilege. See High Lights of the Uniform Evidence Rules, (1955) 33 Tex. L. Rev. 559, 571. The privilege enacted in the recent Virgin Islands Code is based on Rule 27 of the Uniform Rules of Evidence. See Appendix.

[8] See Appendix, herein. The Rule incorporates the provisions of Rules 220 to 223 of the Model Code of Evidence (1942).

Uniform Rules therefore imposes a number of rigid limitations upon the application of the privilege in designated classes of actions and thus, in large measure, it eliminates most of the evils that hitherto have brought into disrepute many physician-patient privilege statutes. It should be noted also that the Uniform Rules of Evidence contain important procedural rules which concern personal privileges generally, including the physician-patient privilege.[9]

---

[9] Rules 37 to 40. See Appendix, herein. The same rules appear in the Model Code of Evidence. (1942) Rules 231 to 234.

CHAPTER IV

Policy of the Privilege

8. *Medical Ethics and the Law: The Duty of Secrecy*

Everywhere medical confidences are regarded as sacred and precious. Unquestionably one of the highest duties of the physician is to keep secret and inviolate the intimate knowledge of his patient's disease, ailment, or physical imperfection, especially that which he learned by means of communication, observation, or examination in the course of his professional employment.[1] Hippocrates (*circa* 400 B.C.), renowned as the "Father of Medicine," was perhaps the first to express the ethical duty of the physician. His Oath, a self-imposed criterion of professional conduct, has come down through the ages. Pledging himself that never would he voluntarily divulge the medical confidences of his patients, Hippocrates vowed, among other things:

---

[1] In England, some physicians seem to have strange notions about the professional duty of secrecy. In C. v. C. (1946) 1 All E. R. 562, a patient, who was preparing to file suit for annulment under the Matrimonial Causes Act, asked her physician to disclose to her the nature of her disease (a venereal one), but he refused. Lewis, J., at 563: "The question which arises out of these circumstances is: 'Is a doctor, when asked by his patient to give him or her particulars of his or her condition and illness to be used in a court of law, when these particulars are vital to the success or failure of the case, entitled to refuse and in effect say: 'Go on with your case in the dark, and I will tell you in court when I am subpoenaed what my conclusions are'? * * * The information should have been given and in all cases where the circumstances are similar, the doctor is not guilty of any breach of confidence in giving the information asked for."

Whatsoever things I see or hear concerning the life of men, in my attendance on the sick or even apart therefrom which ought not to be noised abroad, I will keep silence thereon, counting such things to be as sacred secrets.[2]

Protected by no greater guaranty of secrecy than this, countless generations of men and women, freely and confidently, have entrusted their most intimate and delicate secrets to their medical advisers.

It must be remembered, however, that we are not dealing with a question of medical ethics or professional etiquette pertaining to the conduct of the physician *outside* the courtroom; on the contrary, we are concerned only with a testimonial privilege, created by legislative enactment, which prohibits a disclosure by the physician, when called to testify in a lawful proceeding, of confidential communications made to, or information acquired by, him in the course of his professional attendance upon the patient. It is manifest, of course, that a voluntary disclosure by the physician of medical confidences gained while attending the patient—when not made in the course of his professional duty—is a plain violation of medical ethics and professional propriety, but the physician-patient privilege statute does not prescribe a rule of conduct for the government of physicians in their general intercourse with society. Therefore, if the physician, disregarding the ethical duty of secrecy, should, in conversation or otherwise, reveal the intimate confidences of the patient, he would not violate the statute however reprehensible his conduct would be.[3] As far as the statute goes, the physician may

---

[2] See Foxe, The Oath of Hippocrates, (1945) 19 Psychiatric Q. 17; Brandeis, The Physician and Medical Ethics, (1932) 38 Med. Rev. of Rev. 699; Flannagan, The Spirit of the Oath, (1930) 57 Va. Med. Mo. 538.

For scope and effect of the oath, see Morrison v. Malmquist, (1953) _____ Fla._____, 62 So. 2d 415.

[3] Nelson v. Nederland Life Ins. Co., (1900) 110 Iowa 600, 81 N. W. 807; Simonsen v. Swenson, (1920) 104 Neb. 224, 177 N. W. 831, 9 A. L. R. 1250; Buffalo Loan, Trust and Safe Dep. Co. v. Knights Templar and M. A. Ass'n., (1891) 126 N. Y. 450, 27 N. E. 942; Boyle v. Northwestern Mut. Relief Ass'n., (1897) 95 Wis. 312, 70 N. W. 351.

See DeWitt, Medical Ethics and the Law: the Conflict Between Dual Allegiances. (1953) 5 Western Res. L. Rev. 5; Chafee, Is Justice Served or Obstructed by Closing the Doctor's Mouth on the Witness Stand? (1943) 52 Yale L. J. 607; Purrington, An Abused Privilege, (1906) 6 Col. L. Rev. 388. There is no punishment provided for the

≫→

talk about the ailments of the patient from New York to San Francisco and to every Tom, Dick and Harry on the street or in his club, since the statute merely permits the patient, or the holder of the privilege, to seal the lips of the physician against testifying in a judicial proceeding,[4] or an investigation authorized by law,[5] and is wholly ineffectual to prevent a public disclosure elsewhere.[6]

9. Reasons for the Statute

There has been and is a considerable difference of opinion regarding the purpose and policy of the statute. Various reasons for its enactment have been offered. It will be remembered that the common law afforded no protection whatever for the confidences reposed by sick and injured persons in their physicians.[1] No matter what the confidence or secret was, however intimate or delicate, he who held it was compellable to disclose it in the interests of justice. Yet many persons, especially those of the medical profession, firmly believed that the fact that the physician was bound to reveal to the world in open court, whenever so directed by the judge, every bit of information he had acquired during his professional employment, could not but act as a deterrent so as to cause patients to suffer untold anguish and torment, rather than divulge facts inexorably held secret. That dread, whether the fear of exposure and disgrace, or the recoil from the infliction of humiliation or grief on others, was the real mischief, it was said, which the

---

physician who reveals what has been confided to him. Jacobs v. Cedar Rapids, (1917) 181 Iowa 407, 164 N. W. 891.

[4] Noble v. United Benefit Life Ins. Co., (1941) 230 Iowa 471, 297 N. W. 881. Chafee, infra note 3, at 607.

[5] Matter of New York City Council v. Goldwater, (1940) 284 N. Y. 296, 31 N. E. 2d 31, 133 A. L. R. 728.

[6] American Republic Life Ins. Co. v. Edenfield, (1957) _____ Ark._____, 306 S. W. 2d 321; Maryland Cas. Co. v. Maloney, (1915) 119 Ark. 434, 178 S. W. 387, L. R. A. 1916 A 519; Noble v. United Benefit Life Ins Co., (1941) 230 Iowa 471, 297 N. W. 881; Jacobs v. Cedar Rapids, (1917) 181 Iowa 407, 164 N. W. 891; People v. Shurly, (1902) 131 Mich. 177, 91 N. W. 139; Cramer v. Hurt, (1900) 154 Mo. 112, 55 S. W. 258; State v. Miller, (1919) 105 Wash(475, 178 Pac. 459. See Lipscomb, Privileged Communications Statute—Sword or Shield, (1944) 16 Miss. L. J. 181, 182.

[1] See § 4, herein.

common law did not prevent or abate.[2] It is highly probable, therefore, that it was precisely this presumptive "mischief" that the authors of the early statutes sought to put an end to.

Generally speaking, however, the courts have not been content to base the origin of the statutory privilege upon this ground alone. On the contrary, other purposes and objectives have been attributed to it. Some courts have held that one of its principal objectives is a humane one, since it gives the patient "free conduct and free tongue" with his medical adviser to the end that the latter may have the information necessary to enable him to render as much aid as possible for the restoration of the patient's health and for relief from his pain and discomfort.[3] Others have said that its primary purpose is to protect the patient's right to privacy.[4] Several courts have expressed the novel view that the real purpose of the statute is to protect the patient from his own physician; that frequently the

---

[2] Barton, J., in National Mut. Life Ass'n. v. Godrich, (1909) 10 Comm. L. R. (Australia) 1, 19.

[3] Travelers' Ins. Co. v. Bergeron, (1928) 25 F. 2d 680, cert denied 278 U. S. 638, 73 Law Ed. 553, 49 Su. Ct. 33, 58 A. L. R. 1127; Hartley v. Calbreath, (1907) 127 Mo. App. 559, 106 S. W. 570; Arnold v. Maryville, (1905) 110 Mo. App. 254, 85 S. W. 107; Green v. Metropolitan Street Ry., (1902) 171 N. Y. 201, 63 N. E. 958. In vindication of the novel statute of New York, the revisers stated: "The ground on which communications to *counsel* are privileged, is the supposed necessity of a full knowledge of the facts, to advise correctly, and to prepare for the proper defence or prosecution of a suit. But surely the necessity of consulting a medical adviser, when life itself may be in jeopardy, is still stronger. And unless such consultations are privileged, men will be incidentally punished by being obliged to suffer the consequences of injuries without relief from the medical art, and without conviction of any offence. Besides, in such cases, during the struggle between legal duty on the one hand, and professional honor on the other, the latter, aided by a strong sense of the injustice and inhumanity of the rule, will, in most cases, furnish a temptation to the perversion or concealment of truth, too strong for human resistance. In every view that can be taken of the policy, justice or humanity of the rule, as it exists, its relaxation seems highly expedient. It is believed that the proposition in the section is so guarded, that it cannot be abused by applying it to cases not intended to be privileged." Original Reports of Revisers, Vol. V, 34; N. Y. Rev. Stat. (2d ed. 1836) vol. III, 737.

[4] Studabaker v. Faylor, (1912) 52 Ind. App. 171, 98 N. E. 318; Chaffee v. Kaufman, (1923) 113 Kan. 254, 214 Pac. 618; Culver v. Union Pac. R. R., (1924) 112 Neb. 441, 199 N. W. 794; Davis v. Supreme Lodge, K. of H., (1900) 165 N. Y. 159, 58 N. E. 891; Williams v. State, (1939) 65 Okla. Cr. 336, 86 P. 2d 1015.

If this view be sound, one may well ask why the lawmakers have not enacted a statute which will protect his right to privacy *outside* the courtroom.

patient and his physician do not stand on equal terms and, therefore, the patient may easily be imposed upon by his own physician and induced to make admissions detrimental to his own interests.[5] The Supreme Court of Ohio, in adopting this view, went on to say that this *defensive* feature of the statute is an important one.[6] Another explanation given for the existence of the statute is that the employee-patient may be under the care of a "company doctor" and because of the relationship between employer and physician, the physician, consciously or unconsciously, is inclined to give testimony more favorable to the company which employs him than to the employee-patient whom he has treated.[7] It has also been said that the purpose of the statute is to place the information obtained by the physician from his patient substantially upon the same foot-

[5] Mr. Justice Pitney put forth this view in Arizona & New Mexico v. Clark, (1915) 235 U. S. 669, 59 Law Ed. 415, 35 Su. Ct. 210, L. R. A. 1915 C. 834.

It is submitted, with respect, that this animadversion upon the medical profession is undeserved and grossly unfair. Moreover, it seems well-nigh unbelievable that any legislature would indulge such a low opinion of the medical profession and found upon it a repressive statute.

[6] Baker v. Industrial Comm'n., (1939) 135 Ohio St. 491, 21 N. E. 2d 593.

[7] United States Fid. & Guar. Co. v. Hood, (1920) 124 Miss. 548, 87 So. 115, 15 A. L. R. 605. Burke, J., dissenting in Booren v. McWilliams, (1914) 26 N. D. 558, 588, 145 N. W. 410, Ann. Cas. 1916 A. 388: "At the time of the enactment of most of the statutes, many railway companies, mining corporations, factories, and other large enterprises were establishing hospitals for the treatment of their employees. The physicians in charge of those hospitals were dependent for their positions upon the good will of the corporations, and it was urged that some at least of those physicians were taking advantage of their positions to obtain from the patients information which would tend to defeat a claim for damages. The legislatures of the various states probably felt that injured employees were unable to give a true account of the manner of their injury, and wholly unable to withstand any 'third degree work,' especially by a physician in whom they should have the utmost confidence. That the legislature intended to remedy this evil is apparent to everybody, excepting Mr. Wigmore and the few courts who have followed him."

See author's comment, infra note 5. But even if such a situation did exist, the problem is not of such far-reaching importance as some give it since juries would be alert to it and would measure testimony accordingly. See Burke v. Chicago & N. W. Ry., (1915) 131 Minn. 209, 154 N. W. 960; Ford, The Physician-Patient Privilege, (1949) 14 Mo. L. Rev. 277, 279; Chafee, Is Justice Served or Obstructed by Closing the Doctor's Mouth on the Witness Stand? (1943) 52 Yale L. J. 607, 611: "This argument has the merit of not being abstract, but of asserting a basis of fact. Yet even if it is valid, it might be wiser to admit the evidence of the physicians, trusting in the jury to discount it heavily if an improper attitude towards the patients exists."

ing with the information acquired by an attorney while acting professionally in his client's affair.[8]

The great majority of the courts, however, declare that the primary purpose of the statute, manifest above all others, is to evoke and encourage the utmost confidence between the patient and his physician and to preserve it inviolate,[9] so that the patient will freely and frankly reveal to his physician all of the facts, circumstances, and symptoms of his malady or injury, or lay bare his body for examination, and thus enable his physician to make a correct diagnosis of his condition and treat him more safely and efficaciously.[10]

---

[8] Pierson v. People, (1880) 79 N. Y. 424, 433; Edington v. Mutual Life Ins. Co., (1875) 5 Hun. (N. Y.) 1, 8. Distinguished members of the medical profession in England have long contended there is no logical reason why the professional secrecy accorded to the lawyer should be respected more than the professional secrecy of the physician; that if it is good policy to prohibit the disclosure of confidential communications between lawyer and client, it is also good policy to shield those between physician and patient. Their efforts, however, have produced no tangible results. Although some American courts regard the relationship of attorney and client as indistinguishable from that of physician and patient, a critical examination of each will reveal a marked difference between them. See opinion of Ethridge, J., in Killings v. Metropolitan Life Ins. Co., (1940) 187 Miss. 265, 277, 192 So. 577, 131 A. L. R. 684. See also 8 Wigmore, Evidence, § 2380a; McCormick, Evidence, § 108; Guttmacher and Weihofen, (1952) Psychiatry and the Law 270; Peterson, The Patient-Physician Privilege in Missouri, (1952) 20 U. of Kan. City L. Rev. 122, 136; Ford, The Physician-Patient Privilege, (1949) 14 Mo. L. Rev, 277, 280; Lipscomb, Privileged Communications Statute—Sword and Shield, (1944) 16 Miss. L. J. 181, 182; Chafee, infra note 7 at 608; Morgan, Suggested Remedy for Obstruction to Expert Testimony by Rules of Evidence, (1943) 10 U. of Chic. L. Rev. 285, 290; Curd, Privileged Communications Between Doctor and His Patient, (1938) 44 W. Va. L. Q. 165, 168; Birkenhead, Should a Doctor Tell? (1922) Points of View, Vol. 1, 33, 34-37; Purrington, An Abused Privilege, (1906) 6 Col. L. Rev. 388, 393; Bach, The Medico-Legal Aspect of Privileged Communications, (1892) 10 Medico-Leg. J. 33, 40.

Professional Confidences of Medical Men, (1900) 64 Just. P. 241: "It is clear why the privilege, so called, is not extended to medical advisers. They have nothing to do as such with the administration of justice. The reason of the privilege in relation to legal advisers does not extend to them. It is not absolutely necessary in the interests of justice that inviolable secrecy should attach to all transactions between a man and his medical adviser."

[9] The statutes of California, Colorado, Guam, Idaho, Montana, Oregon and Utah expressly declare this to be the policy of the privilege.

[10] Miller, J., in Edington v. Mut. Life Ins. Co., (1876) 67 N. Y. 185, 194: "To open the door to the disclosure of secrets revealed on the sick bed, or when consulting a physician, would destroy confidence between the physician and the patient, and, it is very easy to see, might tend very much to prevent the advantages and benefits which flow from this confidential relationship."

It seems to be taken for granted that the legislatures which enacted the statute firmly believed that this desirable objective could best be attained by prohibiting physicians to reveal in courts of law the medical confidences imparted to them, especially those pertaining to diseases or physical imperfections which might expose the patient to civil or criminal prosecution, or subject him to humiliation, embarrassment, disgrace, reproach or unfriendly comment.[11]

10. *Public Policy*

Most of the courts still cling to the traditional theory that the statute is designed to promote the health and welfare of the community and, therefore, is founded upon principles of sound public policy.[1] However, a small minority oppose this view on the ground

---

[11] City and County of San Francisco v. Superior Court, (1951) 37 Cal. 2d 227, 232, 231 P. 2d 26, 25 A. L. R. 2d 1418: "The whole purpose of the privilege is to preclude the humiliation of the patient that might follow the disclosures of his ailments". Pierson v. People, (1880) 79 N. Y. 424, 434: "The plain purpose of this statute * * * was to enable a patient to make known his condition to his physician without the danger of any disclosure by him which would annoy the feelings, damage the character, or impair the standing of the patient while living, or disgrace his memory when dead. It could have no other purpose."

Representative cases explaining the purpose and policy of the privilege, are: Maryland Cas. Co. v. Maloney, (1915) 119 Ark. 434, 178 S. W. 387, L. R. A. 1916 A. 519; *In re* Flint, (1893) 100 Cal. 391, 34 Pac. 863; Moreno v. New Guadalupe Mining Co., (1917) 35 Cal. App. 744, 170 Pac. 1088; Brackney v. Fogle, (1901) 156 Ind. 535, 60 N. E. 303; Penn Mut. Life Ins. Co. v. Wiler, (1884) 100 Ind. 92; Howard v. Porter, (1949) 240 Iowa 153, 35 N. W. 2d 837; Jacobs v. Cedar Rapids, (1917) 181 Iowa 407, 164 N. W. 891; Battis v. Chicago, R. I. & P. Ry., (1904) 124 Iowa 623, 100 N. W. 543; Novak v. Chicago Fraternal Life Ass'n., (1932) 136 Kan. 609, 16 P. 2d 507; Powell v. J. J. Newman Lumber Co., (1936) 174 Miss. 685, 165 So. 299; McCaw v. Turner, (1921) 126 Miss. 260, 88 So. 705; Ansnes v. Loyal Protective Ins. Co., (1937) 133 Neb. 665, 276 N. W. 397; Leeds v. Prudential Ins. Co., (1935) 128 Neb. 395, 258 N. W. 672, 96 A. L. R. 1414; Steinberg v. New York Life Ins. Co., (1933) 263 N. Y. 45, 188 N. E. 152, 90 A. L. R. 642; Capron v. Douglass, (1908) 193 N. Y. 11, 85 N. E. 827, 20 L. R. A. (n. s.) 1003; Clifford v. Denver & Rio G. R. R., (1907) 188 N. Y. 349, 80 N. E. 1094; State v. Karcher, (1951) 155 Ohio St. 253, 98 N. E. 2d 308; Industrial Comm'n. v. Warnke, (1936) 131 Ohio St. 140, 2 N. E. 2d 248; Larson, C. J. in Clawson v. Walgreen Drug Co., (1945) 108 Utah 577, 600, 162 P. 2d 759; Randa v. Bear, (1957) _____ Wash. _____ , 312 P. 2d 640; Prudential Ins. Co. v. Kozlowski, (1938) 226 Wis. 641, 276 N. W. 300; *In re* Will of Bruendl, (1899) 102 Wis. 45, 78 N. W. 169; Warnecke v. Equitable Life Assur. Soc., (1906) Victoria L. R. (Australia) 482.

[1] Pennsylvania R. R. v. Durkee, (1906) 147 Fed. 99, 8 Ann. Cas. 790; Carmody v. Capital Traction Co., (1915) 43 App. D. C. 245, Ann. Cas. 1916 D 706; American Re-

≫→

that since the privilege is personal to the patient and can be waived by him at his pleasure, the public interest is not involved; that the public policy of the State does not depend upon the will of individuals who are free to act as circumstances may suggest to them.[2] It has been said that public policy demands that the truth be sometimes sacrificed to the necessity of protecting medical confidences.[3]

Unquestionably, when the revisers drafted the original statute in New York, it was believed that the benefits which would accrue to the general public from its enactment would far outweigh any harm and injustice which litigants might suffer in particular cases

---

← ⃰

public Life Ins. Co. v. Edenfield, (1957) ....Ark........., 306 S. W. 2d 321; Missouri and N. A. R. R. v. Daniels, (1911) 98 Ark. 352, 136 S. W. 651; *In re* Flint, (1893) 100 Cal. 391, 34 Pac. 863; *In re* Estate of Visaxis, (1928) 95 Cal. App. 617, 273 Pac. 165; Brackney v. Fogle, (1901) 156 Ind. 535, 60 N. E. 303; Campau v. North, (1878) 39 Mich. 606; Hobson v. McLeod, (1933) 165 Miss. 853, 147 So. 778; Ossenkop v. State, (1910) 86 Neb. 539, 126 N. W. 72; People v. Bloom, (1908) 193 N. Y. 1, 85 N. E. 824, 18 L. R. A. (n.s.) 898, 15 Ann. Cas. 932; Hoyt v. Hoyt, (1889) 112 N. Y. 493, 20 N. E. 402; *In re* Cashman's Will, (1936) 159 Misc. 881, 289 N. Y. S. 328, a'ffd. (1939) 280 N. Y. 681, 21 N. E. 2d 193; Harpman v. Devine, (1937) 133 Ohio St. 1, 10 N. E. 2d 776, 114 A. L. R. 789; Sumpter v. National Grocery Co., (1938) 194 Wash. 598, 78 P. 2d 1087, 116 A. L. R. 1166; Kiehlhoefer v. Washington Water Power Co., (1908) 49 Wash. 646, 96 Pac. 220; *In re* Will of Bruendl, (1899) 102 Wis. 45, 78 N. W. 169. For discussion of the policy of the privilege in the Province of Quebec and in France, see Mutual Life Ins. Co. v. Jeannotte-Lamarche, [1935] 59 K. B. (Quebec) 510.

2 Adraveno v. Mutual Reserve F. Life Ass'n., (1888) 34 Fed. 870; Schornick v. Schornick, (1923) 25 Ariz. 563, 220 Pac. 397, 31 A. L. R. 159; Metropolitan Life Ins. Co. v. Brubaker, (1908) 78 Kan. 146, 96 Pac. 62, 18 L. R. A. (n.s.) 362, 16 Ann. Cas. 267. It does not follow that because a rule is founded on public policy it, for that reason, cannot be waived. Milbourne v. Robison, (1908) 132 Mo. App. 198, 110 S. W. 598; *In re* Cashman's Will, (1936) 159 Misc. 881, 289 N. Y. S. 328, aff'd (1939) 280 N. Y. 681, 21 N. E. 2d 193.

3 Barton, J., in National Mut. Life Ass'n v. Godrich, [1909] 10 Comm. L. R. (Australia) 1, 21.

In justifying the attorney-client privilege, Shadwell, V. C., in Pearse v. Pearse, (1846) 1 DeGex & S. 12, 28, said: "Truth, like all other good things, may be loved unwisely—may be pursued too keenly—may cost too much. And surely the meanness and the mischief of prying into a man's confidential consultations with his legal adviser, the general evil of infusing reserve and dissimulation, uneasiness, and suspicion, and fear, into those communications which must take place, and which, unless in a condition of perfect security, must take place uselessly or worse, are too great a price to pay for truth itself."

Gilbert, J., in Edington v. Mut. Life Ins. Co., (1875) 5 Hun (N. Y.) 1, 11, expressed the same view with respect to the physician-patient privilege.

resulting from the exclusion of relevant and material medical testimony.[4] How much the theory is the result of observation and experience and how much the result of conjecture and sentiment, are matters upon which there is a wide difference of opinion.[5] Nevertheless, whether the policy of the privilege improves or impairs the administration of justice is a question which only the legislatures, not the courts, must decide. It may well be that the statute prevents the discovery of the true facts in a lawsuit and thereby thwarts justice; but it is for the legislature to amend or repeal the law.[6]

---

[4] Steinberg v. New York Life Ins. Co., (1933) 263 N. Y. 45, 49, 188 N. E. 152, 90 A. L. R. 642. William Laurie Co. v. McCullough, (1910) 174 Ind. 477, 483, 90 N. E. 1014, Ann. Cas. 1913 A 49: "The purposes of this statute are broader than the exigencies of any given lawsuit, and in the legislative judgment the considerations of public policy and the general advantage to mankind from the establishment of inviolable confidence between physician and patient outweigh the private interests of any particular litigant."

    Smart v. Kansas City, (1907) 208 Mo. 162, 184, 105 S. W. 709, 14 L. R. A. (n. s.) 565, 13 Ann. Cas. 932: "Such a rule may and doubtless does work a hardship and an injustice in many cases, but that is greatly overshadowed and outweighed by the benefits it brings to the human family at large and to society in general."

[5] See § 11, herein.

[6] Barton, J., in National Mut. Life Ass'n v. Godrich, [1909] 10 Comm. L. R. (Australia) 1, 21: "In considering the range of the subject matter to be protected the legislature had to weigh in the balance the danger to life and health, arising from the rigidity of the common law, against the loss of material testimony which must, often to the defeat of justice, result from its relaxation by Statute. They have done this duty, with the result, be it right or wrong in the main, that they have secured the safety of an immense range of confidences, and by so doing have necessarily impaired and in many cases prohibited the means of proof in a large class of forensic controversies. * * * It is not for us to say which view is the right one. That is for the legislators, because it is a matter of policy, and our exposition of the laws is not to be turned this way or that by our own opinions on such a matter. If in our view—I do not say it would be a correct view—the humane policy of holding confidences sacred has led the lawmakers to make inroads, fraught with possibilities of disaster, upon the administration of justice, it is their law and not ours, and if it is plain, as I think it is, we must declare and enforce it." See dissent of McGowen, J., in Killings v. Metropolitan Life Ins. Co., (1940) 187 Miss. 265, 192 So. 577, 131 A. L. R. 684. See also Connecticut Mut. Life Ins. Co. v. Union Trust Co., (1884) 112 U. S. 250, 28 Law. Ed. 708, 5 Su. Ct. 119; Tweith v. Duluth, M. and Iron Range Ry., (1946) 66 F. Supp. 427; Jones v. Caldwell, (1911) 20 Idaho 5, 116 Pac. 110, 48 L. R. A. (n. s.) 119; Ost v. Ulring, (1940) 207 Minn. 500, 292 N. W. 207; Hilary v. Minneapolis Street Ry., (1908) 104 Minn. 432, 116 N. W. 933; Provident Life & Acc. Ins. Co. v. Chapman, (1928) 152 Miss. 747, 118

≫→

11. Criticism of the Privilege

The main purpose of a judicial inquiry is to ascertain by rational means where the truth lies upon the issue of fact involved; and the policy of the law is to require the disclosure of all information by witnesses in order that justice may prevail. The primary object of all the laws of evidence, therefore, should be to bring the whole truth of a case before the court and jury. No thoughtful person will deny that the exclusion of relevant and important evidence—oftentimes the best evidence—presents a serious obstacle to the administration of justice. For how otherwise can justice be done unless the judgment rests upon truth, and truth alone? It seems strange, therefore, that a system of law designed to ascertain the truth, should embody rules which permit a litigant to withhold or shut out, at his option, material portions of it. Hence, a statute which prevents a physician, when lawfully summoned as a witness, from testifying to facts within his personal knowledge and relevant and material to the issue on trial, can only be justified by clear and convincing proof, based on reason and experience—not on sentiment or surmise—that the claimed advantage and benefits which may result to the general public from the shielding of confidences arising from the physician-patient relationship, far outweigh the harm and injustice which necessarily results to litigants from the concealment or suppression of the truth in actions in which the public has little or no concern.[1]

Throughout its history, the physician-patient privilege has been the subject of considerable discussion and, admittedly, much

---

←⤙⫸

So. 437; Record v. Saratoga Springs, (1887) 46 Hun 448, aff'd 120 N. Y. 646, 24 N. E. 1102; Weis v. Weis, (1947) 147 Ohio St. 416, 72 N. E. 2d 245, 169 A. L. R. 668; Harpman v. Devine, (1937) 133 Ohio St. 1, 10 N. E. 2d 776, 114 A. L. R. 789; Noelle v. Hoquiam Lumber & S. Co., (1907) 47 Wash. 519, 92 Pac. 372.

[1] Chafee, Is Justice Served or Obstructed by Closing the Doctor's Mouth on the Witness Stand? (1943) 52 Yale L. J. 607, 609: "Secrecy in court is prima facie calamitous, and it is permissible only when we are very sure that frankness will do more harm than good. With doctors' secrets as with any other kind of secrets, the only proper test is the welfare of the community. Courtroom secrecy in the particular case must produce a public good which more than offsets the risks resulting from the concealment of truth and from the lies which can be made with less fear of detection."

See also 8 Wigmore, Evidence, § 2285.

has been said in its favor. Unquestionably, the legislatures which adopted the privilege deemed it a wise one[2] and, as we have seen, many courts have justified its existence on the ground of public policy. But the public policy of one generation may not, under different conditions, be the public policy of another. "Things change, and times change, and men change." Experience, the most dependable of all teachers, has demonstrated that the hopes of the authors of the original statute[3] were illusive. No thoughtful judge or trial lawyer will deny that the privilege, in our day, is much abused. The law reports, federal and state, and the accumulated experience of judges and lawyers in the trial courts furnish ample evidence of this fact.[4] It is not surprising, therefore, that, in recent years, the voices of disapproval have become predominant. Judges, lawyers, textwriters, and teachers have severely criticized the privilege as having but little, if any, justification for its existence,[5] and of effecting great injury to the cause of justice by the concealment

---

[2] The fact, however, that England, Scotland, and most of the other jurisdictions of the British Commonwealth of Nations, as well as seventeen American jurisdictions, have never adopted the privilege, clearly indicates that its wisdom has not been universally apparent.

[3] See § 9, note 3, herein.

[4] Lamm, J., in Epstein v. Pennsylvania R. R., (1913) 250 Mo. 1, 40, 156 S. W. 699, 48 L. R. A. (n. s.) 394, Ann. Cas. 1915 A. 423: "The scandals in beating down the truth arising from a too harsh and literal interpretation of this law * * * every one of us knows by experience and observation in the courtroom."

　　See also Randa v. Bear, (1957) ......Wash....... , 312 P. 2d 640.

[5] Freedman, Medical Privilege, (1954) 32 Can. B. Rev. 1, 4; Duque, Privileged Communications Between Physician and Patient, (1953) 360 Ins. L. J. 19; Peterson, The Patient-Physician Privilege in Missouri, (1952) 20 U. of Kan. City L. Rev. 122, 136; Barnhart, Theory of Testimonial Competency and Privilege, (1950) 4 Ark. L. Rev. 377, 406; Lipscomb, Privileged Communications Statute—Sword and Shield, (1944) 16 Miss. L. J. 181; Chafee, infra note 1; Morgan, Suggested Remedy for Obstructions to Expert Testimony by Rules of Evidence, (1943) 10 U. of Chic. L. Rev. 285, 290; Welch, Another Anomaly—The Patient's Privilege, (1941) 13 Miss. L. J. 137; Curd, Privileged Communications Between the Doctor and his Patient, (1938) 44 W. Va. L. Q. 165; Present Status of Medical Privilege, (1933) 81 U. of Pa. L. Rev. 755; Purrington, An Abused Privilege, (1906) 6 Col. L. Rev. 388; Purrington, A Recent Case of Patient's "Privilege," (1907) 9 Bench and Bar 48; Bach, The Medico-Legal Aspect of Privileged Communications, (1892) 10 Medico-Leg. J. 33.

　　See also 8 Wigmore, Evidence, § 2380a. This is the best yet most severe of all criticisms.

and suppression of useful truth,[6] the disclosure of which ordinarily could harm no one.[7] In denouncing the privilege, some of these have characterized it as a "farce," "parody on justice," "misguided sentimentality," "sop," "instrument of injustice," "perversion of justice," "monumental hoax" and an "obstruction to the administration of justice." Wigmore has described it as "merely a clever legerdemain, loaned by the Law to the parties to suppress the truth,"[8] and two judges have regarded it as one which may oftentimes "cheat" rather than promote justice.[9]

It has been estimated that ninety percent of the litigation in which the privilege is invoked consists of three classes of cases: (a) actions on policies of life, accident or health insurance; (b) actions for damages for personal injury or for wrongful death; (c) testamentary actions where the mental competency of the testator is the principal issue. In nearly all of the cases, the testimony of the physician who attended the patient is generally the best and most reliable evidence. Nevertheless and notwithstanding, the patient, or the holder of the privilege may, at his option, close the door of all courts to the receipt of the physician's testimony no matter how much light it may throw upon the controversy, no matter how much logical connection it may have with the issue of fact to be proved or disproved.[10] In other words, as one court frankly stated,[11] the

---

[6] Greenleaf, Evidence, (16th ed. 1899) § 247a: "In all these cases, the medical testimony is 'the most vital and reliable', 'the most important and decisive,' and is absolutely needed for the purpose of learning the truth."

[7] Boyles v. Cora, (1942) 232 Iowa 822, 848, 6 N. W. 2d 401.

[8] 8 Wigmore, Evidence, § 2389.

[9] Start, C. J., in Olson v. The Court of Honor, (1907) 100 Minn. 117, 123, 110 N. W. 374, 8 L. R. A. (n. s.) 521, 10 Ann. Cas. 622; Owen, J., in Maine v. Maryland Cas Co., (1920) 172 Wis. 350, 359, 178 N. W. 749, 15 A. L. R. 1536.

[10] Travelers Ins. Co. v. Bergeron, (1928) 25 F. 2d 680, 683, Cert. denied, 278 U. S. 638, 73 Law. Ed. 553, 49 Su. Ct. 33; 58 A. L. R. 1127: "In many cases, it will close the door to the best possible evidence on the issue of fact presented for determination." Renihan v. Dennin, (1886) 103 N. Y. 573, 9 N. E. 320; Paxos v. Jarka Co., (1934) 314 Pa. 148, 171 Atl. 468.

It is interesting and very welcome to note that the legislatures of some states have amended their statutes so as to withdraw the privilege from operation in one or more of these classes of cases.

See also statutes of New Zealand and Victoria (Australia).

[11] Record v. Saratoga Springs, (1887) 46 Hun. 448, aff'd. 120 N. Y. 646, 24 N. E. 1102.

statute permits the holder of the privilege to use the testimony of the physician if he thinks the evidence will bolster his case, or exclude it if offered by his adversary, when he thinks it will weaken it. The question of dealing justly between the patient, or the holder of the privilege, and third parties is a secondary consideration.[12]

The principal reasons advanced in support of the privilege are not convincing. The traditional theory that a person suffering from a serious disease or painful injury will hesitate to confide in a physician unless he has complete assurance that his confidences cannot later be revealed by the physician[13] in some future litigation, has been thoroughly discredited and disproved.[14] The basic fallacy of the theory is that one must assume that the prospective patient knows all about the privilege and, specifically, the protection it affords. Of course, such an assumption is utterly unwarranted. There is not one patient in many thousands who knows anything about the privilege or has ever heard of it. It need not be remarked that unless the patient has some knowledge of the protection afforded by the privilege *before* he consults the physician, there can be no reliance upon it; therefore, it can have no effect whatever upon the patient's state of mind and can offer no inducement to him to freely and frankly reveal confidential information which

---

[12] Arizona & New Mexico Ry. v. Clark, (1915) 235 U. S. 669, 59 Law. Ed. 415, 35 Su. Ct. 210, L. R. A. 1915 C. 834; American Bankers' Ins. Co. v. Hopkins, (1917) 67 Okla. 150, 169 Pac. 489.

Some courts have lamented the fact that the privilege gives aid and comfort to unscrupulous litigants in many cases with the result that innocent persons are mulcted of large sums of money; nevertheless, "with face unmoved" and aware of the wrongs being perpetrated, they have enforced the statute to the point of rank absurdity. See Meyer v. Supreme Lodge, K. of P., (1904) 178 N. Y. 63, 70 N. E. 111, aff'd. 198 U. S. 508, 49 Law. Ed. 1146, 25 Su. Ct. 754, 64 L. R. A. 839; Harpman v. Devine, 133 Ohio St. 1, 10 N. E. 2d 776, 114 A. L. R. 789.

[13] The incongruity of the privilege is patent. If it be true that it is designed to encourage persons to consult freely their medical advisers, why, then, is it not extended to psychiatrists, nurses, Christian Science practitioners, and professional men engaged in specialized fields of medical science? Surely the secrets imparted to such persons engaged in the art of healing are often as intimate and sacred as those acquired by physicians engaged in the general practice of medicine. See Guttmacher and Weihofen, (1952) Psychiatry and the Law 271; Hayt, Hayt and Groeschel, (1952) Law of Hospital, Physician and Patient 640; Birkenhead, (1922) Points of View, Vol. 1, 70; Purrington, infra note 5, at 394.

[14] See articles and texts, infra note 5.

he would not otherwise disclose.[15] Furthermore, only a relatively small number of patients would shy at consulting a physician even t rough they knew that he might later be required to disclose their state of health or the nature and effect of their injuries in a court of law. It need hardly be mentioned that as compared with the numerous ailments which affect the human body, those which bring shame and disgrace to the sufferer are inconsiderable. Ordinarily, bodily injuries and disease are attended with neither humiliation nor disgrace and most of them are not kept secret even by the patients themselves, many of whom, if given the chance, being ready and willing to relate to their friends and relatives the details of their maladies, injuries, or surgical operations. In all the range of human ailments there is, perhaps, but one that the sufferer would be prone to conceal, and that is veneral disease. But even in the matter of this loathesome disease, the physician, in practically every state, is required by law to report such cases to the public health authorities where it may become a matter of public record. Nevertheless, experience has shown that even this fearsome but required publicity will not discourage patients from making a full disclosure of their symptoms and distress to their physicians.

Another and, perhaps, the most favored theory is that the injury to the relationship of physician and patient is greater than the injury to the cause of justice; that in the interests of the public health,[16] public policy demands that medical confidences be protected against disclosure. There is not a whit of evidence that the privilege tends to improve the public health.[17] On the other hand,

---

[15] Some courts have disapproved this view. People v. Stout, (1858) 3 Park. Cr. (N. Y.) 670, 679: "It is no valid objection to an application of this statute, that the prisoner [the alleged patient] did not probably know of its existence, and had no opinion whether or not the particulars of that interview would be privileged from disclosure. It is a sufficient answer that the salutary rule of law stands upon the statute book, and is to be dispensed alike to those familiar with or ignorant of its existence and applicability."

[16] Snyker v. Snyker, (1955) 245 Minn. 405, 407, 72 N. W. 2d 357: "This statutory shield is solely for the protection of the patient and is designed to promote health and not truth." See McCormick, Evidence, § 105.

[17] Morgan, Comments on the Proposed Code of Evidence, (1942) 20 Can. B. Rev. 271, 279; Ladd, A Modern Code of Evidence, (1942) 27 Iowa L. Rev. 213, 224; Morgan,

$\ggg\!\!\rightarrow$

there is abundant evidence that it undermines the very foundations of justice. The conjectural social policy behind such privilege is completely overborne by the injustices which too often result from the suppression of relevant and important evidence.[18] It need hardly be observed that the citizens of seventeen states in America and countless persons in the British Commonwealth of Nations freely consult their physicians with no assurance whatever that, should their state of health or their injuries become the subject of litigation, their confidences cannot be revealed by their physicians when relevant to the issues on trial; yet the level of public health in these jurisdictions has not, for lack of a physician-patient privilege, been lowered beyond that of other jurisdictions which have adopted it.[19] Furthermore, no one would contend that the progress of medical science in the great hospitals and medical schools in Baltimore, Boston, and Chicago, for example, has been retarded because their patients do not have the protection of the privilege. Patients attend these renowned institutions not to bring damage suits but to seek medical advice and treatment, and the lack of a physician-patient privilege does not deter a single one of them from disclosing to the physicians and surgeons their most intimate confidences or submitting their naked bodies for examination.

In the vast majority of the reported cases where the privilege has been claimed, the patient or the party objecting to the testimony of the attending physician, did not invoke the privilege in order to protect the patient's right to privacy or to prevent the disclosure of matters which would humiliate or disgrace the patient;[20] rather his

---

Some Observations Concerning a Model Code of Evidence, (1940) 89 U. of Pa. L. Rev. 145, 151.

[18] Larson, C. J., in Clawson v. Walgreen Drug Co., (1945) 108 Utah 577, 602, 162 P. 2d 759.

[19] Morgan, infra note 5 at 291.

[20] Fowler, J., in Prudential Ins. Co. v. Kozlowski, (1938) 226 Wis. 641, 644, 276 N. W. 300: "The reason of the rule, as far as it has any, is that the patients may be afflicted with diseases or have vicious or uncleanly habits necessary for a physician to know in order to treat them properly, disclosure of which would subject them to humiliation, shame or disgrace, and which they might refrain from disclosing to a physician if the physician could be compelled to disclose them on the witness stand. If the disclosures

primary motive was to use the privilege as a procedural device for the single purpose of winning a lawsuit by excluding relevant and material evidence which, were it admitted, would tend to reduce, if not defeat, his chances for a verdict in his favor.[21] The accumulated experience of many decades shows that the privilege has accomplished little but the concealment and suppression of the truth. When a party voluntarily puts in issue his state of health or his bodily injury and discloses the details thereof to serve his own pecuniary ends, any good and sufficient reason for maintaining the silence of the physician no longer obtains. A patient may keep the door of the sick-room closed, but he should not be permitted to open it so as to give an imperfect or false view of what took place there, and promptly shut the door the moment the true facts are about to be revealed. It is a monstrous thing to permit a party to fabricate evidence for himself in this class of cases, and then deny his adversary the right to resort to the only reliable means to elicit the truth. Nevertheless, the law reports are filled with cases where such miscarriages of justice have occurred.[22]

←—◃◃◃

to the physician be such as not to subject the patient to shame or affect his reputation or social standing, there is no reason why a physician should not disclose them, and sound reason why in the interest of truth and justice he should be compelled to disclose them. The physician's exemption from disclosure should in reason be limited to such disclosures as would injure the patient's feelings or reputation."

[21] Purrington, A Recent Case of Patient's Privilege, (1907) 9 Bench and Bar 48, 52: "What is there indelicate or of a nature to humiliate a patient claiming damages for defective vision or a broken leg, or any other injury displayed in evidence, in proving that the condition attributed to a recent accident was of long standing? Such a disclosure might show that the litigation was dishonest; but the physician's testimony * * * would not be in itself humiliating or disgraceful, or reveal any secret except that the injury exhibited as new was in fact old."

Peterson, infra note 5, at 137: "Perhaps the only embarrassment or humiliation which might arise in the ordinary case where the privilege is claimed is that which would arise from the failure to prove a case as pleaded."

[22] Some judges and text writers have unsparingly denounced the abuse of the privilege. Thurman, J., in Dahlquist v. Denver & Rio G. R. R., (1918) 52 Utah 438, 454, 174 Pac. 833: "The whole proceeding, in the opinion of the writer, to say the least, was a perversion of justice, if not an absolute travesty. It was anything but even-handed justice. It was not a square deal, and * * * it was using as a sword against his adversary the privilege which was merely intended for his own protection. If this is the meaning and extent of the statute under which the privilege is claimed, the sooner the statute is re-

⟫⟫→

In the few instances where an honest patient does dread disclosure of his state of health by the physician, his real and most
distressing fear is not that the physician may some day be compelled
to disclose the truth in a court of law, but that he will voluntarily
reveal the facts to some friend or relative on the street or in his club,
or that the physician may make his affliction the subject of an
article in some medical journal or of an address before a group of
medical men. Yet the physician-patient privilege affords him no
protection against this possible danger.[23]

But there are hopeful signs of better things to come. The
mounting waves of protest are inexorably beating down the worn-
out theories which hitherto have sustained the whole policy of
testimonial privilege. The manifest destiny of the laws of evidence
is a lowering of the barriers which have held back the truth.[24] Perhaps the physician-patient privilege is on the way out. It is ironical
indeed that much of the pressure operating against the privilege
is being exerted by the very legislatures which enacted it. They
have all but cancelled out the intended benefits of the statute. Most
of the medical confidences they once saw fit to preserve inviolate
are now required by them to be reported by physicians, and some-

---

pealed the better it will be for the administration of justice."
8 Wigmore, Evidence, § 2389: "The privilege under those circumstances becomes a
burlesque upon logic and justice."

Nelson v. Ackermann, (1957) .... Minn. ...., 83 N. W. 2d 500, 506: "Instead of
accomplishing the purpose for which it was originally intended, the privilege has been
so far corrupted today that it is used, at least in personal injury cases, for the most part
for suppression of the truth."

[23] That this danger is not fanciful can be proved by several reported cases where physicians and hospitals made extra-judicial disclosures, or exhibitions of their patients' ailments or physical imperfections under circumstances constituting an unwarranted invasion of their rights to privacy. See Bazemore v. Savannah Hospital, (1930) 171 Ga.
257, 155 S. E. 194; DeMay v. Roberts, (1881) 46 Mich. 160, 9 N. W. 146; Sullings v.
Shakespeare, (1881) 46 Mich. 408, 9 N. W. 451; Feeney v. Young, (1920) 191 App. Div.
501, 181 N. Y. S. 481; Griffin v. Medical Society, (1939) 11 N. Y. S. 2d 109; Clayman v.
Bernstein, (1940) 38 Pa. D. & C. 543.

[24] McCormick, The Scope of Privilege in the Law of Evidence, (1938) 16 Tex. L. Rev.
447, 469. Judge Jerome Frank has recommended abolition of most of the exclusionary
rules of evidence except those relating to self-incrimination and to evidence obtained
by unlawful search and seizure. Frank, (1949) Courts on Trial 422. See also De Parcq,
The Uniform Rules of Evidence, (1956) 40 Minn. L. Rev. 301, 322-327.

times by hospitals, to the public health authorities and, on some occasions, to particular persons who are likely to come in contact with their patients; moreover, some of these reports are made a matter of public record. It should be noted also that not only is the physician required to report such information but, in many cases, he can be compelled to testify and relate the facts and his conclusions thereon.[25] In most of the states, physicians are now required by law to prepare and file for public record certificates of death which state the causes of death and whether they are accidental, homicidal, or suicidal. In some states the legislatures have enacted laws which require drunken operators of automobiles to submit to blood, saliva, and urine tests; and some compel prostitutes to submit to physical examinations for venereal disease. In a number of states, the legislatures have authorized the courts to appoint physicians to examine and to testify on the mental condition of persons suspected of feeblemindedness or insanity, or of being sexual psychopaths; and there are many more such laws.

As a result of the astounding change in the attitude of the legislatures, there are today few medical confidences that can really be kept secret except, of course, in a court of law where justice cries out for the facts. But why, we ask, should they be protected there? Honest patients have little to fear for they will not hide the truth, whether the privilege exists or not. Except in rare cases, only the dishonest litigant will attempt to shut out truth. It is high time to abolish the physician-patient privilege, but this may not be possible within a reasonable length of time.[26] Perhaps the best solution is to amend the statute along the lines of that of North Carolina.[27] Honest patients will be protected, the dishonest ones exposed.

---

[25] De Witt, Medical Ethics and the Law: the Conflict Between Dual Allegiances, (1953) 5 Western Res. L. Rev. 5, 8.

[26] Welch, infra note 5 at 163: "To repeal the statute entirely would be an almost impossible task for the reason that, at first blush, the statute appeals to those who are uninitiated and unfamiliar with the harm that can flow from such a statutory exemption."

[27] See Appendix, herein.

CHAPTER V

Nature of the Privilege

12. *Statute Relates to Introduction of Evidence*

The statute does not create a rule of substantive law;[1] it is simply a rule of evidence.[2] As we have pointed out earlier, the purpose of the statute is to prevent, within certain limits, any lawful

---

[1] Metropolitan Life Ins. Co. v. McSwain, (1928) 149 Miss. 455, 115 So. 555; New Orleans & N. E. R. R. v. Jackson, (1926) 145 Miss. 702, 110 So. 586.

[2] Connecticut Mut. Life Ins. Co. v. Union Trust Co., (1884) 112 U. S. 250, 28 Law Ed. 708, 5 Su. Ct. 119; Doll v. Equitable Life Assur Soc., (1905) 138 Fed. 705; American Republic Life Ins. Co. v. Edenfield, (1957) _____Ark._____, 306 S. W. 2d 321; Hamilton v. P. E. Johnson & Sons, (1938) 224 Iowa 1097, 276 N. W. 841; Bruington v. Wagoner, (1917) 100 Kan. 10, 164 Pac. 1057; New York Life Ins. Co. v. Newman, (1945) 311 Mich. 368, 18 N. W. 2d 859; Dick v. International Congress, (1904) 138 Mich. 372, 101 N. W. 564; Bernard v. Doctor Nelson Co., (1913) 123 Minn. 468, 143 N. W. 1133; Yazoo & M. V. R. R. v. Decker, (1928) 150 Miss. 621, 116 So. 287; Metropolitan Life Ins Co. v. McSwain, (1928) 149 Miss. 455, 115 So. 555; New Orleans & N. E. R. R. v. Jackson, (1926) 145 Miss. 702, 110 So. 586; Homnyack v. Prudential Ins. Co., (1909) 194 N. Y. 456, 87 N. E. 769; Hoyt v. Hoyt, (1889) 112 N. Y. 493, 20 N. E. 402; John Hancock Mut. Life Ins. Co. v. Jennings, (1934) 17 Ohio Law Abst. 583; State v. Miller, (1919) 105 Wash. 475, 178 Pac. 459; Isaacs, J., in National Mut. Life Ass'n. v. Godrich, [1909] 10 Comm. L. R. (Australia) 1, 34.

tribunal being made the instrument to violate the confidence which a patient has reposed in his medical adviser. Although the medical profession's code of ethics prohibits a physician voluntarily disclosing confidential information to any one, the statute does not. The statute itself relates solely to the *introduction of evidence,* and not to disclosures in any other way. It merely prohibits the physician revealing, without the consent of the patient, confidential communications or information in a court of law, or in some proceeding where he is a witness under oath.[3] The form in which the statements are sought to be introduced is of no consequence, whether as a witness on the stand or through the medium of an affidavit, an office record, or a document. All are equally under the ban of the statute.[4] Likewise, the recordings of privileged matters in the patient's hospital chart and records are inadmissible.[5] And since the physician is prohibited from disclosing the information, it follows necessarily that he cannot introduce in evidence his *opinion* based upon the knowledge acquired in the course of his professional employment. He is no more at liberty to give an opinion based upon such knowledge than he is to detail the facts revealed to him by the patient.[6]

---

[3] The privilege also extends to an examination *before* trial. Woernley v. Electromatic Typewriters, Inc., (1936) 271 N. Y. 228, 2 N. E. 2d 638; Lorde v. Guardian Life Ins. Co., (1937) 252 App. Div. 646, 300 N. Y. S. 721; *In re* Meyer's Estate, (1954) 206 Misc. 368, 132 N. Y. S. 2d 825.

The law is quite clear that the privilege conferring confidentiality upon communications between attorney and client relates only to a privilege *against testimonial compulsion.*

Lanza v. New York State Joint Legislative Committee, (1957) 3 App. Div. 2d 531, 162 N. Y. S. 2d 467; Erlich v. Erlich, (1951) 278 App. Div. 244, 104 N. Y. S. 2d 531.

In the Lanza case, the court held that even though the wiring of the consultation room and the transcribing of a conversation between the prisoner and his attorney was grossly improper, a legislative committee had the right to make public the same since its investigation involved no testimony coming within the protection of the statutory privilege.

[4] Davis v. Supreme Lodge, K. of H., (1900) 165 N. Y. 159, 58 N. E. 891; Buffalo Loan, Trust & Safe Dep. Co. v. Knights Templar & M. M. A. Ass'n., (1891) 126 N. Y. 450, 27 N. E. 942.

[5] Matter of New York City Council v. Goldwater, (1940) 284 N. Y. 296, 31 N. E. 2d 31, 133 A. L. R. 728. See § 64, herein.

[6] United States v. Witbeck, (1940) 113 F. 2d 185; Triangle Lumber Co. v. Acree,

13. *Statute Creates No Positive Prohibition:* *The Patient May Forego Its Protection*

The competency of witnesses is largely controlled by the statutes in that regard. Generally speaking, competency is the rule; incompetency the exception. The statutes which grant testimonial privileges deal only with particular classes of persons whose confidential relationships, in the opinion of the legislatures, require protection from disclosure in court or in some other lawful proceeding. Such statutes, however, *do not disqualify absolutely* such persons as witnesses, but only certain of their testimony. It is not the inherent incompetency of the evidence that precludes it being given, but it is the fact that the evidence comes from a person who occupied a certain relation of confidence to another, by virtue of which the statute says he shall not disclose his information without the consent of the person from whom he obtained it.[1]

Notwithstanding the ostensible prohibitory form of most of the statutes,[2] the courts uniformly have held that such statutes do

---

(1914) 112 Ark. 534, 166 S. W. 958, Ann. Cas. 1916 B. 773; Thompson v. Ish, (1889) 99 Mo. 160, 12 S. W. 510; People v. Murphy, (1886) 101 N. Y. 126, 4 N. E. 326.

The Minnesota and Louisiana statutes expressly prohibit the physician from giving an opinion based on information acquired in his professional capacity.

[1] Metropolitan Life Ins. Co. v. McSwain, (1928) 149 Miss. 455, 115 So. 555; May v. Northern Pac. Ry., (1905) 32 Mont. 522, 81 Pac. 328, 70 L. R. A. 111, 4 Ann. Cas. 605; Milbourne v. Robison, (1908) 132 Mo. App. 198, 203, 110 S. W. 598: "There is a distinction between competent evidence and a competent witness. The evidence may be relevant and applicable to the matter under investigation, but the source through which it is offered may be objectionable and non-competent."

Wells v. New England Mut. Life Ins. Co., (1898) 187 Pa. 166, 169, 40 Atl. 802: "It is the physician, attending a patient, who is prohibited from testifying to information acquired while rendering professional service. * * * No other person who being present at the time when the information was communicated, and heard the same, would be prevented by this act from testifying to the very matter in question. It is only the physician himself who is prohibited, and that is manifestly on account of the professional relation between himself and his patient."

[2] Examples are: "a physician shall not testify * * * "; "physicians cannot be witnesses * * *"; "a physician cannot be examined * * *"; "physicians shall be incompetent to testify * * *"; "physician shall not divulge any communication * * *"; "no physician shall be allowed to disclose * * *"; "a physician shall not be required to disclose * * *"; "physicians shall be protected from testifying as to * * *"; "no physician may be compelled to declare what has been revealed to him * * *."

not make the physician *absolutely incompetent* as a witness in any and all cases in which the patient, in some manner, may be involved. Furthermore, they do not forbid absolutely the introduction in evidence of the confidential matters they were designed to protect from disclosure, but merely grant to the patient a privilege, or right of choice, which entitles him to elect whether such evidence shall be introduced or excluded at the trial. That is a matter over which he has full and complete control.[3] The secrecy imposed upon the medical man by the statute is for the benefit and protection of the patient only; hence, if he consents to the disclosure of confidential matters, no one can insist upon their exclusion.[4] What possible interest can the public have in the exclusion of relevant testimony of the physician, or the records of a hospital, respecting the physical condition of a private individual, when he himself chooses to make public the nature and effect of his malady or injury?[5] It is manifest, therefore, that the statute creates no absolute prohibition,[6] but simply grants a privilege, or option, which the patient may exercise or not as he sees fit.[7] To hold otherwise would, in many cases, result in thwarting justice without subserving the purpose of the statute.[8]

---

[3] Davenport v. State, (1926) 143 Miss. 121, 108 So. 433, 45 A. L. R. 1348; Hoyt v. Cornwall Hospital, (1938) 169 Misc. 361, 6 N. Y. S. 2d 1014.

[4] One must keep clearly in mind the difference between a rule of absolute incompetency and a rule of privilege, whereby the incompetency may be insisted upon or waived by the person in whose favor it exists. Rules of privilege such as those applicable to the relationship of husband and wife, priest and penitent, attorney and client, are examples both of partial and of optional incompetency. See Rowley, The Competency of Witnesses, (1939) 24 Iowa L. Rev. 482, 493.

[5] Adraveno v. Mutual Reserve Fund Life Ass'n., (1888) 34 Fed. 870; Metropolitan Life Ins. Co. v. Brubaker, (1908) 78 Kan. 146, 96 Pac. 62, 18 L. R. A. (n. s.) 362, 16 Ann. Cas. 267.

[6] Hier v. Farmers Mut. Fire Ins. Co., (1937) 104 Mont. 471, 67 P. 2d 831, 110 A. L. R. 1051.

There appears to be but one case which holds that a patient is absolutely prohibited from introducing the testimony of his attending physician as to matters within the scope of the privilege. See Harriman v. Stowe, (1874) 57 Mo. 93. Later cases have ignored this decision.

[7] Schornick v. Schornick, (1923) 25 Ariz. 563, 220 Pac. 397, 31 A. L. R. 159; Stayner v. Nye, (1949) 227 Ind. 231, 85 N. E. 2d 496; Penn Mut. Life Ins. Co. v. Wiler, (1884) 100

》》》→

It may be proper here to point out that, as a general rule, the physician is only prohibited from testifying as to any communications made to him, or to facts learned by him, in the discharge of his professional duties, where they are of a confidential nature and necessary and proper to enable him to prescribe for, or treat, the patient. There are, of course, a variety of facts to which the physician may properly testify without violating the protected secrecy of the sick room or trespassing upon the patient's right to privacy.[9]

14. *Legislature May Modify or Withhold Privilege*

Inasmuch as the privilege is a statutory one, the legislators, at any time, may modify it, or, if in their judgment the interests and welfare of the public would be better served, they can withhold it altogether. In doing so, the legislature does not encroach upon any vested right of an individual and has in no sense taken anything away.[1] No person has a vested right in a rule of evidence. It per-

Ind. 92; Davenport v. Hannibal, (1891) 108 Mo. 471, 18 S. W. 1122; Hoyt v. Hoyt, (1889) 112 N. Y. 493, 20 N. E. 402.

[8] Broaddus, J., in Webb v. Metropolitan Street Ry., (1901) 89 Mo. App. 604, 608: "There never was any question but what a physician, as such, was prohibited from disclosing information obtained while he was treating his patients; and this prohibition, if the statute be literally construed, would exclude him from being a witness on behalf of his patient. But the courts hold that the statute must be construed in the sense as that intended by the Legislature which framed the law; and to hold that the patient was not to have the benefit of the evidence of the person who knew most about his affliction, would be absurd, and would be doing violence to the intention of the legislature. It was, therefore, held that the patient might waive the privilege of the statute in order to obtain the benefit of the physician's evidence."

[9] Kirkpatrick v. Milks, (1950) 257 Wis. 549, 44 N. W. 2d 574. These matters will be discussed in subsequent chapters.

[1] Randolph v. Supreme Liberty Life Ins. Co., (1949) 359 Mo. 251, 221 S. W. 2d 155; Matter of New York City Council v. Goldwater, (1940) 284 N. Y. 296, 31 N. E. 2d 31, 133 A. L. R. 728; McGrath v. State, (1950) 200 Misc. 165, 104 N. Y. S. 2d 882; Bozicevich v. Kenilworth Mercantile Co., (1921) 58 Utah 458, 199 Pac. 406, 17 A. L. R. 346; Wilhelm v. Order of Columbian Knights, (1912) 149 Wis. 585, 136 N. W. 160.

Marshall, C. J., in Spitzer v. Stillings, (1924) 109 Ohio St. 297, 302, 142 N. E. 365: "A rule of evidence seldom ripens into a right of property, and this is necessarily true of the so-called privileged communication between attorney and client. It is in any event clearly a matter of policy, and within the power of legislators to change or even abrogate entirely."

tains to the remedy only and is subject to modification and control by the legislature.[2]

It is well established that the legislature may change a rule of evidence even though such change affects pending actions;[3] therefore, unless expressly declared otherwise,[4] an amendatory act applies as well to cases pending, and to causes of action existing at the date of its taking effect, as to future cases and causes of action.[5] Accordingly, it has been held that when at the time the action was brought a witness would have been incompetent, but an amendatory law in force at the time of trial makes him competent, the amendatory law governs the question.[6]

---

[2] People v. Braun, (1910) 246 Ill. 428, 92 N. E. 917; Wheelock v. Myers, (1902) 64 Kan. 47, 67 Pac. 632; Gile v. Hudnutt, (1937) 279 Mich. 358, 272 N. W. 706; Maki v. Mohawk Mining Co., (1913) 176 Mich. 497, 142 N. W. 780; Matter of Grand Jury of County of Kings, (1955) 286 App. Div. 270, 143 N. Y. S. 2d 501, appeal denied 309 N. Y. 1031; Bozicevich v. Kenilworth Mercantile Co., (1921) 58 Utah 458, 199 Pac. 406, 17 A. L. R. 346.

[3] In re Patterson's Estate, (1909) 155 Cal. 626, 102 Pac. 941, 26 L. R. A. (n. s.) 654; Wilhelm v. Order of Columbian Knights, (1912) 149 Wis. 585, 136 N. W. 160.

[4] Bartlett, J., in Homnyack v. Prudential Ins. Co., (1909) 194 N. Y. 456, 460, 87 N. E. 769: "Where an existing statute is amended as to leave it in full force and effect so far as it goes, and the only amendment consists in the addition of new matter, a limitation in the amendatory statute providing that such statute shall not affect pending suits or proceedings qualifies only the addition which is made to the pre-existing law by the amendatory statute and does not qualify or limit the pre-existing general law itself."

[5] Westerman v. Westerman, (1874) 25 Ohio St. 500. (husband-wife privilege)

[6] Moreno v. New Guadalupe Mining Co., (1918) 35 Cal. App. 744, 170 Pac. 1088; John v. Bridgman, (1875) 27 Ohio St. 22. In Parker v. United States, (1956) 235 F. 2d 21, the defendant appealed from a conviction for a robbery committed in May, 1955. Trial was had in November 1955, and insanity was asserted as a defense. A physician who had treated the defendant both before and after the crime, testified for the government regarding the defendant's mental condition. The Court of Appeals held that the statute which forbids physicians to disclose confidential information did not apply since an amendment thereto, effective August 9, 1955, makes the prohibition in applicable in criminal trials when the accused raises the defense of insanity. In Matter of Boyle's Will, (1955) 208 Misc. 942, 145 N. Y. S. 2d 386, counsel for the proponent in a will contest made a motion to strike out the testimony of the attending physician of the testatrix on the ground of privilege. The Surrogate reserved his ruling on the motion. Subsequently, the Legislature amended the statute and the Surrogate ruled, in accordance therewith, that the evidence was admissible and denied the motion notwithstanding the fact that if a ruling had been made at the time of the physician's testimony, the motion would have been granted.

15. *Privilege Violates No Constitutional Right*

In several cases, the constitutionality of the statute has been questioned. Litigants have claimed that when it is construed so as to permit the patient to call as a witness one of his attending physicians whose testimony is favorable to the patient's version of the case, yet prohibits his adversary from introducing the testimony of another physician who also treated the patient, the statute has the effect of being more than a rule of evidence; that such a construction affects the substantive rights of the adversary, denies him a hearing of his cause on its merits, and is, therefore, violative of the 14th Amendment of the Constitution of the United States. Although one judge has twice expressed some doubt upon the question,[1] the Supreme Court of Mississippi has held that the statute works no abridgement of any substantial right, no invasion of liberty or property, and does not deprive a litigant of due process or the equal protection of the law as guaranteed him by the 14th Amendment of the Federal Constitution.[2]

16. *Privilege Not for Benefit of Physician,*
or Adverse Party

It is plain that the privilege is for the sole benefit of the patient, whose interests, reputation, and sensibilities may be injured and outraged by the disclosure of his bodily ailments or imperfections. The fact that the physician obtained the information in order to prescribe for or treat the patient cannot affect the physician in the least degree unfavorably, nor that he should be compelled to reveal

---

[1] Anderson, J., in Keeton v. State, (1936) 175 Miss. 631, 649, 167 So. 68: "The decisions of our court to the contrary, the writer thinks, ought to be overruled; the construction they put upon the statute comes dangerously near, in a civil case, violating, if it does not actually do so, the equal protection clause of the Federal Constitution."

Anderson, J., in Killings v. Metropolitan Life Ins. Co., (1940) 187 Miss. 265, 274, 192 So. 577, 131 A. L. R. 684: "How far may a statute of this kind go and not come into conflict with the constitutional requirements of due process?"

[2] Yazoo & M. V. R. R. v. Decker, (1928) 150 Miss. 621, 116 So. 287. The proffered testimony of the physician, called as defendant's witness, bore upon the main issue of liability.

New Orleans & N. E. R. R. v. Jackson, (1926) 145 Miss. 702, 110 So. 586; Brookhaven Lumber & M. Co. v. Adams, (1923) 132 Miss. 689, 97 So. 484. In these two cases, the proffered testimony of the physician related to plaintiff's alleged injury.

as a witness the information or knowledge thus acquired. Manifestly, the purpose of the privilege is to protect the patient, to whom protection is so important, and not the physician, to whom it is quite unimportant, from the consequences of such disclosure.[1] The well-established and common sense view is that if the patient consents to his physician making the disclosure, or if the patient, expressly or by implication, waives the privilege,[2] the physician must answer and reveal the confidential information that is sought. The statute gives him no right to refuse to testify and creates no absolute incompetency under such circumstances.[3] Moreover, if he persists in his refusal, he may be adjudged in contempt of court.[4]

It must be noted, however, that several courts have held that the privilege is one which the physician himself may claim even though the patient is in court and consents to the disclosure of his

---

[1] Harpman v. Devine, (1937) 133 Ohio St. 1, 5, 10 N. E. (2d) 776, 114 A. L. R. 789; Markham v. Hipke, (1919) 169 Wis. 37, 171 N. W. 300; Boyle v. Northwestern Mut. Relief Ass'n., (1897) 95 Wis. 312, 70 N. W. 351. A physician cannot, for his own purpose, invoke the privilege in order to prevent disclosure of a patient's name, address and telephone number which appeared in the physician's records. Wolf v. People, (1947) 117 Colo. 279, 187 P. 2d 926.

See also Jones v. Jones, (1955) 208 Misc. 721, 144 N. Y. S. 2d 820.

[2] The patient's waiver may be express, or may be implied from his conduct, whether, in fact, he be willing to waive or not. See c. XVIII, herein.

[3] City and County of San Francisco v. Superior Court, (1951) 37 Cal. 2d 227, 231 P. 2d 26, 25 A. L. R. 2d 1418; Valensin v. Valensin, (1887) 73 Cal. 106, 14 Pac. 397; Penn Mut. Life Ins. Co. v. Wiler, (1884) 100 Ind. 92; State v. Knight, (1927) 204 Iowa 819, 216 N. W. 104; Doty v. Crystal Ice & Fuel Co., (1925) 118 Kan. 323, 235 Pac. 96; Harvey v. Silber, (1942) 300 Mich. 510, 2 N. W. 2d 483; Lincoln v. Detroit, (1894) 101 Mich. 245, 59 N. W. 617; Wells v. Jefferson, (1939) 345 Mo. 239, 132 S. W. 2d 1006; Foerstel v. St. Louis Public Service Co., (1951) |... Mo. App......, 241 S. W. 2d 792; Cromeenes v. Sovereign Camp W. of W., (1920) 205 Mo. App. 419, 224 S. W. 15; Hier v. Farmers Mut. Fire Ins. Co., (1937) 104 Mont. 471, 67 P. 2d 831, 110 A. L. R. 1051; Trieber v. New York & Queens County Ry., (1912) 149 App. Div. 804, 134 N. Y. S. 267; Zimmer v. Third Ave. R. R., (1899) 36 App. Div. 265, 55 N. Y. S. 308; Waldron v. State, (1948) 193 Misc. 113, 82 N. Y. S. 822. 8 Wigmore, Evidence, § 2386.

See interesting discussion of the question in Mutual Life Ins. Co. v. Lamarche, [1935] Quebec Rep. 59 K. B. 510.

The legislature of Washington (1951 Rev. Code, § 10.52.020) has granted to "regular physicians" a *personal* privilege in criminal actions from testifying "as to confessions, or information received from any defendant, by virtue of their profession and character." See State v. Miller, (1919) 105 Wash. 475, 178 Pac. 459.

[4] Markham v. Hipke, (1919) 169 Wis. 37, 171 N. W. 300.

medical confidences or makes no objection to questions which elicit them from the physician-witness.[5] It is respectfully submitted that these courts have misconceived entirely the purpose of the statute. The whole history of the privilege is opposed to such construction.[6]

It will be noted also that the privilege cannot be availed of by the patient's adversary; for the evidence may be received with the consent of the patient.[7] In *Hoyt* v. *Cornwall Hospital*,[8] a former patient claimed she had contracted syphilis as a result of the hospital's negligence. To aid her in preparing her complaint, she moved, before trial, for the production of the hospital's records of her case. In granting her motion, the court held that since the patient herself saw fit to make public the records, the hospital could not refuse to divulge the information on the ground that its disclosure was prohibited by the statute.[9]

A number of courts have held that after the death of the patient, a person expressly authorized by the statute to waive the patient's privilege may introduce the testimony of the deceased's physician notwithstanding an objection by the adverse party that the matters sought to be revealed are prohibited from disclosure.[10]

---

[5] In Blackwell v. Seattle, (1917) 97 Wash. 679, 167 Pac. 53, the defendant called the plaintiff's physician as a witness and sought to elicit confidential information. Plaintiff's counsel said the matter was privileged but if the doctor desired to violate the confidence, plaintiff would not object. The court advised the witness that if he felt he was violating a professional confidence, he had the right to refuse to testify. The witness declined to disclose the information sought. In affirming the judgment for plaintiff, Mount, J., (p. 683) : "[the statute] provides that no physician shall be examined as a witness without the consent of his patient. No consent is given here, and clearly it was not the duty of the court to have required the doctor to testify under the circumstances." The decision is questionable. In Darling v. Pacific Elec. Ry., (1925) 197 Cal.702, 242 Pac. 703, the physician-witness was permitted to claim the privilege for his patient who was not a party and not present at the trial.

[6] See § 130, herein. See also 8 Wigmore, Evidence, § 2386.

[7] Olson v Court of Honor, (1907) 100 Minn. 117, 110 N. W. 374, 8 L. R. A. (n. s.) 521, 10 Ann. Cas. 622. In an action for divorce, defendant cannot, by objection, exclude testimony of plaintiff's physician who testified at plaintiff's request. McCarthy v. McCarthy, (1921) 116 Wash. 360, 199 Pac. 733. See § 13 herein.

[8] (1938) 169 Misc. 361, 6. N. Y. S. 2d 1014. See also *In re* Greenberg's Estate, (1949) 196 Misc. 809, 89 N. Y. S. 2d 807.

[9] See § 64, herein.

[10] Unionaid Life Ins. Co. v. Bank of Dover, (1936) 192 Ark. 123, 90 S. W. 2d 982; Olson

Manifestly, the privilege is granted in deference to the private feelings of the patient, and in deference to the sensibilities of the members of his family. Other litigants have no concern in the supposed indelicacy of exposing such private matters to public hearing.[11] Moreover, it has been held that in an action against the State for damages arising out of an assault committed against the plaintiff by an inmate of a State hospital, the State cannot invoke the privilege of the assailant and thus prevent the plaintiff from introducing the hospital records of the assailant which showed that the hospital's physicians, who made them, well knew of his violent and assaultive disposition.[12]

It is quite generally conceded that a defendant in a prosecution for crime has no right to claim the protection of his victim's privilege and thus exclude relevant and important evidence which the State seeks to elicit from the victim's physician. No confidential

---

← v. The Court of Honor, (1907) 100 Minn. 117, 110 N. W. 374, 8 L. R. A. (n. s.) 521, 10 Ann. Cas. 622; Hier v. Farmers Mut. Fire Ins. Co., (1937) 104 Mont. 471, 67 P. 2d 831, 110 A. L. R. 1051; Matter of Warrington, (1951) 303 N. Y. 129, 100 N. E. 2d 170. See § 89, herein.

[11] Chaffee v. Kaufman, (1923) 113 Kan. 254, 214 Pac. 618. In Waldron v. State, (1948) 193 Misc. 113, 82 N. Y. S. 2d 822, the administrator sued the State for the wrongful death of a prisoner and moved, before trial, to examine the State's medical men who had attended the deceased. The State objected on the ground that their information was privileged under the statute. In granting plaintiff's motion Greenberg, J., (p. 116) said: "The State's interest in now claiming the privilege is not to protect the memory or confidences of the deceased patient, but solely to erect a barrier in the path of his estate to recover damages for the State's negligence. The State cannot claim the privilege in behalf of its physicians and dentists in view of the waiver by the claimant, for the privilege is that of the patient and not that of the physician."

See also § 89, herein.

[12] Scolavino v. State, (1946) 187 Misc. 253, 62 N. Y. S. 2d 17; modified as to damages, 271 App. Div. 618, 67 N. Y. S. 2d 202; aff'd. as modified, 297 N. Y. 460, 74 N. E. 2d 174. Lounsburg, J, (187 Misc. 253, 259) : "It is difficult to view the position of the State on this issue as other than unconscionable. The State, as defendant, seeks, as physician, to invoke a privilege asserted to belong to its patient, J. B. [the assailant] in order to exclude clearly relevant evidence reflecting on the care given by it to another patient, M. S. [the plaintiff] It does not do this to protect, J. B., but to protect itself. Surely the privilege afforded communications between physician and patient was never intended to be used in this manner. In this case the evidence is chiefly within the control of the State and its employees. If important portions thereof can be excluded on the ground of privilege, the State enjoys an advantage over private litigants which is unjust and indefensible."

relation exists between physician and the accused; hence, no privilege exists.[13] In *Davenport* v. *State*,[14] the defendant was convicted of manslaughter. Physicians who had attended the victim testified for the State, over objection by the defendant, as to the nature of his wound, treatment given, and the cause of his death. There was no evidence showing consent or waiver of the privilege by the victim. A majority of the court held that the defendant could not claim the privilege of the victim; therefore, the testimony of the physicians was admissible.[15]

17. Privilege Applies Also to Patient's Testimony

Since the privilege is intended for the protection of the patient in his subjective freedom of consultation, it would be utterly ineffectual if the disclosure of the confidences, though not compellable from the physician, were still obtainable from the patient. On principle alone, it is plain that if a patient could be compelled to

---

[13] Cabe v. State, (1930) 182 Ark. 49, 30 S. W. 2d 855; Wolf v. People, (1947) 117 Colo. 279, 187 P. 2d 926; State v. Bennett, (1907) 137 Iowa 427, 110 N. W. 150; Maddox v. State, (1935) 173 Miss. 799, 163 So. 449; Thrasher v. State, (1912) 92 Neb. 110, 138 N. W. 120, Ann. Cas. 1913 E. 882; People v. Lay, (1938) 254 App. Div. 372, 5 N. Y. S. 2d 325, aff'd. 279 N. Y. 737, 18 N. E. 2d 686; Jasper v. State, (1954) _____Okla. Cr._____, 269 P. 2d 375; State v. Fackrell, (1954) 44 Wash. 2d 874, 271 P. 2d 679. See also notes, 45 A. L. R. 1357; 2 A. L. R. 2d 645, 647. In Wimberly v. State, (1950) 217 Ark. 130, 228 S. W. 2d 991, defendant was charged with shooting his ex-wife. At the trial, the State called as a witness the physician who had attended her. He was asked to testify concerning the nature, extent and location of her wounds. Defendant objected on the ground that the physician's testimony was prohibited by the statute and that the patient had not waived her privilege. The physician also stated that *she had specifically requested him not to testify*. The court, notwithstanding, permitted the physician to testify. Defendant was convicted. The Supreme Court held that since there was nothing in the physician's testimony that would subject his patient to prosecution, damage her reputation, wound her feelings, or disclose to the public any infirmity or condition that she might legitimately wish kept private, the evidence was admissible.

[14] (1926) 143 Miss. 121, 108 So. 433, 45 A. L. R. 1348.

[15] Ethridge, J., (p. 128) : "Manifestly the defendant on trial could not object to the evidence because it is not made incompetent and because he has no kind of privilege or protection afforded by the statute. * * * It was not for him to be heard upon it. As to him, the evidence was competent and admissible and no right of his was violated by the admission of the evidence." Three judges dissented on the ground that the prohibition is for the benefit of the patient and no one but he can waive it. See also State v. Karcher, (1951) 155 Ohio St. 253, 98 N. E. 2d 308. For application of the privilege in criminal cases, see § 70, herein.

disclose the very facts which the physician is prohibited from revealing, the doctrine of privileged communications in this relationship would become farcical.[1]

Although in terms the statute only purports to render the physician an incompetent witness as to matters specified therein, it is quite evident that the intended protection would amount to nothing if the patient could be compelled to make the disclosure.[2] It is universally conceded, therefore, that the patient's testimony is just as much within the protection of the privilege as that of his physician.[3]

18. *Only Patient, or Holder of Privilege, Can Complain of Violation*

Even though evidence pertaining to privileged matters is wrongfully admitted by the trial court, parties other than the patient, or holder of the privilege, cannot complain of the error.[1]

---

[1] Dambmann v. Metropolitan Street Ry., (1907) 55 Misc. 60, 106 N. Y. S. 221.

[2] Aspy v. Botkins, (1903) 160 Ind. 170, 66 N. E. 462; Citizens Street R. R. v. Shepherd, (1902) 30 Ind. App. 193, 65 N. E. 765.

[3] Baum v. Pennsylvania R. R., (1953) 14 F. R. D. 398; Post v. State, (1895) 14 Ind. App. 452, 42 N. E. 1120; Galligano v. Galligano, (1935) 245 App. Div. 743, 280 N. Y. S. 419; Randa v. Bear, (1957) ....Wash........., 312 P. 2d 640. Burgess v. Sims Drug Co., (1901) 114 Iowa 275, 279, 86 N. W. 307, 54 L. R. A. 364: "We think that there is no question but that the patient is privileged from disclosing communications made to his physician, although the statute does not so expressly provide." Likewise, a client cannot be compelled to disclose communications which his attorney will not be permitted to disclose. *In re* Martin, (1943) 141 Ohio St. 87, 47 N. E. 2d 388; 8 Wigmore, Evidence, § 2324.

[1] Chaffee v. Kaufman, (1923) 113 Kan. 254, 214 Pac. 618; Maas v. Midway Chevrolet Co., (1945) 219 Minn. 461, 18 N. W. 2d 233, 158 A. L. R. 215; Vance v. State, (1938) 182 Miss. 840, 183 So. 280.

(1950) La. Rev. Stat. Ann., § 15-478: "The right to exclude the testimony * * * is purely personal, and can be set up only by the person in whose favor the right exists. * * *." Similarly, a defendant cannot complain of error where the trial court disregarded a witness's constitutional privilege against self-incrimination. Samuel v. People, (1897) 164 Ill. 379, 45 N. E. 728.

See also Mathews v. McNeill, (1916) 98 Kan. 5, 157 Pac. 387 (attorney-client) .

Rule 40 of the Uniform Rules of Evidence, (1953) provides: "A party may predicate error on a ruling disallowing a claim of privilege only if he is the holder of the privilege." See also Rule 234, Model Code of Evidence. (1942)

19. Effect of Presence of Third Person

It will be remembered that the policy of the privilege—sometimes expressly declared by the legislatures—is to encourage confidence and preserve it inviolate. It would seem to follow naturally that to render a communication between physician and patient privileged, it must have been received in private;[1] in short, it must have been a *confidential* communication.[2] By this we do not mean that it must have been made under an express promise of secrecy, but rather that the communication was made in confidence, express or implied, that it should not be revealed to anyone without the consent of the patient. The mere fact that a communication is made to a person who is a lawyer, clergyman, or physician should not of itself make it a privileged one. To have that effect, it must have been made in confidence of the relation and under such circumstances as to imply that it should forever remain a secret in the breast of the confidential adviser.[3] The common sense view, therefore, would seem to be that the confidential communication must

---

[1] Among his four fundamental conditions that justify a testimonial privilege against the disclosure of communications between persons standing in a given relation, Wigmore requires: " (1) The communications must originate in a *confidence* that they will not be disclosed; (2) This element of *confidentiality must be essential* to the full and satisfactory maintenance of the relation between the parties." 8 Wigmore, Evidence, § 2285.

[2] Culver v. Union Pac. R. R., (1924) 112 Neb. 441, 449, 199 N. W. 794: "The statute is not intended to conceal relevant facts not communicated confidentially to a physician in his professional capacity." The statutes of District of Columbia, Iowa, Kentucky, and Nebraska expressly limit their operation to "confidential" communications and information. See also Constitution of Louisiana, art. 6, § 12. A few courts have held that the statute cannot be confined to information of a "confidential nature." Marfia v. Great Northern Ry., (1914) 124 Minn. 466, 145 N. W. 385; People v. Decina, (1956) 2 N. Y. 2d 133, 138 N. E. 2d 799; Griffiths v. Metropolitan Street Ry., (1902) 171 N. Y. 106, 63 N. E. 808; Renihan v. Dennin, (1886) 103 N. Y. 573, 9 N. E. 320; Grattan v. Metropolitan Life Ins. Co., (1880) 80 N. Y. 281.

The statute in Indiana makes physicians incompetent witnesses "as to *matters communicated* to them, as such, by patients," but bars attorneys as witnesses only "as to confidential communications made to them * * *." (Italics supplied)

[3] State v. Thomas, (1954) 78 Ariz. 52, 275 P. 2d 408; Hills v. State, (1901) 61 Neb. 589, 85 N. W. 836, 57 L. R. A. 155. In Masonic Mut. Benefit Ass'n. v. Beck, (1876) 77 Ind. 203, it was held that confidentiality will be implied from the mere relationship of physician and patient.

be a secret one. As such, it is inherently private, and it is not intended or contemplated that it shall be known to others.[4]

Just what are confidential communications and what may be privileged will depend upon the circumstances of each case, and will involve questions that can only be determined judicially upon a trial or hearing.[5] Since it is almost universally held that the party who asserts the privilege has the burden of proving in each instance all the facts and circumstances essential to its existence and operation, it would seem that this would necessitate his showing the circumstances indicating confidentiality.[6]

If, then, confidentiality is essential, what is the effect of the presence of a third person upon an occasion when the physician is rendering professional services to his patient?[7] When the patient, under such circumstances, discloses to the physician, or permits the physician to reveal, matters otherwise protected by the statute, should the patient be heard to assert that the confidence, which the statute was intended to maintain inviolate, continues to exist? Has he, by his own act, let down the barriers of secrecy and removed such matters from the operation of the statute? The patient may insist upon secrecy if he chooses, but when he himself renders useless the obligation, should he be entitled to the protection afforded by the statute?[8]

---

[4] State v. Thomas, (1954) 78 Ariz. 52, 275 P. 2d 408; Crawford v. Raible, (1928) 206 Iowa 732, 221 N. W. 474; Clark v. State, (1899) 8 Kan. App. 782, 61 Pac. 814. The Uniform Rules of Evidence define the phrase "confidential communications between physician and patient." See Rule 27 (1) (d), Appendix, herein.

See also Model Code of Evidence, (1942) Rule 220 (d).

[5] Bowles v. Kansas City, (1892) 51 Mo. App. 416.

[6] See § 46, herein.

[7] As to this question, cases involving the physician-patient relationship are few, but there are many which concern that of attorney and client.

See notes: 53 A. L. R. 369; 64 A. L. R. 201.

See also 8 Wigmore, Evidence, § 2311.

It has been said that there is a stronger presumption that the presence of a third party destroys the confidentiality of the occasion in the case of the attorney-client relationship than in that of the physician-patient. Cook, Privileged Communications As Affected By The Presence of Third Parties, (1938) 36 Mich. L. Rev. 641, 654.

[8] Lord Eldon once said: "The moment confidence ceases, privilege ceases." Parkhurst v. Lowten, (1819) 2 Swants. 194, 216.

The questions are important as they are practical. It is a matter of common knowledge that relatives or friends sometimes accompany patients when the latter consult their physicians. Often their presence is necessary, as when the patient is very young, or old and infirm. At other times, however, their presence is quite unnecessary as the patients well know. Moreover, relatives, medical men, nurses, and even neighbors are sometimes present in the sickroom to render such assistance as the attending physician may require. If the patient is unconscious, delirious, or exhausted by pain and suffering, so that he is unable to relate the symptoms and effect of his malady, or the nature and extent of his injury, to the physician, other persons necessarily must be present to furnish the information. It will readily be recognized that if the mere presence of a third person neutralizes the confidentiality of the relationship and destroys the privilege of the patient in each and every instance, regardless of the exigencies of the occasion, the privilege would be of little, if any, value. The courts, therefore, have usually held that *the capacity in which the third person is present* is the determining factor in resolving the question whether the communications between physician and patient retain the necessary attribute of confidentiality, and remain within the protection of the statute.[9]

[9] Kramer v. Policy Holders Life Ins. Ass'n., (1935) 5 Cal. App. 2d 380, 42 P. 2d 665.

There is a considerable conflict of opinion on the subject.[10] There appear to be three lines of decision in this respect, but even these, due to special circumstances, have their exceptions. The minority rule is that where the third person is a casual friend of the patient or the physician, or a mere stranger or bystander, and his presence, as the patient well knows, is in no respect necessary to the consultation, there is no confidence to protect and the statute does not operate. The theory is that the statute applies only to *confidential* communications between physician and patient and that the very nature of the occasion is inconsistent with the idea that the consultation was intended to be confidential. Therefore, the third person and the physician are competent witnesses and may testify to all that was said or done on that occasion, provided, of course, the testimony is otherwise admissible. The third person may testify

[10] See note, 96 A. L. R. 1419.

since the statute does not bar him from so doing.[11] The physician

[11] Iwerks v. People, (1941) 108 Colo. 556, 120 P. 2d 961; Bowles v. Kansas City, (1892) 51 Mo. App. 416.

is permitted to testify, not because the privilege has been waived, but simply because it does not exist since no confidence ever originates which demands, much less deserves, protection.[12]

The majority rule is that the privilege attaches notwithstanding the presence of third persons; and while as to any communications made in the presence of others and such persons be not necessary to enable the patient and the physician to communicate with each other, such third person may testify,[13] yet the privi-

---

[12] State v. Thomas, (1954) 78 Ariz. 52, 275 P. 2d 408 (deputy sheriffs present) ; Matter of Daniels, (1903) 140 Cal. 335, 73 Pac. 1053 (capacity of third parties not stated) ; People v. Dutton, (1944) 62 Cal. App. 2d 862, 145 P. 2d 676 (police officer) ; Horowitz v. Sacks, (1928) 89 Cal. App. 336, 265 Pac. 281 (husband, mother and brother present). *Cf* Kramer v. Policy Holders Life Ins. Ass'n., (1935) 5 Cal. App. 2d 380, 42 P. 2d 665; Murphy v. Board of Police Pension Fund, (1905) 2 Cal. App. 468, 83 Pac. 577 (wife present) ; State v. Knight, (1927) 204 Iowa 819 216 N. W. 104 (aunt and friends present) ; State v. Werner, (1907) 16 N. D. 83, 112 N. W. 60 (state's attorney present) ; *In re* Will of Swartz, (1920) 79 Okla. 191, 192 Pac. 203, 16 A. L. R. 450 (capacity of third persons not stated). Cases involving the attorney-client privilege are in accord. Nebhan v. Monsour, (1932) 162 Miss. 418, 139 So. 166 and 878 (friend present) ; Canty v. Halpin, (1922) 294 Mo. 96, 242 S. W. 94 (wife of attorney and friend of client) ; Baumann v. Steingester, (1915) 213 N. Y. 328, 107 N. E. 578, Ann. Cas. 1916 C. 1071 (companion-housekeeper of client present) ; Matter of Bennett, (1915) 166 App. Div. 637, 152 N. Y. S. 46 (friend present) ; Haley v. Dempsey, (1921) 14 Ohio App. 326 (friend present). The fact that on one or more occasions the communications were made in the presence of a third person whose presence was not necessary, does not prevent communications made later, in the absence of such person, or made on a different occasion, from being confidential and therefore privileged. Matter of Daniels, infra; Murphy v. Board of Police Pension Fund, infra; Haley v. Dempsey, infra.

In State v. Burchett, (1957) .... Mo........, 302 S. W. 2d 9, the testimony of a registered nurse employed by a hospital to which the defendant was removed that she helped him get out of an automobile and that she smelled liquor on his breath and that he slapped her, was not privileged since third persons were present when the transactions occurred.

[13] In Springer v. Byram, (1894) 137 Ind. 15, 36 N. E. 361, 23 L. R. A. 244, an ambulance driver and his assistant overheard the conversation between the injured man and the physician who attended him. The trial court excluded the testimony of the ambulance men on the ground of privilege. Holding this to be reversible error, Dailey, J., (p. 23) : "It is settled law that if parties sustaining confidential relations to each other hold their conversation in the presence of hearing of third persons, whether they be

⟫⟫→

lege still exists so far as to exclude the testimony of the physician,[14] and probably the testimony of the patient as well.[15]

The third rule, briefly stated, is that whenever the presence of a third person is in aid of the sick person, or to assist the physician, and the circumstances are such as to indicate that the patient still regards the occasion as a confidential one, the privilege still exists.[16]

---

necessarily present as officers or indifferent bystanders, such third persons are not prohibited from testifying to what they heard."

Accord: Mullin-Johnson Co. v. Penn Mut. Life Ins. Co., (1933) 2 F. Supp. 203 (wife must disclose treatments given husband by physician in her presence) ; Iwerks v. People, (1941) 108 Colo. 556, 120 P. 2d 961 (deputy sheriff) ; Cincinnati, H. & D. R. R. v. Gross, (1917) 186 Ind. 471, 114 N. E. 962 (claim agents of railroad) ; North American Union v. Oleske, (1917) 64 Ind. App. 435, 116 N. E. 68 (neighbors); Indiana Union Traction Co. v. Thomas, (1909) 44 Ind. App. 468, 88 N. E. 356 (friend); Masons' Union Life Ins. Ass'n. v. Brockman, (1901) 26 Ind. App. 182, 59 N. E. 401 (indifferent bystander) ; Woods v. Lisbon, (1908) 138 Iowa 402, 116 N. W. 143, 16 L. R. A. (n. s.) 886 (defendant's surgeon present when plaintiff's surgeon operated) ; Metropolitan Life Ins. Co. v. Brubaker, (1908) 78 Kan. 146, 96 Pac. 62, 18 L. R. A. (n. s.) 362, 16 Ann. Cas. 267; (dictum) ; Plater v. W. C. Mullins Const. Co., (1928) 223 Mo. App. 650, 17 S. W. 2d 658 (defendant's physician attending pre-trial examination of plaintiff conducted by other physicians) ; Bowles v. Kansas City, (1892) 51 Mo. App. 416 (capacity of witness not stated) ; Leeds v. Prudential Ins. Co., (1935) 128 Neb. 395, 258 N. W. 672, 96 A. L. R. 1414 (Trial court admitted deposition of insured's friend, but excluded testimony of doctor. Supreme Court affirmed but without discussing admissibility of friend's testimony. See case notes: (1935) 15 Bost. U. L. Rev. 846; (1937) 16 Neb. L. Bull. 206) ; Denaro v. Prudential Ins. Co., (1913) 154 App. Div. 840, 139 N. Y. S. 758 (members of family) ; Ryan v. Industrial Comm'n., (1946) 47 Ohio Law Abst. 561, 72 N. E. 2d 907 (fellow workman) ; Wells v. New England Mut. Life Ins. Co., (1898) 187 Pa. 166, 40 Atl. 802 (dictum); Gilham v. Gilham, (1955) 177 Pa. Super. 328, 110 A. 2d 915. (Admissions made by patient to physician in the presence of a nurse, the husband of the patient, and his parents, may be testified to by parents but not by physician or nurse)

[14] Iwerks v. People, (1941) 108 Colo. 556, 120 P. 2d 961; Cincinnati, H. &. D. R. R. v. Gross, (1917) 186 Ind. 471, 114 N. E. 962; Post v. State, (1895) 14 Ind. App. 452, 42 N. E. 1120; Walmer-Roberts v. Hennessey, (1921) 191 Iowa 86, 181 N. W. 798; Bassil v. Ford Motor Co., (1936) 278 Mich. 173, 270 N. W. 258, 107 A. L. R. 1491; Leeds v. Prudential Ins. Co., (1935) 128 Neb. 395, 258 N. W. 672, 96 A. L. R. 1414; People v. Decina, (1956) 2 N. Y. 2d 133, 138 N. E. 2d 799 (Police guard at entrance of prisoner's hospital room) ; Hobbs v. Hullman, (1918) 183 App. Div. 743, 171 N. Y. S. 390; Denaro v. Prudential Ins. Co., (1913) 154 App. Div. 840, 139 N. Y. S. 758; Gilham v. Gilham, (1955) 177 Pa. Super. 328, 110 A. 2d 915.

[15] Indiana Union Traction Co. v. Thomas, (1909) 44 Ind. App. 468, 88 N. E. 356; Post v. State, (1895) 14 Ind. App. 452, 42 N. E. 1120.

[16] Sedgwick, J., in Cahen v. Continental Life Ins Co., (1876) 41 N. Y. Super. 296, 304:

The inquiry usually turns upon the question of how necessary is the presence of the third party to the basic transaction.[17] In this class of cases, the courts universally hold that the physician cannot testify to what was said or done upon that occasion, provided, of course, that the testimony sought to be elicited concerned matters within the protection of the privilege. Generally speaking, the courts exclude also the testimony of the third person, but there is respectable authority to the contrary when the third person is one to whom the privilege is not extended by the statute.

Interpreter. Communications made through the medium of an interpreter are protected by the statute. It might, and often does, happen that a patient who cannot speak the English language takes with him a close friend who can interpret communications between the physician and himself. It is manifest that the presence of the interpreter is required by the exigencies of the occasion, and neither he nor the physician will be permitted, on objection, to testify to the conversation.[18]

Intermediary. Communications made by or through an intermediary other than an interpreter, are usually protected by the statute. Certainly a patient who adopts the indirect, instead of the direct, method of communication without good reason or reasonable necessity for so doing comes perilously near the one who con-

---

"Nor do I think that if the physician gained his knowledge in the presence of a wife of the patient, or of a person nursing the patient, or of an assistant, the physician should be allowed to testify. * * * The presence of third parties could only be used, as allowing the doctor to testify, because such presence was a waiver of the secrcey which is the patient's protection. It should not be deemed a waiver, however, whenever their presence is in aid of the sick man, because then it does not appear that declarations made before them evince that the patient was willing to renounce the secrecy secured by the statute." Rev'd. on other grounds, (1877) 69 N. Y. 300. See also Edington v. Mut. Life Ins. Co., (1875) 5 Hun. (N. Y.) 1, 8.

[17] See Rice, Extension of Privilege to Communications Involving Agents, (1951) 50 Mich. L. Rev. 308, 311.

[18] Leeds v. Prudential Ins. Co., (1935) 128 Neb. 395, 258 N. W. 672, 96 A. L. R. 1414. In this case, however, there was no evidence tending to show that the third person actually acted as interpreter, or that her presence was in any way necessary to the consultation. Cases involving the attorney-client privilege are in accord with the rule stated. Goddard v. Gardner, (1859) 28 Conn. 172; *In re* Busse's Estate, (1947) 332 Ill. App. 258, 75 N. E. 2d 36; Maas v. Bloch, (1855) 7 Ind. 202. See also Cook, infra note 7 at 643.

sults a physician in the presence of a disinterested bystander, thus surrendering the protection of the statute because of the presumption that the communication is not intended to be private and confidential. However, there are occasions where the physical or mental condition of the patient is such that he cannot act for himself, and therefore is obliged to depend upon others to furnish the information the physician needs concerning the origin, history, symptoms, and effect of his ailment or injury. When a physician enters a house for the purpose of consulting or treating a patient, or renders his professional service elsewhere, he is often called upon to make inquiries, not alone of the sick or injured patient, but of those about him who are familiar with the facts and are in attendance upon him because of his own helplessness. Under such circumstances, communications made to the physician by or through those attending the patient should, and usually do, come within the scope of the privilege. The question probably comes down after all to one of whether or not the method employed was intended and understood *to be confidential,* and in deciding that question, the presence or absence of reasonable necessity will be an important, if not controlling, factor. In *People* v. *Brower*,[19] the defendant was convicted of manslaughter. The evidence showed that he went to a physician and urged him to go to the aid of a woman who was in agony following her attempt to procure a miscarriage. Believing that the physician should know all the facts concerning her condition so that he might go prepared to treat her properly, the defendant related the circumstances and cause of her sudden prostration, some of which indicated his participation in the affair. Called as a witness by the State, the physician was permitted, over objection, to relate what the defendant had said to him when he sought his aid. On appeal, the judgment was reversed since the information conveyed to the physician by the defendant was privileged and should not have been received in evidence.[20] And where a wife,

---

[19] (1889) 53 Hun. 217, 6 N. Y. S. 730.

[20] Landon, J., (p. 219): "In this critical moment, with the sole purpose of saving the woman's life, he disclosed the secret to the physician to enable him to act rightly. To have withheld the disclosure would have made the defendant a consenting party to the woman's death. We have no doubt that the statute, both in its letter and spirit, protects the confidence thus reposed in the physician and forbids him to betray it."

discovering her husband unconscious, summoned neighbor women and a physician, and related to him the origin and history of her husband's malady in order that the physician might treat him, it was held that neither the physician nor the wife could be compelled to disclose the information so communicated.[21]

Non-Professional Agent or Assistant. It is a matter of common knowledge that, in the modern practice of medicine, the services of a physician cannot always be satisfactorily performed without the aid of a confidential secretary or office assistant. As a wise precaution, the physician, when making a physical examination of a female patient in his office, usually requires the presence of his secretary or assistant. Sometimes such person is present during a consultation for the purpose of making a stenographic record of the patient's description of his or her ailment or injury, its origin, history, and symptoms. Under such circumstances, the patient has every right to regard the presence of such person as necessary, and to consider the occasion still a confidential one. He is fully justified, therefore, in believing that any communications made, or information given, are just as sacred as if made to the physician privately.[22] Manifestly it would be against the spirit and plain purpose of the statute to allow such employees of the physician to be subpoenaed and be required to testify as to the very matters which the physician himself is not permitted to disclose.[23] In *Hogan* v.

---

[21] North American Union v. Oleske, (1917) 64 Ind. App. 435, 116 N. E. 68. It does not appear that the neighbors were asked to testify, and no ruling was made as to their competency. Springer v. Byram, (1894) 137 Ind. 15, 22, 36 N. E. 361, 23 L. R. A. 244: "Neither can disclosures be made by other persons whose intervention is strictly necessary to enable the parties to communicate with each other." Bassil v. Ford Motor Co., (1936) 278 Mich. 173, 270 N. W. 258, 107 A. L. R. 1491. A wife accompanied her husband when he consulted a physician to ascertain whether he was impotent. Held: the physician could not testify. Evidently the court felt that the subject was one which required her presence also.

See Jayne v. Bateman, (1942) 191 Okla. 272, 129 P. 2d 188. Attorney-client privilege. Wife's presence necessary. Attorney could not testify.

[22] The Iowa statute extends the privilege to the stenographer or confidential clerk of the physician as to any information obtained by reason of her employment. The Puerto Rico statute extends it to the "assistant" of the physician.

[23] The same principle was recognized at common law in cases involving the attorney-client privilege. In several states, the statute provides that, in addition to the usual

Bateman[24] the plaintiff, after his injury and while he was in the hospital, made a statement to his physician which the latter wrote out in longhand, and then had a notary public type the statement, read it to the patient, and witness his signature to the statement. At the trial, the court, over objection, admitted the statement in evidence; also the testimony of the notary. This was clearly error. The confidentiality of the consultation was not destroyed by the act of the physician, particularly as the patient was in great pain at the time and simply acquiesced in what he was asked to do.[25] And where the physician makes an oral and physical examination of the patient, and his findings and observations are taken down by a stenographer, who performs all the duties of an office assistant and acts as agent of the physician, under his direction and supervision, the patient's privilege is neither waived nor destroyed, and the testimony of the physician, on objection, must be excluded.[26] Where the physician's wife acted as his assistant and was present during a conversation between the defendant and the physician, it was held that the confidentiality of the consultation was not destroyed: therefore, she was not permitted to testify to what transpired in her presence.[27]

Professional Assistants: Physicians. It has been uniformly held that the presence of another physician, whose advice or assistance is requested by the patient's physician, will not affect, much less destroy, the confidentiality of the occasion. The presence of such medical man in no way evinces any intention that the patient

---

← ⚞

prohibition against disclosure by the attorney, his secretary, stenographer, or clerk cannot testify concerning any fact, the knowledge of which was gained in that capacity. See Cook, infra note 7, at 648. See also McCormick, Evidence, § 95.

[24] (1931) 184 Ark. 842, 43 S. W. 2d 721.

[25] Mehaffy, J., (p. 845): "If a physician could call any third person and disclose to such person his information and thereby enable her to testify, the statute would be of no effect. The physician could always evade the statute in this way."

[26] Kramer v. Policy Holders' Life Ins. Ass'n., (1935) 5 Cal. App. 2d 380, 42 P. 2d 665. Since the stenographer was not called as a witness, the court felt that it was not required to determine whether she could testify.

[27] Williams v. State, (1939) 65 Okla. Cr. 336, 86 P. 2d 1015. The decision is a curious one, since it is doubtful that the relation of physician and patient existed as to the defendant.

is willing to renounce the secrecy secured by the statute, and certainly he would not be expected to protest to a consultation or an examination of his own person held under such circumstances.[28] It is, therefore, not material in such case that the assisting physician was called by the patient's physician and not by the patient himself.[29] To bring the case within the statute, it is sufficient that the third person attended the consultation or examination as a physician and obtained confidential information in that capacity.[30] Neither the patient's physician nor the invited one can testify to confidential information acquired under such circumstances.[31] Obviously it would be an evasion of the statute to permit the introduction of such matters in evidence since it would always be possible to defeat the purpose of the statute by the simple expedient of a physician inviting others of his profession to be present in the role of assisting or consulting physicians at the time of the consultation or examination.

Professional Assistants: Nurses. Although it is uniformly held that the presence of a nurse will not destroy the confidentiality of the consultation or examination insofar as the testimony of the physician is concerned, the courts are divided on the question whether the testimony of the nurse is also within the prohibition of the statute.[32]

20. Illegality of Purpose

The protection which the law affords to communications between physician and patient has reference to those which are legitimately and properly within the scope of a lawful employment,

---

28 Provident Life & Acc. Ins Co. v. Chapman, (1928) 152 Miss. 747, 118 So. 437.

29 Munz v. Salt Lake City R. R., (1902) 25 Utah 220, 70 Pac. 852.

30 Renihan v. Dennin, (1886) 103 N. Y. 573, 9 N. E. 320.

31 Mutual Life Ins. Co. v. Owen, (1914) 111 Ark. 554, 164 S. W. 720; Prader v. National Masonic Acc. Ass'n., (1895) 95 Iowa 149, 63 N. W. 601; Raymond v. Burlington, Cedar Rapids & N. Ry., (1884) 65 Iowa 152, 21 N. W. 495; Leonczak v. Minneapolis, St. Paul & S. S. M. Ry., (1924) 161 Minn. 304, 201 N. W. 551; Mississippi Power & L. Co. v. Jordan, (1932) 164 Miss. 174, 143 So. 483; Provident Life & Acc. Ins. Co. v. Chapman, (1928) 152 Miss. 747, 118 So. 437; Renihan v. Dennin, (1886) 103 N. Y. 573, 9 N. E. 320. See also § 42, herein.

32 For discussion of this question, see § 31, herein.

and does not extend to communications made for the purpose of aiding or enabling anyone to commit, or to plan to commit, a crime or a tort, or to escape the consequences of such unlawful conduct.[1] In the case of crime, they then partake of the nature of a conspiracy, or attempted conspiracy,[2] and it is not only lawful to divulge such communications, but, under certain circumstances, it may be the moral duty of the physician to reveal them.[3] It is a mistaken notion to think that a physician has the right to assist in the perpetration of a crime or a civil wrong, and a mistaken notion to think that a person having in mind the commission of a crime or a tort can safely entrust this knowledge to a physician any more than to an attorney or anyone else.

It is certain that a patient who consults a physician for assistance in connection with a contemplated violation of law can expect no help from the law. He cannot complain if the truth is allowed to be told. The interests of public justice require that no shield from merited exposure shall be interposed to protect a patient who requests a physician to advance the patient's unlawful purpose. Therefore, communications to, or advice from, a physician looking to the procuring of an illegal abortion are not privileged.[4] Like-

---

[1] This limitation is embodied in Rule 27 (6) of the Uniform Rules of Evidence. See Appendix, herein. The New Zealand statute expressly exempts "any communication made for any criminal purpose." It is well established that communications made by a client to his attorney before the commission of a crime, or proposed infraction of the law, for the purpose of being advised or assisted in its commission, are not privileged. 125 A. L. R. 508; 28 R. C. L., *Witnesses*, § 158. Green, V. C., in Mathews v. Hoagland, (1891) 48 N. J. E. 455, 469, 21 Atl. 1054: "If the client consults the lawyer with reference to the perpetration of a crime, and they cooperate in effecting it, there is no privilege, for it is no part of an attorney's duty to assist in crime—he ceases to be counsel and becomes a criminal. If he refuses to be a party to the act, still there is no privilege, because he cannot properly be consulted professionally for advise to aid in the perpetration of a crime." See *Re* Selser, (1954) 15 N. J. 393, 105 A. 2d 395. Excellent opinion by Vanderbilt, C. J.

[2] McKenzie v. Banks, (1905) 94 Minn. 496, 103 N. W. 497.

[3] See DeWitt, Medical Ethics and the Law: the Conflict Between Dual Allegiances, (1953) 5 Western Res. L. Rev. 5, 11.

[4] Seifert v. State, (1903) 160 Ind. 464, 67 N. E. 100; Sticha v. Benzick, (1923) 156 Minn. 52, 194 N. W. 752; McKenzie v. Banks, 94 Minn. 496, 103 N. W. 497; Smith v. State, (1940) 188 Miss. 339, 194 So. 922; Cramer v. State, (1944) 145 Neb. 88, 15 N. W. 2d 323; State v. Karcher, (1951) 155 Ohio St. 253, 98 N. E. 2d 308.

⟫→

wise, communications from one physician to another, made to secure the aid of the latter in the commission of an abortion are not privileged.[5] It has been held, however, that since it is not unlawful to produce the miscarriage of a pregnant woman if it becomes necessary to do so in order to save her life, in the absence of any showing to the contrary, the presumption must be indulged that the communication was made for a lawful purpose, and is therefore privileged.[6] Where the accused requested a physician to procure a miscarriage of a woman whom he was charged with having raped, and the physician refused to have anything to do with the affair, the physician could testify to the communication made to him by the accused because of the unlawful purpose sought to be accomplished.[7] If the communication was a *post factum* declaration and had nothing to do with the promotion or future commission of a crime, the privilege applies, whether the communication was made by the patient,[8] or by another acting in her behalf.[9] Of course, in the jurisdictions which do not extend the privilege to criminal actions and proceedings, the physician may always testify and disclose the communication made to, or the information acquired by, him in his professional character.[10]

21. Duration of the Privilege

Death of the patient does not end the operation of the statute. Whatever prohibition existed in the patient's lifetime against his physician revealing, as a witness, confidential information as to the patient's state of health or his bodily infirmities, is still in existence

---

Contra: Citizens Street R. R. v. Shepherd, (1902) 30 Ind. App. 193, 65 N. E. 765. The decision is absurd; two judges dissented.

[5] State v. Smith, (1896) 99 Iowa 26, 68 N. W. 428.

[6] Post v. State, (1895) 14 Ind. App. 452, 42 N. E. 1120 (a strange conclusion, from which two judges dissented); Guptil v. Verback, (1882) 58 Iowa 98, 12 N. W. 125 (in the light of the facts, an unwarranted presumption).

[7] Smith v. State, (1940) 188 Miss. 339, 194 So. 922; Hewit v. Prime, (1835) 21 Wend. (N. Y.) 79.

[8] State v. Karcher, (1951) 155 Ohio St. 253, 98 N. E. 2d 308.

[9] People v. Brower, (1889) 53 Hun. 217, 6. N. Y. S. 730.

[10] See § 70, herein.

notwithstanding the patient's death. All of the courts agree that
the privilege does not lapse with death; hence, it is coupled with
the evidence when offered at the trial, or at some other lawful
proceeding.[1]

There still remains, however, the question whether the privilege of the patient can be waived by those who represent him after
his death, or who claim an interest under him. This is an important
question. The decisions of the courts are not in harmony respecting
the matter. They are divided with respect to the existence of the
right of waiver, at all, and also as to who may exercise the right.[2]
It is fortunate, indeed, that, in recent years, the problems of waiver
have been considerably reduced in number and their solution made
more easy. Because of the impressive mass of litigation that resulted
from the lack of express provisions relating to the right of waiver,
many legislatures have amended their statutes by inserting clauses
therein which permit, under certain conditions, personal representatives, heirs, and others to waive the privilege of the deceased
patient. It should not be overlooked, however, that the power
granted to such persons is sometimes not as broad as that of the
patient himself.[3]

---

[1] National Annuity Ass'n. v. McCall, (1912) 103 Ark. 201, 146 S. W. 125, 48 L. R. A.
(n. s.) 418; *In re* Flint, (1893) 100 Cal. 391, 34 Pac. 863; Bassil v. Ford Motor Co.,
(1936) 278 Mich. 173, 270 N. W. 258, 107 A. L. R. 1491; McCaw v. Turner, (1921) 126
Miss. 260, 88 So. 705; Westover v. Aetna Life Ins. Co., (1885) 99 N. Y. 56, 1 N. E. 104;
Grattan v. Metropolitan Life Ins. Co., (1880) 80 N. Y. 281; Edington v. Mutual Life
Ins. Co., (1876) 67 N. Y. 185; State v. Karcher, (1951) 155 Ohio St. 253, 98 N. E. 2d
308; *In re* Will of Hunt, (1904) 122 Wis. 460, 100 N. W. 874; Nat'l. Mut. Life Ass'n. v.
Godrich [1909] 10 Comm. L. R. (Australia) 1; 8 Wigmore, Evidence, § 2387.

[2] See c. XVI and c. XVIII, herein for a full discussion of the multifarious questions
involving the doctrine of waiver.

[3] *In re* Cashman's Will, (1936) 159 Misc. 881, 289 N. Y. S. 328, aff'd. N. Y. 681, 21
N. E. 2d 193.

CHAPTER VI

Construction of the Statute

22. In General

The policy indicated by the physician-patient privilege statute is not one of the fundamental policies coming down to us from the common law. In that particular, it stands upon a different footing than the ancient privilege accorded to the relationship of attorney and client. As it rested with the lawmakers to discover the necessity for, and to effectually impose, some measure of restrictions upon the freedom of the physician to testify, it is for the courts to enforce only those restrictions that have been expressly ordained. In the main, the statutes in the various jurisdictions are all substantially the same with respect to their purpose and scope, yet the meaning and effect of some of them have proved troublesome. The principal difficulty, therefore, lies in the interpretation and application of the rule enacted. Of course, under the general rules of statutory construction, a court has no right to add anything to or take anything from a statute, where the language is plain and unequivocal.[1]

---

[1] One court, however, has seen fit to annex to the physician-patient privilege statute the right of waiver, which the lawmakers overlooked.

Faris, J., in Epstein v. Pennsylvania R. R., (1913) 250 Mo. 1, 21, 156 S. W. 699, 48 L. R. A. (n. s.) 394, Ann. Cas. 1915 A. 423: "It will not avail to say that we are bound to a hard-and-fast construction of our statute—that it is to us an iron-bound law of the Medes and Persians, eternally unchangeable—and that we cannot by construction engraft upon it a single abatement in jot or tittle, by invoking the doctrine of waiver, because, forsooth, there are no waivers or provisos therein expressly written. We have,

⟫→

A statute which is clear, unambiguous, and free from doubt is its own best interpreter and in such cases it is not necessary to resort to any rule of construction to ascertain its meaning. Unfortunately, however, some of the physician-patient privilege statutes are not of this type. Due to the paucity of words, or lack of precise language, their phraseology is far from faultless, with the result that their meaning is doubtful and their limitations are perplexing. Not infrequently, therefore, it becomes the duty of the court to construe a statute of this kind and to apply it to the facts and circumstances of a given case. In doing this, the court may properly observe closely the uses to which the rule has been put,[2] and so control those uses that, while the purpose of the rule shall be fairly fulfilled, it shall be put to no use which has for its purpose the defeat of justice;[3] for in proportion as the sources of the best evidence are closed to courts of justice, will be the inability of those courts to render judgments that are morally satisfactory even to themselves.

The law is well settled that when the highest court in the state construes a statute of that state, the construction so placed thereon becomes as much a part and parcel of the statute as if specifically incorporated therein, and when the legislature re-enacts the statute it adopts the construction so made by the courts.[4] And where the legislature of one state adopts literally the statute of another state, the courts of the adopting state will likely feel constrained to follow the decisions of the highest court of the parent state construing such statute.[5]

Whether the physician-patient privilege statute is to be strictly or liberally construed is a matter concerning which there is a marked difference of opinion. Basically, we believe, this conflict stems from the different attitudes of courts towards the policy of

as has every civilized court where the statute exists, already engrafted, by construction, waivers upon it, which are now so well-settled as not to admit of question or quibble; * * *."

[2] Hamner v. Yazoo Delta Lumber Co., (1911) 100 Miss. 349, 417, 56 So. 466.

[3] Killings v. Metropolitan Life Ins. Co., (1940) 187 Miss. 265, 273, 192 So. 577, 131 A. L. R. 684.

[4] Hamner v. Yazoo Delta Lumber Co., (1911) 100 Miss. 349, 419, 56 So. 466.

[5] Grieve v. Howard, (1919) 54 Utah 225, 180 Pac. 423.

the privilege. On the one hand, the courts which are in sympathy with the purpose of the privilege are fearful lest a strict construction of the statute would fritter away the protection it was designed to provide. On the other hand, those unreconciled to the wisdom of the privilege are apprehensive that a liberal construction would work great mischief in the administration of justice. Between these two views, however, there exists another—the common sense view. If it be admitted that the object of every judicial inquiry is to get at the truth, then no rule of law standing in the way of getting at the truth should be either loosely or mechanically applied. The application of the statute must be with sound reasoning and careful discrimination so that it may have the legislative effect intended for it, and yet the investigation of truth be not unnecessarily thwarted.[5]

23. *Strict Construction*

In the early years of the privilege, many of the courts, unable to foresee the evil uses to which it would be put, were extremely liberal in their decisions involving the interpretation and application of the statutes which created it, with the result that the ban of secrecy was often imposed upon important evidence which, in the opinion of others, was plainly outside the ambit of the privilege. But the tendency of the decisions in the years succeeding has been towards a more rational and less liberal construction. The majority of the courts now hold that, since the statute is in derogation of the common law, it must be *strictly* construed.[1] The reason is obvious.

---

[6] Green v. Terminal R. R. Ass'n., (1908) 211 Mo. 18, 36, 109 S. W. 715: "In other words, the danger of frittering away this statute is not to operate as a scarecrow frightening courts from their duty to give every word of it a due office and meaning—being zealous and astute at all times to see to it that the statute be so construed as not to strike down its obvious purpose."

Flack v. Brewster, (1920) 107 Kan. 63, 67, 190 Pac. 616: "Of course, the prohibition of the statute must be given the effect intended by the legislature, but so far as it is open to interpretation it should be strictly construed instead of reaching for an implication that would operate to suppress the true facts necessary to a just determination of the issue involved."

[1] Rhodes v. Metropolitan Life Ins. Co., (1949) 172 F. 2d 183; cert. denied, 337 U. S. 930, 93 Law Ed. 1737, 69 Su. Ct. 1493; Travelers Ins. Co. v. Bergeron, (1928) 25 F. 2d 680, cert. denied, 278 U. S. 638, 73 Law Ed. 553, 49 Su. Ct. 33, 58 A. L. R. 1127; Mis-

≫→

In many cases, the statute, if loosely interpreted and applied, will close the door to the best possible evidence on the issue of fact presented for determination; therefore, it should not be so construed as to apply to persons, or to matters of evidence, not coming clearly within its language and obvious purpose.[2] As we have pointed out earlier, the general rule of evidence is competency. Incompetency is the exception, and no person should be excluded from testifying, and no testimony should be rejected, unless plainly within the ban of the statute.[3] If construed too strongly in favor of the patient, the beneficial effects intended to result from its enactment will be far more than overcome by the injustice which must, in many cases, result.[4] So far as practicable the courts ought to see to it that the statute is not used as a mere barrier against exposure of falsehood and fraud, and that a rule intended as a shield is not turned into a sword.[5]

←※

souri Pac. Ry. v. Castle, (1909) 172 Fed. 841, aff'd. 224 U. S. 541, 56 Law Ed. 875, 32 Su. Ct. 606; Stayner v. Nye, (1949) 227 Ind. 231, 85 N. E. 2d 496; Myers v. State, (1922) 192 Ind. 592, 137 N. E. 547, 24 A. L. R. 1196; State v. Masters, (1924) 197 Iowa 1147, 198 N. W. 509; Kirsch v. Federal Life Ins. Co., (1939) 149 Kan. 309, 87 P. 2d 591; Flack v. Brewster, (1920) 107 Kan. 63, 190 Pac. 616; Armstrong v. Topeka Ry., (1914) 93 Kan. 493, 144 Pac. 847; Campau v. North, (1878) 39 Mich. 606; Killings v. Metropolitan Life Ins. Co., (1940) 187 Miss. 265, 192 So. 577, 131 A. L. R. 684; Keeton v. State, (1936) 175 Miss. 631, 167 So. 68; Gulf, M. & N. R. R. v. Willis, (1934) 171 Miss. 732, 157 So. 899, 158 So. 551; Green v. Terminal R. R. Ass'n., (1908) 211 Mo. 18, 109 S. W. 715; Smith v. John L. Roper Lumber Co., (1908) 147 N. C. 62, 60 S. E. 717, 15 Ann. Cas. 580; Booren v. McWilliams, (1914) 26 N. D. 558, 145 N. W. 410, Ann. Cas. 1916 A 388; Weis v. Weis, (1947) 147 Ohio St. 416, 72 N. E. 2d 245, 169 A. L. R. 668; Carson v. Beatley, (1948) 86 Ohio App. 173, 82 N. E. 2d 745; Meier v. Peirano, (1945) 76 Ohio App. 9, 62 N. E. 2d 920; Phillips's Estate, (1929) 295 Pa. 349, 145 Atl. 437; *In re* Golder's Estate, (1916) 37 S. D. 397, 158 N. W. 735; State v. Dean, (1927) 69 Utah 268, 254 Pac. 142; Chadwick v. Beneficial Life Ins. Co., (1919) 54 Utah 443, 181 Pac. 448; Randa v. Bear, (1957) _____Wash_____, 312 P. 2d 640; Leusink v. O'Donnell, (1949) 255 Wis. 627, 39 N. W. 2d 675; Prudential Ins. Co. v. Kozlowski, (1938) 226 Wis. 641, 276 N. W. 300.

2 Travelers Ins. Co. v. Bergeron, (1928) 25 F. 2d 680, cert. denied 278 U. S. 638, 73 Law Ed. 553, 49 Su. Ct. 33, 58 A. L. R. 1127; Southwest Metals Co. v. Gomez, (1925) 4 F. 2d 215, 39 A. L. R. 1416; Gulf, M. & N. R. R. v. Willis, (1934) 171 Miss. 732, 157 So. 899, 158 So. 551.

3 Blau v. United States, (1951) 340 U. S. 332, 335, 95 Law Ed. 306, 71 Su. Ct. 301; Haughton v. Aetna Life Ins. Co., (1905) 165 Ind. 32, 73 N. E. 592.

4 Booren v. McWilliams, (1914) 26 N. D. 558, 577, 145 N. W. 410, Ann. Cas. 1916 A 388.

5 Campau v. North, (1878) 39 Mich. 606.

The courts are practically in complete agreement that the statutory privilege must be held to afford protection only to those relationships specifically named therein; that the maxim *expressio unius est exclusio alterius* should be strictly applied; and that unless the witness comes clearly within the class limited by the statute, his testimony must be received.[6]

The statute applies to hospital records,[7] but there is no reason for applying the privilege more liberally when the information is sought from a hospital than when it is sought from the physician.[8] In Louisiana, the statute confines the privilege to criminal cases only; therefore, a court cannot extend it to civil cases.[9] Since the language in the body of the Pennsylvania statute is broader than that used in the title of the Act, the latter will control the scope of the privilege.[10]

24. Liberal Construction

There is respectable authority for the proposition that the statute must receive a broad and liberal construction.[1]   Although

---

[6] Travelers Ins. Co. v. Bergeron, (1928) 25 F. 2d 680, cert. denied, 278 U. S. 638, 73 Law. Ed. 553, 49 Su. Ct. 33, 58 A. L. R. 1127; Southwest Metals Co. v. Gomez, (1925) 4 F. 2d 215, 39 A. L. R. 1416; William Laurie Co. v. McCullough, (1910) 174 Ind. 477, 90 N. E. 1014, Ann. Cas. 1913 A. 49; General Acc., Fire & Life Assur. Co. v. Tibbs, (1936) 102 Ind. App. 262, 2 N. E. 2d 229; Gulf, M. & N. R. R. v. Willis, (1934) 171 Miss. 732, 157 So. 899, 158 So. 551; Goodman v. Lang, (1930) 158 Miss. 204, 130 So. 50; Deutschmann v. Third Ave. R. R., (1903) 87 App. Div. 503, 84 N. Y. S. 887; Weis v. Weis, (1947) 147 Ohio St. 416, 72 N. E. 2d 245, 169 A. L. R. 668; Leusink v. O'Donnell, (1945) 255 Wis. 627, 39 N. W. 2d 675; Prudential Ins. Co. v. Kozlowski, (1938) 226 Wis. 641, 276 N. W. 300.

See also, c. VIII and c. IX, herein.

[7] See § 64, herein.

[8] *In re* Albert Lee Lindley Memorial Hospital, (1953) 115 F. Supp. 643, aff'd. 209 F. 2d 122, cert. denied Cincotta v. United States, 347 U. S. 960, 98 Law. Ed. 1104, 74 Su. Ct. 709.

[9] Rhodes v. Metropolitan Life Ins. Co., (1949) 172 F. 2d 183, cert denied, 337 U. S. 390, 93 Law. Ed. 1737, 69 Su. Ct. 1493.

[10] Phillips's Estate, (1929) 295 Pa. 349, 145 Atl. 437.

[1] Manufacturers' Life Ins. Co. v. Brennan, (1921) 270 Fed. 173; Hirschberg v. Southern Pacific Co., (1919) 180 Cal. 774, 183 Pac. 141; Turner v. Redwood Mut. Life Ass'n., (1936) 13 Cal. App. 2d 573, 57 P. 2d 222; Kramer v. Policy Holders Life Ins. Ass'n., (1935) 5 Cal. App. 2d 380, 42 P. 2d 665; McRae v. Erickson, (1905) 1 Cal. App. 326,

≫→

practically all of these courts apply the rule of strict construction with respect to the *persons* coming under the ban of the statute, they apply the rule of liberal construction with respect to the *information* which is protected by it.

Most of the statutes expressly provide that the privilege shall extend only to that information which was given to, or obtained by, the physician in his professional character and which was necessary to enable him to advise, or to prescribe or act for, the patient.[2] It seems quite clear, therefore, that the legislatures did not intend that *all* information, which is obtained by physicians from their patients, should be privileged, but such information only as may reasonably be necessary to enable the physicians to apply their full professional skill for the benefit of their patients.[3] The decisions, however, are not in complete accord as to just what information or communications actually are within the periphery of this limitation.[4] The question of "necessity" is often a vexing one. Some courts take the view that the statutes are beneficial and based on elevated grounds of policy, and ought not to be frittered away by technical refinements;[5] that, on the contrary, all doubtful points should be resolved against the admission of evidence which even borders on that which should be kept secret.[6] Others have been

---

82 Pac. 209; Cincinnati, H. & D. R. R. v. Gross, (1917) 186 Ind. 471, 114 N. E. 962; Towles v. McCurdy, (1904) 163 Ind. 12, 71 N. E. 129; Penn Mut. Life Ins. Co. v. Wiler, (1884) 100 Ind. 92; Howard v. Porter, (1949) 240 Iowa 153, 35 N. W. 2d 837; Pride v. Inter-State B. M. Acc. Ass'n., (1928) 207 Iowa 167, 216 N. W. 62, 62 A. L. R. 31; Jacobs v. Cedar Rapids, (1917) 181 Iowa 407, 164 N. W. 891; Battis v. Chicago, R. I. & Pac. Ry., (1904) 124 Iowa 623, 100 N. W. 543; Kling v. Kansas, (1887) 27 Mo. App. 231; Leeds v. Prudential Ins. Co., (1935) 128 Neb. 395, 258 N. W. 672, 96 A. L. R. 1414; Matter of New York City Council v. Goldwater, (1940) 284 N. Y. 296, 31 N. E. 2d 31, 133 A. L. R. 728; Buffalo Loan, Trust and Safe Dep. Co. v. Knights Templar and M. Mut. Aid Ass'n., (1891) 126 N. Y. 450, 27 N. E. 942; Renihan v. Dennin, (1886) 103 N. Y. 573, 9 N. E. 320; Edington v. Mutual Life Ins. Co., (1876) 67 N. Y. 185; People v. Decina, (1956) 1 A. D. 2d 592, 152 N. Y. S. 2d 169; aff'd. 2 N. Y. 2d 133, 138 N. E. 2d 799; Boyle v. Northwestern Mut. Relief Ass'n., (1897) 95 Wis. 312, 70 N. W. 351.

2 See § 49, herein.

The phraseology of this limitation varies in the different jurisdictions.

3 Madsen v. Utah Light & Ry., (1909) 36 Utah 528, 105 Pac. 799.

4 These matters are discussed in c. X, herein.

5 Cincinnati, H. & D. R. R. v. Gross, (1917) 186 Ind. 471, 114 N. E. 962.

6 Seifert v. State, (1903) 160 Ind. 464, 67 N. E. 100.

inordinately liberal in construing the statute in favor of the patient, and have held that *all* information obtained by the physician in the course of his professional employment is privileged, however unimportant or unnecessary it may have been in enabling the physician to render his service.[7] The rule of construction enunciated in some of the decisions plainly demonstrates the unyielding determination on the part of the courts to guard the privilege and to save it from being nibbled away because of factual situations which, although they do not come within the letter of the statute, are, nevertheless, embraced within its spirit and intent.[8] It has been held that when the relationship of physician and patient is once established, the court may properly assume that all that was told to the physician, and all that was developed by his examination or came under his observation, was necessary and helpful for his understanding of the condition of his patient.[9]

The courts of Indiana have been very liberal in their construction of the statute, but it should be noted that the statute of that state is much broader than most of the other statutes in this respect,[10] in that it contains no provision relating to the *necessity* of

---

[7] McRae v. Erickson, (1905) 1 Cal. App. 326, 82 Pac. 209; Pennsylvania Co. v. Marion, (1889) 123 Ind. 415, 23 N. E. 973, 7 L. R. A. 687; Battis v. Chicago, R. I. & Pac. Ry., (1904) 124 Iowa 623, 100 N. W. 543; Kling v. Kansas, (1887) 27 Mo. App. 231; Stapleton v. Chicago, B. & Q. R. R., (1917) 101 Neb. 201, 162 N. W. 644; Renihan v. Dennin, (1886) 103 N. Y. 573, 9 N. E. 320; Grattan v. Metropolitan Life Ins. Co., (1880) 80 N. Y. 281; Pride v. Inter-State B. M. Acc. Ass'n., (1928) 207 Iowa 167, 174, 216 N. W. 62, 62 A. L. R. 31: "We have held repeatedly that we will draw no fine lines as to whether a communication is necessary or unnecessary. * * * All our previous cases take a broad general ground upon this subject, and construe the statute liberally, to the protection of the confidence reposed by a patient in his physician."

[8] Kramer v. Policy Holders Life Ins. Ass'n., (1935) 5 Cal. App. 2d 380, 42 P. 2d 665.

[9] McRae v. Erickson, (1905) 1 Cal. App. 326, 82 Pac. 209; Towles v. McCurdy, (1904) 163 Ind. 12, 71 N. E. 129; Hays v. Hays, (1912) 49 Ind. App. 298, 97 N. E. 198; Indiana Union Traction Co. v. Thomas, (1909) 44 Ind. App. 468, 88 N. E. 356; Battis v. Chicago R. I. & Pac. Ry., (1904) 124 Iowa 623, 100 N. W. 543; Keist v. Chicago G. W. Ry., (1899) 110 Iowa 32, 81 N. W. 181.

The courts are divided as to whether the question of necessity is one of which the physician must be regarded as the sole judge. See § 60, herein.

[10] Cincinnati, H. & D. R. R. v. Gross, (1917) 186 Ind. 471, 114 N. E. 962; Towles v. McCurdy, (1904) 163 Ind. 12, 71 N. E. 129.

the information.[11]   Later decisions, however, seem to have abandoned the earlier rule of liberal construction.[12]

Perhaps the most troublesome of all the problems of construction are those that concern the doctrine of Waiver. Since these are many and complex, the rules of construction applicable thereto will be discussed elsewhere.[13]

---

[11] See also Kansas statute. Appendix, herein.

[12] See Stayner v. Nye, (1949) 227 Ind. 231, 85 N. E. 2d 496; Myers v. State, (1922) 192 Ind. 592, 137 N. E. 547, 24 A. L. R. 1196; General Acc., Fire & Life Assur Co. v. Tibbs, (1936) 102 Ind. App. 262, 2 N. E. 2d 229.

[13] See c. XVI and c. XVIII, herein.

CHAPTER VII

What Law Governs

25. *Law of the Forum*

It is everywhere conceded that the law of the forum governs the conduct of proceedings in court, and determines the competency of witnesses and the admissibility of evidence.[1] The principle is that whatever relates merely to the remedy and constitutes part of the procedure is determined by the law of the forum, for such matters must be uniform in the courts of the same state.[2] The physician-patient privilege is not a rule of substantive law;[3] hence, it is applicable in every case where the evidence is offered within a state wherein the statute is in force.[4] The disclosure of medical

---

[1] Restatement of Conflict of Laws, §§ 592, 596, 597. Wigmore points out that there are certain apparent exceptions to the general rule. 1 Wigmore, Evidence, § 5.

[2] Pritchard v. Norton, (1882) 106 U. S. 124, 27 Law. Ed. 104, 1 Su. Ct. 102.

[3] See § 12, herein.

[4] Supreme Lodge, K. of P. v. Meyer, (1904) 198 U. S. 508, 49 Law. Ed. 1146, 25 Su. Ct. 754; Connecticut Mut. Life Ins. Co. v. Union Trust Co., (1884) 112 U. S. 250, 28 Law. Ed. 708, 5 Su. Ct. 119; First Trust Co. v. Kansas City Life Ins. Co., (1935) 79 F. 2d 48; Metropolitan Life Ins. Co. v. Kendall, (1955) 225 Ark. 731, 284 S. W. 2d 863; Standard Oil Co. v. Reddick, (1941) 202 Ark. 393, 150 S. W. 2d 612; Brotherhood of Railroad Trainmen v. Long, (1932) 186 Ark. 320, 53 S. W. 2d 433; Kansas City So. Ry. v. Leslie, (1914) 112 Ark. 305, 167 S. W. 83, Ann. Cas. 1915 B. 834; Metropolitan Life Ins. Co. v. Brubaker, (1908) 78 Kan. 146, 96 Pac. 62, 18 L. R. A. (n. s.) 362, 16 Ann. Cas. 267; Metropolitan Life Ins. Co. v. McSwain, (1927) 149 Miss. 455, 115 So. 555; New Orleans & N. E. R. R. v. Jackson, (1926) 145 Miss. 702, 110 So. 586; Wexler v. Metropolitan Life Ins. Co., (1942) 38 N. Y. S. 2d 889; National Mut. Life Ass'n. v. Godrich, [1909] 10 Comm. L. R. (Australia) 1.

secrets is not permitted on an examination before a commissioner
or referee outside the state any more than on the trial of the action.[5]
The privilege applies even though the events or facts sought to be
proved may have occurred in a state which does not recognize the
privilege.[6] On the other hand, it has been held that if no testimonial
privilege exists in the state where the action is brought, the physician may testify and disclose confidential information even though
he acquired it within a state where such statutory privilege is in full
force and effect.[7]

It is a well established rule that, in actions brought in a state
court to enforce rights granted by a federal statute, the rules of

---

[5] In Lorde v. Guardian Life Ins. Co., (1937) 252 App. Div. 646, 300 N. Y. S. 721, the
court struck out certain proposed interrogatories of the defendant to be submitted
under a commission to the supervising physician of a hospital in Pennsylvania where
the insured had been a patient. "The plain purpose of the statute would be frustrated
if the information acquired by the physician were revealed, as is here suggested, upon
an examination without the state. * * * In a word, the statute contemplates that, in
the absence of the required waiver, the confidential information be shut off at the
source." Accord: *In re* Meyer's Estate, (1954) 206 Misc. 368, 132 N. Y. S. 2d 825. See
also § 79 herein.

It has been held that when the deposition of a witness is taken in Ohio, before a
commissioner who derives his authority from another state in which the deposition is
to be used, the witness may refuse to divulge any information which would infringe a
personal privilege granted by Constitution or statutes of Ohio, or any rule of the common law recognized by the courts of Ohio. *In re* Martin, Jr., (1943) 141 Ohio St. 87,
47 N. E. 2d 388 (attorney-client privilege).

[6] Tri-State Transit Co. v. Mondy, (1943) 194 Miss. 714, 12 So. 2d 920; Wexler v. Metropolitan Life Ins. Co., (1942) 38 N. Y. S. 2d 889; National Mut. Life Ass'n. v. Godrich,
[1909] 10 Comm. L. R. (Australia) 1. *Contra:* Levy v. Mutual Life Ins. Co., (1945) 56
N. Y. S. 2d 32. A New York court issued a commission to take the deposition of a
physician in Georgia who had attended the deceased insured. The insurance contract
was made in Georgia. In his application, the insured waived all provisions of law forbidding any physician who had attended him from disclosing any information which
he thereby acquired. Georgia has no physician-patient privilege statute. The New
York court held that the waiver clause was valid under the Georgia Law and was binding on all who claimed under the insured; hence, the physician's testimony would be
admissible in the New York court. This decision is questionable. The New York
statute requires that a waiver of the privilege be made in open court. Under the law
of the forum, therefore, the waiver was not valid. In Jones v. Jones, (1955) 208 Misc.
721, 144 N. Y. S. 2d 820, the court refused to issue a commission to take the deposition
of defendant's physician in France.

[7] Doll v. Equitable Life Assur. Soc., (1905) 138 Fed. 705; Abety v. Abety, (1950) 10
N. J. Super. 287, 77 A. 2d 291.

evidence of the state court must control unless otherwise provided by a federal law. In the absence of a statute prescribing the rules of evidence upon the subject, the law of the forum will govern.[8]

The question as to what law governs sometimes arises in an action brought to recover the proceeds due upon an insurance policy. The condition of health of the insured may become a primary issue and the insurer may desire to offer the testimony of the insured's attending physician, or to introduce the records of the hospital in which the insured was a patient. Where the contract of insurance was made in a state other than that in which the action was brought, it has been urged that the law and usages of the place of the contract should govern in matters of construction affecting the validity of the contract and the rights of the parties; and that if the contract was made in a state which has enacted a physician-patient privilege statute, that statute should control in the trial of the case. This construction, however, confuses those laws which enter into and form a part of the contract with those which merely govern the remedy and procedure. The privilege statute is a rule of evidence and does not enter into the contract of insurance. The interpretation of the contract does not at all depend upon it. The rule affects the remedy and not the contract. Therefore, in such cases, the law of the forum, and not that of the place of the contract, must govern.[9] Moreover, the interpretation and effect of an alleged waiver of the privilege by the insured in his application for insurance, or in the contract itself, must be determined by the law of the forum, and not of the place of the contract.[10] When the insured, by his act or omission to act, has waived the privilege in a state where

---

[8] Tweith v. Duluth, M. & I. Ry., (1946) 66 F. Supp. 427; Kansas City So. Ry. v. Leslie, (1914) 112 Ark. 305, 167 S. W. 83, Ann. Cas. 1915 B. 834; Yazoo & M. V. R. R. v. Decker, (1928) 150 Miss. 621, 116 So. 287; New Orleans & N. E. R. R. v. Jackson, (1926) 145 Miss. 702, 110 So. 586. (All of these actions were brought under the Federal Employers' Liability Act.)

[9] Doll v. Equitable Life Ins. Soc., (1905) 138 Fed. 705; Metropolitan Life Ins. Co. v. Kendall, (1955) 225 Ark. 731, 284 S. W. 2d 863.

[10] Brotherhood of Railroad Trainmen v. Long, (1932) 186 Ark. 320, 53 S. W. 2d 433; Metropolitan Life Ins. Co. v. Brubaker, (1908) 78 Kan. 146, 96 Pac. 62, 18 L. R. A. (n. s.) 362, 16 Ann. Cas. 267. See also Supreme Lodge, K. of P. v. Meyer, (1904) 198 U. S. 508, 49 Law. Ed. 1146, 25 Su. Ct. 754. *Contra:* Levy v. Mut. Life Ins. Co., (1945) 56 N. Y. S. 2d 32. See infra note 6.

the action is pending, a physician in another state, which also recognizes the privilege, cannot refuse to testify when his deposition is sought for use in the pending case. The question as to whether or not a waiver took place must be determined by the law of the forum, and not by the law of the state where the deposition of the physician is sought.[11]

Injunctive relief will not be granted a defendant merely because the rules of evidence in a foreign state, or the state's procedure, differ from those of the state in which the cause of action arose. In *Tri-State Transit Co.* v. *Mondy,*[12] the plaintiff, a Louisiana corporation, sought to restrain the defendant from prosecuting an action for damages for personal injury sustained by her by reason of the alleged negligence of the plaintiff. She had filed her action in a court of Mississippi although the accident occurred in Louisiana where she, at that time, resided. Service was had upon the corporation in Mississippi. The corporation alleged that the claimant had temporarily absented herself from Louisiana for the purpose of evading the laws of her domicile and to obtain the advantage of trial under the laws and in the courts of Mississippi, which, it was asserted, were more favorable to her case than those of Louisiana. It was said that the claimant Mondy was examined by a physician in Louisiana shortly after her injury and that this physician could testify, over her objection, in that state, but not in Mississippi. The court denied the injunction, since the claimant had the legal right to bring her action in a court of Mississippi.[13]

As pointed out earlier,[14] the general rule is that the scope and effect of the privilege is determined by the statute in force at the time of trial. It has been held, however, that where the deposition of a physician, since deceased, was taken *before* the enactment of the privilege statute, it was admissible in evidence notwithstanding the statute was in force at the time of trial.[15]

---

[11] Metropolitan Life Ins. Co. v. Kaufman, (1939) 104 Colo. 13, 87 P. 2d 758.

[12] (1943) 194 Miss. 714, 12 So. 2d 920.

[13] In a similar case, injunctive relief was denied. Standard Oil Co. v. Reddick, (1941) 202 Ark. 393, 150 S. W. 2d 612.

[14] See § 14, herein.

[15] Wells v. New England Mut. Ins. Co., (1898) 187 Pa. 166, 40 Atl. 802.

26. The Rule in Federal Courts

In *civil* actions, it is the duty of the courts of the United States to enforce—except where the laws of the United States otherwise provide—the rules of evidence prescribed by the state in which they sit.[1] If a state has enacted a physician-patient privilege statute, it is obligatory upon the courts of the United States sitting within that state, and will determine the admissibility of evidence which is objected to as being a privileged communication.[2] Moreover, the federal court must accept the construction the state's highest court

---

[1] 28 U. S. C. § 1652; Fed. R. Civ. P. 43(a) Nashua Savings Bank v. Anglo-American Land, M. & A. Co., (1903) 189 U. S. 221, 47 Law. Ed. 782, 23 Su. Ct. 517; New York Life Ins. Co. v. Anderson, (1933) 66 F. 2d 705; Von Crome v. Travelers Ins. Co., (1926) 11 F. 2d 350, cert. denied 271 U. S. 665, 70 Law. Ed. 1140, 49 Su. Ct. 482.

See also 5 Moore's Federal Practice, c. 43, pp. 1301-1350; 2 Barron and Holtzoff, Federal Practice and Procedure, (Rules Edition) pp. 673-700; Armstrong, State Privilege Rules Applicable in Diversity Actions, (1956) 44 Calif. L. Rev. 949. Pugh, Rule 43(a) and the Communication Privileged Under State Law, (1954) 7 Vand. L. R. 556; Green, Federal Civil Procedure Rule 43(a), (1952) 5 Vand. L. Rev. 560; Conrad, Let's Weigh Rule 43(a) (1952) 38 Va. L. Rev. 985; Green, The Admissibility of Evidence Under the Federal Rules, (1941) 55 Harv. L. Rev. 197.

See able article, Louissell, Confidentiality, Conformity and Confusion: Privileges in Federal Court Today, (1956) 31 Tul. L. Rev. 101.

[2] Ranger, Inc. v. Equitable Life Assur. Soc., (1952) 196 F. 2d 968; Feldman v. Connecticut Mut. Life Ins. Co., (1944) 142 F. 2d 628; Engl v. Aetna Life Ins. Co., (1943) 139 F. 2d 469; First Trust Co. v. Kansas City Life Ins. Co., (1935) 79 F. 2d 48; Federal Mining & S. Co. v. Dalo, (1918) 252 Fed. 356; Doll v Equitable Life Assur. Soc., (1905) 138 Fed. 705; Miller v. Pacific Mut. Life Ins. Co., (1953) 116 F. Supp. 365; aff'd. 209 F. 2d 889; Van Wie v. United States, (1948) 77 F. Supp. 22; Stiles v. Clifton Springs Sanitarium Co., (1947) 74 F. Supp. 907; Munzer v. Swedish American Line. (1940) 35 F. Supp. 493.

See also Moore, *op. cit.* infra note 1, at p. 1332; Barron and Holtzoff, *op. cit.* infra note 1, at p. 690; 8 Cyclopedia of Federal Procedure § 26.50.

The doctrine was well established prior to the adoption of the Federal Rules of Civil Procedure.

Supreme Lodge, K. of P. v. Meyer, (1904) 198 U. S. 508, 49 Law. Ed. 1146, 25 Su. Ct. 754; Connecticut Mut. Life Ins. Co. v. Union Trust Co., (1884) 112 U. S. 250, 28 Law. Ed. 708, 5 Su. Ct. 119; Mutual Ben. Life Ins. Co. v. Robison, (1893) 58 Fed. 723, 22 L. R. A. 325. In South Carolina, there is no physician-patient privilege statute; nevertheless the Supreme Court, in Next of Kin of Clinton Cole v. Anderson Cotton Mills, (1938) 191 S. C. 458, 4 S. E. 2d 908, said, by way of dictum, that the privilege had long been the established law. A federal court sitting in that state felt bound to accept this as the law of that state and therefore recognized the privilege. Holbert v. Chase, (1952) 12 F. R. D. 171. But see § 5, note 4.

See Palmer v. Fisher, (1955) 228 F. 2d 603, involving public accountant's privilege under Illinois statute.

has given the statute.[3]   The application of the privilege to depositions taken under the authority of Rule 26 of the Federal Rules of
Civil Procedure will be discussed elsewhere.[4]

In *criminal* trials, the Federal Rules of Criminal Procedure
govern the procedure in the courts of the United States.[5]   These
rules have the force and effect of law.   The principle rule of evidence in federal criminal trials is contained in Rule 26.[6]   There is
no reason, therefore, to look to the state law.   The determination
of the question whether a matter is privileged is governed by federal
decisions and the state statutes or rules of evidence have no application.[7]   Since there is no federal statute creating a physician-patient
privilege,[8] and since it does not exist at common law,[9] it is not likely

---

[3] Supreme Lodge, K. of P. v. Meyer, (1904) 198 U. S. 508, 49 Law. Ed. 1146, 25 Su. Ct.
754; Ranger, Inc. v. Equitable Life Assur. Soc., (1952) 196 F. 2d 968; Aetna Life Ins. Co.
v. McAdoo, (1939) 106 F. 2d 618; Southwest Metals Co., v. Gomez, (1925) 4 F. 2d 215, 39
A. L. R. 1416; Federal Mining & S. Co. v. Dalo, (1918) 252 Fed. 356; Metropolitan Street
Ry. v. Jacobi, (1901) 112 Fed. 924; Miller v. Pacific Mut. Life Ins. Co., (1953) 116 F. Supp.
365, aff'd. 209 F. 2d 889; Munzer v. Swedish American Line, 35 F. Supp. 493; Mayers
v. Associated Ind. Corp., (1938) 22 F. Supp. 956; Adamos v. New York Life Ins. Co.,
(1937) 22 F. Supp. 162, aff'd. 94 F. 2d 943. See also Halsband v. Columbian National
Life Ins. Co., (1933) 67 F. 2d 863, cert. denied 291 U. S. 681, 78 Law. Ed. 1008, 54 Su.
Ct. 531; Pennsylvania R. R. v. Durkee, (1906) 147 Fed. 99, 8 Ann. Cas. 790. Determination of what evidence is admissible in an income tax investigation is a matter to be
decided according to federal law, and neither state statutes prohibiting the use of
privileged communications in court actions nor the Federal Rules of Civil Procedure
are applicable to federal administrative investigations. *In re* Albert Lindley Lee
Memorial Hospital, (1953) 209 F. 2d 122, cert. denied Cincotta v. United States, 347
U. S. 960, 98 Law. Ed. 1104, 74 Su. Ct. 709. See comment, (1954) 67 Harv. L. Rev. 1272.

[4] See § 82, herein.

[5] See Fed. R. Crim. P., 1.
    See also Louisell, note 1 infra, at 122.

[6] "* * * The admissibility of evidence and the *competency and privileges of witnesses* shall be governed, except when an act of Congress or these rules otherwise provide, by the principles of the *common law* as they may be interpreted by the courts
of the United States in the light of reason and experience" (italics supplied). See also
Wolfle v. United States, (1934) 291 U. S. 7, 78 Law Ed. 617, 54 Su. Ct. 279.

[7] McNabb v. United States, (1943) 318 U. S. 332, 87 Law. Ed. 819, 63 Su. Ct. 608; United
States v. Montgomery, (1942) 126 F. 2d 151; Petition of Borden Co., (1948) 75 F. Supp.
857; United States v. Haynes, (1949) 81 F. Supp. 63.

[8] Neither the Federal Rules of Civil Procedure nor the Federal Rules of Criminal
Procedure create such a privilege.

[9] See § 4, herein.

that such a privilege could be successfully invoked in a federal criminal trial.[10]

---

[10] Petition of Borden Co., (1948) 75 F. Supp. 857. See also 4 Barron and Holtzoff, Federal Practice and Procedure (Rules Edition, 1951) §§ 2151, 2152.

CHAPTER VIII

Medical Persons Protected by the Privilege

Sec.
27. Statutory Designations
28. Who Is a Physician: General and Limited Practitioners
29. Privilege Confined to General Practitioners of Medicine: Proof of License to Practice
30. Healers of the Mind
31. Nurses

27. *Statutory Designations*

As pointed out earlier,[1] practically all courts agree that the statute must be held to afford protection only to those relationships specifically named therein. In most of the statutes, the words "physician" and "surgeon" are used to designate the persons whose disclosures of information acquired in their professional capacity are prohibited.[2] In some, only the word "physician" is used.[3] Others employ terms or phrases such as "licensed physician or surgeon";[4] "regular physician or surgeon";[5] "person authorized to practice physic or surgery";[6] "person duly authorized to practice medicine or surgery";[7] "physician or surgeon, or other regular practitioner of the healing art."[8] In addition to the physician or

---

[1] See § 23, herein.

[2] Alaska, Arizona, Colorado, District of Columbia, Hawaii, Idaho, Iowa, Kansas, Mississippi, Missouri, Nebraska, North Dakota, Oklahoma, Puerto Rico, Utah, Virgin Islands, West Virginia, Wisconsin, New Zealand, Victoria (Australia).

[3]. Indiana, Kentucky, Louisiana, Michigan (criminal code), Ohio, Wyoming, Quebec (Canada).

[4] California, Canal Zone, Guam, Minnesota, Montana, Nevada.

[5] Oregon, Washington.

[6] Arkansas, New Mexico, New York, North Carolina, Pennsylvania.

[7] Michigan (civil code), Philippine Islands. (This adds "or obstetrics.")

[8] South Dakota.

surgeon, a few states have granted the privilege to other persons. Iowa extends it to the "stenographer or confidential clerk" of the physician or surgeon; Puerto Rico, to a physician or surgeon "or the assistant of either of them"; New York, to a dentist, or to a "registered professional or licensed practical nurse"; New Mexico, to a "professional or registered nurse"; and Arkansas, to "trained nurses."

28. *Who Is a Physician: General and Limited Practitioners*

The statutes which create the physician-patient privilege do not define the word "physician" as used therein.[1] Exactly where the line will be drawn in a particular state between those who are physicians within the meaning of the statutory privilege and those who are not, depends largely upon the wording of the state's statute and its laws pertaining to the right to practice medicine.[2]

In common acceptation, a physician is one who is a graduate of an accredited medical school, has met the requirements of a state's board of medical examiners, and has been duly authorized and licensed by it to engage in the general practice of medicine. He is, therefore, one "who practices the art of healing disease and preserving health; a prescriber of remedies for sickness and disease. He is presumed to be familiar with the anatomy of the human body in its entirety; to understand the science of physiology and the laws of hygiene, and to be able to minister, as far as may be, to the relief of pain, disease, and physical ailments of all sorts and kinds whatsoever."[3] Generally speaking, the license issued to a physician entitles the recipient thereof to practice as a physician or surgeon, the two being recognized as members of the same profession—that of practicing medicine.[4]

---

[1] Rule 27 of the Uniform Rules of Evidence (1953) provides: "(1) As used in this rule, * * * (b) 'physician' means a person authorized or reasonably believed by the patient to be authorized, to practice medicine in the state or jurisdiction in which the consultation or examination takes place." The same definition is embodied in Rule 220 (b) of the Model Code of Evidence. (1942) .

[2] Because the licensure statutes differ widely in the various states, that of any particular state should be examined carefully.

[3] State v. Beck, (1899) 21 R. I. 288, 291, 43 Atl. 366.

[4] Joyner v. State, (1938) 181 Miss. 245, 179 So. 573, 115 A. L. R. 954.

There are, of course, certain practitioners who minister to the sick and afflicted without the use of drugs or surgery, each of whom either treats only some particular part of the human body, or all diseases by some special method or system.[5] Perhaps the most common classes of these healers are chiropractors, chiropodists, optometrists, electrotherapists, hydrotherapists, physiotherapists, and naturopaths; but there are others also. The legislatures of most of the states have recognized many of these classes of healers and have created special licensing boards, each acting independently of the others, for the licensing of applicants who have satisfied the examiners that they are qualified to practice in their selected special fields. However, practice outside the scope of the limited license is prohibited,[6] since the legislative grant to certain groups of the right to perform special medical services does not carry with it the unrestricted right to engage in the general practice of medicine.[7] Accordingly, it has been held that a licensed chiropractor,[8] a naturopath,[9] an electrotherapist,[10] a mechanotherapist,[11] a physiotherapist,[12] a massage operator,[13] a dentist,[14] is not entitled to engage in the general practice of medicine. There has been a conflict of opinion as to whether a licensed doctor of osteopathy is authorized to practice medicine and surgery in all its branches.[15] Some courts have held that the practice of osteopathy is a special and limited

---

[5] See Herzog, (1931) Medical Jurisprudence, §§ 112-141; (1936) 16 B. U. L. Rev. 488; L. R. A. 1917 C. 822.

[6] See 70 C. J. S., *Physicians and Surgeons*, § 15 (b) 2, p. 868.

[7] Palmer v. O'Hara, (1948) 359 Pa. 213, 58 A. 2d 574.

[8] Joyner v. State, (1938) 181 Miss. 245, 179 So. 573, 115 A. L. R. 954.

[9] State Board v. Scherer, (1942) 221 Ind. 92, 46 N. E. 2d 602.

[10] Joyner v. State, (1938) 181 Miss. 245, 179 So. 573, 115 A. L. R. 954.

[11] Botkin v. State Board, (1950) ...... Ohio Com. Pleas ......, 96 N. E. 2d 215.

[12] People v. Mari, (1933) 260 N. Y. 383, 183 N. E. 858; O'Neill v. Board of Regents, (1947) 272 App. Div. 1086, 74 N. Y. S. 2d 762, app. denied, (1948) 297 N. Y. 863, 79 N. E. 2d 270.

[13] People v. Dennis, (1946) 271 App. Div. 526, 66 N. Y. S. 2d 912.

[14] Cherokee v. Perkins, (1902) 118 Iowa 405, 92 N. W. 68; State v. Fisher, (1893) 119 Mo. 344, 24 S. W. 167, 22 L. R. A. 799.

[15] See Notes: 86 A. L. R. 626 and 115 A. L. R. 959.

field of the art of healing,[16] but, among the more recent decisions, there is ample authority to the contrary.[17]

Although there have been conflicting points of view,[18] it is now generally held that treatment of a sick person by a Christian Science practitioner, who, in good faith, follows the religious tenets of such church, is not the practice of medicine, and he is not a physician in the sense that term is generally used.[19] Practically all of the states now recognize this and have enacted statutes which expressly exempt Christian Science practitioners from the operation of statutes relating to the practice of medicine.[20] Those who profess to heal the sick by the laying on of hands, or by magnetism, spiritism, hypnotism, mesmerism, or any other method based upon a supernatural agency, are not physicians and their system or method is in no sense the practice of medicine.

---

[16] State v. Johnson, (1911) 84 Kan. 411, 416, 114 Pac. 390, 41 L. R. A. (n. s.) 539: "Osteopathy is carved out as a separate department, and registration and license are required, while its practitioners are prohibited from giving medicine and performing surgical operations—that is, from practicing medicine and surgery as distinguished from osteopathy."

Accord: Mabry v. State Board, (1940) 190 Ga. 751, 10 S. E. 2d 740; State v. Sawyer, (1923) 36 Idaho 814, 214 Pac. 222; State v. Stoddard, (1932) 215 Iowa 534, 245 N. W. 273, 86 A. L. R. 616; Keiningham v. Blake, (1919) 135 Md. 320, 109 Atl. 65, 8 A. L. R. 1066; State v. Wagner, (1941) 139 Neb. 471, 297 N. W. 906; State v. Baker, (1948) 229 N. C. 73, 48 S. E. 2d 61; Palmer v. O'Hara, (1948) 359 Pa. 213, 58 A. 2d 574.

[17] Chicago College of Osteopathy v. Puffer, (1955) 5 Ill. 2d 441, 126 N. E. 2d 26; People v. Siman, (1917) 278 Ill. 256, 115 N. E. 817; Bandel v. Department of Health, (1908) 193 N. Y. 133, 85 N. E. 1067; Vest v. Cobb, (1953) 138 W. Va. 660, 76 S. E. 2d 885. A careful examination of the licensure statute in a given jurisdiction must be made. Some of the modern statutes are very broad, and imply, if not declare, that a licensed osteopath is entitled to practice medicine without limitation. See able discussion of the scope and effect of the modern licensure statutes, McKay, Doctors of Osteopathy and Osteopathic Hospitals, (August, 1956) No. 403 Ins. L. J. 509.

[18] See (1936) 16 B. U. L. Rev. 488.

[19] Estate of Mossman, (1931) 119 Cal. App. 404, 6 P. 2d 576 (also not a physician within the meaning of the privilege statute); Kansas City v. Baird, (1902) 92 Mo. App. 204; People v. Cole, (1916) 219 N. Y. 98, 113 N. E. 790, L. R. A. 1917 C. 816.

[20] *e.g.,* (1955 Supp.) Ark. Stat. Ann., 72-118; (1956 Supp.) La. Rev. Stat., § 37: 1290; (1953) N. M. Stat. Ann. § 65-7-10; (1957) N. Y. *Education Law,* § 6512; (1953) Ohio Rev. Code, § 4731.34.

29. Privilege Confined to General Practitioner of Medicine: Proof of License to Practice

Consideration must now be given to the question: Did the legislatures intend to extend the privilege to those physicians only who are engaged in the *general practice* of medicine and to exclude from its operation any and all persons who are engaged in some *limited* or *special* branch of the healing art? It can hardly be disputed that at the time the early statutes were enacted, a physician was a general practitioner; there were few, if any, "specialists" as that term is used today. It is reasonable to assume, therefore, that the lawmakers could have had no one else in mind than the general practitioner—the traditional "country doctor"—when they used the term "physician" in the statutes creating the testimonial privilege.

The general rule is, therefore, that unless the statute expressly extends the privilege to other classes, the ban of secrecy applies only to the duly authorized or licensed *general practitioner* of medicine and those only whose business as a whole comes fairly within the definition of "physician,"[1] and does not apply to persons employing other curative processes which do not come within the ordinary meaning of the term "practicing medicine."[2]

The following classes or groups have been adjudged outside the scope of the statute, and such persons may testify and disclose information obtained by them in the course of their employment: veterinary surgeon,[3] gymnast,[4] Christian Science practitioner,[5]

---

[1] William Laurie Co. v. McCullough, (1910) 174 Ind. 477, 90 N. E. 1014, Ann. Cas. 1913 A. 49; People v. DeFrance, (1895) 104 Mich. 563, 62 N. W. 709, 28 L. R. A. 139.

[2] William Laurie Co. v. McCullough, (1910) 174 Ind. 477, 90 N. E. 1014, Ann. Cas. 1913 A. 49. It has been noticed (§ 27, herein) that some of the privilege statutes limit their application to those persons only who are authorized or licensed to practice medicine or surgery. In many states, the legislatures have defined the practice of medicine, *e.g.*, (1956) Ariz. Rev. Stat. § 32-1402; (1947) Ark. Stat. Ann., § 72-617; (1955 Supp.) La. Rev. Stat., § 37:1261; (1953) N. M. Stat. Ann., § 67-5-10; (1929) Nev. Comp. Laws, § 4102; (1953) Ohio Rev. Code, § 4731.34; (1955) W. Va. Code Ann., § 2867.

[3] Hendershot v. Western Union Tel. Co., (1898) 106 Iowa 529, 76 N. W. 828.

[4] William Laurie Co. v. McCullough, (1910) 174 Ind. 477, 90 N. E. 1014, Ann. Cas. 1913 A. 49.

[5] Estate of Mossman, (1931) 119 Cal. App. 404, 6 P. 2d 576.

dentist,[6] chiropractor,[7] x-ray operator,[8] undertaker,[9] pharmacist,[10] hospital dietitian,[11] army medical corps sergeant in prophylaxis station,[12] interne,[13] medical student,[14] laboratory technician.[15] It

[6] People v. DeFrance, (1895) 104 Mich. 563, 62 N. W. 709, 28 L. R. A. 139; Gulf, M. & N. R. R. v. Willis, (1934) 171 Miss. 732, 157 So. 899, 158 So. 551; Howe v. Regensburg, (1912) 75 Misc. 132, 132 N. Y. S. 837; Carrington v. St. Louis, (1886) 89 Mo. 208, 1 S. W. 240 (question not decided).
The New York statute now expressly includes a dentist.
Art. 6, § 12 of the Constitution of Louisiana authorizes a privilege for dentists, but the legislature has never enacted one.

[7] S. H. Kress & Co. v. Sharp, (1930) 156 Miss. 693, 126 So. 650, 68 A. L. R. 167. See Clayton v. St. Louis Public Service Co., (1955) _____Mo. App._____, 276 S. W. 2d 621, which seems to regard a chiropractor as a physician within the meaning of the privilege statute. O'Brien v. General Acc. Fire & Life Assur. Co., (1930) 42 F. 2d 48 (question not decided).

[8] Leusink v. O'Donnell, (1949) 255 Wis. 627, 39 N. W. 2d 675; Prudential Ins. Co. v. Kozlowski, (1938) 226 Wis. 641, 276 N. W. 300.

[9] Chadwick v. Beneficial Life Ins. Co., (1919) 54 Utah 443, 181 Pac. 448.

[10] Brown v. Hannibal & St. J. R. R., (1877) 66 Mo. 588; *In re* Miner's Will, (1954) 206 Misc. 234, 133 N. Y. S. 2d 27; Deutschmann v. Third Ave. R. R., (1903) 87 App. Div. 503, 84 N. Y. S. 887. Art. 6, § 12 of the Constitution of Louisiana authorizes a privilege for druggists, but the legislature has never enacted one.

[11] First Trust Co. v. Kansas City Life Ins. Co., (1935) 79 F. 2d 48.

[12] Culver v. Union Pac. R. R., (1924) 112 Neb. 441, 199 N. W. 794.

[13] Frederick v. Federal Life Ins. Co., (1936) 13 Cal. App. 2d 585, 57 P. 2d 235; Borosich v. Metropolitan Life Ins. Co., (1926) 191 Wis. 239, 210 N. W. 829. See Shepard v. Whitney National Bank, (1938) _____La. App._____ , 177 So. 825. Although it did not appear that an interne was a student and not a licensed physician, the privilege was denied.
Contra: Eureka-Maryland Assur. Co. v. Gray, (1941) 74 App. D. C. 191, 121 F. 2d 104, 107, cert. denied 314 U. S. 613, 86 Law. Ed. 494, 62 Su. Ct. 114. "The interne is himself a physician. He is a graduate of a medical school with a doctor's degree, though, it may be, not licensed to practice his profession in the ordinary way by so holding himself out to the public. But it is common knowledge that a part of his duty is to get the medical history of the patient, and in this respect he is the attending physician. Not only this, but in many instances he does the work of the physician and, in other respects, relieves the physician of professional services which he would ordinarily perform. It would be straining the law to hold that disclosures made to him by the patient are not equally privileged as those made to the physician in charge."
In Greenbaum v. Columbian National Life Ins. Co., (1932) 62 F. 2d 56, cert. denied 293 U. S. 616, 79 Law. Ed. 705, 55 Su. Ct. 148, the testimony of an interne was excluded as privileged.
For discussion of medical practice by internes, see Hayt, Hayt and Groeschel, (1952) Law of Hospital, Physician, and Patient, pp. 410-411.

[14] Frederick v. Federal Life Ins. Co., (1936) 13 Cal. App. 2d 585, 57 P. 2d 235; Sparer

⟫⟶

has been held that a licensed optometrist is a physician within the meaning of the statutory privilege;[16] also an oculist.[17]

Whether or not a licensed osteopath is within the scope of the privilege has been questioned.[18] The early statutes governing the licensing of osteopaths usually limited their professional activities to that particular branch of the art of healing and the courts generally denied to them the right to engage in the general practice of medicine. The more recent statutes, however, are very broad and in most states now an osteopath appears to be entitled to practice in all the fields of medicine and surgery. Therefore, unless the courts stubbornly cling to the old notion that an osteopath is a limited practitioner only, there seems to be no valid reason why he should not be considered a "physician" within the meaning and intent of the physician-patient privilege statutes.

It has been held that a witness who states he is a physician, but also admits he is not a licensed physician, does not come within the prohibition of a privilege statute which limits its operation to persons "duly authorized to practice physic and surgery."[19] However, the failure of a licensed physician to register his license will not exclude him from the operation of the statute.[20] As a general rule,

---

v. Travelers' Ins. Co., (1919) 185 App. Div. 861, 173 N. Y. S. 673.

In Barnes v. Harris, (1851) 61 Mass. 576, the relation of attorney and client did not exist where a person seeking professional advice consulted a law student whom he believed to be a lawyer in the office of an attorney.

[15] Block v. People, (1951) 125 Colo. 36, 240 P. 2d 512. See also Prudential Ins. Co. v. Kozlowski, (1937) 226 Wis. 641, 276 N. W. 300.

[16] State v. Viola, (1947) _____ Ohio App. _____, 82 N. E. 2d 306, app. dismissed 148 Ohio St. 712, 76 N. E. 2d 715, cert. denied 334 U. S. 816, 92 Law. Ed. 1746, 68 Su. Ct. 1070.

[17] Arizona & New Mexico Ry. v. Clark, (1913) 207 Fed. 817, aff'd. (1915) 235 U. S. 669, 59 Law. Ed. 415, 35 Su. Ct. 210, L. R. A. 1915 C. 834. It may be questioned, however, whether the court actually decided that an oculist is a "physician," and therefore within the ban of the statute. It seems certain that the fact that defendant was guilty of bad faith in sending the injured man to a specialist of its own choice for the purpose of gaining information to be used against the claimant, was the most compelling reason for the court's refusal to allow the oculist to testify.

[18] Brennan v. Manufacturers' Life Ins. Co., (1919) 11 Puerto Rico Fed. 203.

[19] State v. Fouquette, (1950) 67 Nev. 505, 221 P. 2d 404; Wiel v. Cowles, (1887) 45 Hun. (N. Y.) 307; People v. Stout, (1858) 3 Park. Cr. (N. Y.) 670.

[20] McGillicuddy v. Farmers' Loan & Trust Co., (1899) 26 Misc. 55, 55 N. Y. S. 242.

a physician, when called as a witness in an action to which he is not a party, need not produce his license. Proof that he practiced as a physician raises the presumption that he was qualified to do so.[21] In any event, the question cannot be raised for the first time on appeal.[22]

30. Healers of the Mind

Throughout countless centuries there have been healers of the mind, but it is only in comparative recent years that diagnosis and treatment of mental illness have been placed upon a scientific basis and become recognized as a limited and special branch of the medical art. Whether or not practitioners in the field of mental disease and disorders, such as psychiatrists, psychoanalysts, psychotherapists, and psychologists are "physicians"[1] within the meaning of the privilege statutes, has not, until recent years, received much attention. A correct determination of the question would seem to depend on whether such a person can properly be classified as a duly authorized physician entitled to engage in the general practice of medicine.

Insofar as the psychologist is concerned, it is clear that in no sense is he a physician; therefore, he is not within the purview of the physician-patient privilege statute.[2] The legislatures of a few states, however, have granted him a special testimonial privilege. They have placed the confidential relations and communications between a licensed applied psychologist and his client upon the same basis as those provided by law between attorney and client,

---

[21] Golder v. Lund, (1897) 50 Neb. 867, 70 N. W. 379; *In re* Halsey's Estate, (1890) 9 N. Y. S. 441. See also Leggat v. Gerrick, (1907) 35 Mont. 91, 88 Pac. 788; Thompson and Boynton v. Sayre, (1845) 1 Denio (N. Y.) 175.

[22] Record v. Saratoga Springs, (1887) 46 Hun. 448, aff'd. 120 N. Y. 646, 24 N. E. 1102.

[1] The differences between psychiatrists, psychoanalysts, and psychologists are clarified in Guttmacher and Weihofen, (1952) Psychiatry and The Law, pp. 6-9.

[2] Guttmacher and Weihofen, Privileged Communications Between Psychiatrist and Patient, (1952) 28 Ind. L. J. 32, 37: "A psychologist * * * is not a doctor of medicine; he is not a graduate of a medical school. If he holds a doctorate, it is from a liberal arts college, that is, he may be a Ph.D., but he is not an M.D. He is therefore not within the privilege."

See also Louisell, The Psychologist in Today's Legal World, (1955) 39 Minn. L. Rev. 235; Part II, Confidential Communications, (1957) 41 Minn. L. Rev. 731.

and the psychologist cannot be required to disclose them.[3] In Montana, a qualified privilege of non-disclosure is extended to any person engaged in teaching psychology in any school, or who acting as such is engaged in the study and observation of child mentality.[4]

The question as it relates to psychiatrists, psychoanalysts, and psychotherapists is in some respects a troublesome one. Are these professional consultants and advisers "physicians" in the sense that term is used in the privilege statutes? Probably the answer in each case will depend upon the language used in the licensure act of the state in which such person practices his particular profession.[5] Psychiatrists are medical graduates—they are M.D.'s.[6] Since they are possessors of a license to practice medicine, it is likely they will be within the ban of the privilege statute on that ground alone;[7] yet it has been pointed out that it is at least arguable that possession of a physician's license bears no relation to a person's advice or counsel as a psychiatrist, psychotherapist or psychologist.[8] However, some of the statutes relating to the practice of medicine are broad enough to include the diagnosis and treatment of mental and

---

[3] (1956 Supp.) Ark. Stat. Ann. § 71-1516; (1955) Ga. Code Ann. § 84-3118; (1955) Ky. Rev. Stat. Ann. § 319.110 (See Appendix herein); (1956) N. Y. *Education Law* § 7611; (1955) Tenn. Code Ann. § 63-1117; (1955 Supp.) Wash. Rev. Code § 18.83.110. Perhaps it should be noted that there is no physician-patient privilege in Georgia or in Tennessee.

[4] (1947) Mont. Rev. Code Ann., § 93-701-4 (6).

[5] For informative discussions of such statutes and the problem in general, see Legal Protection of the Confidential Nature of the Physician-Patient Relationship, (1952) 52 Col. L. Rev. 383, 391-393; Guttmacher and Weihofen, (1952) Privileged Communications Between Psychiatrist and Patient, (1952) 28 Ind. L. J. 32; Confidential Communications to a psychotherapist: A New Testimonial Privilege, (1952) 47 N. W. U. L. Rev. 384.

Psychiatric Technicians may be licensed to practice as such in Arkansas. (1953) Acts of Arkansas: Act 124, p. 427.

[6] Guttmacher and Weihofen, (1952) Psychiatry and The Law 6.

[7] Taylor v. United States, (1955) 95 App. D. C. 373, 222 F. 2d 398. See comments: (1956) 54 Mich. L. Rev. 423; (1956) 40 Minn. L. Rev. 621; (1955) Wash. U. L. Q. 405. See also Kendall v. Gore Properties, Inc., (1956) 236 F. 2d 673.

[8] Legal Protection of the Confidential Nature of the Physician-Patient Relationship, (1952) 52 Col. L. Rev. 383, 392; Confidential Communications to a Psychotherapist: A New Testimonial Privilege, (1952) 47 N. W. U. L. Rev. 384, 386: "The psychotherapist-patient relationship seems much more analogous to that of the priest-penitent rather than to the physician-patient."

emotional disorders as well as those of a physical nature.[9] If, on the other hand, the professional consultant possesses only a limited license, he is not entitled to practice medicine and is not a "physician" within the meaning of the privilege statute.[10] Usually a psychoanalyst is a licensed physician, but even a layman can call himself a psychoanalyst.[11] Obviously the latter is not within the scope of the privilege statute.

Two courts appear to have assumed that a psychiatrist is within the statutory privilege,[12] and one has expressly declared him so.[13] Although a physician-patient privilege statute has never been enacted in Illinois, a trial court extended a new testimonial privilege to a psychiatrist. Called to testify as a witness in a civil action, he refused to disclose information revealed to him by his patient during a series of psychiatric consultations on the ground that such matters were strictly confidential and could not be divulged by him without his patient's consent. The court upheld his claim of privilege and excused the psychiatrist from testifying.[14]

It may be proper here to point out that if it be true that the primary purpose of the statutory privilege is to encourage confi-

---

[9] Legal protection of the Confidential Nature of the Physician-Patient Relationship, infra note 8, at pp. 392-393.

In Davis v. Davis, (1955) 1 A. D. 2d 675, 146 N. Y. S. 2d 630, the court regarded the testimony of plaintiff's psychiatrists as within the physician-patient privilege, but held that she had waived the privilege and therefore could not preclude them from testifying at the instance of defendant.

[10] See § 29, herein.

[11] Guttmacher and Weihofen, Privileged Communications Between Physician and Patient, (1952) 28 Ind. L. Rev. 32, 37.

[12] San Francisco v. Superior Court, (1951) 37 Cal. 2d 227, 231 P. 2d 26, 25 A. L. R. 2d 1418; People v. Dutton, (1944) 62 Cal. App. 2d 862, 145 P. 2d 676. In neither case, however, was treatment contemplated; hence, the relation of physician and patient did not exist.

[13] Jackson v. Jackson, (1953) 175 Kan. 418, 264 P. 2d 1087. It is not entirely clear, however, that the so-called "psychiatrist" was not also a licensed physician and therefore privileged on that ground alone.

[14] Binder v. Ruvell, Civil Docket 52C2535, Circuit Court of Cook County, Ill., June 24, 1952. See comment, (1952) 47 N. W. U. L. Rev. 384; also Chicago Sun-Times, June 25, 1952.

The case is also discussed in Guttmacher and Weihofen, Privileged Communications Between Psychiatrist and Patient, (1952) 28 Ind. L. J. 32.

dence between the patient and his medical adviser, then certainly
a persuasive argument can be made for extending a similar privilege to the relationship of practitioner in the limited field of mental
illness and his patient.[15]   This, however, should be accomplished
by legislation, not by judicial decision.

31. Nurses

At common law, a nurse is no more a privileged witness than
is a physician, and she may be compelled to testify as to what she
sees or learns in her contacts with patients, and as to communications made to her by them.   However, in jurisdictions where the
statutory physician-patient privilege is in force, the question frequently arises as to whether the testimony of a nurse is within the
protection of such privilege.   As later indicated, some of the statutes
expressly extend the privilege to nurses; but there is a conflict on
the question whether the statutes which merely extend the privilege to physicians include nurses also by implication.[1]   Admittedly,
nurses render essential services in the care and treatment of patients
and it is often urged that if such persons are not privileged on the
same basis as physicians, there is a well-founded danger of disclosure

---

[15] Guttmacher and Weihofen, (1952) Psychiatry and The Law 272: "The psychiatrist
must insist on very personal data, and must explore the relationship of the patient's
acts to his basic drives, which can only be adequately revealed by his deepest and most
secret thoughts and feelings.   This is true not only in psychoanalysis but in all pscho-
therapy.   The possibly neurotic nature of even such patently criminal acts as forgery
or theft cannot be determined without exploring the patient's attitudes and behavior
in regard to * * *, homosexuality, etc.

What is more, the patient's statements may reveal to his therapist much more
than the patient intends or realizes.   The psychiatric patient confides more utterly
than anyone else in the world.   He exposes to the therapist not only what his words
directly express; he lays bare his entire self, his dreams, his fantasies, his sins, and his
shame.   Most patients who undergo psychotherapy know that this is what will be expected of them, and that they cannot get help except on that condition. * * * It
would be too much to expect them to do so if they knew that all they say—and all that
the psychiatrist learns from what they say—may be revealed to the whole world from
a witness stand."

See Taylor v. United States, (1955) 95 App. D. C. 373, 222 F. 2d 398, 401, quoting a
portion of the above.

[1] See excellent note, 47 A. L. R. 2d 742.

of confidential communications and intimate information which the privilege statute is purposely designed to keep secret.[2]

Every state now recognizes nursing as a necessary branch of the healing art, and laws have been enacted creating boards of examiners with which properly accredited nurses, both professional and practical, may register after passing an examination.[3] In no sense, however, are they physicians;[4] in fact, some of the statutes authorizing the licensing of nurses, expressly prohibit them from engaging in the practice of medicine.[5]

Except in jurisdictions which expressly include nurses within the provisions of the physician-patient privilege statutes,[6] the general rule is that a nurse who acts as an *independent* person is competent to testify as to communications made to her by the patient and to disclose all that she sees, hears, or learns concerning the patient in the performance of her duties, however confidential and intimate such communications or information may be.[7]

---

[2] Legal Protection of the Confidential Nature of the Physician-Patient Relationship, (1952) 52 Col. L. Rev. 383, 393.

[3] For definitions of "professional nurse" and "practical nurse," see Hayt, Hayt and Groeschel, (1952) Law of Hospital, Physician, and Patient 374.

[4] Wills, Adm'r. v. National Life & Acc. Ins. Co., (1928) 28 Ohio App. 497, 162 N. E. 822; Borosich v. Metropolitan Life Ins. Co., (1926) 191 Wis. 239, 210 N. W. 829.

[5] e.g., (1950) La. Rev. Stat., § 37:938; (1956 Supp.) Mo. Stat. Ann., § 335:190; (1953) N. Y. *Education Law*, § 6909; (1956 Supp.) Ohio Rev. Code, § 4723.21; (1956 Supp.) Pa. Stat. Ann., Tit. 63, § 214.

[6] Arkansas includes "trained nurses"; New Mexico "a professional or registered nurse"; New York "a registered professional or licensed practical nurse." If the witness does not come strictly within the class of nurses designated in the statute, she may testify. Hobbs v. Hullman, (1918) 183 App. Div. 743, 171 N. Y. S. 390. See Homnyack v. Prudential Ins. Co., (1909) 194 N. Y. 456, 87 N. E. 769, for effect of amendment of 1906 on pending actions.

See also Hurd v. Republic Steel Corp., (1949) 275 App. Div. 725, 87 N. Y. S. 2d 64, involving the question whether an order may be made requiring the plaintiff to submit or authorize the submittal of x-ray photographs and examination reports made by physicians and nurses in their attendance upon the plaintiff.

[7] Life and Casualty Ins. Co. v. Walters, (1937) 180 Miss. 384, 177 So. 47; Mississippi Power & L. Co. v. Jordan, (1932) 164 Miss. 174, 143 So. 483; Culver v. Union Pac. R. R., (1924) 112 Neb. 441, 199 N. W. 794; Meyer v. Russell, (1926) 55 N. D. 546, 214 N. W. 857; Wills, Adm'r. v. National Life & Acc. Ins. Co., (1928) 28 Ohio App. 497, 162 N. E. 822 (public health nurse). See also dissent of Hilton, J., in State v. Voges, (1936) 197 Minn. 85, 89, 266 N. W. 265.

There is a conflict of opinion, however, as to the admissibility of her testimony where the nurse attending the patient acts as one of the necessary assistants or agents of the attending physician, or is an employee of the hospital in which the afflicted person is a patient. Most of the courts take the view that, even under such circumstances, the privilege does not apply to the nurse; that the statute is in derogation of the common law and should be strictly construed, and therefore limited to those persons specifically named therein.[8]   Several courts have pointed out that if public policy demands that the privilege of the physician should be extended to nurses and other attendants who are not physicians, the change should be made by the legislature, not by judicial construction.[9]

---

[8] First Trust Co. v. Kansas City Life Ins. Co., (1935) 79 F. 2d 48; Southwest Metals Co. v. Gomez, (1925) 4 F. 2d 215, 39 A. L. R. 1416; Estate of Budan, (1909) 156 Cal. 230, 104 Pac. 442. (Nurse allowed to testify but question of privilege apparently was not raised.) Kramer v. Policy Holders' Life Ins. Ass'n., (1935) 5 Cal. App. 2d 380, 42 P. 2d 665. (question not decided but it was intimated that a nurse was not covered by the privilege) ; Block v. People, (1951) 125 Colo. 36, 240 P. 2d 512, cert. denied 343 U. S. 978, 96 Law. Ed. 1370, 72 Su. Ct. 1074; State v. Bounds, (1953) 74 Idaho 136, 258 P. 2d 751; General Acc., Fire & Life Assur. Co. v. Tibbs, (1936) 102 Ind. App. 262, 2 N. E. 2d 229; Gorman v. Hickey, (1937) 145 Kan. 54, 64 P. 2d 587; Goodman v. Lang, (1930) 158 Miss. 204, 130 So. 50; Weis v. Weis, (1947) 147 Ohio St. 416, 72 N. E. 2d 245, 169 A. L. R. 668; Wills v. National Life & Acc. Ins. Co., (1928) 28 Ohio App. 497, 162 N. E. 822; Prudential Ins. Co. v. Kozlowski, (1938) 226 Wis. 641, 276 N. W. 300; Borosich v. Metropolitan Life Ins. Co., (1926) 191 Wis. 239, 210 N. W. 829.

[9] Southwest Metals Co. v. Gomez, (1925) 4 F. 2d 215, 39 A. L. R. 1416; General Acc., Fire & Life Assur. Co. v. Tibbs, (1936) 102 Ind. App. 262, 2 N. E. 2d 229; Weis v. Weis, (1947) 147 Ohio St. 416, 72 N. E. 2d 245, 169 A. L. R. 668; Prudential Ins. Co. v. Kozlowski, (1938) 226 Wis. 641, 276 N. W. 300. In Minnesota, the legislature has seen fit to include within the attorney-client privilege "any employee" of the attorney, but has not extended a similar privilege to a nurse assisting the physician. A federal court considered this omission. Stone, J., in First Trust Co. v. Kansas City Life Ins. Co., (1935) 79 F. 2d 48, 52: "It is significant that subdivision 2 [attorney-client privilege] is the only one in which there is an extension of the privilege to those outside the privileged relation who might normally acquire knowledge in connection therewith, and it is also significant that at to physicians and surgeons there is no such extension to similar persons such as nurses. Defendant argues, and it seems with telling force, that when the entire section is considered it should not be said that the Legislature overlooked an express extension of subdivision 4 [physician-patient privilege] to cover nurses, dietitians, and others connected with the treatment of a patient under the supervision of a doctor, or that it intended such an extension by the language used." See also Southwest Metals Co. v. Gomez, (1925) 4 F. 2d 215, 39 A. L. R. 1416; and comment on the Iowa statute, (1927) 13 Iowa L. Rev. 118.

In a few jurisdictions, the courts have taken the view that the privilege statute includes *by implication* nurses who are assisting the physician, or acting under his direction, in his treatment of the patient. It has been pointed out that a nurse is often necessarily present at conversations between the patient and the physician, or during a physical examination of the patient, or a surgical operation, and little good would be subserved if the lips of the physician might be sealed by the statute as to such communications and information, but the nurse might freely testify to all that was said or done in her presence.[10]

It should be noticed, however, that, even in those states which expressly include a nurse within the statutory privilege, the prohibition against disclosure is only applicable and operative as a bar

---

10 Ethridge, P. J., in Mississippi Power & L. Co. v. Jordan, (1932) 164 Miss. 174, 185, 143 So. 483: "We think where information and knowledge of a nurse are gained by being present and assisting a physician in treatment and hearing communications between the physician and the patient, then her testimony would be incompetent, for the reason that it is a part of the knowledge of the physician himself. A physician, in many cases, must have the assistance of a nurse or another physician where the work must be done quickly and skillfully, and to permit a nurse, under such circumstances, to testify as to facts or communications made to the physician by the patient, would be to annul the statute. As to all matters learned when not assisting a physician, a nurse is a competent witness."

Luce v. Service Life Ins. Co., (1939) 227 Iowa 532, 288 N. W. 681 (implies nurse was privileged but a waiver permitted her to testify); State v. Anderson, (1956) 247 Minn. 469, 78 N. W. 2d 320; Ostrowski v. Mockbridge, (1954) 242 Minn. 265, 65 N. W. 2d 185, 47 A. L. R. 2d 733; Culver v. Union Pac. Ry., (1924) 112 Neb. 441, 199 N. W. 794; Meyer v. Russell, (1926) 55 N. D. 546, 214 N. W. 857; Humble v. John Hancock Mut. Life Ins. Co., (1931) 28 Ohio N. P. (n. s.) 481, aff'd......Ohio App......, 31 N. E. 2d 887; Jasper v. State, (1954) ......Okla. Cr......, 269 P. 2d 375; Clapp v. State, (1941) 73 Okla. Cr. 261, 120 P. 2d 381, reversed on other grounds (1942) 74 Okla. Cr. 144, 124 P. 2d 267; Williams v. State, (1939) 65 Okla. Cr. 336, 86 P. 2d 1015; American Bankers Ins. Co. v. Hopkins, (1917) 67 Okla. 150, 169 Pac. 489; Gilham v. Gilham, (1955) 177 Pa. Super. 328, 110 A. 2d 915. See opinion of O'Connor, J., in National Mut. Life Ass'n. v. Godrich, [1909] 10 Comm. L. R. (Australia) 1, 29. See also Rarogiewicz v. Brotherhood of American Yeomen, (1926) 242 N. Y. 590, 152 N. E. 440. In State v. Bounds, (1953) 74 Idaho 136, 258 P. 2d 751, the question was left undecided.

In State v. Burchett, (1957) ......Mo......, 302 S. W. 2d 9, a registered nurse employed by a hospital was permitted to testify that the defendant was intoxicated when brought to the hospital. It was unnecessary to decide whether there may be circumstances under which a nurse may be rendered incompetent by the statute, since her observation of the defendant's condition and his conduct at the time took place when four other persons were present.

if the testimony sought to be elicited from the nurse would disclose confidential information which was acquired in attending the patient and was necessary to enable the nurse to care for and treat the patient, or was acquired as a necessary incident of such care or treatment. Certainly, not *all* information which a nurse may acquire is privileged, but only that which is necessary and germane to the treatment process.[11] Thus, in an action by a surgeon on an account for services rendered, a trained nurse, attending the patient at the time of the operation, may testify that she heard the patient's father tell the surgeon that he would pay all charges for the operation.[12] In a lunacy hearing, a nurse was properly permitted to testify to matters of description relating to or concerning the physical surroundings of the patient, and to those in attendance upon her, and to conversations between third persons and the patient, and to the reactions of the patient to the acts and conduct of third persons, since all of these were matters to which any layman could have testified and were not barred merely because the witness happened to be a registered nurse.[13] It has also been held that the nurse may testify that the patient was under the influence of intoxicating liquor.[14]

A general objection to the testimony of a nurse is not sufficient; the objection should be made to each question eliciting information that appears to be privileged so that the court can determine whether or not the information was acquired by the nurse while actually assisting the physician or acting as his agent.[15]

---

[11] Meyer v. Russell (1926) 55 N. D. 546, 214 N. W. 857.

[12] Cleveland v. Maddox, (1922) 152 Ark. 538, 239 S. W. 370.

[13] *In re* Schermerhorn, (1950) 98 N. Y. S. 2d 361, rev'd on other grounds in 277 App. Div. 845, 98 N. Y. S. 2d 367, aff'd. 302 N. Y. 660, 98 N. E. 2d 475. See also *In re* Avery's Estate, (1948) 76 N. Y. S. 2d 790.

[14] State v. Townsend, (1937) 146 Kan. 982, 73 P. 2d 1124; Goodman v. Lang. (1930) 158 Miss. 204, 130 So. 50.

Contra: Clapp v. State, (1941) 73 Okla. Cr. 261, 120 P. 2d 381, reversed on other grounds 74 Okla. Cr. 144, 124 P. 2d 267.

[15] Meyer v. Russell, (1926) 55 N. D. 546, 214 N. W. 857.

CHAPTER IX

Relationship of Physician and Patient

32. *Essential That Relationship Exist*

The privilege statute applies only to communications made to, or information acquired by, the physician during the existence of the relationship of physician and patient;[1] therefore, in order to render information or knowledge acquired by a physician privileged, the relationship of physician and patient must first be estab-

---

[1] Travelers Ins. Co. v. Bergeron, (1928) 25 F. 2d 680, cert. denied 278 U. S. 638, 73 Law. Ed. 553, 49 Su. Ct. 33, 58 A. L. R. 1127; Herries v. Waterloo, (1901) 114 Iowa 374, 86 N. W. 306; State v. Newsome, (1928) 195 N. C. 552, 143 S. E. 187; Dubcich v. Grand Lodge, (1903) 33 Wash. 651, 74 Pac. 832; *In re* Will of Williams, (1925) 186 Wis. 160, 202 N. W. 314.

Information gained in social or business contacts is not obtained in the professional relationship of physician and patient and is not privileged. See § 55, herein.

lished.[2] A physician is free to testify regarding matters which transpired or which he observed or learned about the patient *before* the inception of the relation[3] and *after* the relation has ceased.[4] In all probability, communications made by a prospective patient to a physician with a view to engaging him would be protected even though the physician declined to accept the person as a patient, or the person decided not to engage the physician. The relation, however brief, would seem to exist during such negotiations.[5] Of

---

[2] Cherokee v. Aetna Life Ins. Co., (1933) 215 Iowa 1000, 247 N. W. 495. In Smoot v. Kansas City, (1906) 194 Mo. 513, 92 S. W. 363, a police surgeon summoned to the scene of an accident, saw plaintiff sitting on the sidewalk. At the trial, defendant called him as a witness and asked whether he saw plaintiff spit blood while on the sidewalk or in the street before getting into the ambulance. On objection by plaintiff on the ground of privilege, the court excluded the answer. Held: error. "It is sufficient to say upon this proposition that upon the retrial of the cause if it appears that the relation of physician and patient had been established and that the plaintiff had submitted himself for examination by Dr. M., then any information acquired by observation after that time would be incompetent. But on the other hand, if prior to the establishment of this relationship the doctor observed the patient and acquired information from such observation, we know of no rule of evidence that would make such information privileged."

[3] Travelers Ins. Co. v. Bergeron, (1928) 25 F. 2d 680, cert. denied 278 U. S. 638, 73 Law. Ed. 553, 49 Su. Ct. 33, 58 A. L. R. 1127; Conner v. First National Bank, (1948) 118 Ind. App. 173, 76 N. E. 262, 77 N. E. 2d 598; Herries v. Waterloo, (1901) 114 Iowa 374, 86 N. W. 306; Leifson v. Henning, (1941) 210 Minn. 311, 298 N. W. 41; Keeton v. State, (1936) 175 Miss. 631, 167 So. 68; Smoot v. Kansas City, (1906) 194 Mo. 513, 92 S. W. 363; Crawford v. State, (1927) 116 Neb. 125, 216 N. W. 294; Nichols v. State, (1922) 109 Neb. 335, 191 N. W. 333; *In re* Will of Williams, (1925) 186 Wis. 160, 202 N. W. 314. *cf.* Chicago, South Bend Lake Shore & Ry. v. Walas, (1922) 192 Ind. 369, 135 N. E. 150, 22 A. L. R. 1212.

[4] Travelers Ins. Co. v. Bergeron, (1928) 25 F. 2d 680, cert. denied 278 U. S. 638, 73 Law. Ed. 553, 49 Su. Ct. 33, 58 A. L. R. 1127; Bressan v. Herrick, (1922) 35 Idaho 217, 205 Pac. 555; Bower v. Bower, (1895) 142 Ind. 194, 41 N. E. 523; Arnold v. Fort Dodge, Des Moines & S. R. R., (1919) 186 Iowa 538, 173 N. W. 252; Smith v. Davis, (1949) 168 Kan. 210, 212 P. 2d 322; Hamilton v. Crowe, (1903) 175 Mo. 634, 75 S. W. 389; People v. Koerner, (1897) 154 N. Y. 355, 48 N. E. 730; Fisher v. Fisher, (1892) 129 N. Y. 654, 29 N. E. 951; Edington v. Aetna Life Ins. Co., (1879) 77 N. Y. 564; Matter of Loewenstine's Will, (1893) 2 Misc. 323, 21 N. Y. S. 931; Jahns v. Clark, (1926) 138 Wash. 288, 244 Pac. 729; Strafford v. Northern Pac. Ry, (1917) 95 Wash. 450, 164 Pac. 71; *In re* Will of Williams, (1925) 186 Wis. 160, 202 N. W. 314; McGinty v. Brotherhood of Railway Trainmen, (1917) 166 Wis. 83, 164 N. W. 249.

[5] Kansas City Southern Ry. v. Miller, (1915) 117 Ark. 396, 175 S. W. 1164. It has been so held in cases involving the attorney-client relation. Lew Moy v. United States,

⫸→

course, a different rule would apply to communications made to the physician after he had informed the prospective patient that no employment would or could be accepted.[6]

In cases where the relationship has ceased to exist, and the physician is called as a witness by the adverse party and asked to disclose information concerning his former patient's condition of health, it being claimed that such information was acquired when the witness was no longer acting as physician for the patient, the courts usually require the witness to state precisely and without equivocation whether he can segregate the information acquired by him during his professional attendance upon the patient from that acquired after his employment had ceased. This, of course, is essential to his competency to testify at all. If he cannot do this, his testimony cannot be received.[7] It is within the discretion of the trial court who has the opportunity to judge of the witness and observe him while he is testifying to say whether the witness can in truth separate his knowledge gained during the existence of the relation from that acquired after it has terminated. The witness is not the final and conclusive judge as to this.[8] Obviously, in many cases, the line of demarcation will be exceedingly difficult to draw.

Generally speaking, when it is made to appear to the trial court that the relationship of physician and patient existed, the bar of the statute is applicable and the physician cannot testify without the consent of the patient.[9] If, for any reason, the relation

---

←

(1916) 237 Fed. 50; Denver Tramway Co. v. Owens, (1894) 20 Colo. 107, 36 Pac. 848; Fimple v. State, (1920) 104 Neb. 471, 177 N. W. 798; State v. Snowden, (1901) 23 Utah 318, 65 Pac. 479. The principle was not applied where the negotiations failed because they were had with a view to employing the physician to perform an illegal operation upon another person. McKenzie v. Banks, (1905) 94 Minn. 496, 103 N. W. 497.

[6] State v. Wade, (1929) 197 N. C. 571, 150 S. E. 32. See also State v. Snowden, (1901) 23 Utah 318, 65 Pac. 479.

[7] Travelers Ins. Co. v. Bergeron, (1928) 25 F. 2d 680, cert. denied 278 U. S. 638, 73 Law. Ed. 553, 49 Su. Ct. 33, 58 A. L. R. 1127; Estes v. McGehee, (1923) 133 Miss. 174, 97 So. 530; Acree v. North, (1923) 110 Neb. 92, 192 N. W. 947; Jahns v. Clark, (1926) 138 Wash. 288, 244 Pac. 729. *cf.* Jones v. Caldwell, (1913) 23 Idaho 467, 130 Pac. 995.

[8] Dabbs v. Richardson, (1924) 137 Miss. 789, 102 So. 769.

[9] National Benevolent Soc. v. Barker, (1922) 155 Ark. 506, 244 S. W. 720; Gardner v. Hobbs, (1949) 69 Idaho 288, 206 P. 2d 539; Cross v. Equitable Life Assur. Soc., (1940) 228

⋙→

did not exist at the time the communication was made or the information was acquired, then the testimony of the physician is admissible.[10] Whether the relation ever existed, or, having existed, still continues at any particular moment, is, in every case, a question of fact.[11] Until the relationship is made known, there is no confidence to be protected. The court, therefore, must find that the confidential relation of physician and patient existed before it would be justified in ruling that the physician cannot testify, and the court can only so find after hearing evidence on the subject in open

---

Iowa 800, 293 N. W. 464; Battis v. Chicago, R. I. & Pac. Ry., (1904) 124 Iowa 623, 100 N. W. 543; United States Fid. & Guar. Co. v. Hood, (1920) 124 Miss. 548, 87 So. 115, 15 A. L. R. 605; Dubcich v. Grand Lodge, (1903) 33 Wash. 651, 74 Pac. 832. While it is clear that to bring the case within the operation of the statute, it must appear that the relationship existed, yet even that alone is not sufficient. In practically every jurisdiction which has enacted the privilege, it must also appear that the information so obtained was necessary to enable the physician to prescribe or act for the patient in his professional capacity. State v. Newsome, (1928) 195 N. C. 552, 560, 143 S. E. 187. "It is only when the relationship of physician or surgeon and patient has been established between the parties, and statements are made by the latter to the former, in reliance upon this relationship, for the purpose of affording information to the physician to enable him to prescribe treatment for the patient or to enable the surgeon to do some act for him as a surgeon, that the statute renders the statements inadmissible as evidence against the patient."

This essential yet troublesome element of the privilege is discussed in c.X, herein.

[10] Travelers Ins. Co. v. Bergeron, (1928) 25 F. 2d 680, cert. denied 278 U. S. 638, 73 Law. Ed. 553, 49 Su. Ct. 33, 58 A. L. R. 1127 (autopsical examination); Estate of Baird, (1916) 173 Cal. 617, 160 Pac. 1078 (physician attended birth of illegitimate child; admissions of paternity by father not privileged) ; Bower v. Bower, (1895) 142 Ind. 194, 41 N. E. 523 (physician called upon patient to collect a bill); Cherokee v. Aetna Life Ins. Co. (1933) 215 Iowa 1000, 247 N. W. 495 (physical examination of applicant for pension); Woods v. Lisbon, (1908) 138 Iowa 402, 116 N. W. 143, 16 L. R. A. (n. s.) 886 (uninvited physician observed operation on another's patient); Smith v. Davis, (1949) 168 Kan. 210, 212 P. 2d 322 (information acquired on social visits); State v. Lyons, (1904) 113 La. 959, 37 So. 890 (physician made friendly call on accused in hospital); Cromeenes v. Sovereign Camp, (1920) 205 Mo. App. 419, 224 S. W. 15 (physician attending baby acquires information from father regarding his own venereal disease); Hamilton v. Crowe, (1903) 175 Mo. 634, 75 S. W. 389 (former patient consults physician regarding a will) ; Bowers v. Industrial Comm'n., (1939) _____ Ohio App._____ , 30 Ohio Law Abst. 353 (physical examination of applicant for admission to State School for the Blind). Additional cases will be cited in appropriate sections of this chapter.

[11] Griffith, J., in National Mut. Life Ass'n v. Godrich, [1909] 10 Comm. L. R. (Australia) 1, 11.

court.[12] It is not always easy to determine when the relation exists, and there has been some difference of opinion on the subject; but the courts generally hold that whenever the circumstances are such that the relation can reasonably and consistently be held to exist, that view of the case will be taken.[13]

33. *Creation of the Relation: In General*

The relation of physician[1] and patient[2] which the privilege statutes are designed to protect, may be said to begin when the physician, in his professional character, first attends the sick or injured person and undertakes to advise, prescribe for or treat him;[3] and this is true whether such attendance results from the voluntary call of the person upon the physician, or from the exigencies of the person's situation.[4] So far as the statute is concerned,

---

[12] Cincinnati, H. & D. R. R. v. Gross, (1917) 186 Ind. 471, 114 N. E. 962; Pennsylvania R. R. v. Hough, (1929) 88 Ind. App. 601, 161 N. E. 705; Smoot v. Kansas City, (1906) 194 Mo. 513, 92 S. W. 363; Bowles v. Kansas City, (1892) 51 Mo. App. 416; Meyer v. Supreme Lodge, K. of P., (1904) 178 N. Y. 63, 70 N. E. 111, 64 L. R. A. 839, aff'd. 198 U. S. 508, 49 Law. Ed. 1146, 25 Su. Ct. 754; Morris v. New York, Ontario & W. Ry., (1895) 148 N. Y. 88, 42 N. E. 410; Kelly v. Dykes, (1916) 174 App. Div. 786, 161 N. Y. S. 551, app. dismissed, 220 N. Y. 653, 115 N. E. 1042; Willig v. Prudential Ins. Co., (1942) 71 Ohio App. 255, 49 N. E. 2d 421.

[13] Cincinnati, H. & D. R. R. v. Gross, (1917) 186 Ind. 471, 114 N. E. 962; Norwood v. State, (1930) 158 Miss. 550, 130 So. 733. In Palmer v. United Commercial Travelers, (1932) 187 Minn. 272, 245 N. W. 146, two physicians were summoned to resuscitate a man found lying under his automobile in his garage. Their efforts were in vain. Was it a dead body—with which no confidential relation could exist—or a live man? The physicians could not be sure. Held: the privilege attached.

[1] For meaning of "physician" as used in statutes, see §29, herein.

[2] For definition of "patient," see Rule 27 (1) (2) of the Uniform Rules of Evidence (1953), Appendix, herein.

A fetus may be a patient. Jones v. Jones, (1955) 208 Misc. 721, 144 N. Y. S. 2d 820.

A dead body is not a patient. Travelers Ins. Co. v. Bergeron, (1928) 25 F. 2d 680, cert. denied 278 U. S. 638, 73 Law. Ed. 553, 49 Su. Ct. 33, 58 A. L. R. 1127. See § 44, herein.

[3] Matter of Freeman, (1887) 46 Hun. (N. Y.) 458, 461: "Attendance on a patient means more than being in the same room; and acting in a professional capacity means acting in reference to that patient."

[4] Epstein v. Pennsylvania R. R., (1913) 250 Mo. 1, 156 S. W. 699, 48 L. R. A. (n. s.) 394, Ann. Cas. 1915 A. 423 (physician voluntarily aiding victims of train wreck); Meyer v. Supreme Lodge, K. of P., (1904) 178 N. Y. 63, 70 N. E. 111, aff'd. 198 U. S. 508, 49 Law.

the relation springs from the fact of professional care and treatment irrespective of the causes which led to the physician's attendance upon the afflicted person.[5]   An examination made in order to advise or prescribe establishes the same relation.[6]   The relation may exist regardless of the time element.   One interview,[7] or even a few moment's employment, is enough.[8]

But where a party *denies,* even on cross-examination, that the relation of physician and patient ever existed, that settles the question—at least for that trial—and this is true even though the physician testifies the relation did exist.   Thus, where the plaintiff in a personal injury action testified that he had never consulted any physician prior to his injury in question, he thereby asserts that no physician exists against whom he might lodge the objection of incompetency to disclose confidential communications occurring prior to such injury.   In other words, such declaration opens wide the door to any physician to testify fully to any professional treatment furnished by said physician to said party, prior to the alleged injury in question.[9]

Ed. 1146, 25 Su. Ct. 754, 64 L. R. A. 839 (house physician tried to save hotel guest, over his protest, from death by poison taken with suicidal intent). A few courts appear to have held that where the physician gratuitously renders only emergency first aid treatment, the relation does not exist. Hanlon v. Woodhouse, (1945) 113 Colo. 504, 160 P. 2d 998; Griffiths v. Metropolitan Street Ry., (1902) 171 N. Y. 106, 63 N. E. 808; Dewert v. Cincinnati Milling Mach Co., (1938) 38 Ohio Law Rep. 318, 15 Ohio Law Abst. 268; Ballard v. Yellow Cab Co., (1944) 20 Wash. 2d 67, 72, 145 P. 2d 1019 (dictum). It is respectfully submitted that this view is narrow and unsound. See Malone v. Industrial Comm'n., (1940) 18 Ohio O. 317, 32 Ohio Law Abst. 231, aff'd. 140 Ohio St. 292, 43 N. E. 2d 266.

[5] Tweith v. Duluth, M. & I. R. Ry., (1946) 66 F. Supp. 427; Cherokee v. Aetna Life Ins. Co., (1933) 215 Iowa 1000, 427 N. W. 495; Battis v. Chicago, R. I. & Pac. Ry., (1904) 124 Iowa 623, 100 N. W. 543; Obermeyer v. Logeman Chair Mfg. Co., (1906) 120 Mo. App. 59, 96 S. W. 673, aff'd. 229 Mo. 97, 129 S. W. 209; Meyer v. Supreme Lodge, K. of P., (1904) 178 N. Y. 63, 70 N. E. 111, aff'd. 198 U. S. 508, 49 Law. Ed. 1146, 25 Su. Ct. 754, 64 L. R. A. 839; Munz v. Salt Lake City R. R., (1902) 25 Utah 220, 70 Pac. 852.

[6] Meyer v. Supreme Lodge, K. of P., (1904) 178 N. Y. 63, 70 N. E. 111, aff'd. 198 U. S. 508, 49 Law. Ed. 1146, 25 Su. Ct. 754, 64 L. R. A. 839.

[7] Grattan v. Metropolitan Life Ins. Co., (1883) 92 N. Y. 274.

[8] Harvey v. Silber, (1942) 300 Mich. 510, 2 N. W. 2d 483 (physician looked at person's x-ray plate).

[9] Jacobs v. Cedar Rapids, (1917) 181 Iowa 407, 164 N. W. 891. But see Hirschberg v.

34. Necessity of Contract

There is authority for the view that the relationship of physician and patient arises in contract, either express or implied, and can be created in no other way.[1] However, it has been said that there is no necessity for the existence of an express or even an implied contractual relation for hire.[2] Ordinarily, the relation is a consensual one wherein the patient knowingly seeks the medical advice and assistance of the physician and the physician knowingly accepts him as a patient. But it is not indispensable to the existence of the relation that the afflicted person himself select and hire the physician.[3] It is quite common for physicians to be summoned by persons other than the sick or injured person, and certainly the privilege statute would be robbed of much of its virtue if a physician thus called were to be excluded from its operation merely because he was not selected and employed by the afflicted person.[4] It is generally held, therefore, that it is not necessary that any con-

---

Southern Pac. Co., (1919) 180 Cal. 774, 183 Pac. 141. Such denial, if made in an application for insurance, will not have the same effect if the evidence at the trial clearly shows that the relation did exist. Cross v. Equitable Life Assur. Soc., (1940) 228 Iowa 800, 293 N. W. 464.

[1] Smart v. Kansas City, (1907) 208 Mo. 162, 189, 105 S. W. 709, 14 L. R. A. (n. s.) 565, 13 Ann. Cas. 932; Matter of Freeman, (1887) 46 Hun. (N. Y.) 458, 461; Bowers v. Santee, (1919) 99 Ohio St. 361, 124 N. E. 238; Lumpkin v. Metropolitan Life Ins. Co., (1945) 75 Ohio App. 310, 62 N. E. 189, aff'd. 146 Ohio St. 25, 64 N. E. 63 (but the Supreme Court declined to consider this question); Dewert v. Cincinnati Milling Mach Co., (1933) 38 Ohio Law Rep. 318, 15 Ohio Law Abst. 268 (criticized and not followed in Malone v. Industrial Comm'n., (1940) 18 Ohio O. 317, 32 Ohio Law Abst. 231, aff'd. 140 Ohio St. 292, 43 N. E. 2d 266).

[2] Epstein v. Pennsylvania R. R., (1913) 250 Mo. 1, 156 S. W. 699, 48 L. R. A. (n. s.) 394, Ann. Cas. 1915 A. 423.

[3] Arizona & New Mexico Ry v. Clark, (1913) 207 Fed. 817, aff'd. (1915) 235 U. S. 669, 59 Law. Ed. 415, 35 Su. Ct. 210, L. R. A. 1915 C. 834; Union Pac. R. R. v. Thomas, (1907) 152 Fed. 365; Brayman v. Russell & Pugh Lumber Co., (1917) 31 Idaho 140, 169 Pac. 932; Louisville & S. Indiana Traction Co. v. Snead, (1911) 49 Ind. App. 16, 93 N. E. 177; Walmer-Roberts Co. v. Hennessey, (1921) 191 Iowa 86, 181 N. W. 798; Russell v. Penn Mutual Life Ins. Co., (1941) 70 Ohio App. 113, 41 N. E. 2d 251; People v. Murphy, (1886) 101 N. Y. 126, 4 N. E. 326.

[4] Renihan v. Dennin, (1886) 103 N. Y. 573, 9 N. E. 320; Duggan v. Phelps, (1903) 82 App. Div. 509, 81 N. Y. E. 916.

tractual relation should be expressly created between them.[5] If, upon request of others or upon his own motion the physician assumes to advise or administer treatment to the afflicted person and the latter in any way acquiesces therein, the relation is thereby established.[6] The mere fact of the physician's attendance upon a person needing medical assistance will in most cases be sufficient evidence of the relationship.[7] It is, therefore, a matter of no consequence that the physician was summoned by a member of the patient's family,[8] by a lawyer's "runner,"[9] by another physician,[10] by the person who injured him,[11] or by friends or utter strangers.[12] Moreover, since professional attendance upon a sick or

---

[5] O'Connor, J., in National Mutual Life Ass'n v. Godrich, [1909] 10 Comm. L. R. Australia) 1, 28. *Accord:* Cherokee v. Aetna Life Ins. Co., (1933) 215 Iowa 1000, 247 N. W. 495; Linscott v. Hughbanks, (1934) 140 Kan. 353, 37 P. 2d 26; Epstein v. Pennsylvania R. R., (1913) 250 Mo. 1, 156 S. W. 699; 48 L. R. A. (n. s.) 394, Ann. Cas. 1915 A. 423; Meyer v. Supreme Lodge, K. of P., (1904) 178 N. Y. 63, 70 N. E. 111, aff'd. 198 U. S. 508, 49 Law. Ed. 1146, 25 Su. Ct. 754, 64 L. R. A. 839. In Jones v. Jones, (1955) 208 Misc. 721, 144 N. Y. S. 2d 820, it was held that an obstetrician attending an expectant mother does in fact treat the child as well as the mother and, from the viewpoint of the physician-patient privilege, the viable fetus becomes the patient of the mother's obstetrician although he, of course, cannot be directly engaged by the viable fetus even when later born. For comments on this case, see (1956) 20 Albany L. Rev. 242; (1956) 31 N. Y. U. L. Rev. 1545; (1956) 28 Rocky Mt. L. Rev. 425; (1956) 7 Syracuse L. Rev. 347; (1956) 17 U. Pitt. L. Rev. 723.

[6] Battis v. Chicago, R. I. & Pac. Ry., (1904) 124 Iowa 623, 100 N. W. 543.

[7] O'Connor, J., in National Mut. Life Ass'n. v. Godrich, [1909] 10 Comm. L. R. (Australia) 1, 28; Epstein v. Pennsylvania R. R., (1913) 250 Mo. 1, 156 S. W. 699, 48 L. R. A. (n. s.) 394, Ann. Cas. 1915 A. 423; Weitz v. Mound City Ry., (1893) 53 Mo. App. 39. Of course, there may be cases in which the prima facie inference from that fact may be rebutted.

[8] Palmer v. United Commercial Travelers, (1932) 187 Minn. 272, 245 N. W. 146.

[9] Michaels v. Harvey, (1915) _____ Mo. App. _____, 179 S. W. 735.

[10] Arizona & New Mexico Ry. v. Clark, (1913) 207 Fed. 817, aff'd. (1915) 235 U. S. 669, 59 Law. Ed. 415, 35 Su. Ct. 210, L. R. A. 1915 C. 834; Tweith v. Duluth, M. & I. R. R., (1946) 66 F. Supp. 427; Leonczak v. Minneapolis, St. P. & S. S. M. Ry., (1924) 161 Minn. 304, 201 N. W. 551; Provident Life & Acc. Ins. Co. v. Chapman, (1928) 152 Miss. 747, 118 So. 437; Renihan v. Dennin, (1886) 103 N. Y. 573, 9 N. E. 320.

[11] Union Pac. R. R. v. Thomas, (1907) 152 Fed. 365; Colorado Midland Ry. v. McGarry, (1907) 41 Colo. 398, 92 Pac. 915; Battis v. Chicago, R. I. & Pac. Ry., (1904) 124 Iowa 623, 100 N. W. 543; Walmer-Roberts v. Hennessey, (1921) 191 Iowa 86, 181 N. W. 798; Yazoo & M. V. R. R. v. Messina, (1915) 109 Miss. 143, 67 So. 963.

[12] Freeberg v. State, (1912) 92 Neb. 346, 138 N. W. 143, Ann. Cas. 1913 E 1101; People

injured person is the decisive test, the relation may exist notwithstanding such person was unconcious or incapable of acting for himself,[13] or that he was treated without his consent, and vigorously protested or resisted the physician's assistance.[14]

The fact that the person receiving medical advice or treatment neither paid nor agreed to pay the physician is immaterial.[15] The relation may still exist even though the services of the physician were gratuitous,[16] or were paid for by a third person,[17] or were not paid at all.[18] The mere fact that the afflicted person is a charity patient in a hospital will not deprive him of the full protection of the privilege; the relationship may exist notwithstanding he is a free patient.[19]

←

v. Decina, (1956) 2 N. Y. 2d 133, 138 N. E. 2d 799; Meyer v. Supreme Lodge, K. of P., (1904) 178 N. Y. 63, 70 N. E. 111, aff'd. 198 U. S. 508, 49 Law. Ed. 1146, 25 Su. Ct. 754, 64 L. R. A. 839; Munz v. Salt Lake City R. R., (1902) 25 Utah 220, 70 Pac. 852.

[13] Battis v. Chicago, R. I. & Pac. Ry., (1904) 124 Iowa 623, 100 N. W. 543; Meyer v. Supreme Lodge, K. of P., (1904), (1904) 178 N. Y. 63, 70 N. E. 111, aff'd. 198 U. S. 508, 49 Law. Ed. 1146, 25 Su. Ct. 754, 64 L. R. A. 839; Edington v. Mutual Life Ins. Co., (1875) 5 Hun. 1, rev'd. on other grounds, (1876) 67 N. Y. 185; Nugent v. Cudahy Packing Co., (1905) 126 Iowa 517, 102 N. W. 442 (considered but not decided) The relation may exist between an insane person and a physician. Taylor v. United States, (1955) 95 App. D. C. 373, 222 F. 2d 398.

[14] Union Pacific R. R. v. Thomas, (1907) 152 Fed. 365; Meyer v. Supreme Lodge, K. of P., (1904) 178 N. Y. 63, 70 N. E. 111, aff'd. 198 U. S. 508, 49 Law. Ed. 1146, 25 Su. Ct. 754, 64 L. R. A. 839.

[15] Battis v. Chicago, R. I. & Pac. Ry., (1904) 124 Iowa 623, 100 N. W. 543; Provident Life & Acc. Ins. Co. v. Chapman, (1928) 152 Miss. 747, 118 So. 437.

[16] Hallenberg v. Hallenberg, (1919) 144 Minn. 39, 174 N. W. 443; Taylor v. Shields, (1951) _____Ohio App._____, 64 Ohio Law Abst. 193, 111 N. E. 2d 595.

[17] Union Pac. R. R. v. Thomas, (1907) 152 Fed. 365; Colorado Midland Ry. v. McGarry, (1907) 41 Colo. 398, 92 Pac. 915; New York, Chicago & St. L. R. R. v. Mushrush, (1894) 11 Ind. App. 192, 37 N. E. 954; Walmer-Roberts v. Hennessey, (1921) 191 Iowa 86, 181 N. W. 798; Battis v. Chicago, R. I. & Pac. Ry., (1904) 124 Iowa 623, 100 N. W. 543; Yazoo & M. V. R. R. v. Messina, (1915) 109 Miss. 143, 65 So. 963; Noble v. Kansas City, (1902) 95 Mo. App. 167, 68 S. W. 969; Stapleton v. Chicago, B. & Q. R. R., (1917) 101 Neb. 201, 162 N. W. 644; People v. Murphy, (1886) 101 N. Y. 126, 4 N. E. 326; Malone v. Industrial Comm'n., (1940) 18 Ohio O. 317, 32 Ohio Law Abst. 231, aff'd. (1942) 140 Ohio St. 292, 43 N. E. 2d 266; 28 R. C. L., *Witnesses*, § 130.

[18] Hallenberg v. Hallenberg, (1919) 144 Minn. 39, 174 N. W. 443. *cf.* Hanlon v. Woodhouse, (1945) 113 Colo. 504, 160 P. 2d 998.

[19] Metropolitan Life Ins. Co. v. McSwain, (1927) 149 Miss. 455, 115 So. 555: Smart v.

⟫→

35. *Curative Treatment Must Be Contemplated*

As a general rule, the relationship of physician and patient does not exist unless the physician's consultation with, or attendance upon, the prospective patient is with a view to protective, alleviative, or curative treatment.[1] Moreover, it is clear that the statutory privilege pertains only to matters germane to the physician's diagnosis and treatment of the patient.[2] There is no privilege as to information acquired by a physician through the physical or mental examination of a person unless it is made in contemplation of, and as a preparation for, medical care and treatment;[3] hence, if the physician's examination of, or conference with, the person is for a purpose other than prescribing or doing any act for him in the way of medical care or treatment, the physician is not disqualified

---

Kansas City, (1907) 208 Mo. 162, 190, 105 S. W. 709, 14 L. R. A. (n. s.) 565, 13 Ann. Cas. 932: "It makes no difference in principle so far as the physician's disqualification is concerned, whether he acquires the confidential communications from a poor or pay patient, in a private residence or hospital, or from a charity patient in a public hospital."

Bauch v. Schultz, (1919) 109 Misc. 548, 180 N. Y. S. 188.

[1] San Francisco v. Superior Court, (1951) 37 Cal. 2d 227, 231 P. 2d 26, 25 A. L. R. 2d 1418; Clark v. State, (1899) 8 Kan. App. 782, 61 Pac. 814; Krueger v. Henschke, (1941) 210 Minn. 307, 298 N. W. 44; Racine v. Woiteshek, (1947) 251 Wis. 404, 29 N. W. 2d 752; Casson v. Schoenfeld, (1918) 166 Wis. 401, 166 N. W. 23, L. R. A. 1918 C. 162. The circumstances may be such that the inference may arise that, if curative or remedial measures were available, such were contemplated. Bassil v. Ford Motor Co., (1936) 278 Mich. 173, 270 N. W. 258, 107 A. L. R. 1491. See Rule 27 (1) (a) Uniform Rules of Evidence (1953), Appendix, herein; Rule 220 (a) Model Code of Evidence (1942). See also note, 107 A. L. R. 1495.

[2] Smith v. Davis, (1949) 168 Kan. 210, 212 P. 2d 322.

[3] Browne v. Brooke, (1956) 236 F. 2d 686; Taylor v. United States, (1955) 95 App. D. C. 373, 222 F. 2d 398; Travelers Ins. Co. v. Bergeron, (1928) 25 F. 2d 680, cert. denied 278 U. S. 638, 73 Law. Ed. 553, 49 Su. Ct. 33, 58 A. L. R. 1127; Krueger v. Henschke, (1941) 210 Minn. 307, 298 N. W. 44; Arnold v. Maryville, (1905) 110 Mo. App. 254, 85 S. W. 107; Nichols v. State, (1922) 109 Neb. 335, 191 N. W. 333.

See Rule 27 (2) (b) Uniform Rules of Evidence (1953), Appendix, herein; Rule 221 (b) Model Code of Evidence (1942).

Cf. Livingston v. Omaha & Council Bluffs St. Ry., (1919) 104 Neb. 118, 175 N. W. 662. (female physician of Juvenile Court not permitted to disclose condition of girl when brought to her for physical examination only).

Stapleton v. Chicago, B. & Q. R. R., (1917) 101 Neb. 201, 162 N. W. 644. (privilege applicable where defendant's physician made repeated examinations of claimant but did not prescribe for or treat him).

as a witness and may disclose any information so acquired concerning such person, since the relation of physician and patient does not exist under such circumstances.[4]

Where, in an action for damages for personal injury, a physician is requested by the plaintiff's attorney to examine his client for the sole purpose of aiding the attorney in his preparation of a lawsuit, the relation of physician and patient does not exist;[5] nor where the examination is made for the sole purpose of qualifying the examining physician to be a witness at the trial.[6] The relation

_____ __ __

[4] Hopkins v. State, (1951) 212 Miss. 772, 55 So. 2d 467; Arnold v. Maryville, (1905) 110 Mo. App. 254, 85 S. W. 107; Kelly v. Dykes, (1916) 174 App. Div. 786, 161 N. Y. S. 551, app. denied 220 N. Y. 653, 115 N. E. 1042. Suetta v. Carnegie-Illinois Steel Co., (1955) ....Ohio App.........., 144 N. E. 2d 292.

A mere casual examination will not create the relation. Edington v. Aetna Life Ins. Co., (1878) 13 Hun. 543. In this case, the witness, a physician, was also the county clerk and on an occasion when the insured, an attorney, was in the clerk's office, he requested the witness to look at an eruption on his skin, and the witness did so on that occasion only, and gratuitously. At the trial, the witness expressed an opinion as to the character and cause of the eruption. In holding this proper, the court said: (p. 552) "It can hardly be said that he attended [the assured] as a patient in a professional character, certainly not that the information acquired by him was to enable him to prescribe for him as a physician. It does not appear that any prescription was made or asked for. Ordinarily, perhaps, it is to be presumed, in the absence of proof to the contrary, that when a physician attends a person as a patient, in a professional character, he does so for the purpose of prescribing for him, but here we think the presumption does not arise, for the reason that the relation of physician and patient contemplated by the statute did not exist." Rev'd. on other grounds, (1879) 77 N. Y. 564.

Hospital records made in connection with examinations made of decedent by physicians employed by his employer are not privileged where such examinations did not include treatment nor advice and clearly were not for the purpose of alleviating decedent's pain nor curing his malady. Suetta v. Carnegie-Illinois Steel Co., (1955) ....Ohio App.........., 144 N. E. 2d 292.

[5] San Francisco v. Superior Court, (1951) 37 Cal. 2d 227, 231 P. 2d 26, 25 A. L. R. 2d 1418. The court disapproved a contrary view expressed in Webb v. Francis J. Lewald Coal Co., (1931) 214 Cal. 182, 4 P. 2d 532, 77 A. L. R. 675; however, it was held that the attorney-client privilege would bar the disclosure. Jacobs v. Cross, (1872) 19 Minn. 454; McMillen v. Industrial Comm'n., (1941) ....Ohio App.........., 34 Ohio Law Abst. 435, 37 N. E. 2d 632.

[6] Taylor v. United States, (1955) 95 App. D. C. 373, 222 F. 2d 398; Nesbit v. People, (1894) 19 Colo. 441, 36 Pac. 221; McGuire v. Chicago & Alton R. R., (1915) ....Mo. ...., 178 S. W. 79, L. R. A. 1915 F 888; Arnold v. Maryville, (1905) 110 Mo. App. 254, 85 S. W. 107; Kelly v. Dykes, (1916) 174 App. Div. 786; 161 N. Y. S. 551, appeal dis-

》》》→

does not exist where an employer sends an employee to its physician, not to treat or cure him, but for the single purpose of enabling the employer to intelligently decide whether it could safely and properly continue him as one of its employees.[7] The examination of an applicant for insurance by a medical examiner of the company to ascertain whether he is an insurable risk, does not create the relation of physician and patient since no curative treatment is contemplated.[8]

Where the examination is solely for the purpose of determining a person's mental competency with a view to an application for his release from guardianship and not for the purpose of curing or helping her, the relation does not exist;[9] nor where the examination is made at the request of the attorney of a woman for the purpose of ascertaining whether she has the mental capacity to make a will.[10] An examination made for the purpose of determining an applicant's eligibility for admission to a school for the blind does not create the relation.[11] Where, in a bastardy proceeding, the prosecutrix submitted to an examination, at the request of the defendant,

<hr />

missed 220 N. Y. 653, 115 N. E. 1042; Henry v. New York, Lake Erie & W. R. R., (1890) 57 Hun. 76, 10 N. Y. S. 508.

  Contra: Doran v. Cedar Rapids & M. C. Ry., (1902) 117 Iowa 442, 90 N. W. 815.

[7] Cherpeski v. Great Northern Ry., (1915) 128 Minn. 360, 150 N. W. 1091; New York Central R. R. v. Wiler, (1931) 124 Ohio St. 118, 177 N. E. 205; Moutzoukos v. Mutual Ben. Health & Acc. Ass'n., (1927) 69 Utah 309, 254 Pac. 1005.

[8] Bouligny v. Metropolitan Life Ins. Co., (1939) _____Mo. App_____, 133 S. W. 2d 1094; Lynch v. Germania Life Ins. Co., (1909) 132 App. Div. 571, 116 N. Y. S. 998. No confidences are entrusted to the physician since it is plain he is acting for the company, not the applicant. The New Zealand statute expressly exempts from its operation communications made to a physician "in or about the effecting by any person of an insurance on the life of himself or any other person."

[9] *In re* Will of Bruendl, (1899) 102 Wis. 45, 78 N. W. 169. See also People v. Sliney, (1893) 137 N. Y. 570, 33 N. E. 150. In Mulvena v. Alexander, (1936) 278 Mich. 265, 270 N. W. 291, two physicians were appointed by the probate court to examine a woman and to report whether she should be committed to an asylum. Held: no relation of physican and patient existed.

  Where the purpose of the examination is to enable the physician to prepare a report on a person's mental condition in connection with proceedings to appoint a conservator for her, no relation exists. Browne v. Brooke, (1956) 236 F. 2d 686.

[10] Matter of Freeman, (1887) 46 Hun. (N. Y.) 458. One judge dissented.

[11] Bowers v. Industrial Comm'n., (1939) _____Ohio App._____, 30 Ohio Law Abst. 353.

to discover the period of her pregnancy and not for the purpose of professional advice or treatment, the relation does not exist and the physician may testify to all that was said or done upon that occasion.[12] The relation does not exist where the physician interviewed his one-time patient about the payment of his fee for services rendered.[13] No relation exists between a physician, acting for the federal government, and an applicant for a pension, where the sole purpose of the physician's examination of the applicant is to determine whether he is entitled to a pension as a disabled veteran, and no treatment was given or contemplated;[14] nor did it exist where the only purpose of the physician's examination was to exempt the person from a poll tax or from working on the highways of the county.[15]

While it is true that to create the relation of physician and patient, curative or remedial measures must be contemplated, still it does not follow necessarily that the physician must actually prescribe for or treat the afflicted person.[16] Although the statute implies that the physician is to do some act in his professional character, this may properly be negative, that is, the physician may decide that no medical care or treatment is needed.[17] There are many instances where the physician is convinced that medicine or surgery will do no good and that there is no advice to give; and it certainly would be unreasonable to suppose that the lawmakers intended to deny the patient the protection of the privilege merely because his condition as revealed to the physician is not subject to

---

[12] Clark v. State, (1899) 8 Kan. App. 782, 61 Pac. 814.

[13] Seifert v. State, (1903) 160 Ind. 464, 67 N. E. 100; Chlandla v. St. Louis Transit Co., (1908) 213 Mo. 244, 112 S. W. 249 (1908).

[14] Cherokee v. Aetna Life Ins. Co., (1933) 215 Iowa 1000, 247 N. W. 495. But when the examination was made with a view to sending the veteran to an army hospital, it was held that the relation existed. Cruce v. Missouri Pac. Ry., (1926) 171 Ark. 1074, 287 S. W. 583.

[15] Woods v. National Aid Life Ass'n., (1935) ......Mo. App ......, 87 S. W. 2d 698.

[16] Beave v. St. Louis Transit Co., (1909) 212 Mo. 331, 111 S. W. 52; Smart v. Kansas City, (1907) 208 Mo. 162, 105 S. W. 709, 14 L. R. A. (n. s.) 565, 13 Ann. Cas. 982.

[17] People v. Decina, (1956) 2 N. Y. 2d 133, 138 N. E. 2d 799; Matter of Freeman, (1887) 46 Hun. (N. Y.) 458; Grattan v. Metropolitan Life Ins. Co., (1881) 24 Hun. (N. Y.) 43.

treatment.[18] It has been held that the relation exists where an afflicted person requests a diagnostician to examine and advise him as to his condition, although the physician did not prescribe for him.[19]

36. *Medical Examination at Instance of Third Person: Civil Actions*

Except in a few jurisdictions,[1] a party, in a civil action, may be required to submit to a medical examination, before or during the trial, by a physician selected by his adversary or appointed by the court, whenever the physical or mental condition of such party is one of the matters in dispute. Where, in such case, the physician is openly acting in the discharge of his duty and it is clearly understood by the person examined that the physician is acting as an investigator at the instance of the adverse party or the court, and that the purpose of the examination is to obtain information as to the cause, nature and extent of the party's malady or injury, and not for the purpose of affording him medical advice or administering treatment, the confidential relationship of physician and patient does not exist, and the physician may testify to any information he may have gained by observation, communications, or otherwise during the course of such examination.[2]

---

[18] Bassil v. Ford Motor Co., (1936) 278 Mich. 173, 270 N. W. 258, 107 A. L. R. 1491. (patient sought advice as to whether he was impotent).

See also Lombard v. Columbia National Life Ins. Co., (1917) 50 Utah 554, 168 Pac. 269.

[19] Lande v. Travelers Ins. Co., (1934) 241 App. Div. 96, 271 N. Y. S. 551, aff'd. 265 N. Y. 655, 193 N. E. 430.

[1] See § 77, herein.

[2] Browne v. Brooke, (1956) 236 F. 2d 686; Freel v. Market Street Cable Ry., (1892) 97 Cal. 40, 31 Pac. 730 (In this case, however, the privilege attached, since the examining physician went further and undertook to prescribe for and treat the person); Chicago, I. & L. Ry. v. Gorman, (1911) 47 Ind. App. 432, 94 N. E. 730; Battis v. Chicago, R. I. & Pac. Ry., (1904) 124 Iowa 623, 100 N. W. 543 (privilege attached, however, since the physician went further and treated the person); Mulvena v. Alexander, (1936) 278 Mich. 265, 270 N. W. 291; Hierl v. McClure, (1953) 238 Minn. 335, 56 N. W. 2d 721; Krueger v. Henschke, (1941) 210 Minn. 307, 298 N. W. 44; Metropolitan Life Ins. Co. v. Evans, (1938) 183 Miss. 859, 185 So. 426; McGuire v. Chicago & Alton R. R., (1915) _____ Mo._____, 178 S. W. 79, L. R. A. 1915 F. 888; Heath v. Broadway & Seventh Ave.

》》→

Occasionally, novel situations occur in connection with such examinations. In *Michaels* v. *Harvey*,[3] the court refused to allow the examining physician to testify, not because the relation of physician and patient existed, but because the examination was made pursuant to an attempt to compromise or settle the plaintiff's claim. In *Plater* v. *W. C. Mullins Construction Co.*,[4] counsel for plaintiff consented to a physical examination by *two* physicians selected by defendants. They, however, sent three, one of whom was not known by plaintiff to be a physician. At the trial, defendants called the third physician as a witness. Plaintiff objected and contended that the agreement of her counsel that she might be examined by two physicians was tantamount to an agreement on the part of defendants that they would not use any other physician as a witness. The trial court refused to allow him to testify. This was error. With or without a previous agreement, plaintiff voluntarily permitted a third person to be present and take part in an examination which was calculated to reveal her physical condition. In *Strafford* v. *Northern Pac. R.R.*,[5] defendant's physicians had treated the injured plaintiff at a hospital for three weeks, but later, at the request of defendant, one of them made two examinations of plaintiff, not as her physician for the purpose of treating her, but for the sole purpose of enabling him to testify as to her condition. Called as a wit-

---

R. R., (1890) 8 N. Y. S. 863; State, *ex rel* Galloway v. Industrial Comm'n., (1938) 134 Ohio St. 496, 17 N. E. 2d 918. Examination under Workmen's Compensation Law. Suetta v. Carnegie-Illinois Steel Corp., (1955) .... Ohio App....... , 144 N. E. 2d 292. In McGuire v. Chicago & Alton R. R., infra, the plaintiff conceded that defendant's physician could disclose any information his examination revealed concerning his physical condition, but contended that since the examination was compulsory, the physician could not reveal any communications made to him relating to the history of plaintiff's condition. Since the record did not disclose that the communications were not "perfectly voluntary," the Supreme Court declined to consider whether the physician would have the right to testify, over objection of plaintiff, to any statements of plaintiff elicited by the physician under assumed authority from the trial court in such circumstances. See also c. c. XIII, XIV, herein.

[3] (1915) ....Mo. App......., 179 S. W. 735. *Cf.* Plater v. W. C. Mullins Const. Co., (1929) 223 Mo. App. 650, 17 S. W. 2d 658.

[4] (1929) 223 Mo. App. 650, 17 S. W. 2d 658.

[5] (1917) 95 Wash. 450, 164 Pac. 71.

ness by defendant, he was permitted to testify fully to what these examinations revealed. This was not error.[6]

37. Same: Criminal Actions

There seems to be no dissent anywhere from the proposition that where a physician is directed by law enforcement officers, the court, or by counsel to make an examination of a person in order to ascertain his physical or mental condition for the purposes of a criminal prosecution or proceeding and the person so examined then and there knows, or the facts are such as to reasonably give knowledge, that the examination is solely for the purposes aforesaid, the confidential relationship of physician and patient contemplated by the statute does not exist.[1] Where a person, charged with committing a lewd act upon a little girl, submits without objection to a physical examination, with knowledge that such examination is for the purpose alone of searching for physical symptoms bearing upon his guilt or innocence and not for diagnosis and treatment, the relation of physician and patient does not exist, and the physician may testify to what the examination revealed.[2] Communications by the prosecuting witness to a physician on his examination

---

[6] Per Curiam (p. 453): "As to these examinations, he was as competent to testify as any other physician or surgeon would be under the same circumstances; the fact that he had previously treated her did not preclude him from testifying to matters he had subsequently learned as to her condition under circumstances not precluding his right to testify. In order to render a physician incompetent, the information which he is called upon to disclose must have been acquired while he was attending the patient in a professional capacity for the purpose of treating her ailments; there is no privilege when the examination is made by the physician for the express purpose of publishing the results—such, for example, as testifying in an action for personal injuries." The decision seems unsound. Did the patient fully understand that the examinations were made solely for the benefit of the company? Could the physician-witness really segregate the information he had previously obtained during his professional attendance upon the injured woman?

For other cases involving examinations made at instance of third persons, see § § 37, 38, 39, herein.

[1] Taylor v. United States, (1955) 95 App. D. C. 373, 222 F. 2d 398; Norwood v. State, (1930) 158 Miss. 550, 130 So. 733.

The Louisiana statute expressly excludes from its operation a physician who is appointed by the court to examine the accused's physical or mental condition. See Appendix, herein. See also c. c. XIII, XIV, herein.

[2] Skidmore v. State, (1939) 59 Nev. 320, 92 P. 2d 979.

of her to determine the duration of her pregnancy were held to be competent in a bastardy proceeding, since she was not his patient and the examination was not made for the purpose of professional advice or treatment.[3]

The courts usually insist, however, that the physician, or whoever employs him, fairly and frankly make known the purpose of the examination and that the person's mind be carefully disabused at the outset of any notion of it being made solely for his benefit. If it appears that the physician, by what he said to the accused, led him to believe that he was there to prescribe for him, or that he was induced to accept the physician as *his* physician and consequently to disclose to him information that perhaps would not otherwise have been given, the relation of physician and patient will undoubtedly be held to exist.[4]

Physical examinations of persons involved in the crime of rape, or other sexual offenses, are not uncommon. The victim may have contracted a venereal disease and the prosecuting attorney or other law enforcement officers may want to ascertain whether the person suspected of, or charged with, the crime is similarly afflicted. Where a physical examination is made, without objection by the accused, for the express purpose of proving or disproving his guilt of the crime charged, the relation of physician and patient does not exist and evidence of the result of such examination may be introduced at the trial.[5] Where a physical examination of the raped woman or child is made by a physician, at the request of the state, for the purpose of ascertaining whether she then had a venereal

---

[3] Clark v. State, (1899) 8 Kan. App. 782, 61 Pac. 814.

[4] Leyra v. Denno, (1954) 347 U. S. 556, 98 Law. Ed. 948, 74 Su. Ct. 716; People v. Decina, (1956) 1 A. D. 592, 152 N. Y. S. 2d 169, aff'd. 2 N. Y. 2d 133, 138 N. E. 2d 799; People v. Leyra, (1951) 302 N. Y. 353, 363, 98 N. E. 2d 553; People v. Austin, (1910) 199 N. Y. 446, 452, 93 N. E. 57; People v. Stout, (1858) 3 Park. Cr. (N. Y.) 670; State v. Moore, (1925) 52 N. D. 633, 204 N. W. 341. See also dissent of Bazelon, J., in Browne v. Brooke, (1956) 236 F. 2d. 686.

[5] Garcia v. State, (1929) 35 Ariz. 35, 274 Pac. 166; People v. Glover, (1888) 71 Mich. 303, 38 N. W. 874; Norwood v. State, (1930) 158 Miss. 550, 130 So. 733; State v. Dean, (1927) 69 Utah 268, 254 Pac. 142; Smits v. State, (1911) 145 Wis. 601, 130 N. W. 525. In Angeloff v. State, (1914) 91 Ohio St. 361, 110 N. E. 936, the question of privilege does not appear to have been raised.

⟫→

disease, or of establishing the crimes of assault and rape, no relation exists and the physician may testify to any information obtained by him during such examination.[6]

It has been held, however, that, even though the relation did not exist, where an examination of the accused was made without his consent and against his protest, such compulsory examination was in violation of the "due process" clause of the state's constitution and all evidence with reference to information so obtained was inadmissible.[7] Other courts regard such an examination as a violation of the accused's constitutional rights not to be a witness against himself.[8]

Frequently, for the purposes of the trial, it becomes necessary to ascertain the mental condition of the accused, particularly where the defense of insanity is made, or is likely to be made.[9] The general rule is that no confidential relation exists precluding a disclosure of information, where a physician, appointed by the court, or employed by the state, or by counsel, makes an examination of a person accused of crime, in order to pass on his sanity and not for diagnosis

---

← ⚞

In State v. Moore, (1925) 52 N. D. 633, 204 N. W. 341, the relation was held to exist, since the accused was led to believe the physician was acting for him.

[6] State v. Fackrell, (1954) 44 Wash. 2d 874, 271 P. 2d 679; State v. Thomas, (1939) 1 Wash. 2d 298, 95 P. 2d 1036; State v. Winnett, (1907) 48 Wash. 93, 92 Pac. 904; James v. State, (1905) 124 Wis. 130, 102 N. W. 320. See notes, 2 A. L. R. 2d 645; 45 A. L. R. 1357. In Leard v. State, (1925) 30 Okla. Cr. 191, 235 Pac. 243, a physician examined the prosecutrix at the request of the state. The prosecuting attorney, however, did not call him as a witness. Over objection by the state, defendant called the physician as a witness and he was permitted to testify since the relation of physician and patient did not exist; moreover, the prosecuting attorney was present at the examination.

[7] State v. Height, (1902) 117 Iowa 650, 91 N. W. 935, 59 L. R. A. 437.

[8] State v. Horton, (1913) 247 Mo. 657, 153 S. W. 1051; State v. Newcombe, (1909) 220 Mo. 54, 119 S. W. 405. A discussion of these constitutional questions is outside the scope of this treatise.

[9] In many states, the legislatures have authorized the trial court to appoint physicians to examine the accused, and to report their findings to the court. They may also testify to the results of their examinations. *e.g.*, (1947) Ark. Stat. Ann., § 43-1302. See Veatch v. State, (1952) 221 Ark. 44, 251 S. W. 2d 1015; Gerlach v. State, (1950) 217 Ark. 102, 229 S. W. 2d 37; Hall v. State, (1945) 209 Ark. 180, 189 S. W. 2d 917. See also note, 32 A. L. R. 2d 434. In State v. Cochran, (1947) 356 Mo. 778, 203 S. W. 2d 707, it was held that when a defendant puts his sanity in issue, he waives the protection of the physician-patient privilege statute.

with a view to treatment.[10] If, therefore, in the course of such examination, the accused makes statements to the physician in the nature of an admission of guilt, such statements are not privileged and the physician may testify thereto.[11] In no event, however, will representatives of the state be allowed to employ the relationship of physician and patient in a deliberate attempt to obtain a confession out of the accused's own mouth.[12] As previously stated, it has been held that whether the examination be compulsory or not, to permit the physician to testify to what he observes or hears concerning the accused during the examination is a violation of his constitutional right not to be a witness against himself, but, generally, the courts have held otherwise.[13]

---

[10] Taylor v. United States, (1955) 95 App. D. C. 373, 222 F. 2d 398; Catoe v. United States, (1942) 131 F. 2d 16; People v. Dutton, (1944) 62 Cal. App. 2d 862, 145 P. 2d 676; Nesbit v. People, (1894) 19 Colo. 441, 36 Pac. 221; Hopkins v. State, (1951) 212 Miss. 772, 50 So. 2d 467; Keeton v. State, (1936) 175 Miss. 631, 167 So. 68; State v. Fouquette, (1950) 67 Nev. 505, 221 P. 2d 404; People v. Austin, (1910) 199 N. Y. 446, 93 N. E. 57; People v. Furlong, (1907) 187 N. Y. 198, 79 N. E. 978; People v. Hoch, (1896) 150 N. Y. 291, 44 N. E. 976; People v. Sliney, (1893) 137 N. Y. 570, 33 N. E. 150; People v. Kemmler, (1890) 119 N. Y. 580, 24 N. E. 9; State v. Litteral, (1947) 227 N. C. 527, 43 S. E. 2d 84; State v. Miller, (1934) 177 Wash. 442, 32 P. 2d 535; State v. Coleman, (1924) 96 W. Va. 544, 123 S. E. 580; Simecek v. State, (1943) 243 Wis. 439, 10 N. W. 2d 161; State v. Riggle, (1956) 76 Wyo._____, 298 P. 2d 349. Where the accused's attorney requires a psychiatrist's aid in interpreting her mental condition, she is entitled to have the psychiatrist examine her in private, without the presence of the sheriff or other represenative of the state. *In re* Ochse, (1951) 38 Cal. 2d 230, 238 P. 2d 561.

[11] State v. Newsome, (1928) 195 N. C. 552, 143 S. E. 187; People v. Sliney, (1893) 137 N. Y. 570, 33 N. E. 150; Simicek v. State, (1943) 243 Wis. 439, 10 N. W. 2d 161.

The textual statement assumes, of course, the absence of a special statute, such as 18 U. S. C. A. § 4244, which restricts the examining physician's testimony.

[12] People v. Leyra, (1951) 302 N. Y. 353, 98 N. E. 2d 553; Leyra v. Denno, (1954) 347 U. S. 556, 98 Law. Ed. 948, 74 Su. Ct. 716. The accused was charged with the murder of his parents. The district attorney sent a physician-psychiatrist to interview him in a police station. The accused was not informed of the purpose of the visit nor of the fact that the conversation was being recorded on a tape recorder. The physician made deceptive offers of friendship and help, his assurance being given in a pseudo-confidential atmosphere of physician and patient. See also People v. Decina, (1956) 1 A. D. 2d 592, 152 N. Y. S. 2d 169, aff'd. 2 N. Y. 2d 133, 138 N. E. 2d 799.

[13] Commonwealth v. Di Stasio, (1936) 294 Mass. 273, 1 N. E. 2d 189; State v. Genna, (1927) 163 La. 701, 112 So. 655, 714: "We fail to see wherein the accused was forced to give evidence against himself. He was forced to do nothing. He was looked at and spoken to; but even a cat may look at a queen, and no one need answer when spoken to unless he wishes to do so."

It has become a common practice of law enforcement officers to require a person suspected of driving an automobile while intoxicated to submit to a blood, urine, or saliva test by a physician selected by the officers, for the purpose of determining whether the alleged offender was actually intoxicated.[14] It is generally held that the taking of such fluids from the body of the person for analysis and test does not involve the relation of physician and patient since there is no intention to prescribe for or treat such person;[15] nor, as a general rule, will it be regarded as a violation of his constitutional right not to be a witness against himself.[16]

Ordinarily, the relation of physician and patient does not exist between a jail physician and a prisoner in such manner as to make communications between them privileged.[17]

38. *Medical Treatment by Physician Employed by Third Person*

As pointed out earlier, the relationship of physician and patient does not depend upon the source of the physician's employment.[1] The real test is: Did the physician actually advise, prescribe for, or treat the afflicted person in his professional character? It is a matter of common knowledge that persons injured by the wrongful acts of other persons are treated by medical men not of their own choice, but by those employed by others. Although an afflicted person is at liberty to refuse and might have declined the assistance of the physician employed by another person, yet, if he accepts it,

---

[14] In some states, such practice, under proper circumstances, is authorized by statute.

[15] Hanlon v. Woodhouse, (1945) 113 Colo. 504, 160 P. 2d 998; People v. Barnes, (1950) 197 Misc. 477, 98 N. Y. S. 2d 481; People v. Cram, (1945) 176 Ore. 577, 160 P. 2d 283, 164 A. L. R. 952; Racine v. Woiteshek, (1947) 251 Wis. 404, 29 N. W. 2d 752. In this case, the examination was not made with a view to treatment, but the physician testified he would have given defendant emergency treatment had it been necessary.

[16] People v. Cram, (1945) 176 Ore. 577, 160 P. 2d 283, 164 A. L. R. 952; State v. Riggle, (1956) 76 Wyo.____, 298 P. 2d 349. See excellent note on this question: 164 A. L. R. 967.

[17] People v. Schuyler, (1887) 106 N. Y. 298, 12 N. E. 783; Commonwealth v. Sykes, (1946) 353 Pa. 392, 45 A. 2d 43, cert. denied 328 U. S. 847, 90 Law. Ed. 1620, 66 Su. Ct. 1021; Commonwealth v. Edwards, (1935) 318 Pa. 1, 178 Atl. 20; State v. Miller, (1934) 177 Wash. 442, 32 P. 2d 535. There may be circumstances, however, which will create the relationship. See People v. Stout, (1858) 3 Park. Cr. (N. Y.) 670

[1] See §§ 33, 34, herein.

he has the right to deem him *his* physician and to place full confidence in the relationship thus established. The reason is obvious. If the physician assumes to advise or treat the injured person, or to examine him with the view to treatment, he should be put in possession of all facts necessary or proper to enable him to perform his professional service efficiently. Furthermore, if the patient acquiesce, he should have the right to communicate freely and fully without fear of exposure or of having his confidence made common property. The protection of this confidence cannot be frustrated by proof that, at the time of rendering professional service, the physician was under a contract of employment to serve the interest of the person charged with responsibility for the identical injury he is called upon or assumes to treat.[2] The general rule is, therefore, that where a person responsible for an accident by which another is injured sends a physician, employed and paid by him, to examine and to render medical assistance to the injured person, if necessary, the relation of physician and patient is established and the privilege applies.[3]

---

[2] Battis v. Chicago, R. I. & Pac. Ry., (1904) 124 Iowa 623, 100 N. W. 543.

[3] Arizona & New Mexico Ry. v. Clark, (1915) 235 U. S. 669, 59 Law. Ed. 415, 35 Su. Ct. 210, L. R. A. 1915 C. 834; Union Pac. R. R. v. Thomas, (1907) 152 Fed. 365; Tweith v. Duluth, Missabbe & I. R. Ry., (1946) 66 F. Supp. 427; Inspiration Cons. Copper Co. v. Mendez, (1917) 19 Ariz. 151, 166 Pac. 278 and 1183, 250 U. S. 400, 63 Law. Ed. 1058, 39 Su. Ct. 553; Breece-White Mfg. Co. v. Green, (1926) 171 Ark. 968, 287 S. W. 173; Kansas City Southern R. R. v. Miller, (1915) 117 Ark. 396, 175 S. W. 1164; Colorado Midland Ry. v. McGarry, (1907) 41 Colo. 398, 92 Pac. 915; Chicago & Erie R. R. v. Schenkel, (1914) 57 Ind. App. 175, 104 N. E. 50; Louisville & Southern Indiana Trac. Co. v. Snead, (1911) 49 Ind. App. 16, 93 N. E. 177; New York, C. & St. Louis R. R. v. Mushrush, (1894) 11 Ind. App. 192, 37 N. E. 954; Walmer-Roberts v. Hennessey, (1921) 191 Iowa 86, 181 N. W. 798; Battis v. Chicago, R. I. & Pac. Ry., (1904) 124 Iowa 623, 100 N. W. 543; Keist v. Chicago Great Western R. R., (1899) 110 Iowa 32, 81 N. W. 181; Raymond v. Burlington, Cedar Rapids & N. Ry., (1884) 65 Iowa 152, 21 N. W. 495; Polin v. St. Paul Union Depot Co., (1924) 159 Minn. 410, 199 N. W. 87; Tonkel v. Yazoo & M. V. R. R., (1934) 170 Miss. 321, 154 So. 351; Newton Oil Mill v. Spencer, (1918) 116 Miss. 568, 77 So. 605; Yazoo & M. V. R. R. v. Messina, (1915) 109 Miss. 143, 67 So. 963; Obermeyer v. Logeman Chair Mfg. Co., (1910) 229 Mo. 97, 129 S. W. 209; Holtzen v. Missouri Pac. Ry., (1911) 159 Mo. App. 370, 140 S. W. 767; Haworth v. Kansas City Southern Ry., (1902) 94 Mo. App. 215, 68 S. W. 111; Malone v. Industrial Comm'n., (1942) 140 Ohio St. 292, 43 N. E. 2d 266; Munz v. Salt Lake City R. R., (1902) 25 Utah 220, 70 Pac. 852; Sumpter v. National Grocery Co., (1938) 194 Wash. 598, 78 P. 2d 1087, 116 A. L. R. 1166; Cohodes v. Menominee & Mari- ⟫⟫→

While it is true, as a general rule, that where a physician is employed and sent by a third person to make an examination of an injured person with a view to ascertaining the nature and extent of his injury and not for the purpose of treatment, the relation of physician and patient does not exist,[4] yet, if the physician undertakes to advise, prescribe for, or treat such person the relation will attach and the rule of privilege applies. Unquestionably a person whose negligence might have been the cause of injury to another may, with the utmost propriety, send a physician to examine the injured person and to ascertain, if possible, the manner, nature, and extent of his injury. But this can avail nothing unless the physician shall strictly retain his character as an employee of the person who sent him. If, upon request or upon his own motion, such physician undertakes to advise, prescribe for, or treat the injured person, and the latter in any manner acquiesces therein, the physician thereby steps out of his role as investigator for the person who sent him and transfers his allegiance to the injured party. In such instances, a case is presented where one cannot serve two masters at one and the same time. The moment the physician begins to advise or treat the injured person in his professional character—even though in so doing he disobeys the specific instructions of the person who sent him—the relation of physician and patient exists and he will not be permitted, on objection by the patient, to testify to any information he may have obtained under such circumstances.[5]

39. *Effect of Person's Belief That Physician Is Acting in His Behalf*

It is not always indispensable that the technical relation of physician and patient exist. There may be a case of circumstances

---

nette L. & T. Co., (1912) 149 Wis. 308, 135 N. W. 879.

In Grossnickle v. Avery, (1926) 96 Ind. App. 479, 152 N. E. 288, defendant, himself a physician, treated plaintiff's injury. Held: the relation of physician and patient existed, but the testimony offered by defendant was not within the scope of the privilege.

[4] See § 36, herein.

[5] Freel v. Market Street Cable Ry., (1892) 97 Cal. 40, 31 Pac. 730; Cincinnati, H. & D. R. R. v. Gross, (1917) 186 Ind. 471, 114 N. E. 962; Battis v. Chicago, R. I. & Pac. Ry., (1904) 124 Iowa 623, 100 N. W. 543; Weitz v. Mound City Ry., (1893) 53 Mo. App. 39.

which falls short of constituting the technical relation, but which presents a proper case for the operation of the physician-patient privilege statute.[1] As previously stated, it is not uncommon for a sick or injured person to be examined by a physician not of his own choice; and where the physician has dealt frankly and openly with the afflicted person and has made known that he is not acting for his benefit but in the interest of another, no confidence exists and the relation does not attach[2] But there may be occasions when the physician makes no mention of the fact that he is acting solely in the interest of another and the person acquiesces in the examination in the mistaken yet reasonable belief that the physician is acting in his behalf alone. In such cases, it is generally held that if the physician attends upon a sick or injured person under circumstances calculated to induce the belief that his visit is of a professional nature and the afflicted person assumes that the examination is being made for the purpose of advising or treating him, it is wholly immaterial what the secret purpose of the physician was in making it and the relation of physician and patient contemplated by the statute is created by implication; and, as a consequence thereof, the physician, in the absence of consent or waiver by the patient, will not be permitted to testify to any information so acquired.[3] The person examined, if capable of forming a judgment on the subject, must understand that the physician is not attending or treating him. If not capable of forming such judgment the question of the physician's status must be determined objectively.[4] The question is one of fact, and it may readily be seen

---

[1] People v. Stout, (1858) 3 Park. Cr. (N. Y.) 670.

[2] See §§ 36, 37, herein.

[3] People v. Stout, (1858) 3 Park. Cr. (N. Y.) 670, 676: "The injury to him is as great, in the divulgement of information thus obtained, as it would be if the relation had technically existed: for it is plain that the opportunities for gaining the information would not have been voluntarily afforded had it not been for an entire confidence in the fact of such relation existing."

See also People v. Decina, (1956) 2 N. Y. 2d 133, 138 N. E. 2d 799; People v. Leyra, (1951) 302 N. Y. 353, 98 N. E. 2d 553, Leyra v. Denno, (1954) 347 U. S. 556, 98 Law. Ed. 948, 74 Su. Ct. 716.

See also § 40, herein.

[4] Browne v. Brooke, (1956) 236 F. 2d 686. This was an action in which the jury found
$\ggg\rightarrow$

that no precise rule can be formulated which will control every case.[5]

In *Arizona & New Mexico Ry. v. Clark*,[6] the plaintiff, having sustained a serious injury to his eye, was taken to a hospital where Dr. D, the physician in attendance, informed him that they had no eye specialist and advised him to have one examine his eye. Plaintiff permitted Dr. S, a specialist obtained by Dr. D, to examine him supposing that Dr. S was acting with Dr. D and not knowing that Dr. S was making the examination in behalf of the defendant who employed and paid him. At the trial, defendant called Dr. S as a

---

that the decedent, at the time of making a purported will, was mentally incompetent. Some ten months prior to the date of the purported will, a physician had been directed to examine the decedent in connection with proceedings to appoint a conservator for her. In the present trial, the physician was permitted to testify to her mental condition. The trial judge made preliminary inquiries to ascertain whether the witness had attended or treated her or if she could have so believed, and then ruled that the relation of physician and patient did not exist. This ruling was upheld by a majority of the Court of Appeals. Bazelon, J., dissented (p. 689): " * * * Here the psychiatrist's purpose was unquestionably testimonial, but it does not appear that the decedent was aware of that fact. Her normal assumption would have been that the doctor who was examining her was doing so qua doctor, not qua bank investigator. To admit the doctor's testimony in these circumstances would make the patient's rights dependent on the doctor's intentions. The statute, however, is designed for the patient's protection. Her frame of mind, therefore, rather than the doctor's, should determine whether the statute applies. Unless it appears that she submitted to examination with knowledge that the doctor might broadcast his findings, her confidence should be respected."

[5] For application of the principle, see Kramer v. Policy Holders' Life Ins. Ass'n., (1935) 5 Cal. App. 2d 380, 42 P. 2d 665; Colorado Fuel & Iron Co. v. Cummins, (1896) 8 Colo. App. 541, 46 Pac. 875; Pennsylvania R. R. v. Hough, (1929) 88 Ind. App. 601, 161 N. E. 705; Patterson v. Cole, (1903) 67 Kan. 441, 73 Pac. 54; State v. Anderson, (1956) 247 Minn. 469, 78 N. W. 2d 320; Smart v. Kansas City, (1907) 208 Mo. 162, 105 S. W. 709, 14 L. R. A. (n. s.) 565, 13 Ann. Cas. 932; Weitz v. Mound City Ry., (1893) 53 Mo. App. 39; Neice v. Farmers Coop. Creamery & S. Co., (1911) 90 Neb. 470, 133 N. W. 878; People v. Leyra, (1951) 302 N. Y. 353, 98 N. E. 2d 553, Leyra v. Denno, (1954) 347 U. S. 556, 98 Law. Ed. 948, 74 Su. Ct. 716; Madsen v. Utah Light & Ry., (1909) 36 Utah 528, 105 Pac. 799. Of contrary import, see *In re* Williams Estate, (1925) 186 Wis. 160, 202 N. W. 314.

[6] (1913) 207 Fed. 817, aff'd. (1915) 235 U. S. 669, 59 Law. Ed. 415, 35 Su. Ct. 210, L. R. A. 1915 C. 834.

witness in his behalf but, on objection by plaintiff, the court refused to permit him to testify.[7]

In *Ballard* v. *Yellow Cab Co.*,[8] plaintiff, after an accident, was taken to a hospital. Dr. H came into her room in the company of a floor nurse and the doctor in charge of the case, and straightway began to examine her at the instance of the company for whom he examined persons at times. She assumed him to be a member of the hospital staff as indeed he was, although, unbeknownst to her, he was not then acting in that capacity. She submitted to his examination and accepted him as her physician. It was held that the relation of physician and patient existed since, on her side at least, there was that confidence which the statute was designed to protect; hence the examining physician was prohibited from testifying to any information he had so acquired.

In *Sumpter* v. *National Grocery Co.*,[9] the defendant called as a witness a physician who had been employed by it to make a special examination of plaintiff and to testify in court as to the results thereof. Plaintiff had been his patient and he had examined her at the time of her injury. Although in the meantime he had been employed by defendant for the purpose of the special examination, she had submitted thereto under the impression that he was still her physician and that the second examination was necessary to enable him to act for her. She had no knowledge to the contrary. The court properly held that he continued to be her physician and she his patient within the purview of the statute, and refused to allow him to testify.

In *People* v. *Stout*,[10] the prisoner, charged with murder, was committed to jail. His condition required medical attention and

---

[7] Ross, J., (p. 823): "The real purpose, as practically conceded by counsel for [defendant] of Dr. S.'s examination of the plaintiff being to obtain information to be used against any claim on his part for damages, good faith required that the plaintiff should have been frankly told that Dr. S. came as the representative of the company, and not left to infer that he came as his own physician, as he very well might from the statement of Dr. D., according to the plaintiff's testimony, that he needed an oculist to consult with."

[8] (1944) 20 Wash. 2d 67, 145 P. 2d 1019.

[9] (1938) 194 Wash. 598, 78 P. 2d 1087, 116 A. L. R. 1166.

[10] (1859) 3 Park. Cr. (N. Y.) 670.

the jail physician was called in. He did not prescribe for him at the time, but told him that he was going to act for him as his physician. Shortly after this visit, two physicians appeared at the prisoner's cell and stated that they had been requested by the coroner to examine him and see what injuries there were about his person. They made a thorough examination of him and conducted themselves, as to their manner, precisely as if they had been examining one of their own patients with a view to ascertaining his injuries and administering whatever treatment was necessary. The prisoner consented to the examination, granted every request and answered all questions. Upon this state of facts, one of the physicians, a witness for the state, was asked to describe what he learned in the course of the examination. Defendant objected on the ground of privilege and it was held that the relation of physician and patient existed; therefore, the witness could not testify.

In *Kansas City Southern Ry.* v. *Miller*,[11] it was held that information acquired by a physician employed by a company to treat its employees was privileged. The plaintiff, not knowing of the physician's relation to the company, consulted him about his injury and permitted an examination to be made, with a view to engaging his professional services; but, upon discovering that the physician was employed by the company, declined to engage him to treat his injury.

In *State* v. *Moore*,[12] the defendant was convicted of rape upon a child who developed signs of syphilis. While defendant was in jail, the sheriff heard rumors to this effect and called in a physician to examine defendant in order that he might protect himself as well as the prisoners if defendant was so affected. The physician told defendant that he could not divulge any information he might obtain. Thereupon he took a blood sample, and a Wasserman test showed defendant was infected. Subsequently the physician treated him. Defendant believed the examination was had with a view to treating him if that proved necessary. It was held that the relation of physician and patient existed and that it was reversible error to have

---

[11] (1915) 117 Ark. 396, 175 S. W. 1164.

[12] (1925) 52 N. D. 633, 204 N. W. 341. Two judges dissented. See note, (1925) 11 Corn. L. Q. 92.

permitted the physician to disclose information obtained by him as the result of such relationship.

40. Hospital Physician

Generally speaking, staff physicians and other physicians in the employ of a hospital,[1] public or private, enter into the relationship of physician and patient with every person who enters the hospital for the purpose of care and treatment.[2] The principle applies as fully and effectually to a sick or injured person who is brought to a hospital unconscious, or in a helpless state mentally, as it does to one who enters of his own volition.[3] Under and by virtue of their appointment, contract, or whatever arrangement they may have made with the hospital, every physician serving it becomes the physician of each and every patient; and they have no legal or moral right or authority to view, treat, or operate upon any patient therein, except by virtue of that appointment or contract.[4]

It is a matter of common knowledge that a hospital patient may be examined or cared for at times by medical men whom he has never seen before and may never see again, submitting to their professional services in the confident belief that they are his physicians and that their examinations or ministrations are for the purpose of enabling them to properly prescribe for or treat his malady or injury. It is altogether right and proper, therefore, that the principles of medical ethics[5] and the rule of privilege, applicable to the indi-

---

[1] The term "hospital," as used here, includes a clinic also; but, generally, it does not include a state hospital for the mentally ill. The latter is discussed in § 41 herein.

[2] Beave v. St. Louis Transit Co., (1908) 212 Mo. 331, 111 S. W. 52; Smart v. Kansas City, (1907) 208 Mo. 162, 105 S. W. 709, 14 L. R. A. (n. s.) 565, 13 Ann. Cas. 932; People v. Decina, (1956) 2 N. Y. 2d 133, 138 N. E. 2d 799.

[3] Cradick v. John Hancock Mut. Life Ins. Co., (1923) _____ Mo. App. _____, 256 S. W. 501, 504: "Those who are the victims of sickness and misfortune incapable at times of selecting those whom they most desire to treat them should be, in an exceptional degree, entitled to the protection which the law affords them." Bauch v. Schultz, (1919) 109 Misc. 548, 180 N. Y. S. 188.

[4] Smart v. Kansas City, (1907) 208 Mo. 162, 105 S. W. 709, 14 L. R. A. (n. s.) 565, 13 Ann. Cas. 932.

[5] American Medical Ass'n., (1937) Principles of Medical Ethics, c. I., § 2: "The ethical principles actuating and governing a group or clinic are exactly the same as those

⋙→

vidual physician selected by the patient, should apply with equal force and effect to the group of physicians selected and employed by the hospital of which the sick or injured person is a patient. Accordingly, it may be regarded as a general rule that a patient, unless fully and frankly informed to the contrary, has a perfect right to assume, and to rely upon the assumption, that any physician who enters his ward or room is rightfully there and has authority to act in his behalf and to examine his person or question him concerning his disease or injury; and the physician will not afterwards be heard to say that he was not connected with the hospital and had no authority to examine or interrogate him.[6] The moment he undertakes to consult with or examine the hospital's patient, the relationship of physician and patient exists, and whatever confidential information the physician may have so acquired is privileged and may not be disclosed in court without the consent of the holder of the privilege.[7]

---

applicable to the individual. As a group or clinic is composed of individual doctors, each of whom, whether employer, employee or partner, is subject to the principles of ethics herein elaborated, the uniting into a business or professional organization does not relieve them either individually or as a group from the obligation they assume when entering the profession."

[6] Smart v. Kansas City, (1907) 208 Mo. 162, 193, 105 S. W. 709, 14 L. R. A. (n. s.) 565, 13 Ann. Cas. 932: "If such a thing as that could be done, then the privilege could be taken from him by trick or fraud." However, in Woods v. Lisbon, (1908) 138 Iowa 402, 116 N. W. 143, 16 L. R. A. (n. s.) 886, defendant's surgeon visited the hospital and, though uninvited, observed plaintiff's operation, and it was held that no relation of physician and patient existed as to him.

[7] Poinsett Lumber & Mfg. Co. v. Longino, (1919) 139 Ark. 69, 213 S. W. 15; Gerick v. Brock, (1949) 120 Colo. 394, 210 P. 2d 214; Cincinnati, H. & D. R. R. v. Gross, 186 Ind. 471, 114 N. E. 962; New York, Chicago & St. Louis R. R. v. Shields, (1916) 185 Ind 704, 112 N. E. 762; Mathews v. Rex Health & Acc. Ins. Co., (1927) 86 Ind. App. 335, 157 N. E. 467; Price v. Standard Life & Acc. Ins. Co., (1903) 90 Minn. 264, 95 N. W. 1118; Metropolitan Life Ins. Co. v. McSwain, (1927) 149 Miss. 455, 115 So. 555; Vermillion v. Prudential Ins. Co., (1936) 230 Mo. App. 993, 93 S. W. 2d 45; Owens v. Kansas City, C. C. & S. Ry., (1920) _____Mo. App._____, 225 S. W. 234; Garrett v. Butte, (1923) 69 Mont. 214, 221 Pac. 537 (relation existed, but the information was not within purview of statute); Woernley v. Electromatic Typewriters, Inc., (1936) 271 N. Y. 228, 2 N. E. 2d 638; Lorde v. Guardian Life Ins. Co., (1937) 252 App. Div. 646, 300 N. Y. S. 721; Sparer v. Travelers Ins. Co., (1919) 185 App. Div. 861, 173 N. Y. S. 673; Duggan v. Phelps, (1903) 82 App. Div. 509, 81 N. Y. S. 916; Hammerstein v. Hammerstein, (1911) 74 Misc. 567, 134 N. Y. S. 473; Mehegan v. Faber, (1914) 158 Wis. 645, 149 N. W. 397 (patient's

A few selected cases will serve to show the application of the principle. In *Smart* v. *Kansas City*,[8] neither the physician in charge of the hospital, his assistant, nor a physician who, for his own clinical purposes, visited the hospital and examined the patients with the permission of those in charge, was a competent witness to testify regarding the information acquired by him during his examination of, or attendance upon, a patient of the hospital. In each case, the relation of physician and patient exists.

In *Beave* v. *St. Louis Transis Co.*[9] the court refused to permit the physician in charge of the hospital to which the plaintiff was taken after an accident, to reveal the nature and extent of plaintiff's injury or his condition while in the hospital. The witness testified that he had examined the plaintiff every day or so, but did not prescribe for or treat him; that his assistant physicians, under his supervision treated and operated upon him. The court held that the knowledge acquired by the witness was within the spirit, if not the letter, of the statute and could not be disclosed.

In *Grossman* v. *Supreme Lodge, K. and L. of Honor*,[10] the testimony of a physician as to the condition of the patient's health was excluded. The witness testified that he and the attending physician made the rounds of the hospital together, but that he did not prescribe for the patient. It was held that whether the witness was actuated by curiosity or by a higher motive made no difference.

In *Chicago, Lake Shore & S. B. Ry.* v. *Walas*,[11] the court held that the fact that a hospital surgeon, at the time he observed the condition of the patient concerning which he was asked to testify, had not been informed that he was to operate on such patient, did not remove him from the ban of the statute.[12]

←

hospital record privileged). See comment, Disqualification of Hospital Physician to Testify, (1938) 72 U. S. L. Rev. 619.

See People v. Decina, (1956) 2 N. Y. 2d 133, 138 N. E. 2d 799.

8 (1907) 208 Mo. 162, 105 S. W. 709, 14 L. R. A. (n. s.) 565, 13 Ann. Cas. 932.

9 (1908) 212 Mo. 331, 111 S. W. 52.

10 (1889) 53 Hun. 637, 6 N. Y. S. 821.

11 (1922) 192 Ind. 369, 135 N. E. 150, 22 A. L. R. 1212.

12 A novel view of a similar situation was expressed by Griffith, C. J., in National Mut. Life Ass'n. v. Godrich, [1909] 10 Comm. L. R. (Australia) 1, 11: "In the case of a person

≫→

In *Johnson* v. *Missouri Pac. Ry.*,[13] it was held that the relation of physician and patient existed between the physician in charge of a railroad hospital, whose services were compensated by assessments upon the wages of the railroad's employees, and an injured employee who was sent to the hospital for examination.

In *Holtzen* v. *Missouri Pac. Ry.*,[14] a personal injury suit, the court held that the relation of physician and patient existed between a passenger and a physician in the hospital maintained by the railroad company who treated him; hence, the physician could not testify to the patient's condition.

In *Kramer* v. *Policy Holder's Life Ins. Co.*,[15] the defendant, in an action on a policy of insurance issued on a woman's life, offered the testimony of a physician. It appeared that some time after the issuance of the policy, the insured visited the C-F Clinic which was maintained by funds donated by the Kellogg Foundation. At that time and place, Dr. H took the insured's case history and made a physical examination which disclosed that she had an extensive spread of cancer, which, in his opinion, had been in existence for years. Dr. H testified that he was there as an "observer" for the Kellogg Foundation and took no part in the treatment of the clinic's patients; that his duty was to assist the Foundation in observ-

---

who undergoes an operation at a public hospital, when the necessity and nature of the operation has already been decided upon, I do not think that the person operated upon is, necessarily, within the meaning of the [privilege statute], the patient of the surgeon who there saw him for the first time. Such a surgeon is, therefore, I think, not necessarily prohibited from divulging what he sees in the course of the operation."

[13] (1925) 167 Ark. 660, 269 S. W. 67.

In Colorado Fuel & Iron Co. v. Cummings, (1896) 8 Colo. App. 541, 46 Pac. 875, the plaintiff was attended by a surgeon in a hospital supported by employees' contributions. The court said (p. 552): "The plaintiff's contributions may have been slight, but the circumstances of the situation were such as to lead him to put himself implicitly under the care of the surgeon and to trust himself in his hands for care to the same extent and under the same circumstances as though he had sent out for another physician and put himself in his charge." The testimony of the surgeon was therefore excluded. See also McRae v. Erickson, (1905) 1 Cal. App. 326, 82 Pac. 209.

[14] (1911) 159 Mo. App. 370, 140 S. W. 767.

[15] (1935) 5 Cal. App. 2d 380, 42 P. 2d 665. *Contra:* Frederick v. Federal Life Ins. Co., (1936) 13 Cal. App. 2d 585, 57 P. 2d 235, since the internes who took the patient's case history did not prescribe or act for her.

ing some 400 patients, so as to be able to report on the efficiency of an extract used by the physicians of the clinic. When taking the insured's history and making an examination of her, Dr. H said nothing to her about the purpose of the examination or whom he was representing. The testimony of Dr. H was excluded on the ground of privilege. The court held that the relation of physician and patient existed since the insured had every right to believe that the information she gave Dr. H was necessary for the diagnosis and proper treatment of her malady.

In *Lamarand* v. *National Life & Acc. Ins. Co.,*[16] the testimony of an interne of a public hospital, who made a routine examination and took the case history of a woman on her admission to the hospital, was held inadmissible since the relation then existing made such examination and communications privileged. In a later case, however, it was held that a physician employed by a public hospital could testify to the condition of a patient therein, since the physician did not bear the relation of a private physician employed by the patient; her contractual relation, the court said, was with the hospital and not with its physician.[17] This distinction had been made in earlier cases.[18]

---

[16] (1937) 58 Ohio App. 415, 16 N. E. 2d 701. As to the relationship of a hospital's ambulance surgeon to an injured person, see Green v. Metropolitan Street Ry., (1902) 171 N. Y. 201, 63 N. E. 958; Duggan v. Phelps, (1903) 82 App. Div. 509, 81 N. Y. S. 916; Bauch v. Schultz, (1916) 109 Misc. Rep. 548, 180 N. Y. S. 188.

[17] Lumpkin v. Metropolitan Life Ins. Co., (1945) 75 Ohio App. 310, 63 N. E. 2d 189, aff'd. 146 Ohio St. 25, 64 N. E. 2d 63. The Supreme Court, however, declined to consider this question.

[18] Nelson v. Western & Southern Ins. Co., (1936) ......Ohio App....,.... 23 Ohio Law Abst. 117. No relation existed between hospital's patient and its pathologist.

Dewert v. Cincinnati Milling Mach. Co., (1933) ...... Ohio App......., 38 Ohio Law Rep. 318, 15 Ohio Law Abst. 268. No relation existed where injured employee was treated by defendant's physician in its own hospital.

Wills, Adm'r. v. National Life & Acc. Ins. Co., (1928) 28 Ohio App. 497, 162 N. E. 822. No relation exists between patient in a municipal tuberculosis hospital and a physician employed by it. These decisions, however, are in conflict with the great weight of authority.

41. *Physician Employed by Hospital for Patients Mentally Ill*

There has been considerable controversy as to whether the relationship of physician and patient exists between medical men employed by hospitals for the insane or mentally ill and the inmates thereof. In New York, it has been held that the public policy of the state demands the maintenance of such institutions and the furnishing of proper care and treatment of the inmates, which necessarily involve their physical and mental examination and the making of public records relative to their condition; hence, the relationship arising by operation of law between a person committed by legal process to a state institution for the insane and the official physician in charge thereof is not the same as that contemplated by the physician-patient privilege statute.[1] The Supreme Court of Iowa has held that physicians employed by a state hospital for the insane were not disqualified from testifying as to their observations concerning the mental condition of an inmate, notwithstanding the fact that they may have attended him professionally while there.[2]

The weight of authority, however, and the better view we think, is to the effect that the fact that the afflicted person is an inmate of a hospital for the insane or mentally ill, public or private, does not deprive him of the protection of the statutory privilege.[3] It has been

---

[1] Liske v. Liske, (1912) 135 N. Y. S. 176.

Accord: Scolavino v. State, (1946) 187 Misc. 253, 62 N. Y. S. 2d 17, modified as to damages 271 App. Div. 618, 67 N. Y. S. 2d 202, aff'd. as modified 297 N. Y. 460, 74 N. E. 2d. 174; Munzer v. Blaisdell, (1944) 183 Misc. 773, 49 N. Y. S. 2d 915, aff'd. 269 App. Div. 970, 58 N. Y. S. 2d 359; McKeever v. Teachers' Retirement Board, (1950) 99 N. Y. S. 2d 884. The courts of New York are not in harmony on this question. Decisions opposed to this view are cited in note 3, infra.

[2] State v. Murphy, (1928) 205 Iowa 1130, 217 N. W. 225; *In re* Harmsen, (1918) ____ Iowa ____ , 167 N. W. 618, L. R. A. 1918 E. 973.

See also *In re* Insanity of Fleming. (1923) 196 Iowa 639, 195 N. W. 242.

[3] Taylor v. United States, (1955) 95 App. D. C. 373, 22 F. 2d 398; *cf.* Kendall v. Gore Properties, Inc., (1956) 236 F. 2d 673; Panella v. United States, (1956) 139 F. Supp. 159; Linscott v. Hughbanks, (1934) 140 Kan. 353, 37 P. 2d 26; Massachusetts Mutual Life Ins. Co. v. Board of Trustees of Michigan Asylum of the Insane, (1913) 178 Mich. 193, 144 N. W. 538, 51 L. R. A. (n. s.) 22, Ann. Cas. 1915 D. 146; *In re* Coddington's Will, (1954) 307 N. Y. 181, 120 N. E. 2d 777; Petition of Maryland Casualty Co., (1948) 274 App. Div. 211, 80 N. Y. S. 2d 181; Westphal v. State, (1948) 191 Misc. 688, 79 N. Y. S. 2d 634;

⟫→

said that in regard to mental patients, the policy behind such a statute is particularly strong; that many physical ailments might be
treated with some degree of effectiveness by a physician whom the
patient did not trust, but a psychiatrist must have his patient's confidence or he cannot help him.[4] Since the relation of physician and
patient does not necessarily spring from contract, it is immaterial
that the entry of the patient into the hospital was an involuntary
act.[5] There is nothing in the statute which distinguishes cases involving private patients from those of public institutions, state or
otherwise.[6] The fact that a public record is required to be kept by
the physician or institution does not affect the rule. A legislative
provision for the filing of certain documents as public reports by
physicians is not a legislative declaration that the secrecy required
of the physician by the statute has been relaxed.[7]

42. *Assisting or Consulting Physician*

The relation of physician and patient applies as fully to the
assistant physician as it does to the physician in chief. A physician
who is called upon to assist the attending physician in examining
the patient's injury, diagnosing his disease, or treating him, is as
much the physician of the patient as the attending physician himself. The assistant's participation in the case clearly brings him
within the spirit of the statutory privilege, and prohibits him from

---

Greff v. Havens, (1946) 186 Misc. 914, 66 N. Y. S. 2d 124; McGrath v. State, (1950) 200
Misc. 165, 104 N. Y. S. 2d 882; *In re* Handwerger, (1947) 79 N. Y. S. 2d 634; Matter of
Baird, (1887) 11 N. Y. St. Rep. 263; Casson v. Schoenfield, (1918) 166 Wis. 401, 166 N.
W. 23, L. R. A. 1918 C. 162.

4 Taylor v. United States, (1955) 95 App. D. C. 373, 222 F. 2d 398.

5 Taylor v. United States, (1955) 95 App. D. C. 373, 222 F. 2d 398; Linscott v. Hughbanks, (1934) 140 Kan. 353, 37 P. 2d 26.

6 Taylor v. United States, (1955) 95 App. D. C. 373, 222 F. 2d 398, 402: "The statute
does not say or imply that the privilege it creates may be withheld from patients who
have been committed to a public mental hospital. Most courts that have considered
the matter hold, as we do, that such patients are entitled to the protection of such a
statute." Westphal v. State, (1948) 191 Miss. 688, 79 N. Y. S. 2d 634. See also § 34
herein.

7 Casson v. Schoenfield, (1918) 166 Wis. 401, 166 N. W. 23, L. R. A. 1918 C. 162.
But cf. Motley v. State, (1936) 174 Miss. 568, 165 So. 296.

disclosing any knowledge of the patient's condition thus acquired.[1]
The rule has been applied to a hospital's pathologist who performed
an autopsy at the request of the attending physician.[2] Where, however, the assistant is not a physician legally admitted to practice, his
testimony may be received.[3]

The relation of physician and patient applies also to the consulting physician. When a physician is called to treat a patient, and
he finds a condition which he regards as serious or unusual and calls
another physician for consultation with a view to obtaining additional medical opinion to his own in dealing with the situation, he
is the agent of his patient in doing so and the consulting physician
is for this occasion an attending physician and therefore precluded
from revealing any information thus acquired;[4] and this is true even
though he took no part in the examination of the patient and did

---

[1] Mutual Life Ins. Co. v. Owen, (1914) 111 Ark. 554, 164 S. W. 720; Shaw v. Nampa,
(1918) 31 Idaho 347, 171 Pac. 1132; Jones v. Caldwell, (1911) 20 Idaho 5, 116 Pac. 110,
48 L. R. A. (n. s.) 119; Arnold v. Fort Dodge, Des Moines & S. R. R., (1919) 186 Iowa
538, 173 N. W. 252; MacEvitt v. Maas, (1901) 33 Misc. Rep. 553, 67 N. Y. S. 817, aff'd.
64 App. Div. 382, 72 N. Y. S. 158; Lamarand v. National Life & Acc. Ins. Co., (1937) 58
Ohio App. 415, 16 N. E. 2d 701.

The Puerto Rico statute expressly includes an assistant of the physician or surgeon. It has been held, therefore, that a bacteriologist, who assisted the attending
physician by examining the sputum of the patient, could not testify. Manufacturers'
Life Ins. Co. v. Brennan, (1921) 270 Fed. 173. See also § 19, herein.

[2] Mathews v. Rex Health & Acc. Ins. Co., (1927) 86 Ind. App. 335, 349, 157 N. E. 467:
"The doctor had no more right to make this examination, and to disclose the information thus received, than he would have had if he had gone into the sick room prior to
the boy's death and made an examination to ascertain the cause of the boy's illness,
and to then go into court and testify as to the information thus acquired. He should
be treated as an assistant of the physician in charge prior to the boy's death."

[3] Borosich v. Metropolitan Life Ins. Co., (1926) 191 Wis. 239, 210 N. W. 829.

See also § 29, herein.

[4] Tweith v. Duluth, Missabe & I. R. Ry., (1946) 66 F. Supp. 427; Prader v. National
Masonic Acc. Ass'n., (1895) 95 Iowa 149, 63 N. W. 601; Raymond v. Burlington, Cedar
Rapids & N. Ry., (1884) 65 Iowa 152, 21 N. W. 495; Leonczak v. Minneapolis, St. Paul
& S. St. M. Ry., (1924) 161 Minn. 304, 201 N. W. 551; Provident Life & Acc. Ins. Co. v.
Chapman, (1928) 152 Miss. 747, 118 So. 437; Epstein v. Pennsylvania R. R., (1913) 250
Mo. 1, 156 S. W. 699, 48 L. R. A. (n. s.) 394, Ann. Cas. 1915 A 423; Smart v. Kansas City,
(1907) 208 Mo. 162, 105 S. W. 709, 14 L. R. A. (n. s.) 565, 13 Ann. Cas. 932; Baker v.
Mardis, (1928) 221 Mo. App. 1185, 1 S. W. 2d 223; Morris v. New York, Ontario & W.
Ry., (1895) 148 N. Y. 88, 41 N. E. 410; Renihan v. Dennin, (1886) 103 N. Y. 573, 9 N. E.
320; Green v. Nebagamain, (1902) 113 Wis. 508, 89 N. W. 520.

not prescribe for him.[5] It is believed that the policy of the privilege would be best promoted by leaving the attending physician free to secure additional medical opinion for the benefit of the patient, and that his act would be attributed to the patient in inviting other medical aid for consultation.[6]

A partner of the attending physician, who obtains confidential information regarding the condition of the patient by reason of his association, comes clearly within the spirit, if not the letter, of the statute.[7]

43. Relationship Between Physician and Person Not Seeking Medical Advice or Treatment for Himself

As a general rule, the relation of physician and patient does not exist between a person who, strictly for his own benefit, consults a physician not about his own condition of health but rather that of another person, especially where the latter neither seeks nor receives medical assistance.[1]

Not infrequently a physician acquires information concerning the physical condition of a person while attending another person in his professional character. The fact that the physician obtained the information, however confidential, while performing his duties in the household of the patient or while attending him elsewhere, does not alter the rule that the statute protects only such information as is acquired by the physician by reason of the existence of the relation of physician and patient and which concerns the patient only. Thus, in an action involving the right of inheritance, the physician who attended the mother at the birth of an illegitimate

---

[5] Green v. Nebagamain, (1902) 113 Wis. 508, 89 N. W. 520.

[6] Provident Life & Acc. Ins. Co. v. Chapman, (1928) 152 Miss. 747, 118 So. 437.

[7] Aetna Life Ins. Co. v. Deming, (1889) 123 Ind. 384, 24 N. E. 86, 24 N. E. 375; Raymond v. Burlington, Cedar Rapids & N. Ry., (1884) 65 Iowa 152, 21 N. W. 495; Mississippi Power & L. Co. v. Jordan, (1932) 164 Miss. 174, 143 So. 483.

[1] State v. Bennett, (1908) 137 Iowa 427, 110 N. W. 150; Smith v. State, (1940) 188 Miss. 339, 194 So. 922; Babcock v. People, (1878) 15 Hun. (N. Y.) 347; Hewit v. Prime, (1835) 21 Wend. (N. Y.) 79. See also Wood v. State, (1941) 72 Okla. Cr. 347, 116 P. 2d 734. Cf. Williams v. State, (1939) 65 Okla. Cr. 336, 86 P. 2d 1015. The decision seems questionable not only because the relation of physician and patient did not exist between the physician and the defendant, but also because the purpose of the consultation was plainly an illegal one.

child, was permitted to testify to an admission made by a person there present that he was the father of the child. No confidential relation existed between such third person and the physician as to render it a privileged communication.[2] Statements disclosing his own misconduct made by the defendant to a physician who was then attending defendant's wife were not privileged, since no professional relationship existed between the physician and the defendant.[3]

44. *Physician Performing Autopsy*

It is well established that, in the absence of express statutory prohibition, the performance of an autopsy to discover the cause of death, in both civil and criminal cases, is a recognized and legitimate proceeding, and that a provision in an insurance policy that the insurer shall have the right to make an autopsy in case of death, is a valid and enforceable one.[1] However, there may still remain the

---

[2] Estate of Baird, (1916) 173 Cal. 617, 160 Pac. 1078. In an action on an insurance certificate, defended on the ground that the insured misrepresented that he had not suffered from a venereal disease, the testimony of a physician who was treating the eyes of a baby suffering from such an infection, that the insured had told him that he had had a venereal disease was excluded. *Held:* Error. The statement of the insured was not privileged since it was not made to the physician in his professional character, the baby, not the insured, being the patient. Cromeenes v. Sovereign Camp, W. of W., (1920) 205 Mo. App. 419, 224 S. W. 15. See also Jennings v. Supreme Council, L. A. B. A., (1903) 81 App. Div. 76, 81 N. Y. S. 90; Keeton v. State, (1936) 175 Miss. 631, 167 So. 68.

[3] People v. Harris, (1893) 136 N. Y. 423, 33 N. E. 65. In Nichols v. State, (1922) 109 Neb. 335, 191 N. W. 333, the defendant was convicted of murdering his wife. A physician was called to the scene of the tragedy to attend the wife but arrived a few minutes after she died. The defendant was beside her suffering from self-inflicted wounds. The physician asked him what the shooting was about and defendant said he had shot her and himself. Called as a witness by the state, the physician was permitted to testify to what defendant said. *Held:* No error. The evidence was not privileged since the conversation took place when the relation of physician and patient did not exist. The fact that later the physician, prompted by humane consideration, voluntarily rendered medical aid to the defendant did not alter the principle.

[1] See note, 88 A. L. R. 984. But the demand for an autopsy must be seasonably made, or a reasonable excuse for delay be proven. Whether a court should authorize the disinterment of a body for purposes of an autopsy depends upon the peculiar circumstances arising in each case. Gath v. Travelers Ins. Co., (1925) 113 Ohio St. 369, 149 N. E. 389.

question? Are the facts coming to the knowledge of the physician, as the result of an autopsical examination, within the protection of the physician-patient privilege statute?[2] There is a conflict of opinion on this matter, but it appears to stem from the different circumstances under which the post mortem examination was made. In some cases, the physician who performed the autopsy was also the attending physician during the lifetime of the deceased; in others, he had never attended or even seen the person before his death.

The weight of authority is to the effect that where the deceased person had not in his lifetime been attended and treated by the particular physician performing or observing the autopsy, the relation of physician and patient contemplated by the statute does not exist; therefore the privilege does not attach. A deceased body is not a patient.[3] To hold that facts discovered through an autopsy are privileged communications within the meaning of the statute will not effectuate what is conceived to be its manifest purpose, namely, to obtain full disclosure to the physician in order to enable him to properly treat the patient. Treatment cannot avail after death.[4]

---

[2] Where the deceased person has no physician and dies under suspicious circumstances, the public authorities are likely to require an autopsy, and facts disclosed as a result thereof are, of course, not privileged. Travelers Ins. Co. v. Bergeron, (1928) 25 F. 2d 680, cert. denied 278 U. S. 638, 73 Law Ed. 553, 49 Su. Ct. 33, 58 A. L. R. 1127.

[3] Harrison v. Sutter Street Ry., (1897) 116 Cal. 156, 166, 47 Pac. 1019: "A dead man is not a 'patient,' capable of sustaining the relation of confidence toward his physician which is the foundation of the rule given in the statute, but is a mere piece of senseless clay which has passed beyond the reach of human prescription, medical or otherwise." Carmody v. Capital Traction Co., (1915) 43 App. D. C. 245, 249, Ann. Cas. 1916 D. 706: "The relation between a surgeon performing an autopsy and the body of a dead person is not the relation of a physician and patient."

[4] Travelers Ins. Co. v. Bergeron, (1928) 25 F. 2d 680, cert. denied 278 U. S. 638, 73 Law. Ed. 553, 49 Su. Ct. 33, 58 A. L. R. 1127. Chadwick v. Beneficial Life Ins. Co., (1919) 54 Utah 443, 448, 181 Pac. 448: "Just how information acquired by means of an autopsy can be said to have been acquired to enable the physician to prescribe or act for the patient presents to our minds an insoluble question. When the patient is dead he is no longer a patient. The only functionaries that can thereafter be said to act for him are the undertaker and the gravedigger, and as to them the statute is silent."

In a leading case,[5] the autopsy was performed by the pathologist

[5] Travelers Ins. Co. v. Bergeron, (1928) 25 F. 2d 680, cert. denied 278 U. S. 638, 73 Law. Ed. 553, 49 Su. Ct. 33, 58 A. L. R. 1127.

at the hospital where the insured died. He did not see the insured during his illness and had nothing to do with the treatment administered. It was held that the relation of physician and patient did not exist at the time of the autopsy,[6] and that the pathologist could testify to what the autopsy revealed concerning the cause of the insured's death. Other courts have approved this view.[7] Moreover, it is a matter of no consequence that the physician who performed the autopsy was employed to do so by the holder of the privilege or by his adversary; in either case the physician may be compelled to testify, at the instance of either party, to the facts coming to his knowledge as the result of such autopsy. Thus, in an action for negligently causing the death of plaintiff's intestate, it was held that two physicians, who made an autopsical examination of the deceased at the instance of plaintiff's counsel, were properly allowed to testify as witnesses for the defense, over plaintiff's objection, as to the results of their examination into the cause of death.[8] In a criminal

[8] Carmody v. Capital Traction Co., (1915) 43 App. D. C. 245, Ann. Cas. 1916 D. 706.

case, it appeared that after the homicide the accused employed a physician to make a post mortem examination of the victim and to report the result. Subsequently, the state employed the same physician to make another examination, and at the trial he testified on behalf of the state, over defendant's objection, as to the conditions disclosed. The court held that the testimony was properly received since it did not come within the protection of the privilege statute.[9]

---

[6] "The relation of physician and patient ends when the death of the patient ensues." Cross v. Equitable Life Assur. Soc., (1940) 228 Iowa 800, 293 N. W. 464; Felska v. John Hancock Mut. Life Ins. Co., (1932) 144 Misc. 508, 259 N. Y. S. 35.

[7] Carmody v. Capital Traction Co., (1915) 43 App. D. S. 245, Ann. Cas. 1916 D. 706; Harrison v. Sutter Street Ry., (1897) 116 Cal. 156, 47 Pac. 1019; Price v. Metropolitan Life Ins. Co., (1939) 235 Mo. App. 168, 129 S. W. 2d 5; Key v. Cosmopolitan Life. H. & Acc. Ins. Co., (1937) _____Mo. App._____ , 102 S. W. 2d 797; Ossenkop v. State, (1910) 86 Neb. 539, 126 N. W. 72; Felska v. John Hancock Mut. Life Ins. Co., (1932) 144 Misc. 508, 259 N. Y. S. 35; Chadwick v. Beneficial Life Ins. Co., (1919) 54 Utah 443, 181 Pac. 448; Borosich v. Metropolitan Life Ins. Co., (1926) 191 Wis. 239, 210 N. W. 829.

[9] Ossenkop v. State, (1910) 86 Neb. 539, 550, 126 N. W. 72: "Defendant contends that knowledge of all of the facts of which the physician testified was obtained as a result of confidential communications properly entrusted to him by the defendant. * * * In the present case the physician was not employed to examine or treat defendant or any member of his family. The relation of physician and patient did not exist between ⟫⟫→

Occasionally the physician who examined and treated the deceased in his lifetime has been called upon to perform an autopsy on the body of his former patient, in order to ascertain the cause of his death, and the question has arisen whether he could testify, without the consent of the holder of the privilege, as to the results of his post mortem examination.[10] Of course, such physician, in disclosing the facts obtained through the autopsy, must not be permitted either directly or indirectly to reveal facts which he learned when he attended and treated the person in his lifetime.[11] But he can testify to the facts discovered by the autopsy or, as an expert, give an opinion based on such facts concerning the cause of death, provided he can completely segregate the information acquired by him while attending the deceased in his lifetime from that which he obtained as a result of the autopsy.[12]

As we have previously indicated, the rule stated above is not universally followed. In two cases, the courts have held that information obtained by an autopsical examination is within the protec-

---

them. The exhumed body contained no secrets which could be kept within the exclusive knowledge of defendant and the physician. The means of ascertaining the condition of the body was equally within the reach of defendant and the state. The court is entitled to know the truth."

[10] In actions on insurance policies where it is claimed that the insured misrepresented his condition of health in his application for insurance, and in actions for wrongful death where the real cause of death is the principal matter in dispute, it is obvious that medical testimony based upon facts disclosed by the autopsy would be highly important and probative. There would seem to be no reason for suppressing such facts except to conceal fraud.

[11] Travelers Ins. Co. v. Bergeron, (1928) 25 F. 2d 680, cert. denied 278 U. S. 638, 73 Law. Ed. 553, 49 Su. Ct. 33, 58 A. L. R. 1127.

[12] Sprouse v. Magee, (1928) 46 Idaho 622, 634, 269 Pac. 993: "As to evidence obtained from an autopsy, we have no hesitancy in saying that such is not privileged, when not dependent upon, and when capable of being by the physician segregated from, information which he received as an attending physician."

Accord: Cross v. Equitable Life Assur. Soc., (1940) 228 Iowa 800, 293 N. W. 464; Martin v. Metropolitan Life Ins. Co., (1943) ....Mo. App........ , 174 S. W. 2d 222; Chadwick v. Beneficial Life Ins. Co., (1926) 54 Utah 443, 181 Pac. 448.

Of course, if it had been necessary for the witness to supplement the information he obtained at the autopsy by information he acquired during his attendance upon the patient, in order to determine the cause of his death, a very different question would be presented. Chadwick v. Beneficial Life Ins. Co., infra.

tion of the statute. In *Thomas* v. *Byron Township*,[13] an action for wrongful death, an autopsy was performed by the physician who had attended the deceased after the accident and until the time of her death. He was called as a witness by defendant and, over objection related in minute detail, what conditions he found as the result of the autopsy. Holding this to be reversible error, the court stressed the fact that on account of the relation which had existed between the witness and deceased, it was possible for him to proceed within a few hours after her death to hold an autopsy. It was felt, therefore, that to allow the testimony of the physician as to the autopsy, and his conclusions therefrom, would operate to take away the barrier of secrecy erected by the statute.

In *Mathews* v. *Rex Health & Acc. Ins. Co.*,[14] the plaintiff, as beneficiary, sued on a policy issued by defendant on the life of her son. At the time of his death and for some time prior thereto, the insured was a patient at the City Hospital. After his death, the pathologist of of the hospital performed an autopsy. Defendant contended that the autopsy revealed facts which voided the policy. At the trial, the pathologist, over objection, was permitted to testify concerning the condition of the internal organs. He had never seen the insured before his death and, of course, had never treated him; however, he was in the employ of the hospital where he performed the autopsy. It was held that the pathologist should be regarded as an assistant to the attending physician and that his testimony, therefore, was within the ban of the privilege statute and should have been excluded.[15]

---

[13] (1912) 168 Mich. 593, 134 N. W. 1021, 38 L. R. A. (n. s.) 1186, Ann. Cas. 1913 C. 686.

[14] (1927) 86 Ind. App. 335, 157 N. E. 467. See notes: (1928) 3 Ind. L. J. 724; (1928) 12 Minn. L. Rev. 390.

[15] McMahan, J., (p. 347): "The fact that the boy was a patient at the hospital provided the opportunity for having the autopsical examination. It was the outgrowth of the relationship existing between the patient and the hospital, and it would not have been performed except for the fact of that relationship. * * * Can a physician, after the death of his patient, through his consent or connivance, allow another physician to take the dead body of his patient, and, in the absence of friends and relatives, and without the consent of anyone, hold a post mortem examination, and thus give to the public the information which the physician in charge could not? Can a hospital, immediately after the death of one of its patients, discharge the physician who
》》》→

45. *Physician Testifying as an Expert:* *Effect of Privilege*

Where an issue of a particular case, civil or criminal, involves matters such as the nature, origin, and duration of a person's malady or injury and the probable effect thereof, his mental condition, or the cause of his death, the opinion of one or more medical men would seem to be indispensable to its proper determination. Jurors, as a rule, have neither the knowledge nor the experience necessary to equip them to decide such matters without the assistance of medical experts, even though they may have had an abundance of facts presented to them upon which to base their own conclusions.

It is everywhere conceded that, in jurisdictions which recognize the physician-patient privilege, the holder of the privilege may call as a witness the physician who attended the patient, and elicit from him his opinion upon matters pertaining to the patient's physical or mental condition, or the cause of his death.[1] The privilege is his to claim or to waive as he chooses.[2] But can the adverse party call

---

had attended the patient up to the time of death, and thereafter rush the dead body to the morgue and direct the physician at the head of the pathological department to perform an autopsy, and thus evade the statute which sealed the lips of the first physician? We think these questions should be answered in the negative, and that a physician under such circumstances steps into the shoes of the attending physician, and must be treated as if he were the assistant of the attending physician holding the autopsy at the direction of the latter, and that the information acquired by him through the autopsy is privileged."

The facts in this case are essentially the same as those in Travelers Ins. Co. v. Bergeron, (1928) 25 F. 2d 680, cert. denied 278 U. S. 638, 73 Law. Ed. 553, 49 Su. Ct. 33, 58 A. L. R. 1127 and in Felska v. John Hancock Mut. Life Ins. Co., (1932) 144 Misc. 508, 259 N. Y. S. 35, wherein the courts reached a different conclusion.

[1] Questions pertaining to the duty of a physician to testify as an expert, and to his right to special compensation therefor, are outside the scope of this treatise. For discussion of these matters, see 8 Wigmore, Evidence, § 2203; Rogers, (1941) Expert Testimony, §§ 317, 318; Herzog, (1931) Medical Jurisprudence, §§ 103, 104; 58 Am. Jur., Witnesses, §§ 874-883; 2 A. L. R. 1576, Power to Compel Expert to Testify; Expert Witness Fees, (1953) 43 J. of Crim. L. and Criminology 777; Porterfield, The Right To Subpoena Expert Testimony And The Fees Required To Be Paid Therefor, (1953) 5 Hast. L. J. 50; Bomar, The Compensation of Expert Witnesses, (1935) 2 Law and Contemp. Prob. 510; Hutchins, The Compensation of Medical Witnesses, (1906) 4 Mich. L. Rev. 413.

See also Johns-Manville Co. v. Cather, (1950) 208 Miss. 268, 44 So. 2d 405.

[2] See §§ 13, 16, herein.

such physician as an expert witness and, over the objection of the holder of the privilege, elicit an opinion upon such matters which may prove to be unfavorable to the cause of the party holding the privilege? The courts are at odds on some aspects of this question.

It appears to be universally recognized that, without the consent of the holder of the privilege, a physician cannot testify as an expert and base his opinion upon any matters confided to him by his patient, or upon information acquired by him in his professional capacity which was necessary to enable him to prescribe or act for the patient.[3] The witness being prohibited from disclosing detailed information, he certainly cannot render an opinion based upon his knowledge thus acquired.[4] Nor can he base it on facts which are inadmissible in evidence for any other reason.[5]

However, a physician who has attended the patient professionally is not thereby prohibited from testifying as an expert for the adverse party and giving his opinion in response to proper questions, provided, of course, he bases it upon facts or information

---

The mere fact that the patient cannot afford to pay his physician extra compensation to testify as an expert does not entitle him to offer hearsay evidence as to what his physician told him. Johns-Manville Products Corp v. Cather, (1950) 208 Miss. 268, 44 So. 2d 405.

[3] Labofish v. Berman, (1932) 60 App. D. C. 397, 55 F. 2d 1022; Manufacturers' Life Ins. Co. v. Brennan, (1921) 270 Fed. 173; Inspiration Consolidated Copper Co. v. Mendez, (1917) 19 Ariz. 151, 166 Pac. 278, 1183, aff'd. 250 U. S. 400, 63 Law. Ed. 1058, 39 Su. Ct. 553; Triangle Lumber Co. v. Acree, (1914) 112 Ark. 534, 166 S. W. 958, Ann. Cas. 1916 B. 773; In re Ross, (1916) 173 Cal. 178, 159 Pac. 603; Jones v. Caldwell, (1913) 23 Idaho 467, 130 Pac. 995; Gilchrist v. Mystic Workers of the World, (1915) 188 Mich. 466, 154 N. W. 575, Ann. Cas. 1918 C. 757; In re Mansbach's Estate, (1907) 150 Mich. 348, 114 N. W. 65; Polin v. St. Paul Union Depot Co., (1924) 159 Minn. 410, 199 N. W. 87; Mississippi Power & L. Co. v. Jordan, (1932) 164 Miss. 174, 143 So. 483; Thompson v. Ish, (1889) 99 Mo. 160, 12 S. W. 510; People v. Murphy, (1886) 101 N. Y. 126, 4 N. E. 326; Brigham v. Gott, (1889) 51 Hun. 636, 3 N. Y. S. 518.

[4] Thompson v. Ish, (1889) 99 Mo. 160, 173, 12 S. W. 510: "He is no more at liberty to give an opinion upon such knowledge than he is to detail the facts revealed to him by the patient."

The Minnesota and Louisiana statutes expressly prohibit a physician-witness giving his opinion based on information acquired while attending the patient.

[5] People v. Murphy, (1886) 101 N. Y. 126, 4 N. E. 326; Baker v. Industrial Comm'n., (1939) 135 Ohio St. 491, 21 N. E. 2d 593. But cf. McEvitt v. Maas, (1901) 33 Misc. 552, 67 N. Y. S. 817, aff'd. 64 App. Div. 382, 72 N. Y. S. 158.

which are outside the ambit of the privilege statute,[6] or upon testimony or documentary evidence properly introduced at the trial,[7] or upon his general knowledge of the subject without reference to the patient,[8] or upon facts which were open to the observation of any layman who had seen or conversed with the patient.[9]

A number of courts have held that a physician who has treated a person professionally is not thereby disqualified or precluded from giving expert testimony in response to proper *hypothetical* questions, provided that in answering them he separates and disregards what he learned and observed while attending the patient and his own opinion formed thereon, and founds his answers solely upon the premises related in the hypothetical question.[10] It has

---

[6] Triangle Lumber Co. v. Acree, (1914) 112 Ark. 534, 166 S. W. 958, Ann. Cas. 1916 B. 773; Wheeler v. State, (1902) 158 Ind. 687, 63 N. E. 975; Keeton v. State, (1936) 175 Miss. 631, 167 So. 68; Dabbs v. Richardson, (1924) 137 Miss. 789, 102 So. 769; Estes v. McGehee, (1923) 133 Miss. 174, 97 So. 530; Price v. Metropolitan Life Ins. Co., (1939) 235 Mo. App. 168, 129 S. W. 2d 5; Fisher v. Fisher, (1892) 129 N. Y. 654, 29 N. E. 951; Hoyt v. Hoyt, (1889) 112 N. Y. 493, 20 N. E. 402; People v. Schuyler, (1887) 106 N. Y. 298, 12 N. E. 783; Edington v. Aetna Life Ins. Co., (1879) 77 N. Y. 564; Meyer v. Standard Life & Acc. Ins. Co., (1896) 8 App. Div. 74, 40 N. Y. S. 419; Chadwick v. Beneficial Life Ins. Co., (1919) 54 Utah 443, 181 Pac. 448; Strafford v. Nothern Pac. Ry., (1917) 95 Wash. 450, 164 Pac. 71; Boyle v. Robinson, (1906) 129 Wis. 567, 109 N. W. 623.

[7] Valensin v. Valensin, (1887) 73 Cal. 106, 14 Pac. 397; Hauck v. Fritch, (1934) 99 Ind. App. 65, 189 N. E. 639; Motley v. State, (1936) 174 Miss. 568, 165 So. 296; Price v. Metropolitan Life Ins. Co., (1939) 235 Mo. App. 168, 129 S. W. 2d 5; Meyer v. Standard Life & Acc. Ins. Co., (1896) 8 App. Div. 74, 40 N. Y. S. 419; Russell v. Penn Mut. Life Ins. Co., (1941) 70 Ohio App. 113, 41 N. E. 2d 251; Gillen v. Industrial Comm'n., (1938) 59 Ohio App. 241, 17 N. E. 2d 663; Chadwick v. Beneficial Life Ins. Co., (1919) 54 Utah 443, 181 Pac. 448.

[8] Ranger, Inc. v. Equitable Life Assur. Soc., (1952) 196 F. 2d 968; Whitmore v. Herrick, (1928) 205 Iowa 621, 218 N. W. 334; Price v. Metropolitan Life Ins. Co., (1896) 8 App. Div. 74, 40 N. Y. S. 419; Dovich v. Chief Consolidated Mining Co., (1918) 53 Utah 522, 174 Pac. 627.

[9] Steele v. Ward, (1883) 30 Hun. (N. Y.) 555; Staunton v. Parker, (1879) 19. Hun. (N. Y.) 55; *In re* Williams' Will, (1950) 256 Wis. 338, 41 N. W. 2d 191.

See also § 53, herein.

[10] Butler v. Rule, (1926) 29 Ariz. 405, 242 Pac. 436; Hauck v. Fritch, (1934) 99 Ind. App. 65, 189 N. E. 639; Whitmore v. Herrick, (1928) 205 Iowa 621, 218 N. W. 334; Crago v. Cedar Rapids, (1904) 123 Iowa 48, 98 N. W. 354; Maetzold v. Walgreen Co., (1957) _____Minn._____, 83 N. W. 2d 233; Watkins v. Watkins, (1926) 142 Miss. 210, 106 So. 753; People v. Schuyler, (1887) 106 N. Y. 298, 12 N. E. 783; Meyer v. Standard Life & Acc. Ins. Co., (1896) 8 App. Div. 74, 40 N. Y. S. 419; Strizak v. Industrial Comm'n.,

⟫→

been said that testimony of this character is not inhibited by the privilege statute because "communications" between the physician and his patient are excluded from the questions asked and from the opinions expressed in response thereto.[11] Even though the hypothetical question incorporates facts similar to those of which he gained knowledge while treating the patient, the witness still may answer.[12]

But one may well ask: Is it possible for the attending physician to answer the question solely upon its hypothetical basis wholly uninfluenced by his personal knowledge of his patient's condition? And who is to decide whether the witness can really perform this intellectual feat? Shall it be the witness? Or must it be the court?

It has been said that the human mind is not competent to separate the facts of which it is cognizant into two classes—those that were obtained professionally and those not so obtained—and distinguish an opinion derived from one set of facts from an opinion derived from another.[13] In some instances, the physician-witness, realizing the difficulty and danger of attempting to segregate knowledge and information acquired in attending the patient, has frankly confessed his inability to make the separation.[14] Of course, where the physician admits that he cannot segregate and disregard the knowledge of the patient's condition and base his opinion solely upon the assumed facts presented to him in the hypothetical ques-

---

(1953) 159 Ohio St. 475, 112 N. E. 2d 529.

See also Triangle Lumber Co. v. Acree, (1914) 112 Ark. 534, 166 S. W. 958, Ann. Cas. 1916 B, 773; Wheeler v. State, (1902) 158 Ind. 687, 63 N. E. 975.

[11] Strizak v. Industrial Comm'n., (1953) 159 Ohio St. 475, 112 N. E. 2d 529.

[12] Olmstead v. Webb, (1894) 5 App. D. C. 38; *In re* Flint, (1893) 100 Cal. 391, 34 Pac. 863. However, in *Re* Ross, (1916) 173 Cal. 178, 184, 159 Pac. 603, the court said: "It cannot be disputed but that if the hypothetical question correctly stated the truth, it was a direct effort to elicit from the testator's family physician in violation of the confidential relationship a statement which of necessity would be based, not upon the facts stated in the question, but on the facts as known to and believed by the physician himself—facts which the law forbade him to disclose. In other words, under the thinnest of disguises the question was an effort to have the witness declare that which the law has said he should not declare. The ruling excluding the inquiry was proper."

[13] Larson v. State, (1912) 92 Neb. 24, 137 N. W. 894.

[14] Jones v. Caldwell, (1913) 23 Idaho 467, 130 Pac. 995; Polin v. St. Paul Union Depot Co., (1924) 159 Minn. 410, 199 N. W. 87.

tion without relation to the patient, the court is bound to exclude his answer.[15] On the other hand, if the witness has attended the patient professionally, but states that he can segregate and disregard all privileged information and form an opinion founded upon the hypothetical statement of facts alone, it is within the discretion of the trial judge, who has the opportunity to judge of the witness and observe him while he is testifying, to say whether the witness can in fact separate and disregard his knowledge acquired professionally and base his answers exclusively upon hypothetical facts, or upon information not within the scope and protection of the privilege statute.[16] Obviously, the witness is not the final and conclusive judge as to whether he can do this.[17] The ruling of the trial judge is not an easy one to make and the line of demarcation in many cases will be a shadowy one at best.

The general rule seems to be that if the court is satisfied that the witness can separate and disregard all knowledge of the patient's condition, it may permit him to answer after admonishing him to base his opinion on the hypothetical facts alone.[18] It has been held, however, that although the knowledge acquired while attending the patient might to some extent influence the witness in his answer to the question, still that fact will not render such answer incompetent, but will merely affect its weight.[19]

It has been noticed that, in some cases, physicians, who had attended and treated patients, have willingly appeared as expert witnesses for their patients' adversaries and that their testimony has been against the interests of their former patients. Most of the

---

[15] Jones v. Caldwell, (1913) 23 Idaho 467, 130 Pac. 995; Polin v. St. Paul Union Depot Co., (1924) 159 Minn. 410, 199 N. W. 87; Mississippi Power & L. Co. v. Jordan, (1932) 164 Miss. 174, 143 So. 483; Salts v. Prudential Ins. Co., (1909) 140 Mo. App. 142, 120 S. W. 714; Jahns v. Clark, (1926) 138 Wash. 288, 244 Pac. 729.

[16] Butler v. Rule, (1926) 29 Ariz. 405, 242 Pac. 436; Mississippi Power & L. Co. v. Jordan, (1932) 164 Miss. 174, 143 So. 483; Dabbs v. Richardson, (1924) 137 Miss. 789, 102 So. 769.

[17] Hutchins v. Hutchins, (1919) 48 App. D. C. 495; Dabbs v. Richardson, (1924) 137 Miss. 789, 102 So. 769.

[18] See cases in note 10, infra.

[19] People v. Schuyler, (1887) 106 N. Y. 298, 12 N. E. 783; Meyer v. Standard Life & Acc. ins. Co., (1896) 8 App. Div. 74, 40 N. Y. S. 419.

courts have made no mention of the matter. To others, however, the circumstances suggest an ethical problem: Is it indelicate for a physician, who has at some time treated a patient, to permit himself to be hired by another person for the purpose of testifying as an expert against his former patient? Two courts have said emphatically it is.[20]

Where the plaintiff, in a personal injury action against a hospital and certain physicians who had treated her there, cross-examined the physicians while they were defendants, no waiver resulted so as to entitle the hospital, after the physicians had been eliminated as defendants, to call them as expert witnesses in its behalf to show by their testimony the condition of the plaintiff while a patient in said hospital.[21]

46. Burden of Establishing Relation of Physician and Patient

The object of the privilege statute is not to make the physician absolutely incompetent as a witness. He is only prohibited from testifying as to communications made to him, or to facts learned by him, during the existence of the relationship of physician and patient when they are of a confidential nature and necessary to enable him to prescribe or act for the patient.[1]

---

[20] Matter of Gates, (1915) 170 App. Div. 921, 154 N. Y. S. 782; Bauch v. Schultz, (1919) 109 Misc. 548, 551, 180 N. Y. S. 188: "A more serious question presented for the consideration of the Associations of the Bar and medical societies is whether such deliberate and flagrant disregard of the ethics of the medical and legal professions should go unchecked, or whether steps should be taken, by statutory amendment or otherwise, to prevent a recurrence of such incidents."

[21] Von Eye v. Hammes et al., (1956) 147 F. Supp. 174, 184: "To permit attending physicians to testify as contended for would be but an end to the means of commercializing knowledge thus obtained, and destroy the intent of the legislative branch of the State. There is nothing in the record that can be spelled into waiver of that privilege by plaintiff. The defendant doctors were eliminated as parties long prior to their being tendered as expert witnesses for defendant hospital. No longer was the propriety of their treatment of plaintiff questioned. Cross-examination under the Rules, while they were defendants, did not constitute waiver within the meaning of the controlling statute."

[1] State v. Masters, (1924) 197 Iowa 1147, 198 N. W. 509; Allen v. Allen, (1933) _____Mo. App._____, 60 S. W. 2d 709, 711. See also § 13, herein.

It is clear that the mere assertion of the privilege, without any showing of facts or circumstances from which the court can see the necessity for the application of the statute under which the privilege is claimed, is not sufficient to warrant the court in rejecting the proffered evidence.[2] Therefore, when the testimony of a physician is sought to be excluded on the ground of privilege, the burden is upon the party seeking to exclude it to bring the case within the purview of the statute. Accordingly, by the great weight of authority, the objector must show the circumstances justifying the application of the statute; in other words, he must make it appear not only that the information he seeks to exclude was acquired by the witness during the relation of physician and patient,[3] but also, in most jurisdictions, that it was necessary to enable him to perform some professional act.[4] Certainly it is not the duty of the party

---

[2] Vermillion v. Prudential Ins. Co., (1936) 230 Mo. App. 993, 93 S. W. 2d 45.

[3] Keeton v. State, (1936) 175 Miss. 631, 651, 167 So. 68: "The person claiming the privilege must show that the relation of physician and patient existed, and must show, further, the existence of all the conditions of exclusion."

Linz v. Massachusetts Mut. Life Ins. Co., (1880) 8 Mo. App. 363, 369: "It is the relation of physician and patient that is the reason and the basis of the whole exclusion. * * * When this relation is not involved,—and the burden is on the objector to show that it is,—the first condition is not met."

Accord: Chicago, Indianapolis & L. Ry. v. Gorman, (1911) 47 Ind. App. 432, 94 N. E. 730; State v. Masters, (1924) 197 Iowa 1147, 198 N. W. 509; State v. Lyons, (1904) 113 La. 959, 37 So. 890; State v. Anderson, (1956) 247 Minn. 469, 78 N. W. 2d 320; Hopkins v. State, (1951) 212 Miss. 772, 55 So. 2d 467; Bouligny v. Metropolitan Life Ins. Co., (1939) _____ Mo. App. _____, 133 S. W. 2d 1094; Schermer v. McMahon, (1904) 108 Mo. App. 36, 82 S. W. 535; People v. Decina, (1956) 2 N. Y. 2d 133, 138 N. E. 2d 799; People v. Austin, (1910) 199 N. Y. 446, 93 N. E. 57; Griffiths v. Metropolitan Street Ry., (1902) 171 N. Y. 106, 63 N. E. 808; People v. Koerner, (1897) 154 N. Y. 355, 48 N. E. 730; People v. Schuyler, (1887) 106 N. Y. 298, 12 N. E. 783; Edington v. Aetna Life Ins. Co., (1879) 77 N. Y. 564; Mulligan v. Sinski, (1913) 156 App. Div. 35, 140 N. Y. S. 835, aff'd. 214 N. Y. 678, 108 N. E. 1101; Henry v. New York, Lake Erie & W. R. R., (1890) 57 Hun. 76, 10 N. Y. S. 508; Wiel v. Cowles, (1887) 45 Hun. 307; People v. Barnes, (1950) 197 Misc. 477, 98 N. Y. S. 2d 481; Heath v. Broadway & Seventh Ave. R. R., (1890) 8 N. Y. S. 863; Stowell v. American Cooperative Relief Ass'n., (1889) 52 Hun 613, 5 N. Y. S. 233; Booren v. McWilliams, (1914) 26 N. D. 558; 145 N. W. 410, Ann. Cas. 1916 A. 388; Forrest v. Portland Ry., L. & P. Co., (1913) 64 Ore. 240, 129 Pac. 1048; Smits v. State, (1911) 145 Wisc. 601, 130 N. W. 525; Boyle v. Robinson, (1906) 129 Wis. 567, 109 N. W. 623. The principle is also applied in cases involving the attorney-client privilege. Bloodgood v. Lynch, (1944) 293 N. Y. 308, 56 N. E. 2d 718; *In re* Martin, (1943) 141 Ohio St. 87, 47 N. E. 2d 388; Hurt v. State, (1957) _____ Okla. Cr._____, 303 P. 2d 476.

[4] The burden of proof as to this requirement is discussed in § 60, herein.

offering the testimony to show that the relation of physician and patient did *not* exist and, therefore, that the statute does not apply.[5]

It is requisite that, in every instance, it shall be judicially determined whether the relation existed at the time the witness acquired the information which is sought to be disclosed, and, in order that such primary determination may advisedly be made, it is indispensable that the court shall be apprised, through preliminary inquiry, of the characterizing circumstances.[6] The witness himself may testify on the subject, but it is peculiarly within the province of the trial judge to determine from the examination of the witness and from other relevant evidence whether the relation existed.[7] Upon request, the objector should be given leave to interrogate the witness so that his relationship be defined.[8] On the other hand, if

---

[5] Henry v. New York, Lake Erie & W. R. R., (1890) 57 Hun. 76, 10 N. Y. S. 508. *But cf.* Tracey v. Metropolitan Street Ry., (1900) 49 App. Div. 197, 63 N. Y. S. 242, aff'd 168 N. Y. 653, 61 N. E. 1135.

See also Vermillion v. Prudential Life Ins. Co., (1936) 230 Mo. App. 993, 1001, 93 S. W. 2d 45.

[6] Bowles v. Kansas City, (1892) 51 Mo. App. 416, 421: "We cannot tell whether the witness was competent or not. The court does not seem to have instituted an inquiry into his competency as was proper before passing upon that question. The facts which under the statute would render the witness incompetent were not shown in any way, and until so shown it is difficult to understand why the witness was incompetent. Certainly, though a physician, he was not incompetent to testify unless rendered so by reason of the facts which the statute declares shall render a physician incompetent. These facts, though possibly existing, were not before the court, and until they were in some way brought to its attention, the witness could not be properly adjudged incompetent to testify." See also Phelps Dodge Corp. v. Guerrero, (1921) 273 Fed. 415; Peoples Bank v. Brown, (1902) 112 Fed. 652 (attorney-client privilege). It has been held that even when the preliminary examination of the witness is conducted by the court in the absence of the jury, the inquiry should be confined to the single question: Did the relation of physician and patient exist? If it did, the evidence should be excluded. United States Fidelity & Guar. Co. v. Hood, (1920) 124 Miss. 548, 87 So. 115, 15 A. L. R. 605.

[7] Cincinnati, Hamilton & D. R. R. v. Gross, (1917) 186 Ind. 471, 114 N. E. 962; Chicago & Erie R. R. v. Schenkel, (1914) 57 Ind. App. 175, 104 N. E. 50; Meyer v. Supreme Lodge K. of P., (1904) 178 N. Y. 63, 70 N. E. 111, aff'd 198 U. S. 508, 49 Law. Ed. 1146, 25 Su. Ct. 754, 64 L. R. A. 839; Griffiths v. Metropolitan Street Ry., (1902) 171 N. Y. 106, 63 N. E. 808; Booren v. McWilliams, (1914) 26 N. D. 558, 145 N. W. 410, Ann. Cas. 1916 A. 388.

[8] Van Wie v. United States, (1948) 77 F. Supp. 22; Nugent v. Cudahy Packing Co.,

the court refuses to allow the witness to testify in behalf of the patient's adversary on the ground that the matters which are the subject of the inquiry are privileged, the party seeking his testimony must be permitted to show, if he can, that the relation of physician and patient did not exist.[9] The trial judge may participate in the preliminary examination and question the witness to determine whether or not the relation existed.[10] Moreover, he has a broad discretion as to the extent of the cross-examination of the witness and the right of the judge himself to participate therein.[11] Upon a conflict of evidence, the decision of the trial court must be deemed conclusive and the discretion exercised by that court is seldom subject to review.[12]

Where a physician examined a person and that physician was later called by another person to testify to what the examination revealed, it was held that the party objecting to such testimony was entitled to the benefit of a *presumption* that the relation of physician and patient existed.[13] It has also been held that entries in a

---

(1905) 126 Iowa 517, 102 N. W. 442; Ballard v. Yellow Cab Co., (1944) 20 Wash. 2d 67, 145 P. 2d 1019.

Proof laying a foundation for the exercise of the privilege does not constitute a waiver of the privilege. Hicks v. Metropolitan Life Ins. Co., (1916) 196 Mo. App. 162, 190 S. W. 661.

[9] Kelly v. Dykes, (1916) 174 App. Div. 786, 161 N. Y. S. 551, app. dismissed 220 N. Y. 653, 115 N. E. 1042. See also People's Bank v. Brown, (1902) 112 Fed. 652 (attorney-client privilege). If the trial judge refuses to hear such preliminary evidence and rules that the answer called for was privileged, error should probably be predicated on his refusal. Arizona Copper Co. v. Burciaga, (1918) 20 Ariz. 85, 177 Pac. 29.

[10] Richter v. Hoglund, (1943) 132 F. 2d 748; Gardner v. Hobbs, (1949) 69 Idaho 288, 206 P. 2d 539; Dotton v. Albion, (1885) 57 Mich. 575, 24 N. W. 786; Ballard v. Yellow Cab Co., (1944) 20 Wash. 2d 67, 145 P. 2d 1019.

[11] Richter v. Hoglund, (1943) 132 F. 2d 748.

[12] Ranger, Inc. v. Equitable Life Assur. Soc., (1952) 196 F. 2d 968; Phelps Dodge Corp. v. Guerrero, (1921) 273 Fed. 415; Valleroy v. Knights of Columbus, (1908) 135 Mo. App. 574, 116 S. W. 1130; Hurt v. State, (1957) ⸺Okla. Cr.⸺, 303 P. 2d 476 (attorney-client). In Meyer v. Supreme Lodge, K. of P., (1904) 178 N. Y. 63, 70 N. E. 111, aff'd 198 U. S. 508, 49 Law. Ed. 1146, 25 Su. Ct. 754, 64 L. R. A. 839, the Court of Appeals did review the trial court's ruling.

[13] Munz v. Salt Lake City R. R., (1902) 25 Utah 220, 70 Pac. 852. The decision is questionable. In Phelps Dodge Corp. v. Guerrero, (1921) 273 Fed. 415, where the evidence was evenly balanced, the trial judge made use of the presumption.

hospital record itself constituted a prima facie showing that the information was of a confidential and privileged character and that the burden was on the party offering them to produce evidence to satisfy the court that such hospital record was not made for the purpose of advancing a professional relationship.[14]

---

[14] Vermillion v. Prudential Ins. Co., (1936) 230 Mo. App. 993, 93 S. W. 2d 45. There are many situations that might fit this rule.

CHAPTER X

What Communications and Information Are Privileged

47. *In General*[1]

The purpose of the legislatures which have adopted the privilege is manifest on the face of the enactment. Generally speaking, the statute does not prohibit a physician from testifying in any and all cases in which his patient may be involved.[2] It seems quite clear that the legislatures did not intend that *all* information, whether by communication or otherwise, which is obtained by physicians from their patients, should be privileged, but such information

---

[1] It is essential, of course, that the relation of physician and patient exist. Without this there is no privilege anyway. For the purposes of this chapter, therefore, it should be assumed that the relation exists. The only question is: Does the communication, or information, come within the scope of the physician-patient privilege statute?

[2] See § 13, herein.

145

only as may reasonably be necessary to enable the physicians to
apply their full skill for the benefit of their patients.[3]

Non-confidential matters obviously are not privileged. There
are a variety of facts to which the physician may properly testify
without violating the protected secrecy of the sick-room or trespassing upon the patient's right to privacy. A physician is free to
testify as to the fact of his employment by, or that he treated, the
patient,[4] the fact that the patient was sick,[5] the place[6] and duration

---

[3] Madsen v. Utah Light & Ry., (1909) 36 Utah 528, 537, 105 Pac. 799. See also Rule 27
(2) of the Uniform Rules of Evidence, (1953), Appendix, herein.

The Puerto Rico statute says "conveniently to prescribe."

[4] Such facts are not secret and confidential, but may be, and usually are, known by
other persons.

In re Albert Lindley Lee Memorial Hospital, (1953) 115 F. Supp. 643, aff'd. 209
F. 2d 122, cert. denied Cincotta v. United States, 347 U. S. 960, 98 Law. Ed. 1104, 74
Su. Ct. 709; Miller v. Pacific Mutual Life Ins. Co., (1953) 116 F. Supp. 365, aff'd. 228
F. 2d 889; Eureka-Maryland Assur. Co. v. Gray, (1941) 74 App. D. C. 191, 121 F. 2d
104, cert. denied 314 U. S. 613, 86 Law. Ed. 494, 62 Su. Ct. 114; Kavakos v. Equitable
Life Assur. Soc., (1936) 88 F. 2d 762; Labofish v. Berman, (1932) 60 App. D. C. 397,
55 F. 2d 1022; Lincoln National Life Ins. Co. v. Hammer, (1930) 41 F. 2d 12; Wolf
v. People, (1947) 117 Colo. 279, 187 P. 2d 926; Haughton v. Aetna Life Ins. Co.,
(1905) 165 Ind. 32, 73 N. E. 592; Metropolitan Life Ins. Co. v. Head, (1927) 86 Ind.
App. 326, 157 N. E. 448; Cross v. Equitable Life Assur. Soc., (1940) 228 Iowa 800,
293 N. W. 464; Nelson v. Nederland Life Ins. Co., (1900) 110 Iowa 600, 81 N. W.
807; In re Nickel's Estate, (1948) 321 Mich. 519, 32 N. W. 2d 733 (hospital records
admissible to show fact that patient was treated, but not what diagnosis indicated); Polish Roman Catholic Union v. Palen, (1942) 302 Mich. 557, 5 N. W. 2d 463;
McKinney v. Liberty Life Ins. Co., (1933) 263 Mich. 490, 248 N. W. 881; Dittrick v.
Detroit, (1893) 98 Mich. 245, 57 N. W. 125; Brown v. Metropolitan Life Ins. Co.,
(1887) 65 Mich. 306, 32 N. W. 610; Sorenson v. New York Life Ins. Co., (1935) 195 Minn.
298, 262 N. W. 868; Stone v. Sigel, (1933) 189 Minn. 47, 248 N. W. 285; Marfia v. Great
Northern Ry., (1914) 124 Minn. 466, 145 N. W. 385; Price v. Standard Life & Acc. Ins.
Co., (1903) 90 Minn. 264, 95 N. W. 1118; Sproles v. State, (1936) 176 Miss. 810, 170 So.
293 (physician was permitted to deny he had attended the accused); State v. Carryer,
(1915)   Mo. ...... , 180 S. W. 850; Leeds v. Prudential Ins. Co., (1935) 128 Neb. 395,
258 N. W. 672, 96 A. L. R. 1414; Livingston v. Omaha & C. B. St. Ry., (1919) 104 Neb.
118, 175 N. W. 662; Sovereign Camp W. of W. v. Grandon, (1902) 64 Neb. 39, 89 N. W.
448; Klein v. Prudential Ins. Co., (1917) 221 N. Y. 449, 117 N. E. 942; Patten v. United
Life & Acc. Ins. Ass'n., (1892) 133 N. Y. 450, 31 N. E. 342; Feeney v. Long Island R. R.,
(1889) 116 N. Y. 375, 22 N. E. 402, 5 L. R. A. 544; Dana v. Commercial Trav. Mut. Acc.
Ass'n., (1934) 241 App. Div. 812, 271 N. Y. S. 952; Denaro v. Prudential Ins. Co., (1913)
154 App. Div. 840, 139 N. Y. S. 758; Deutschmann v. Third Ave. R. R., (1903) 87 App.
Div. 503, 84 N.Y.S.887; McGrath v. State, (1950) 200 Misc. 165, 104 N.Y.S.2d 882; West-
$\gg\!\!\!\to$

← ⚞

phal v. State, (1948) 191 Misc. 688, 79 N. Y. S. 2d 634; Entian v. Provident Mutual Life Ins. Co., (1935) 155 Misc. 227, 279 N. Y. S. 580; Palmer v. John Hancock Mut. Life Ins. Co., (1934) 150 Misc. 669, 270 N. Y. S. 10 (hospital record admissible to show fact that deceased was treated).... Felska v. John Hancock Mut. Life Ins. Co., (1932) 144 Misc. 508, 259 N. Y. S. 35; Hammerstein v. Hammerstein, (1911) 74 Misc. 567, 134 N. Y. S. 473; Sambles v. Metropolitan Life Ins. Co., (1952) 158 Ohio St. 233, 108 N. E. 2d 321; Willig v. Prudential Ins. Co., (1942) 71 Ohio App. 255, 49 N. E. 2d 421; Russell v. Penn Mutual Life Ins. Co., (1941) 70 Ohio App. 113, 41 N. E. 2d 251; American Bankers Ins. Co. v. Hopkins, (1917) 67 Okla. 150, 169 Pac. 489; Freedman v. Mutual Life Ins. Co., (1941) 342 Pa. 404, 21 A. 2d 81, 135 A. L. R. 1249; Sweeney v. Green, (1935) 116 Pa. Super. 190, 176 Atl. 849; Eklund v. Metropolitan Life Ins. Co., (1936) 89 Utah 273, 57 P. 2d 362; Chadwick v. Beneficial Life Ins. Co., (1919) 54 Utah 443, 181 Pac. 448; Willhelm v. Order of Columbian Knights, (1912) 149 Wis. 585, 136 N. W. 160, but *cf* McGowan v. Supreme Court of Independent Order of Foresters, (1899) 104 Wis. 173, 80 N. W. 603, to the effect that a physician cannot testify that he treated a person since he must obtain his knowledge from his professional relationship.

See also Masson v. Metropolitan Life Ins. Co., (1930) 225 Mo. App. 925, 36 S. W. 2d 118.

[5] First Trust Co. v. Kansas City Life Ins. Co., (1935) 79 F. 2d 48; Steinberg v. New York Life Ins. Co., (1933) 263 N. Y. 45, 188 N. E. 152, 90 A. L. R. 642; Klein v. Prudential Ins. Co., (1917) 221 N. Y. 449, 117 N. E. 942; Patten v. United Life & Acc. Ins. Co., (1892) 133 N. Y. 450, 31 N. E. 342; Rubin v. Equitable Life Assur. Soc., (1945) 269 App. Div. 677, 53 N. Y. S. 2d 351; Dana v. Commercial Trav. Mut. Acc. Ass'n, (1934) 241 App. Div. 812, 271 N. Y. S. 952; Keck v. Metropolitan Life Ins. Co., (1933) 238 App. Div. 538, 264 N. Y. S. 892, aff'd. 264 N. Y. 422, 191 N. E. 495; Cirrincioni v. Metropolitan Life Ins. Co., (1928) 223 App. Div. 461, 228 N. Y. S. 354; Denaro v. Prudential Ins. Co., (1913) 154 App. Div. 840, 139 N. Y. S. 758; Rossetti v. Metropolitan Life Ins. Co., (1939) 10 N. Y. S. 2d 437.

Under certain circumstances, the physician cannot disclose whether the patient was sick or well. Lande v. Travelers Ins. Co., (1934) 241 App. Div. 96, 271 N. Y. S. 551, aff'd. 265 N. Y. 655, 193 N. E. 430.

[6] Patten v. United Life & Acc. Ins. Ass'n., (1892) 133 N. Y. 450, 31 N. E. 342; Dana v. Commercial Trav. Mut. Acc. Ass'n., (1934) 241 App. Div. 812, 271 N. Y. S. 952; Deutschmann v. Third Ave. R. R., (1903) 87 App. Div. 503, 84 N. Y. S. 887; Felska v. John Hancock Mut. Life Ins. Co., (1932) 144 Misc. 508, 259 N. Y. S. 35; American Bankers Ins. Co. v. Hopkins, (1917) 67 Okla. 150, 169 Pac. 489; Michaels v. Metropolitan Life Ins. Co., (1930) 26 Luz. (Pa.) 79; Eklund v. Metropolitan Life Ins. Co., (1936) 89 Utah 273, 57 P. 2d 362. In Rush v. Metropolitan Life Ins. Co., (1933) ....Mo. App........., 63 S. W. 2d 453, hospital records of the insured showing that he had been a patient at various hospitals were excluded as privileged. It is not clear, however, whether the records also contained other information entitled to protection from disclosure, which could not be shielded if the records were shown to the jury for the sole purpose of proving his admittance to several hospitals for treatment. See also Martin v. Metropolitan Life Ins. Co., (1943) ....Mo. App........., 174 S. W. 2d 222; Masson v. Metropolitan Life Ins. Co., (1930) 225 Mo. App. 925, 36 S. W. 2d 118.

of the treatment,[7] and the dates and number of his visits.[8] The physician also may testify to the dates of the patient's entry into and his departure from a hospital,[9] that he made an examination

[7] Eureka-Maryland Assur Co. v. Gray, (1941) 74 App. D. C. 191, 121 F. 2d 104, cert. denied 314 U. S. 613, 86 Law. Ed. 494, 62 Su. Ct. 114; Dana v. Commercial Trav. Mut. Acc. Ass'n., (1934) 241 App. Div. 812, 271 N. Y. S. 952; Becker v. Metropolitan Life Ins. Co., (1904) 99 App. Div. 5, 90 N. Y. S. 1007; Deutschmann v. Third Ave. R. R., (1903) 87 App. Div. 503, 84 N. Y. S. 887; Hammerstein v. Hammerstein, (1911) 74 Misc. 567, 134 N. Y. S. 473; Eklund v. Metropolitan Life Ins. Co., (1936) 89 Utah 273, 57 P. 2d 362.

[8] Ranger, Inc., v. Equitable Life Assur. Soc., (1952) 196 F. 2d 698; Eureka-Maryland Assur. Soc., (1941) 74 App. D. C. 191, 121 F. 2d 104, cert. denied 314 U. S. 613, 86 Law. Ed. 494, 62 Su. Ct. 114; Kavakos v. Equitable Life Assur. Soc., (1936) 88 F. 2d 762; Miller v. Pacific Mutual Life Ins. Co., (1953) 116 F. Supp. 365, aff'd. 228 F. 2d 889; Baum v. Pennsylvania R. R. (1953) 14 F. R. D. 398; Metropolitan Life Ins. Co. v. Head, (1927) 86 Ind. App. 326, 157 N. E. 448; Cross v. Equitable Life Assur Soc., (1940) 228 Iowa 800, 293 N. W. 464; Nelson v. Nederland Life Ins. Co., (1900) 110 Iowa 600, 81 N. W. 807; Polish Roman Catholic Union v. Palen, (1942) 302 Mich. 557, 5 N. W. 2d 463; Briesenmeister v. Supreme Lodge, K. of P., (1890) 81 Mich. 525, 45 N. W. 977, 8 L. R. A. 682; Price v. Standard Life & Acc. Ins. Co., (1903) 90 Minn. 264, 95 N. W. 1118; Leeds v. Prudential Ins. Co., (1935) 128 Neb. 395, 258 N. W. 672, 96 A. L. R. 1414; Travelers Ins. Co. v. Pomerantz, (1927) 246 N. Y. 63, 158 N. E. 21; Patten v. United Life & Acc. Ins. Ass'n., (1892) 133 N. Y. 450, 31 N. E. 342; Rubin v. Equitable Life Assur. Soc., (1945) 269 App. Div. 677, 53 N. Y. S. 2d 351; Lorde v. Guardian Life Ins. Co., (1937) 252 App. Div. 646, 300 N. Y. S. 721; Dana v. Commercial Trav. Mut. Acc. Ass'n., (1934) 241 App. Div. 812, 271 N. Y. S. 952; Keck v. Metropolitan Life Ins. Co., (1933) 238 App. Div. 538, 264 N. Y. S. 892, aff'd. 264 N. Y. 422, 191 N. E. 495; Cirrincioni v. Metropolitan Life Ins. Co., (1928) 223 App. Div. 461, 228 N. Y. S. 354; Denaro v. Prudential Ins. Co., (1913) 154 App. Div. 840, 139 N. Y. S. 758; Becker v. Metropolitan Life Ins. Co., (1904) 99 App. Div. 5, 90 N. Y. S. 1007; McGillicuddy v. Farmers Loan & Trust Co., (1899) 26 Misc. 55, 55 N. Y. S. 242; Sambles v. Metropolitan Life Ins. Co., (1952) 158 Ohio St. 233, 108 N. E. 2d 321; Willig v. Prudential Ins. Co., (1942) 71 Ohio App. 255, 49 N. E. 2d 421; Russell v. Penn Mutual Life Ins. Co., (1941) 70 Ohio App. 113, 41 N. E. 2d 251; American Bankers Ins. Co. v. Hopkins, (1917) 67 Okla. 150, 169 Pac. 489; McKeehan Estate, (1948) 358 Pa. 548, 57 A. 2d 907; Eklund v. Metropolitan Life Ins. Co., (1936) 89 Utah 273, 57 P. 2d 362; Chadwick v. Beneficial Life Ins. Co., (1919) 54 Utah 443, 181 Pac. 448.

[9] Ranger, Inc., v. Equitable Life Assur. Soc., (1952) 196 F. 2d 968; First Trust Co. v. Kansas City Life Ins. Co., (1935) 79 F. 2d 48; Cross v. Equitable Life Assur. Soc., (1940) 228 Iowa 800, 293 N. W. 464; *In re* Nickel's Estate, (1948) 321 Mich. 519, 32 N. W. 2d 733; Rubin v. Equitable Life Assur Soc., (1945) 269 App. Div. 677, 53 N. Y. S. 2d 351; Lorde v. Guardian Life Ins. Co., (1937) 252 App. Div. 646, 300 N. Y. S. 721; McGrath v. State, (1950) 200 Misc. 165, 104 N. Y. S. 2d 882; Westphal v. State, (1948) 191 Misc. 688, 79 N. Y. S. 2d 634; Palmer v. John Hancock Mut. Life Ins. Co., (1934) 150 Misc. 669, 270 N. Y. S. 10 (hospital record admissible to show date of entry and discharge of

of the patient,[10] that a diagnosis was made,[11] that he recommended the taking of x-ray photographs,[12] that he performed an operation on the patient,[13] the date when treatment ceased,[14] and he may state whether or not he discharged the patient as being well.[15]

While it is true that the names and addresses of a physician's patients,[16] or those of a hospital,[17] are not privileged,[18] a creditor of

---

←※ patient); Felska v. John Hancock Mut. Life Ins. Co., (1932) 144 Misc. 508, 259 N. Y. S. 35; Willig v. Prudential Ins. Co., (1942) 71 Ohio App. 255, 49 N. E. 2d 421; American Bankers Ins. Co. v. Hopkins, (1917) 67 Okla. 150, 169 Pac. 489.

The physician may also disclose the means of patient's conveyance to the hospital. Garrett v. Butte, (1923) 69 Mont. 214, 221 Pac. 537 (dictum).

Hospital records are admissible to show entry and discharge of the patient, but not if they show also the nature of his disease or injury, or the treatment given him. Ranger, Inc. v. Equitable Life Assur. Soc., infra; *In re* Nickel's Estate, infra; Rubin v. Equitable Life Assur Soc., infra; Lorde v. Guardian Life Ins Co., infra. Willig v. Prudential Ins. Co., infra, p. 258: "Objection was made to the introduction in evidence of a portion of a hospital record. The part admitted showed the name of the patient who was the insured, the date of admittance to the hospital, and the name of the attending physician. We think this was competent for the reasons given for the competency of the physician to testify to the same matters."

[10] Dana v. Commercial Trav. Mut. Acc. Ass'n., (1934) 241 App. Div. 812, 271 N. Y. S. 952; Van Allen v. Gordon, (1894) 83 Hun. 379, 31 N. Y. S. 907.

[11] First Trust Co. v. Kansas City Life Ins. Co., (1935) 79 F. 2d 48; Van Allen v. Gordon, (1894) 83 Hun. 379, 31 N. Y. S. 907.

Of course, the physician cannot reveal what the diagnosis was or the nature of the treatment. Travelers Ins. Co. v. Pomerantz, (1927) 246 N. Y. 63, 158 N. E. 21.

[12] Entian v. Provident Mut. Life Ins. Co., (1935) 155 Misc. 227, 279 N. Y. S. 580. In Willig v. Prudential Ins. Co., (1942) 71 Ohio App. 255, 49 N. E. 2d 421, a physician was permitted to testify that an assisting physician had treated their patient with x-rays. See also Eklund v. Metropolitan Life Ins. Co., (1936) 89 Utah 273, 57 P. 2d 362. In Aspy v. Botkins, (1903) 160 Ind. 170, 66 N. E. 462, however, it was held that a patient could not be compelled to testify that her physician made an x-ray picture of her knee.

[13] Sparer v. Travelers Ins. Co., (1919) 185 App. Div. 861, 173 N. Y. S. 673; Van Allen v. Gordon, (1894) 83 Hun. 379, 31 N. Y. S. 907; Willig v. Prudential Ins. Co., (1942) 71 Ohio App. 255, 49 N. E. 2d 421; Eklund v. Metropolitan Life Ins. Co., (1936) 89 Utah 273, 57 P. 2d 362.

[14] American Bankers Ins. Co. v. Hopkins, (1917) 67 Okla. 150, 169 Pac. 489; Eklund v. Metropolitan Life Ins. Co., (1936) 89 Utah 273, 57 P. 2d 362.

[15] Dittrick v. Detroit, (1893) 98 Mich. 245, 57 N. W. 125; Edington v. Aetna Life Ins. Co., (1879) 77 N. Y. 564.

[16] Wolf v. People, (1947) 117 Colo. 279, 187 P. 2d 926; Garrett v. Butte, (1923) 69 Mont. 214, 221 Pac. 537; Mutual Life Ins. Co. v. Dame Jeannotte-Lamarche, [1935] 59 K. B. (Quebec) 510. See also cases in note 4, infra.

⋙→

a physician cannot have access to the latter's books and records for the purpose of ascertaining who owes him money, if these contain information concerning the nature of his patients' maladies.[19] In an action for malpractice for alleged improper diagnosis and treatment of cancer, the court refused to allow the defendant-physician to name another of his patients who had similar results, since the name was immaterial and its disclosure would violate the patient's right to secrecy.[20]

It is generally conceded that the ban of the statute is aimed at confidential communications of the patient regarding his state of health, and also such information as the physician may acquire by an examination of the patient. Except in one state,[21] the statute is not concerned with any particular kind of ailment, whether loathesome or otherwise,[22] nor, except in two jurisdictions,[23] is it designed

---

[17] *In re* Albert Lindley Lee Memorial Hospital, (1953) 115 F. Supp. 643 aff'd. 209 F. 2d 122, cert. denied Cincotta v. United States, 347 U. S. 960, 98 Law. Ed. 1104, 74 Su. Ct. 709. See comment, (1954) 67 Harv. L. Rev. 1272.

[18] See note in this question with reference to the attorney-client privilege, 114 A. L. R. 1321.

[19] Kelley v. Levy, (1890) 8 N. Y. S. 849.

In Mott v. Consumers' Ice Co., (1877) 2 Abb. N. C. (N. Y.) 143, a physician sued defendant for personal injury and claimed damages for loss of business. Defendant made application for inspection of plaintiff's records in order to ascertain his income for the two years period preceding the accident. The application was denied because the information sought would necessarily involve the revealment of his patients' ailments.

In Snyker v. Snyker, (1955) 245 Minn. 405, 72 N. W. 2d 357, where evidence was necessary to fix the amount of alimony, the trial court ordered defendant, a physician, to submit his log books to an accountant who was charged by the court to abstract therefrom nonprivileged information relating to the physician's income. Defendant's application for a writ of prohibition was denied. It was held that where records and documents, which are the object of discovery and inspection procedures, contain both privileged and non-privileged evidence, the trial court, in the exercise of a sound discretion, may permit their inspection "subject to express conditions and requirements which reasonably shield and protect the person for whose benefit the privilege exists."

[20] Costa v. Regents of Univ. of California, (1953) 116 Cal. App. 2d 445, 254 P. 2d. 85.

[21] The New Mexico statute restricts the privilege, except in Workmen's Compensation cases, to any communication made with reference to any real or supposed venereal or loathesome disease.

[22] Harpman v. Devine, (1937) 133 Ohio St. 1, 10 N. E. 2d 776, 114 A. L. R. 789. *But cf.*

to exclude only such information as tends to disgrace or humiliate the patient, but rather any necessary confidential[24] information intrusted to the physician in his professional capacity.

In some states, the legislatures have expressly denied to persons the right to invoke the privilege in certain classes of actions and proceedings. In Missouri[25] and Wisconsin,[26] in a criminal prosecution involving an illegal abortion, the physician who later attended or prescribed for the woman is a competent witness and may testify concerning any facts relevant to the issue therein. In Minnesota,[27] in a bastardy proceeding, the physician may testify concerning the fact and probable date of inception of the pregnancy of his patient. In Michigan,[28] in a criminal prosecution based on a violation of the marriage laws, any physician who has attended or prescribed for any husband or wife suffering from syphilis or gonorrhea may be compelled to testify to any facts found by him from such attendance. In North Carolina,[29] even a privileged communication may be disclosed if, in the opinion of the presiding judge of a superior

---

Prudential Ins. Co. v. Kozlowski, (1938) 226 Wis. 641, 276 N. W. 300. See § 9, herein, note 23.

[23] The statutes of Pennsylvania and the Philippine Islands confine the privilege strictly to matters "which shall tend to blacken the character of the patient." Federal and Pennsylvania courts have construed and applied this limitation in the following cases: Adamos v. New York Life Ins. Co., (1937) 22 F. Supp. 162, aff'd 94 F. 2d 943; Skruch v. Metropolitan Life Ins. Co., (1925) 284 Pa. 299, 131 Atl. 186; Massich v. Keystone Coal & Coke Co., (1939) 137 Pa. Super. 541, 10 A. 2d 98; Soltaniuk v. Metropolitan Life Ins. Co., (1938) 133 Pa. Super. 139, 2 A. 2d 501; Sweeney v. Green, (1935) 116 Pa. Super. 190, 176 Atl. 849; Michaels v. Metropolitan Life Ins. Co.. (1930) 26 Luz. (Pa.) 79; Dyer v. Dyer, (1929) 78 Pitts. L. J. 348; Reid v. Reid, (1920) 50 Pa. C. C. 601; Peters v. Peters, (1915) 4 D. & C. (Pa.) 287.

[24] State v. Masters, (1924) 197 Iowa 1147, 1150, 198 N. W. 509: "He is only prohibited from testifying to any *confidential communication* properly intrusted to him in his professional capacity * * *, and to facts which are learned by him in the discharge of his duties, where they are of a *confidential nature* * * *." (Italics supplied.)

Some courts, however, believe that confidentiality is not essential. See § 19 herein.

[25] (1953) Mo. Stat. Ann., § 546.310.

[26] (1953) Wis. Stat., § 325.26.

[27] (1947) Minn. Stat. Ann., § 257.30.

[28] (Rev. Vol. 1957) Mich. Stat. Ann., § 25.6.

[29] (Recomp. Vol. 1953) N. C. Gen. Stat. Ann., § 8-53.

court, the same is necessary to a proper administration of justice.[30] Other examples will be discussed elsewhere.

Although the courts have not always been in harmony in concretely applying the statute, it now seems to be conceded almost everywhere that, in order to bring the information referred to in the statute within its protection, three elements must coincide: (a) that the relation of physician and patient existed; (b) that the information was acquired during the existence of the relation; and (c) that the information, however acquired, was necessary to enable the physician to prescribe or act professionally for the patient.[31]

48. The Statutory Limitation: Construction of Words and Phrases

Although the language of the various statutes differs in some respects, yet there is a sufficient similarity in the words and phrases used as to admit of a general discussion of the constructions that have been put upon them by the courts. The statutes of Idaho[1] and Missouri[2] may be taken as typical examples of those which forbid

---

[30] The judge must enter his finding on the record. Sawyer v. Weskett, (1931) 201 N. C. 500, 160 S. E. 575; State v. Newsome, (1928) 195 N. C. 552, 143 S. E. 187; Metropolitan Life Ins. Co. v. Boddie, (1927) 194 N. C. 199, 139 S. E. 228. Only the presiding judge of a Superior Court in term has authority to rule upon the application of the privilege. Yow v. Pittman, (1954) 241 N. C. 69, 84 S. W. 2d 297.

[31] Ranger, Inc. v. Equitable Life Assur. Soc., (1952) 196 F. 2d 968; Green v. Terminal R. R. Ass'n., (1908) 211 Mo. 18, 109 S. W. 715; Garrett v. Butte, (1923) 69 Mont. 214, 221 Pac. 537; Griffiths v. Metropolitan Street Ry., (1902) 171 N. Y. 106, 63 N. E. 808; Edington v. Aetna Life Ins. Co., (1879) 77 N. Y. 564; Westphal v. State, (1948) 191 Misc. 688, 79 N. Y. S. 2d 634; Booren v. McWilliams (1914) 26 N. D. 558, 145 N. W. 410, Ann. Cas. 1916 A 388; Madsen v. Utah Light & Ry., (1909) 36 Utah 528, 105 Pac. 799.

[1] See Appendix, herein.

[2] See Appendix, herein.

Statutes closely resembling these examples with respect to the limitation "which was necessary to enable him to prescribe or act for the patient," are those of Alaska, Arizona (criminal code), Arkansas, California, Canal Zone, Colorado, District of Columbia, Guam, Hawaii, Idaho, Michigan (civil and criminal codes), Minnesota, Montana, Nebraska, Nevada, New York, New Zealand, North Carolina, North Dakota, Oregon, Pennsylvania, Philippine Islands, Puerto Rico, South Dakota, Utah, Victoria (Australia), Virgin Islands, Washington (civil code), West Virginia, Wisconsin.

The statutes of Ohio and Wyoming forbid a physician to testify to "a communication made to him by his patient in that relation." It has been held that when the

the attending physician to testify to information acquired by him which was necessary to enable him to prescribe or act for the patient.

"To testify" ordinarily means the making of any statement under oath in a judicial proceeding. It should be noticed, however, that practically all courts have so construed the statute as to extend the privilege not only to the testimony of the physician, but also to hospital records that disclose information which would be privileged if one sought to elicit it as testimony from the physician himself.[3]

The word "information," as used in the statute, comprehends the knowledge which the physician acquired in any manner while attending the patient, whether by his own examination or observation, or by verbal or written statements of the patient, or from members of his household, or from nurses or strangers, given in aid of the physician in the performance of his professional duty.[4] Knowledge, however communicated, is "information."[5] It has been held, therefore, that an x-ray picture taken of an afflicted person contains "information" acquired in attending the patient and its introduction in evidence, without the consent of the patient, would be a violation of the statute.[6]

←

words "in that relation" were used, the legislature intended to follow the generally accepted limitation expressed in the statutes mentioned above. (1945) Meier v. Peirano, 76 Ohio App. 9, 62 N. E. 2d 920. See also Carson v. Beatley, (1948) 86 Ohio App. 173, 82 N. E. 2d 745.

It may be noted also that the attorney-client privilege statutes in Arkansas, Kansas, Missouri, and Nebraska contain the words "in that relation."

[3] See § 64, herein.

[4] The statute of the District of Columbia expressly includes information which "shall have been obtained from the patient or from his family or from the person or persons in charge of him." See also the Louisiana statute which implies the same.

[5] Edington v. Mutual Life Ins. Co., (1876) 67 N. Y. 185. Isaacs, J., in National Mut. Life Ass'n. v. Godrich, [1909] 10 Comm. L. R. (Australia) 1, 36: "The word 'information' primarily denotes knowledge from any source; the word 'acquired,' in itself, regards the matter from the doctor's standpoint, and indicates the fact of his possession of the information howsoever obtained, and reading the two in conjunction, as the legislature has used them, they comprehend as well the perception of facts by the doctor as the statement of them by the patient."

[6] Tonkel v. Yazoo & M. V. R. R., (1934) 170 Miss. 321, 154 So. 351; Stapleton v. Chicago, B. & Q. R. R., (1917) 101 Neb. 201, 162 N. W. 644; Hurd v. Republic Steel Corp.,

⟫→

In lieu of the word "information," some of the statutes use the word "communication," or the words "matters communicated." Strictly speaking, the word "information" is broader than "communication,"[7] but, except in Pennsylvania,[8] the courts generally have held that, as used in the statute, the words mean much the same.[9] It has been held that the words "matters communicated" may be defined as information obtained in the sick room, heard or observed by the physician, or of which he is otherwise informed pertaining to the patient and upon which he is persuaded to do some act or give some direction or advice in the discharge of his professional obligation.[10]

The word "act," as used in the statute, connotes a professional service rendered the patient which is intended to prevent, palliate, or cure an ailment. A physician cannot be said to act for a plaintiff where he never prescribed for or treated him as a patient, but merely examined him as the agent of the plaintiff's attorneys for the sole purpose of aiding them in the preparation of the plaintiff's lawsuit.[11]

The word "prescribe" embodies the purpose of cure, remedy, or alleviation, and usually means "to advise, appoint, or designate

---

(1949) 275 App. Div. 725, 87 N. Y. S. 2d 64; Clawson v. Walgreen Drug Co., (1945) 108 Utah 577, 162 P. 2d 759; Hansen v. Sandvik, (1924) 128 Wash. 60, 222 Pac. 205.

[7] Clawson v. Walgreen Drug Co., (1945) 108 Utah 577, 162 P. 2d 759.

[8] The title of the Pennsylvania statute relates to "communications made to them [physicians] by their patients." In the body of the statute, however, the words "any information" are used. The Supreme Court has held that a communication from one person to another, necessarily excludes the idea of information obtained only in some other way; therefore, since the language used in the body of the statute is broader than that used in the title, the latter must control. Hence, the statute excludes only communications made by the patient to the physician and does not render incompetent the testimony of an attending physician regarding facts which he ascertained by an examination of the patient. Phillips's Estate, (1929) 295 Pa. 349, 145 Atl. 437.

[9] Howard v. Porter, (1949) 240 Iowa 153, 35 N. W. 2d 837; Battis v. Chicago, R. I. & Pac. Ry., (1904) 124 Iowa 623, 100 N. W. 543; Prader v. National Masonic Acc. Ass'n., (1895) 95 Iowa 149, 63 N. W. 601; Briggs v. Briggs, (1870) 20 Mich. 34; Clawson v. Walgreen Drug Co., (1945) 108 Utah 577, 162 P. 2d 759.

[10] Myers v. State, (1922) 192 Ind. 592, 137 N. E. 547, 24 A. L. R. 1196.

[11] City and County of San Francisco v. Superior Court, (1951) 37 Cal. 2d 227, 231 P. 2d 26, 25 A. L. R. 2d 1418, overruling, on this point, Webb v. Francis J. Lewald Coal Co., (1931) 214 Cal. 182, 4 P. 2d 532, 77 A. L. R. 675.

as a remedy for disease."[12] It has been said that in order to prescribe, a physician must diagnose.[13] The meaning of "serve," as used in the Wisconsin statute, is equivalent to that of "prescribe."[14]

49. Same: "Necessary" Information

As pointed out earlier, it is a mistake to assume that the statute prohibits a physician from testifying in any and all cases in which his patient may be a party. According to the great weight of authority, he is only prohibited from testifying to any confidential communication properly intrusted to him in his professional capacity, and necessary and proper to enable him to perform his service, and to facts which are learned by him in the discharge of his duties from his observation and examination of the patient, where they are of a confidential nature, and necessary and proper to enable him to act or prescribe for the patient.[1] It has always been recognized that there may exist a different character of evidence arising from independent events which may come to the knowledge of a physician, such as evidence of acts or admissions not at all necessary to enable

---

12 *In re* Will of Bruendl, (1899) 102 Wis. 45, 78 N. W. 169.

Isaacs, J., in National Mut. Life Ass'n. v. Godrich, [1909] 10 Comm. L. R. (Australia) 1, 37: "Probably 'prescribe' refers to treatment as a physician, and 'act' to treatment as a surgeon; though the same person may act in both capacities and be covered by both words. But 'prescribe' and 'act' are used in the widest sense to denote anything that the practitioner may do professionally for the cure or relief of the patient." See also § 35, herein.

13 West, J., in Perry v. Hannagan, (1932) 257 Mich. 120, 241 N. W. 232, 79 A. L. R. 1127.

14 Racine v. Woiteshek, (1947) 251 Wis. 404, 29 N. W. 2d 752.

1 A study of the cases discloses a clear line of demarcation between information obtained by a physician not necessary to enable him to act and information required by the physician to prescribe for and treat the patient. The distinction is well stated in Edington v. Aetna Life Ins. Co., (1879) 77 N. Y. 564, 569: "Before information can be excluded under this statute, it must appear that it was such as the physician acquired in some way while professionally attending a patient; and it must also be such as was necessary to enable him to prescribe as a physician, or to do some act as a surgeon. It is not sufficient to authorize the exclusion that the physician acquired the information while attending his patient; *but it must be the necessary information mentioned.* If the physician has acquired any information which was not necessary to enable him to prescribe, or to act as a surgeon, such information he can be compelled to disclose, although he acquired it while attending the patient; and before the exclusion is authorized, the facts must in some way appear upon which such exclusion can be justified." (Italics supplied.)

him to perform his professional duty to his patient. It seems clear that that kind of evidence does not come under the ban of the statute.[2]

The meaning of the word "necessary," as used in the statute, has long been the subject of controversy. The lack of harmony among the courts which have construed the word may be attributed in large part, we believe, to the diverse views courts have entertained towards the basic policy of the privilege. Those which favor the privilege naturally have construed it liberally; those which are not in sympathy with it have construed it strictly.[3] Ordinarily the word "necessary" means "essential to an end: indispensable." It has been questioned, however, whether the legislatures contemplated such an uncompromising construction. Thus despite the use of the word "necessary" in the statutes, a number of courts have felt that something less than "necessary" was meant. It has been suggested that the legislatures were attempting only to limit the operation of the statute to facts communicated in confidence to a physician as a physician.[4] It has been said that the word "necessary" must be construed in a wide sense, so as to include any information which is, or is likely to be, relevant in determining the proper treatment of the patient; and that it is not material whether the information given is actually followed by any treatment or not.[5] Moreover, it has been held that the word "necessary" should not be

---

[2] Kirkpatrick v. Milks, (1950) 257 Wis. 549, 44 N. W. 2d 574.

[3] Legal Protection Of The Confidential Nature Of The Physician-Patient Relationship, (1952) 52 Col. L. Rev. 383, 395: "In this area courts often claim to be interpretating the word ["necessary"] in accordance with a finding that a particular statute is remedial, and therefore to be liberally construed, or in derogation of common law, and therefore to be strictly construed. At least in cases of first impression, such a formula is probably no more than a cloak for a judge's feeling that the privilege does or does not represent a valid social judgment. In any event, wide disparate standards for determining necessity have been evolved."

[4] Krislov, Physician-Patient Privilege As Affected By Mode Of Gaining Information, (1949) 1 West. Res. L. Rev. 142, 144.

[5] Griffith, C. J., in National Mut. Life Ass'n. v. Godrich, [1909] 10 Comm. L. R. (Australia) 1, 8.

After examining a patient, the physician may decide that neither medicine nor advice will do any good, hence neither are given. Grattan v. Metropolitan Life Ins. Co., (1881) 24 Hun (N. Y.) 43.

so restricted as to permit testimony of statements or information in good faith asked for by, or given to, the physician to enable intelligent treatment, although it may appear that the physician might have diagnosed the malady or injury and prescribed for it without certain of the information, so that it was not in fact strictly necessary.[6] It is well known that the modern physician, when undertaking to diagnose a difficult or unusual case, requires and usually receives a complete medical history of the patient, including any and all diseases, disorders, and symptoms which the patient, at any time, may have had. Some courts and commentators have pointed out that it would be quite unreasonable to require of the patient the exercise of any judgment with reference to the propriety of the questions asked by his physician, or to facts which he could, without prejudice to his right of secrecy, disclose to his physician,[7] except,

---

[6] McRae v. Erickson, (1905) 1 Cal. App. 326, 82 Pac. 209; Briesenmeister v. Supreme Lodge, K. of P., (1890) 81 Mich. 525, 45 N. W. 977, 8 L. R. A. 682; In re Will of Bruendl, (1899) 102 Wis. 45, 78 N. W. 169. See also Lombard v. Columbia National Life Ins. Co., (1917) 50 Utah 554, 168 Pac. 269.

[7] McRae v. Erickson, (1905) 1 Cal. App. 326, 83 Pac. 209; Pennsylvania Co. v. Marion, (1889) 123 Ind. 415, 23 N. E. 973, 7 L. R. A. 687; Pride v. Inter-State Business Mens' Ass'n., (1928) 207 Iowa 167, 216 N. W. 62, 62 A. L. R. 31. Williams v. Alexander, (1955) 309 N. Y. 283, 288, 129 N. E. 2d 417; People v. Runion (1957) 3 A. D. 2d 982, 162 N. Y. S. 2d 640, aff'd 3 N. Y. 2d 637, 148 N. E. 2d 165.

Chafee, Jr., The Progress of the Law, (1922) 35 Harv. L. Rev. 673, 691: "Logically, it may be that facts leading up to a physical condition are often not 'necessary to enable the physician to act in a professional capacity' and consequently are not protected by the statute, but practically it is very unjust to a patient, consulting a physician in a state where the law insists that the utmost confidence shall be preserved, if his conversation with the physician can be sifted out by the law into two classes of utterances and one class will be kept secret. One sentence will be necessary for treatment but the next, dealing only with the cause of the ailment, receives no protection. The dividing line may fall in the middle of a sentence. What sort of confidence is secured by the statute if a sick and perhaps hysterical patient must be constantly on the alert, every time a question is asked him, to determine at his peril whether it is necessary for treatment, and, even if it is, must be watchful lest he add something to his answer which is not necessary? * * * A patient should not be forced to tell his story to the doctor with the circumspection of a lawyer."

See also Legal Portection Of The Confidential Nature Of The Physician-Patient Relationship, (1952) 52 Col. L. Rev. 383, 397.

In Obermeyer v. Logeman Chair Mfg. Co., (1910) 229 Mo. 97, 129 S. W. 209, the court refused to split the interview between physician and patient into parts and de-

⟫→

perhaps, where their irrelevancy is obviously apparent.[8]

There are a few statutes which appear to prohibit the physician from disclosing *any* information which he may have obtained while in attendance upon the patient, whether such information was necessary to enable the physician to prescribe or act for the patient, or not. For example, the Quebec statute—the shortest of all—provides:

> No physician may be compelled to declare what has been revealed to him in his professional character.[9]

There are other statutes equally, if not more, comprehensive in

---

termine what parts were and were not necessary to enable the physician to act for the plaintiff, but held the physician incompetent to testify to any portion of the interview.

[8] It must be recognized, however, that information which the legal profession may deem utterly irrelevant is often regarded by the medical profession as extremely helpful and as a professional secret meriting protection. In an address on Professional Secrecy, delivered by Lord Dawson of Penn at a meeting of the Medico-Legal Society in London (1922), the renowned British surgeon said: "In the course of an illness the doctor asks about, or the patient tells him, many intimate things; indeed, a patient often tells things which are, scientifically, irrelevant. But those things, however irrelevant, are very real things to him. He thinks they have a bearing on his case, and unless and until he can unburden them upon the doctor he feels that all the facts relevant to his case are not before his medical adviser, and he has not that full confidence which he has when they have been disclosed. It follows that the doctor gains deep and intimate knowledge into the lives of his patients. Is it to be seriously contended that this knowledge is to be at the service of the cross-examining counsel in courts of justice? I find it difficult to think that anybody could seriously contend that it should be. Permit me to give an example. A woman, now in middle life, happily married, with three or four children, in a previous period in her life, when she was eighteen, got into trouble and had an illegitimate child. That disaster was, by good fortune, known to perhaps only two people, one of them being her medical man. Is her former doctor to be liable to answer questions in a court of law concerning her early misfortune which he only knew of as her medical adviser? Further, a patient weakened by illness will sometimes unburden to his doctor a load of care which has been disturbing his mind and prejudicing his recovery. It may concern some phase of wrong-doing in earlier life. Such a disclosure, made when the patient was suffering from sickness and weakness, might never have been made if the patient had been in health; during the period of convalescence the patient half regrets that he made it, and asks his doctor to make sure that it will never be revealed. Is the law to have the power to take advantage of this patient's illness and to compel the doctor to a disclosure should occasion necessitate? If so, all honour is at an end."

[9] For an excellent discussion of this statute, see Mutual Life Ins. Co. v. dame Jeannotte-Lamarche, [1935] 59 K. B. (Quebec) 510.

their wording.[10] In some of the early cases, a few courts held that
if the relation of physician and patient furnished the physician
merely the opportunity to obtain any information whatsoever, it
was privileged. The fact that the information had nothing to do
with the physical condition of the patient and therefore was not
necessary for diagnosis or treatment, did not remove it from the
ban of the statute.[11] We respectfully submit, however, that this
construction of the statute is unsound since it disregards the plain
purpose of the privilege.[12]

At long last, however, the basic policy of the privilege has
become better understood with the result that the doctrine of broad
and liberal construction is on the way out. The courts now recognize, as one New York court did more than fifty years ago, that
theirs is a judicial function, not a legislative one, and that the
provisions of the statute must be strictly enforced as written.[13]
Practically all courts now hold that to bring the communication,

---

[10] Indiana, Kansas, Louisiana, Mississippi, Ohio, Oklahoma, and Wyoming. See Appendix, herein.

[11] Pennsylvania Co. v. Marion, (1889) 123 Ind. 415, 23 N. E. 973, 7 L. R. A. 687; Doran
v. Cedar Rapids & M. C. Ry., (1902) 117 Iowa 442, 90 N. W. 815.

[12] Smith v. John L. Roper Lumber Co., (1908) 147 N. C. 62, 64, 60 S. E. 717, 15 Ann.
Cas. 580; "Many of the courts have been very liberal in construing this statute in favor
of the protection afforded the patient, some of them going to the extent of holding
that, whenever a question has been asked by an attending physician with a view to prescribing, the answer is privileged, however unimportant or irrelevant such answer may
prove to be, but we do not think that such a position can be sustained."

See also Myers v. State, (1922) 192 Ind. 592, 137 N. E. 547, 24 A. L. R. 1196; Green
v. Metropolitan Street Ry., (1902) 171 N. Y. 201, 63 N. E. 958; Edington v. Aetna Life
Ins. Co., (1879) 77 N. Y. 564.

[13] Griebel v. Brooklyn Heights R. R., (1902) 68 App. Div. 204, 207, 74 N. Y. S. 126:
"We have no right thus to nullify an act of the Legislature or any portion thereof. If
the law-making power desires to extend the privilege of secrecy to all statements of
every kind made by an injured person to his medical attendant, it is very easy to say
so in plain and unmistakable language. Up to the present time, however, the Legislature has refused to go as far as that. It has limited the privilege to information
necessary to enable the physician or surgeon to act in the capacity of physician or surgeon; and when in any case it is perfectly plain that the information given is not of
this character, there is no reason why the courts should be sedulous to create a protection which the Legislature has not seen fit to bestow." The case was tried four
times. This portion of the opinion was approved in (1904) 95 App. Div. 214, 88 N. Y. S.
767, aff'd. 184 N. Y. 528, 76 N. E. 1096.

or information, within the protection of the statute, it must affirmatively appear that it was necessary or proper to enable the physician
to prescribe or act for the patient;[14] and this is true even though
the statute in question may not, in express terms, so provide.[15] It

---

[14] Representative decisions are:

Van Wie v. United States, (1948) 77 F. Supp. 22; Cooper v. State, (1949) 215 Ark.
732, 223 S. W. 2d 507; Burris v. State, (1925) 168 Ark. 1145, 273 S. W. 19; Cleveland v.
Maddox. (1922) 152 Ark. 538, 239 S. W. 370; Collins v. Mack, (1877) 31 Ark. 684; Estate
of Black, (1901) 132 Cal. 392, 64 Pac. 695; Harris v. Zanone, (1892) 93 Cal. 59, 28 Pac.
845; Hanlon v. Woodhouse, (1945) 113 Colo. 504, 160 P. 2d 998; Continental Inv. Co.
v. Garcher, (1928) 83 Colo. 239, 264 Pac. 723; Cook v. People, (1915) 60 Colo. 263, 153
Pac. 214; Myers v. State, (1922) 192 Ind. 592, 137 N. E. 547, 24 A. L. R. 1196; State v.
Johnston (1936) 221 Iowa 933, 267 N. W. 698; State v. Masters, (1924) 197 Iowa 1147, 198
N. W. 509; Blossi v. Chicago & N. W. Ry., (1909) 144 Iowa 697, 123 N. W. 360, 26
L. R. A. (n. s.) 255; Yager v. Yager, (1946) 313 Mich. 300, 21 N. W. 2d 138; Perry v.
Hannagan, (1932) 257 Mich. 120, 241 N. W. 232, 79 A. L. R. 1127; Steketee v. Newkirk,
(1912) 173 Mich. 222, 138 N. W. 1034; People v. Cole, (1897) 113 Mich. 83, 71 N. W. 455;
Lincoln v. Detroit, (1894) 101 Mich. 245, 59 N. W. 617; Cooley v. Foltz, (1891) 85 Mich.
47, 48 N. W. 176; Campau v. North, (1878) 39 Mich. 606; Cherpeski v. Great Northern
Ry., (1915) 128 Minn. 360, 150 N. W. 1091; Marfia v. Great Northern Ry., (1914) 124
Minn. 466, 145 N. W. 385; Burgdorf v. George J. Keeven, (1943) 351 Mo. 1003; 174 S. W.
2d 816; State v. Carryer, (1915) ___Mo.___, 180 S. W. 850; Chlanda v. St. Louis Transit
Co., (1908) 213 Mo. 244, 112 S. W. 249; Green v. Terminal R. R. Ass'n., (1908) 211 Mo.
18, 109 S. W. 715; Hamilton v. Crowe, (1903) 175 Mo. 634, 75 S. W. 389; Baker v. Lyell,
(1922) 210 Mo. App. 230, 242 S. W. 703; Arnold v. Maryville, (1905) 110 Mo. App. 254,
85 S. W. 107; Garrett v. Butte, (1923) 69 Mont. 214, 221 Pac. 537; Cramer v. State, (1944)
145 Neb. 88, 15 N. W. 2d 323; Koskovich v. Rodestock, (1921) 107 Neb. 116, 185 N. W.
343; Skidmore v. State, (1939) 59 Nev. 320, 92 P. 2d 979; Klein v. Prudential Ins. Co.,
(1917) 221 N. Y. 449, 117 N. E. 942; People v. Austin, (1910) 199 N. Y. 446, 93 N. E. 57;
Green v. Metropolitan Street Ry., (1902) 171 N. Y. 201, 63 N. E. 958; People v. Schuyler,
(1887) 106 N. Y. 298, 12 N. E. 783; Edington v. Aetna Life Ins. Co., (1879) 77 N. Y. 564;
Smith v. John L. Roper Lumber Co., (1908) 147 N. C. 62, 60 S. E. 717, 15 Ann. Cas. 580;
Booren v. McWilliams, (1914) 26 N. D. 558, 145 N. W. 410, Ann. Cas. 1916 A 388; Higgs
v. Bigelow, (1917) 39 S. D. 359, 164 N. W. 89; Eklund v. Metropolitan Life Ins. Co.,
(1936) 89 Utah 273, 57 P. 2d 362; Dovich v. Chief Consolidated Mining Co., (1918) 53
Utah 522, 174 Pac. 627; Madsen v. Utah Light & Ry., (1909) 36 Utah 528, 105 Pac. 799;
Schwartz v. Schneuriger, (1955) 269 Wis. 535, 69 N. W. 2d 756; Kirkpatrick v. Milks,
(1950) 257 Wis. 549, 44 N. W. 2d 574; Racine v. Woiteshek, (1947) 251 Wis. 404, 29 N. W.
2d 752; Smits v. State, (1911) 145 Wis. 601, 130 N. W. 525; James v. State, (1905) 124
Wis. 130, 102 N. W. 320; *In re* Will of Bruendl, (1899) 102 Wis. 45, 78 N. W. 169;
National Mutual Life Ass'n. v. Godrich, [1909] 10 Comm. L. R. (Australia) 1.

[15] The Indiana statute contains no provision relating to the *necessity* of the information; yet the Supreme Court has held: "This statute * * * should not be enlarged by
intendment to include as privileged information entirely aside from that 'necessary

≫→

follows, therefore, that if the physician has acquired any information that was not necessary to enable him to prescribe or act for the patient, such information he can be compelled to disclose although he acquired it while attending his patient.[16]

50. Selected Cases Showing Application of the Rule

Obviously courts must be alert to safeguard the purpose of the privilege, but they must be equally alert to see that it is not enforced in such a blind and sweeping manner that it unnecessarily becomes a means for the suppression of material evidence which is not privileged. A few selected cases, which cannot readily be classified factually, may perhaps be helpful to a better understanding of the application of the statute under various and unusual circumstances.

In *Cook* v. *People*,[1] defendant was convicted of murder. At the trial, it was shown that on the night of the crime, he was taken to a hospital suffering from a gunshot wound. The state called as a wit-

---

to enable the physician to act or prescribe.' Nor does it assume to do so merely because the relation of physician and patient exists." Myers v. State, (1922) 192 Ind. 592, 137 N. E. 547, 24 A. L. R. 1196.

The Kansas statute also is quite broad and contains no provision relating to the *necessity* of the information; nevertheless, the courts have confined the privilege to "matters germane to the physician's diagnosis and treatment." Smith v. Davis, (1949) 168 Kan. 210, 212 P. 2d 322; State v. Aguirre, (1949) 167 Kan. 266, 206 P. 2d 118; State v. Townsend, (1937) 146 Kan. 982, 73 P. 2d 1124.

[16] In Arkansas, the privilege is extended to a nurse, yet she may testify to hearing the defendant say to the plaintiff, a physician, that he would pay for the operation; obviously, the communication was not privileged. Cleveland v. Maddox, (1922) 152 Ark. 538, 239 S. W. 370.

In an action for damages for personal injuries arising out of an assault and battery inflicted upon the plaintiff, the court excluded the proffered testimony of the physician, who had treated the plaintiff's injuries, when he was called as a witness by the defendant. The defense was that plaintiff was the aggressor and that the blows struck by defendant were in self-defense. Defendant sought to show by the witness that when he was treating plaintiff for his injuries, he told him "that he [plaintiff] pulled his revolver and snapped it several times, but that the blamed thing would not go off." Held: reversible error. The communication was not privileged. "It is difficult to imagine how the fact that the plaintiff had a revolver in his hand, and snapped it several times but that it would not go off, as narrated by him, would throw any possible light on, or assist in any manner, the proper treatment of his injuries * * *." Koskovich v. Rodestock, (1921) 107 Neb. 116, 185 N. W. 343.

[1] (1915) 60 Colo. 263, 153 Pac. 214.

ness the physician who attended him and, over objection, he was permitted to testify that the defendant refused to allow him to remove the bullet or to tell him how he received the wound. The ruling was proper. How he came to be shot or that he would not consent to have the bullet removed was not information necessary to enable the physician to prescribe or act for his patient.

In a breach of promise suit, defendant called as a witness the physician who had attended the plaintiff in her confinement, and offered to show by him that during his attendance upon her, she told him that the defendant had never promised to marry her. The trial court erred in excluding this evidence since it was not information necessary to enable the physician to prescribe for or treat his patient.[2]

In *Campau* v. *North*,[3] plaintiff, a nurse, sought damages for injuries and among them for a rupture caused, as she alleged, by defendant's acts of violence against her. After she had left the defendant, she was attended by a physician. At the trial, defendant called the physician as a witness and sought to show by him that his patient had admitted to him that she had been ruptured before she went to live with the defendant and had not been ruptured by him. The court excluded the proffered testimony. This was reversible error since the information was not necessary to enable the physician to discharge his professional duties.

In a personal injury action, defendant pleaded a full and complete settlement of all claims for damages by the plaintiff. Defendant's claim agent, plaintiff's physician, his clergyman, and a friend were present during the negotiations. Each testified as to the circumstances surrounding the discussion and execution of the release. A verdict was directed for the defendant. On appeal, it was held that the physician was a competent witness since the information he acquired on this subject was in no way necessary to enable him to prescribe or act for his patient.[4]

---

[2] Collins v. Mack, (1877) 31 Ark. 684.

　　See also Booren v. McWilliams, (1914) 26 N. D. 558, 145 N. W. 410, Ann. Cas. 1916 A 388.

[3] (1878) 39 Mich. 606.

[4] Blossi v. Chicago & N. W. Ry., (1909) 144 Iowa 697, 123 N. W. 360, 26 L. R. A. (n. s.) 255. A similar ruling was made regarding the testimony of the plaintiff's clergyman.

In a bastardy proceeding, the attending physician, called as a witness by the defendant, was asked if his patient told him who was the father of her child. The question was ruled out as eliciting a confidential communication. This was error. The information was not necessary to enable the physician to prescribe or act for the patient.[5]

In a personal injury case, one of plaintiff's physicians, called as a witness by the defendant, testified that after he had examined her, she told him that she was going to file a lawsuit, and that she would want him as a witness. The testimony was competent since it had no reference to her condition.[6]

In *Cooper* v. *State*,[7] defendant was convicted of murder. He claimed his wife was killed when a truck she was driving backed into a ravine and crushed her. He also was injured. The state claimed that he had deliberately planned to kill her in such a way as to make it appear that her death was the result of an accident. While his physician was examining him, defendant described the "accident." The physician testified for the state and, over objection, related the story as told to him by the defendant. This contained admissions which were very damaging to the defense. Affirming the judgment, the court held that the privilege statute did not apply since the admissions were not made for the purpose of supplying the physician with information necessary to any treatment.

In a personal injury action, defendant alleged it had settled with the plaintiff. The latter testified that when signing an alleged release, he was "bothered with chloroform" administered two days before in a surgical operation. It was held improper to sustain objections to questions asked his physician by defendant's counsel as to how long the plaintiff was under the anaesthetic and whether,

---

[5] People v. Cole, (1897) 113 Mich. 83, 71 N. W. 455. See also State v. Lassieur, (1922) _____Mo._____, 242 S. W. 900; People v. Abrahams, (1904) 96 App. Div. 27, 88 N. Y. S. 924. *But cf.* Harris v. Rupel, (1860) 14 Ind. 209. Later decisions of the Supreme Court of Indiana undoubtedly have nullified the ruling on this point.

[6] Cooley v. Foltz, (1891) 85 Mich. 47, 48 N. W. 176.

See also Holloway v. Kansas City (1904) 184 Mo. 19, 82 S. W. 89.

[7] (1949) 215 Ark. 732, 223 S. W. 2d 507.

on the date of signing, he was still under the effects of the anaesthetic. The questions did not seek, nor could they possibly elicit, any information acquired by the physician which was necessary to enable him to prescribe or act for the patient.[8]

In *Fitzhugh* v. *Baird,*[9] plaintiff claimed that defendant rented a house from her. The evidence was highly conflicting. On cross-examination, plaintiff, over her objection, was required to answer a question concerning the advice of her physician about moving into the house. The question was proper since it did not elicit information concerning her condition of health and was in no respect necessary to enable the physician to discharge his professional duties.

In *Hewit* v. *Prime,*[10] plaintiff sued for seduction of his daughter. She was delivered of a child. Over objection, plaintiff proved by a physician that the defendant had applied to him for drugs to produce an abortion, and told the physician that the pregnant girl was the plaintiff's daughter. It was held that, aside from the question whether the relation of physician and patient existed between the physician and defendant, it was certain that the information was not essential to enable the physician to prescribe for the girl; hence it was not privileged.

In an action against an estate on a promissory note executed by the decedent while in a hospital and payable to the claimant who had worked on decedent's farm, the defense was that the deceased was mentally incompetent and the victim of undue influence. The attending physician was a witness to the note and took part in the transaction resulting in its execution. It was held that he could testify to what took place so far as his testimony related to information not necessary to enable him to professionally serve his patient.[11]

In an action to recover damages for the death of a passenger in an automobile collision, defendant's statement to his physician that he drove the colliding car was not privileged.[12]

---

8 Dovich v. Chief Consolidated Mining Co., (1918) 53 Utah 522, 174 Pac. 627.

9 (1901) 134 Cal. 570, 66 Pac. 723.

10 (1835) 21 Wend. (N. Y.) 79.

11 Kirkpatrick v. Milks, (1950) 257 Wis. 549, 44 N. W. 2d 574.

12 Munson v. McDonald et al., (1948) 273 App. Div. 1039, 78 N. Y. S. 2d 629, appeal denied 298 N. Y. 935, 84 N. E. 2d 639.

In *Yager* v. *Yager*,[13] it was held that the testimony of the physician, who had attended the defendant at the birth of her child, as to its length and condition at birth was admissible in the husband's suit for annulment on the ground of fraudulent misrepresentation that he was the child's father, since the testimony disclosed no information which was necessary to enable him to prescribe for or treat the patient.

In several cases where suits have been brought on policies of insurance, the insurer has sought to avoid liability on the ground that the insured committed suicide. To prove this fact, the attending physician has been called as a witness by the insurer to testify to threats of suicide made by the insured. In *Griffith* v. *Continental Casualty Co.*,[14] a suit on an accident policy, the physician of the insured was not incompetent to testify that the insured, while he was treating him for tuberculosis, had said that he did not think life worth living and that he might as well jump in the river. The information was not necessary to enable the physician to prescribe for the insured as a patient.

Where the physician knew that his patient had attempted suicide and knew what to treat his patient for before any statement was made by him, and it made no difference in treatment whether poison was taken by mistake or with suicidal intent, the physician's testimony that the deceased patient told him that he did not care to live was properly admitted over objection that it was a privileged communication.[15] However, where the information was necessary

---

[13] (1946) 313 Mich. 300, 21 N. W. 2d 138. *But cf.* Van Bergen v. Catholic Relief & Ben. Ass'n., (1904) 99 App. Div. 72, 91 N. Y. S. 362.

[14] (1923) 299 Mo. 426, 253 S. W. 1043.

[15] Bolts v. Union Central Life Ins. Co., (1940) 20 N. Y. S. 2d 675. See also Modern Woodmen of America v. Watkins, (1942) 132 Fed. 2d 352 (attorney-client privilege).

Contra: Pride v. Inter-State Business Mens Acc. Ass'n., (1928) 207 Iowa 167, 216 N. W. 62, 62 A. L. R. 31. This case seems to have been decided on the unsound theory that *any and all* information is protected. Evans, C. J., (p. 174): "We have held repeatedly that we will draw no fine lines as to whether a communication is necessary or unnecessary."

Scheiner v. Metropolitan Life Ins. Co., (1932) 236 App. Div. 24, 257 N. Y. S. 783. This decision may, perhaps, be justified on the ground that the physician's testimony as to the patient's suicidal tendencies and threats was not separated from, but, on the contrary, was intermingled with facts which were plainly privileged.

to enable the physician to properly treat the patient, it must be excluded. In *Meyer* v. *Supreme Lodge, K. of P.*,[16] a physician was summoned to attend a man *in extremis,* suffering agony and incapable of acting or deciding for himself. The physician, at first, did not know how to treat the patient. It was only because the patient told him that he had taken poison and wanted to die, that the physician was enabled to administer any proper treatment.

Of course, any information, however unnecessary it may be, which involves, or is likely to involve, a disclosure of the nature of the patient's disease or malady, cannot be testified to by his physician.[17] Thus, in an action for divorce on the ground of adultery, defendant's physician cannot, as a witness for the wife, testify that his patient told him he had had intercourse with a woman on board his boat and had contracted a venereal disease from her.[18]

In an action involving the question of the deceased's domicile, a physician who had attended her was not permitted to give his opinion as to whether the patient's condition prevented her from returning to New Orleans, since a responsive answer might have included a statement that the deceased was suffering from a disease of such a nature as would prevent her from travelling.[19]

In a personal injury case, a physician was not allowed to testify to any information acquired by him in attending the plaintiff which concerned the cause of her condition, since he could not well have testified to such cause without throwing some light on her condition; and the same might be said of the medicine prescribed for her by the witness. He cannot tell indirectly that which the statute forbade him to tell directly.[20]

---

[16] (1904) 178 N. Y. 63, 70 N. E. 111, aff'd. 198 U. S. 508, 49 Law. Ed. 1146, 25 Su. Ct. 754, 64 L. R. A. 839.

[17] Briesenmeister v. Supreme Lodge, K. of P., (1890) 81 Mich. 525, 45 N. W. 977, 8 L. R. A. 682.

[18] Hunn v. Hunn, (1873) 1 Thom. & C. (N. Y.) 499.

[19] Matter of Newcomb, (1908) 192 N. Y. 238, 84 N. E. 950.

[20] Streeter v. Breckenridge, (1886) 23 Mo. App. 244.

The admissibility of a physician's prescriptions was questioned in Nelson v. Nederland Life Ins. Co., (1900) 110 Iowa 600, 81 N. W. 807, but was held proper in Deutschmann v. Third Avenue R. R. (1903) 87 App. Div. 503, 84 N. Y. S. 887 because no objection was made thereto on the ground of privilege. In Travelers Ins. Co. v. Pomerantz,

In *Brayman* v. *Russell & Pugh Lumber Co.,*[21] a personal injury suit, defendant offered to prove by a physician that while he was attending plaintiff's injury, the witness said it would be necessary to operate on the injured arm, but plaintiff refused to submit to an operation and stated that if the witness would amputate the arm so that plaintiff could recover more from the defendant, he would consent, and when the witness insisted upon an operation, plaintiff refused saying he intended to get a life pension out of the defendant. The offer of proof was rejected on the ground that it was a privileged communication.

In *Resor* v. *Schaefer,*[22] plaintiffs sought specific performance of the deceased's oral contract. By the terms of the alleged contract, plaintiff and his wife were to nurse, care for and maintain him in their home as long as he lived, and for this he agreed to devise all his property to them. He died without having made provision for plaintiffs. At the trial, plaintiffs called as a witness the physician who had attended the deceased and he testified that the deceased had told him of the arrangement with plaintiffs. The physician admitted, however, that these statements were elicited from his patient in the course of his prescribing for him and in response to his suggestion that his patient go to a hospital where he could receive proper care. It was held that the evidence was inadmissible as privileged, and should have been excluded.[23]

(1927) 246 N. Y. 63, 158 N. E. 21, a physician testified that he had administered digitalis to his patient, but it does not appear that an objection was made to such disclosure.

[21] (1917) 31 Idaho 140, 169 Pac. 932. The decision is questionable. Was the information necessary to enable the physician to properly apply his skill in the treatment of plaintiff's injury?

[22] (1937) 193 Wash. 91, 74 P. 2d 917.

[23] Steinert, C. J. (p. 97): "The statement made by [the deceased] to the physician was not an incidental one nor was it extraneous to the duty required of the physician. [The deceased] was giving his reasons why it was unnecessary for him to go to the hospital. The care that he would receive from the Resors was a substitute for the care he would receive in a hospital, and the conditions under which the Resors were to render him care and treatment would undoubtedly be a factor in the determination by the doctor whether their services would be both lasting and sufficient."

In *Hays* v. *Hays*,[24] the administrator of the estate of the deceased sued for compensation rendered the defendant in the management of his store. It was held that statements made by the deceased to her physician concerning her financial condition, and made while he was advising her about her health and the necessity of her going away for a rest, were privileged communications and inadmissible in evidence over objection by the plaintiff.

Where a woman who had suffered an abortion told her physician that it had been performed with her consent by a third person not named, such statement was inadmissible in evidence against the accused indicted for the procuration of such abortion, since it was privileged information.[25]

In a proceeding before a grand jury charging the defendant with criminal negligence arising from his operation of a motor vehicle, a physician, who previously had treated him as a patient suffering from epilepsy, was held incompetent to testify that he had warned the defendant never to drive alone since he might lose momentary consciousness or suffer a dizzy spell; neither should the defendant be compelled to disclose his awareness of danger, since the warning was given during the relation of physician and patient and was necessary for his protection.[26]

Other situations which can be more readily classified will be discussed in subsequent sections.

51. *Information as to Ailment Not the Subject of Physician's Attendance or Treatment*

When the information obtained by a physician extends to the existence of an ailment, although not the subject of his attendance or treatment but is acquired through an examination of the patient in attending him in a professional capacity and the discovery of which was a necessary incident to the investigation made to enable him to act in his professional capacity, it is clearly within the spirit and purpose of the statutory privilege.[1] A surgical operation may

---

[24] (1912) 49 Ind. App. 298, 97 N. E. 198.

[25] State v. Karcher, (1951) 155 Ohio St. 253, 98 N. E. 2d 308.

[26] People v. Eckert, (1955) 208 Misc. 93, 142 N. Y. S. 2d 657.

[1] Klein v. Prudential Ins. Co., (1917) 221 N. Y. 449, 117 N. E. 942; Nelson v. Oneida,

result in the discovery of a condition of which neither the patient nor the physician was aware, such as the existence of a malignant tumor or some other internal disease or malformation. Certainly the protection of the privilege should extend to the condition so discovered. A disclosure by the physician under such circumstances would render the statute a mere pretense.[2]

52. Information Acquired by Observation and Examination

It must be regarded as settled that the protection afforded by the statute extends not only to information given the physician orally or in writing by the patient, but also to information and knowledge acquired by the physician in his professional capacity through his observation, examination, diagnosis and treatment of the patient as well as all inferences and conclusions therefrom;[1]

←《《

(1898) 156 N. Y. 219, 50 N. E. 802; See also Kling v. Kansas City, (1887) 27 Mo. App. 231; Barton, J., in National Mutual Life Ass'n. v. Godrich, [1909] 10 Comm. L. R. (Australia) 1, 23; Krislov, Physician-Patient Privilege as Affected by Mode of Gaining Information, (1949) 1 West. Res. L. Rev. 142, 144.

In Ohio, however, it has been held that the physician may testify to the *mental* condition of his patient where his knowledge thereof was acquired while examining or treating him for a *physical* ailment only. See § 57, note 6, therein.

[2] In Nelson v. Oneida, (1898) 156 N. Y. 219, 50 N. E. 802, a personal injury case, the injuries plaintiff claimed to have suffered were an umbilical hernia, a prolapsus of the uterus, and several bruises. The defendant attempted to show by the plaintiff's physician that she had an umbilical hernia before the accident. He had attended the plaintiff at childbirth and had discovered the hernia. He did not treat her for this and the knowledge of its existence was of no assistance to him in delivering the child; nevertheless it was an incident of his professional service. It was held, therefore, that the matter was privileged and that the physician could not testify to his discovery of the hernia.

In Jones v. Caldwell, (1913) 23 Idaho 467, 130 Pac. 995, a personal injury case, it appeared that some time *after* an operation had been performed on the injured plaintiff, the surgeon examined the affected and injured parts that had been removed. The defendant called the surgeon as a witness and asked him to describe the material so removed and to give his opinion as to the *real* cause which led to the operation. The evidence was excluded. One judge dissented.

[1] Representative decisions are: Sher v. DeHaven, (1952) 91 App. D. C. 257, 199 F. 2d 777, cert. denied 345 U. S. 936, 97 Law. Ed. 1363, 73 Su. Ct. 797, 36 A. L. R. 2d 937; Labofish v. Berman, (1932) 60 App. D. C. 397, 55 F. 2d 1022; Colorado Fuel & Iron Co.,

》》》→

provided always that the information and knowledge so obtained was necessary to enable the physician to prescribe or act professionally in attending him.[2]

Information concerning the actual condition of a patient may be much more readily communicated to or acquired by a physician through a physical examination than by statements of the patient.[3]

←※

v. Cummings (1896) 8 Colo. App. 541, 46 Pac. 875; Myers v. State, (1922) 192 Ind. 592, 137 N. E. 547, 24 A. L. R. 1196; Towles v. McCurdy, (1904) 163 Ind. 12, 71 N. E. 129; Springer v. Byram, (1894) 137 Ind. 15, 36 N. E. 361, 23 L. R. A. 244; Howard v. Porter, (1949) 240 Iowa 153, 35 N. W. 2d 837; Battis v. Chicago, R. I. & Pac. Ry., (1904) 124 Iowa 623, 100 N. W. 543; Prader v. National Masonic Acc. Ass'n., (1895) 95 Iowa 149, 63 N. W. 601; Oldenburg v. Leiberg, (1913) 177 Mich. 150, 142 N. W. 1076; Briggs v. Briggs, (1870) 20 Mich. 34; Yazoo & M. V. R. R. v. Messina, (1915) 109 Miss. 143, 67 So. 963; Gartside v. Connecticut Mutual Life Ins. Co., (1882) 76 Mo. 446; James v. Kansas City, (1900) 85 Mo. App. 20; Kling v. Kansas City, (1887) 27 Mo. App. 231; Matter of Coddington's Will, (1954) 307 N. Y. 181, 120 N. E. 2d 777; Barker v. Cunard Steamship Co., (1895) 91 Hun 495, 36 N. Y. S. 256, aff'd. 157 N. Y. 693, 51 N. E. 1089; Grattan v. Metropolitan Life Ins. Co., (1883) 92 N. Y. 274; Edington v. Mutual Life Ins. Co., (1876) 67 N. Y. 185; Sparer v. Travelers Ins. Co., (1919) 185 App. Div. 861, 173 N. Y. S. 673; McGrath v. State, (1950) 200 Misc. 165, 104 N. Y. S. 2d 882; Creech v. Sovereign Camp, (1937) 211 N. C. 658, 191 S. E. 840; Smith v. John L. Roper Lumber Co., (1908) 147 N. C. 62, 60 S. E. 717, 15 Ann. Cas. 580; Baker v. Industrial Comm'n., (1939) 135 Ohio St. 491, 21 N. E. 2d 593; Ausdenmoore v. Holzback, (1914) 89 Ohio St. 381, 106 N. E. 41; McKee v. New Idea, Inc., (1942) ⸺ Ohio App. ⸺ , 36 Ohio Law Abst. 563, 44 N. E. 2d 697; Robertson v. State, (1952) 95 Okla. Cr. 223, 243 P. 2d 367; Munz v. Salt Lake City R. R., (1902) 25 Utah 220, 70 Pac. 852; Randa v. Bear, (1957) ⸺ Wash. ⸺ , 312 P. 2d 640; Wesseler v. Great Northern Ry., (1916) 90 Wash. 234, 155 Pac. 1063, 157 Pac. 461; Shafer v. Eau Claire, (1900) 105 Wis. 239, 81 N. W. 409; Stack v. Stack, [1905] 25 New Zealand L. R. 209; F. v. F., [1950] Victoria (Australia) L. R. 352; National Mut. Life Ass'n. v. Godrich, [1909] 10 Comm. L. R. (Australia) 1, at pp. 17-18 and 27; Warnecke v. Equitable Life Assur. Soc., [1906] Victoria (Australia) L. R. 482.

See also Krislov, Physician-Patient Privilege as Affected by Mode of Gaining Information, (1949) 1 West. Res. L. Rev. 142.

[2] State v. Masters, (1924) 197 Iowa 1147, 198 N. W. 509; Arnold v. Maryville, (1905) 110 Mo. App. 254, 85 S. W. 107; Henry v. New York, L. E. & W. R. R., (1890) 57 Hun 76, 10 N. Y. S. 508. See also § 37, herein. Sometimes courts have not observed this essential requirement. See § 49, herein.

[3] Isaacs, J., in National Mutual Life Ass'n. v. Godrich, [1909] 10 Comm. L. R. (Australia) 1, 36: "When we recollect that a patient consults a doctor to gain and not to give authentic knowledge of his condition, and that the doctor's knowledge of his patient's condition is acquired much more by means of his professional skill and experience than by any words of the patient, it is plain that the suggested construction [that the statute

⸺⸺→

In many cases exact knowledge can only be obtained by means of such examination, and it is plain that it is as much to the interest of the patient to have the information so obtained treated as confidential as it would be had he known and communicated it verbally.[4] His attendance upon a patient may enable the experienced and skillful practitioner to discern more of the patient's condition and of the cause thereof than the patient could himself tell, or would be willing to reveal; therefore, whether the information which the physician gets is obtained in one way or the other should make no difference in the application of the statute.[5] Information derived from the observations of the patient's appearance and symptoms is as much within the statute as if it had been oral and reached the physician's ear.[6] Even if the patient could not speak, or his mental capacity was so affected that he could not accurately relate the nature of his ailment, the experienced medical man observing or

---

←◀

protects only communications, oral or written] would reduce the legislative provision almost to a nullity. A patient in submitting his body for examination is presenting a human document as legible to the eye of medical science as is an instrument of title to the practiced eye of a legal adviser, or any ordinary printed matter to a general reader. It is a much more distinct, complete and certain presentation of the actual facts of his condition than any verbal statement by him could possibly convey, and, without the most violent restriction of the ordinary and natural sense of the words 'information acquired,' the suggested limitation is impossible."

Bissell, J., in Colorado Fuel & Iron Co. v. Cummings, (1896) 8 Colo. App. 541, 551, 46 Pac. 875: "The inhibition is broad enough to exclude an examination of the surgeon as to any information which he has acquired while attending a patient, whether this information is deduced from statements or gathered from his professional or surgical examination. It is a common knowledge that the eye and finger of the attending surgeon is vastly more expert in locating cause or trouble than the tongue of the most astute patient."

4 Prader v. National Masonic Acc. Ass'n., (1895) 95 Iowa 149, 63 N. W. 601. It has been said that the examination need not be private. Grattan v. Metropolitan Life Ins. Co., (1880) 80 N. Y. 281. This, however, is questionable. See § 19, herein.

5 Masonic Mut. Ben. Ass'n. v. Beck, (1881) 77 Ind. 203.

6 Rose v. Supreme Court, O. of P., (1901) 126 Mich. 577, 85 N. W. 1073; Westphal v. State, (1948) 191 Misc. 688, 79 N. Y. S. 2d 634.

It has been held that the principle does not apply to observations pertaining to the mental condition of the patient. State v. Murphy, (1928) 205 Iowa 1130, 217 N. W. 225; Re Fleming, (1923) 196 Iowa 639, 195 N. W. 242; Re Harmsen, (1918) ...... Iowa......, 167 N. W. 618, L. R. A. 1918 E. 973.

examining him would readily comprehend his condition. Information so obtained should certainly come within the protection of the statute.[7]

Some of the legislatures have expressly prohibited a physician from testifying as to any knowledge he may have acquired by personal examination of the patient.[8] As previously stated,[9] the Pennsylvania statute does not render incompetent the testimony of a physician in regard to facts which he learned by an examination of the patient. It excludes only communications from the patient to the physician which disclose facts that would tend to blacken the character of the patient.[10]

53. Facts Plain to Anyone

There is substantial authority for the doctrine that the statute is not intended to prohibit a physician from testifying to such ordinary incidents and facts as are plain to the observation of anyone having no expert or professional knowledge, and without tacitly or otherwise inviting or receiving confidences by which the incidents and facts are, or may be, brought to light and obtained.[1] Of course,

---

[7] Grattan v. Metropolitan Life Ins. Co., (1880) 80 N. Y. 281; Edington v. Mutual Life Ins. Co., (1876) 67 N. Y. 185. See excellent discussion of New York cases in Matter of Coddington's Will, (1954) 307 N. Y. 181, 120 N. E. 2d 777.

[8] See statutes of Arizona, Kansas, Louisiana, New Mexico and Oklahoma. Appendix, herein.

[9] See § 48, note 8.

[10] Adamos v. New York Life Ins. Co., (1937) 22 F. Supp. 162, aff'd. 94 F. 2d 943; Massich v. Keystone Coal & Coke Co., (1939) 137 Pa. Super. 541, 10 A. 2d 98.

In Michaels v. Metropolitan Life Ins. Co., (1930) 26 Luz. (Pa.) 79, physicians who attended the patient were permitted to testify that, *from their observations*, she had syphilis.

[1] Klein v. Prudential Ins. Co., (1917) 221 N. Y. 449, 117 N. E. 942. *Cf.* Lande v. Travelers Ins. Co., (1934) 241 App. Div. 96, 271 N. Y. S. 551, aff'd. 265 N. Y. 655, 193 N. E. 430. *Accord:* Linz v. Massachusetts Mut. Life Ins. Co., (1880) 8 Mo. App. 363; Lorde v. Guardian Life Ins. Co., (1937) 252 App. Div. 646, 300 N. Y. S. 721; Staunton v. Parker, (1879) 19 Hun (N. Y.) 55; Westphal v. State, (1948) 191 Misc. 688, 79 N. Y. S. 2d 634; *In re* Strong's Estate, (1938) 168 Misc. 716, 6 N. Y. S. 2d 300, aff'd. 256 App. Div. 971, 11 N. Y. S. 2d 225; *In re* Meyer's Estate, (1954) 206 Misc. 368, 132 N. Y. S. 2d 825; McGrath v. State, (1950) 200 Misc. 165, 104 N. Y. S. 2d 882; *In re* Avery's Estate, (1948) 76 N. Y. S. 2nd 790; See also Matter of Coddington's Will, (1954) 307 N. Y. 181, 120 N. E. 2d 777.

one would hardly contend that such a thing as a plainly visible scar or wound on the face or hand, if shown to a physician, is the subject of confidence as to its existence. Things that are obvious to all cannot be confidentially communicated.[2]

It may reasonably be assumed that the prohibition of the statute does not extend to matters of description relating to the physical surroundings of the patient, or to his companions, or to those in attendance upon him, or to conversations between third persons and the patient, or to the reaction of the patient to the acts and conduct of third persons.[3] In a will contest, where the mental capacity of the testatrix was in issue, the attending physician was permitted to testify that her gestures, conversation and language impressed him as coming from a person of sane mind.[4] In another will contest, it appeared that the physician who had attended the testatrix was present, together with others, when she signed her will. He was permitted to testify that she was suffering from jaundice at the time.[5] A physician may testify that he observed his

---

[2] State v. Thomas, (1954) 78 Ariz. 52, 275 P. 2d 408; Linz v. Massachusetts Mutual Life Ins. Co., (1880) 8 Mo. App. 363; F. v. F., [1950] Victorian (Australia) L. R. 352; Barton, J., in National Mutual Life Ins. Co. v. Godrich, [1909] 10 Comm. L. R. (Australia) 1, 18. See Krislov, Physician-Patient Privilege as Affected by Mode of Gaining Information, (1949) 1 West. Res. L. Rev. 142.

[3] In re Schermerhorn, (1950) 98 N. Y. S. 2d 361, rev'd. on other grounds, 277 App. Div. 845, 98 N. Y. S. 2d 367, aff'd. 302 N. Y. 660, 98 N. E. 2d 475.

[4] Steele v. Ward, (1883) 30 Hun. (N. Y.) 555.

[5] In re Will of Swartz, (1920) 79 Okla. 191, 193, 192 Pac. 203, 16 A. L. R. 450: "The matters testified to by the physician were not obtained by reason of his knowledge as a physician, but rather by a knowledge equally possessed by the laity. All the physician testified to was as to her condition, that she was suffering with jaundice; the other parties in the room knew just as well as the physician that the testatrix was suffering with this disease. The average man or woman can as easily tell when one is suffering from jaundice as they can when the party is suffering from an ordinary cold." The court, moreover, felt that the presence of third persons had rendered the privilege, if one existed, inapplicable anyway. In Lande v. Travelers Ins. Co. (1934), 241 App. Div. 96, 271 N. Y. S. 551, 97, aff'd. 265 N. Y. 655, 193 N. E. 430, the court said: "If, on the contrary, it was intended to prove that on this occasion the deceased was in a condition of sickness which would have been 'plain to the observation of anyone without expert or professional knowledge,' then the information was not privileged."

See also Matter of Loewenstine's Will, (1893) 2 Misc. 323, 21 N. Y. S. 931.

patient walking on the street or on his farm.[6] Observations made
of the outward, visible facts that were seen by the physician on
occasions when he was not attending the patient in his professional
capacity and which were open and visible to the sight of any person
are not privileged.[7] In an action for divorce, the issue was adultery.
The manager of a sanatorium, where the defendant was a patient,
was permitted to testify that she entered the sanatorium without a
child and took one away with her.[8]

54. Family Affairs and Relations

As a general rule the statute does not forbid a physician to
testify to matters observed by him, or to communications incidentally made to or overheard by him, pertaining to family affairs,
events, and relations, while professionally attending the patient.
Usually such information has no connection whatever with the illness or injury of the patient, nor can it be said that it was reasonably
necessary to the rendering of the physician's professional service.[1]
A physician, therefore, may testify to a person's mental and physical
condition as he observed it while attending other members of the
family.[2] In a will contest, physicians who had attended a testator
were permitted to testify as to interviews with their patient upon
the subject of his daughter's mental condition, since the information so obtained was not such as was necessary to enable them to act
in a professional capacity towards their patient.[3] In an action

---

[6] Pence v. Waugh, (1893) 135 Ind. 143, 34 N. E. 860. See also Haworth v. Kansas
City Southern Ry., (1902) 94 Mo. App. 215, 68 S. W. 111.

[7] Burley v. Barnhard, (1887) 9 N. Y. St. Rep. 587, 45 Hun. 588.

[8] Hammerstein v. Hammerstein, (1911) 74 Misc. 567, 134 N. Y. S. 473.

[1] *In re* Schermerhorn, (1950) 98 N. Y. S. 2d 361, rev'd. on other grounds 277 App.
Div. 845, 98 N. Y. S. 2d 367, aff'd. 302 N. Y. 660, 98 N. E. 2d 475; Matter of Boury,
(1887) 8 N. Y. St. Rep. 809. In Estate of Chase, (1940) ___ Ohio App. ___ , 31 Ohio
Law Abst. 111, a physician was properly permitted to testify that, while attending
the patient, she told him, in the presence of others, that she was having difficulty
with her husband and a nurse; that she (the patient) had concealed two bank pass-
books which they sought; and that she wanted to give them to her mother and
sister.

[2] Jennings v. Supreme Council, (1903) 81 App. Div. 76, 81 N. Y. S. 90.

[3] Hoyt v. Hoyt, (1889) 112 N. Y. 493, 20 N. E. 402.

brought by a physician to recover his fee for services rendered to the defendant's adult son, a nurse may testify, without violating the statutory privilege,[4] that she overheard the defendant say to the physician that he would pay the physician's fee.[5] In a prosecution for murder, defended on the ground of self-defense, testimony by a physician who had treated the deceased that he on one occasion, when leaving the sickroom and was in the hallway outside, overheard him make threats against defendant's life, was not privileged.[6]

There have been several instances where a suit has been filed by a member of a family, or by a nurse, attendant, or housekeeper against the estate of a deceased person to obtain compensation for services rendered the deceased in caring for or nursing him. In this class of actions, the plaintiff, of course, could not testify;[7] consequently her case rested upon the testimony of others. Not infrequently, the plaintiff has called upon the attending physician to aid her in proving her case. In such actions the physician is a competent witness to testify to what he has seen or heard concerning the character of the plaintiff's services and the patient's intention to pay therefor, where the information so acquired was not essential to enable the physician to prescribe or act for the patient. Such evidence is plainly outside the ambit of the statutory privilege. Thus, where the plaintiff sued the estate of the deceased patient for services rendered in caring for and nursing him, two attending physicians were permitted to testify as to the character and value of such services.[8] Moreover, a physician may testify that, while performing

---

4 A nurse is a privileged witness under the Arkansas statute.

5 Cleveland v. Maddox, (1932) 152 Ark. 538, 239 S. W. 370.

6 Myers v. State, (1922) 192 Ind. 592, 601, 137 N. E. 547, 24 A. L. R. 1196: "It cannot reasonably be claimed that the statements proposed to be proved by the witness tended to reveal that which should be kept inviolate, nor were they such as would enable him to give advice, treat or prescribe for the patient, nor can it be said that they were made to or that they were intended for him."

7 Because of the dead man statute.

8 Keller v. Gerber, (1920) 49 Cal. App. 515, 193 Pac. 809. *Accord:* Bick v. Mueller, (1940) 346 Mo. 746, 142 S. W. 2d 1021; McQueen's Estate, (1891) 13 N. Y. S. 705, 59 Hun. 625; Higgs v. Bigelow, (1917) 39 S. D. 359, 164 N. W. 89.

his professional duties, his patient told him that the nurse should be paid and well paid for the work she was doing in caring for her.[9]

Obviously, testimony of this character must be carefully screened by the trial court so as to avoid the possibility of any disclosure of the patient's malady or its cause, and if the testimony which concerns the character and value of the claimant's services is so intermingled with that which is clearly privileged and inadmissible so that one is not readily separable from the other, all of the testimony must be excluded.[10]

The mere presence of the attending physician will not preclude other competent witnesses from relating communications made by the patient where they were not directed to the physician and were not in any way connected with his professional duties.[11]

55. Social and Business Visits

Information concerning the physical or mental condition of a person, which is received by a physician outside the course of his professional practice and is not confidential in its nature, is not within the ban of the statute. Hence, observations made and impressions formed by a physician on social or business visits or in casual meetings with an afflicted person who may be at the time, or later become, his patient, are generally not privileged from disclosure. On such occasions, the physician is not acting in his professional character, and is not seeking information for the purpose of enabling him to prescribe or administer medical treatment. Moreover, the afflicted person himself is not seeking medical assist-

---

[9] Miller v. Miller, (1911) 47 Ind. App. 239, 94 N. E. 243. *Accord:* Minnis v. Steele, (1921) 79 Ind. App. 45, 132 N. E. 702; Baker v. Lyell, (1922) 210 Mo. App. 230, 242 S. W. 703.

[10] *In re* Johnson, (1898) 32 App. Div. 634, 52 N. Y. S. 1081. See also Bick v. Mueller, (1940) 346 Mo. 746, 142 S. W. 2d 1021.

[11] Sutcliffe v. Iowa State Traveling Men's Ass'n., (1903) 119 Iowa 220, 93 N. W. 90, was an action brought by the beneficiary of a policy of insurance. The insured had sustained a bullet wound from which he died the next day. The question was whether it was an accident or suicide. His widow testified that her husband had told her, in the presence of his mother and sister, that he had shot himself. The plaintiff-beneficiary contended that the insured's statement should be excluded because of the presence of the physician who was treating the insured at the time. The evidence was not privileged; hence, admissible.

ance; in fact, no mention is made of his malady or injury. No confidential relationship arises on such occasions; therefore, there is no need for the application of the statutory privilege, particularly when the things observed are equally observable by others.[1]

56. *Intoxication or Odor of Liquor*

In a criminal proceeding, or in an action for damages for personal injury or for wrongful death, the condition of a person with respect to his sobriety or insobriety upon a particular occasion, may become an important issue. The testimony of the physician who rendered him medical aid would certainly be most helpful in resolving this particular issue. But the question of privilege may intervene. Is the physician, over objection by the holder of the privilege, competent to testify to the insobriety of the person as he observed it when he was first summoned to attend him? The courts are not in harmony upon this question, but the weight of authority supports the view that the physician, although not called upon to treat a patient on account of his intoxicated condition, may not testify that he observed that the patient was in a state of intoxication,[1] or that he detected the odor of liquor on his breath or about

---

[1] Ranger, Inc. v. Equitable Life Assur. Soc., (1952) 196 F. 2d 968; Bower v. Bower, (1895) 142 Ind. 194, 41 N. E. 523; Pence v. Waugh, (1893) 135 Ind. 143, 34 N. E. 860; Minnis v. Steele, (1921) 79 Ind. App 45, 132 N. E. 702; Herries v. Waterloo, (1901) 114 Iowa 374, 86 N. W. 306; Smith v. Davis, (1949) 168 Kan. 210, 212 P. 2d 322; Watkins v. Watkins, (1926) 142 Miss. 210, 106 So. 753; Dabbs v. Richardson, (1924) 137 Miss. 789, 102 So. 769; Estes v. McGehee, (1923) 133 Miss. 174, 97 So. 530; Faris, J., in Epstein v. Pennsylvania R. R., (1913) 250 Mo. 1, 20, 156 S. W. 699, 48 L. R. A. (n. s.) 394, Ann. Cas. 1915 A 423; Chlanda v. St. Louis Transit Co., (1908) 213 Mo. 244, 112 S. W. 249; Hamilton v. Crowe, (1903) 175 Mo. 634, 75 S. W. 389; Fisher v. Fisher, (1892) 129 N. Y. 654, 29 N. E. 951; Edington v. Aetna Life Ins. Co., (1879) 77 N. Y. 564; *In re* Meyer's Estate, (1954) 206 Misc. 368, 132 N. Y. S. 2d 825; Loewenstine's Will, (1893) 2 Misc. 323, 21 N. Y. S. 931; Burley v. Barnhard, (1887) 45 Hun. 588, 9 N. Y. State Rep. 587.

Before allowing the attending physician to testify, the judge must determine whether the witness can in fact separate his knowledge gained in a business or social way from his knowledge acquired professionally. Dabbs v. Richardson, infra; Estes v. McGehee, infra. See also § 32, herein.

[1] Pittsburgh, Cincinnati, C. & St. L. Ry. v. O'Connor, (1909) 171 Ind. 686, 85 N. E. 969; Burns v. Waterloo, (1919) 187 Iowa 922, 173 N. W. 16, 174 N. W. 644; Finnegan v. Sioux City, (1900) 112 Iowa 232, 83 N. W. 907; Kling v. Kansas City, (1887) 27 Mo.

》》》→

his person,[2] or that he found a bottle of whiskey in his pocket;[3] and it has been held that this is true even though the observation was made before the physician had been notified that he was to treat him for his injury.[4] In none of these cases does it affirmatively appear that the physician's observations were necessary to enable him to properly prescribe for or treat the patient.[5] The courts seem to stress the fact that the *opportunity* to make such observations results solely from the relationship of physician and patient; therefore, the physician's observations of the patient's intoxicated condition come within the protection of the statutory privilege.[6]

On the other hand, there is respectable authortity for the view that such evidence is admissible notwithstanding an objection on the ground of privilege. Some courts, adhering strictly to the doctrine that the privilege protects only that information as is necessary to enable the physician to prescribe or act for the patient, have held that he is not prohibited to testify to the fact that the patient came, or was brought, to him in an intoxicated condition, or that his breath smelled of liquor.[7]

←⑃ App. 231. *But cf.* Linz v. Massachusetts Mut. Life Ins. Co., (1880) 8 Mo. App. 363.

[2] New York, Chicago & St. L. Ry. v. Shields, (1916) 185 Ind. 704, 112 N. E. 762; Owens v. Kansas City, C. C. & S. Ry., (1920) ....Mo. App. ...., 225 S. W. 234; Freeburg v. State, (1912) 92 Neb. 346, 138 N. W. 143, Ann. Cas. 1913 E. 1101; Clapp v. State, (1941) 73 Okla. Cr. 261, 120 P. 2d 381, (1942) 74 Okla. Cr. 144, 124 P. 2d 267.

[3] Yazoo & M. V. R. R. v. Decker, (1928) 150 Miss. 621, 116 So. 287.

[4] Chicago, South Bend & L. S. Ry. v. Walas, (1922) 192 Ind. 369, 135 N. E. 150, 22 A. L. R. 1212.

[5] In Burns v. Waterloo, (1919) 187 Iowa 922, 173 N. W. 16, 174 N. W. 644, the court indulges in inferences that do not seem to be warranted by the facts.

[6] New York, Chicago & St. L. R. R. v. Shields, (1916) 185 Ind. 704, 112 N. E. 762. This however, is not the sole test. See §§ 49, 52, herein.

[7] Perry v. Hannagan, (1932) 257 Mich. 120, 241 N. W. 232, 79 A. L. R. 1127. Plaintiff sued defendant for damages for personal injuries resulting from a collision on the highway, and claimed that defendant was under the influence of liquor. After the accident defendant was taken to the office of a physician for first aid treatment for cuts and bruises he had sustained. Plaintiff called the physician as a witness in his behalf and, over objection, he was permitted to testify that when defendant came to his office, he noticed an odor of liquor on his breath. The evidence was properly admitted since the information was not necessary to enable the physician to treat defendant's cuts and bruises and defendant did not seek treatment or advice on account

⑄→

A significant feature of this type of case, which the courts seem to overlook, is the fact that, ordinarily, the condition observed is not at all of a confidential nature. Drunkenness is seldom a secret affliction. Any layman witnessing an accident, or event of any kind, might observe a participant's state of intoxication or perhaps smell liquor on his breath or about his person. When an intoxicated person appears before a physician, he communicates nothing more to him with respect to this condition than what any layman could as easily have perceived. It is well-recognized that where the facts sought to be elicited are such, and so superficially apparent, that in regard to them no confidence could have been reposed, the basis of exclusion does not exist.[8]

Where a motorist, charged with driving while intoxicated, was examined by a physician at the instance of the police, only to determine whether he was drunk, it was error to exclude the testimony of the physician as to the motorist's condition since the information was not obtained for the purpose of enabling the physician to prescribe or act for him, barring an emergency.[9]

Of course, where the physician has treated the patient for alcoholism, he may not testify to his observations as regards the patient's appearance or symptoms since such information would properly be necessary to enable the physician to advise or treat the patient for that affliction.[10] For the same reason, the patient's hospital record would be inadmissible.[11]

← ⚞

of his intoxicated condition. See also State v. Aguirre, (1949) 167 Kan. 266, 206 P. 2d 118; State v. Townsend, (1937) 146 Kan. 982, 73 P. 2d 1124; Lincoln v. Detroit, (1894) 101 Mich. 245, 59 N. W. 617; Linz v. Massachusetts Mutual Life Ins. Co., (1880) 8 Mo. App. 363.

[8] See § 53, herein.

[9] Racine v. Woiteshek, (1947) 251 Wis. 404, 29 N. W. 2d 752. An additional reason might be that the relation of physician and patient did not exist.

See also Hanlon v. Woodhouse, (1945) 113 Colo. 504, 160 P. 2d 998. See Ladd and Gibson, The Medico-Legal Aspects of the Blood Test to Determine Intoxication, (1939) 24 Iowa L. Rev. 191, 251.

[10] Gerick v. Brock, (1949) 120 Colo. 394, 210 P. 2d 214; Matter of Hoyt, (1887) 46 Hun 677, 20 Abb. N. C. (N. Y.) 162. See also Finnegan v. Sioux City, (1900) 112 Iowa 232, 83 N. W. 907.

[11] Ost v. Ulring, (1940) 207 Minn. 500, 292 N. W. 207.

⚟→

In a prosecution for driving an automobile while intoxicated, a highway patrol officer may not testify to statements made to him by the attending physician concerning the condition of the accused shortly after the time of the alleged offense. Such evidence is not only privileged, but hearsay also.[12]

57. Mental Condition of the Patient

In all but a few jurisdictions the statute makes no distinction between a confidential communication which relates to the patient's *physical* condition and one which concerns his *mental* condition.[1] The general rule is, therefore, that a physician cannot, without the consent of the holder of the privilege, reveal on the witness stand any information concerning the mental condition of his patient which was acquired by him while attending the patient in his professional capacity.[2] Except, perhaps, in New Mexico, the disqualifi-

---

← ⁘

     In Reed v. Order of United Commercial Travelers, (1941) 123 F. 2d 252, the patient's hospital record was admissible as a proper business entry, but the question of privilege was not considered. In Soltaniuk v. Metropolitan Life Ins. Co., (1938) 133 Pa. Super. 139, 2 A. 2d 501, the patient's hospital record was admissible in evidence since the Pennsylvania statute is restricted to communications made by the patient to the physician which tend to blacken the character of the patient, and not to information obtained by the physician by observation or examination.

     See also note, 38 A. L. R. 2d 778.

[12] Robertson v. State, (1952) 95 Okla. Cr. 223, 243 P. 2d 367.

[1] The statutes of Arizona (Civil Code only), Kansas, and Oklahoma appear to restrict the privilege to communications relating to "any physical or supposed physical disease." The courts, however, construe the statute liberally and hold that communications relating to the mental illness of a patient are within the protection of the privilege.

     In New Mexico, the privilege is restricted to communications relating to "any real or supposed venereal or loathsome disease."

     The Louisiana statute protects "any investigation made into the patient's physical or mental condition * * *."

[2] In some of the following cases, the courts, conceding that the physician's testimony came within the ban of the statute, held the evidence admissible since the privilege was lawfully waived.

     McCartney v. Holmquist, (1939) 70 App. D. C. 334, 106 F. 2d 855, 126 A. L. R. 375; Labofish v. Berman, (1932) 60 App. D. C. 397, 55 F. 2d 1022; Stafford v. American Security & Trust Co., (1931) 60 App. D. C. 380, 55 F. 2d 542; Hutchins v. Hutchins, (1919) 48 App. D. C. 495; Schornick v. Schornick, (1923) 25 Ariz. 563, 220 Pac. ⟫→

cation imposed by the statute unquestionably extends to cases where the patient's mental condition was the subject of the physician's attendance and treatment. A physician, therefore, will not be permitted to testify that he prescribed for or treated the patient for a

←—◅◅

397, 31 A. L. R. 159; Hyatt v. Wroten, (1931) 184 Ark. 847, 43 S. W. 2d 726; Schirmer v. Baldwin, (1930) 182 Ark. 581, 32 S. W. 2d 162; Poinsett Lumber & Mfg. Co. v. Longino, (1919) 139 Ark. 69, 213 S. W. 15; *In re* Ross, (1916) 173 Cal. 178, 159 Pac. 603 (facts not clear); Estate of Budan, (1909) 156 Cal. 230, 104 Pac. 442; Estate of Nelson, (1901) 132 Cal. 182, 64 Pac. 294; *In re* Flint, (1893) 100 Cal. 391, 34 Pac. 863; Estate of Visaxis, (1928) 95 Cal. App. 617, 273 Pac. 165; *Re* Shapter's Estate, (1906) 35 Colo. 578, 85 Pac. 688, 6 L. R. A. (n. s.) 575; Marker v. McCue, (1931) 50 Idaho 462, 297 Pac. 401; Stayner v. Nye, (1949) 227 Ind. 231, 85 N. E. 2d 496; Pence v. Myers, (1913) 180 Ind. 282, 101 N. E. 716; Towles v. McCurdy, (1904) 163 Ind. 12, 71 N. E. 129; Gurley v. Park, (1893) 135 Ind. 440, 35 N. E. 279; Morris v. Morris, (1889) 119 Ind. 341, 21 N. E. 918; Heuston v. Simpson, 1888) 115 Ind. 62, 17 N. E. 261; Sager v. Moltz, (1923) 80 Ind. App. 122, 139 N. E. 687; Long v. Garey Investment Co., (1906) ...... Iowa ......, 110 N. W. 26; Shuman v. Supreme Lodge, K. of H., (1900) 110 Iowa 480, 81 N. W. 717; Winters v. Winters, (1897) 102 Iowa 53, 71 N. W. 184; Stayton v. Stayton, (1938) 148 Kan. 172, 81 P. 2d 1; Gorman v. Hickey, (1937) 145 Kan. 54, 64 P. 2d 587; Chaffee v. Kaufman, (1923) 113 Kan. 254, 214 Pac. 618; Flack v. Brewster, (1920) 107 Kan. 63, 190 Pac. 616; Bruington v. Wagoner, (1917) 100 Kan. 10, 164 Pac. 1657; Fish v. Poorman, (1911) 85 Kan. 237, 116 Pac. 898; Oldenberg v. Leiberg, (1913) 177 Mich. 150, 142 N. W. 1076; *Re* Mansbach's Estate, (1907) 150 Mich. 348, 114 N. W. 65; Fraser v. Jennison, (1879) 42 Mich. 206, 3 N. W. 882; Estate of Cunningham, (1944) 219 Minn. 80, 17 N. W. 2d 85; Hunter v. Hunter, (1921) 127 Miss. 683, 90 So. 440; Thompson v. Ish, (1889) 99 Mo. 160, 12 S. W. 510; Estate of Mary Gray, (1911) 88 Neb. 835, 130 N. W. 746, 33 L. R. A. (n. s.) 319, Ann. Cas. 1912 B 1037; Parker v. Parker, (1907) 78 Neb. 535, 111 N. W. 119; Matter of Coddington's Will, (1954), 307 N. Y. 181, 120 N. E. 2d 777; Matter of Cashman, (1939) 280 N. Y. 681, 21 N. E. 2d 193; Roche v. Nason, (1906) 185 N. Y. 128, 77 N. E. 1007; Matter of Myer, (1906) 184 N. Y. 54, 76 N. E. 920, 6 Ann. Cas. 26; Matter of Coleman, (1888) 111 N. Y. 220, 19 N. E. 71; Renihan v. Dennin, (1886) 103 N. Y. 573, 9 N. E. 320; Westover v. Aetna Life Ins. Co., (1884) 99 N. Y. 56, 1 N. E. 104; *Re* Cleveland's Will, (1948) 273 App. Div. 623, 78 N. Y. S. 2d 897; Scheiner v. Metropolitan Life Ins. Co., (1932) 236 App. Div. 24, 257 N. Y. S. 783; Matter of Gates, (1915) 170 App. Div. 921, 154 N. Y. S. 782; Matter of Preston, (1906) 113 App. Div. 732, 99 N. Y. S. 312; Beil v. Supreme Lodge, K. of H., (1903) 80 App. Div. 609, 80 N. Y. S. 751; Van Orman v. Van Orman, (1890) 58 Hun. 606, 11 N. Y. S. 931; *Re* Darragh's Estate, (1889) 52 Hun. 591, 5 N. Y. S. 58; Brigham v. Gott, (1889) 51 Hun. 636, 3 N. Y. S. 518; Wilcox v. Wilcox, (1887) 46 Hun. 32; Auld v. Cathro, (1910) 20 N. D. 461, 128 N. W. 1025, 32 L. R. A. (n. s.) 71, Ann. Cas. 1913 A 90; Estate of Chase, (1940) ...... Ohio App......, 31 Ohio Law Abst. 111 (questioned); Estate of Van Alstine, (1903) 26 Utah 193, 72 Pac. 942; *Re* Thomas's Estate, (1931) 165 Wash. 42, 4 P. 2d 837, 7 P. 2d 1119; *Re* Quick's Estate, (1931) 161 Wash. 537, 297 Pac. 198; *Re* Will of Hunt, (1904) 122 Wis. 460, 100 N. W. 874.

mental disorder;[3] and, where he attended the patient and treated him for both mental and physical ailments, he can not testify to either condition.[4]

Although the courts are not in harmony on the question, the decided weight of authority is to the effect that the statute precludes the physician from testifying as to the patient's mental condition, even though his knowledge thereof may not have come from communications made by the patient to him, but was the result of his own observations,[5] and notwithstanding the fact that he was treating the patient for some ailment or injury wholly unconnected with or unrelated to his mental condition.[6] Likewise, the patient's hospital

---

[3] *Re* Flint, (1893) 100 Cal. 391, 34 Pac. 863; McCaw v. Turner, (1921) 126 Miss. 260, 88 So. 705; Mulligan v. Sinski, (1913) 156 App. Div. 35, 140 N. Y. S. 835, aff'd. 214 N. Y. 678, 108 N. E. 1101; *Re* Myer, (1906) 184 N. Y. 54, 76 N. E. 920, 6 Ann. Cas. 26; Casson v. Schoenfeld, (1918) 166 Wis. 401, 166 N. W. 23, L. R. A. 1918 C 162.

[4] Shuman v. Supreme Lodge, K. of H., (1900) 110 Iowa 480, 81 N. W. 717; Wilcox v. Wilcox, (1887) 46 Hun (N. Y.) 32.

[5] Labofish v. Berman, (1932) 60 App. D. C. 397, 55 F. 2d 1022; Estate of Redfield, (1897) 116 Cal. 637, 48 Pac. 794; Fritcher v. Kelley, (1921) 34 Idaho 471, 201 Pac. 1037; Towles v. McCurdy, (1904) 163 Ind. 12, 71 N. E. 129; Gurley v. Park, (1893) 135 Ind. 440, 35 N. E. 279; Heuston v. Simpson, (1888) 115 Ind. 62, 17 N. E. 261; Matter of Coddington's Will, (1954) 307 N. Y. 181, 120 N. E. 2d 777; Renihan v. Dennin, (1886) 103 N. Y. 573, 9 N. E. 320; Beil v. Supreme Lodge, K. of H., (1903) 80 App. Div. 609, 80 N. Y. S. 751; Brigham v. Gott, (1889) 51 Hun. 636, 3 N. Y. S. 518; Auld v. Cathro, (1910) 20 N. D. 461, 128 N. W. 1025, 32 L. R. A. (n. s.) 71, Ann. Cas. 1913 A 90; Estate of Van Alstine, (1903) 26 Utah 193, 72 Pac. 942; *Re* Will of Hunt, (1904) 122 Wis. 460, 100 N. W. 874.

See also § 52, herein.

In Estate of Johnson, (1927) 200 Cal. 299, 252 Pac. 1049, a physician of the State Hospital for Insane was not allowed to relate a conversation he had with the decedent at the hospital, but was permitted to give his opinion as to his mental condition based on his observations at the time of the conversation. The decision on this point seems questionable.

In Bahl v. Byal, (1914) 90 Ohio St. 129, 106 N. E. 766, the attending physician of the testator was permitted to give his opinion as to the mental competency of the testator, but the question of privilege was not raised.

[6] Poinsett Lumber & Mfg. Co. v. Longino, (1919) 139 Ark. 69, 213 S. W. 15; Estate of Nelson, (1901 132 Cal. 182, 64 Pac. 294; Estate of Redfield, (1897) 116 Cal. 637, 48 Pac. 794; Fritcher v. Kelley, (1921) 34 Idaho 471, 201 Pac. 1037; Preston's Will, (1906) 113 App. Div. 732, 99 N. Y. S. 312.

See also § 51, herein.

Several Ohio courts have held that where the only purpose of the physician's

≫≫→

record is privileged and matters stated therein concerning his mental condition cannot be disclosed.[7]

It has been held, however, that the physician may testify to the mental condition of the patient when the information sought to be elicited was acquired by him outside the professional relationship,[8] or was not necessary to enable the physician to prescribe or act for

←※

professional attendance was for examination and treatment of a bodily ailment, which was in no way related to a mental condition, the physician is competent to testify as to the patient's mental condition as he observed it during the course of his professional employment. Carson v. Beatley, (1948) 86 Ohio App. 173, 82 N. E. 2d 745; Meier v. Peirano, (1945) 76 Ohio App. 9, 62 N. E. 2d 920; Olney v. Schurr, (1936) ...... Ohio App......... , 21 Ohio Law Abst. 630, appeal dismissed 131 Ohio St. 398, 3 N. E. 2d 43; Heiselmann v. Franks, (1934) 48 Ohio App. 536, 194 N. E. 604. This decision seems to be based on the theory that the physician's observations were such as any layman could make; therefore, they did not pertain to confidential matters. See also Krislov, Physician-Patient Privilege as Affected by Mode of Gaining Information, (1949) 1 West. Res. L. Rev. 142. For criticism of the decision in Heiselmann v. Franks, *supra,* see note, (1935) 2 Ohio O. 389. See also Burris v. State, (1925) 168 Ark. 1145, 273 S. W. 19; Estate of Casarotti, (1920) 184 Cal. 73, 192 Pac. 1085; Buck v. Buck, (1914) 126 Minn. 275, 148 N. W. 117. It is respectfully submitted that the Ohio decisions are violative of the spirit, if not the letter of the privilege statute; if not, they are dangerously near to it.

[7] *Re* Nickel's Estate, (1948) 321 Mich. 519, 32 N. W. 2d 733; *Re* Coddington's Will, (1954) 307 N. Y. 181, 120 N. E. (2d) 777; Greff v. Havens, (1946) 186 Misc. 914, 66 N. Y. S. 2d 124; Eikenberry v. McFall, (1941)......Ohio App........ , 33 Ohio Law Abst. 525, 36 N. E. 2d 27. See also § 64, herein.

[8] Wheeler v. State, (1902) 158 Ind. 687, 63 N. E. 975; Bower v. Bower, (1895) 142 Ind. 194, 41 N. E. 523; Conner v. First National Bank, (1948) 118 Ind. App. 173, 76 N. E. 2d 262, 77 N. E. 2d 598; Smith v. Davis, (1949) 168 Kan. 210, 212 P. 2d 322; Leifson v. Henning, (1941) 210 Minn. 311, 298 N. W. 41; Estes v. McGehee, (1923) 133 Miss. 174, 97 So. 530; Fisher v. Fisher, (1892) 129 N. Y. 654, 29 N. E. 951; Matter of Loewenstine's Will, (1893) 2 Misc. 323, 21 N. Y. S. 931; Matter of Freeman, (1887) 46 Hun. (N. Y.) 458; State v. Miller, (1934) 177 Wash. 442, 32 P. 2d 535; *Re* Will of Williams, (1925) 186 Wis. 160, 202 N. W. 314; Boyle v. Robinson, (1906) 129 Wis. 567, 109 N. W. 623.

Some courts are unwilling to believe that the human mind is capable of separating the facts obtained professionally from those not so obtained but coming within the observation of the witness. See § 45.

It has been held that the attending physician, testifying as an expert, may answer a hypothetical question calling for an opinion regarding his patient's mental condition. Watkins v. Watkins, (1926) 142 Miss. 210, 106 So. 753; *Re* Flint, (1893) 100 Cal. 391, 34 Pac. 863.

Contra: Re Ross, (1916) 173 Cal. 178, 159 Pac. 603.

the patient.[9] Moreover, the physician, or a nurse who comes within the statutory privilege, may testify to the mental condition of the patient when his or her testimony is based on observations which would be equally apparent to any lay person.[10] Where an attorney representing the accused requires the aid of a psychiatrist in interpreting his client's mental condition, the accused is entitled to have the psychiatrist examine her in private, and the court will order the sheriff to afford her this right.[11]

58. Manner or Cause of Patient's Injury or Ailment

As stated earlier,[1] practically all courts now concede that not *all* information which is obtained by physicians from their patients is privileged, but only such confidential communications entrusted to them which are necessary and proper to enable them to perform their professional duties.[2]

Ordinarily, the time, place, manner, and circumstances of an accident or the cause of injury to a person, are not confidential matters.[3] They neither reveal nor concern the nature of his injury or ailment. There is no secrecy, or intimacy, or privacy about them.[4]

---

[9] Burris v. State, (1925) 168 Ark. 1145, 273 S. W. 19; Estate of Black, (1901) 132 Cal. 392, 64 Pac. 695; Smith v. Davis, (1949) 168 Kan. 210, 212 P. 2d 322; Steketee v. Newkirk, (1912) 173 Mich. 222, 138 N. W. 1034; Herrington v. Winn, (1891) 60 Hun. 235, 14 N. Y. S. 612; Matter of Freeman, (1887) 46 Hun. (N. Y.) 458; *Re* Will of Bruendl, (1899) 102 Wis. 45, 78 N. W. 169. See also § 49. In Estate of Budan, (1909) 156 Cal. 230, 104 Pac. 442, necessity for the information was presumed.

[10] See § 53, herein.

[11] Ex Parte Ochse, (1951) 38 Cal. 2d 230, 238 P. 2d 561.

[1] § 47, herein.

[2] Green v. Terminal R. R. Ass'n., (1908) 211 Mo. 18, 109 S. W. 715; Koskovich v. Rodestock, (1921) 107 Neb. 116, 185 N. W. 343; Green v. Metropolitan St. Ry., (1902) 171 N. Y. 201, 63 N. E. 958; Smith v. John L. Roper Lumber Co., (1908) 147 N. C. 62, 60 S. E. 717, 15 Ann. Cas. 580. See also §§ 49, 50, herein. Whether or not the information was necessary and proper is usually a question for the court, not the witness. Koskovitch v. Rodestock, infra; Griffiths v. Metropolitan St. Ry., (1902) 171 N. Y. 106, 63 N. E. 808; Madsen v. Utah Light & Ry., (1909) 36 Utah 528, 105 Pac. 799.
See also § 60, herein.

[3] The Kansas statute, however, arbitrarily classifies them with confidential matters with which they may be associated.

[4] Armstrong v. Topeka Ry., (1914) 93 Kan. 493, 144 Pac. 847; Kansas City, Fort Scott & M. R. R. v. Murray, (1895) 55 Kan. 336, 40 Pac. 646. Of course, where the witness

≫→

Moreover, except in rare instances, it is difficult to imagine how a patient's statement of facts concerning the manner or circumstances in which he sustained bodily injury would throw any possible light upon, or assist in any way, the proper treatment of his injury. Usually the nature of the injury is self-evident, and the treatment would be the same regardless of what the patient was doing when he received it.[5] Accordingly, the great weight of authority supports the view that communications made by a patient to his physician concerning the manner or circumstances of the accident or occurrence in which he sustained injury, or incurred his ailment, are not within the protection of the statute; and this is true, whether the information was voluntarily given by the patient, or was elicited by the physician.[6] For the same reason, a portion of the patient's hos-

---

←

cannot relate what the patient said concerning the cause of his condition without, at the same time, throwing some light on the nature of the patient's injury or ailment, the matter would likely be privileged. Streeter v. Breckenridge, (1886) 23 Mo. App. 244.

[5] Van Wie v. United States, (1948) 77 F. Supp. 22; Missouri Pac. Ry. v. Castle, (1909) 172 Fed. 841, 845, aff'd. 224 U. S. 541, 56 Law. Ed. 875, 32 Su. Ct. 606: "In the case at bar there was beyond question a crushed right leg about four inches above the ankle. * * * Whether the injury was caused by plaintiff's or defendant's negligence was the pivotal question in the case. It is impossible to imagine anything that Castle, the injured person, could say to the physician in reference to the cause of the injury that would in any way throw any light upon the manner of treating the same. How the leg came to be crushed was for the purpose of treatment absolutely immaterial. What plaintiff told the witness was of no assistance whatsoever to enable him to discharge the functions of his office." Green v. Terminal R. R. Ass'n., (1908) 211 Mo. 18, 109 S. W. 715; Koskovich v. Rodestock, (1921) 107 Neb. 116, 185 N. W. 343; DeJong v. Erie R. R., (1899) 43 App. Div. 427, 428, 60 N. Y. S. 125: "The disclosures prohibited by the statute are only such as were necessary to enable the medical man to act as physician or surgeon. The prohibition does not extend to admissions, made by a party to an action, of facts which have and can have no possible relation to the professional conduct of the medical or surgical practitioner. Nothing that the plaintiff could say in regard to his observation of the train which struck him, or his failure to observe it, could, by any possibility, have been either material or useful to Dr. M in his treatment of the plaintiff as a patient. Whatever statement the plaintiff made on that subject was wholly outside the case in its medical or surgical aspects."

Madsen v. Utah Light & Ry., (1909) 36 Utah 528, 105 Pac. 799.

[6] Van Wie v. United States, (1948) 77 F. Supp. 22; Missouri Pac. Ry. v. Castle, (1909) 172 Fed. 841, aff'd. 224 U. S. 541, 56 Law. Ed. 875, 32 Su. Ct. 606; Cooper v. State,

⟫→

pital record showing the manner of the accident in which he received his injury, has been held admissible in evidence.[7]

Among the earlier cases there are a few in which the courts liberally construed the statute in favor of the patient, some of them going so far as to prohibit the disclosure of *any* communication made by the patient to the physician notwithstanding it was neither necessary nor proper to enable the physician to prescribe for or treat the patient. Accordingly, it has been held that the physician cannot reveal what the patient told him concerning the manner in which he received his injury or incurred his ailment,[8] particularly when the information was elicited by the physician.[9] These views appear

---

←≪

(1949) 215 Ark. 732, 223 S. W. 2d 507; Grosnickle v. Avery, (1926) 96 Ind. App. 479, 152 N. E. 288, rehearing denied 154 N. E. 395 (elicited by physician); State v. Johnston, (1936) 221 Iowa 933, 267 N. W. 698 (elicited by physician); Kansas City, Fort Smith & M. R. R. v. Murray, (1895) 55 Kan. 336, 40 Pac. 646; Campau v. North, (1878) 39 Mich. 606; Leifson v. Henning, (1941) 210 Minn. 311; 298 N. W. 41; State v. Carryer, (1915) ____Mo.____, 180 S. W. 850; Green v. Terminal R. R. Ass'n., (1908) 211 Mo. 18, 109 S. W. 715; Garrett v. Butte, (1923) 69 Mont. 214, 221 Pac. 537; Koskovich v. Rodestock, (1921) 107 Neb. 116, 185 N. W. 343; Green v. Metropolitan Street Ry., (1902) 171 N. Y. 201, 63 N. E. 958; Munson v. Model Taxi Corp., (1948) 273 App. Div. 1039, 78 N. Y. S. 2d 629, appeal denied 298 N. Y. 935, 84 N. E. 2d 639; Gray v. New York, (1910) 137 App. Div. 316, 122 N. Y. S. 118; Travis v. Haan, (1907) 119 App. Div. 138, 103 N. Y. S. 973; Benjamin v. Tupper Lake, (1905) 110 App. Div. 426, 97 N. Y. S. 512; Griebel v. Brooklyn Heights R. R., (1902) 68 App. Div. 204, 74 N. Y. S. 126; DeJong v. Erie R. R., (1899) 43 App. Div. 427, 60 N. Y. S. 125; Brown v. Rome, Watertown & O. R. R., (1887) 45 Hun. 439, aff'd. 121 N. Y. 669, 24 N. E. 1094; Smith v. John L. Roper Lumber Co., (1908) 147 N. C. 62, 60 S. E. 717, 15 Ann. Cas. 580 (elicited by physician); Madsen v. Utah Light & Ry., (1909) 36 Utah 528, 105 Pac. 799 (elicited by physician). The same rule has been applied to the clergyman-penitent privilege. Christenson v. Pestorious, (1933) 189 Minn. 548, 250 N. W. 363.

[7] Hodge v. Lyford, (1948) 298 N. Y. 651, 82 N. E. 2d 40.

[8] Cincinnati, Hamilton & D. R. R. v. Gross, (1917) 186 Ind. 471, 114 N. E. 962; Chicago & Erie R. R. v. Schenkel, (1914) 57 Ind. App. 175, 104 N. E. 50; Indiana Union Traction Co. v. Thomas, (1909) 44 Ind. App. 468, 88 N. E. 356; Pride v. Inter-State Business Mens Acc. Ass'n., (1928) 207 Iowa 167, 216 N. W. 62, 62 A. L. R. 31; Arnold v. Fort Dodge, Des Moines & S. R. R., (1919) 186 Iowa 538, 173 N. W. 252; Battis v. Chicago, R. I. & Pac. Ry., (1904) 124 Iowa 623, 100 N. W. 543; Keist v. Chicago Great W. R. R., (1899) 110 Iowa 32, 81 N. W. 181; E. Patterson & Son v. Cole, (1903) 67 Kan. 441, 73 Pac. 54.

[9] McRae v. Erickson, (1905) 1 Cal. App. 326, 82 Pac. 209; Pennsylvania Co. v. Marion, (1889) 123 Ind. 415, 23 N. E. 973, 7 L. R. A. 687; New York, Chicago & St. L. R. R. v.

≫→

unsound,[10] and, in some instances, later decisions of the same courts seem to have repudiated them.[11]

There are cases, however, where a statement by the injured person to his physician, regarding the manner in which he received his injury, was held privileged because the information was plainly necessary in order to enable the physician to treat the patient in an intelligent and safe manner.[12] Some of the courts, which approve the general rule, are frank to concede that there may be unusual circumstances where such information is truly necessary and is therefore entitled to protection from revealment by the physician.[13]

59. *Narcotic Drugs*

The Uniform Narcotic Drug Act was adopted by the National Conference of Commissioners on Uniform State Laws in 1932. Section 17(2) of the original act provides that "information communicated to a physician in an effort to unlawfully procure a narcotic drug, or unlawfully to procure the administration of any such drug, shall not be deemed a privileged communication."

Mushrush, (1894) 11 Ind. App. 192, 37 N. E. 954; Obermeyer v. Logeman Chair Mfg. Co., (1910) 229 Mo. 97, 129 S. W. 209.

See also dissent of Straup, C. J., in Madsen v. Utah Light & Ry., (1909) 36 Utah 528, 554, 105 Pac. 799.

10 Griebel v. Brooklyn Heights R. R., (1902) 68 App. Div. 204, 74 N. Y. S. 126; Smith v. John L. Roper Lumber Co., (1908) 147 N. C. 62, 60 S. E. 717, 15 Ann. Cas. 580.

11 See § 49, herein.

12 Raymond v. Burlington, Cedar Rapids & N. Ry., (1884) 65 Iowa 152, 21 N. W. 495; Norton v. Moberly, (1885) 18 Mo. App. 457; Meyer v. Supreme Lodge, K. of P., (1904) 178 N. Y. 63, 70 N. E. 111, aff'd. 198 U. S. 508; 49 Law. Ed. 1146, 25 Su. Ct. 754, 64 L. R. A. 839; People v. Runion, (1957) 3 A. D. 2d 982, 162 N. Y. S. 2d 640, aff'd 3 N. Y. 2d 637, 148 N. E. 2d 165; Kenyon v. Mondovi, (1897) 98 Wis. 50, 73 N. W. 314.

13 Green v. Terminal R. R. Ass'n., (1908) 211 Mo. 18, 44, 109 S. W. 715: "A case might be imagined where the method by which a man lost his arm was an element essential to correct surgical or medical treatment * * *." Griffiths v. Metropolitan Street Ry., (1902) 171 N. Y. 106, 112, 63 N. E. 808: "There may be circumstances in which it is necessary for a physician to inquire of a patient how an accident happened in order to properly treat him."

Griebel v. Brooklyn Heights R. R., (1902) 68 App. Div. 204, 207, 74 N. Y. S. 126: "It is easy of course to imagine cases * * * where a disclosure by the injured person of the manner in which the accident occurred might well be deemed necessary to the furtherance of proper surgical or medical treatment."

This act has been adopted[1] by practically every state which, prior thereto, had enacted the physician-patient privilege statute. Unless a state's statute otherwise provides, in all situations mentioned in the section cited above, the Uniform Narcotic Act unquestionably will determine the competency of the physician to testify,[2] the physician-patient privilege statute being, to this extent, impliedly repealed thereby.[3]

60. Burden of Proof

It is almost universally established that where a party to litigation seeks to exclude the testimony of a witness on the ground that it is privileged by statute or otherwise, the burden rests upon him to bring or show it within the terms of the law establishing the privilege. This rule is consonant with common sense and justice.[1] The general rule of evidence is competency. Incompetency is the exception, and to bring one within the exception, one must come within the reason for it. In any event the burden is on the one claiming a privilege to show the existence of circumstances justifying its recognition.[2] As stated earlier, the general rule is that the physician-patient privilege statute protects only such information as was acquired by the physician in his professional capacity and which was necessary to enable him to prescribe or act for the patient.[3] To hold that all communications made to, or any information acquired by, the physician during his professional employment come within the ban of the statute would be to repeal by judicial fiat the express qualification imposed by the lawmakers upon the application of the privilege by rendering the phrase "which was necessary to enable

---

[1] In some instances with a few changes.

[2] Mississippi has omitted this section from its law. Missouri has expressly denied its application when the relation of physician and patient exists and the information is necessary to prescribe or act for the patient. (1952) Mo. Stat. Ann., 195, 170 (2).

[3] See 50 Am. Jr., *Statutes*, § 563.

[1] Booren v. McWilliams, (1914) 26 N. D. 558, 145 N. W. 410, Ann. Cas. 1916 A 388.

[2] Myers v. State, (1922) 192 Ind. 592, 137 N. E. 547, 24 A. L. R. 1196; Bloodgood v. Lynch, (1944) 293 N. Y. 308, 56 N. E. 2d 718. But this principle does not require the objector to prove the law of a foreign country with respect to privileged communications. Jones v. Jones, (1955) 208 Misc. 721, 144 N. Y. S. 2d 820.

[3] § 49, herein.

him to prescribe or act for the patient" totally ineffective.[4] The general rule is, therefore, that where a party seeks to exclude the testimony of a physician on the ground of privilege, the burden is upon such party to bring the case within the statute, and he must make it appear not only that the information which he seeks to exclude was acquired by the witness in attending the patient in a professional capacity, but also that it was necessary to enable him to perform some professional act.[5] The trial court is not at liberty to assume that to be the fact.[6] Furthermore, the mere assertion of the privilege, without any showing of facts or circumstances from which the court can see the necessity for the application of the statute, is not sufficient to warrant the court in rejecting the offered evidence; neither is the mere relationship of physician and patient alone sufficient to warrant a court in rejecting on the ground of privilege,

---

[4] Green v. Terminal R. R. Ass'n., (1908) 211 Mo. 18, 109 S. W. 715; Koskovich v. Rodestock, (1921) 107 Neb. 116, 185 N. W. 343; Booren v. McWilliams, (1914) 26 N. D. 558, 145 N. W. 410, Ann. Cas. 1916 A 388.

[5] Continental Investment Co. v. Garcher, (1928) 83 Colo. 239, 264 Pac. 723; Myers v. State, (1922) 192 Ind. 592, 137 N. E. 547, 24 A. L. R. 1196 (a significant departure from the rule established by earlier Indiana decisions); State v. Masters, (1924) 197 Iowa 1147, 198 N. W. 509; Campau v. North, (1878) 39 Mich. 606; State v. Anderson, (1956) 247 Minn. 469, 78 N. W. 2d 320; Brown v .St. Paul City Ry., (1954) 241 Minn. 15, 62 N. W. 2d 688; Green v. Terminal R. R. Ass'n., (1908) 211 Mo. 18, 109 S. W. 715; Schermer v. McMahon, (1904) 108 Mo. App. 36, 82 S. W. 535; James v. Kansas City, (1900) 85 Mo. App. 20; People v. Decina, (1956) 2 N. Y. 2d 133, 138 N. E. 2d 799; Green v. Metropolitan Street Ry., (1902) 171 N. Y. 201, 63 N. E. 958; Griffiths v. Metropolitan Street Ry., (1902) 171 N. Y. 106, 63 N. E. 808; People v. Koerner, (1897) 154 N. Y. 355, 48 N. E. 730; People v. Schuyler, (1887) 106 N. Y. 298, 12 N. E. 783; Edington v. Aetna Life Ins. Co., (1879) 77 N. Y. 564; Kelly v. Dykes, (1916) 174 App. Div. 786, 161 N. Y. S. 551, app. dismissed 220 N. Y. 653, 115 N. E. 1042; Jennings v. Supreme Council, L. A. B. Ass'n., (1903) 81 App. Div. 76, 81 N. Y. S. 90; Herrington v. Winn, (1891) 60 Hun. 235, 14 N. Y. S. 612; Van Heuverzwyn v. State, (1954) 206 Misc. 896, 134 N. Y. S. 2d 922; People v. Barnes, (1950) 197 Misc. 477, 98 N. Y. S. 2d 481; Carson v. Beatley, (1948) 86 Ohio App. 173, 82 N. E. 2d 745; Smits v. State, (1911) 145 Wis. 601, 130 N. W. 525.

Likewise, it is not the duty of the party offering the testimony to show that the relation of physician and patient did not exist.

See § 46, herein.

[6] Of course, the objector also has the burden of proving that the relation of physician and patient existed when the information was acquired. See § 46, herein.

evidence which would otherwise be competent.[7] If, therefore, the objector fails to meet the burden of proof, the testimony of the physician must be received.[8] It is not incumbent on the party who seeks information from a physician who has been in attendance upon a patient, to show that the information was *not* acquired as specified in the statute; but the party objecting must in some way make it appear, if it does not otherwise appear, that the information is within the statutory exclusion.[9]

It must be admitted, however, that the decisions cited in support of these doctrines are, under varying circumstances, opposed by others, and, sometimes, in the same jurisdictions. A few courts, construing the statute most liberally, go so far as to hold that, once the relation of physician and patient has been established, there is a presumption that all information communicated by, or acquired in attendance upon, the patient, was necessary for the treatment of the patient; hence, the objector has met the necessary burden of proof when he has shown the relationship to exist.[10] It has also been held

---

[7] Brown v. St. Paul City Ry., (1954) 241 Minn. 15, 62 N. W. 2d 688; Vermillion v. Prudential Ins. Co., (1936) 230 Mo. App. 993, 93 S. W. 2d 45; Bowles v. Kansas City, (1892) 51 Mo. App. 416; Edington v. Aetna Life Ins. Co., (1879) 77 N. Y. 564; People v. Barnes, (1950) 197 Misc. 477, 98 N. Y. S. 2d 481; See also Robertson v. Commonwealth, (1943) 181 Va. 520, 540, 25 S. E. 2d 352, 146 A. L. R. 966 (attorney-client privilege).

It is respectfully submitted that this is the better rule, but there is ample authority to the contrary. See cases in note 10 infra.

[8] Campau v. North, (1878) 39 Mich. 606; State v. Anderson, (1956) 247 Minn. 469, 78 N. W. 2d 320; Green v. Terminal R. R. Ass'n., (1908) 211 Mo. 18, 109 S. W. 715; Schermer v. McMahon, (1904) 108 Mo. App. 36, 82 S. W. 535; Bowles v. Kansas City, (1892) 51 Mo. App. 416; Griffiths v. Metropolitan Street Ry., (1902) 171 N. Y. 106, 63 N. E. 808; Carson v. Beatley, (1948) 86 Ohio App. 173, 82 N. E. 2d 745; Smits v. State, (1911) 145 Wis. 601, 130 N. W. 525.

[9] Edington v. Aetna Life Ins. Co. (1879) 77 N. Y. 564. *Contra:* Wesseler v. Great Northern Ry., (1916) 90 Wash. 234, 155 Pac. 1063, 157 Pac. 461. See also Stafford v. American Security and Trust Co., (1931) 60 App. D. C. 380, 55 F. 2d 542; Jacobs v. Cedar Rapids, (1917) 181 Iowa 407, 164 N. W. 891.

[10] Stafford v. American Security and Trust Co., (1931) 60 App. D. C. 380, 55 F. 2d 542; Estate of Budan, (1909) 156 Cal. 230, 104 Pac 442; McRae v. Erickson, (1905) 1 Cal. App. 326, 82 Pac. 209; Pennsylvania Co. v. Marion, (1889) 123 Ind. 415, 23 N. E. 973, 7 L. R. A. 687; Battis v. Chicago, R. I. & Pac. Ry., (1904) 124 Iowa 623, 100 N. W. 543; State v. Kennedy, (1903) 177 Mo. 98, 75 S. W. 979; Feeney v. Long Island

⟫→

that entries in a hospital record itself constituted a prima facie showing that the information contained therein was of a confidential and privileged character, and that the burden was on the party offering the evidence to satisfy the court that such information was not given by the patient to the hospital physicians for the purpose of enabling them to prescribe for and treat her, especially in view of the claim of privilege on that ground.[11] Of course, where it is self-evident that the question seeks information plainly within the protection of the statute, there is no need for further proof.[12]

Although there is a lack of harmony among the courts, the better view seems to be that the question whether information communicated to, or acquired by, the physician in attending a patient was necessary for treatment, is one of fact to be determined pri-

---

R. R., (1889) 116 N. Y. 375, 22 N. E. 402, 5 L. R. A. 544; Grattan v. Metropolitan Life Ins. Co., (1880) 80 N. Y. 281; Edington v. Mutual Life Ins. Co., (1876) 67 N. Y. 185; Dambmann v. Metropolitan Street Ry. (1907) 55 Misc. 60, 106 N. Y. S. 221; *In re* Darragh's Estate, (1889) 52 Hun. 591, 5 N. Y. S. 58; *In re* Halsey's Estate, (1890) 9 N. Y. S. 441; Munz v. Salt Lake City R. R., (1902) 25 Utah 220, 70 Pac. 852 (Rolapp, J., rendered a strong dissent as to the presumption of necessity); State v. Miller, (1919) 105 Wash. 475, 178 Pac. 459.

There is, however, substantial opposition to this view. Madsen v. Utah Light & Ry. Co., (1909) 36 Utah 528, 538, 105 Pac. 799: "A moment's reflection will show that the law does not raise a presumption either way, but leaves the question as one of fact." The court criticized the decisions on this point in State v. Kennedy, (1903) 177 Mo. 98, 75 S. W. 979, and in Munz v. Salt Lake City R. R., (1902) 25 Utah 220, 70 Pac. 852.

See also Myers v. State, (1922) 192 Ind. 592, 137 N. E. 547, 24 A. L. R. 1196; Green v. Metropolitan Street Ry., (1902) 171 N. Y. 201, 63 N. E. 958; Smith v. John L. Roper Lumber Co., (1908) 147 N. C. 62, 60 S. E. 717, 15 Ann. Cas. 580.

[11] Vermillion v. Prudential Ins. Co., (1936) 230 Mo. App. 993, 93 S. W. 2d 45.

In Hurd v. Republic Steel Corp., (1949) 275 App. Div. 725, 87 N. Y. S. 2d 64, it was held that the appellate court may take judicial notice and must presume that x-rays and reports made by hospital physicians and nurses were made to enable them to treat the patient.

[12] Estate of Budan, (1909) 156 Cal. 230, 104 Pac. 442; Meyer v. Supreme Lodge, K. of P., (1904) 178 N. Y. 63, 70 N. E. 111, aff'd. 198 U. S. 508, 49 Law. Ed. 1146, 25 Su. Ct. 754, 64 L. R. A. 839; Grattan v. Metropolitan Life Ins. Co., (1880) 80 N. Y. 281; Sloan v. New York Central R. R., (1871) 45 N. Y. 125; Jones v. Brooklyn, B. & West End R. R., (1888) 3 N. Y. S. 253, aff'd. 121 N. Y. 683, 24 N. E. 1098; State v. Miller, (1919) 105 Wash. 475, 178 Pac. 459.

marily by the trial court,[13] taking into consideration all the circumstance and, if necessary, the opinion of the physician, and the belief of the patient.[14] Usually counsel is permitted to conduct a preliminary examination of the witness to ascertain whether or not the information sought to be elicited was necessary to enable him to prescribe or act for the patient.[15] Moreover, to this end, the court itself may interrogate the witness.[16] Of course, every precaution should be taken to make sure that no privileged matters be dis-

---

[13] Stafford v. American Security & Trust Co., (1931) 60 App. D. C. 380, 55 F. 2d 542; Phelps Dodge Corporation v. Guerrero, (1921) 273 Fed. 415; Hutchins v. Hutchins, (1919) 48 App. D. C. 495; Estate of Casarotti, (1920) 184 Cal. 73, 192 Pac. 1085; Estate of Redfield (1897) 116 Cal. 637, 48 Pac. 794; Dabbs v. Richardson, (1924) 137 Miss. 789, 102 So. 769; Koskovich v. Rodestock, (1921) 107 Neb. 116, 185 N. W. 343; Meyer v. Supreme Lodge, K. of P., (1904) 178 N. Y. 63, 70 N. E. 111, aff'd. 198 U. S. 508, 49 Law. Ed. 1146, 25 Su. Ct. 754, 64 L. R. A. 839; Booren v. McWilliams, (1914) 26 N. D. 558, 145 N. W. 410, Ann. Cas. 1916 A 388; Madsen v. Utah Light & Ry., (1909) 36 Utah 528, 105 Pac. 799. For the rule in North Carolina, see Creech v. Sovereign Camp W. of W., (1937) 211 N. C. 658, 191 S. E. 840; State v. Newsome, (1928) 195 N. C. 552, 143 S. E. 187; Metropolitan Life Ins. Co. v. Boddie, (1927) 194 N. C. 199, 139 S. E. 228.

[14] Van Wie v. United States, (1948) 77 F. Supp. 22; Green v. Terminal R. R. Ass'n., (1908) 211 Mo. 18, 109 S. W. 715; Smith v. John L. Roper Lumber Co., (1908) 147 N. C. 62, 60 S. E. 717, 15 Ann. Cas. 580; Booren v. McWilliams, (1914) 26 N. D. 558, 145 N. W. 410, Ann. Cas. 1916 A 388; Madsen v. Utah Light & Ry., (1909) 36 Utah 528, 105 Pac. 799. See also Burley v. Barnhard, (1887) 45 Hun. 588, 9 N. Y. St. 587, where court relied on physician's statement.

[15] Phelps Dodge Corporation v. Guerrero, (1921) 273 Fed. 415; People's Bank v. Brown, (1902) 112 Fed. 652, 654: "It is requisite that in every instance it shall be judicially determined whether the particular communication in question be really privileged, and, in order that such primary determination may be advisedly made, it is indispensable that the court shall be apprised, through preliminary inquiry, of the characterizing circumstances." (Involving attorney-client privilege).

Van Wie v. United States, (1948) 77 F. Supp. 22; Burris v. State, (1925) 168 Ark. 1145, 273 S. W. 19; Stewart v. Douglass, (1909) 9 Cal. App. 712, 100 Pac. 711 (attorney-client); Green v. Terminal R. R. Ass'n., (1908) 211 Mo. 18, 109 S. W. 715.

In Herrington v. Winn, (1891) 60 Hun 235, 14 N. Y. S. 612, after plaintiff's objection to physician's testimony was sustained, defendant recalled the witness and asked him questions to ascertain whether the information he acquired was necessary for treatment. The questions were objected to and excluded. This was error.

[16] Richter v. Hoglund, (1943) 132 F. 2d 748; Burris v. State, (1925) 168 Ark. 1145, 273 S. W. 19; Gardner v. Hobbs, (1949) 69 Idaho 288, 206 P. 2d 539; Hays v. Hays, (1912) 49 Ind. App. 298, 97 N. E. 198; Hughes v. Boone, (1889) 102 N. C. 137, 9 S. E. 286 (attorney-client).

closed, even though the preliminary examination be conducted in the absence of the jury.[17]

Although there are a few decisions to the contrary,[18] the trend of modern authority is to the effect that the physician-witness is not the final and conclusive judge as to the application of the privilege, and the fact that he testifies that the information he acquired was, or was not, necessary to enable him to prescribe or act for the patient is not binding on the trial court in determining whether the information sought is within, or without, the ban of the statute.[19] To

---

[17] Powell v. J. J. Newman Lumber Co., (1936) 174 Miss. 685, 165 So. 299; United States Fidelity & Guar. Co. v. Hood, (1920) 124 Miss. 548, 87 So. 115, 15 A. L. R. 605; *In re* Contempt of Emil Swenson, (1931) 183 Minn. 602, 237 N. W. 589 (clergyman-penitent); Sloan v. New York Central R. R., (1871) 45 N. Y. 125; Jones v. Brooklyn, B. & West End R. R., (1888) 3 N. Y. S. 253, 255, aff'd 121 N. Y. 683, 24 N. E. 1098: "It is unreasonable that the secrets must first be told to enable the court to determine that they were necessary to the physician's action in his professional capacity, and therefore were privileged, and could not be used in evidence. This would accomplish as much good as did the locking of the stable after the horse was stolen." See also People v. Austin, (1910) 199 N. Y. 446, 93 N. E. 57.

[18] State v. Kennedy, (1903) 177 Mo. 98, 129, 75 S. W. 979: "We take it that the physician or surgeon must, as a general rule, under the statute, determine for himself whether the information acquired by him from his patient is necessary for him to prescribe for such patient. * * * To rule otherwise would be to usurp the prerogative of a physician, learned in his profession, which we have no inclination or right to do * * *."

Van Bergen v. Catholic Relief & Ben. Ass'n., (1904) 99 App. Div. 72, 91 N. Y. S. 362; *In re* Halsey's Estate, (1890) 9 N. Y. S. 441. See also McRae v. Erickson, (1905) 1 Cal. App. 326, 82 Pac. 209; Madsen v. Utah Light & Ry., (1909) 36 Utah 528, 105 Pac. 799 (giving qualified approval to State v. Kennedy, infra).

[19] Hutchins v. Hutchins, (1919) 48 App. D. C. 495; People's Bank v. Brown, (1902) 112 Fed. 652, 654: "The witness declines to answer, not after inquiry and adjudication by the court, but upon his own mere declaration that the matters to which his declination relates were privileged communications, and thus both of the facts and the law he constitutes himself the exclusive judge. The province of the court cannot be thus usurped. If it could be, it is obvious that the rule under consideration, which is designed to promote the administration of justice, might readily be misused for its obstruction, and become, in consequence, too pernicious to be tolerated."

Larson v. State, (1912) 92 Neb. 24, 137 N. W. 894. See also Dabbs v. Richardson, (1924) 137 Miss. 789, 102 So. 769.

Griffiths v. Metropolitan Street Ry., (1902) 171 N. Y. 106, 113, 63 N. E. 958: "Where the party seeking to exclude the evidence shows facts which indicate that the information was necessary for professional treatment, the trial judge is the sole judge of its admissibility, notwithstanding the physician's statement to the contrary."

$\ggg\!\!\rightarrow$

allow the rule to be evaded by the physician swearing that the information obtained was not necessary to enable him to act, would place it in his power to violate the statute at will.[20]

Some latitude must necessarily be given the trial court in determining whether the evidence offered does or does not come within the protection of the statute.[21] Furthermore, since the trial court has the distinct advantage of judging of the witness and observing him while he is testifying, it is not likely that an appellate court will interfere with his ruling upon the question of privilege where there is a conflict of evidence.[22]

On the other hand, the physician's unqualified statement that the information enabled him to care for the patient is persuasive evidence that it was necessary. *In re* Estate of Redfield, (1897) 116 Cal. 637, 48 Pac. 794.

[20] Bach, The Medico-Legal Aspect of Privileged Communications, (1892) 10 Medico-Leg. J. 33, 61. Madsen v. Utah Light & Ry., (1909) 36 Utah 528, 538, 105 Pac. 799: " * * * , the testimony of the physician may not, in all cases and under all circumstances, be conclusive, and the court may still be justified in holding the information necessary, the statement of the physician to the contrary notwithstanding. If the rule were otherwise, the physician would have it in his power to either enforce the statute with respect to all information, or to ignore it with respect to all. This would be unreasonable."

For a discussion of this element of the privilege in the province of Quebec, influenced by the French Civil Law, see Gagne v. Alliance Nationale, [1946] 13 I. L. R. 13; Mutual Life Ins. Co. v. dame Jeannotte-Lamarche, [1935] Quebec 59 K. B. 510.

[21] Chicago & Erie R. R. v. Schenkel, (1914) 59 Ind. App. 175, 104 N. E. 50.

[22] Richter v. Hoglund, (1943) 132 F. 2d 748; Stewart v. Douglass, (1909) 9 Cal. App. 712, 100 Pac. 711 (attorney-client); Dabbs v. Richardson, (1924) 137 Miss. 789, 102 So. 769; Valleroy v. Knights of Columbus, (1908) 135 Mo. App. 574, 116 S. W. 1130.

See also Phelps Dodge Corp. v. Guerrero, (1921) 273 Fed. 415.

CHAPTER XI

Mode of Attempted Introduction Immaterial

61. In General

Where communications between physician and patient are protected from disclosure by a statutory privilege, the form in which they are sought to be introduced in evidence is generally of no consequence.[1] Although the statutory privilege is usually couched in the language of a prohibition and forbids *the physician from testifying,* it is given a broad and liberal construction to carry out its policy.[2] While there is a conflict of opinion on some of the questions, most of the courts have so construed the statute as to extend its application not merely to the testimony of the physician on the witness stand, but also, in many cases, to a pleading, affidavit, proof of death, certificate of death, hospital record, or, sometimes, a public record, if any of these tends in any degree, however remote or in-

---

[1] Davis v. Supreme Lodge, K. of P., (1900) 165 N. Y. 159, 163, 58 N. E. 891; Poses v. Travelers Ins. Co., (1935) 245 App. Div. 304, 281 N. Y. S. 126 (affidavit of physician); Schamberg v. Whitman, (1912) 75 Misc. 215, 135 N. Y. S. 262, aff'd 151 App. Div. 939, 135 N. Y. S. 1141.

[2] Buffalo Loan, Trust & Safe Deposit Co. v. Knights Templar and Masonic Mut. Aid Ass'n., (1891) 126 N. Y. 450, 27 N. E. 942.

direct, to disclose information or matters within the protection of the privilege, unless, of course, the seal of secrecy is expressly or impliedly removed by the patient himself or by the holder of the privilege.[3]

62. Pleadings

The statute prohibits a physician from disclosing privileged matters in a pleading as well as on the witness stand. Therefore, allegations in a petition to recover the value of services rendered by the plaintiff as a surgeon, which disclose confidential information obtained by the physician while attending the defendant and which was necessary to enable him to prescribe or act for the defendant, are improper and should be stricken out on motion.[1]

---

[1] Schamberg v. Whitman, (1912) 75 Misc. 215, 135 N. Y. S. 262, aff'd 151 App. Div. 939, 135 N. Y. S. 1141.

63. Hospital Records and Physicians' Office Records as Evidence: Apart From Physician-Patient Privilege

The term "hospital records" generally means the records, charts, and memoranda which relate to the hospitalization, diagnosis, and treatment of the patient; also data obtained from laboratory tests and x-ray examinations, and, in general, the medical history of the patient, past and present. These usually cover a wide range of information concerning the patient. If he was brought to the hospital as the result of an accident, his statement, or perhaps that of someone with him, as to the manner and place of the accident is sometimes recorded. These records and entries usually are made, in the course of the routine business of the hospital, by physicians, nurses, internes, or by other persons acting under the direction of the management or members of the hospital staff.

Hospital records have long been the subject of controversy in the law of evidence.[1] At first, the courts were reluctant to regard them in the same category as regular business entries and therefore

---

[3] These are discussed separately in subsequent sections. Questions pertaining to waiver are discussed in c.c. XVI, XVIII, herein.

[1] See excellent annotations: 75 A. L. R. 378; 120 A. L. R. 1124; 38 A. L. R. 2d 778, 44 A. L. R. 2d 553. See also 26 Am. Jur., Hospitals and Asylums, § 6.

excluded them as evidence.[2] The chief objection, of course, is that such records are mere hearsay. In the course of time, however, many courts have come to realize that hospital records, made in the regular course of business by those who have a competent knowledge of the facts recorded and a self-interest to be served through the accuracy of the entries made and kept with knowledge that they will be relied upon in a systematic conduct of such business, are accurate and trustworthy;[3] and, to avoid the necessity and thereby the expense, inconvenience and sometimes the impossibility of calling as witnesses the attendants, nurses and physicians who have collaborated to make the hospital record of a patient, a respectable number of courts have admitted such record in evidence under certain conditions or qualifications.[4]

Today the liberal trend towards the recognition that hospital records are entitled to admission under the common law exception for Regular Business Entries has been notably advanced by the wide-spread adoption of the federal Model Act,[5] and the Uniform Business Records as Evidence Act.[6] These have greatly simplified

---

[2] McCormick, The Use of Hospital Records as Evidence, (1952) 26 Tulane L. Rev. 371; Hale, Hospital Records as Evidence, (1941) 14 So. Calif. L. Rev. 99.

For discussion of the common law rule, see Austin, Hospital Records in Evidence, (1935) 13 Chi-Kent L. Rev. 347.

In all fairness, it should be remembered that "early records were meager in their information and were not kept in today's orderly and systematic manner; they were not as reliable as the modern medical record in the hospital." Hayt, Hayt and Groeschel, Law of Hospital, Physician and Patient, (2d ed. 1952) p. 676.

[3] Globe Indemnity Co. v. Reinhart, (1927) 152 Md. 439, 137 Atl. 43 (splendid discussion).

[4] Weis v. Weis, (1947) 147 Ohio St. 416, 72 N. E. 2d 245, 169 A. L. R. 668. See also 6 Wigmore, Evidence, § 1707; McCormick, Evidence, § 290.

[5] 28 U. S. C. § 1732 (as amended 1951).

"The statute was designed to bring the realities of business and professional practice into the courtroom in usable form." Korte v. New York, N. H. & H. R. R., (1951) 191 F. 2d 86, cert. denied 342 U. S. 868, 96 Law Ed. 952, 72 Su. Ct. 108.

[6] e.g., (1953) Ohio Rev. Code, § 2317.40. More than one-third of the states have enacted laws patterned after the Model Act, or the Uniform Act.

For differences between these two acts, see Norville, the Uniform Business Records as Evidence Act, (1948) 27 Ore. L. Rev. 188.

See also Rule 62 (13) of the Uniform Rules of Evidence (1953), and Rule 514 of the Model Code of Evidence (1943).

The English statute, Evidence Act, [1938] 1 & 2 Geo. VI, c. 28, is broader in scope than the American statutes.

the common law requirements for the admission of such records. Moreover, they embody a definition of "business" so broad as to leave no doubt that hospital records come within their terms.[7]

There is considerable conflict among the cases, however, with respect to the content of hospital records that is properly admissible under the Model and the Uniform Acts.[8] Various hospital records, or portions thereof, have been held inadmissible on the ground, either that they did not record observable facts or conditions, or that they were records of opinion and speculation, or that they included events or narrations such as those pertaining to the cause of a patient's injury and the circumstances attending the accident, and having no reference to his treatment or medical or surgical history in the hospital. There is a lamentable lack of harmony in the decisions involving some of these matters.[9] However, one rule that seems to be fairly well established is that hospital records and charts, properly identified and supported by a proper foundation, are admissible, when not privileged, to prove diagnosis, treatment, or medical history of the patient pertinent to the medical and surgical aspects of the case;[10] but the fact that hearsay and self-serving statements concerning the manner in which a patient sustained an injury are contained in a hospital record does not render them admissible in evidence under the Model Act or the Uniform Act, at least when they are offered by the patient.[11] Nor, generally speak-

---

[7] Ulm v. Moore-McCormack Lines, (1940) 115 F. 2d 492, cert. denied 313 U. S. 567, 85 Law Ed. 1525, 61 Su. Ct. 941; Loper v. Morrison, (1944) 23 Cal. 2d 600, 145 P. 2d 1; Borucki v. MacKenzie Bros. Inc., (1938) 125 Conn. 92, 3 A. 2d 224.

[8] See note, 38 A. L. R. 2d 778, for admissibility of hospital record relating to intoxication or sobriety of patient.

[9] The following articles or case notes discuss many of these conditions and qualifications.

Green, Business Records as Evidence, (1954) 16 Georgia B. J. 383; Admissibility of Hospital Records, (1953) 3 DePaul L. Rev. 134; McCormick, infra note 2; Ginsburg, The Admissibility of Business Records as Evidence, (1950) 29 Neb. L. Rev. 60; Scallen, Hospital Records in Evidence—Some Limitations on Their Use, (1948) 15 Ins. Counsel J. 73; Norville, infra note 6; Admissibility of Hospital Records in Evidence: Federal Shop Book Statute, (1945) 54 Yale L. J. 868; Brock, Hospital Records as Evidence Under the Federal Business Records Act, (1945) 23 Tex. L. Rev. 178; Hale, infra note 2. See also Hayt, Hayt and Groeschel, op. cit. infra note 2, at pp. 676-690.

[10] Weis v. Weis, (1947) 147 Ohio St. 416, 72 N. E. 2d 245, 169 A. L. R. 668.

[11] A large number of cases involve this problem. Representative decisions are: New

ing, will the fact that it may be important for a physician to know how an injury occurred in order to diagnose the case properly, make the patient's statements to him as recorded in the hospital records admissible in evidence as proof by the injured person of the circumstances of the accident.[12] But hospital records may be admitted in evidence where it is possible to cover up or eliminate the inadmissible portions relating to the circumstances of the accident.[13]

The records of a practicing physician, made in the course of his professional service, are, when not privileged, admissible as documentary evidence under the Business Records Acts in the same manner, to the same effect and subject to the same restrictions as hospital records. The fact that the person who made the record is available to testify does not make the written proof inadmissible. Thus, memoranda or records of a physician made at the time of consultation and including a statement of the patient's complaints, the results of his examination, and the treatment prescribed, were held admissible as evidence of the facts therein contained under the Business Records Act.[14] The act applies as well to the records of

York Life Ins. Co. v. Taylor, (1944) 147 F. 2d 297, (1946) 158 F. 2d 328. See also notes in (1945) 23 Tex. L. Rev. 178 and (1944) 18 So. Calif. L. Rev. 60; Watts v. Delaware Coach Co., (1948) 44 Del. 283, 58 A. 2d 689; Valenti v. Mayer, (1942) 301 Mich. 551, 4 N. W. 2d 5; Melton v. St. Louis Pub. Service Co., (1952) 363 Mo. 474, 251 S. W. 2d 663; Brown v. Saint Paul City Ry., (1954) 241 Minn. 15, 62 N. W. 2d 688, 44 A. L. R. 2d 535; Williams v. Alexander, (1955) 309 N. Y. 283, 129 N. E. 2d 417; Hodge v. Lyford, (1948) 298 N. Y. 651, 82 N. E. 2d 40; Roberto v. Neilson, (1942) 288 N. Y. 581, 42 N. E. 2d 27; Geroeami v. Fancy Fruit & Produce Corp., (1936) 249 App. Div. 221, 291 N. Y. S. 837; Perry v. Industrial Comm'n., (1954) 160 Ohio St. 520, 117 N. E. 2d 34; Green v. Cleveland, (1948) 150 Ohio St. 441, 83 N. E. 2d 63; Commonwealth v. Harris, (1945) 351 Pa. 325, 41 A. 2d 688.

For other cases see notes in 44 A. L. R. 2d 553; 38 A. L. R. 2d 778; 144 A. L. R. 727.

[12] Brown v. Saint Paul City Ry., (1954) 241 Minn. 15, 62 N. W. 2d 688, 44 A. L. R. 2d 535. *Cf.* Watts Delaware Coach Co., (1948) 44 Del. 283, 58 A. 2d 689; Melton v. St. Louis Pub. Service Co., (1952) 363 Mo. 474, 251 S. W. 2d 663.

[13] Brown v. Saint Paul City Ry., (1954) 241 Minn. 15, 62 N. W. 2d 688, 44 A. L. R. 2d 535.

[14] Freedman v. Mutual Life Ins. Co., (1941) 342 Pa. 404, 21 A. 2d 81, 135 A. L. R. 1249. Drew, J., (p. 413): "Those by whom the records were made are not parties to this action and have no interest in its termination or incentive to falsify the relevant facts. They personally examined the insured and prescribed for him. They heard his statements of symptoms made for the purpose of medical treatment. These facts were recorded at the time they transpired and in the course of the professional business of

》》》→

prescriptions prepared by a pharmacist, and to a cardiogram prepared under proper circumstances by a physician, and such records are competent documentary evidence.[15] A physician's office record, when verified and adopted by him as a witness, is admissible as a past recollection recorded, without the necessity of invoking the federal act.[16] A physician's office record concerning the condition of his patient was held admissible even though in some instances he may have delayed for as long as two weeks in transcribing his notes from his daily memoranda to his office records.[17]

A hospital record or chart, a physician's office record, or a nurse's memoranda, whether admissible or not as evidence, may, under proper circumstances, be used by a physician or nurse, when testifying as a witness, to refresh his or her recollection of the matters therein stated.[18].

64. Same: As Affected by Privilege

As previously stated, in most of the jurisdictions hospital records and physicians' office records, when properly made and

---

←≪

physicians. They were fully as competent to compile these records as those by whom the records of the usual hospital are prepared."

Physician's office memoranda and records were held admissible in Croll v. John Hancock Mut. Life Ins. Co., (1952) 198 F. 2d 562; Ettelson v. Metropolitan Life Ins. Co., (1947) 164 F. 2d 660; Adler v. New York Life Ins. Co., (1929) 33 F. 2d 827; Weis v. Weis, (1947) 147 Ohio St. 416, 72 N. E. 2d 245, 169 A. L. R. 668; Glickman v. Prudential Ins. Co., (1942) 151 Pa. Sup. 52, 29 A. 2d 224. See note, 135 A. L. R. 1258.

[15] Freedman v. Mutual Life Ins. Co., (1941) 342 Pa. 404, 21 A. 2d 81, 135 A. L. R. 1249. Cardiograms are also admissible under the federal Model Act. Croll v. John Hancock Mut. Life Ins. Co., (1952) 198 F. 2d 562; Ettelson v. Metropolitan Life Ins. Co., (1947) 164 F. 2d 660.

But cf. Fries v. Goldsby, (1956) 163 Neb. 424, 80 N. W. 2d 171 and note, (1957) 36 Neb. L. Rev. 600.

[16] Ettelson v. Metropolitan Life Ins. Co., (1947) 164 F. 2d 660.

[17] Croll v. John Hancock Mut. Life Ins. Co., (1952) 198 F. 2d 562. Depending upon the circumstances, letters passing between the plaintiff's physicians and the railroad's medical examiner may or may not be admissible as regular business entries. See Korte v. New York, New Haven & H. R. R., (1951) 191 F. 2d 86, cert. denied 342 U. S. 868, 96 Law Ed. 952, 72 Su. Ct. 108. See notes: (1952) 37 Corn. L. Q. 290; (1952) 5 U. of Fla. L. Rev. 112.

See also Masterson v. Pennsylvania R. R., (1950) 182 F. 2d 793.

[18] See § 105, herein.

identified, may be admitted in evidence on behalf of a patient,[1] but, as a general rule, they are inadmissible against a patient or his privy in interest, in jurisdictions which have enacted laws prohibiting the disclosure of confidential communications between physician and patient. In the absence of consent or waiver by the patient or by the holder of the privilege, such records are plainly within the scope and spirit, if not the letter, of such statutes. It would be ironical indeed to hold that a physician might make up a hospital or office record pertaining to the nature and treatment of a patient's ailment or injury and present such record to be introduced in evidence and yet hold that the same physician, because of the privilege statute, would not be permitted to disclose the same confidential information on the witness stand.[2] On the other hand, in those states where there is no privilege and the common law rule is still in force, a hospital record when properly made and identified and otherwise admissible, cannot be excluded on the ground of privilege.[3] It should, perhaps, be noticed that in many cases the courts have admitted hospital records in evidence despite a possible privilege but have usually held that the privilege was not claimed, or that it did not exist, or, if it existed, that it had been waived.[4] Furthermore,

---

[1] § 63, herein.

[2] Smart v. Kansas City, (1907) 208 Mo. 162, 198, 105 S. W. 709, 14 L. R. A. (n. s.) 565, 13 Ann. Cas. 932: "It seems that it must follow as a natural sequence that when the physician subsequently copies that privileged communication upon the record of the hospital, it still remains privileged. If that is not true, then the law which prevents the hospital physician from testifying to such matters could be violated both in letter and spirit and the statute nullified by the physician copying into the record all the information acquired by him from his patient, and then offer or permit the record to be offered in evidence containing the diagnosis, and thereby accomplish, by indirection, that which is expressly prohibited in a direct manner."

See also Matter of Coddington, (1954) 307 N. Y. 181, 120 N. E. 2d 777; Lorde v. Guardian Life Ins. Co., (1937) 252 App. Div. 646, 300 N. Y. S. 721; Vilardi v. Vilardi, (1951) 200 Misc. 1043, 107 N. Y. S. 2d 342; Kinbacher v. Schneider, (1949) 194 Misc. 969, 89 N. Y. S. 2d 350; Eikenberry v. McFall, (1941) _____ Ohio App. _____, 33 Ohio Law Abst. 525, 36 N. E. 2d 27.

[3] Florida Power & L. Co. v. Bridgeman, (1938) 133 Fla. 195, 182 So. 911.

[4] Hospital records made in connection with physical examinations made of decedent by his employer's physicians are not privileged where such examinations did not include treatment or advice and were not made to alleviate his pain or cure his malady.

Suetta v. Carnegie Illinois Steel Co., (1955) _____ Ohio App. _____, 144 N. E. 2d 292.

⟫→

in a number of jurisdictions, the legislatures have denied the right to exercise the privilege in actions for damages for personal injury, malpractice, or for the death of the patient; in actions brought under Workmens' Compensation laws; in criminal prosecutions; and in other designated classes of actions. Hence, hospital records and physicians' office records may be introduced in evidence in such actions, unless otherwise inadmissible.

It is generally conceded by the courts, federal and state, that hospital records concerning diagnosis or treatment of the patient are plainly within the scope and purpose of the physician-patient privilege statutes.[5] However, there are some variations in state doctrines.

Other citations are unnecessary here since the questions involved are dealt with elsewhere.

[5] Ferguson v. Quaker City Life Ins. Co., (1957) ......D. C.......,, 129 A. 2d 189; Buckminster's Estate v. Commissioner of Internal Revenue, (1944) 147 F. 2d 331; Kaplan v. Manhattan Life Ins. Co., (1939) 71 App. D. C. 250, 109 F. 2d 463; Munzer v. Swedish American Line, (1940) 35 F. Supp. 493; Young v. McLaughlin, (1952) 126 Colo. 188, 247 P. 2d 813; Metropolitan Life Ins. Co. v. Kaufman, (1939) 104 Colo. 13, 87 P. 2d 758; Stalker v. Breeze, (1917) 186 Ind. 221, 114 N. E. 968; In re Nickel's Estate, (1948) 321 Mich. 519, 32 N. W. 2d 733; Harvey v. Silber, (1942) 300 Mich. 510, 2 N. W. 2d 483; Massachusetts Mut. Life Ins. Co. v. Board of Trustees, (1913) 178 Mich. 193, 144 N. W. 538, 51 L. R. A. (n. s.) 22, Ann. Cas. 1915 D 146; Ost v. Ulring, (1940) 207 Minn. 500, 292 N. W. 207; Price v. Standard Life & Acc. Ins. Co., (1903) 90 Minn. 264, 95 N. W. 1118; Metropolitan Life Ins. Co. v. McSwain, (1927) 149 Miss. 455, 115 So. 555; Fitzgerald v. Metropolitan Life Ins. Co., (1941) ......Mo. App......., 149 S. W. 2d 389; Gilpin v. Aetna Life Ins. Co., (1939) 234 Mo. App. 566, 132 S. W. 2d 686; Key v. Cosmopolitan Life, H. & Acc. Ins. Co., (1937) ......Mo. App......, 102 S. W. 2d 797; Vermillion v. Prudential Ins. Co., (1936) 230 Mo. App. 993, 93 S. W. 2d 45; Rush v. Metropolitan Life Ins. Co., (1933) ......Mo. App......, 63 S. W. 2d 453; O'Donnell v. O'Donnell, (1943) 142 Neb. 706, 7 N. W. 2d 647; Matter of Coddington, (1954) 307 N. Y. 181, 120 N. E. 2d 777; Matter of New York City Council v. Goldwater, (1940) 284 N. Y. 296, 31 N. E. 2d 31, 133 A. L. R. 728; Rarogiewicz v. Brotherhood of American Yeomen, (1926) 242 N. Y. 590, 152 N. E. 440; Hurd v. Republic Steel Corp., (1949) 275 App. Div. 725, 87 N. Y. S. 2d 64; Thompson v. Prudential Ins. Co., (1943) 266 App. Div. 783, 41 N. Y. S. 2d 621; Sparer v. Travelers Ins. Co., (1919) 185 App. Div. 861, 173 N. Y. S. 673; Griebel v. Brooklyn Heights R. R., (1904) 95 App. Div. 214, 88 N. Y. S. 767, aff'd 184 N. Y. 528, 76 N. E. 1096; Palmer v. John Hancock Mut. Life Ins. Co., (1934) 150 Misc. 669, 270 N. Y. S. 10; Vilardi v. Vilardi, (1951) 200 Misc. 1043, 107 N. Y. S. 2d 342; In re Erickson's Will, (1951) 200 Misc. 1005, 106 N. Y. S. 2d 203; In re Handwerger, (1947) 79 N. Y. S. 2d 634; Weis v. Weis, (1947) 147 Ohio St. 416, 72 N. E. 2d 245, 169 A. L. R. 668; McLaughlin v. Massachusetts Indemnity Ins. Co., (1948) 85 Ohio App. 511, 84 N. E. 2d 114 (veteran's medical record in possession of Veterans' Administration); Lamarand v. National Life & Acc. Ins. Co., (1937) 58 Ohio App. 415, 16 N. E. 2d 701; Prudential

In Pennsylvania the record or chart of a hospitalized patient is usually admissible in evidence since the statute of that state is restricted to communications made by the patient to the physician which "tend to blacken his character," and does not prohibit the disclosure of information obtained by the physician by his personal examination.[6] In Louisiana, hospital records may be introduced in civil cases only.[7] In Mississippi, the statutory privilege does not apply to hospital records where the law itself requires the disclosure of the condition of patients.[8] The Supreme Court of Ohio has held that hospital records which do not contain any diagnosis or report on the condition of the patient by the attending physician or any record of communications between him and the patient are not privileged,[9] especially where no evidence is offered showing that the records were made from statements made by the patient to the

---

Ins. Co. v. Heaton, (1935) _____ Ohio App._____, 20 Ohio Law Abst. 454; Randa v. Bear, (1957) _____Wash._____, 312 P. 2d 640; Toole v. Franklin Inv. Co., (1930) 158 Wash. 696, 291 Pac. 1101; Hansen v. Sandvik, (1924) 128 Wash. 60, 222 Pac. 205; Mehegan v. Faber, (1914) 158 Wis. 645, 149 N. W. 397.

[6] Soltaniuk v. Metropolitan Life Ins. Co., (1938) 133 Pa. Super. 139, 2 A. 2d 501. In Platt v. John Hancock Mut. Life Ins. Co., (1949) 361 Pa. 652, 66 A. 2d 266, hospital records of the insured were introduced in evidence by defendant to show the facts of hospitalization, diagnosis, treatment prescribed and symptoms given, but it does not appear affirmatively that the question of privilege was considered.

[7] Shepard v. Whitney National Bank, (1938) _____La. App._____, 177 So. 825. The privilege statute appears in the criminal code and does not apply in civil cases.

[8] Motley v. State, (1936) 174 Miss. 568, 165 So. 296. The hospital for the insane was created by law and its Board of Trustees was required to visit it twice a year and, at each visitation, to carefully examine the hospital register containing the diagnosis of the case of each patient. In an earlier case the records of a *general* hospital were held privileged. Metropolitan Life Ins. Co. v. McSwain, (1927) 149 Miss. 455, 115 So. 555.

[9] Weis v. Weis, (1947) 147 Ohio St. 416, 72 N. E. 2d 245, 169 A. L. R. 668. The records contained facts which seem perilously near, if not within, the ban of secrecy since they tended to disclose the mental condition of the patient, and, to some degree, his physical condition also. Hart, J., (p. 428): "The hospital records * * * consisted of the entrance slip, the physician's directions for the medication to be administered and treatment to be given the patient by the nurses, record of the analysis of the blood and urine of the patient and the day-to-day charts made and kept by the nurses who had charge of the patient while at the hospital. These charts recorded the food and medicines given and the condition and behavior of the patient to the effect that he was irrational at times; that he left his bed at unreasonable hours; * * * and that on several occasions he became unruly."

physician.[10] In Wisconsin, the ban of secrecy extends only to the testimony of the physician, not to that of nurses and hospital technicians; hence, hospital records made by the attending physician are privileged, but confidential notes and records made by a nurse, and x-ray plates made by a hospital x-ray operator which are used by the physician in treating the patient, are not privileged.[11] However, the records of a *maternity* hospital are expressly declared to be within the protection of the physician-patient privilege statute.[12]

Although the question has been raised in only a few cases,[13] it seems reasonably clear that the physician-patient privilege statutes are neither repealed nor altered by the later Business Records as Evidence Acts.[14]

In several cases it has been held that the fact that the state legislature has enacted a law, or that a city council has enacted an ordinance, which requires hospitals, public or private, to keep records of each patient, does not remove such records from the ban of secrecy

---

[10] Perry v. Industrial Comm'n., (1954) 160 Ohio St. 520, 117 N. E. 2d 34.

[11] Leusink v. O'Donnell, (1949) 255 Wis. 627, 39 N. W. 2d 675; Prudential Ins. Co. v. Kozlowski, (1938) 226 Wis. 641, 276 N. W. 300. In accord as to nurses' records, Weis v. Weis, (1947) 147 Ohio St. 416, 72 N. E. 2d 245, 169 A. L. R. 668. See also § 31, herein.

[12] (1953) Wis. Stat. § 48.44(4).

[13] Matter of Coddington, (1954) 307 N. Y. 181, 120 N. E. 2d 777; Poses v. Travelers Ins. Co., (1935) 245 App. Div. 304, 281 N. Y. S. 126; Palmer v. John Hancock Mut. Life Ins. Co., (1934) 150 Misc. 669, 270 N. Y. S. 10; Weis v. Weis, (1947) 147 Ohio St. 416, 72 N. E. 2d 245, 169 A. L. R. 668; Eikenberry v. McFall, ___ Ohio App.___, 33 Ohio Law Abst. 525, 36 N. E. 2d 27.

In Lumpkin v. Metropolitan Life Ins. Co., (1945) 75 Ohio App. 310, 62 N. E. 2d 189, it was held that hospital records were admissible under the Business Records Act notwithstanding the privilege statute. The judgment was affirmed by the Supreme Court (146 Ohio St. 25, 64 N. E. 2d 63), but the court did not find it necessary to pass on this question. Subsequently, in Weis v. Weis, infra, the court ruled that such records, under proper circumstances, are still entitled to the protection of the privilege statute.

[14] Conway, Jr., in Matter of Coddington, infra note 13 (p. 195): "Undoubtedly, parts of the hospital records were the result of 'confidential communications' and, therefore, the doctors could not have testified to such matters had they been called to the stand. We perceive no valid reason why the rule should be different merely because the objectionable matter has been reduced to writing. The purpose of section 374-a of the Civil Practice Act [Business Records Act] was to overcome the objection of the hearsay rule, not to destroy or weaken the privilege existing between physician and patient."

imposed by the privilege statute.[15] In New York, the rule is well established that the hospital records of patients of *general* hospitals, public and private, are clearly within the scope of the privilege statute, and are inadmissible in evidence when proper and timely objection is made thereto.[16] However, there has been a notable lack of harmony among the courts concerning the application of the privilege statute to the records of patients and physicians of state hospitals for the mentally ill. Some courts have held that the privilege does not apply, since the confidential relationship contemplated by the statute does not exist between the official physicians of such institutions and their patients.[17] Others have opposed this

---

[15] Smart v. Kansas City, (1907) 208 Mo. 162, 199, 105 S. W. 709, 14 L. R. A. (n. s.) 565, 13 Ann. Cas. 932: "The mere fact that the ordinance of the city requires such a record to be kept is no reason on earth why the statute regarding privileged communications should be violated. That record is required to be kept for the benefit of the institution and not for the benefit of outside litigants. It is not the object or purpose of the ordinance to repeal the statute in question, but even if it were it would be null and void, because in conflict with the statute."

Massachusetts Mut Life. Ins Co. v. Board of Trustees, (1913) 178 Mich. 193, 144 N. W. 538, 51 L. R. A. (n. s.) 22, Ann. Cas. 1915 D. 146; Galli v. Wells, (1922) 209 Mo. App. 460, 239 S. W. 894; Connor v. Metropolitan Life Ins. Co., (1899) 78 Mo. App. 131; Greff v. Havens, (1946) 186 Misc. 914, 66 N. Y. S. 2d 124; Casson v. Schoenfeld, (1918) 166 Wis. 401, 413, 166 N. W. 23, L. R. A. 1918 C. 162: "That a public record is required to be kept by such physician or institution does not affect the rule. A legislative provision for the filing of certain documents as public reports by physicians is not a legislative declaration that the secrecy of section 4075 [privilege statute] as to physicians has been relaxed."

Contra: Allen v. American Life & Acc. Ins. Co., (1938) _____Mo. App_____, 119 S. W. 2d 450; Wills, Adm'r. v. National Life & Acc. Ins. Co., (1928) 28 Ohio App. 497, 162 N. E. 822. Records of the Cleveland City Hospital showing that the insured died of tuberculosis were admitted in evidence over objection that they were privileged. The decision is unsound and was not followed in Lamarand v. National Life &. Acc. Ins. Co., (1937) 58 Ohio App. 415, 16 N. E. 2d 701.

[16] See New York cases cited in note 5, infra.

The insurance carrier of a patient against whom a hospital lien has been filed is not entitled to examine the records of the hospital as to the care, treatment, and maintenance of the patient, if this would result in the disclosure of confidential communications. Matter of Larchmont Gables, Inc., (1946) 188 Misc. 164, 64 N. Y. S. 2d 623.

[17] Scolavino v. State, (1946) 187 Misc. 253, 62 N. Y. S. 2d 17, modified as to damages 271 App. Div. 618, 67 N. Y. S. 2d 202, aff'd. as modified 297 N. Y. 460, 74 N. E. 2d 174; Munzer v. Blaisdell, (1944) 183 Misc. 773, 49 N. Y. S. 2d 915, aff'd. 269 App. Div. 970, 58 N. Y. S. 2d 359; Liske v. Liske, (1912) 135 N. Y. S. 176; Matter of Maryland

>>>→

view.[18] But the conflict now appears to be completely resolved and there can be no longer any doubt that information obtained by a physician employed by a state institution for the mentally ill in the course of a diagnosis and treatment of a patient committed to its care, and the hospital records of such patient, are privileged communications within the broad meaning of the physician-patient privilege statute.[19]

The New York rule relating to the *availability* of such records is not so clear. The Mental Hygiene Law makes accessible for inspection under proper safeguards, the hospital records of patients of state hospitals and institutions for the care and treatment of the insane; notwithstanding their privileged character and the statutory rule of testimonial privilege.[20] In the light of its provisions, such records enjoy no such absolute privilege against disclosure that only the patient can waive it. The Mental Hygiene Law clearly provides that case records may be *accessible* to anyone,[21] without consulting the patient, but only after the commissioner or judge of a court of record has passed upon the propriety of the requested inspection.[22] It will be observed that the law treats the contents of the case records as privileged communications, and that it imposes a duty upon officials in charge of the institutions not to make such records available to anyone, except in accordance with its provisions.[23] Thus, the

---

←

Casualty Co., (1948) 274 App. Div. 211, 80 N. Y. S. 2d 181. (hospital records admissible at a hearing of a claim prosecuted under Workmens' Compensation Law.)

[18] Westphal v. State, (1948) 191 Misc. 688, 79 N. Y. S. 2d 634; Greff v. Havens, (1946) 186 Misc. 914, 66 N. Y. S. 2d 124; McGrath v. State, (1950) 200 Misc. 165, 104 N. Y. S. 2d 882; Munzer v. State, (1943) 41 N. Y. S. 2d 98.

[19] Matter of Coddington (1954) 307 N. Y. 181, 120 N. E. 2d 777; La Plante v. Garrett, (1953) 282 App. Div. 1096, 126 N. Y. S. 2d 470; Eder v. Cashin, (1953) 281 App. Div. 456, 120 N. Y. S. 2d 165; Jaffe v. New York, (1949) 196 Misc. 710, 94 N. Y. S. 2d 60; Kinbacher v. Schneider, (1949) 194 Misc. 969, 89 N. Y. S. 2d 350; *In re* Grabau's Will, (1948) 193 Misc. 859, 85 N. Y. S. 2d 748; *In re* Handwerger, (1947) 79 N. Y. S. 2d 634.

[20] Pertinent sections of the law are § 20 and § 34(9).

[21] We are not here concerned *with evidence offered upon a trial or examination.*

[22] Scolavino v. State, (1946) 187 Misc. 253, 62 N. Y. S. 2d 17, modified as to damages 271 App. Div. 618, 67 N. Y. S. 2d 202, aff'd. as modified 297 N. Y. 460, 74 N. E. 2d 174; *In re* Grabau's Will, (1948) 193 Misc. 859, 85 N. Y. S. 2d 748.

[23] The Code of Hospital Ethics adopted by the American Hospital Association and

⟫→

intent and purpose of the Mental Hygiene Law, with respect to this subject, appears to be two-fold: to make the records of state hospitals for the mentally ill accessible, under close supervision of the commissioner or the court, when they are needed for the discovery of the truth and a proper determination of the matter in issue;[24] to prevent officials of such institutions from disclosing information imparted to them for the purpose of care and treatment, and thus save patients from humiliation, embarrassment, and disgrace.[25]

The Mental Hygiene Law does not repeal or vitiate the physician-patient privilege statute; on the contrary, it indicates the intention of the legislature to keep and protect state hospital records as privileged communications to be made accessible only when the provisions of the law as to release are met.[26] Moreover, it does not apply to *private or general* hospitals,[27] nor to institutions other than state hospitals for the insane.[28]

←⧼

the American College of Surgeons stipulates that "it is the responsibility of the hospital and its personnel to safeguard the clinical records of the patients and to see that such records are available only to properly authorized individuals or bodies." Hayt, Hayt and Groeschel, Law of Hospital, Physician and Patient, (2d ed. 1952) p. 641.

[24] *In re* Grabau's Will, (1948) 193 Misc. 859, 85 N. Y. S. 2d 748.

[25] Munzer v. Blaisdell, (1944) 183 Misc. 773, 49 N. Y. S. 2d 915, aff'd. 269 App. Div. 970, 58 N. Y. S. 2d 359, holding that where the statutory duty is violated, the patient is entitled to redress; therefore, an action for damages will lie for the wrongful disclosure of the contents of the patient's case record.

[26] Matter of Warrington, (1951) 303 N. Y. 129, 100 N. E. 2d 170; La Plante v. Garrett, (1953) 282 App. Div. 1096, 126 N. Y. S. 2d 470; Jaffe v. New York, (1949) 196 Misc. 710, 94 N. Y. S. 2d 60; Kinbacher v. Schneider, (1949) 194 Misc. 969, 89 N. Y. S. 2d 350; Westphal v. State, (1948) 191 Misc. 688, 79 N. Y. S. 2d 634; Greff v. Havens, (1946) 186 Misc. 914, 66 N. Y. S. 2d 124; McGrath v. State, (1950) 200 Misc. 165, 104 N. Y. S. 2d 882; Munzer v. State, (1943) 41 N. Y. S. 2d 98.

[27] Matter of Maryland Casualty Co., (1948) 274 App. Div. 211, 213, 80 N. Y. S. 2d 181: "Subdivision 9 of section 34 of the Mental Hygiene Law has no application to Bellevue Hospital. * * * Bellevue Hospital is not a state institution and its records, even if they relate to the mental condition of a patient, do not come within the purview of this section of the Mental Hygiene Law."

Matter of Fitzgerald, (1954) 133 N. Y. S. 2d 779.

[28] Lee v. State, (1944) 183 Misc. 615, 49 N. Y. S. 2d 836. The Mental Hygiene Law does not apply to an application for inspection of records by an inmate of a school for mental defectives.

Generally speaking, the privilege belongs to the patient; it is his to control as he sees fit.[29] The state cannot invoke it for its own benefit.[30] If the patient is unable to act for himself, his committee, or, if the patient has died, any other authorized person, may act in his stead to enforce the right to an inspection of the patient's hospital records. Where the committee of an incompetent person confined in a state hospital applied to the Court of Claims for an order permitting inspection of hospital records to determine whether the state or any of its employees were guilty of negligence when the patient fell in the hospital and sustained injuries, the court had authority, under the Mental Hygiene Law, to enter the order.[31] In an action by a public administrator against the state to recover damages for the death of plaintiff's decedent as the result of a fall while a patient in a state hospital, a judge of the Court of Claims had authority to issue an order permitting plaintiff to inspect the hospital records even though such records were privileged for the benefit of the patient.[32] Where, however, an action for damages for personal injury was brought against the state by a patient who was brutally assaulted by another patient, it was held that the plaintiff's right to inspect the records of the state hospital extended only

---

[29] Matter of Warrington, (1951) 303 N. Y. 129, 100 N. E. 2d 170; Matter of Weiss, (1955) 208 Misc. 1010, 147 N. Y. S. 2d 455;Becker v. New York, (1955) 208 Misc. 744, 145 N. Y. S. 2d 22; Hoyt v. Cornwall Hospital, (1938) 169 Misc. 361, 6 N. Y. S. 2d 1014; Romano v. Mount Sinai Hospital, (1956) 150 N. Y. S. 2d 246; In re Handwerger, (1947) 79 N. Y. S. 2d 634. See also § 16, herein. The guardian ad litem of an infant may waive the privilege in an action brought by him for damages for personal injuries suffered by the infant resulting from the alleged negligence of the state. Van Heuverzwyn v. State, (1954) 206 Misc. 896, 134 N. Y. S. 2d 922.

[30] Matter of Warrington, (1951) 303 N. Y. 129, 100 N. E. 2d 170; Matter of Weiss, (1955) 208 Misc. 1010, 147 N. Y. S. 2d 455; Hoyt v. Cornwall Hospital, (1938) 169 Misc. 361, 6 N. Y. S. 2d 1014. In Kinbacher v. Schneider, (1949) 194 Misc. 969, 89 N. Y. S. 2d 350, objection by the state was sustained, but the request for inspection was not made by a proper person.

[31] Matter of Warrington, (1951) 303 N. Y. 129, 100 N. E. 2d 170. See also Matter of Weiss, (1955) 208 Misc. 1010, 147 N. Y. S. 2d 455; Romano v. Mount Sinai Hospital, (1956) 150 N. Y. S. 2d 246.

[32] Mulligan v. State, (1951) 303 N. Y. 129, 100 N. E. 2d 170. This case was argued in conjunction with the Warrington Case, infra note 31. See also Matter of Greenberg, (1949) 196 Misc. 809, 89 N. Y. S. 2d 807; Buchalter v. State, (1939) 172 Misc. 420, 15 N. Y. S. 2d 244; McGrath v. State, (1950) 200 Misc. 165, 104 N. Y. S. 2d 882.

to his own records and not to those of his assailant, except as to such facts in the latter's records which were not confidential and therefore outside the protection of the privilege statute.[33]

Of course, if the statutory privilege is the only bar to the admissibility of a hospital record in evidence, a waiver of the privilege will permit its introduction.[34]

Not all recitals in a hospital record or in a physician's office record are privileged from disclosure, but only those, generally speaking, that disclose information regarding the nature and extent of the patient's injury or ailment, or the symptoms, diagnosis, and treatment thereof. Non-confidential facts are no more within the protection of the statute than is the testimony of the physician himself concerning them.[35] Hospital records, therefore, may be admitted in evidence to show the name, age and address of the patient,[36] dates of entry and discharge;[37] name of attending physician;[38] facts obvious to anyone;[39] time or times the physician attended the patient;[40] that

---

[33] Panella v. United States, (1956) 139 F. Supp. 159; Westphal v. State, (1948) 191 Misc. 688, 79 N. Y. S. 2d 634; McGrath v. State (1950) 200 Misc. 165, 104 N. Y. S. 2d 882.

[34] Questions relating to waiver of the privilege are discussed in c. c. XVI, XVIII, herein.

[35] See § 47, herein.

[36] In re Albert Lindley Lee Memorial Hospital, (1953) 209 F. 2d 122, cert. denied Cincotta v. United States, 347 U. S. 960, 98 Law. Ed. 1104, 74 Su. Ct. 709; Kaplan v. Manhattan Life Ins. Co., (1939) 71 App. D. C. 250, 109 F. 2d 463; Matter of Meyer, (1954) 206 Misc. 368, 132 N. Y. S. 2d 825; Willig v. Prudential Ins. Co., (1942) 71 Ohio App. 255, 49 N. E. 2d 421.

[37] In re Albert Lindley Lee Memorial Hospital, infra note 36; Ranger, Inc. v. Equitable Life Assur. Soc., (1952) 196 F. 2d 968; In re Nickel's Estate, (1948) 321 Mich. 519, 32 N. W. 2d 733; Rubin v. Equitable Life Assur. Soc., (1945) 269 App. Div. 677, 53 N. Y. S. 2d 351; Lorde v. Guardian Life Ins. Co., (1937) 252 App. Div. 646, 300 N. Y. S. 721; Westphal v. State, (1948) 191 Misc. 688, 79 N. Y. S. 2d 634; McGrath v. State, (1950) 200 Misc. 165, 104 N. Y. S. 2d 882; Willig v. Prudential Ins. Co., (1942) 71 Ohio App. 255, 49 N. E. 2d 421.

[38] In re Albert Lindley Lee Memorial Hospital, (1953) 209 F. 2d 122, cert. denied Cincotta v. United States, 347 U. S. 960, 98 Law. Ed. 1104, Su. Ct. 709; Lorde v. Guardian Life Ins. Co., (1937) 252 App. Div. 646, 300 N. Y. S. 721; Westphal v. State, (1948) 191 Misc. 688, 79 N. Y. S. 2d 634; McGrath v. State, (1950) 201 Misc. 165, 104 N. Y. S. 2d 882; Willig v. Prudential Ins. Co., (1942) 71 Ohio App. 255, 49 N. E. 2d 421.

[39] In re Albert Lindley Lee Memorial Hospital, (1953) 209 F. 2d 122, cert. denied Cincotta v. United States, 347 U. S. 960, 98 Law. Ed. 1104, 74 Su. Ct. 709; Matter of Coddington, (1954) 307 N. Y. 181, 120 N. E. 2d 777; Lorde v. Guardian Life Ins. Co., (1937) 252 App. Div. 646, 300 N. Y. S. 721; Westphal v. State, (1948) 191 Misc. 688, 79 N. Y. S.

➤

an operation was performed;[41] whether the patient was sick[42] what an autopsy revealed;[43] date of birth of the patient's child, its weight, length and condition at time of birth;[44] prior escapes and previous assaults made by a patient of a state hospital.[45] Of course, all precautions must be taken which are necessary to insure that confidential communications and information contained in the records, which are plainly within the protection of the privilege, are not disclosed at the time that the non-privileged matters are introduced in evidence.

65. Public Records: In General

The well-established rule is that official records and written reports of a public nature which public officers are required by law to keep, made either by the officers themselves or under their supervision, are ordinarily admissible in evidence as proof of the facts recorded therein, so far as they are relevant and material to the issue on trial, although their authenticity be not confirmed by the usual and ordinary tests of truth, the obligation of an oath and the power of cross-examining the parties on whose authority the truth of the record or report depends.[1] Such records do not, as a general rule, import absolute verity, but are treated as prima facie evidence of the truth of that which they purport to state.

2d 634; McGrath v. State, (1950) 200 Misc. 165, 104 N. Y. S. 2d 882.

[40] In re Albert Lindley Lee Memorial Hospital, (1953) 209 F. 2d 122, cert. denied Cincotta v. United States, 347 U. S. 960, 98 Law. Ed. 1104, 74 Su. Ct. 709; Ranger, Inc. v. Equitable Life Assur. Soc., (1952) 196 F. 2d 968; In re Nickel's Estate, (1948) 321 Mich. 519, 32 N. W. 2d 733; Rubin v. Equitable Life Assur. Soc., (1945) 269 App. Div. 677, 53 N. Y. S. 2d 351; Lorde v. Guardian Life Ins. Co., (1937) 252 App. Div. 646, 300 N. Y. S. 721; Westphal v. State, (1948) 191 Misc. 688, 79 N. Y. S. 2d 634; McGrath v. State, (1950) 200 Misc. 165, 104 N. Y. S. 2d 882.

[41] Sparer v. Travelers Ins. Co., (1919) 185 App. Div. 861, 173 N. Y. S. 673.

[42] Rubin v. Equitable Life Assur. Soc., (1945) 269 App. Div. 677, 53 N. Y. S. 2d 351.

[43] Eureka-Maryland Assur. Co. v. Gray, (1941) 74 App. D. C. 191, 121 F. 2d 104, cert. denied 314 U. S. 613, 86 Law. Ed. 494, 62 Su. Ct. 114. See also § 44, herein.

[44] Yager v. Yager, (1946) 313 Mich. 300, 21 N. W. 2d 138.

[45] Westphal v. State, (1948) 191 Misc. 688, 79 N. Y. S. 2d 634.

[1] 20 Am. Jur., Evidence, § 1023.

66. Public Health Records

It is everywhere conceded that one of the primary duties of the state is to take all necessary steps for the promotion and protection of the health and safety of its inhabitants, and whatever reasonably tends to preserve the public health is a subject upon which the legislature may take action. So well have the lawmakers kept pace with the almost incredible advance in preventive medicine and public health that it is difficult to conceive of any type of serious or infectious disease which the physician is not required by law to report to a duly constituted public health bureau or officer. In many states, the physician is required to report not only cases of communicable diseases coming under his observation or care, but also various maladies, injuries and physical defects which, however serious and dangerous to the persons afflicted, are not necessarily dangerous to the public at large.

In a broad sense, such reports and records may be classified as "public records" or "official documents," yet it seems unreasonable to suppose that the legislatures intended to make them available as such to any member of the public who might choose to make use thereof to advance some personal interest of his own. It may rightly be assumed that such records and reports are intended to aid governmental agencies and officers in the control and prevention of disease, and ought not to be open for inspection, or made available for use, by private persons.[1]

---

[1] Buffalo Loan, Trust & Safe Deposit Co. v. Knights Templar Masonic Mut. Aid Ass'n., (1891) 126 N. Y. 450, 27 N. E. 942. Mark's Appeal, (1936) 121 Pa. Super. 181, 192, 183 Atl. 432: "These records are in no true sense of the words 'public records'; they are departmental records. To thwart the important functions of the Health Department by placing their confidential data in the hands of the general public would effectively impair the important work performed by this Department in the prevention, control and treatment of infectious diseases. It is earnestly submitted that the interests of the public in protecting itself and those afflicted with dangerous infectious diseases far outweighs any benefit that insurance companies or other litigants might gain by reason of ready access to departmental records."

McGowan v. Metropolitan Life Ins. Co., (1932) 234 App. Div. 366, 367, 255 N. Y. S. 130, appeal dismissed 259 N. Y. 454, 182 N. E. 81: "To induce those who are afflicted with a communicable disease to submit to examination and treatment in an effort to eradicate such diseases and protect the public who might come in contact with those suffering from same, the department of health has established clinics for their use,

≫→

In many states, the legislatures have expressly declared certain records privileged from disclosure and have prohibited their use as evidence in any action or proceeding, except, in some instances, where their disclosure is authorized under the supervision of a court of record.[2] On the other hand, a number of states have enacted laws which make official reports and public records open to inspection by the public,[3] and prima facie evidence of the facts stated therein.[4] But the question still remains whether reports made by physicians to public boards and agencies concerning the health and condition of their patients are admissible in evidence in actions between private persons, when objection is made thereto on grounds of public policy or because such a disclosure would be a violation of the physician-patient privilege statute. There is a conflict of opinion on this subject. In *Tinsley* v. *Washington National Ins Co.,*[5]

---

with the assurance that the information thus obtained will not be divulged and that the records containing such information will not be open for inspection by the public. If that assurance cannot be relied upon, those so afflicted may refuse such aid with the result that they may endanger the health of the public at large. The security inspired by such a rule gives confidence to those requiring treatment and encourages them to cooperate with the department of health in an effort to control or eradicate such diseases." See notes, 136 A. L. R. 856; 165 A. L. R. 1302.

[2] *e. g.*, (1949) Iowa Code Ann. § 140.28: (1953) Ohio Rev. Code § 3701.25; (1953) Wis. Stat. § 140.05(11). See also Matter of Bakers Mutual Ins. Co., (1950) 301 N. Y. 21, 92 N. E. 2d 49.

There are a number of Federal statutes which relate to the disclosure or divulgence of information by specified officials or employees. The records of the Veterans' Bureau and of the War Risk Insurance Bureau, containing information concerning the physical condition of veterans, are public or quasi-public documents, but the Federal statutes protect these as privileged and confidential and under various circumstances, no disclosure of same can be made except (a) to a claimant or his representative, or (b) when required by process of a Federal court. See Chytracek v. United States, (1932) 60 F. 2d 325; Young v. Terminal R. R. Ass'n., (1947) 70 F. Supp. 106 (Selective Service files). See also note, 165 A. L. R. 1302, 1344; Kassow v. Robertson, (1957) .... Ohio Com. Pleas ...., 143 N. E. 2d 926.

[3] *e. g.*, (1956 Re-issue) Neb. Rev. Stat. § 25-1280.

[4] *e. g.*, (1948) Idaho Code § 9-322.

[5] (1936) .... Mo. App. ...., 97 S. W. 2d 874. See also McGowan v. Metropolitan Life Ins. Co., (1932) 234 App. Div. 366, 255 N. Y. S. 130, appeal dismissed 259 N. Y. 454, 182 N. E. 81. A city's health department records showing insured's treatment for a communicable disease were excluded on the ground of public policy. The physician-patient privilege was not discussed, yet the reasoning of the court appears to be based

records of the public health department made from reports submitted by the attending physician which showed that seventeen months before the insured's policies were issued he was afflicted with tuberculosis, were excluded on the ground that they were privileged communications between physician and patient.

There is, however, respectable authority to the contrary. In an action for damages for the death of plaintiff's intestate from typhoid fever as the result of the alleged negligent conduct of defendant who was, to her own knowledge, a "typhoid carrier," plaintiff was entitled to have produced at the trial the records of the county and state health departments showing defendant's condition. The court expressly held that the statutory privilege did not apply thereto even though the information was furnished to the health authorities by defendant's own physician, since it was transmitted to them in obedience to the express command of the Public Health Law.[6]

In *People* v.*Nisonoff*,[7] the defendants were convicted of manslaughter as the result of performing an abortion on a patient who

---

on the confidential relationship of physician and patient and its right to privacy. The decision in this case was approved and followed in Mark's Appeal, (1936) 121 Pa. Super. 181, 183 Atl. 432.

In Pence v. Myers, (1913) 180 Ind. 282, 101 N. E. 716, a will contest, plaintiff offered in evidence a record kept by a county health officer. This was prepared from the attending physician's death certificate, and contained the date and cause of his death. The fact of death was not disputed, and the evident purpose of the health officer's record was to present to the jury the statement of the attending physician as to the cause of such death. Held: the admission in evidence of the record was error.

6 Thomas v. Morris, (1941) 286 N. Y. 266, 36 N. E. 2d 141, 136 A. L. R. 854. The court also observed that a legislative intention that the records as to communicable diseases should not be kept confidential was shown by the fact that the Public Health Law provided that records as to four named diseases, not including typhoid fever, should not be divulged or made public, the inference being that records as to other communicable diseases were not so privileged. Rule 27(5) of the Uniform Rules of Evidence (1953) and Rule 223(4) of the Model Code of Evidence (1942) provide that "There is no privilege * * * as to information which the physician or patient is required to report to a public official or as to information required to be recorded in a public office, unless the statute requiring the report or record specifically provides that the information shall not be disclosed."

7 (1944) 293 N. Y. 597, 59 N. E. 2d 420, cert. denied 326 U. S. 745, 90 Law. Ed. 445, 66 Su. Ct. 368. See also Iovino v. Green Bus Lines, (1950) 277 App. Div. 1002. Report of toxicologist as to quantity of alcohol found in brain of deceased admissible as a public record.

died. The state was permitted to introduce in evidence the autopsy findings of the medical examiner, who had died prior to the trial of the defendants, notwithstanding the fact that the Charter of the city of New York provided that "such records shall not be open to public inspection." It was still admissible in evidence as a public record, even though only public officers had access thereto.

67. Certificates of Death: In General

In most of the jurisdictions, the legislatures have enacted laws which specify the contents of a death certificate, or authorize the department of public health to prescribe them,[1] and have also made such certificate prima facie evidence in all courts and places of the facts therein stated.[2] The legislature has the right to determine what facts shall be stated in a death certificate and to make such matters prima facie evidence, and the certificate is not therefore inadmissible on the theory that it invades the province of the jury and cuts off the right of cross-examination.[3] It appears to be everywhere conceded that a certificate of death may be introduced in evidence to show the *fact* of death, but the decisions are in conflict as to the admissibility of a public record containing the certificate of a physician reciting the *cause* of the death of a person. Some

---

[1] *e. g.*, (1956) Ariz. Rev. Stat., § 36-334; (1949) Iowa Code Ann. § 141.4; (1954) N. Y. *Public Health Law* § 4141; (1952) N. C. Stat. § 130-79; (1943) N. D. Rev. Code § 23-0230; (1953) Ohio Rev. Code, § 3705.26: "A certificate of death shall contain such items and information as may be required by the United States bureau of the census, and such additional items and information as the public health council, by regulation, may prescribe * * *."

A number of states have enacted laws identical with, or similar to, the Uniform Vital Statistics Act. See 9A. Uniform Laws Ann., p. 392.

[2] *e. g.*, (1956) Ariz. Rev. Stat., § 12-2264; (1948) Idaho Code § 9-322; (1949) Iowa Code Ann. § 144.48; (1943) N. D. Rev. Code § 23-0240: "A registrar's * * * certified copy of any birth or death certificate issued by the state registrar of vital statistics shall be prima facie evidence of the facts therein stated and shall be accepted as such proof in any court or before any commission, bureau, board, or agency in this state."

Some of the states have enacted laws which preclude the inspection of death certificates by curious busybodies. *e. g.*, (1949) Okla. Stat. Ann. Tit. 63, § 560.8(c).

[3] Massachusetts Mut. Life Ins. Co. v. Bush, (1930) 236 Ky. 400, 33 S. W. 2d 351; Simpson v. Wells, (1922) 292 Mo. 301, 237 S. W. 520; Seater v. Penn Mut. Life Ins. Co., (1945) 176 Ore. 542, 156 P. 2d 386, 159 P. 2d 826; Bozicevich v. Kenilworth Mercantile Co., (1921) 58 Utah 458, 199 Pac. 406, 17 A. L. R. 346.

courts have held that such a record, or a certified copy thereof, is admissible for such purpose if the certificate is made pursuant to a statute and the record is properly kept as required by law; but there are decisions to the contrary. These are based on the theory that the records are required to be kept under police regulations for local and specific purposes only, and that a statute making a death certificate evidence is not to be construed as making the certificate a public record in the sense that it is evidence in controversies between private parties.[4]

Admittedly there is a conflict of opinion on the question, but the weight of authority is to the effect that the statutes making death certificates admissible as evidence, relate only to the facts as contained in such certificate, and not to any statement therein that is purely and clearly an opinion or conclusion, especially when it is founded on hearsay.[5] The distinction between a statement of fact and an opinion or conclusion as to the cause of death, is sometimes difficult to draw.[6]

---

[4] See notes in 17 A. L. R. 359; 42 A. L. R. 1454; 96 A. L. R. 324.

[5] New York Life Ins. Co. v. Miller, (1935) 81 F. 2d 263; Equitable Life Assur. Soc. v. Stinnett, (1926) 13 F. 2d 820; Levy v. Vaughn, (1914) 42 App. D. C. 146; Henninger v. Inter-Ocean Cas. Co., (1920) 217 Ill. App. 542; Morton v. Equitable Life Ins. Co., (1934) 218 Iowa 846, 254 N. W. 325, 96 A. L. R. 315; Marion v. Frank R. Messers & Sons, Inc., (1948) 306 Ky. 743, 209 S. W. 2d 321; Kentucky Home Mut. Life Ins. Co. v. Watts, (1944) 298 Ky. 471, 183 S. W. 2d 499; Gilchrist v. Mystic Workers of the World, (1915) 188 Mich. 466, 154 N. W. 575, Ann. Cas. 1918 C 757; Backstrom v. New York Life Ins. Co., (1931) 183 Minn. 384, 236 N. W. 708; Massachusetts Protective Ass'n. v. Cranford, (1924) 137 Miss. 876, 102 So. 171; Callahan v. Connecticut General Life Ins. Co., (1947) 357 Mo. 187, 207 S. W. 2d 279; Lynde v. Western & Southern Life Ins. Co., (1956) _____ Mo. App._____ , 293 S. W. 2d 147; Killip v. Rochester General Hospital, (1955) 1 Misc. 2d 349, 146 N. Y. S. 2d 164; Perry v. Industrial Comm'n., (1954) 160 Ohio St. 520, 117 N. E. 2d 34; Carson v. Metropolitan Life Ins. Co., (1951) 156 Ohio St. 104, 100 N. E. 2d 197, 28 A. L. R. 2d 344; Stough v. Industrial Comm'n., (1944) 142 Ohio St. 446, 52 N. E. 2d 992; Oklahoma Aid Ass'n. v. Thomas, (1927) 125 Okla. 190, 256 Pac. 719; Seater v. Penn Mutual Life Ins. Co., (1945) 176 Ore. 542, 156 P. 2d 386, 159 P. 2d 826; Heffron v. Prudential Ins. Co., (1939) 137 Pa. Super. 69, 8 A. 2d 491.

Contra: Guardian Life Ins. Co. v. Kissner, (1940) 111 F. 2d 532; California State Life Ins. Co. v. Fuqua, (1932) 40 Ariz. 148, 10 P. 2d 958; Hillman v. Utah Power & L. Co., (1935) 56 Idaho 67, 51 P. 2d 703; Massachusetts Mut. Life Ins. Co. v. Bush, (1930) 236 Ky. 400, 33 S. W. 2d 351; Dow v. United States Fid. & Guar. Co., (1937) 297 Mass. 34, 7 N. E. 2d 426; Scott v. Empire State Degree of Honor, (1923) 204 App. Div. 530, 198 N. Y. S. 535.

[6] Rath v. Industrial Comm'n., (1954) 99 Ohio App. 261, 266, 129 N. E. 2d 525: "In the

⟫→

When admitted in evidence, the certificate becomes prima facie, not conclusive, evidence of the cause of death.[7] If the party against whom it is offered is not satisfied with the statement contained in the certificate of death, he may contradict the record by any proper evidence. The field is open for any other testimony which may tend to disprove any or all of the subject matter of the certificate.[8] Moreover, either party may call the attending physician

←⋘

case of suicide the question is not whether a gunshot wound or a strangulation or a drowning or death under the wheels of a railroad train was the immediate cause of death, but as to whether the particular individual willfully caused the same to be done. This is a question of a state of mind and of a motivating cause. To the writer of this opinion, this involves a guess of the mental process of the decedent and, in accordance with the Supreme Court's decision, becomes a matter of opinion based on many facts unrelated to the field of medicine. However, when a doctor states that the cause of death is due to a gunshot wound, tuberculosis, a rupturing of a blood vessel in the brain, commonly known as a stroke, coronary thrombosis, heat exhaustion, hemorrhage, or any other *primary* cause of death, such statement is a statement of fact and not of opinion. It is true that the statement of fact results from an opinion formed from many sources. This diagnosis may be from considerations arrived at from long treatment; it may be from short treatment and a history of the case; it may also be from an examination of a body after death. * * * Physical appearance and previous symptoms might well enter into the ultimate conclusion. In any event, however, it is a fact stated by the doctor which has to do with a primary physical cause and not with a mental motivation.

(Distinguishing Carson v. Metropolitan Life Ins. Co., (1951) 156 Ohio St. 104, 100 N. E. 2d 197, 28 A. L. R. 2d 344 and Perry v. Industrial Comm'n., (1954) 160 Ohio St. 520, 117 N. E. 2d 34).

[7] Aetna Life Ins. Co. v. Ward, (1891) 140 U. S. 76, 35 Law. Ed. 371, 11 Su. Ct. 720; Kirsch v. Federal Life Ins. Co., (1939) 149 Kan. 309, 87 P. 2d 591; Harrington v. Interstate Business Mens Acc. Ass'n., (1925) 232 Mich. 101, 205 N. W. 116; Swigerd v. Ortonville, (1956) 246 Minn. 339, 75 N. W. 2d 217; Krema v. Great Northern Life Ins. Co., (1938) 204 Minn. 186, 282 N. W. 822; Johnson v. Missouri Ins. Co., (1932) _____ Mo. App._____ , 46 S. W. 2d 959; Rath v. Industrial Comm'n., (1954) 99 Ohio App. 261, 129 N. E. 2d 525; Griffin v. National Mining Co., (1937) 127 Pa. Super. 588, 193 Atl. 447; Borgon, v. John Hancock Mut. Life Ins. Co., (1930) 99 Pa. Super. 377; McGinty v. Brotherhood of Railway Trainmen, (1917) 166 Wis. 83, 164 N. W. 249; 20 Am. Jur., Evidence, § 1034.

[8] Harris v. Wood, (1943) 214 Minn. 492, 8 N. W. 2d 818; Milleren v. Federal Life Ins. Co., (1932) 185 Minn. 614, 242 N. W. 290; Rath v. Industrial Comm'n., (1954) 99 Ohio App. 261, 129 N. E. 2d 525; Borgon v. John Hancock Mut. Life Ins. Co., (1930) 99 Pa. Super. 377; Bozicevich v. Kenilworth Mercantile Co., (1921) 58 Utah 458, 199 Pac. 406, 17 A. L. R. 346; Milwaukee Elec. Ry. & L. Co. v. Industrial Comm'n., (1936) 222 Wis. 111, 267 N. W. 62; McGinty v. Brotherhood of Railway Trainmen, (1917)

⋙→

who made and signed it and have him explain it, if explanation is deemed necessary.[9] Where the evidence is conflicting, the question of fact must be submitted to the jury.[10] In civil actions in the Federal courts, the admissibility of a certificate of death is determined by the law of the state where the trial is had.[11]

The question of the admissibility of the death certificate and the weight to be accorded it is procedural and the law of the forum prevails.[12]

68. Same: Effect of Privilege

The plain purpose of the physician-patient privilege statute is to enable a patient to fully and frankly reveal the nature of his disease or ailment without fear that his feelings will be shocked or his reputation tarnished by its disclosure by his physician without his consent. But what becomes of the reason and purpose of the statute when, by subsequent legislation, the attendant physician is compelled to make this very disclosure in a certificate of death which becomes a matter of public record and prima facie evidence in all courts and places of the facts recited therein? Obviously, such

---

166 Wis. 83, 164 N. W. 249. The certificate cannot be contradicted, however, by the hearsay statement of the physician who signed it. Krug v. Mutual Ben. Health & Acc. Ass'n., (1941) 120 F. 2d 296; Estate of Scott, (1942) 55 Cal. App. 2d 780, 131 P. 2d 613.

[9] Kirsch v. Federal Life Ins. Co., (1939) 149 Kan. 309, 87 P. 2d 591; Metropolitan Life Ins. Co. v. Cleveland's Adm'r., (1928) 226 Ky. 621, 11 S. W. 2d 434; Harrington v. Interstate Business Men's Acc. Ass'n., (1925) 232 Mich. 101, 205 N. W. 116; Krema v. Great Northern Life Ins. Co., (1938) 204 Minn. 186, 282 N. W. 822; Milleren v. Federal Life Ins. Co., (1932) 185 Minn. 614, 242 N. W. 290; Johnson v. Missouri Ins. Co., (1932) ...... Mo. App ......, 46 S. W. 2d 959; Randolph v. Supreme Liberty Life Ins. Co., (1949) 359 Mo. 251, 221 S. W. 2d 155; Borgon v. John Hancock Mut. Life Ins. Co., (1930) 99 Pa. Super. 377; Bozicevich v. Kenilworth Mercantile Co., (1921) 58 Utah 458, 199 Pac. 406, 17 A. L. R. 346; McGinty v. Brotherhood of Railway Trainmen, (1917) 166 Wis. 83, 164 N. W. 249.

[10] Krema v. Great Northern Life Ins. Co., (1938) 204 Minn. 186, 282 N. W. 822; Johnson v. Missouri Ins. Co., (1932) ......Mo. App......, 46 S. W. 2d 959; Rath v. Industrial Comm'n., (1954) 99 Ohio App. 261, 129 N. E. 2d 525.

[11] Parfet v. Kansas City Life Ins. Co., (1942) 128 F. 2d 361; Guardian Life Ins. Co. v. Kissner, (1940) 111 F. 2d 532; New York Life Ins. Co. v. Anderson, (1933) 66 F. 2d 705; Von Crome v. Travelers Ins. Co., (1926) 11 F. 2d 350.

[12] Lynde v. Western & Southern Ins. Co., (1956) ......Mo. App......, 293 S. W. 2d 147.

legislation requires the physician, in making out his certificate, to reveal information which he would not only have acquired from his patient while attending him professionally, but which would have been necessary to enable him to properly prescribe for or treat him. It has been urged, therefore, that the later enactments abolish all pretense of preserving the secrecy that the privilege statute enjoins, and consequently that the physician should no longer be prohibited from divulging on the witness stand the information he acquired while attending the patient. Admittedly there appears to be a conflict between the statute which requires the physician to prepare and file a death certificate as a public record and the statute which protects confidential communications between physician and patient. In other words, the physician's certificate of death, reporting facts concerning the disease, ailment, or injury which caused, or contributed to, the patient's death, appears to be as much in conflict with the privilege statute as if the physician testified to such facts in person.

It is generally conceded, however, that the repeal of a statute by implication is not favored,[1] and the courts have properly held that the legislatures, in making death certificates public records and prima facie evidence, did not intend thereby to repeal the physician-patient privilege statute in its entirety. Notwithstanding such legislation, the privilege still exists and the physician will not be permitted, over objection, to testify and disclose the medical secrets of the patient.[2] Furthermore, it has been held that even though the certificate of death is admissible in evidence, the physician who made it is prohibited by the privilege statute from testifying to the facts therein stated because acquired in his professional capacity.[3]

---

[1] Davis v. Supreme Lodge, K. of H., (1900) 165 N. Y. 159, 58 N. E. 891.

[2] Polish Roman Catholic Union v. Palen, (1942) 302 Mich. 557, 5 N. W. 2d 463; Davis v. Supreme Lodge, K. of H., (1900) 165 N. Y. 159, 58 N. E. 891; Prudential Ins. Co. v. Vozzella, (1934) 242 App. Div. 800, 274 N. Y. S. 774; Robinson v. Supreme Commandery, (1902) 77 App. Div. 215, 79 N. Y. S. 13, aff'd. 177 N. Y. 564, 69 N. E. 1130; Bozicevich v. Kenilworth Mercantile Co., (1921) 58 Utah 458, 199 Pac. 406, 17 A. L. R. 346; Cohodes v. Menominee & M. Light & Traction Co., (1912) 149 Wis. 308, 135 N. W. 879.

Contra: Randolph v. Supreme Liberty Life Ins. Co., (1949) 359 Mo. 251, 221 S. W. 2d 155; National Benevolent Society v. Russell, (1935) 173 Okla. 331, 48 P. 2d 1047.

[3] Polish Roman Catholic Union v. Palen, (1942) 302 Mich. 557, 5 N. W. 2d 463; Krapp

≫→

The courts are not in harmony as to the question whether the certificate itself is admissible in evidence in those states where the privilege statute is in force. According to the clear weight of present authority, where subsequent legislation requires physicians to file death certificates in a public office, such certificates become public records and their contents being thus published to the world are no longer treated as privileged; hence, they are admissible in evidence.[4]

On the other hand, the courts of several states have held that the privilege to exclude the physician's testimony on the witness stand necessarily implies the withholding of his testimony by cer-

---

v. Metropolitan Life Ins. Co., (1906) 143 Mich. 369, 106 N. W. 1107.

Contra: National Benevolent Soc. v. Russell, (1935) 173 Okla. 331, 334, 48 P. 2d 1047: "About the facts stated in the certificate, the physician making the statement should be allowed to testify, for to that extent the privileged communication doctrine does not apply." See also McGinty v. Brotherhood of Railway Trainmen, (1917) 166 Wis. 83, 164 N. W. 249.

[4] State v. Flory, (1924) 198 Iowa 75, 79, 199 N. W. 303: "The rule which protects privileged communications has no application to public records. The requirements of the law that a public record be kept could not be complied with if the privilege extended thereto, and statutes authorizing the introduction of certified copies thereof in evidence would be a nullity." In Cowan v. Allamakee County Benevolent Soc., (1943) 232 Iowa 1387, 8 N. W. 2d 433, the question was not decided. Other cases holding that the privilege statute does not preclude the introduction of death certificates in evidence, are: Polish Roman Catholic Union v. Palen, (1942) 302 Mich. 557, 5 N. W. 2d 463; Krapp v. Metropolitan Life Ins. Co., (1906) 143 Mich. 369, 106 N. W. 1107; Life & Casualty Ins. Co. v. Walters, (1937) 180 Miss. 384, 177 So. 47; Randolph v. Supreme Liberty Life Ins. Co., (1949) 359 Mo. 251, 221 S. W. 2d 155, overruling Key v. Cosmopolitan Life, H. & Acc. Ins. Co., (1937) ___Mo. App.___, 102 S. W. 2d 797; Perry v. Industrial Comm'n., (1954) 160 Ohio St. 520, 524, 117 N. E. 2d 34: "In view of the fact that of the two Ohio statutes the one relating to death certificates is the more recent and since the latter is specific while the older staute [physician-patient privilege] is merely general, the specific and more recent enactment must prevail."

See also Life & Casualty Ins. Co. v. Walters, infra. National Benevolent Soc. v. Russell, (1935) 173 Okla. 331, 48 P. 2d 1047; Bozicevich v. Kenilworth Mercantile Co., (1921) 58 Utah 458, 199 Pac. 406, 17 A. L. R. 346; Milwaukee Elec. Ry. & L. Co. v. Industrial Comm'n., (1936) 222 Wis. 111, 267 N. W. 62; State v. Pabst, (1909) 139 Wis. 561, 121 N. W. 351.

Wigmore favors this view. 8 Wigmore, Evidence, § 2385a.

Perhaps it should be mentioned that there are numerous reported cases, in jurisdictions which recognize the privilege, where certificates of death were admitted in evidence, but it does not appear that any objections were made thereto on the ground of privilege.

tificate,[5] and that to permit the introduction in evidence of a certificate of death would be to evade the statutory privilege by indirection.[6] Moreover, some of the courts have held that legislation, whether it be in the form of local charters or ordinances,[7] or state statutes,[8] requiring physicians to make and file certificates of death, are police regulations,[9] enacted for the purpose of aiding public health officers, city and state, in gathering information essential to the effective control and prevention of disease,[10] and, within those objects and purposes, such a record is proper evidence; but that such legislation does not interfere with private rights or create a new rule of evidence. It is the considered judgment of these courts that the lawmakers did not intend to repeal or alter the well-established rules

---

[5] Buffalo Loan, Trust & Safe Deposit Co. v. Knights Templar and M. Mut. Aid Ass'n., (1891) 126 N. Y. 450, 455, 27 N. E. 942: "The [privilege] statute should have a broad and liberal construction to carry out its policy. By reasonable construction it excludes a physician from giving testimony in a judicial proceeding in any form, whether by affidavit or oral examination, involving a disclosure of confidential information acquired in attending a patient, unless the seal of secrecy is removed by the patient himself."

[6] Sovereign Camp, W. of W. v. Grandon, (1902) 64 Neb. 39, 48, 89 N. W. 448: "That a record of this character, reciting privileged communications, may be used in evidence against a party where the testimony of the physician making it could not be received, is a proposition so inconsistent with reason and natural rules of justice that we cannot give our consent thereto. The court properly refused to allow the certificate [of death] in evidence."

The Kentucky statute expressly provides that the privilege shall prevail. See Appendix, herein.

[7] Sovereign Camp, W. of W. v. Grandon, (1902) 64 Neb. 39, 89 N. W. 448; Davis v. Supreme Lodge, K. of H., (1900) 165 N. Y. 159, 58 N. E. 891; Buffalo Loan, Trust and Safe Deposit Co. v. Knights Templar & Masonic Mut. Aid Ass'n., (1891) 126 N. Y. 450, 27 N. E. 942; Robinson v. Supreme Commandery, (1902) 77 App. Div. 215, 79 N. Y. S. 13, aff'd. 177 N. Y. 564, 69 N. E. 1130; Painton v. Cavanaugh, (1912) 151 App. Div. 372, 135 N. Y. S. 418.

[8] Beglin v. Metropolitan Life Ins. Co., (1903) 173 N. Y. 374, 66 N. E. 102.

[9] Brotherhood of Painters, Decorators & Paperhangers v. Barton, (1910) 46 Ind. App. 160, 92 N. E. 64 (two judges dissented); Sovereign Camp, W. of W. v. Grandon, (1902) 64 Neb. 39, 89 N. W. 448; Beglin v. Metropolitan Life Ins. Co., (1903) 173 N. Y. 374, 66 N. E. 102; Davis v. Supreme Lodge, K. of H., (1900) 165 N. Y. 159, 58 N. E. 891; Buffalo Loan, Trust and Safe Deposit Co. v. Knights Templar and M. Mut. Aid Ass'n., (1891) 126 N. Y. 450, 27 N. E. 942.

[10] Steele v. Campbell, (1948) 118 Ind. App. 549, 82 N. E. 2d 274; Brotherhood of Painters, Decorators & Paperhangers v. Barton, (1910) 46 Ind. App. 160, 92 N. E. 64; Oklahoma Aid Ass'n. v. Thomas, (1927) 125 Okla. 190, 256 Pac. 719.

of evidence which protect from disclosure confidential communications between physician and patient, in controversies between private parties;[11] that the proper and rational rule, therefore, is that an authenticated copy of a certificate of death is admissible only when the records themselves are relevant and admissible according to the existing rules of evidence.[12]

Of course, where there is no proof to show that the person who signed the certificate is a physician, the privilege statute would have no application.[13] A certificate of death may be admitted in evidence under the provisions of the Business Records Act if no claim of privilege is made,[14] or when the privilege is lawfully waived.[15] In an action upon a policy of insurance, defendant's motion was granted to the extent of allowing a commission to issue upon written interrogatories upon specified matters including the fact that the attending physician made and filed as a public record a certificate in which no external or accidental injury was assigned as either the direct or contributing cause of death, and to exhibit a copy of same; but it was also held that if the answers of the physician elicited any-

---

11 Pence v. Myers, (1913) 180 Ind. 282, 101 N. E. 716; Steele v. Campbell, (1948) 118 Ind. App. 549, 82 N. E. 2d 274; Brotherhood of Painters, Decorators & Paperhangers, (1910) 46 Ind. App. 160, 92 N. E. 64; Omaha & Council Bluffs Street Ry. v. Johnson, (1922) 109 Neb. 526, 191 N. W. 691; Sovereign Camp, W. of W. v. Grandon, (1902) 64 Neb. 39, 89 N. W. 448; Beglin v. Metropolitan Life Ins. Co., (1903) 173 N. Y. 374, 66 N. E. 102; Davis v. Supreme Lodge, K. of H., (1900) 165 N. Y. 159, 58 N. E. 891; Buffalo Loan, Trust & Safe Deposit Co. v. Knights Templar and M. Mut. Aid Ass'n., (1891) 126 N. Y. 450, 27 N. E. 942; Robinson v. Supreme Commandery, (1902) 77 App. Div. 215, 79 N. Y. S. 13, aff'd. 177 N. Y. 564, 69 N. E. 1130; Oklahoma Aid Ass'n. v. Thomas, (1927) 125 Okla. 190, 256 Pac. 719.

See comments on some of these cases in Bozicevich v. Kenilworth Mercantile Co., (1921) 58 Utah 458, 199 Pac. 406, 17 A. L. R. 346.

For cases involving Birth Certificates, see State v. Worden, (1932) 331 Mo. 566, 56 S. W. 2d 595; *In re* Billings' Estate, (1949) 196 Misc. 141, 91 N. Y. S. 2d 665; *In re* Meyers, (1954) 206 Misc. 368, 132 N. Y. S. 2d 825.

12 This seems to be the view of the Court of Appeals of New York. See Buffalo Loan, Trust & Safe Deposit Co. v. Knights Templar and M. Mut. Aid. Ass'n., (1891) 126 N. Y. 450, 27 N. E. 942.

13 Naudzius v. Metropolitan Life Ins. Co., (1929) 136 Misc. 167, 238 N. Y. S. 702.

14 Duffy v. 42nd Street, M. & S. Ave. Ry., (1943) 266 App. Div. 865, 42 N. Y. S. 2d 534.

15 *In re* Monroe's Will, (1946) 270 App. Div. 1039, 63 N. Y. S. 2d 141.

thing prohibited by the privilege statute, an objection could be made thereto on the trial of the action.[16]

Where the Sanitary Code of the city of New York required a medical report of the cause of a death to be filed but provided further that such report should be treated as a privileged communication and not subject to subpoena or open to inspection other than for scientific purposes, it was held, in an action brought by the widow of a deceased employee under the Workmen's Compensation Act, that the City Department of Health properly refused the demand of the employer's carrier to produce such report at a hearing held by a referee of the Workmens Compensation Board upon her claim for death benefits.[17]

There have been several cases where attending physicians, for one reason or another, have made and signed affidavits or certificates, *not required by law,* for the purpose of showing the cause of the patient's death, and the question has been raised: Are such documents admissible in evidence when they plainly disclose information within the scope of the privilege statute? In an action to recover death benefits under a policy of insurance issued by the defendant, it was held that the admission in evidence of a certificate issued by the insured's physician to another insurance company wherein he stated that he believed the insured had a cardiac condition, violated the privilege statute and constituted prejudicial error.[18] In an action brought by an insurance company to cancel a policy of insurance on the ground that the insured misrepresented his physical condition at the time the policy was issued, the trial court excluded the record of the Bureau of Vital Statistics offered by the company. The document contained a certificate of death and affidavits of the attending physicians which disclosed confiden-

---

[16] Dana v. Commercial Travelers Mut. Acc. Ass'n., (1934) 241 App. Div. 812, 271 N. Y. S. 952. In one respect, the decision seems unsound. The disclosure should be cut off at the source; otherwise, the secret is out and a ruling at the time of trial would come too late.

[17] *In re* Bakers Mutual Ins. Co., (1950) 301 N. Y. 21, 92 N. E. 2d 49. The court held that, by act of the legislature, the Sanitary Code of the city of New York has within that city the force and effect of state law, while elsewhere in the state, the state Sanitary Code and Public Health Law are supreme. Two judges dissented.

[18] Epstein v. Metropolitan Life Ins. Co., (1937) 250 App. Div. 854, 294 N. Y. S. 919.

tial information acquired by them in their professional capacity. These were made during the insured's illness but were attached to the certificate of death. It was held that since the affidavits were not required by law and were in violation of the privilege statute, the certificate of death to which they were attached was not admissible in evidence and was properly excluded by the trial court.[19] In an action to recover double indemnity under life insurance policies and the principal issue was whether the insured died from carbon monoxide poisoning or from heart trouble, it was prejudicial error to admit in evidence an affidavit of the insured's physician, not required by law but given to avoid the necessity of an autopsy, in which he stated the cause of death was heart trouble. The introduction in evidence of such affidavit was a violation of the privilege statute.[20]

69. Proofs of Death and Proofs of Loss

The phrases "proof of death" and "proof of loss" which appear in contracts of insurance are somewhat general terms, their precise subject matter varying perhaps with the type of policy[1] and the circumstances involved, as well as with the express requirements of the particular insurer. They are used generally, however, to denote the notice of the claim of the beneficiary under the policy, and include all documents required of him which, in the opinion of the insurer, are necessary for it to form an intelligent estimate of its rights and liabilities, to afford it an opportunity for investigation, and to prevent fraud and imposition upon it.[2] In a sense, therefore, a "proof of death" comprehends not only the individual statement of the beneficiary, but all documents required of, or furnished by,

---

[19] Northwestern Mutual Life Ins. Co. v. New Fisheries Co., (1925) ....Ohio App........, 3 Ohio Law Abst. 716.

[20] Poses v. Travelers Ins. Co., (1935) 245 App. Div. 304, 281 N. Y. S. 126. See also American National Ins. Co. v. White, (1916) 126 Ark. 483, 191 S. W. 25; Fidelity & Casualty Co. v. Meyer, (1912) 106 Ark. 91, 152 S. W. 995, 44 L. R. A. (n. s.) 493.

[1] The phrases are often used interchangeably. It would seem, however, the "proof of loss" more appropriately describes the formal proof required by the insurer to support the insured's claim for *disability benefits* to which he may be entitled under the policy.

[2] 29 Am. Jur., *Insurance*, § 1100. See also note, 1 A. L. R. 2d 366.

him to the insurer to establish his claim under the policy, such as the statement of the physician who last attended the insured, the statement of the undertaker, a certified copy of the certificate of death filed by the physician with the Health Department or the Bureau of Vital Statistics, or a certified copy of the official report of the coroner.[3] Usually, a proof of death is required by the insurer as a condition precedent to liability, and no obligation is imposed upon it until such condition has been performed, unless performance is waived. The same is true, in general, with reference to a "proof of loss" where the claim is for disability benefits under the policy.[4]

In many jurisdictions where the physician-patient privilege statute is in force, the question has been raised as to whether an insurer, in its defense to an action brought by the beneficiary to recover the proceeds of an insurance policy, may introduce as evidence in its behalf the proof of death furnished the insurer where such proof includes a statement signed by the insured's physician and disclosing the nature, extent, or duration of the insured's ailment, disease, or injury, or the cause, or contributing cause, of his death.

The general rule is that where the physician's statement, containing information plainly within the scope of the privilege statute and which, if true, would vitiate the policy, is furnished to the insurer by the beneficiary as part of the proof of death, such statement, even though it may not be admissible as *original* evidence of the facts recited therein, is admissible in an action against the insurer when introduced in evidence by it as an admission against the interest of the plaintiff-beneficiary.[5]

---

[3] Sometimes, the insured's hospital record, or permission to inspect it, is required by the insurer.

[4] Appleman, (1941) Insurance Law and Practice, § 1395. See also Acee v. Metropolitan Life Ins. Co., (1927) 219 App. Div. 246, 219 N. Y. S. 152.

[5] From the multitude of cases in jurisdictions which recognize the privilege, the following are selected:

Haughton v. Aetna Life Ins. Co., (1905) 165 Ind. 32, 73 N. E. 592; Noble v. United Benefit Life Ins. Co., (1941) 230 Iowa 471, 297 N. W. 881; Michalek v. Modern Brotherhood, (1917) 179 Iowa 33, 161 N. W. 125; Nelson v. Nederland Life Ins. Co., (1900) 110

⁍→

The statement of the physician, which is a part of the proof of death or the proof of loss, cannot be excluded on the ground of privilege arising from the confidential relation between the physician and his patient. This is so because it is admitted in evidence as an admission by the beneficiary, not as the testimony of the physician.[6] Its character as proof is not derived from what the physi-

←

Iowa 600, 81 N. W. 807; Mexicott v. Prudential Ins. Co., (1933) 263 Mich. 420, 248 N. W. 856; Harrington v. Interstate Business Mens Acc. Ass'n., (1925) 232 Mich. 101, 205 N. W. 116; Haapa v. Metropolitan Life Ins. Co., (1907) 150 Mich. 467, 114 N. W. 380, 16 L. R. A. (n. s.) 1165; Krapp v. Metropolitan Life Ins. Co., (1906) 143 Mich. 369, 106 N. W. 1107; John Hancock Mut. Life Ins. Co. v. Dick, (1898) 117 Mich. 518, 76 N. W. 9, 44 L. R. A. 846; Elness v. Prudential Ins. Co., (1933) 190 Minn. 169, 251 N. W. 183; Laury v. Northwestern Mutual Life Ins. Co., (1930) 180 Minn. 205, 230 N. W. 648, 231 N. W. 824; Portell v. Metropolitan Life Ins. Co., (1952) ....Mo. App. .... , 246 S. W. 2d 546; Metropolitan Life Ins. Co. v. Ryan, (1943) 237 Mo. App. 464, 172 S. W. 2d 269; Mayhew v. Travelers Protective Ass'n., (1932) ....Mo. App. .... , 52 S. W. 2d 29; Grohmann v. The Maccabees, (1922) ....Mo. App. .... , 237 S. W. 875; Stephens v. Metropolitan Life Ins. Co., (1915) 190 Mo. App. 673, 176 S. W. 253; Schroeder v. Metropolitan Life Ins. Co., (1937) 103 Mont. 547, 63 P. 2d 1016; Strang v. Prudential Ins. Co., (1933) 263 N. Y. 71, 188 N. E. 161; Rudolph v. John Hancock Mut. Life Ins. Co., (1929) 251 N. Y. 208; 167 N. E. 223; Hanna v. Connecticut Mutual Life Ins Co., (1896) 150 N. Y. 526, 44 N. E. 1099; Spencer v. Citizens Mutual Life Ins. Ass'n., (1894) 142 N. Y. 505, 37 N. E. 617; Buffalo Loan, Trust & Safe Deposit Co. v. Knights Templar and Masonic Mut. Aid Ass'n., (1891) 126 N. Y. 450, 27 N. E. 942; Scheiner v. Metropolitan Life Ins. Co., (1932) 236 App. Div. 24, 257 N. Y. S. 783; Cirrincioni v. Metropolitan Life Ins. Co., (1928) 223 App. Div. 461, 228 N. Y. S. 354; Blandin v. Benefit Ass'n. of Railway Employees, (1956) ....N. D. .... , 75 N. W. 2d 135; National Benevolent Soc. v. Russell, (1935) 173 Okla. 331, 48 P. 2d 1047; Beard v. Royal Neighbors, (1909) 53 Ore. 102, 99 Pac. 83, 19 L. R. A. (n. s.) 798, 17 Ann. Cas. 1199; Felix v. Fidelity Mutual Life Ins. Co., (1906) 216 Pa. 95, 64 Atl. 903; Palyo v. Western & Southern Life Ins. Co., (1934) 114 Pa .Super. 583, 174 Atl. 640; Eklund v. Metropolitan Life Ins. Co., (1936) 89 Utah 273, 57 P. 2d 362; Askey v. New York Life Ins. Co., (1918) 102 Wash. 27, 172 Pac. 887, L. R. A. 1918 F. 267.

See notes, 17 A. L. R. 359; 42 A. L. R. 1454; 96 A. L. R. 324; Ann. Cas. 1918 C. 761.

Generally speaking, admissions do not come in on the ground that the party making them is speaking from his own knowledge, but upon the ground that a party will not make admissions against himself unless they are true. Unquestionably, it is evidence of a very unsatisfactory character, depending altogether on the circumstances under which it is made; but it is competent nevertheless.

See 8 Wigmore, Evidence, § 2390.

[6] In some instances, the courts have characterized the physician's statement in a proof of death as "direct evidence," "affirmative testimony," or "competent testimony," but it may be assumed, we believe, that the courts intended no more than that such proofs were admissible in evidence because they were in the nature of admissions against

⋙→

cian declared,[7] but from what the beneficiary has admitted to be the fact, and the privilege which he might assert to exclude the evidence of the physician, does not extend to evidence of what he himself has admitted.[8] Where, however, the physician's statement, or any other privileged document, is furnished to the insurer in pursuance of the beneficiary's contractual obligation to file a proof of death or a proof of loss, but its correctness is, at the same time, denied by the beneficiary, such statement or document cannot be treated as an admission against interest.[9] It would seem, therefore,

←—«

interest by the beneficiary, not because they were original evidence of the physician's testimony.

[7] Nelson v. Nederland Life Ins. Co., (1900) 110 Iowa 600, 606, 81 N. W. 807: "The affidavit [of the physician] was presented to the company by the beneficiary as a part of her proofs of loss, and was a communication to it of facts indicating the invalidity of the policy. * * * But it is said that this was in violation of the [privilege] statute already mentioned. That does not prescribe any rule of professional conduct. * * * It is 'giving testimony' in a judicial proceeding that such disclosures are prohibited by statute, and doubtless this may no more be done by affidavit than orally. But here the information ascertained professionally had been revealed in an affidavit, not for use in such a proceeding, and *it was not offered nor received as evidence of the physician, or of what he said*, as in that event it would have been incompetent, but as an admission by the plaintiff that its contents were true." (Italics supplied)

   Scheiner v. Metropolitan Life Ins. Co., (1932) 236 App. Div. 24, 257 N. Y. S. 783: "The legal theory is that the evidence is received, not as the declaration of the physician, but as the admission of the party who furnished them."

[8] Martin v. Metropolitan Life Ins. Co., (1943) ⸺Mo. App.⸺, 174 S. W. 2d 222; Metropolitan Life Ins. Co. v. Ryan, (1943) 237 Mo. App. 464, 172 S. W. 2d 269; Hicks v. Metropolitan Life Ins. Co., (1916) 196 Mo. App. 162, 190 S. W. 661; Rudolph v. John Hancock Mut. Life Ins. Co., (1929) 251 N. Y. 208, 167 N. E. 223; Buffalo Loan, Trust & Safe Deposit Co. v. Knights Templar and Masonic Mut. Aid Ass'n., (1891) 126 N. Y. 450, 27 N. E. 942; Emanuele v. Metropolitan Life Ins. Co., (1930) 137 Misc. 542, 242 N. Y. S. 715; Naudzius v. Metropolitan Life Ins. Co., (1929) 136 Misc. 167, 238 N. Y. S. 702; Carmichael v. John Hancock Mut. Life Ins. Co., (1904) 45 Misc. 597, 90 N. Y. S. 1033; Phillips v. New York Life Ins. Co., (1890) 56 Hun. 649, 9 N. Y. S. 836. See also Dreier v. Continental Life Ins. Co., (1885) 24 Fed. 670 (the physician's statement was offered as *original* evidence, not as an admission by plaintiff); Repala v. John Hancock Mut. Life Ins. Co., (1924) 229 Mich. 463, 201 N. W. 465. The decision seems to be out of line with other Michigan cases.

[9] Binder v. Commercial Travelers Mut. Acc. Ass'n., (1947) 165 F. 2d 896; Justice v. Interocean Casualty Co., (1930) 108 Cal. App. 267, 291 Pac. 436; Craiger v. Modern Woodmen, (1907) 40 Ind. App. 279, 80 N. E. 429; Howard v. Metropolitan Life Ins. Co., (1896) 18 Misc. 74, 41 N. Y. S. 33; Fisher v. Fidelity Mutual Life Ass'n., (1898) 188 Pa. 1, 41 Atl. 467.

since neither the statement nor the document is admissible as *original* evidence nor as an admission against interest, they should not be allowed in evidence at all.[10]

The physician's statement, furnished as part of the proof of death, has been held admissible in evidence as an admission by the beneficiary, even though it included matters not required by the policy,[11] or was based on hearsay only.[12] Furthermore, the rule seems to apply with equal force to admissions contained in a proof of death, or proof of loss, furnished by the beneficiary to some company other than the one defending the suit. In other words, if the admissions so made to one company are of such a nature as to preclude recovery against another company, then the latter is entitled to rely upon and use them.[13]

Admissions made by the beneficiary in the proofs furnished by him as an individual will be regarded as adopted by him where, without furnishing any proofs at all, he later brings suit upon the policy in a representative capacity,[14] or where he has adopted as his own the proofs filed by other claimants.[15] But an infant beneficiary is not bound by admissions gratuitously made by his guardian in proofs furnished by the latter as a condition precedent to the infant's right to recover on the policy.[16] In a suit by an insurer

---

[10] Connecticut Mutual Life Ins. Co. v. Lanahan, (1940) 112 F. 2d 375; Craiger v. Modern Woodmen, (1907) 40 Ind. App. 279, 80 N. E. 429; Shiovitz v. New York Life Ins. Co., (1937) 281 Mich. 382, 275 N. W. 181; Goldschmidt v. Mutual Life Ins. Co., (1886) 102 N. Y. 486, 7 N. E. 408.

In Emmanuele v. Metropolitan Life Ins. Co., (1930) 137 Misc. 542, 242 N. Y. S. 715, it was held that it is the duty of a claimant, if he does not wish to have the proof of death used as evidence against his claim, to submit with the proofs a protest that the facts therein alleged are untrue.

[11] Helwig v. Mutual Life Ins. Co., (1892) 132 N. Y. 331, 30 N. E. 834; Buffalo Loan, Trust & Safe Deposit Co. v. Knights Templar and Masonic Mut. Aid Ass'n., (1891) 126 N. Y. 450, 27 N. E. 942.

[12] Mayhew v. Travelers Protective Ass'n., (1932) _____ Mo. App._____, 52 S. W. 2d 29.

[13] Cope v. Central States Life Ins. Co., (1933) _____ Mo. App._____, 56 S. W. 2d 602; Scheiner v. Metropolitan Life Ins. Co., (1932) 236 App. Div. 24, 257 N. Y. S. 783.

[14] Strang v. Prudential Ins. Co., (1933) 263 N. Y. 71, 188 N. E. 161; Vechio v. Metropolitan Life Ins. Co., (1928) 224 App. Div. 301, 230 N. Y. S. 131; Cirrincioni v. Metropolitan Life Ins. Co., (1928) 223 App. Div. 461, 228 N. Y. S. 354.

[15] Kirk v. Metropolitan Life Ins. Co., (1935) 336 Mo. 765, 81 S. W. 2d 333.

[16] Nichols v. Supreme Tribe of Ben Hur, _____Mo. App._____, 274 S. W. 868; Queatham

≫→

to cancel a policy of disability insurance, statements of the physician furnished by the insured's wife as part of the proofs of the insured's disability were held inadmissible as admissions on the part of the insured who was insane, particularly where the insured's guardian *ad litem* had not adopted, but repudiated such proofs.[17]

Generally speaking, a certified copy of a certificate of death made and signed by the attending physician and filed as a public record as required by law, is competent evidence in the nature of an admission by the beneficiary when it is made a part of the proof of death;[18] but there is authority for the proposition that unless it is made a part thereof, it is not admissible in evidence when offered by the insurer to prove the cause of death.[19] An affidavit, statement, or a letter of the insured's physician, which was not included in the proof of death or the proof of loss furnished the insured by the claimant, is not admissible in evidence when offered by the insurer.[20]

v. Modern Woodmen, (1910) 148 Mo. App. 33, 127 S. W. 651; Buffalo Loan, Trust & Safe Deposit Co. v. Knights Templar and Masonic Mut. Aid Ass'n., (1891) 126 N. Y. 450, 27 N. E. 942.

[17] Metropolitan Life Ins. Co. v. Ryan, (1943) 237 Mo. App. 464, 172 S. W. 2d 269.

[18] Greenbaum v. Columbian National Ins. Co., (1932) 62 F. 2d 56; Wagner v. Orden Allemania, (1911) 71 Misc. 448, 128 N. Y. S. 629; Wilmer v. Industrial Health, Acc., & Life Ins. Co., (1931) 101 Pa. Super. 366.

In Carson v. Metropolitan Life Ins. Co., (1951) 156 Ohio St. 104, 100 N. E. 2d 197, 28 A. L. R. 2d 344, the physician's certificate of death was furnished to the insurer as part of the proof of death. Because this was required by the insurer, it was held that it did not constitute an admission against interest by the plaintiff. See also Mar Shee v. Maryland Assur. Corp., (1922) 190 Cal. 1, 210 Pac. 269.

[19] Beglin v. Metropolitan Life Ins. Co., (1903) 173 N. Y. 374, 66 N. E. 102; Davis v. Supreme Lodge, K. of H., (1900) 165 N. Y. 159, 58 N. E. 891; Buffalo Loan, Trust & Safe Deposit Co. v. Knights Templar and Masonic Mut. Aid Ass'n., (1891) 126 N. Y. 450, 27 N. E. 942; Flynn v. Metropolitan Life Ins. Co., (1937) 252 App. Div. 78, 297 N. Y. S. 349; Cirrincioni v. Metropolitan Life Ins. Co., (1928) 223 App. Div. 461, 228 N. Y. S. 354. See also § 68, herein.

[20] Richardson v. North American Life & Casualty Co., (1919) 142 Minn. 295, 172 N. W. 131; Salts v. Prudential Ins. Co., (1909) 140 Mo. App. 142, 120 S. W. 714; Poses v. Travelers Ins. Co., (1935) 245 App. Div. 304, 281 N. Y. S. 126; Prudential Ins. Co. v. Vozzella, (1934) 242 App. Div. 800, 274 N. Y. S. 774.

Where physicians' statements, or other documents, included in the proofs of death or proofs of loss, are treated as admissions against interest by the party furnishing them, they are, like other admissions, not conclusive but are subject to explanation, correction, or contradiction; and evidence may be presented to show that they are erroneous.[21] Ordinarily, they create no estoppel.[22] Any other rule might result in great injustice to the claimant in many cases. Reputable physicians frequently disagree as to the cause of death or disability, and in some cases the attending physician may be unable to diagnose the case. Moreover, additional causes of death or disability may be discovered after the claim has been filed.[23] The preponderance of modern authority, therefore,

---

This is especially true where the proofs tendered were rejected by the insurer. Masson v. Metropolitan Life Ins. Co., (1930) 225 Mo. App. 925, 36 S. W. 2d 118.

But a letter written to the insurer by a physician at its request, although not binding on the plaintiff who had never seen it, may be used by the insurer to impeach the testimony of the physician if it contains anything in the nature of an admission by him. Aldridge v. Aetna Life Ins. Co., (1912) 204 N. Y. 83, 97 N. E. 399, 38 L. R. A. (n. s.) 343.

21 Wachtel v. Equitable Life Assur. Soc., (1935) 266 N. Y. 345, 194 N. E. 850. "Explanation * * * may completely destroy the effect of the admission."

22 Aetna Life Ins. Co. v. Ward, (1891) 140 U. S. 76, 35 Law. Ed. 371, 11 Su. Ct. 720; Denver Life Ins. Co. v. Price, (1902) 18 Colo. App. 30, 69 Pac. 313; Michalek v. Modern Brotherhood, (1917) 179 Iowa 33, 161 N. W. 125; Wildey Casualty Co. v. Sheppard, (1900) 61 Kan. 351, 59 Pac. 651, 47 L. R. A. 650; Ligrow v. Abraham Lincoln Life Ins. Co., (1932) 260 Mich. 444, 245 N. W. 498; John Hancock Mut. Life Ins. Co. v. Dick, (1898) 117 Mich. 518, 76 N. W. 9, 44 L. R. A. 846; Elness v. Prudential Ins. Co., (1933) 190 Minn. 169, 251 N. W. 183; Bentz v. Northwestern Aid Ass'n., (1889) 40 Minn. 202, 41 N. W. 1037, 2 L. R. A. 784; Coscarella v. Metropolitan Life Ins. Co., (1913) 175 Mo. App. 130, 157 S. W. 873; Hanna v. Connecticut Mutual Life Ins. Co., (1896) 150 N. Y. 526, 44 N. E. 1099; Cushman v. United States Life Ins. Co., (1877) 70 N. Y. 72; Wilmer v. Industrial Health, Acc. & Life Ins. Co., (1931) 101 Pa. Super. 366; Borgon v. John Hancock Mut. Life Ins. Co., (1930) 99 Pa. Super. 377; Baldi v. Metropolitan Life Ins. Co., (1904) 24 Pa. Super. 275.

23 Wade v. Metropolitan Life Ins. Co., (1936) 179 S. C. 70, 183 S. E. 589. See also West v. National Council K. & L. of Security, (1920) _____ Mo. App. _____ , 221 S. W. 391; Santos v. John Hancock Mut. Life Ins. Co., (1935) 245 App. Div. 198, 281 N. Y. S. 35; Baldi v. Metropolitan Life Ins. Co., (1904) 24 Pa. Super. 275; Monaghan v. Prudential Ins. Co., (1927) 90 Pa. Super. 392, 394: "It would be a harsh rule that would bind the claimant to a statement made by a doctor which would prevent recovery notwithstanding the claimant would be in possession of facts, the proof of which would show that the doctor's statement was either falsely or inaccurately made."

strongly favors the view that physicians' statements, reports, certificates, or affidavits, when made a part of, or used in connection with proofs of death or proofs of loss, although admissible in evidence as admissions against the party furnishing them to the insurer under a policy, are not conclusive against him, but may be nullified or overcome by other evidence tending to explain, contradict, impair or relieve against adverse statements or admissions therein, as that they were the result of inadvertence, mistake, or misinformation and were erroneous.[24]

---

[24] Aetna Life Ins. Co. v. Ward, (1891) 140 U. S. 76, 35 Law Ed. 371, 11 Su. Ct. 720; Walther v. Mutual Life Ins. Co., (1884) 65 Cal. 417, 4 Pac. 413; Justice v. Interocean Casualty Co., (1930) 108 Cal. App. 267, 291 Pac. 436; Metropolitan Life Ins. Co. v. Lanigan, (1924) 74 Colo. 386, 222 Pac. 402; Haughton v. Aetna Life Ins. Co., (1905) 165 Ind. 32, 73 N. E. 592; Wildey Casualty Co. v. Sheppard, (1900) 61 Kan. 351, 59 Pac. 651, 47 L. R. A. 650; Mexicott v. Prudential Ins. Co., (1933) 263 Mich. 420, 248 N. W. 856; Ferris v. Loyal Americans, (1908) 152 Mich. 314, 116 N. W. 445; Cooper v. Progressive Assur. Co., (1931) 182 Minn. 434, 234 N. W. 645; Bentz v. Northwestern Aid Ass'n., (1889) 40 Minn. 202, 41 N. W. 1037, 2 L. R. A. 784; Eagan v. Prudential Ins. Co., (1937) ___ Mo. App.___, 107 S. W. 2d 133, rev'd on other grounds 119 S. W. 2d 309; Otto v. Metropolitan Life Ins. Co., (1934) 228 Mo. App. 742, 72 S. W. 2d 811; Ryan v. Metropolitan Life Ins. Co., (1930) ___ Mo. App.___, 30 S. W. 2d 190; Bultralik v. Metropolitan Life Ins. Co., (1921) ___ Mo. App.___, 233 S. W. 250; West v. National Council, K. L. S., (1920) ___ Mo. App.___, 221 S. W. 391; Coscarella v. Metropolitan Life Ins. Co., (1913) 175 Mo. App. 130, 157 S. W. 873; Frazier v. Metropolitan Life Ins. Co., (1911) 161 Mo. App. 709, 141 S. W. 936; Hinnenkamp v. Metropolitan Life Ins. Co., (1938) 134 Neb. 846, 279 N. W. 784; Rudolph v. John Hancock Mut. Life Ins. Co., (1929) 251 N. Y. 208, 167 N. E. 223; Redmond v. Industrial Benefit Ass'n., (1896) 150 N. Y. 167, 44 N. E. 769; Hanna v. Connecticut Mutual Life Ins., (1896) 150 N. Y. 526, 44 N. E. 1099; Spencer v. Citizens Mutual Life Ins. Ass'n., (1894) 142 N. Y. 505, 37 N. E. 617; Cushman v. United States Life Ins. Co., (1877) 70 N. Y. 72; Hirsch v. New York Life Ins. Co., (1944) 267 App. Div. 404, 45 N. Y. S. 2d 892; Santos v. John Hancock Mut. Life Ins. Co., (1935) 245 App. Div. 198, 281 N. Y. S. 35; Boylan v. Prudential Ins. Co., (1896) 18 Misc. 444, 42 N. Y. S. 52; Fields v. Equitable Life Assur. Soc., (1928) 195 N. C. 262, 141 S. E. 743; Fagerlie v. New York Life Ins. Co., (1929) 129 Ore. 485, 278 Pac. 104; Robinson v. Knights and Ladies of Security, (1918) 88 Ore. 516, 172 Pac. 116; Evans v. Penn Mutual Life Ins. Co., (1936) 322 Pa. 547, 186 Atl. 133; Felix v. Fidelity Mutual Life Ins. Co., (1906) 216 Pa. 95, 64 Atl. 903; Dischner v. Piqua Mutual Aid & Acc. Ass'n., (1901) 14 S. D. 436, 85 N. W. 998; Pagni v. New York Life Ins. Co., (1933) 173 Wash. 322, 23 P. 2d 6, 93 A. L. R. 1325; Rohloff v. Aid Ass'n. for Lutherans, (1906) 130 Wis. 61, 109 N. W. 989.
    See excellent note, 93 A. L. R. 1342.
    Conceding that the physician's statement may be rebutted or explained, it was held that this could not be accomplished by the hearsay statement of the physician

⋙→

While it is true that the physician's statements in a proof of death, or in a proof of loss, are prima facie only and are not to be treated as conclusive in every case where other facts are brought forward to explain or refute them so as to relieve against the baneful effect of such admission, they are, nevertheless, binding and conclusive until corrected or explained. Proofs of death or proofs of loss are presented to the insurer as preliminary to the payment of the insurance money. They are intended for the action of the insurer, and upon their truth it has a right to rely. Good faith and fair dealing require that the beneficiary or other claimant should be held to the representations made therein until it is shown that they were made under a misapprehension of facts, or in ignorance of matters subsequently ascertained. Therefore, when no effort is made to explain, impeach, or contradict the statements of the physician in the proofs furnished and such are sufficient as an admission to defeat the right of recovery under the law, they will be treated accordingly—that is, as if such facts be true. There is, then, no determinative issue for the jury, but only a question for the court.[25] On the other hand, where there is any evidence produced which conflicts with the alleged admissions and tending to show a

---

who made and filed a certificate of death as a public record. Krug v. Mutual Benefit Health & Acc. Ass'n., (1941) 120 F. 2d 296.

[25] National Reserve Life Ins. Co. v. Jeffries, (1938) 147 Kan. 16, 75 P. 2d 302; Harrington v. Interstate Business Men's Acc. Ass'n., (1925) 232 Mich. 101, 205 N. W. 116; Haapa v. Metropolitan Life Ins. Co., (1907) 150 Mich. 467, 114 N. W. 380, 16 L. R. A. (n. s.) 1165; Kirk v. Metropolitan Life Ins. Co., (1935) 336 Mo. 765, 81 S. W. 2d 333; Turner v. Central Mutual Ins. Ass'n., (1944) 238 Mo. App. 425, 183 S. W. 2d 347; Eagan v. Prudential Ins. Co., (1937) _____ Mo. App. _____, 107 S. W. 2d 133; Smiley v. John Hancock Mut. Life Ins. Co., (1932) _____ Mo. App. _____, 52 S. W. 2d 12; Grohmann v. The Maccabees, (1922) _____ Mo. App. _____, 237 S. W. 875; Stephens v. Metropolitan Life Ins. Co., (1915) 190 Mo. App. 673, 176 S. W. 253; Schroeder v. Metropolitan Life Ins. Co., (1937) 103 Mont. 547, 63 P. 2d 1016; Rudolph v. John Hancock Mut. Life Ins. Co., (1929) 251 N. Y. 208, 167 N. E. 223; Hanna v. Connecticut Mutual Life Ins. Co., (1896) 150 N. Y. 526, 44 N. E. 1099; Trudden v. Metropolitan Life Ins. Co., (1900) 50 App. Div. 473, 64 N. Y. S. 183; Leonard v. John Hancock Mut. Life Ins. Co., (1912) 76 Misc. 529, 135 N. Y. S. 564; Proppe v. Metropolitan Life Ins. Co., (1895) 13 Misc. 266, 34 N. Y. S. 172; Palyo v. Western & Southern Life Ins. Co., (1934) 114 Pa. Super. 583, 174 Atl. 640. See note, 93 A. L. R. 1349.

contrary state of facts, a question arises to be determined by the jury on the credibility of witnesses and the weight of evidence.[26].

It should, perhaps, be noticed that there is some support for the view that where the beneficiary is *required* by the insurer to furnish proof of death as a condition precedent to his right to recover the proceeds of the policy, statements made by the physician concerning the insured's ailment or the cause of his death, which are a necessary part of such proof, cannot be treated as admissions against the interest of the beneficiary furnishing them. The theory is that the beneficiary has no option, since the physician's statement is extracted from the beneficiary by the terms of the policy; that while he did agree to *furnish* it, he did not agree to *adopt* it. Moreover, the beneficiary cannot know how the physician will answer the questions, or whether he can agree that they are true.[27] Accordingly, statements in a physician's affidavit to make proof of death in an action upon the policy, are not competent as evidence to establish an affirmative defense, as that the disease from which the insured died existed before the renewal of the policy.[28] In an

[26] Wright v. John Hancock Mut. Life Ins. Co., (1941) _____Mo. App._____, 153 S. W. 2d 747; Ryan v. Metropolitan Life Ins. Co., (1930) _____Mo. App._____, 30 S. W. 2d 190; Bultralik v. Metropolitan Life Ins. Co., (1921) _____Mo. App._____, 233 S. W. 250; West v. National Council K. L. S., (1920) _____Mo. App._____, 221 S. W. 391; Bruck v. John Hancock Mut. Life Ins. Co., (1916) 194 Mo. App. 529, 185 S. W. 753; Clarkston v. Metropolitan Life Ins. Co., (1915) 190 Mo. App. 624, 176 S. W. 437; Coscarella v. Metropolitan Life Ins. Co., (1913) 175 Mo. App. 130, 157 S. W. 873; Spencer v. Citizens Mutual Life Ins. Co., (1894) 142 N. Y. 505, 37 N. E. 617; Fields v. Equitable Life Assur. Soc., (1928) 195 N. C. 262, 141 S. E. 743; Osche v. New York Life Ins. Co., (1936) 324 Pa. 1, 187 Atl. 396; Evans v. Penn Mutual Life Ins. Co., (1936) 322 Pa. 547, 186 Atl. 133; Felix v. Fidelity Mutual Life Ins. Co., (1906) 216 Pa. 95, 64 Atl. 903; Borgon v. John Hancock Mut. Life Ins. Co., (1930) 99 Pa. Super. 377; Dischner v. Piqua Mutual Aid & Acc. Ass'n., (1901) 14 S. D. 436, 85 N. W. 998; Askey v. New York Life Ins. Co., (1918) 102 Wash. 27, 172 Pac. 887, L. R. A. 1918 F 267.

[27] Hubbs, J., dissenting, in Rudolph v. John Hancock Mut. Life Ins. Co., (1929) 251 N. Y. 208, 214, 167 N. E. 223: "Under the circumstances, it is a misuse of the word 'admission' to say that by filing the statement [of the physician] which she was obliged to file, she admitted the truth of the statements it contains." Crane and Kellogg, JJ., concurred.

[28] American Assurance Co. v. Early, (1912) 23 Ohio C. C. (n. s.) 418, aff'd 91 Ohio St. 367, 110 N. E. 1053.

See also Binder v. Commercial Travelers Mutual Acc. Ass'n., (1947) 165 F. 2d 896;

action for additional death benefits upon a claim that the insured's death was caused by accident, defendant claimed that the insured committed suicide. It was reversible error to admit in evidence, at the instance of the defendant, copies of the coroner's report and the physician's certificate of death which were furnished to the defendant as parts of the proof of death. The plaintiff could not be bound by them since they were required by the insurer and, therefore, did not constitute admissions against interest by the plaintiff.[29] The general rule, however, is that statements of the physician in the proof of death or in the proofs of loss are, unless their correctness is denied at the time, admissible in evidence as admissions against interest whether they are furnished voluntarily or because they are required by the terms of the policy, and this is usually true even though the claimant may have no actual knowledge of their contents.[30]

←

Mar Shee v. Maryland Assurance Corp., (1932) 190 Cal. 1, 210 Pac. 269 (coroner's verdict); Cushman v. United States Life Ins. Co., (1877) 70 N. Y. 72. Kundiger v. Metropolitan Life Ins. Co., (1944) 218 Minn. 273, 285, 15 N. W. 2d 487: "It [physician's statement as to cause of death] was required by the insurance company as part of the proofs of loss, and cannot be considered as the voluntary act or admission of plaintiff."

[29] Carson v. Metropolitan Life Ins. Co., (1951) 156 Ohio St. 104, 100 N. E. 2d 197, 28 A. L. R. 2d 344.

[30] An appreciable number of courts have questioned the wisdom and fairness of the rule. Some follow it with obvious reluctance. Others have declined to enforce it where the statement of the physician has been procured by the insurer without the intervention of the claimant; or where it was based not on the physician's own personal knowledge, but on hearsay only; or where the statements went beyond those required by the insurer; or where the claimant signed the proof at the request of an agent of the insurer without knowing its contents; or where his attention was not called by the insurer to the inconsistency of his own statement and that of the physician; or where the claimant referred the insurer to the physician but was given no opportunity to inspect the physician's report to the insurer.

However, these and other problems equally important involve questions which are more appropriately discussed in textbooks relating to the law of Evidence and to the law of Insurance. Perhaps the following selected cases will be helpful to the solution of some of them:

New York Life Ins. Co. v. Taylor, (1945) 79 App. D. C. 66, 147 F. 2d 297, aff'd 158 F. 2d 328; Triple Tie Benefit Ass'n v. Wheatley, (1907) 76 Kan. 251, 91 Pac. 59; Metropolitan Life Ins. Co. v. Dabudka, (1925) 232 Mich. 36, 204 N. W. 771; Bentz v. Northwestern Aid Ass'n., (1889) 40 Minn. 202, 41 N. W. 1037, 2 L. R. A. 784; Masson v. Metropolitan Life Ins. Co., (1931) 225 Mo. App. 925, 36 S. W. 2d 118; McHenry v.

⋙→

When the proof of death or the proof of loss admits facts supporting a defense to the plaintiff's action on an insurance policy, the burden is on him to introduce evidence explaining or contradicting such proofs and unless he does so, the insurer is entitled to a verdict. The plaintiff having furnished them has vouched for their truth. He must show they are not correct.[31] On the other hand, where the claimant denied the correctness of the proofs which he was required to furnish the insurer, the burden of proof rested with the insurer since the proofs contained no admission by the claimant which changed this burden.[32]

Whether or not by furnishing a proof of death or a proof of loss to the insurer, or by its introduction in evidence, the beneficiary or claimant has waived the protection of the physician-patient privilege is a troublesome question as to which there is a conflict of opinion. This subject will be discussed in a subsequent chapter.[33]

Royal Neighbors, (1922) 211 Mo. App. 230, 242 S. W. 147; Frazier v. Metropolitan Life Ins. Co., (1911) 161 Mo. App. 709, 141 S. W. 936; Neudeck v. Grand Lodge Am. O. of U. W., (1895) 61 Mo. App. 97; Aldridge v. Aetna Life Ins. Co., (1912) 204 N. Y. 83, 97 N. E. 399, 38 L. R. A. (n. s.) 343; Cushman v. United States Life Ins. Co., (1877) 70 N. Y. 72; Tennenbaum v. Metropolitan Life Ins. Co., (1931) 141 Misc. 394, 252 N. Y. S. 599; Montgomery v. John Hancock Mut. Life Ins. Co., (1931) 140 Misc. 233, 250 N. Y. S. 403; Muller v. Orden Germania, (1892) 18 N. Y. S. 794; John Hancock Mut. Life Ins. Co. v. Jennings, (1934) _____Ohio App._____, 17 Ohio Law Abst. 583; Federal Life Ins. Co. v. Maples, (1951) 204 Okla. 195, 228 P. 2d 363; Robinson v. Knights and Ladies of Security, (1918) 88 Ore. 516, 172 Pac. 116; Cox v. Royal Tribe of Joseph, (1903) 42 Ore. 365, 71 Pac. 73, 60 L. R. A. 620.

[31] Turner v. Central Mutual Ins. Ass'n., (1944) 238 Mo. App. 425, 183 S. W. 2d 347; Fields v. Equitable Life Assur. Co., (1928) 195 N. C. 262, 141 S. E. 743; Felix v. Fidelity Mutual Life Ins. Co., (1906) 216 Pa. 95, 64 Atl. 903.

[32] Goldschmidt v. Mutual Life Ins. Co., (1886) 102 N. Y. 486, 7 N. E. 408.

[33] See § 137, herein.

CHAPTER XII

Actions and Proceedings in Which Privilege May or May Not Be Invoked

70. Criminal Cases

At common law, communications between physician and patient are not privileged,[1] and, unless a statute creates such a privilege, a physician is a competent witness and may testify thereto in a criminal action or proceeding and his testimony must be received, if not otherwise objectionable.[2]

Where a statute creating the privilege exists, it is necessary, of course, to examine it carefully in order to ascertain the scope and limitations of the privilege, since its wording usually will determine whether the rule is applicable to civil actions, or to criminal actions, or to both. It will be remembered that the first statute in America[3] was expressed in broad terms which, beyond reasonable question, applied to all actions whether civil or criminal.[4] Some of

---

[1] See § 4, herein.

[2] e.g., Dyer v. State, (1941) 241 Ala. 679, 4 So. 2d 311; Bonewald v. State, (1952) 157 Tex. Cr. 521, 251 S. W. 2d 255; Dodd v. State, (1918) 83 Tex. Cr. 160, 201 S. W. 1014; Rex v. Gibbons, (1823) 1 Car. & P. 97.

[3] New York, (1828). See § 5, herein.

[4] People v. Murphy, (1886) 101 N. Y. 126, 4 N. E. 326.

the statutes subsequently enacted in other jurisdictions followed this pattern.[5] Others have restricted the privilege to civil cases only.[6] In Arizona and Washington, the legislature has enacted the privilege in the civil code of procedure and in the criminal code also.[7] In Minnesota, the statute expressly provides that the privilege applies to both civil and criminal actions. In Mississippi, it applies "in any legal proceeding."[8] In Louisiana, the privilege is a part of the criminal code and applies to criminal cases only.[9]

Some of the statutes, although applicable to civil and criminal cases generally, are limited and therefore inoperative with respect to specified classes of criminal prosecutions. In the District of Columbia, the privilege does not apply in criminal cases where the accused is charged with the death of, or inflicting injuries upon, a human being, and the disclosure is necessary in the interests of public justice.[10] In New York, the privilege is a general one, except that it does not apply where the patient is a child under the

---

[5] Arkansas, Colorado, Indiana, Iowa, Kansas, Michigan, Missouri, Nebraska, Nevada, New Mexico, North Carolina, North Dakota, Ohio, Oklahoma, West Virginia, Wyoming, Province of Quebec.
See Appendix, herein.

[6] Alaska, California, Canal Zone, Guam, Hawaii, Idaho, Montana, Oregon, Pennsylvania, Philippine Islands, Puerto Rico, South Dakota, Utah, Virgin Islands, New Zealand, Victoria (Australia). See Appendix, herein.
Under Rule 27(2) of the Uniform Rules of Evidence (1953) the privilege, except when denied under specified circumstances, is applicable in a civil action or in a prosecution for a misdmeanor. See Appendix, herein.

[7] It should be noted, however, that in each state the wording of the statute in the civil code differs from that in the criminal code. In Washington, it has been held that the civil statute protects the patient in both civil and criminal actions, while that in the criminal code protects the physician. State v. Miller, (1919) 105 Wash. 475, 178 Pac. 459. In Michigan, the privilege is applicable in proceedings before a grand jury, and in an authorized inquiry about crime before trial. (1954 Repl. Vol.) Mich. Stat. Ann. § 28.945(1).

[8] One writer has remarked that it cannot be said with certainty that the privilege applies to criminal actions. For a discussion of the Mississippi decisions, see Welch, Another Anomaly—The Patient's Privilege, (1941) 13 Miss. L. J. 137, 145.

[9] Rhodes v. Metropolitan Life Ins. Co., (1949) 172 F. 2d 183, cert. denied 337 U. S. 930, 93 Law Ed. 1737, 69 Su. Ct. 1493. No statute appears in the *civil* code with respect to communications between physician and patient.

[10] The application of the criterion "public justice" is a matter of discretion with the trial judge. Catoe v. United States, (1942) 131 F. 2d 16.

age of sixteen and has been the victim or the subject of a crime in which the commission of such crime is a subject of inquiry. In North Carolina the physician may be compelled to testify if the trial judge rules that disclosure is necessary for the proper administration of justice. In Wisconsin, the privilege does not apply in trials for homicide when the disclosure relates directly to the fact or the immediate circumstances of a homicide, nor in criminal actions against the physician for malpractice.

Perhaps it should be stated here that, in some states, separate statutes have been enacted which authorize a physician to testify, without the consent of the patient, in certain classes of criminal prosecutions, or quasi-criminal proceedings. In Minnesota,[11] a physician may testify in a bastardy case concerning the fact and probable date of the inception of the pregnancy of his patient. In Missouri,[12] in a prosecution for abortion or for manslaughter occasioned by an abortion, or by an attempt to produce either, a physician who has attended the woman is a competent witness and may be compelled to testify concerning any facts relative to the issue therein. In Wisconsin,[13] a physician must testify in a prosecution for abortion when ordered by a judge of a court of record so to do.

As pointed out earlier, the privilege does not apply when the patient requests the physician to commit a crime, or solicits his aid or advice to advance his own unlawful purpose.[14] The seal of professional confidence cannot be used to cover a transaction which is in itself a crime.[15]

Notwithstanding the fact that in most of the jurisdictions the statute creating the privilege appears in the civil code of procedure and is expressly restricted to civil actions only, the legislatures of

---

[11] (1947) Minn. Stat. Ann., § 257.30.

[12] (1953) Mo. Stat. Ann., § 546.310.

[13] (1953) Wis. Stat., § 325.26.

See also Bonich v. State, (1930) 202 Wis. 523, 232 N. W. 873; State v. Law, (1912) 150 Wis. 313, 136 N. W. 803, 137 N. W. 457.

[14] See § 20, herein.

[15] People v. Farmer, (1909) 194 N. Y. 251, 87 N. E. 457. See also Rule 27(6) of the Uniform Rules of Evidence (1953).

many states have, in later years, enacted statutes—as a part of the Code of Criminal Procedure—which provide that the rules of evidence in civil actions shall apply in criminal cases also.[16] Yet, in spite of the apparent purpose of such statutes, the courts of several states have declined to apply the privilege in criminal cases.[17]

It may safely be assumed, we believe, that the privilege under proper circumstances, extends to all criminal actions and proceedings,[18] in the following jurisdictions:[19] Arizona,[20] Arkansas,[21]

---

[16] There are slight differences in the wording of the statutes.

e.g., (1949) Cal. Penal Code, § 1321: "The rules for determining the competency of witnesses in civil actions are applicable to criminal actions and proceedings, except as otherwise provided in this code."

(1954 Repl. Vol.) Mich. Stat. Ann., § 28.1045: "The rules of evidence in civil actions, insofar as the same are applicable, shall govern in all criminal and quasi criminal proceedings except as otherwise provided by law." Similar statutes are in effect in Arizona, Arkansas, Canal Zone, Idaho, Indiana, Iowa, Kansas, Montana, Nevada, New York, North Dakota, Ohio, Oklahoma, Oregon, South Dakota, Utah, Washington. In two jurisdictions, criminal trials are conducted in accordance with the common law rules except as otherwise provided by law. (1949) Alaska Comp. Laws Ann., § 66-13-52; (1953) Colo. Rev. Stat. Ann., § 39-7-13.

[17] People v. Griffith, (1905) 146 Cal. 339, 80 Pac. 68; People v. West, (1895) 106 Cal. 89, 39 Pac. 207; People v. Lane, (1894) 101 Cal. 513, 36 Pac. 16; People v. Dutton, (1944) 62 Cal. App. 2d 862, 145 P. 2d 676; State v. Bounds, (1953) 74 Idaho 136, 258 P. 2d 751; State v. Dean, (1927) 69 Utah 268, 254 Pac. 142.

In Arizona and Washington, the lawmakers apparently considered such a statute not sufficient to bring the civil privilege into the criminal practice, since the criminal code in each state contains a statute expressly extending the privilege to criminal actions. On the other hand, several courts have held that such a statute carries the civil code privilege into the criminal code of procedure. People v. Murphy, (1886) 101 N. Y. 126, 4 N. E. 326; In the Matter of the Investigation of Criminal Abortions in the County of Kings, (1954) 286 App. Div. 270, 143 N. Y. S. 2d 501, appeal denied 309 N. Y. 1031; State v. Moore, (1925) 52 N. D. 633, 204 N. W. 341.

See also State v. Miller, (1919) 105 Wash. 475, 178 Pac. 459.

[18] Except, of course, as previously indicated, where a special statute expressly withholds the privilege from certain classes of criminal prosecutions.

[19] The specific question has not often been decided. In most of the cases it seems to be taken for granted that the privilege applies, and the questions which the courts have been called upon to decide usually concern the existence or non-existence of one or more of the essential elements of the privilege: *e.g.,* Did the relation of physician and patient exist? Was the information necessary to enable the physician to prescribe or act for the patient? Was the information given for a lawful purpose? Was there a waiver of the privilege? Did the objector have the right to claim the privilege? Did the objector successfully meet the burden of proof?

[20] Garcia v. State, (1929) 35 Ariz. 35, 274 Pac. 166.

⋙→

Canal Zone, Colorado,[22] Indiana,[23] Iowa,[24] Kansas,[25] Louisiana,[26] Michigan,[27] Minnesota,[28] Mississippi,[29] Missouri,[30] Montana, Nebraska,[31] Nevada,[32] New York,[33] North Carolina,[34] North Dakota,[35] Ohio,[36] Oklahoma,[37] Washington,[38] Wisconsin.[39] In a few

[21] Wimberly v. State, (1950) 217 Ark. 130, 228 S. W. 2d 991; Cooper v. State, (1949) 215 Ark. 732, 223 S. W. 2d 507; Burris v. State, (1925) 168 Ark. 1145, 273 S. W. 19.

[22] Wolf v. People, (1947) 117 Colo. 279, 187 P. 2d 926.

[23] Myers v. State, (1922) 192 Ind. 592, 137 N. E. 547, 24 A. L. R. 1196; Seifert v. State, (1903) 160 Ind. 464, 67 N. E. 100; Wheeler v. State, (1902) 158 Ind. 687, 63 N. E. 975; Hauk v. State, (1897) 148 Ind. 238, 46 N. E. 127; Post v. State, (1895) 14 Ind. App. 452, 42 N. E. 1120.

[24] State v. Johnston, (1936) 221 Iowa 933, 267 N. W. 698; State v. Murphy, (1928) 205 Iowa 1130, 217 N. W. 225; State v. Masters, (1924) 197 Iowa 1147, 198 N. W. 509; State v. Adams, (1924) 197 Iowa 331, 197 N. W. 64; State v. Grimmell, (1901) 116 Iowa 596, 88 N. W. 342; State v. Smith, (1896) 99 Iowa 26, 68 N. W. 428.

[25] State v. Aguirre, (1949) 167 Kan. 266, 206 P. 2d 118; State v. Townsend, (1937) 146 Kan. 982, 73 P. 2d 1124.

[26] See note 9, infra.

[27] People v. Kayne, (1934) 268 Mich. 186, 255 N. W. 758.

[28] State v. Voges, (1936) 197 Minn. 85, 266 N. W. 265.

[29] Hopkins v. State, (1951) 212 Miss. 772, 55 So. 2d 467; Smith v. State, (1940) 188 Miss.

[29] Hopkins v. State, (1951) 212 Miss. 772, 55 So. 2d 467; Smith v. State, (1940) 188 Miss. 339, 194 So. 922; Vance v. State, (1938) 182 Miss. 840, 183 So. 280; Keeton v. State, (1936) 175 Miss. 631, 167 So. 68; Maddox v. State, (1935) 173 Miss. 799, 163 So. 449; Davenport v. State, (1926) 143 Miss. 121, 108 So. 433, 45 A. L. R. 1348. But see note 8, infra.

[30] State v. Sapp, (1947) 356 Mo. 705, 203 S. W. 2d 425; State v. Cochran, (1947) 356 Mo. 778, 203 S. W. 2d 707; State v. Lassieur, (1922) .... Mo. ...., 242 S. W. 900; State v. Carryer, (1915) ....Mo......., 180 S. W. 850; State v. Long, (1914) 257 Mo. 199, 165 S. W. 748.

[31] Cramer v. State, (1944) 145 Neb. 88, 15 N. W. 2d 323; Crawford v. State, (1927) 116 Neb. 125, 216 N. W. 294; Nichols v. State, (1922) 109 Neb. 335, 191 N. W. 333; Freeberg v. State, (1912) 92 Neb. 346, 138 N. W. 143, Ann. Cas. 1913 E 1101; Larson v. State, (1912) 92 Neb. 24, 137 N. W. 894; Thrasher v. State, (1912) 92 Neb. 110, 138 N. W. 120, Ann. Cas. 1913 E 882; Ossenkop v. State, (1910) 86 Neb. 539, 126 N. W. 72.

[32] State v. Fouquette, (1950) 67 Nev. 505, 221 P. 2d 404; Skidmore v. State, (1939) 59 Nev. 320, 92 P. 2d 979; State v. Depoister, (1891) 21 Nev. 107, 25 Pac. 1000.

[33] People v. Austin, (1910) 199 N. Y. 446, 93 N. E. 57; People v. Koerner, (1897) 154 N. Y. 355, 48 N. E. 730; People v. Hoch, (1896) 150 N. Y. 291, 44 N. E. 976; People v. Murphy, (1886) 101 N. Y. 126, 4 N. E. 326; People v. Stout, (1858) 3 Park. Cr. (N. Y.) 670; People v. Eckert, (1955) 208 Misc. 93, 142 N. Y. S. 2d 657.

[34] State v. Newsome, (1928) 195 N. C. 552, 143 S. E. 187. But the presiding judge may compel disclosure if in his opinion the same is necessary to a proper administration of justice. See statute, Appendix herein.

[35] State v. Moore, (1925) 52 N. D. 633, 204 N. W. 341; State v. Werner, (1907) 16 N. D. 83, 112 N. W. 60.

⟫→

jurisdictions, the courts have held that the privilege does not apply in criminal actions and proceedings.[40]

It is interesting to note that in many jurisdictions where the privilege ordinarily applies in criminal actions, the courts have held that, on the ground of public policy, a defendant in a prosecution for murder, abortion, rape, and the like, is not entitled to invoke the privilege belonging to his victim.[41] The weight of authority supports the view that the privilege is intended for the benefit of the patient only and that the defendant in a criminal prosecution has no right to object to the testimony of a physician concerning communications made by the victim of the crime to such physician, or to information acquired by him during his professional attendance upon the victim.[42] In Ohio, however, the rule appears to be

---

[36] State v. Karcher, (1951) 155 Ohio St. 253, 98 N. E. 2d 308. See also State v. Nevius, (1946) 147 Ohio St. 263, 71 N. E. 2d 258, concerning rules of evidence in criminal cases.

[37] Jasper v. State, (1954) _____ Okla. Cr._____, 269 P. 2d 375; Williams v. State, (1951) _____ Okla. Cr._____, 226 P. 2d 989; Hudman v. State, (1949) 89 Okla. Cr. 160, 205 P. 2d 1175; Clapp v. State, (1942) 74 Okla. Cr. 144, 124 P. 2d 267; Howe v. State, (1926) 34 Okla. Cr. 33, 244 Pac. 826.

[38] State v. Miller, (1919) 105 Wash. 475, 178 Pac. 459; State v. Stapp, (1911) 65 Wash. 438, 118 Pac. 337.

[39] Simecek v. State, (1943) 243 Wis. 439, 10 N. W. 2d 161; *cf.* Smits v. State, (1911) 145 Wis. 601, 130 N. W. 525 (not decided). There appears to be some doubt as to the application of the rule in certain types of criminal actions. See State v. Law, (1912) 150 Wis. 313, 136 N. W. 803, 137 N. W. 457.

[40] See cases in note 17, infra. See also Commonwealth v. Sykes, (1946) 353 Pa. 392, 45 A. 2d 43, cert. denied 328 U. S. 847, 90 Law Ed. 1620, 66 Su. Ct. 1021; Commonwealth v. Edwards, (1935) 318 Pa. 1, 178 Atl. 20; Commonwealth v. Townsley, (1937) 30 D. & C. (Pa.) 209; National Mutual Life Ass'n. v. Godrich, [1909] 10 Comm. L. R. 1 (Australia); *In re* St. Helens Hospital, [1913] 32 New Zealand 682.

[41] State v. Grimmell, (1901) 116 Iowa 596, 600, 88 N. W. 342: "This, as will be observed, is a criminal case, and it surely will not do to hold that a statute intended to protect a patient should operate as a shield for one who is charged with murder. Such a construction, while perhaps technically correct, is evidently so foreign to the purpose and object of the act, and so subversive of public justice, that it ought not to be adopted, except for the most imperative reasons. The safety of the public is the supreme law of the commonwealth, and we do not think the legislature, in passing the act in question, intended it to operate as a barrier to the enforcement of the criminal laws of the state. * * * The purpose of the statute, as we have said, is to protect the patient, and not to shield one who feloniously takes his life."

[42] Representative decisions are: Wimberly v. State, (1950) 217 Ark. 130, 228 S. W. 2d

otherwise. In *State* v. *Karcher*,[43] the defendant was charged with committing a criminal abortion on a woman who died as a result thereof. The State called as a witness the physician who attended her and he testified that she told him she had had an abortion performed but did not disclose who had performed it. Objection to the physician's testimony was made by the defendant on the ground that it was both hearsay and a privileged communication. Defendant was convicted. The Supreme Court held it was reversible error to have allowed this evidence to be admitted.

It has been held that where the victim is also a party to the crime, as, for example, where the victim has consented to an abortion and survives, then the testimony of the physician who attended her is inadmissible. In such case the objection of the defendant is permissible and must be sustained.[44] Other courts, however, have

---

←≪≪

991; Cabe v. State, (1930) 182 Ark. 49, 30 S. W. 2d 855; Hauk v. State, (1897) 148 Ind. 238, 46 N. E. 127; Vance v. State, (1938) 182 Miss. 840, 183 So. 280; Maddox v. State, (1935) 173 Miss. 799, 163 So. 449; Davenport v. State, (1926) 143 Miss. 121, 108 So. 433, 45 A. L. R. 1348; Thrasher v. State, (1912) 92 Neb. 110, 138 N. W. 120, Ann. Cas. 1913 E. 882; State v. Depoister, (1891) 21 Nev. 107, 25 Pac. 1000; People v. Brecht, (1907) 120 App. Div. 769, 105 N. Y. S. 436, aff'd. 192 N. Y. 581, 85 N. E. 1114; People v. Harris, (1893) 136 N. Y. 423, 33 N. E. 65; Pierson v. People, (1880) 79 N. Y. 424; People v. Lay, (1938) 254 App. Div. 372, 5 N. Y. S. 2d 325, aff'd 279 N. Y. 737, 18 N. E. 2d 686; State v. Martin, (1921) 182 N. C. 846, 109 S. E. 74; Jasper v. State, (1954) _____ Okla. Cr. _____, 269 P. 2d 375; State v. Fackrell, (1954) 44 Wash. 2d 874, 271 P. 2d 679.

In State v. DeZeler, (1950) 230 Minn. 39, 41 N. W. 2d 313, 15 A. L. R. 2d 1137, the question was left undecided. In Wisconsin, except as to prosecutions for abortion (State v. Law, (1912) 150 Wis. 313, 136 N. W. 803, 137 N. W. 457), the question appears to be undecided. See Smits v. State, (1911) 145 Wis. 601, 130 N. W. 525; James v. State, (1905) 124 Wis. 130, 102 N. W. 320.

In People v. Weiss, (1932) 147 Misc. 595, 261 N. Y. S. 646, defendant was charged with homicide resulting from a criminal abortion. The attending physicians of the victim were allowed to testify to her statements to them and to their statements to her, the purpose of which was to lay a foundation for the admission, as a dying declaration, of her written statement to the coroner about the facts of the abortion. The dying declaration was ruled out, but the question of privilege does not appear to have been raised.

43 (1951) 155 Ohio St. 253, 98 N. E. 2d 308.

44 People v. Murphy, (1885) 101 N. Y. 126, 4 N. E. 326. In departing from the rule announced in Pierson v. People, (1879) 79 N. Y. 424, Finch, J. said: (p. 129) "In that decision the statute was construed, and we held it did not cover a case where it was invoked for the protection of a criminal, and not at all for the benefit of the patient;

≫→

declined to follow this decision where the disclosure by the physician would not subject the woman to prosecution, damage her reputation, or wound her feelings.[45]

Even though the testimony of a physician as to information
acquired by him in his professional capacity is inadmissible in the
criminal trial of the patient, such testimony can be included for
consideration by the trial judge in deciding whether such person
is mentally competent to stand trial.[46]

71. *Testamentary Actions and Probate Proceedings*

In testamentary actions and in probate proceedings, two questions are usually in issue, *viz.*, whether the document purporting to
be a will is the result of undue influence and whether the testator

---

and where the latter was dead so that an express waiver of the privilege had become
impossible. The present is a different case. Here the patient was living, and the
disclosure which tended to convict the prisoner inevitably tended to convict her of
a crime, or cast discredit and disgrace upon her." The decision has been criticized.
See Bach, The Medico-Legal Aspect of Privileged Communications, (1892) 10 Medico-
Leg. J. 33, 51.

In State v. Grimmell, (1901) 116 Iowa 596, 88 N. W. 342, it was held that a
defendant charged with murder could not invoke the privilege of his victim, but
the court went on to say: (p. 601) "If the patient were alive, perhaps no one but she
could waive the prohibition. But in this case she is dead and unable to speak." See
also State v. Martin, (1921) 182 N. C. 846, 109 S. E. 74.

[45] People v. Lay, (1938) 254 App. Div. 372, 5 N. Y. S. 2d 325, aff'd 279 N. Y. 737, 18 N.
E. 2d 686. Defendant was charged with shooting a woman with intent to kill. The
conviction was based in part upon the relevant testimony of the physician who, upon
examination and treatment of her, found a bullet wound in her body and extracted
the bullet.

In Wimberly v. State, (1950) 217 Ark. 130, 228 S. W. 2d 991, the facts were similar
to those in People v. Lay, supra, except that in the Wimberly case *the woman specifically requested the physician not to testify.* Over her objection and that of the
defendant, the court permitted the physician who had treated the woman to describe
the location, nature and extent of her wounds. The Supreme Court held the testimony
admissible since there was nothing in it which would subject her to prosecution or
disclose to the public any infirmity or condition which she might legitimately wish
kept private.

Annotations concerning the various problems discussed in this section will be
found in 2 A. L. R. 2d 645; 45 A. L. R. 1357; Ann. Cas. 1913 E. 884. See also (1956)
2 Underhill's Criminal Evidence, §§ 336-339.

[46] Taylor v. United States, (1955) 95 App. D. C. 373, 222 F. 2d 398. See also United
States v. Everett, (1956) 146 F. Supp. 54.

was competent to make it. In such cases the testator's attorney and the attending physician are usually in a position to give important and reliable testimony bearing directly upon these issues. It is not surprising, therefore, that frequently one or both of them have testified as to such matters without objection, and that the courts, in some instances, have commented on the peculiar value of their testimony.[1] However, the question still remains whether the privilege statute excludes such testimony if proper and timely objection is made thereto. The question appears to have been first decided by a surrogate court in New York, and it was held that testamentary cases are not within the reason or intention of the statute.[2] This was the rule in that state for many years.[3] In 1886, however, the Court of Appeals rejected it and held that the privilege is applicable in testamentary actions and proceedings.[4]

---

[1] Estate of Bean, (1914) 159 Wis. 67, 81, 149 N. W. 745: "Her family physician should know more about her condition than any one else, and there is nothing to show that he had any interest or bias in the matter. The experience and training of physicians is such that they ought to be able to form reasonably correct conclusions on the condition of a person's mind."

[2] Allen v. Public Administrator, (1850) 1 Bradf. (N. Y.) 221.

[3] Pearsall v. Elmer, (1881) 5 Redf. (N. Y.) 181, 190: "I feel constrained to hold with Judge Bradford in *Allen* v. *Public Administrator,* that the statute does not apply to a probate case, in respect to instructions given by decedent to his attorney for the drawing of his will, and the circumstances connected with its execution, nor to the testimony of an attending physician, where he had occasion to treat the patient at or about the time when the will was executed, where the question of mental capacity is the subject of the inquiry; for to hold otherwise would make the statute, in many cases, a hindrance to the ascertainment of the most important facts bearing upon the issue to be tried."

It should, perhaps, be noted here that at common law the privilege between attorney and client ordinarily does not prevail where the question arises in a will contest. *In re* Young's Estate, (1908) 33 Utah 382, 94 Pac. 731, 17 L. R. A. (n. s.) 108, 14 Ann. Cas. 596. In such cases, the general rule seems to be that the attorney is at liberty to disclose all that affects the execution and tenor of the will. See 8 Wigmore, Evidence, § 2314.

However, it has been pointed out that the privilege statute is not declaratory of the common law rule. Spitzer v. Stillings, (1924) 109 Ohio St. 297, 142 N. E. 365.

See also Platz, The Competency of Attorneys and Physicians to Disclose Privileged Communications in Testamentary Cases, (1939) Wis. L. Rev. 339.

[4] Renihan v. Dennin, 103 N. Y. 573, 579, 9 N. E. 320: "But it is claimed that the statute should be held not to apply to testamentary cases. There is just as much reason for applying it to such cases as to any other, and the broad and sweeping

≫→

In the early history of the privilege, the statutes generally were couched in broad and all-embracing language and seldom designated the classes of actions or proceedings in which the privilege might not be invoked. Later enactments, to a large extent, have removed all doubts in this respect. To determine whether the privilege applies in testamentary actions and in probate proceedings, obviously one should first examine the statute of the particular jurisdiction in which the question may arise. It has been observed that most of the modern statutes restrict the operation of the privilege statute to *civil* actions, but a proceeding to probate a will, or an action to contest one, would seem to partake of the nature of a civil action. Several courts have so held,[5] but there are decisions to the contrary.[6] According to the great weight of authority, the statutory privilege is applicable to testamentary actions and to probate proceedings. The specific question is seldom discussed, and it appears to be taken for granted that the privilege applies to such cases.[7]

←≪≪

language of the two sections cannot be so limited as to exclude such cases from their operation. There is no more reason for allowing the secret ailments of a patient to be brought to light in a contest over his will than there is for exposing them in any other case where they become the legitimate subject of inquiry." See also Mason v. Williams, (1889) 53 Hun. 398, 6 N. Y. S. 479; *In re* Halsey's Estate, (1890) 9 N. Y. S. 441.

[5] *Re* Flint, (1893) 100 Cal. 391, 34 Pac. 863; Niemes v. Niemes, (1918) 97 Ohio St. 145, 119 N. E. 503; Miller v. Livingstone, (1906) 31 Utah 415, 88 Pac. 338.

The Mississippi privilege statute applies "in any legal proceeding."

[6] In Estate of Joseph, (1897) 118 Cal. 660, 50 Pac. 768, it was held that an action to revoke the probate of a will is a *special proceeding,* not a civil action.

In Golder's Estate, (1916) 37 S. D. 397, 158 N. W. 735, it was held that a will contest is not a civil action; hence, the statutory privilege, which extends only to *civil* actions, ought not to have been enforced and the physicians should have been allowed to testify.

[7] The following selected cases are sufficient to sustain the textual statement: Hyatt v. Wroten, (1931) 184 Ark. 847, 43 S. W. 2d 726; Schirmer v. Baldwin, (1930) 182 Ark. 581, 32 S. W. 2d 162; Estate of Johnson, (1927) 200 Cal. 299, 252 Pac. 1049; Estate of Casarotti, (1920) 184 Cal. 73, 192 Pac. 1085; *In re* Ross, (1916) 173 Cal. 178, 159 Pac. 603. (Subsequent amendments of the California statute, however, have nullified the privilege in will contests.) *In re* Shapter's Estate, (1906) 35 Colo. 578, 85 Pac. 688, 6 L. R. A. (n. s.) 575; McCartney v. Holmquist, (1939) 70 App. D. C. 334, 106 F. 2d 855, 126 A. L. R. 375; Thompson v. Smith, (1939) 70 App. D. C. 65, 103 F. 2d 936, 123 A. L. R. 76; Labofish v. Berman, (1932) 60 App. D. C. 397, 55 F. 2d 1022; Hutchins v. Hutchins, (1919) 48 App. D. C. 495; Marker v. McCue, (1931) 50 Idaho 462, 297 Pac.

≫≫→

Therefore, in the absence of waiver, or of a specific statutory exemption, the attending physician may not testify, against objection, as to the mental or physical condition of the testator, where his information was acquired while attending him and was necessary to enable him to prescribe or act for him in his professional capacity.[8] It may be noted in passing that most of the decisions concern the right of an attending physician to testify to the testator's mental condition and turn upon the question by whom the privilege may be waived.[9]

←《

401; Pence v. Myers, (1913) 180 Ind. 282, 101 N. E. 716; Scott v. Smith, (1908) 171 Ind. 453, 85 N. E. 774; Heaston v. Krieg, (1906) 167 Ind. 101, 77 N. E. 805; Towles v. Mc-Curdy, (1904) 163 Ind. 12, 71 N. E. 129; Barry v. Walker, (1911) 152 Iowa 154, 128 N. W. 386; Winters v. Winters, (1897) 102 Iowa 53, 71 N. W. 184; Stayton v. Stayton, (1938) 148 Kan. 172, 81 P. 2d 1; Gorman v. Hickey, (1937) 145 Kan. 54, 64 P. 2d 587; Chaffee v. Kaufman, (1923) 113 Kan. 254, 214 Pac. 618; *In re* Nickel's Estate, (1948) 321 Mich. 519, 32 N. W. 2d 733; Oldenberg v. Leiberg, (1913) 177 Mich. 150, 142 N. W. 1076; *In re* Mansbach's Estate, (1907) 150 Mich. 348, 114 N. W. 65; *In re* Estate of Cunningham, (1944) 219 Minn. 80, 17 N. W. 2d 85; Watkins v. Watkins, (1926) 142 Miss. 210, 106 So. 753; Dabbs v. Richardson, (1924) 137 Miss. 789, 102 So. 769; McCaw v. Turner, (1921) 126 Miss. 260, 88 So. 705; Spurr v. Spurr, (1920) 285 Mo. 163, 226 S. W. 35; Thompson v. Ish, (1889) 99 Mo. 160, 12 S. W. 510; Estate of Mary Gray, (1911) 88 Neb. 835, 130 N. W. 746, 33 L. R. A. (n. s.) 319, Ann. Cas. 1912 B. 1037; Parker v. Parker, (1907) 78 Neb. 535, 111 N. W. 119; Matter of Coddington, (1954) 307 N. Y. 181, 120 N. E. 2d 777; Matter of Elizabeth Cashman, (1939) 280 N. Y. 681, 21 N. E. 2d 193; Roche v. Nason, (1906) 185 N. Y. 128, 77 N. E. 1007; Loder v. Whelpley, (1888) 111 N. Y. 239, 18 N. E. 874; Auld v. Cathro, (1910) 20 N. D. 461, 128 N. W. 1025, 32 L. R. A. (n. s.) 71, Ann. Cas. 1913 A 90; Weis v. Weis, (1947) 147 Ohio St. 416, 72 N. E. 2d 245, 169 A. L. R. 668; Carson v. Beatley, (1948) 86 Ohio App. 173, 82 N. E. 2d 745; *In re* Porter's Estate, (1953) 208 Okla. 475, 257 P. 2d 517; *In re* Will of Swartz, (1920) 79 Okla. 191, 192 Pac. 203, 16 A. L. R. 450; Grieve v. Howard, (1919) 54 Utah 225, 180 Pac. 423; *In re* Thomas' Estate, (1931) 165 Wash. 42, 4 P. 2d 837, 7 P. 2d 1119; *In re* Quick's Estate, (1931) 161 Wash. 537, 297 Pac. 198; *In re* Peterson's Estate, (1947) 250 Wis. 158, 26 N. W. 2d 553; Estate of Gallun, (1934) 215 Wis. 314, 254 N. W. 542; *In re* Will of Bruendl, (1899) 102 Wis. 45, 78 N. W. 169.

See also 28 R. C. L., Witnesses, § 131; 58 Am. Jur., Witnesses, § 433; note, 32 L. R. A. (n. s.) 72.

In re Shapter's Estate, *infra*, appears to regard the privilege inapplicable in a will contest, but it seems fair to assume that the evidence was admitted not on this ground, but because the privilege was waived by a party entitled to waive it.

[8] See c. X, herein.

[9] Questions concerning how, when, and by whom the privilege may be waived are discussed c. c. XVI, XVIII herein. See also 8 Wigmore, Evidence, § 2391.

In California, Guam and in Nevada, the statute now specifically provides that either before or after probate, upon the contest of any will, the attending physician may testify to the mental condition of the deceased patient and may disclose information acquired by him in his professional capacity. In Kentucky, Louisiana, New Mexico[10] and West Virginia the privilege is a limited one and does not apply in testamentary actions and in probate proceedings. In North Carolina the privilege applies, but the court may admit the testimony of the physician if, in the court's opinion, the same is necessary to a proper administration of justice. In Pennsylvania and in the Philippine Islands, the privilege would seldom apply in the cases here under discussion, since the statute excludes only disclosures which shall tend to blacken the character of the patient. In Hawaii, New Zealand, and in Victoria (Australia) the privilege applies "unless the sanity of the patient be the matter in dispute."[11] According to the Model Code of Evidence[12] and the Uniform Rules of Evidence,[13] there is no privilege upon an issue as to the validity of a document as a will of the patient, or upon an issue between parties claiming by testate or intestate succession from a deceased patient.

72. *Lunacy Inquisitions*

In the absence of an express limitation in the statute,[1] it seems reasonable to assume that the statutory privilege extends to lunacy inquisitions,[2] and that, in the absence of waiver, the ban of the statute will preclude a physician from testifying as to his patient's mental and physical condition where the facts enabling him to do so

---

[10] The prohibition in New Mexico is limited to any real or supposed venereal or loathesome disease.

[11] See Appendix, herein, for statutes mentioned in the text.

[12] (1942) Rule 223 (2)(b), (c).

[13] (1953) Rule 27 (3)(b), (c). See Appendix, herein.

[1] The Wisconsin statute expressly excludes the privilege "in all lunacy inquiries." In Hawaii, New Zealand, and Victoria (Australia), the privilege does not apply in any civil action or proceeding where the sanity of the patient is the matter of dispute.

[2] The Mississippi statute extends the privilege to "any legal proceeding."

were gained in the course of his professional attendance.[3] However, there is respectable authority for the view that the rule is not applicable in such proceedings.[4]

It should, perhaps, be observed that, in most of the states, statutes dealing with cases of mental illness and hidden disorders of the mind usually require the probate judge, before whom the determination is made, to appoint two or more reputable physicians to examine the individual involved concerning the nature, duration, and probable consequences of his mental affliction. It becomes the duty of a physician so appointed to make, and certify under oath, a report of the case and to file the same with the court; moreover, he may be required to testify to the facts and information he acquired in the course of his examination of the person. Obviously, the relation of physician and patient contemplated by the statute does not exist, and the privilege, therefore, has no application to the physicians appointed by the court in such proceedings.[5]

[3] Matter of Gates, (1915) 170 App. Div. 921, 154 N. Y. S. 782; Matter of Baird, (1887) 11 N. Y. St. Rep. 263.

[4] *In re* Fleming, (1923) 196 Iowa 639, 195 N. W. 242; *In re* Harmsen, (1918) .... Iowa ......, 167 N. W. 618, L. R. A. 1918 E. 973; *In re* Benson, (1891) 16 N. Y. S. 111, 112: "I do not think the section applies to a proceeding of this character. No physician can be better qualified to testify to the sanity or insanity of a person than he who has for some time attended such person in a professional capacity. Indeed, the cases are not rare where none but the attending physician could intelligently testify to a person's mental condition." It should be pointed out, however, that no objection was raised to the admission of the physician's testimony.

See also Metropolitan Life Ins. Co. v. Ryan, (1943) 237 Mo. App. 464, 172 S. W. 2d 269.

In Hawkyard v. People, (1946) 115 Colo. 35, 39, 169 P. 2d 178, Alter, J., said: "We do not believe that in a lunacy inquisition, which is a statutory proceeding by the state for the protection of an unfortunate individual and his property, the [attorney-client privilege] statute has any application. A lunacy inquisition is not instituted for the purpose of punishing a mental incompetent or to deprive him of any property rights, but is a proceeding to protect him from the impositions of unscrupulous persons and to conserve his property for his use and benefit. It is in no sense adversary, and an attorney who has had charge of his legal business may be in much better position than any other person to give evidence as to the unfortunate person's inability to properly manage his affairs."

According to the Model Code of Evidence, (1942) Rule 223(2)(a), and to the Uniform Rules of Evidence, (1953) Rule 27 (3)(a), there is no privilege in lunacy inquisitions. See Appendix, herein, for the latter rule.

[5] See c. IX, herein.

73. *Actions for Malpractice*

An action for damages for medical malpractice is a civil action;[1] hence, generally speaking, the statutory privilege is applicable thereto.[2] In some jurisdictions, however, the statute expressly debars the privilege in actions for malpractice.[3] In others, the privilege is expressly withheld from actions for damages for personal injury or for wrongful death.[4] If, then, an action for malpractice can be treated as an action for personal injury, or for wrongful death if the patient dies, it would seem that the privilege would not apply to actions for malpractice brought in the courts of these jurisdictions. There is a conflict of opinion, however, as to the nature and form of an action for malpractice.[5] Theoretically, it may be regarded as one essentially tortious in its nature growing out of the breach of duty incident to the relationship of physician and patient.[6] Some courts, however, have emphasized the contract theory of the relationship and have held that, where the facts are properly pleaded, the plaintiff may elect to sue on contract and waive the tort.[7] It has

---

[1] The liability of a physician for malpractice may be civil and criminal. In State v. Lester, (1914) 127 Minn. 282, 149 N. W. 297, L. R. A. 1915 D. 201, a physician was held guilty of manslaughter where his patient's death resulted from his gross negligence.

[2] In a number of jurisdictions, the legislature has so restricted the application of the privilege as to render it virtually, if not entirely, ineffectual in actions for malpractice. *e. g.*, New Mexico, North Carolina, Pennsylvania, Philippine Islands. In Louisiana, the privilege extends to criminal cases only. In West Virginia, it is limited to actions before a Justice of the Peace. In Kentucky, its operation is strictly limited and it does not apply to an action for malpractice. Williams v. Tartar, (1941) 286 Ky. 717, 151 S. W. 2d 783.

[3] Colorado, Nevada, Puerto Rico, Wisconsin. In Michigan, if a patient brings an action for malpractice and calls as a witness a physician who treated him for a condition with reference to which such malpractice is alleged, he waives the privilege as to any other physician who may have treated him for the same condition. Rule 223 (3) of the Model Code of Evidence (1942) and Rule 27 (4) of the Uniform Rules of Evidence (1953) exclude the privilege in actions for malpractice.

[4] California, Canal Zone, Guam, Hawaii, Nevada.

[5] For a general discussion of the nature of the action, see Regan, (1956) Doctor and Patient and the Law, § 3; Regan, (1943) Medical Malpractice, § 3; Herzog, (1931) Medical Jurisprudence, § 195; 41 Am. Jur., Physicians and Surgeons, § 120. See also note, Ann. Cas. 1912 D. 866.

[6] Carpenter v. Walker, (1910) 170 Ala. 659, 54 So. 60, Ann. Cas. 1912 D. 863.

[7] Carpenter v. Walker, supra note 6; Lane v. Boicourt, (1891) 128 Ind. 420, 27 N. E. 1111. In Bernard v. Doctor Nelson Co., (1913) 123 Minn. 468, 143 N. W. 1133, plaintiff sued in assumpsit.

been held, however, that an action for malpractice is an action for personal injury.[8]

Regardless of the form of the action, the doctrine of waiver has practically nullified the privilege in malpractice cases.[9] If the plaintiff calls another physician to testify to his condition as he found it when he treated him, he thereby lifts the bar of privilege from all communications between himself and the witness, and makes it possible for the defendant to examine the witness fully and at length, as to all relevant matters with respect to the condition of the patient at the time of his professional attendance upon him.[10] Of course, the privilege is waived as to the defendant if the patient, or his representative, calls him a witness.[11] But even though the plaintiff does not call the defendant as a witness, the latter, in all fairness, should have the right to defend himself on the witness stand. Being a party, the necessity of the matter makes him competent to testify in his own behalf concerning confidential communications between himself and his patient, notwithstanding the statutory privilege; otherwise, the defendant might be without the means of protecting himself.[12] It has been said, therefore, that where a patient directly attacks his physician, as by an action for malpractice, he abandons the protection afforded by the statutory privilege, for he thereby challenges the defendant to disprove the patient's contention as to the character of his injury or malady, or of his treatment.[13]

---

[8] Phillips v. Powell, (1930) 210 Cal. 39, 290 Pac. 441; Aspy v. Botkins, (1903) 160 Ind. 170, 66 N. E. 462.

[9] Of course, the privilege belongs to the patient, not the physician, and the patient, or, if he be dead, the holder of the privilege may, as a general rule, waive it. Sprouse v. Magee, (1928) 46 Idaho 622, 269 Pac. 993; Harvey v. Silber, (1942) 300 Mich. 510, 2 N. W. 2d 483; Markham v. Hipke, (1916) 169 Wis. 37, 171 N. W. 300. We are here concerned with the question whether the defendant-physician can insist that the privilege has been waived by the plaintiff. For particular questions involving the doctrine of waiver, see c. c. XVI and XVIII, herein.

[10] Albers v. Wilson, (1922) 201 App. Div. 775, 195 N. Y. S. 145; McDonnell v. Monteith, (1930) 59 N. D. 750, 231 N. W. 854.

[11] See § 131, herein.

[12] Cramer v. Hurt, (1899) 154 Mo. 112, 55 S. W. 258; Hartley v. Calbreath, (1907) 127 Mo. App. 559, 106 S. W. 570.

[13] May v. Northern Pac. Ry., (1905) 32 Mont. 522, 81 Pac. 328, 70 L. R. A. 111, 4 Ann. Cas. 605.

≫→

Surely there is no sound basis for enforcing the privilege where the patient himself, for the purpose of monetary gain, voluntarily makes public the details of his injury, ailment, or disease. When secrecy ends, the privilege ends.[14] There also is authority for the proposition that when a patient brings an action against his physician for alleged malpractice in the treatment of his injury or ailment, the privilege is thereby waived as to all matters connected with the treatment in which the defendant participated.[15] It would

---

←—

In actions between attorneys and clients, wherein charges of malpractice have been made against the attorney, it has generally been held that the rule as to privileged communications does not apply. If the disclosure of confidential matters becomes necessary to protect the reputation, integrity, and rights of the attorney, he is released from the obligations of secrecy which the law ordinarily imposes upon him. Pierce v. Norton, (1909) 82 Conn. 441, 74 Atl. 686; Nave v. Baird, (1859) 12 Ind. 318; State v. Madigan, (1896) 66 Minn. 10, 12, 68 N. W. 179: "If the client does not wish a repulse, he should not attack. If he does not wish the obligation of secrecy released, he should not divulge the matter himself."

Mitchell v. Bromberger, (1866) 2 Nev. 345; Stern v. Daniel, (1907) 47 Wash. 96, 91 Pac. 522; State v. Markey, (1951) 259 Wis. 527, 49 N. W. 2d 437.

[14] Whitmore v. Herrick, (1928) 205 Iowa 621, 630, 218 N. W. 334: "Many physicians, as well as the appellant herself, had related to the jury a description of the injury, together with the revelation of its nauseating aspect; and moreover she (appellant) had previously voluntarily exposed the member to the jury. Waiver lifts the bar of the legislative enactment, and the circumstances here related constituted such relinquishment."

Lane v. Boicourt, (1891) 128 Ind. 420, 423, 27 N. E. 1111: "The testimony given by the witnesses of the appellee broke the seal of privacy, and gave publicity to the whole matter. The plaintiff waived the statutory rule. Nothing was privileged, since all was published. The statute was not meant to apply to such a case as this, nor is it within the letter or the spirit of the law."

Capron v. Douglass, (1908) 193 N. Y. 11, 17, 85 N. E. 827, 20 L. R. A. (n. s.) 1003: "This action * * * was for malpractice. The plaintiff both in his complaint and in his testimony has fully disclosed all of the details of his affliction as it existed both at his home and in the hospital. * * * He, himself, has, therefore, given to the public the full details of his case, thereby disclosing the secrets which the statute was designed to protect, thus removing it from the operation of the statute."

[15] Becknell v. Hosier, (1893) 10 Ind. App. 5, 37 N. E. 580; Polin v. St. Paul Union Depot Co., (1924) 159 Minn. 410, 199 N. W. 87 (dictum); Marfia v. Great Northern Ry., (1914) 124 Minn. 466, 145 N. W. 385 (dictum); Cramer v. Hurt, (1899) 154 Mo. 112, 55 S. W. 258 (dictum); Terier v. Dare, (1911) 146 App. Div. 375, 377, 131 N. Y. S. 51: "By bringing an action against his regular physician, who had been treating him for a disease, claiming that the subsequent treatment was malpractice, the plaintiff waived the professional privilege and the defendant was permitted to show any facts he knew

⟫—→

be manifestly most unfair to establish any other rule,[16] since it would leave a physician absolutely at the mercy of an unscrupulous patient.[17] The waiver extends both to the physician and to such others who acted or consulted with him.[18] Some courts, however, have held that the waiver does not extend to a physician who consulted with or treated the patient at another time and independently of the defendant-physician,[19] unless, it may be, the patient voluntarily discloses his communications to such other physician.[20] However, where such are elicited by the defendant on cross-examination, the disclosure is not voluntary and the privilege is not waived.[21] But where the plaintiff called the family physician of the

---

bearing upon the present condition of the plaintiff. (Two judges dissented); Van Allen v. Gordon, (1894) 83 Hun. 379, 31 N. Y. S. 907.

16 Becknell v. Hosier, (1893) 10 Ind. App. 5, 37 N. E. 580; Capron v. Douglass, (1908) 193 N. Y. 11, 85 N. E. 827, 20 L. R. A. (n. s.) 1003. See also Hethier v. Johns, (1922) 233 N. Y. 370, 135 N. E. 603.

17 Capron v. Douglass, (1908) 193 N. Y. 11, 85 N. E. 827, 20 L. R. A. (n. s.) 1003.

18 Lane v. Boicourt, (1891) 128 Ind. 420, 27 N. E. 1111; Becknell v. Hosier, (1893) 10 Ind. App. 5, 37 N. E. 580; Whitmore v. Herrick, (1928) 205 Iowa 621, 218 N. W. 334; Hartley v. Calbreath, (1907) 127 Mo. App. 559, 106 S. W. 570; Capron v. Douglass, (1908) 193 N. Y. 11, 85 N. E. 827, 20 L. R. A. (n. s.) 1003.

See also Hennessy v. Kelly, (1900) 30 Misc. 703, 64 N. Y. S. 562. This case was reversed in (1900) 55 App. Div. 441, 66 N. Y. S. 871, but the decision of the County Court is in accord with the rule later established by the Court of Appeals in Capron v. Douglass, infra.

19 Aspy v. Botkins, (1903) 160 Ind. 170, 66 N. E. 462. Wigmore characterizes this case as a "mockery of justice." Wigmore, Evidence, § 2385, note 3.

Linscott v. Hughbanks, (1934) 140 Kan. 353, 37 P. 2d 26; Hartley v. Calbreath, (1907) 127 Mo. App. 559, 106 S. W. 570; Gunn v. Robinson, (1918) 103 Misc. 547, 171 N. Y. S. 692, rev'd on other grounds 188 App. Div. 948, 176 N. Y. S. 901; Packard v. Coberly, (1928) 147 Wash. 345, 265 Pac. 1082. There is a conflict of opinion on this question. See § 140, herein. In New York, the rule previously established by a long line of decisions was altered by the decision in Capron v. Douglass, (1908) 193 N. Y. 11, 85 N. E. 827, 20 L. R. A. (n. s.) 1003, and in Hethier v. Johns, (1922) 233 N. Y. 370, 135 N. E. 603.

20 Hartley v. Calbreath, (1907) 127 Mo. App. 559, 106 S. W. 570; Gunn v. Robinson, (1918) 103 Misc. 547, 171 N. Y. S. 692, rev'd on other grounds 188 App. Div. 948, 176 N. Y. S. 901.

21 Linscott v. Hughbanks, (1934) 140 Kan. 353, 37 P. 2d 26.

Wigmore regards this case as "another mockery of justice." Wigmore, Evidence, § 2385, note 3. Gunn v. Robinson, (1918) 103 Misc. 547, 171 N. Y. S. 692, rev'd on other grounds 188 App. Div. 948, 176 N. Y. S. 901; Packard v. Coberly, (1928) 147 Wash. 345, 265 Pac. 1082.

deceased as a witness and he testified to the patient's condition as he found it after the defendant had discontinued his efforts, it was held that the privilege was waived by the plaintiff and that the defendant could call as a witness in his behalf another physician who attended the deceased as a consulting physician.[22] Of course, where the information sought from another physician was not such as was necessary to enable him to act for the patient, but to obtain his opinion on the facts of the case so as to better enable plaintiff's attorney to conduct the action, the privilege does not apply and the witness may be compelled, at the instance of the defendant, to disclose what the patient said to him about his condition.[23]

In an action by the husband for damages sustained as the result of alleged malpractice performed by the defendant upon the plaintiff's wife, it was held that the privilege of the wife against the testimony of her physician was not waived by her husband calling her as a witness in the action brought by him alone.[24]

The defendant in a malpractice case, when being examined adversely before trial, cannot refuse, on the ground of privilege, to disclose information received by him while treating the plaintiff as a patient, where the plaintiff expressly waives the statutory privilege. The privilege belongs to the patient, not to the physician.[25] But the plaintiff cannot seek to make out her case in chief by expert testimony evidence elicited from the defendant on cross-examination over his protest.[26]

74. *Actions by Physicians for Services Rendered*

The right to compensation for medical services rendered is not in its general sense peculiar to the law of physicians and surgeons.

[22] Denny v. Robertson, (1944) 352 Mo. 609, 179 S. W. 2d 5.

[23] Jacobs v. Cross, (1872) 19 Minn. 454.

[24] Cramer v. Hurt, (1899) 154 Mo. 112, 55 S. W. 258. But where plaintiff's wife and her physician were called by plaintiff and they testified to the wife's condition, defendant was entitled to examine the attending physician. The privilege may not be waived in part and retained in part. Demonbrun v. McHaffie, (1941) 348 Mo. 1120, 156 S. W. 2d 923.

[25] Markham v. Hipke, (1919) 169 Wis. 37, 171 N. W. 300.

[26] Osborn v. Carey, (1913) 24 Idaho 158, 132 Pac. 967; Wiley v. Wharton, (1941) 68 Ohio App. 345, 41 N. E. 2d 255; Forthofer v. Arnold, (1938) 60 Ohio App. 436, 21 N. E. 2d 869. *Contra:* Lawless v. Calaway, (1944) 24 Cal. 2d 81, 147 P. 2d 604.

Ordinarily, it involves the law of contracts, and the legal obligations which the law imposes when the employment of a physician is procured by persons other than the patient.[1] But a physician who sues his patient for the value of his professional services may find that certain rules of evidence severely hinder, if not entirely bar, his chances of recovering a judgment. If he sues the personal representative of a deceased patient, the dead man statute will prevent him from taking the witness stand, if timely objection is made to his competency.[2] If he sues a living patient, the privilege statute, if its protection is claimed by the patient, may prevent the physician from testifying to the nature and extent of the patient's malady or injury, and his treatment thereof.[3] Obviously the statute does not deprive the physician of a right of action, but, to succeed, he must establish his case without offending its provisions.[4] Moreover, the allegations of the complaint filed by a physician, which disclose privileged information acquired while attending the defendant, may be stricken out on motion.[5] Furthermore, the law will not permit another physician, or a nurse who is within the privilege[6] to testify at the instance of the physician-plaintiff if either of them has attended the

---

[1] See 41 Am. Jur., Physicians and Surgeons, §§ 140-150; 70 C. J. S., Physicians and Surgeons, §§ 68-70; McClenahan v. Keyes, (1922) 188 Cal. 574, 206 Pac. 454.

[2] Kennedy v. Mulligan, (1916) 173 App. Div. 859, 160 N. Y. S. 105; Titus v. Spencer, (1915) 151 N. Y. S. 515; McGillicuddy v. Farmers' Loan & Trust Co., (1899) 26 Mis. 55, 55 N. Y. S. 242. The incompetency may be waived by the personal representative, and is waived where the latter took the deposition of the physician-plaintiff, although he did not use it at the trial. McClenahan v. Keyes, (1922) 188 Cal. 574, 206 Pac. 454.

[3] Hobbs v. Hullman, (1918) 183 App. Div. 743, 744, 171 N. Y. S. 390: "It is against public policy to permit a physician to make such disclosures, even in an action to recover for his services." Kennedy v. Mulligan, (1916) 173 App. Div. 859, 160 N. Y. S. 105; Van Allen v. Gordon, (1894) 83 Hun. 379, 31 N. Y. S. 907; MacEvitt v. Maas, (1901) 33 Misc. 552, 67 N. Y. S. 817, aff'd 64 App. Div. 382, 72 N. Y. S. 158.

[4] Schamberg v. Whitman, (1912) 75 Misc. 215, 135 N. Y. S. 262, aff'd. 151 App. Div. 939, 135 N. Y. S. 1141; McGillicuddy v. Farmers' Loan & Trust Co., (1899) 26 Misc. 55, 55 N. Y. S. 242.

[5] Schamberg v. Whitman, (1912) 75 Misc. 215, 135 N. Y. S. 262, aff'd. 151 App. Div. 939, 135 N. Y. S. 1141.

[6] But a nurse, not within the privilege, can testify to conversations between the physician, the patient and the patient's husband concerning the patient's condition and its cause. Hobbs v. Hullman, (1918) 183 App. Div. 743, 171 N. Y. S. 390.

For competency of a nurse, see § 31, herein.

patient and their testimony would disclose confidential information which they acquired in the performance of their duties.[7]

It has been urged that if the physician-plaintiff, or his professional assistant or consultant, is not permitted to describe the injury or ailment from which the patient suffered, he will not be able to show the character and value of his services and thus he will be deprived of the only evidence upon which a jury could rightfully return a verdict in his favor.[8] However, it has been pointed out that such a result does not necessarily follow.[9]

The ban of the statute is equally effective where the patient pleads malpractice defensively, or by way of setoff or counterclaim, in an action for compensation. In doing this, the patient does not waive the benefit of the statute even though he might be deemed to

---

[7] MacEvitt v. Maas, (1901) 33 Misc. 552, 67 N. Y. S. 817, aff'd 64 App. Div. 382, 72 N. Y. S. 158; McGillicuddy v. Farmers' Loan & Trust Co., (1899) 26 Misc. 55, 55 N. Y. S. 242.

[8] This is no fanciful argument. See McGillicuddy v. Farmers' Loan & Trust Co., (1899) 26 Misc. 55, 55 N. Y. S. 242; Titus v. Spencer, (1915) 151 N. Y. S. 515.

It is submitted, with respect, that the lawmakers should consider the plight of the physician in such cases, and absolve him from the inflexible ban of the statute.

[9] Van Allen v. Gordon, (1894) 83 Hun. 379, 380, 31 N. Y. S. 907: "The physician can still testify to his employment, to the number of visits made, to the examinations, prescriptions, and operations, and, if the defendant objects to his describing them, the physician may then testify as to the value. It may be that the plaintiff [assignee of the physician's claim] would be unable to corroborate the physician's testimony as to the value of the services for the reasons that he would not be permitted to disclose to other physicians the character of the services rendered, but the defendant would meet the same embarrassment when he undertook to dispute the value of such services."

In MacEvitt v. Maas, (1901) 33 Misc. 552, 67 N. Y. S. 817, aff'd 64 App. Div. 382, 72 N. Y. S. 158, an action for professional services rendered defendant's wife, the plaintiff and two surgeons who assisted in the operation were not allowed to testify concerning the patient's ailment. Over objection by the defendant, however, the two surgeons were permitted to testify as experts as to the value of the plaintiff's services. Gaynor, J., (p. 554): "There was evidence that a capital surgical operation was performed, of the time it took, and of the number of visits the plaintiff made to the patient before and after it; but there was none to show what the operation really was. But while there were no particulars before the jury to serve as a basis for the value of the surgical operation, the witnesses knew the particulars. The statute excluding such particulars cannot justly be held to exclude such evidence of value by the surgeons who saw them. It was the best evidence which the nature of the case admitted of; and that has been held to justify the admission of evidence. The operation of the statute having created an exceptional case, it had to be treated in an exceptional manner."

have abandoned the privilege had he brought an original action against the physician alleging misconduct or malpractice.[10]

In Ohio, in an action by a physician to recover the value of professional services rendered the defendant, it is proper for the physician to testify to whatever is necessary to protect or maintain his rights and he may disclose facts which show his employment and the services he performed.[11] In Pennsylvania, in an action brought by a physician to recover compensation for services rendered a deceased patient, the testimony of the plaintiff's secretary and his records made in the course of his professional conduct, were held admissible to prove the number of visits made by him and the treatment prescribed; also the records of the hospital.[12]

75. Non-judicial Proceedings and Investigations

Although the principle of testimonial privilege usually is associated with judicial proceedings, it does not necessarily follow that a privilege of this type is inapplicable in a proceeding or investigation not strictly of a judicial character.[1]

---

[10] Van Allen v. Gordon, (1894) 83 Hun. 379, 31 N. Y. S. 907 (by interposing a general denial, patient does not waive privilege). McGillicuddy v. Farmers' Loan & Trust Co., (1899) 26 Misc. 55, 55 N. Y. S. 242.

[11] Petrucelli v. Steinharter, (1926) 24 Ohio App. 471, 157 N. E. 803. A sensible and just decision. This view has long been recognized in suits for compensation brought by attorneys against their clients. e. g., Pierce v. Norton, (1909) 82 Conn. 441, 74 Atl. 686; Weinshenk v. Sullivan, (1937) ...... Mo. App. ......, 100 S. W. 2d 66; Mitchell v. Bromberger, (1866) 2 Nev. 345; Stern v. Daniel, (1907) 47 Wash. 96, 91 Pac. 552.

It may be that the statute of Puerto Rico excludes the privilege in actions of this character.

[12] McKeehan Estate, (1948) 358 Pa. 548, 57 A. 2d 907. The question of privilege does not appear to have been raised, due, probably, to the fact that the statutory privilege in that state is a very limited one.

[1] See note, 133 A. L. R. 732.

In McMann v. Securities and Exchange Comm'n., (1937) 87 F. 2d 377, cert. denied 301 U. S. 684, 81 Law. Ed. 1342, 57 Su. Ct. 785, 109 A. L. R. 1445, an action involving an investigation by defendant, the court assumed for the purposes of the opinion that the conduct of investigations under the Securities Act of 1933 was "subject to the same testimonial privileges as judicial proceedings," referring particularly to the traditional privileges touching communications made in certain confidential relationships. In Matter of Hirschfield v. Hanley, (1920) 228 N. Y. 346, 127 N. E. 252, it was held that, in an examination of the accounts of designated public officials conducted by the Commissioner of Accounts under authority of law, wherein persons are summoned to

⤷

Doubtless, the primary purpose of the physician-patient privilege statute was to declare a rule that would govern the examination of a physician as a witness in a judicial proceeding;[2] but under a broad and liberal construction, it seems reasonable to assume that it was intended to extend also to any lawful examination of a physician as a witness under oath.[3] In *New York City Council* v. *Goldwater*,[4] an order of the lower courts granting an application for the commitment of certain officials of a city hospital to jail until they should produce books, papers, and records specified in subpoenas served upon them in a councilmanic investigation of charges of negligence and maladministration in the treatment of patients at such hospital, was reversed and the application denied. It was held that the statutory privilege may be asserted in *legislative* investigations, as well as in purely judicial proceedings.[5] The privilege ex-

←꿕
testify, those who are thus made witnesses are entitled to all the privileges and protection extended by the law to witnesses in judicial proceedings. The husband-wife privilege may properly be invoked in a proceeding conducted by a Special Inquiry Officer of the office of the Immigration and Naturalization Service and in a hearing before the Board of Immigration Appeals. Gilles v. Del Guercio, (1957) 150 F. Supp. 864.

[2] Buffalo Loan, Trust & Safe Deposit Co. v. Knights Templar & Masonic Mut. Aid Ass'n., (1891) 126 N. Y. 450, 27 N. E. 942.

[3] The Minnesota statute extends the privilege to "any action or proceeding, civil or criminal, in court or before any person who has authority to receive evidence."

[4] (1949) 284 N. Y. 296, 31 N. E. 2d 31, 133 A. L. R. 728.

See also *In re* St. Helen's Hospital, [1913] 32 New Zealand 682, to the same effect.

[5] Two judges dissented, believing that it is not unreasonable to require that the protection of the individual by privilege must bow to the welfare and protection of the public. A number of commentators share this view.

See (1941) 26 Corn. L. Q. 482; (1941) 4 U. Det. L. J. 173; (1941) 54 Harv. L. Rev. 705; (1941) 16 Ind. L. J. 592; (1941) 39 Mich. L. Rev. 1258; (1941) 89 U. Pa. L. Rev. 981. It should be remembered that the statutory privilege is a testimonial privilege only. Accordingly, it has been held that the attorney-client privilege cannot be invoked to prevent a legislative committee from publicly revealing a surreptitiously obtained tape-recording of a conversation between a prisoner and his attorney in the county jail. Lanza v. New York State Joint Legislative Committee, (1957) 3 N. Y. 2d 92, 164 N. Y. S. 2d 9: "The committee in the instant case does not seek to compel the attorney or the client to testify as to the confidential communication and is not, as in New York City Council v. Goldwater, supra, invoking the power of the court to compel plaintiffs or anyone else to disclose information they are forbidden to disclose. It is seeking to make a part of the public record of its investigation informa-

꿕→

tends also to an investigation by a grand jury of certain types of cases in a public hospital.[6] In *People* v. *Sellick*,[7] an indictment for abortion was set aside on the ground that during the investigation by the grand jury of the alleged offense, two physicians were permitted to testify to information they had acquired while professionally attending the woman upon whom the alleged abortion was performed.[8]

There is authority for the view that the statutory privilege is applicable in a proceeding before a *private* tribunal. In an action on a fraternal benefit certificate issued by the defendant, it appeared that upon the hearing of plaintiff's claim before the Supreme Body, whose decisions as to the validity of such claims was final, an affidavit signed by a physician who had attended the deceased was received and considered. The tribunal rejected the claim. The Supreme Court held that the physician-patient privilege statute was intended by the legislature to be applicable to any judicial proceedings which it had the power to regulate; that the hearing before defendant's Supreme Body was a judicial hearing to which the privi-

---

tion which has come to it in the course thereof." (Three judges dissented.) Of course, the lawyer can not subsequently be compelled to testify and to answer questions based on the recording and concerning contact with a third person within his professional employment. *Re* Lanza, (1957) 4 A. D. 2d 252, 164 N. Y. S. 2d 534.

[6] Application of Grand Jury of County of Kings, (1955) 286 App. Div. 270, 143 N. Y. S. 2d 501, appeal denied 309 N. Y. 1031. Provisions of the Sanitary Code of the city of New York require that information regarding criminal abortions be turned over to the Health Department. It was held, however, that these do not modify or repeal the privilege statute. The superintendent of the hospital was therefore justified in refusing to obey a subpoena issued by the grand jury which required him to produce all papers, charts and records of all persons treated at such hospital during specified periods of time.

[7] (1886) 4 N. Y. Crim. Rep. 329.

[8] The court pointed out that a section of the Criminal Code provides: "The grand jury can receive nothing but legal evidence."

However, in Wickline v. Alvis, Warden, (1957) 103 Ohio App. 1, 144 N. E. 2d 207, a habeas corpus action, petitioner's conviction of murder was upheld notwithstanding the fact that the indictment was based in part upon evidence given to the grand jury by the wife of the petitioner in violation of the husband-wife privilege.

See also People v. Eckert, (1956) 2 N. Y. 2d 126, 138 N. E. 2d 794. For application of the attorney-client privilege to an investigation before a grand jury, see United States v. Lee, (1901) 107 Fed. 702; People ex rel. Vogelstein v. Warden, (1934) 150 Misc. 714, 270 N. Y. S. 362, aff'd. 242 App. Div. 611, 271 N. Y. S. 1059.

lege applied; and that the rejection of plaintiff's claim, which was based upon the affidavit of the insured's physician, was improper.[9]

The state of the law pertaining to the right of a patient or a hospital to invoke the protection of the physician-patient privilege statute in an income tax investigation authorized by 28 U. S. C. A. § 3614 (a) is not entirely clear. It has been held that an investigatory inquiry by a Government agent is not a judicial proceeding and that the determination of what evidence is admissible is a matter to be decided according to federal law.[10] This does not mean, however, that the Government agent can use the records of a hospital to learn the nature of a patient's illness or the character of his surgical operation. It may well be he cannot.[11] If the government is entitled to inspect the records, some feasible and practical method of concealing this particular information should be adopted so as to seal off and keep secret any confidential information plainly within the scope of the privilege and not essential to the determination of the matter under investigation.[12]

---

[9] Dick v. Supreme Body of the International Congress, (1904) 138 Mich. 372, 101 N. W. 564, overruled on other grounds in Palmer v. Patrons' Mut. F. Ins. Co., (1922) 217 Mich. 292, 186 N. W. 511.

In the Dick Case, Carpenter, J., (p. 377) said: "There is nothing in the [privilege] statute to limit its operation to any particular judicial tribunal or to any particular class of judicial proceedings. * * * This statute was, therefore, in my judgment, violated when the physician's affidavit was used as testimony." Three judges dissented, holding that the defendant had the right to make its own rules of evidence for its tribunal and, in the absence of fraud or oppression, the judgment of such tribunal ought to stand.

[10] *In re* Albert Lindley Lee Memorial Hospital, (1953) 209 F. 2d 122, cert. denied Cincotta v. United States, 347 U. S. 960, 98 Law. Ed. 1104, 74 Su. Ct. 709; Falsone v. United States, (1953) 205 F. 2d 734, cert. denied 346 U. S. 864, 98 Law. Ed. 375, 74 Su. Ct. 103 (State accountant-client privilege not recognized in tax investigation); Gretsky v. Basso, (1955) 136 F. Supp. 640.

[11] *In re* Albert Lindley Lee Memorial Hospital, supra. The case is not decisive, however, since the information sought was not privileged anyway. See note, (1954) 67 Harv. L. Rev. 1272. Gretsky v. Basso, (1955) 136 F. Supp. 640. Petition for order requiring a hospital to produce certain records, which revenue agent desired to examine, was granted, but confidential information relating to patients was protected from disclosure.

[12] It was so ordered in the cases cited in note 11, infra.

76. Proceedings Under Workmen's Compensation Acts

Workmen's Compensation Acts have been enacted in every state of the Union.[1] Each Act embodies a plan to compensate workmen, or their dependents, for loss of earnings because of personal injuries received by the workman, arising under the circumstances designated in the Act. Necessarily, in proceedings conducted under the auspices of a workmen's compensation board or commission, the inquiry in every case concerns the nature and extent of the physical injury produced by the accident, which includes, of course whether the injury, or the death, was caused by the accident or resulted from other causes. This ordinarily is essentially a medical question which can be determined best by the testimony of the physician or physicians who examined or treated the workman. Indeed, without such medical testimony, it would be very difficult to fairly and equitably administer a compensation law or, with any reasonable degree of accuracy, determine the actual facts involved in a compensation claim. It would seem, therefore, not only proper but imperative that any physician who has examined or treated the injured workman be permitted to testify at the instance of either party to the controversy. It need hardly be stated that the testimony of the medical man would be most useful, if not essential, in establishing the nature and extent of the injury and, to a large degree, in determining the amount of compensation the claimant will be entitled to receive. Of course, in the jurisdictions which do not recognize the physician-patient privilege at all, there is no problem in this regard. The attending physician is a competent witness and his testimony, however damaging it may be to the interests of his patient, is admissible in evidence.[2] On the other hand, among the jurisdictions which have enacted the privilege, there appears to be a conflict of opinion as to whether, or to what extent, it is applicable in hearings conducted by workmen's compensation commissions, or in compensation trials in courts of record.

---

[1] Also in Alaska, Hawaii, and Puerto Rico. Congress has enacted a compensation law pertaining to employees of the United States. See 5 U. S. C. A. § 751 et seq.

[2] H. H. Waegner & Co. v. Moock, (1946) 303 Ky. 222, 197 S. W. 2d 254. In a few of these jurisdictions, the legislatures have seen fit to expressly deny the privilege in workmen's compensation proceedings, e. g., (1953) Del. Code Ann., Tit. 19, § 2343 (c).

In practically all of the jurisdictions, a workman injured in the course of his employment, who seeks to recover compensation under a Workmen's Compensation Act, is required, at the request of the employer or when ordered by the commission, to submit himself to a physical examination when such examination is necessary to determine the character and extent of his injury and the probable duration of his disability. Usually, he is given the right to have a physician, provided and paid for by himself, present at such examination. If the workman refuses to submit to any such examination, or obstructs the same, his right to compensation may be suspended until such examination has taken place.[3] Some of the Acts provide that any physician who makes or is present at any such examination may be required to testify as to the results thereof.[4] Obviously, if

---

[3] There is a notable lack of uniformity in the statutes governing medical examinations. The Michigan statute is a typical example of such statutes. Mich. Sta. Ann., § 17.169 (1955 Cum. Supp.): "After an employee has given notice of an injury, as provided by this act, and from time to time thereafter during the continuance of his disability, he shall, if so requested by the employer, or the insurance company carrying such risk, or the commissioner of insurance, as the case may be, submit himself to an examination by a physician or surgeon authorized to practice medicine under the laws of the state, furnished and paid for by the employer, or the insurance company carrying such risk, or the commissioner of insurance, as the case may be. If such an examination be made the employee or his attorney shall be furnished, within 15 days from date of a request therefor, a complete and correct copy of the report of every such physical examination performed by the physician making the examination on behalf of the employer or the insurance company or the commissioner of insurance, as the case may be. The employee shall have the right to have a physician provided and paid for by himself present at the examination. If he refuses to submit himself for the examination, or in any way obstructs the same, his right to compensation shall be suspended, and his compensation during the period of suspension may be forfeited. Any physician who shall make or be present at any such examination may be required to testify under oath as to the results thereof." Similar provisions appear in the Workmen's Compensation Acts of Alaska, Arizona, Arkansas, California, Colorado, Hawaii, Idaho, Indiana, Iowa, Kansas, Minnesota, Mississippi, Missouri, Montana, Nebraska, Nevada, New Mexico, New York, North Carolina, North Dakota, Ohio, Oklahoma, Oregon, Pennsylvania, Puerto Rico, South Dakota, Utah, Washington, West Virginia, Wisconsin, Wyoming.

Since we are concerned with the application of the physician-patient privilege in workmen's compensation cases, the statutes mentioned above, and others that follow, are restricted to those states only which recognize the privilege. For the statutes of other states, see 8 Wigmore, Evidence, § 2220(7).

[4] Provisions of this type appear in the Acts of Alaska, Arizona, California, Colorado,

the information acquired by a physician in the course of such examination is not available to the employer, the examination would serve no practical purpose.[5] Independently of such a provision, however, it would seem that any information so acquired by the examining physician, or any communication made to him by the workman, may be disclosed by the physician if he be called upon to testify. The relation of physician and patient contemplated by the privilege statute does not exist under such circumstances; hence, no confidence results which needs or is entitled to protection.[6] In some jurisdictions, the employer or the commission has the right in any case of death to require an autopsy.[7]

A very different question is presented, however, where in a hearing conducted by the commission, or in the trial of a compensation case in a court of record, a physician, who at some time or other, has *treated* the injured workman, is called as a witness to testify in behalf of the employer, the insurance carrier, or the commission and his competency as a witness is challenged by the injured workman or, in the event of his death, by the holder of the privilege. Unlike the examining physician, the confidential relationship of physician and patient exists between the physician and the workman whom he has attended with the view to treatment; therefore, unless the statutory privilege is not applicable to workmen's compensation trials and proceedings, the attending physician's testimony, in the absence of waiver, is clearly within its ban.

Indiana, Michigan, Minnesota, Missouri, Montana, New Mexico, North Carolina, North Dakota, Pennsylvania, South Dakota, Washington, Wisconsin, Wyoming.

In Kansas, unless the employee's physician be given a reasonable opportunity to participate in the examination made by the employer's physician, the latter cannot give evidence of the condition of the employee at the time such examination was made. Kan. Gen. Stat. Ann., § 44-515(c) (1955 Cum. Supp.).

In New York, certain physicians, employed by the Board to make examinations of injured workmen, are disqualified from testifying in proceedings before the Board. See (1950) N. Y. *Workmen's Compensation Law*, § 19-a.

[5] Hamilton v. P. E. Johnson & Sons, (1938) 224 Iowa 1097, 276 N. W. 841.

[6] State, *ex rel* Galloway v. Industrial Comm'n., (1938) 134 Ohio St. 496, 17 N. E. 2d 918. See §§ 35, 36, herein.

[7] Alaska, California, Indiana, Minnesota, Missouri, Nebraska, North Carolina. Ordinarily, information gained by a physician as the result of an autopsical examination is not privileged. See § 44, herein.

Where a Workmen's Compensation Act contains no provision annulling the statutory physician-patient privilege in compensation hearings and trials, it has been held that the privilege is applicable thereto, and that a physician cannot, without the consent of the holder of the privilege, reveal confidential information acquired by him while attending the injured workman in his professional character.[8] There is, however, authority to the contrary.[9] But it should be remembered that where the privilege is applicable to workmen's compensation cases, the burden rests upon the objector[10] to show that the relation of physician and patient existed and that the information sought to be elicited from the witness was necessary to enable him to prescribe or act for the patient.[11] Of course, the doctrine of waiver applies also.[12] Generally speaking, it may be said that where the workman, or his representative, introduces evidence pertaining to his injury and the consequences thereof and thus

---

[8] Malone v. Industrial Comm'n., (1942) 140 Ohio St. 292, 43 N. E. 2d 266; Baker v. Industrial Comm'n., (1939) 135 Ohio St. 491, 21 N. E. 2d 593; Hasbrouck v. Goodyear Tire & Rubber Co., (1951) _____Com. Pleas_____, 60 Ohio Law Abst. 138, 99 N. E. 2d 329. But cf. Matter of Maryland Casualty Co., (1948) 274 App. Div. 211, 80 N. Y. S. 2d 181.

[9] Skelly v. Sunshine Mining Co., (1941) 62 Idaho 192, 109 P. 2d 622 (doctors jointly employed); Hamilton v. P. E. Johnson & Sons, (1938) 224 Iowa 1097, 276 N. W. 841.

In Doty v. Crystal Ice & Fuel Co., (1925) 118 Kan. 323, 325, 235 Pac. 96, it was held that the privilege "has no application to the testimony of physicians in claims for compensation under the workmen's compensation act." A provision to this effect is now embodied in the Kansas Act.

In Winthrop v. Industrial Acc. Comm'n., (1933) _____ Cal. App._____, 22 P. 2d 579, it was held that the privilege does not apply to the testimony of a surgeon who performed an operation on a compensation claimant to remove his disability.

In New Mexico, the statutory privilege is expressly made applicable to workmen's compensation cases except in instances where the physician has examined or treated the patient at the expense of the employer, and such payment is consented to by the patient. See Appendix, herein.

[10] See § 60, herein.

[11] Continental Investment Co. v. Garcher, (1928) 83 Colo. 239, 264 Pac. 723; McMillan v. Industrial Comm'n., (1941) _____Ohio App._____, 34 Ohio Law Abst. 435, 37 N. E. 2d 632; Bowers v. Industrial Comm'n., (1939) _____ Ohio App._____, 30 Ohio Law Abst. 353. See also Massich v. Keystone Coal & Coke Co., (1939) 137 Pa. Super. 541, 10 A. 2d 98. See also §§ 49, 50, herein.

[12] See c. c. XVI, XVIII, herein.

makes public matters which he might have kept secret, he will be deemed to have waived the privilege.[13]

Throughout the country, in recent years, Workmen's Compensation Acts have been thoroughly re-examined and revised. One of the important changes relates to the application of the physician-patient privilege. In many jurisdictions, the legislatures have virtually rejected the entire doctrine of privilege and authorize any physician who has examined *or treated* the injured workman to testify as a witness in a hearing before the commission, or in an action at law brought to recover damages against an employer who is subject to the compensation provisions of the Workmen's Compensation Act.[14] It should be noted, however, that some of these

[13] Cases involving the doctrine of waiver in compensation proceedings are few, and some are out of line with the generally recognized rules. La Count v. Von Platen-Fox Co., (1928) 243 Mich. 250, 220 N. W. 697; Petition of Maryland Cas. Co., (1948) 274 App. Div. 211, 80 N. Y. S. 2d 181; Baker v. Industrial Comm'n., (1939) 135 Ohio St. 491, 21 N. E. 2d 593; Gillen v. Industrial Comm'n., (1938) 59 Ohio App. 241, 17 N. E. 2d 663; Industrial Comm'n. v. Willoughby, (1936) _____ Ohio App._____ , 21 Ohio Law Abst. 588; Goodyear Tire & Rubber Co. v. Motz, (1935) _____ Ohio App._____ , 19 Ohio Law Abst. 14; Strebeck v. Eagle Picher Mining & S. Co., (1953) _____Okla._____ , 259 P. 2d 536.

[14] There are some interesting variations in the language of the statutes. *e. g.*, (1949) Alaska Comp. Laws Ann., § 43-3-27: "* * * No fact communicated to, or otherwise learned by any physician or surgeon who may have attended or examined the employee, or who may have been present at any examination, shall be privileged, either in the hearings provided for in this Act, or any action to recover damages against any employer who is subject to the compensation provisions of this Act * * *."

(1956) Ariz. Rev. Stat., § 23-908(c): "Information obtained by the attending physician or surgeon while in attendance on the injured person shall not be considered a privileged communication, if such information is required by the commission for a proper understanding of the case and a determination of the rights involved."

(1953) Colo. Rev. Stat. Ann., § 81-12-12: "* * * Any physician having attended an employee in a professional capacity may be required to testify before the commission when it shall so direct. A physician will not be required to disclose confidential communications imparted to him for the purpose of treatment and which are unnecessary to a proper understanding of the case * * *."

See also: Ind. Stat. Ann., § 40-1227 (1952 Repl.); (1955 Supp.) Kan. Gen. Stat. Ann., § 44-515 (expressly authorizing physician to testify to information acquired "prior to or after an injury"); (1956 Supp.) Minn. Stat. Ann., § 176.155 (5) (authorizing physician designated by the commission or furnished by the employer, who treats or examines an injured employee, to testify "relative to the injury or disability re-

⟫→

statutes appear to confine the abrogation to instances where the physician's attendance upon the patient was *subsequent* to the accident which is the basis of the claim,[15] or, exclusively, to hearings before the commission.[16]

In a number of States,[17] the Act provides that in hearings conducted by the commission it shall not be bound by the common law or statutory rules of evidence, or by any technical or formal rules of procedure, but may make the investigation in such manner as in its judgment is best calculated to ascertain the substantial rights of the parties and to carry out the spirit of the Act. This, however, does not authorize a commission, under its rule-making power, to require an applicant for compensation to waive his rights under the privilege statute as a condition precedent to a consideration of his claim.[18] Moreover, a commission cannot ignore the rule against the admission of hearsay evidence as proof of a fact, and thus make use of a letter written by a physician, deceased at the time of the hearing, to an insurance carrier, to overthrow a prima-facie showing of a right of recovery on the part of the claimant.[19]

Some of the Workmen's Compensation Acts expressly authorize the use in evidence of a physician's report concerning the injured workmen's injury and his condition of health; also the records of the hospital in which he was a patient.[20] A physician's certificate of

---

sulting therefrom."); Miss. Code Ann., § 6998.08 (1952 Recomp. Vol. 5a); (1952) Mo. Stat. Ann., § 287.140 (5); (1949 Supp.) Nev. Comp. Laws, § 2680.52; (1950 Recomp. Vol 2c) N. C. Gen. Stat., § 97-27; (1943) N. D. Rev. Code, § 65-0530 (filing of a claim constitutes consent to physician testifying); (1951) Wash. Rev. Code, § 51.04.050; (1953) Wis. Stat., § 102.13; (1955 Supp.) Wyo. Comp. Stat. Ann., § 72-182. See also (1953) Uniform Rules of Evidence, Rule 27(4), and (1942) Model Code of Evidence, Rule 223(3).

[15] *e. g.,* Alaska, Arizona, supra note 14.

[16] *e. g.,* Arizona, Colorado, Nevada, supra note 14.

[17] Arizona, Arkansas, Idaho, Indiana, Iowa, Minnesota, Mississippi, Missouri, Montana, New York, North Dakota, Ohio, Pennsylvania, West Virginia.

[18] State *ex rel* Galloway v. Industrial Comm'n., (1938) 134 Ohio St. 496, 17 N. E. 2d 918.

[19] Swim v. Central Iowa Fuel Co., (1927) 204 Iowa 546, 215 N. W. 603.

[20] *e. g.,* Ark. Stats. Ann., § 81-1323(c) (1955 Supp.): "At such hearing the claimant and the employer may each present evidence in respect of such claim. * * * Such evidence may include verified medical reports which shall be accorded such weight as may be

death is admissible in evidence to show that the death of the workman was due to natural causes and not the result of an industrial accident.[21] If, in a compensation proceeding, the injured workman fails to call as a witness the physician who attended him after the accident, without any explanation of his failure in this respect, the commission may presume that his testimony would have been unfavorable to the claimant's case.[22] The rule applies with equal force to a defendant who fails to produce medical evidence within its control.[23]

←—⟪

warranted from all the evidence of the case." See Foster v. Ft. Smith Cotton Oil Co., (1954) 224 Ark. 394, 273 S. W. 2d 529. (1953) Colo. Rev. Stat. Ann., § 81-14-3: "* * * The commission may receive as evidence and use as proof of any fact in dispute the following matters, in addition to sworn testimony presented at open hearings: (1) Reports of attending or examining physicians. * * * (4) Hospital records in the case of an injured or deceased employee."

(1952) Mo. Stat. Ann., § 287.140 (6): "Every hospital or other person furnishing the employee with medical aid shall permit its record to be copied by and shall furnish full information to the commission, the employer, the employee or his dependents * * *, and certified copies of such records shall be admissible in evidence in any such proceedings. Similar provisions are embodied in the Workmen's Compensation Acts of California, Kansas, Minnesota, Nebraska, Pennsylvania. See also Schaefer v. Lowell-Krekeler Grocery Co., (1932) ____ Mo. App.____, 49 S. W. 2d 209; Matter of Maryland Cas. Co., (1948) 274 App. Div. 211, 80 N. Y. S. 2d 181; Miller v. Pittsburgh Coal Co., (1937) 129 Pa. Super. 1, 195 Atl. 151. But *cf.* Matter of Lanham, (1955) 1 Misc. 2d 264, 144 N. Y. S. 2d 401.

21 Elleman v. Industrial Comm'n., (1937) 100 Colo. 120, 66 P. 2d 323; Griffin v. National Mining Co., (1937) 127 Pa. Super. 588, 193 Atl. 447.

See also §§ 67, 68, herein.

22 Guillory v. Union Sulphur Co., (1941) ____La. App.____, 3 So. 2d 197; Law v. Kansas City Bridge Co., (1940) ____La. App.____, 199 So. 155; Marotto v. George D. Ellis & Sons, Inc., (1942) 149 Pa. Super. 221, 28 A. 2d 339; Hilton v. Edwards Memorial Church, (1944) 50 Pa. D. & C. 341.

23 Anders v. Employers' Liability Assur. Corp., (1951) ____ La. App.____, 50 So. 2d 87; Agresta v. Western Elec. Co., (1949) 1 N. J. Super. 177, 63 A. 2d 290; Mosely v. Jones & Laughlin Steel Co., (1944) 155 Pa. Super. 598, 39 A. 2d 161.

CHAPTER XIII

Pre-Trial Proceedings: State Courts

Sec.
77. Physical Examination of a Party: In General
78. Same: Testimony and Report of Examining Physician
79. Depositions and Interrogatories

77. *Physical Examination of a Party: In General*

The authorities are in conflict upon the question whether, in an action to recover damages for personal injury, the court has inherent power to require the injured person to submit to a physical examination.[1] It need hardly be stated that the primary purpose of allowing an examination is to ascertain the true character and extent of the plaintiff's injury and thus prevent a defendant from being subjected to feigned, fraudulent and dishonest claims. A defendant should be protected in every way from any imposition which may be perpetrated by plaintiffs in suits of this character, and any plaintiff whose injury is real ought to welcome a thorough scrutiny of it by a competent physician.[2] Unquestionably, the great

---

[1] See notes, 108 A. L. R. 142; 51 A. L. R. 183. 14 R. C. L., *Inspection and Physical Examination,* § 14-25.

Power of Court to Order Physical Examination in Personal Injury Cases, (1938) 25 Va. L. Rev. 73. In Greenhow v. Whitehead's, Inc., (1946) 67 Idaho 262, 175 P. 2d 1007, the court discusses many cases, pro and con, pertaining to the rule in various jurisdictions. See note, 37 A. L. R. 2d 586, concerning appealability of order pertaining to pre-trial examination and discovery.

[2] Chicago, Rock Island & Pac. Ry. v. Hill, (1912) 36 Okla. 540, 545, 129 Pac. 13, 43 L. R. A. (n. s.) 622: "In an action for personal injuries, it is manifest that the jurors are entitled to all the information which can be produced, not only upon the cause of the injuries, but also the extent of the injuries, in order to determine whether the plaintiff should recover at all, and, if so, the amount of his recovery. Would an examination of the injuries by competent and disinterested physicians, appointed by the court and

⇛→

weight of authority supports the view that, in actions to recover damages for personal injury, trial courts have an inherent discretionary power to order a reasonable physical examination of the plaintiff to be made before trial by a competent physician whenever such examination is necessary to ascertain the nature and extent of his injury.[3] The character, extent, and conduct of the examination is usually set forth in the order of the court.[4] In a number of juris-

←

acting under his supervision, aid the jury in ascertaining these facts? Manifestly it would, and the jury would doubtless rely more upon the testimony of such a physician than they would upon one employed as an expert by one of the interested parties. Would the plaintiff be prejudiced by such an examination? Manifestly he would not, if his case was a *bona fide* one; and if it was not *bona fide* the law should not exert itself to assist him in concealing the bad faith. Such an examination, it is manifest, would be in the interest of truth and justice. If the plaintiff declined to submit to it for good reason, he, of course, could explain his reason to the jury. If he declined to submit to it without reason, that fact would doubtless have its influence as affecting his good faith; and it seems to us that such a question [whether he would submit to an examination] would tend to assist the court and jury in arriving at the truth, and would result in no harm to any party asserting a *bona fide* claim."

[3] 17 Am. Jur., *Discovery and Inspection,* § 55; 8 Wigmore, Evidence, § 2220.

Wanek v. Winona, (1899) 78 Minn. 98, 100, 80 N. W. 851, 46 L. R. A. 448: "Any other rule in these personal injury cases would often result in an entire denial of justice to the defendant, and leave him wholly at the mercy of the plaintiff's witnesses."

For power of a court to require a physical examination of the insured in an action for disability and accident benefits, see note, 163 A. L. R. 923.

In Herskovitz v. Travelers Ins. Co., (1947) 272 App. Div. 584, 73 N. Y. S. 2d 851, appeal denied 297 N. Y. 863, 79 N. E. 2d 278, an action upon an insurance policy, it was held that the court lacked power to order such examination; that a personal injury action is the only type of action in which a physical examination is authorized by § 306 of the Civil Practice Act.

By virtue of court rule, in an action for personal injuries, defendant's motion for an order requiring plaintiffs to produce before a named expert and for inspection, x-rays of the plaintiff in his possession, was granted.

Schnur v. Gajewski, (1957) 6 Misc. 2d 206, 163 N. Y. S. 2d 259.

[4] By exercising its control of the examination, the court is in a position to protect the rights of the plaintiff and to prohibit an examination which is unreasonable, untimely, or fraught with danger. *e.g.,* Depfer v. Walker, (1935) 125 Fla. 189, 169 So. 660; Greenhow v. Whitehead's, Inc., (1946) 67 Idaho 262, 175 P. 2d 1007; Carrig v. Oakes, (1940) 259 App. Div. 138, 18 N. Y. S. 2d 917; Gimerez v. Great Atlantic & Pac. Tea Co., (1932) 236 App. Div. 804, 259 N. Y. S. 597; Gilbert v. Klar, (1928) 223 App. Div. 200, 228 N. Y. S. 183; Hollister v. Robertson, (1924) 208 App. Div. 449, 203 N. Y. S. 514; Hayt v. Brewster, Gordon & Co., (1921) 199 App. Div. 68, 191 N. Y. S. 176; Cardinal v. University of Rochester, (1947) 188 Misc. 823, 71 N. Y. S. 2d 614, aff'd 271

dictions, statutes have been enacted which confer discretionary authority upon the trial court to order a physical examination of the plaintiff in an action to recover damages for personal injury.[5] Needless to say, such examinations are usually requested.[6]

Furthermore, it has been held that in divorce and annulment proceedings, the court has power to order a physical examination of either party, whenever such examination is necessary to determine the fact of sexual capacity.[7] In paternity cases, the court may

---

←‹‹‹

App. Div. 1048, 71 N. Y. S. 2d 617; Myers v. Travelers Ins. Co., (1946) 353 Pa. 523, 46 A. 2d 224, 163 A. L. R. 919.

See note, 135 A. L. R. 883; 17 Am. Jur., *Discovery and Inspection*, §§ 58-66.

For power of court to stay proceedings or to dismiss action if plaintiff refuses to submit to a physical examination, see 17 Am. Jur., Discovery and Inspection, § 70.

For admissibility of evidence of party's refusal to permit physical examination, see note, 175 A. L. R. 234.

[5] *e.g.*, N. Y. Civil Prac. Act, § 306: "In an action to recover damages for personal injuries, if the defendant shall present to the court satisfactory evidence that he is ignorant of the nature and extent of the injuries complained of, the court, by order, shall direct that the plaintiff submit to a physical examination by one or more physicians or surgeons to be designated by the court or judge, and such examination shall be had and made under such restrictions and directions as to the court or judge shall seem proper. If the party to be examined shall be a female she shall, if she desire, be entitled to have such examination in the presence of her own personal physician and such relative or other person as the court may direct. The order for such physical examination, upon the application of the defendant, may also direct that the testimony of such party be taken by deposition pursuant to this article."

See also (1945) Rev. Laws of Hawaii § 9922; (1953) Wis. Stat. § 269.57(2). For application of the Wisconsin statute, see Thompson v. Roberts, (1955) 269 Wis. 472, 69 N. W. 2d 482; Leusink v. O'Donnell, (1949) 255 Wis. 627, 39 N. W. 2d 675.

Perhaps it should be noted that since the adoption of the Federal Rules of Civil Procedure, a number of states and territories have adopted procedural rules patterned upon, though not always identical with, them. A number of states have adopted some of the rules, and other states are currently giving consideration to the subject.

See Weinstein, Gleit, and Kay, Procedures for Obtaining Information Before Trial, (1957) 35 Tex. L. Rev. 481; Discovery Practice in States Adopting the Federal Rules of Civil Procedure, (1955) 68 Harv. L. Rev. 673, note 2; Hein, Discovery and the Physician-Patient Privilege, (1955) 34 Neb. L. Rev. 507.

See also Randa v. Bear, (1957) ......Wash......., 312 P. 2d 640.

[6] Black v. Bisgier, (1931) 139 Misc. 100, 101, 248 N. Y. S. 555: "The trial judge of today finds that negligence cases are in a great majority upon his calendar. Orders for the physical examination of plaintiffs by defendants in personal injury actions are stipulated or ordered in nearly every case."

[7] Trovato v. Trovato, (1941) 262 App. Div. 276, 28 N. Y. S. 2d 55; White v. White,

›››→

order that blood tests be made of either or both of the parties and the child.[8]

In connection with a claim for compensation pending before the Workmen's Compensation Board, an application made on behalf of the insurance carrier of the employer for an order authorizing the director of a State hospital for the insane to permit a physical examination of the claimant, a patient therein, will not be granted where there is no showing that a committee has been appointed to act for such claimant in the selection of a physician who can attend such examination in behalf of the claimant.[9]

78. *Same: Testimony and Report of Examining Physician*

In jurisdictions which recognize the physician-patient privilege, the question may arise whether the information acquired by the examining physician may be barred from disclosure upon the trial of the action. As pointed out earlier, the general rule is that where a physical or mental examination of a party is made by a physician employed for that purpose by his adversary, or by a neu-

---

(1938) 255 App. Div. 718, 6 N. Y. S. 2d 512; Boscia v. Boscia, (1943) 49 N. Y. S. 2d 597, aff'd 267 App. Div. 993, 49 N. Y. S. 2d 671; Sucher v. Burger, (1912) 13 Ohio N. P. (n. s.) 161, 12 Ohio Dec. 385 (action for breach of promise). *cf.* Welch v. Verduin, (1923) 121 Misc. 545, 201 N. Y. S. 324, 14 L. R. A. 466. A physical examination may not be had of the wife in a divorce case for the purpose of establishing pregnancy by another. Ortiz v. Ortiz, (1954) 205 Misc. 295, 128 N. Y. S. 2d 354.

In Geis v. Geis, (1925) 116 App. Div. 362, 101 N. Y. S. 2d 845, and in Cowen v. Cowen, (1925) 125 Misc. 755, 211 N. Y. S. 840, plaintiff's application for an order requiring defendant to submit to a physical examination was denied on condition that defendant waive the statutory privilege in relation to the testimony of the physicians who had treated her. See also Galligano v. Galligano, (1935) 245 App. Div. 743, 280 N. Y. S. 419; Yelin v. Yelin, (1929) 142 Misc. 533, 255 N. Y. S. 708.

[8] In a number of states, the legislature has authorized the court to order that such tests be made. *e.g.*, N. Y. Civil Practice Act § 306-a; (1953) Ohio Rev. Code § 2317.47; (1939) S. D. Code § 36.0602. See also Jordan v. Davis, (1948) ____ Me.____, 57 A. 2d 209; Cortese v. Cortese, (1950) 10 N. J. Super. 152, 76 A. 2d 717; Anthony v. Anthony, (1950) 9 N. J. Super. 411, 74 A. 2d 919; Kwartler v. Kwartler, (1943) 291 N. Y. 689, 52 N. E. 2d 588; State, *ex rel.* Walker v. Clark, (1944) 144 Ohio St. 305, 58 N. E. 2d 773; State v. Damm, (1936) 64 S. D. 309, 266 N. W. 667. See note, Power of Court to Order Blood Tests to Determine Non-Paternity, (1935) 44 Yale L. J. 508. For discussion of physical and mental examinations of persons accused of crime, see § 37, herein.

[9] Matter of Lanham, (1955) 1 Misc. 2d 264, 144 N. Y. S. 2d 401.

tral physician appointed by the court, to determine the character of his injury, ailment, or disability, and not with a view to curative treatment or medical advice, the confidential relationship of physician and patient, contemplated by the statute, does not exist and the privilege does not apply.[1] The examining physician, therefore, may testify to any information gained by him in the course of the examination, and, sometimes, to voluntary communications made to him by the party examined.[2] Some of the statutes which empower the court to order a physical examination of a party, expressly authorize the physician to testify,[3] or plainly infer that it is so intended.[4]

There is a conflict of opinion upon the question whether the party examined is entitled to a copy of the written report of the examining physician. In the states which, by statute or court rule, have adopted the federal rule,[5] the examining physician's report must be made available to the person examined if he requests it.

---

[1] See §§ 36, 37, herein.

[2] Metropolitan Life Ins. Co. v. Evans, (1938) 183 Miss. 859, 184 So. 426; Dixie Greyhound Lines, Inc. v. Mathews, (1936) 177 Miss. 103, 170 So. 686, 108 A. L. R. 134; McGuire v. Chicago & Alton R. R., (1915) ...... Mo. ...... , 178 S. W. 79, L. R. A. 1915 F 888; Plater v. W. C. Mullins Const. Co., (1929) 223 Mo. App. 650, 17 S. W. 2d 658; Kelman v. Union Ry., (1922) 202 App. Div. 487, 195 N. Y. S. 313; Schulze v. Schulze, (1942) 35 N. Y. S. 2d 218; Sucher v. Burger, (1912) 13 Ohio N. P. (n. s.) 161, 12 Ohio Dec. 385.

It has been held that the examining physician may ask the plaintiff such questions as are necessary to enable him, as a physician, to ascertain the nature and extent of the injuries complained of, and the manner in which they were received.

Wunsch v. Weber, (1894) 31 Abb. N. C. 365, 29 N. Y. S. 1100. See also Young v. Kennedy, (1951) 106 N. Y. S. 2d 274.

Contra: Hess v. Lake Shore & M. S. R. R., (1890) 7 Pa. Co. Ct. 565, 567: "To interrogate the plaintiff as to his condition, the nature of the injury, or the manner in which it was sustained, thus, perhaps, eliciting declarations from him which may be used in evidence against him, would be highly improper, when the circumstances attending the examination are considered."

In McGuire v. Chicago & Alton R. R., infra, the voluntary statements of the plaintiff to the physician were testified to by the latter, but the court declined to decide whether the physician could testify, against objection by the plaintiff, to statements elicited by him under assumed authority from the court in such circumstances.

[3] *e.g.,* (1945) Hawaii Rev. Laws § 9922: " * * * Any information which may be acquired by such physicians or any of them by making an examination under order of the court may be divulged without the consent of the person examined."

[4] *e.g.,* (1952) Mo. Stat. Ann. § 510.040.

[5] Federal Rules of Civil Procedure, Rule 35. See § 81, herein.

In the absence of such a statute or rule, the weight of authority supports the view that the party requesting the examination is under no duty to deliver a copy of his own physician's report to the party examined;[6] however, the examining physician would be subject to having his deposition taken at the instance of the party examined if the latter so desired.[7]

79. Depositions and Interrogatories

The statutory privilege applies as well to confidential matters sought to be elicited from the patient or his physician by deposition or by interrogatories, as it does when such matters are sought to be

---

[6] Callan v. Adams, (1941) 176 Misc. 292, 27 N. Y. S. 2d 93: "There is no statutory requirement that the physician make any report whatsoever. * * * The physician is paid, not by the plaintiff or the court, but by the defendant, and remains his employee throughout. The defendant should not be required to disclose before trial what the physical examination of the plaintiff by his physician reveals any more than he should be forced to disclose what he expects to prove by any other witness."

Accord: Feinberg v. Fairmont Holding Corp., (1947) 272 App. Div. 101, 69 N. Y. S. 2d 414; Kelman v. Union Ry., (1922) 202 App. Div. 487, 195 N. Y. S. 313; Valentine v. State, (1950) 197 Misc. 972, 95 N. Y. S. 2d 827; Stoczynski v. Croft, (1938) 166 Misc. 553, 2 N. Y. S. 2d 740; Mizak v. Carborundum Co., (1912) 75 Misc. 205, 132 N. Y. S. 1104, aff'd 151 App. Div. 899, 135 N. Y. S. 1128; Giordano v. Harding, (1942) 38 N. Y. S. 2d 1009; *In re* Bates, (1957) 167 Ohio St. 46, 146 N. E. 2d 306; Theetge v. Cincinnati Street Ry., (1955) _____ Ohio Com. Pleas _____ , 139 N. E. 2d 365; Schroeder v. Cincinnati Street Ry., (1949) _____ Com. Pleas_____ , 74 Ohio Law Abst. 412, 139 N. E. 2d 129.

Contra: Fred Howland, Inc. v. Morris, (1940) 143 Fla. 189, 196 So. 472; Rooney v. Colson, (1957) 3 A. D. 2d 410, 161 N. Y. S. 2d 445; Del Ra v. Vaughn, (1956) 2 A. D. 2d 156, 154 N. Y. S. 2d 336; Tutone v. New York Cons. R. R., (1919) 180 App. Div. 954, 178 N. Y. S. 924 (no reasons assigned for decision); Goldstein v. Feinerman, (1956) 2 Misc. 2d 554, 150 N. Y. S. 2d 287; Swiatlowsi v. Kasprzyk, (1956) 2 Misc. 2d 707, 154 N. Y. S. 2d 543; Martin v. La Fonte, (1945) 53 N. Y. S. 2d 415; Horowitz v. B. Q. T. Corp., (1939) 171 Misc. 321, 12 N. Y. S. 2d 41; Williams v. Chattanooga Iron Works, (1915) 131 Tenn. 683, 176 S. W. 1031, Ann. Cas. 1916 B 101.

It will be observed that the New York courts are not in agreement on this question. See Di Salvo v. Di Giacomo, (1956) 2 Misc. 2d 1068, 154 N. Y. S. 2d 705.

[7] Carpenter v. Dawson, (1954) _____ Ohio Com. Pleas_____ , 138 N. E. 2d 172.

In State, *ex rel* Berge v. Superior Court, (1929) 154 Wash. 144, 281 Pac. 335, it was held that where a person voluntarily submits to an examination by a physician at the instance of the adverse party, he may call the physician as a witness and interrogate him not only as to the facts which he discovered, but also as to his opinion as to the nature and extent of the injury. Moreover, the physician is entitled to no compensation other than the ordinary witness fees.

Contra: In re Bates, (1957) 167 Ohio St. 46, 146 N. E. 2d 306.

disclosed by their testimony at the trial of the action. The plain purpose of the privilege is to preserve inviolate the confidential communications between the physician and his patient; hence, the mode of the attempted disclosure is of no importance.[1] The same reasons which prohibit disclosure of privileged matters at the trial apply with equal force to their disclosure in a deposition or in an answer to an interrogatory. Were this not so, the privilege would be a useless and farcical one.[2] The better rule, therefore, is that in the absence of consent or waiver, the disclosure must be shut off at the source.[3] There is some authority for the view that because there is a possibility that the privilege may be waived by the holder thereof on the trial of the action, the physician should answer questions put to him by interrogatories or upon the taking of his deposition and the admissibility thereof should be determined when and if the evidence is offered at the trial.[4] It has been said that questions of waiver cannot be decided until the case is tried; therefore the adversary should not be placed in the position of having the privilege waived and then have no means of producing the evidence

---

[1] See § 61, herein.

[2] Ragland, (1932) Discovery Before Trial, p. 146: "Every objection which would be tenable as of right at the trial is tenable when the examination is held before trial. It is as well a futile as an unjust thing to allow the discovery of evidence which can be excluded at the trial on the ground that it is privileged."

[3] Woernley v. Electromatic Typewriters, Inc., (1936) 271 N. Y. 228, 2 N. E. 2d 638; Equitable Life Assur. Soc. v. Mpasstas, (1939) 256 App. Div. 878, 9 N. Y. S. 2d 221; Lorde v. Guardian Life Ins. Co., (1937) 252 App. Div. 646, 300 N. Y. S. 721 (interrogatories whereby defendant sought production of record of insured's medical treatment and x-ray pictures made by physicians attending him while at a hospital in another state, should have been stricken out on plaintiff's motion as calling for privileged information); Rodner v. Buchman, (1935) 246 App. Div. 777, 284 N. Y. S. 99 (patient not party to action); Matter of Mayer S. Ames, (1955) 207 Misc. 746, 139 N. Y. S. 2d 327; Matter of Meyer's Estate, (1954) 206 Misc. 368, 132 N. Y. S. 2d 825; Kinbacher v. Schneider, (1949) 194 Misc. 969, 89 N. Y. S. 2d 350; Jones v. Jones, (1955) 208 Misc. 721, 144 N. Y. S. 2d 820; Kriebel v. Commercial Travelers Mut. Acc. Ass'n, (1946) 63 N. Y. S. 2d 282; Wexler v. Metropolitan Life Ins. Co., (1942) 38 N. Y. S. 2d 889. See also McGowan v. Metropolitan Life Ins. Co., (1932) 234 App. Div. 366, 255 N. Y. S. 130, appeal dismissed 259 N. Y. 454, 182 N. E. 81.

[4] In Dana v. Commercial Travelers Mut. Acc. Ass'n, (1934) 241 App. Div. 812, 271 N. Y. S. 952, it was held that if the answers to interrogatories disclose anything prohibited by the statute or decisions, an objection may be made thereto on the trial of the action. The decision is unsound. Why let the secret out at all?

sought to be made available, as would be the case if the refusal of medical witnesses to answer were allowed to control.[5] This view appears to be unsound. If the privilege be waived in the trial of the case, the adversary may apply, in the light of the waiver, for suspension for a reasonable length of time in which to produce and examine the physician who attended the patient or to produce the records of any hospital in which he was maintained.[6]

In practically all jurisdictions, statutes exist which permit any party in a civil action to take the depositions of persons whose evidence he may desire to use;[7] moreover, some expressly authorize the taking of the deposition of a physician under certain circumstances.[8] Such a statute, however, does not contemplate the taking of a deposition of a person disqualified to give evidence in the case and confers no right to investigate or inquire into matters which the court could not investigate or inquire into at the actual trial. A statute authorizing the taking of depositions must, therefore, be considered in connection with the physician-patient privilege statute.[9] In New York, in a personal injury action, the testimony of a physician, or of professional or registered nurse attached to any hospital, dispensary, or other charitable institution as to information which he or she acquired in attending a patient at such institution, *must* be taken before a referee; but a judge, in his discretion, notwithstanding such deposition, may require the attendance and

---

[5] State v. Osborne, ... Ohio Com. Pleas ...., 25 Ohio Law Abst. 543; Lazzell v. Harvey, (1935) 174 Okla. 86, 49 P. 2d 519. These decisions practically abrogate the privilege. Even though the evidence is excluded at the trial, the harm is done when the disclosure is once made. See Percival v. Richardson, (1917) 165 N. Y. S. 1.

[6] Rubin v. Equitable Life Assur. Soc., (1945) 269 App. Div. 677, 53 N. Y. S. 2d 351; Lorde v. Guardian Life Ins. Co., (1937) 252 App. Div. 646, 300 N. Y. S. 721; Jaffe v. New York, (1949) 196 Misc. 710, 94 N. Y. S. 2d 60. In Brown v. Brown, (1946) 65 N. Y. S. 2d 602, it was held that where it was impossible to determine on opposition to an application for leave to examine physicians whether defendant had waived the privilege by testifying to his ailment, the application would be granted with leave to defendant to make appropriate objection to the testimony either upon examination or upon the trial.

[7] *e.g.,* (1943) N. C. Gen. Stat. Ann., § 8-71.

[8] *e.g.,* (1948) Idaho Code § 9-906; (1946 Replacement) Ind. Stat. Ann. 2-1506; (1951) La. Rev. Stat., § 13:3667; (1952) Mo. Stat. Ann., § 492.400.

[9] Edington v. Mutual Life Ins. Co., (1876) 67 N. Y. 185; Yow v. Pittman, (1954) 241 N. C. 69, 84 S. E. 2d 297.

examination of such professional person upon the trial of the action.[10] This, however, does not abrogate the provisions of the statute forbidding a physician or nurse to disclose information acquired in attending a patient in a professional capacity.[11]

The law of the forum governs the taking of a deposition; hence, the rules of evidence applicable thereto are those prescribed by the laws of the state wherein the action is pending, not those in force where the deposition is to be taken.[12]

A witness who, on the taking of his deposition, claims that the information sought from him is privileged and refuses to answer questions put to him, runs the risk of being adjudged guilty of contempt if he is not able to prove that the matters sought to be elicited are within the scope and protection of the privilege statute.[13] A physician, who is the defendant in an action to recover damages for malpractice, cannot refuse, when his deposition is taken at the instance of the patient, to disclose information acquired by him from the patient when he treated him. The privilege belongs to the patient, not the physician, and if the witness persists in his refusal he may be adjudged guilty of contempt.[14]

---

[10] (1957) N. Y. Civil Practice Act § 296-a.

[11] Woernley v. Electromatic Typewriters, Inc., (1936) 271 N. Y. 228, 232, 2 N. E. 2d 638: "Section 354 [now 296-a] permitting the examination of hospital physicians before a referee was undoubtedly enacted to protect physicians and the institutions where they are engaged from the annoyance of being compelled to attend trials as witnesses. The section extends to them a privilege because of the nature of their services which is not extended to others." See also Friedman v. State, (1937) 164 Misc. 400, 299 N. Y. S. 127; Paparone v. Ader, (1931) 139 Misc. 281, 248 N. Y. S. 321.

[12] Matter of Meyer's Estate, (1954) 206 Misc. 368, 370, 132 N. Y. S. 2d 825: "The purpose of taking the deposition is to procure evidence for use at the hearing, and the exclusion of the testimony on the hearing in this court cannot depend upon the residence of the physician or the place where he attended the patient. It would be illogical to compel disclosure at the examination before trial and to forbid such disclosure at the actual hearing." See also § 25, herein.

[13] Matter of King v. Ashley, (1904) 96 App. Div. 143, 89 N. Y. S. 482, aff'd 179 N. Y. 281, 72 N. E. 106 (attorney-client privilege); Re Martin, Jr., (1943) 141 Ohio St. 87, 47 N. E. 2d 388 (attorney-client privilege).

[14] Markham v. Hipke, (1919) 169 Wis. 37, 171 N. W. 300. See also § 16, herein.

CHAPTER XIV

Pre-Trial Proceedings: Federal Courts

80. Federal Rules of Civil Procedure: In General

In this chapter we shall have occasion to examine generally the use a litigant may make of the "discovery" provisions of the Federal Rules of Civil Procedure,[1] and to consider particularly the extent to which the right of discovery is limited by the application of the physician-patient privilege.[2] It is plain that the Rules relating

---

[1] The Federal Rules of Civil Procedure became effective September 16, 1938, and supersede all statutes inconsistent with them.

[2] It is not our purpose to enter into an exhaustive discussion of the subject. Authoritative treatises exist which, we believe, will better serve the purposes of the reader. See Moore, (1951) Federal Practice; (1951) Cyclopedia of Federal Procedure; Barron and Holtzoff, (1951) Federal Practice and Procedure; Ohlinger, (1948) Federal Practice.

The following articles and notes also may be helpful: Discovery Practice in States Adopting the Federal Rules of Civil Procedure, (1955) 68 Harv. L. Rev. 673; Jordan, Assertion of Privilege in Deposition Proceedings, (1952) 6 Sw. L. J. 228; Denecke, Discovery in State and Federal Courts, (1952) 31 Ore. L. Rev. 197; Conrad, Let's Weigh Rule 43 (a), (1952) 38 Va. L. Rev. 985; Speck, The Use of Discovery in United States District Courts, (1951) 60 Yale L. J. 1132; Tactical Use and Abuse of Depositions Under the Federal Rules, (1949) 59 Yale L. J. 117; Holtzoff, Instruments of Discovery Under Federal Rules of Civil Procedure, (1942) 41 Mich. L. Rev. 205; Pike and Willis, Federal Discovery in Operation, (1940) 7 U. Chic. L. Rev. 297; Sunderland, Discovery Before Trial Under the New Federal Rules, (1939) 15 Tenn. L. Rev. 737; Pike, The New Federal Deposition-Discovery Procedure and the Rules of Evidence, (1939) 34 Ill. L. Rev. 1.

⟫→

to depositions, interrogatories, production and inspection of documents and objects, physical and mental examinations, and requests for admissions were formulated with the view of granting the widest latitude in ascertaining before trial facts concerning the real issues in dispute. Discovery procedure simply advances the stage at which disclosure can be compelled from the time of the trial to the period preceding it.[3] Generally speaking, the privilege which protects confidential matters from discovery under the Rules is the same as that applicable under the rules of evidence.[4]

81. *Physical and Mental Examinations of Persons*

Rule 35 of the Federal Rules of Civil Procedure governs physical and mental examinations of persons in the course of civil[1] actions in federal trial courts.[2] It is obvious that the rule introduced

←※

See also A Symposium on the Use of Depositions and Discovery Under the Federal Rules, (1951) 12 F. R. D. 131; note, Pre-Trial Disclosures Under Federal Rules, 166 A. L. R. 1442.

[3] Bergstrom Paper Co. v. Continental Ins. Co., (1947) 7 F. R. D. 548. See 2 Barron and Holtzoff, (1951) Federal Practice and Procedure, § 641. See note, 37 A. L. R. 2d 586, concerning appealability of order pertaining to pre-trial examination and discovery.

[4] See able article, Louisell, Confidentiality, Conformity and Confusion: Privileges in Federal Court Today, (1956) 31 Tul. L. Rev. 101.

[1] Under the Federal Rules, there is but one form of action, namely, a "civil" action. This combines the practices formerly known as "law" and "equity."

[2] Text of Rule 35 follows:

"(a) ORDER FOR EXAMINATION

In an action in which the mental or physical condition of a party is in controversy, the court in which the action is pending may order him to submit to a physical or mental examination by a physician. The order may be made only on motion for good cause shown and upon notice to the party to be examined and to all other parties and shall specify the time, place, manner, conditions, and scope of the examination and the person or persons by whom it is to be made.

(b) REPORT OF FINDINGS

(1) If requested by the person examined, the party causing the examination to be made shall deliver to him a copy of a detailed written report of the examining physician setting out his findings and conclusions. After such request and delivery the party causing the examination to be made shall be entitled upon request to receive from the party examined a like report of any examination, previously or thereafter made, of the same mental or physical condition. If the party examined refuses to deliver such report the court on

»»→

an innovation into federal practice. Prior to its adoption, federal courts could not subject plaintiffs in actions for damages for personal injury to physical examination except in states where such examinations were authorized by statute.[3] It should be noted also that Rule 35 has a wider application than that usually found in states authorizing physical examination where this type of discovery is limited to personal injury cases only.[4] The rule is sensible and salutary; it furnishes a perfectly fair way to obtain evidence of the physical or mental condition of a party without resorting to witnesses against whom the claim of privilege may be made.[5] The rule does not violate a person's right to privacy and does not transgress rights guaranteed to him by the Constitution of the United States.[6]

---

motion and notice may make an order requiring delivery on such terms as are just, and if a physician fails or refuses to make such a report the court may exclude his testimony if offered at the trial.

(2) By requesting and obtaining a report of the examination so ordered or by taking the deposition of the examiner, the party examined waives any privilege he may have in that action or any other involving the same controversy, regarding the testimony of every other person who has examined or may thereafter examine him in respect of the same mental or physical condition."

The Advisory Committee, in October, 1955, recommended to the Supreme Court amendments which, if adopted, will broaden Rule 35. See 2 Barron and Holtzoff, Federal Practice and Procedure, § 821 (1956 Pocket Part).

[3] See note, 131 A. L. R. 810.

[4] Beach v. Beach, (1940) 72 App. D. C. 318, 114 F. 2d 479, 131 A. L. R. 304. Suit by wife for maintenance. Paternity of child was an issue. Order of trial court requiring wife and child to submit to blood grouping tests approved. See also Lue Chow Kon v. Brownell, (1955) 220 F. 2d 187.

Countee v. United States, (1940) 112 F. 2d 447, cert. denied 317 U. S. 628, 87 Law Ed. 508, 63 Su. Ct. 44. Examination of plaintiff ordered in action to recover benefits under a war risk insurance policy.

In Wadlow v. Humberd, (1939) 27 F. Supp. 210, a libel action, the court denied defendant's motion for an order to require plaintiff to submit to a mental and physical examination because his condition was not "immediately and directly in controversy." The decision seems unsound. See Beach v. Beach, (1940) 72 App. D. C. 318, 114 F. 2d 479, 131 A. L. R. 304.

[5] Tweith v. Duluth, Missabe & I. R. Ry., (1946) 66 F. Supp. 427.

[6] Sibbach v. Wilson & Co., (1940) 312 U. S. 1, 85 Law Ed. 479, 61 Su. Ct. 422; Countee v. United States, (1940) 112 F. 2d 447, cert. denied 317 U. S. 628, 87 Law Ed. 508, 63 Su. Ct. 44.

Nevertheless, since the rule is in derogation of statutory privilege, it should be strictly construed.[7]

Even though a state court may be without power to order a party to submit to a physical or mental examination, that fact will not prevent a federal court, sitting in the state, requiring such an examination. The matter is one of procedure and the federal rule will govern.[8] But the right to an order for the examination of a party is not absolute; the matter is addressed to the sound discretion of the court.[9] The right under the rule does not go so far as to require the court to designate a physician selected by either party, and it may designate one of its own choice. That also is a matter which is left to the sound discretion of the court.[10] The court may fix the time, place, manner, conditions and scope of the examination, and will, of course, take every precaution against subjecting the party to an examination that may unnecessarily be painful or fraught with danger.[11] An order for physical examination is interlocutory and not appealable.[12]

Rule 35 impliedly recognizes that an examination made on behalf of the party to be examined is privileged unless the privilege is waived by pursuing the course referred to in the rule.[13] It is

[7] Sher v. DeHaven, (1952) 91 App. D. C. 257, 199 F. 2d 777, cert. denied 345 U. S. 936, 97 Law Ed. 1363, 73 Su. Ct. 797, 36 A. L. R. 2d 937.

[8] Rule 35 supersedes the state rules of practice regarding physical examination of parties in civil actions. Sibbach v. Wilson & Co., (1941) 312 U. S. 1, 85 Law Ed. 479, 61 Su. Ct. 422; Beach v. Beach, (1940) 72 App. D. C. 318, 114 F. 2d 479, 131 A. L. R. 804; Leach v. Greif Bros. Cooperage Corp., (1942) 2 F. R. D. 444.

[9] Bucher v. Krause, (1952) 200 F. 2d 576, cert. denied 345 U. S. 997, 97 Law Ed. 1404, 73 Su. Ct. 1141. Court declined to hold that the trial judge abused his discretion in denying a motion for a physical examination of a plaintiff suing for damages for a bullet wound.

Teche Lines, Inc. v. Boyette, (1940) 111 F. 2d 579; Gitto v. Societa Anonima Di Navigazione, (1939) 27 F. Supp. 785.

[10] Warren v. Weber & Heidenthaler, (1955) 134 F. Supp. 524; Gale v. National Transportation Co., Inc., (1946) 7 F. R. D. 237; Pierce v. Brovig, (1954) 16 F. R. D. 569; Klein v. Yellow Cab Co., (1944) 7 F. R. D. 169; Leach v. Greif Bros. Cooperage Co., (1942) 2 F. R. D. 444; Gitto v. Societa Anonima Di Navigazione, (1939) 27 F. Supp. 785.

[11] Klein v. Yellow Cab Co., (1944) 7 F. R. D. 169; Strasser v. Prudential Life Ins. Co., (1939) 1 F. R. D. 125. See note, 135 A. L. R. 883.

[12] Bowles v. Commercial Casualty Ins. Co., (1939) 107 F. 2d 169.

[13] Holbert v. Chase, (1952) 12 F. R. D. 171, 172: "Apparently the drafters of this rule

obvious that the rule has introduced an entirely new feature calling for an exchange of physicians' reports procured by the examining party and the party examined. However, the rule must be reasonably construed. It does not place upon a party the burden of procuring copies of the records of hospitals or of the office records of physicians. It is limited to medical examinations conducted at the request of the party, and the reports, copies of which are subject to production, are the reports made by the examining physician as the result of such an examination.[14]

A plaintiff who submits to a physical examination at the instance of the defendant in a personal injury case is entitled to have the defendant produce the findings of the examining physician and permit the plaintiff to receive, or to make, a copy of same.[15] The fact that the plaintiff waives the right to compel the defendant to apply for an order requiring an examination of the plaintiff by the defendant's physician and voluntarily submits to an examination, will not defeat his right to receive a copy of the physician's report.[16] It should be noted, however, that Rule 35 also provides

---

considered the medical examinations made on behalf of the party to be examined privileged since they provided for their disclosure *only* if the adverse party took advantage of this rule and obtained an independent examination and the party examined obtained a report of the last. There would, therefore, seem to be sound authority behind the claim of privilege." The court refused to allow defendant to take the deposition of plaintiff's physician who had examined and treated plaintiff after the accident, but pointed out that, under Rule 35, defendant could apply to the court and obtain the right to have a physical examination of plaintiff and thereby ascertain his condition. See Lewis v. United Air Lines Transport Corp., (1940) 32 F. Supp. 21.

See also note, 36 A. L. R. 2d 946.

14 Butts v. Sears, Roebuck & Co., (1949) 9 F. R. D. 58. See also note, 36 A. L. R. 2d 946.

15 Gillig v. Bymart-Tintair, Inc., (1954) 16 F. R. D. 393; Keil v. Himes, (1952) 13 F. R. D. 451; Dumas v. Pennsylvania R. R., (1951) 11 F. R. D. 496. See also 4 Moore, Federal Practice, § 35.06.

16 Keil v. Himes, (1952) 13 F. R. D. 451; Dumas v. Pennsylvania R. R., (1951) 11 F. R. D. 496; Nedimyer v. Pennsylvania R. R., (1946) 6 F. R. D. 21; Lipshitz v. Bleyhl, (1946) 5 F. R. D. 225; Rutherford v. Alben, (1940) 1 F. R. D. 277; Kelleher v. Cohoes Trucking Co., (1938) 25 F. Supp. 965.

See also Coriell v. Cosmopolitan Tourist Co., (1950) 10 F. R. D. 442; Dugger v. Baltimore & O. R. R., (1946) 5 F. R. D. 334; Barreca v. Pennsylvania R. R., (1946) 5 F. R. D. 391; Gordon v. Pennsylvania R. R., (1946) 5 F. R. D. 510; Jones v. Pennsylvania R. R., (1947) 7 F. R. D. 662; Williams v. New Jersey-New York Transit Co., (1940) 1 F. R. D. 138.

that by requesting and obtaining a copy of the examining physician's report, the party examined waives any privilege he may have regarding the testimony *of any other person* who has examined or may thereafter examine him in respect of the same mental or physical condition.[17] It is only by requesting and obtaining the report of an examination made of him by his adversary's physician or by the taking of his deposition that a party waives the physician-patient privilege as to examinations made by his own physicians. Accordingly, in a personal injury suit, the defendant's mere willingness to furnish the plaintiff a copy of the defendant's medical examiner's report on his examination of the plaintiff after the accident — a report which the plaintiff had neither requested nor received — did not entitle the defendant under Rule 35 to demand reports of other examinations which the plaintiff had undergone on his own account.[18]

If the defendant causes a physical examination to be made of the plaintiff and a report of such examination is furnished to both parties but the defendant does not call the examining physician as a witness, counsel for the plaintiff may comment on the failure of the defendant to produce such witness at the trial.[19]

A party who refuses to submit to a mental or physical examination when ordered by the court, may be subjected to the procedural consequences of Rule 37(b), but the court has no power to order his arrest; this by virtue of the exception in (iv) of the same rule.[20]

82. *Depositions and Interrogatories*
Rule 26 of the Federal Rules of Civil Procedure authorizes the taking of a deposition of any person, including a party, and governs

---

[17] Lindsay v. Prince, (1948) 8 F. R. D. 233.

[18] Sher v. DeHaven, (1952) 91 App. D. C. 257, 199 F. 2d 777, cert. denied 345 U. S. 936, 97 Law Ed. 1363, 73 Su. Ct. 797, 36 A. L. R. 2d 937.
  See note, 36 A. L. R. 2d 946.

[19] Pitcairn v. Perry, (1941) 122 F. 2d 881, cert. denied 314 U. S. 697, 86 Law Ed. 557, 62 Su. Ct. 414. See note, 5 A. L. R. 2d 893, 919-927.

[20] Sibbach v. Wilson & Co., (1940) 312 U. S. 1, 85 Law Ed. 479, 61 Su. Ct. 422.
  See note, 4 A. L. R. 2d 378. See also § 85, herein.

its use as evidence in any civil action pending in a federal court.[1] The rule affords an equal right to all the parties to take depositions before trial. However, Rule 26(b) expressly declares that the deponent may not be examined regarding any matter that is privileged from disclosure. But, of course, the privilege may be waived under certain circumstances.[2] As stated elsewhere,[3] "privilege" is determined by the rules of evidence applicable to the trial of the action.[4] Therefore, the same rules which, at the trial, exclude evidence pertaining to confidential communications within the scope of the physician-patient privilege statute, will exclude it also at the examination by deposition.[5]

The Rules of Civil Procedure provide ample opportunity to raise the claim of privilege during the taking of depositions and to press objections based on the ground of a claimed privilege at the

---

[1] Pertinent portions of the Rule are:

(a) WHEN DEPOSITIONS MAY BE TAKEN

Any party may take the testimony of any person, including a party, by deposition upon oral examination or written interrogatories for the purpose of discovery or for use as evidence in the action or for both purposes. * * *

(b) SCOPE OF EXAMINATION

Unless otherwise ordered by the court as provided by Rule 30(b) or (d), the deponent may be examined regarding any matter, not privileged, which is relevant to the subject matter involved in the pending action, * * *.

It should be noted that Rule 30 governs the taking of depositions *upon oral examination* and that Rule 31 governs the taking of depositions *upon written interrogatories.*

For thoroughgoing discussions of Rule 26, see 2 Barron and Holtzoff, Federal Practice and Procedure, c. 9; 4 Moore, Federal Practice, c. 26.

[2] Brockway Glass Co. v. Hartford-Empire Co., (1941) 36 F. Supp. 470.

See also c.c. XVI, XVII, XVIII, herein.

[3] § 26, herein.

[4] Wild v. Payson, (1946) 7 F. R. D. 495; Humphries v. Pennsylvania R. R., (1953) 14 F. R. D. 177, 181.

[5] Engl v. Aetna Life Ins. Co., (1943) 139 F. 2d 469; Munzer v. Swedish American Line, (1940) 35 F. Supp. 493; McCarthy v. Benton, (1952) 13 F. R. D. 454. Of course, a witness, on the taking of his deposition, cannot properly refuse to answer questions eliciting information that is plainly not within the protection of the privilege. Mullin-Johnson Co. v. Penn Mutual Life Ins. Co., (1933) 2 F. Supp. 203.

Although the plaintiff may not be compelled to divulge information received from his physician, he is obliged to disclose whether he was treated professionally and the name of his physician and the dates of his visits. Baum v. Pennsylvania R. R., (1953) 14 F. R. D. 398.

trial;[6] but it does not follow that Rule 26, limiting the scope of examination before trial to relevant matters not privileged, has such an extensive application as to control and largely nullify another federal rule, namely, Rule 56, concerning summary judgments.[7]

By virtue of Rule 33, any party may serve upon any adverse party written interrogatories to be answered by the party served.[8] Obviously the testimony of a person not a party must be obtained under Rule 26. Moreover, Rule 26 and Rule 33 provide alternative remedies and the remedies cannot be availed of concurrently against the same party or parties.[9]

It has been generally recognized that "privilege" as an objection applies to interrogatories under Rule 33 just as it may be the basis of an objection to questions on the examination of a party whose deposition is being taken under Rule 26. In other words, the scope of interrogatories under Rule 33 is as broad as the scope of examination by deposition, as provided in Rule 26(b), which permits an examination "regarding any matter, not privileged, which is relevant to the subject matter involved in the pending action."[10] Therefore, the right of a party to require answers to interrogatories under Rule 33 is not an absolute right, but is one which can be secured and must be exercised only under definitely restricted circumstances as permitted by Rule 26(b), and subject always to such

---

[6] Lewis v. United Airlines T. Corp., (1939) 27 F. Supp. 946.

[7] Engl v. Aetna Life Ins. Co., (1943) 139 F. 2d 469.

[8] Pertinent portions of Rule 33 are:

"Any party may serve upon any adverse party written interrogatories to be answered by the party served, * * *.

Interrogatories may relate to any matters which can be inquired into under Rule 26(b), and the answers may be used to the same extent as provided in Rule 26(d) for the use of the deposition of a party. * * *

The provisions of Rule 30(b) are applicable for the protection of the party from whom answers to interrogatories are sought under this rule."

See § 84, herein.

[9] Isbrandsten v. Moller, (1947) 7 F. R. D. 188.

[10] Munzer v. Swedish American Line, (1940) 35 F. Supp. 493; Auer v. Hershey Creamery Co., (1939) 1 F. R. D. 14.

See 4 Moore's Federal Practice, § 33.10, p. 2289.

limitations as the court may direct for the protection of the parties under Rule 30(b).[11]

83. *Production and Inspection of Documents: Admissions*

Rule 34 of the Federal Rules of Civil Procedure governs the right of a party to require any party to the action to produce certain documents, papers, books, or tangible things for inspection.[1] Under this rule and the related Rule 26(b), if the moving party shows good cause[2] for the production of the documents or things he seeks, and if these are not privileged[3] and constitute or contain evidence relating to the subject matter involved in the action, the court may order the party who has possession, custody, or control of the desired documents or things to produce them, and to permit the movant to inspect, and copy or photograph them.[4] It is not necessary to

---

[11] Herbst v. Chicago, R. I. & Pac. Ry., (1950) 10 F. R. D. 14.

See § 84, herein.

[1] Pertinent portions of Rule 34 are:

"Upon motion of any party showing good cause therefor and upon notice to all other parties, and subject to the provision of Rule 30(b), the court in which an action is pending may (1) order any party to produce and permit the inspection and copying or photographing, by or on behalf of the moving party, of any designated documents, papers, books, accounts, letters, photographs, objects, or tangible things, not privileged, which constitute or contain evidence relating to any of the matters within the scope of the examination permitted by Rule 26(b) and which are in his possession, custody, or control; * * *."

See 2 Barron and Holtzoff, Federal Practice and Procedure, c. 9; 4 Moore, Federal Practice, c. 34.

[2] For meaning of "good cause," see Scourtes v. Fred W. Albrecht Grocery Co., (1953) 15 F. R. D. 55, 59; Hirshhorn v. Mine Safety Appliances Co., (1948) 8 F. R. D. 11, 21.

See also 4 Moore, Federal Practice, 34.08.

[3] The term "not privileged" as used in Rule 34, refers to privileges as that term is used in the law of evidence. United States v. Reynolds, (1952) 345 U. S. 1, 6, 97 Law Ed. 727, 75 Su. Ct. 528, 32 A. L. R. 2d 382.

Documents, records, or objects which disclose privileged matters need not be produced. Sher v. DeHaven, (1952) 91 App. D. C. 257, 199 F. 2d 777, cert. denied 345 U. S. 936, 97 Law Ed. 1363, 73 Su. Ct. 797, 36 A. L. R. 2d 937; Gillig v. Bymart-Tintair, Inc., (1954) 16 F. R. D. 393.

[4] Perhaps counsel desiring the information should first make use of interrogatories to require the other party to furnish a list of documents, papers, records, or other things within the description contained in Rule 34, *not privileged*, and, upon being furnished such a list, to then move for production of the particular items which it is desired to inspect and copy. Lindsay v. Prince, (1948) 8 F. R. D. 233. See also Sheffield Corp. v. George F. Alger Co., (1954) 16 F. R. D. 27.

take his deposition.[5]

The right of a party to require the production of documents, records, and other matters, and to inspect, copy and use them under Rule 34, is not an absolute right, but is one which can be exercised under the restrictions imposed by Rule 26(b) and subject always to such limitations as the court may direct for the protection of the parties under Rule 30(b).[6]

The report of a physician who examined the plaintiff in a personal injury action is, generally speaking, not within the scope and purpose of the physician-patient privilege statute;[7] hence, if the plaintiff has been examined by the defendant's physician, he is entitled to a copy of the physician's report to the defendant.[8] It has been held that the defendant is entitled to inspect and copy the report of the physician who examined the plaintiff at the latter's request.[9]

Rule 36 of the Federal Rules of Civil Procedure provides a means whereby either party may request his adversary to admit for the purpose of the pending action, (a) the genuineness of any relevant documents, and (b) the truth or existence of any relevant facts. However, timely objection will prevent the disclosure of confidential communications or information within the scope and purpose of the physician-patient privilege statute.[10]

84. *Orders for the Protection of Privileged Matters*

Rule 30(b) of the Federal Rules of Civil Procedure provides that, for good cause shown, timely application may be made to the court in which the action is pending for an order limiting the scope

---

[5] Hawaiian Airlines v. Trans-Pacific Airlines, (1948) 8 F. R. D. 449.

[6] Herbst v. Chicago, R. I. & Pac. Ry., (1950) 10 F. R. D. 14. See § 87, herein.

[7] See §§ 36, 81, herein.

[8] Gordon v. Pennsylvania R. R., (1946) 5 F. R. D. 510; Barreca v. Pennsylvania R. R., (1946) 5 F. R. D. 391; Dugger v. Baltimore & O. R. R., (1946) 5 F. R. D. 334.

[9] Cox v. Pennsylvania R. R., (1949) 9 F. R. D. 517. The decision appears unsound. See Sher v. DeHaven, (1952) 91 App. D. C. 257, 199 F. 2d 777, cert. denied 345 U. S. 936, 97 Law Ed. 1363, 73 Su. Ct. 797, 36 A. L. R. 2d 937.

[10] See 2 Barron and Holtzoff, Federal Practice and Procedure, c. 9, § 833; Moore, Federal Practice, c. 36, § 36.06.

of the deposition of the proposed witness and prohibiting inquiry into matters that are privileged from disclosure.[1] It is plain that Rule 30(b) relates to motions for protection made prior to the taking of the deposition.[2] If a party or the person to be examined believes that the examination will include inquiry into matters which are within the ban of the physician-patient privilege statute and are, therefore, improper subjects of discovery, the court, upon motion reasonably made by the party or the person to be examined, may order that the deposition shall not be taken, or may limit the scope of the examination by prohibiting any inquiry regarding such privileged matters. The court is given a wide discretion in determining what safeguards are necessary for the protection of parties and witnesses. As pointed out earlier, this protection may be invoked where the privileged matter is sought to be disclosed by any other means for discovery.

85. *Refusal to Make Discovery: Consequences*

Rule 37 of the Federal Rules of Civil Procedure sets forth the procedure by which the court may compel a party or other person to make discovery, and prescribes the various penalties which the court may impose upon a party or other person for refusal to comply with the order of the court requiring him to make discovery.[1] This rule provides the means whereby the procedure of discovery may be enforced and made effective.[2]

---

[1] Pertinent portions of Rule 30(b) are:

"After notice is served for taking a deposition by oral examination, upon motion reasonably made by any party or by the person to be examined and upon notice and for good cause shown, the court in which the action is pending may make an order that the deposition shall not be taken, * * * or that it may be taken only on written interrogatories, or that certain matters shall not be inquired into, or that the scope of the examination shall be limited to certain matters, * * *; or the court may make any other order which justice requires to protect the party or witness from annoyance, embarrassment, or oppression."

See 2 Barron and Holtzoff, Federal Practice and Procedure, c. 9, § 715; 4 Moore, Federal Practice, c. 30, § 30.04.

[2] Rule 30(d) relates to similar motions made during the taking of the deposition.

[1] See 2 Barron and Holtzoff, Federal Practice and Procedure, c. 9, § 851; 4 Moore, Federal Practice, c. 37, § 37.02.

[2] Rule 37 is applicable to all rules relating to depositions and discovery, namely Rules 26-36.

Failure to comply with the order of the court may be considered a contempt of that court. Moreover, other consequences may follow. The court is authorized to make such orders in regard to the refusal as are just. It may issue orders establishing facts or excluding evidence or striking pleadings. It may also issue orders staying further proceedings, or dismissing the action, or rendering a judgment by default against the disobedient party. In lieu of any of the foregoing orders or in addition thereto, the court may order the arrest of any party for disobeying any of such orders except an order to submit to a physical or mental examination. It is clear that a broad discretion is vested in the court within the bounds of Rule 37 to make whatever disposition is just in the light of the facts of the particular case.[3] However, the sanctions imposed by the Rule may not be used to elicit information which is plainly within the protection of a recognized privilege.[4]

---

[3] Valenstein v. Bayonne Bolt Corp., (1946) 6 F. R. D. 363.

The rule presupposes an opportunity to comply followed by a failure to comply with the order of the court. O'Toole v. William J. Meyer Co., (1957) 243 F. 2d 765.

[4] McCarthy v. Benton, (1952) 13 F. R. D. 454.

CHAPTER XV

Trial Practice

86. *Offer of Proof of Privileged Matters*

It is the policy of the law to admit relevant evidence, when properly offered, unless some valid reason exists for its exclusion.[1] Generally speaking, it is not only the right but also the duty of a

---

[1] For a general discussion of this subject, see McCormick, Evidence, c. 6.

Rule 43(a) of the Federal Rules of Civil Procedure favors the admissibility of evidence. The Rule, however, has nothing to do with what should be excluded.

party to introduce, in the first instance, all the evidence upon which he relies to establish his claim or defense. The fact that the evidence, if offered, may be excluded on the ground of privilege does not, as a general rule, deprive a party of the right to offer it.[2] The right to call an attending physician as a witness is not limited to the patient. The physician may be called as a witness by any party to the action, but whether he shall or shall not be permitted to testify concerning confidential communications or information is a question which, usually, only the patient, or his representative, may decide.[3] The court, in the presence of the jury, has no right to criticize or impugn the motives of counsel for producing the physician in court as a witness, nor has he the right to intimate, much less assert, that the physician is guilty of a breach of the code of medical ethics by becoming a witness against his former patient.[4] The statute is not violated by merely asking the physician-witness a question which elicits information acquired by him in his professional character. The statutory privilege is not a prohibition of inquiry; hence, the mere offer of testimony which is competent and material in itself, but may be excluded on the ground of privilege, does not, ordinarily at least, afford any ground for the assignment of error.[5] If a party desires the testimony of a physician who attended the patient, he may produce him in court and the question of the adversary objecting on the ground of privilege will then

---

[2] Booren v. McWilliams, (1914) 26 N. D. 558, 145 N. W. 410, Ann. Cas. 1916 A 388. See also Nelson v. Ackerman, (1957) ....Minn........, 83 N. W. 2d 500.

[3] State Farm Mutual Automobile Ins. Co. v. Kramer, (1938) 105 Ind. App. 591, 14 N. E. 2d 741.

[4] Batchoff v. Craney, (1946) 119 Mont. 157, 172 P. 2d 308. Later in the case, the court instructed the jury to disregard his remarks. The Supreme Court held that this was sufficient to remove the effects of the remarks upon the jury. The decision, in this respect, seems unsound. The criticism of the physician was very damaging to the defendant who called him, and it is doubtful whether any instruction could cure the error. In Booren v. McWilliams, (1914) 26 N. D. 558, 145 N. W. 410, Ann. Cas. 1916 A 388, an acrimonious criticism by the court of counsel for the defendant and, by indirection, of the plaintiff's physician who testified for the defendant, resulted in a reversal of a judgment for the plaintiff.

[5] State v. Booth, (1903) 121 Iowa 710, 97 N. W. 74. What might be the rule in exceptional cases where the offer is made in evident bad faith merely to force a party into apparent discredit before the jury, the court declined to consider.

have to be presented in the presence of the court and jury.[6] There is always the possibility that the holder of the privilege may elect to forego its protection.[7] A mere verbal suggestion for invoking a ruling, or a promissory announcement of what is intended to be proved is, generally speaking, not sufficient to constitute an offer of evidence.[8]

It is not reversible error for a party to keep on trying to introduce the testimony of a physician after the court rules it inadmissible if, in fact, the evidence is not privileged but truly admissible.[9] But it is gross misconduct on the part of counsel to persist in putting questions to the patient's physician which he knows are not proper.[10] Where a witness has already answered a proper question, it is not error to exclude it when asked a second time.[11]

Where an offer of evidence contains matter which is clearly privileged, it is not error to reject it, although a part of the matter embraced in the offer is competent.[12] The court is not bound to

---

[6] Dent v. Springfield Traction Co., (1910) 145 Mo. App. 61, 129 S. W. 1044.

The principle has been applied to other testimonial privileges. In People v. Chand, (1953) 116 Cal. App. 2d 242, 253 P. 2d 499, a murder case, the State called the defendant's wife as a witness and thereby compelled him to assert her disqualification as a witness against him. Held: No error. Prejudice cannot be predicated upon this ground. The State had the right to offer the spouse as a witness, subject to the claim of privilege by the defendant. It has been held, however, that it is not an abuse of discretion for the trial court to permit a question of privilege, regarding an offer of a physician's testimony, to be raised and argued in the absence of the jury. Howard v. Porter, (1949) 240 Iowa 153, 35 N. W. 2d 837; Johnson v. Kinney, (1942) 232 Iowa 1016. 7 N. W. 2d 188, 144 A. L. R. 997. See note, p. 1007.

[7] Gulf, Mobile & O. R. R. v. Smith, (1951) 210 Miss. 768, 777, 50 So. 2d 898: "The privileged communication statute is no prohibition against the offering of a physician as a witness since the patient may or may not waive the statute."

[8] Chicago City R. R. v. Carroll, (1903) 206 Ill. 318, 68 N. E. 1087. (physician-patient privilege not involved).

See 1 Wigmore, Evidence, § 17.

[9] Posner v. New York Life Ins. Co., (1940) 56 Ariz. 202, 106 P. 2d 488.

[10] Thomas v. Byron, (1912) 168 Mich. 593, 134 N. W. 1021, 38 L. R. A. (n. s.) 1186, Ann. Cas. 1913 C. 686. See also Van Hartesveldt v. Westrate, (1933) 264 Mich. 538, 250 N. W. 302; In re Fine's Estate, (1933) 249 Mich. 391, 228 N. W. 687. See note, 109 A. L. R. 1089.

[11] McConnell v. Osage, (1890) 80 Iowa 293, 45 N. W. 550, 8 L. R. A. 778.

[12] Matter of Newcomb, (1908) 192 N. Y. 238, 84 N. E. 950; Eikenberry v. McFall, (1941) _____ Ohio App. _____ , 33 Ohio Law Abst. 525, 36 N. E. 2d 27.

separate the competent part from the incompetent and admit such part which is competent; that is the duty of counsel making the offer.[13] This rule applies to a deposition as well as to an offer of testimony at the trial.[14]

87. *Proffer of Evidence After Its Exclusion by Trial Judge:* **In State Courts**

It is generally conceded that a judgment will not be reversed for error unless it be shown by the record that the error actually was prejudicial and harmful to the rights of the complaining party. Consonant with this principle, when a party would seek a reversal because of excluded testimony, he must either place the witness on the stand, ask the questions, and have the answers made a matter of record, or else the witness must be presented, and there must be a specific statement at the time of what the testimony of the witness would be, if allowed, so that the reviewing court may see from the record itself whether the offered evidence would be material and of benefit to the merits of the case, and whether its exclusion was actually harmful and prejudicial to the offerer; and, generally speaking, this is true even where it is claimed that the matter sought to be elicited is privileged from disclosure.[1] When, on appeal, com-

---

13 Mutual Life Ins. Co. v. Good, (1913) 25 Colo. App. 204, 136 Pac. 821; Bresson v. Herrick, (1922) 35 Idaho 217, 205 Pac. 555; Indianapolis & M Rapid Transit Co. v. Hall, (1905) 165 Ind. 557, 76 N. E. 242; Matter of Newcomb, (1908) 192 N. Y. 238, 84 N. E. 950; National Mutual Life Ass'n. v. Godrich, [1909] 10 Comm. L. R. 1 (Australia).

14 Bresson v. Herrick, (1922) 35 Idaho 217, 205 Pac. 555.

1 Continental Investment Co. v. Garcher, (1928) 83 Colo. 239, 264 Pac. 723; Mannix v. Cooper, (1917) 66 Ind. App. 226, 117 N. E. 932; Pearson v. Butts, (1938) 224 Iowa 376, 276 N. W. 65; Arnold v. Fort Dodge, Des Moines & So. R. R., (1919) 186 Iowa 538, 173 N. W. 252; Jacobs v. Cedar Rapids, (1917) 181 Iowa 407, 164 N. W. 891; State v. DeZeler, (1950) 230 Minn. 39, 41 N. W. 2d 313, 15 A. L. R. 2d 1137; Gulf, Mobile & N. R. R. v. Willis, (1934) 171 Miss. 732, 157 So. 899, 158 So. 551; New Orleans & N. E. R. R. v. Scarlet, (1917) 115 Miss. 285, 76 So. 265; Williams v. Wabash R. R., (1915) ......Mo........, 175 S. W. 900; Salts v. Prudential Ins. Co., (1909) 140 Mo. App. 142, 120 S. W. 714; Zimmer v. Third Ave. R. R., (1899) 36 App. Div. 265, 55 N. Y. S. 308; New York Life Ins. Co. v. Hansen, (1941) 71 N. D. 383, 2 N. W. 2d 163; Packard v. Coberly, (1928) 147 Wash. 345, 265 Pac. 1082.

It may be reversible error for the trial judge to refuse to allow a party to make a proffer of evidence. Gulf, Mobile & N. R. R. v. Willis, (1934) 171 Miss. 732, 157 So.

plaint is made of the exclusion of evidence, it must appear that the relevant probative force of the excluded evidence is such that, if admitted, it would be materially effective towards the production of a different result; otherwise there would be no real or practical use for the excluded evidence.[2] The court, of course, will not imagine the testimony that would have been given and therefrom presume prejudice.[3] In some states, a court rule requires a proffer of the evidence excluded.[4]

←〰️
899, 158 So. 551; Philadelphia Record Co. v. Sweet, (1936) 124 Pa. Super. 414, 188 Atl. 631.

In Triangle Lumber Co. v. Acree, (1914) 112 Ark. 534, 166 S. W. 958, Ann. Cas. 1916 B. 773, after the court had excluded the testimony of certain physicians on the ground of privilege, it was agreed by the parties, and the court, that appellant need not actually place said witnesses on the stand, but might prepare questions and answers, and insert them in the record, and that all of said questions and answers should be considered objected to, and the objections sustained, just as though each witness was put on the stand and the questions actually asked.

[2] Bradley v. Howell, (1931) 161 Miss. 346, 354, 133 So. 660, 134 So. 843; Gulf, Mobile & N. R. R. v. Willis, (1934) 171 Miss. 732, 739, 157 So. 899, 158 So. 551: "There should have been a sufficient disclosure of this witness' testimony to show that it might have resulted in a different verdict in the case."

Buck v. Buck, (1914) 126 Minn. 275, 279, 148 N. W. 117: "We need not stop to consider whether the objection was well taken * * *, for the ruling was not followed by any offer to show that the ailment which the doctor was treating had any relation to testator's mental condition. The question did not indicate that the answer would be pertinent to the issue and an offer showing materiality was necessary."

Zimmer v. Third Ave. R. R., (1899) 36 App. Div. 265, 55 N. Y. S. 308; In re Johnson, (1898) 32 App. Div. 634, 52 N. Y. S. 1081 (no offer of proof that privilege was waived); Romanant v. White Star Bus Line, Inc., (1932) 43 Puerto Rico 901 (no specific offer of what was intended to be proved).

[3] Pearson v. Butts, (1938) 224 Iowa 376, 276 N. W. 65; Jacobs v. Cedar Rapids, (1917) 181 Iowa 407, 164 N. W. 891; Trieber v. New York & Queen's County Ry., (1912) 149 App. Div. 804, 134 N. Y. S. 267.

[4] e. g., Rule 26 of the Supreme Court of Pennsylvania provides: "In cases of jury trial, when the error alleged is the admission or rejection of evidence * * * the assignment must quote verbatim the question or offer, the objection thereto, the ruling of the court thereon, and the evidence admitted, rejected, or stricken out, or which the court refused to strike out, and the exception * * *. Alleged error in the exclusion of evidence will not be considered, unless the record shows what such evidence would have been or otherwise preserves such evidence for the consideration of the reviewing court, either literally or in substance, and shows that it was offered and actually excluded, the grounds urged for its admission * * * and unless the record shows that such evidence would have been favorable to appellant and material

〰️→

It has been observed that it is not enough that the general tenor or trend of the offered evidence shall be shown, nor in any case is it sufficient merely to put questions to the witness or witnesses. The showing must be specific to the extent that the court may see that the proposed evidence would actually be responsive in terms of facts and not of mere conclusions; that it would be believable; and that, if believed, it would be sufficiently definite and substantial to sustain the issue.[5] Moreover, the offer to prove must not be a general one which includes evidence which is plainly incompetent.[6] Where the testimony of a physician is erroneously excluded on the ground of privilege and the materiality of it is perfectly obvious, no offer of proof of its materiality is necessary.[7] Notwithstanding the trial court might have erred in excluding the testimony of a physician called by the defendant, the error was not necessarily prejudicial and reversible where the record disclosed that the defendant was allowed to and did introduce by the uncontradicted testimony of another physician the same facts which it offered to prove by the testimony of the witness whose testimony was wrongfully excluded.[8]

The practice of stating proposed evidence after an adverse ruling is highly improper when the statement is made by counsel in the hearing of the jury,[9] and an alert and conscientious judge will so rule.

---

and relevant." For rules in other jurisdictions, see 1 Wigmore, Evidence, § 20(3) and 1953 Supplement.

[5] Martin v. Gill, (1938) 182 Miss. 810, 181 So. 849.

[6] Indianapolis & M Rapid Transit Co. v. Hall, (1905) 165 Ind. 557, 76 N. E. 242.

[7] Phillips v. Powell, (1930) 210 Cal. 39, 290 Pac. 441. See also Patten v. United Life & Acc. Ins. Ass'n., (1892) 133 N. Y. 450, 31 N. E. 342.

[8] Hassing v. Mutual Life Ins. Co., (1945) 108 Utah 198, 159 P. 2d 117.

[9] In re Fine's Estate, (1930) 249 Mich. 391, 228 N. W. 687 (attorney-client privilege involved).

In some states, a statute so provides e. g., (1939) S. D. Code § 36.0209: "If an objection to a question propounded to a witness is sustained by the court, the examining attorney may make a specific offer of what he expects to prove by the answer of the witness. In jury trials the court shall require the offer to be made out of the hearing of the jury. * * * In the absence of the jury the court, upon request, may take and report the evidence in full, unless it clearly appears that the evidence is not admissible on any ground or that the witness is privileged."

For federal practice, see § 88, herein.

Some courts recognize a few exceptions to the general rule requiring a proffer of the evidence excluded, and one of these is when the witness is tendered and it is sought to examine him regarding confidential matters which the law forbids him to disclose. In such case, the offerer cannot state into the record—even in the absence of the jury—what he expects to prove by that witness since the law denies the right to prove by him anything of the matters sought to be disclosed. If it appears that the information sought to be placed in the record was acquired during the existence of the relationship which makes such information privileged, then the inquiry is not permitted to proceed further than to show the actual existence of the privileged relationship.[10] In *Powell v. J. J. Newman Lumber Co.*,[11] it was held that permitting a physician, in the absence of the jury, but over objection of the plaintiff, to testify to his examination of the plaintiff, and permitting framing of a hypothetical question to be asked the physician as an expert before the jury, embracing matters testified to by him, was error.[12] The court, while disapproving a proffer of the physician's testimony, indicates that a statement by counsel is acceptable.[13]

---

[10] Gulf, Mobile & N. R. R. v. Willis, (1934) 171 Miss. 732, 157 So. 899, 158 So. 551; United States Fidelity & Guar. Co. v. Hood, (1920) 124 Miss. 548, 87 So. 115, 15 A. L. R. 605.

See also (1939) S. D. Code § 36.0209, infra note 9.

[11] (1936) 174 Miss. 685, 165 So. 299.

[12] The error, however, did not require a reversal of the judgment since substantial justice lay in the jury's verdict.

A statute which requires a party to produce, upon the hearing of a motion for a new trial, any excluded evidence, by the affidavit or deposition of the witness, cannot apply to a physician who claims a privilege from testifying, which claim was sustained. Doty v. Crystal Ice & Fuel Co., (1925) 118 Kan. 323, 235 Pac. 96.

[13] (p. 694): "The well-known practice is for counsel to state what he expects to prove by a physician, if permitted. This is quite different from having the physician mount the witness stand in the presence of the court, attorneys, and audience, and disclose all private and privileged matters covered by the statute giving the patient the right of privileged communications. * * * A statement by counsel to the court as to what he expects to prove will carry to the legal and judicial mind the purpose of the evidence as freely as though it would if testified to, but it makes a very different impression upon the popular and nonlegal mind. Such statements are often termed 'lawyers' talk,' and do not carry to the popular mind the full truth of the purported testimony, and are less prejudicial than would be the testimony of a physician who would probably disclose in full the privileged matters."

When documentary evidence, such as a hospital record, physician's office record, report of autopsy, certificate of death, proof of death, and the like, is offered and excluded, the contents of the writing, or so much thereof as is necessary to show that error has been committed, should be set forth in the record. Statements of counsel, made to the court at the time of the offer, will not, ordinarily, supply the lack of the document itself or so much thereof as may be sufficient to enable the appellate court to determine whether the rejection of the offered writing was prejudicial to any substantial right of the party claiming that its exclusion was error.[14]

The rule requiring a proffer of the evidence excluded usually has no application where the witness is upon cross-examination.[15] Questions upon cross-examination are largely exploratory and it would be unreasonable to require an offer of proof since counsel often cannot know what pertinent facts might be elicited. The general rule, therefore, is that no proffer is necessary in order to obtain a review of rulings which exclude evidence sought on the cross-examination of a witness.[16] Moreover, it has been pointed out that the value of a cross-examination, as a test of truth, would be lost in the case of a crafty and unreliable witness, if the examiner were bound to disclose the purpose and intent of every question asked.[17] But where the question indicates that the matter proposed to be proved is not proper cross-examination, it is not subject to the rule that a party need not, on legitimate cross-examination, disclose what he proposes to prove by the witness; therefore, if it does not reasonably appear that the evidence sought may be relevant and

---

[14] Turner v. Redwood Mutual Life Ass'n., (1936) 13 Cal. App. 2d 573, 57 P. 2d 222; People v. Bray, (1919) 42 Cal. App. 465, 183 Pac. 712; Fitzgerald v. Metropolitan Life Ins. Co., (1941) _____ Mo. App. _____ , 149 S. W. 2d 389. See also dissent by Vinson, J., in Eureka-Maryland Assur. Co., (1941) 74 App. D. C. 191, 121 F. 2d 104, cert. denied 314 U. S. 613, 86 Law. Ed. 494, 62 Su. Ct. 114.

[15] Brock v. Cato, (1947) 75 Ga. App. 79, 42 S. E. 2d 174.

[16] Tossman v. Newman, (1951) 37 Cal. 2d 522, 233 P. 2d 1; Cohen v. Cohen, (1943) 196 Ga. 562, 27 S. E. 2d 28; Hyland v. Milner, (1884) 99 Ind. 308; Stevens v. William S. Howe Co., (1931) 275 Mass. 398, 176 N. E. 208; Etheridge v. Atlantic Coast Line R. R., (1936) 209 N. C. 326, 183 S. E. 539.

 Contra: Gibson v. Pennsylvania R. R., (1951) 14 N. J. Super. 425, 82 A. 2d 635.

 See 1 Wigmore, Evidence, § 20 and 1953 Supplement.

[17] Martin v. Elden, (1877) 32 Ohio St. 282, 289.

material, the court may in its discretion require of counsel a sufficient intimation of the purpose to be served.[18] But nothing further
than a bare intimation should generally be required, since, in many
cases, to state the precise object of a cross-examination would be to
defeat it.[19]

As a general rule, if the testimony of a witness is erroneously
rejected by the trial court upon the sole ground of his incompetency
and not upon the ground of the incompetency of the testimony
itself, it will be *presumed* by an appellate court that the testimony
of such witness would have been material without any statement
to that effect in the record and without a proffer having been made
of what it was expected to prove by him.[20]

Where the court refused to hear preliminary evidence as to
whether the physician-witness was attending the plaintiff at the
time concerning which it was sought to have him testify, but error
was assigned only to the exclusion of ultimate testimony as to the

---

[18] Cox v. Norris, (1944) 70 Ga. App. 580, 584, 28 S. E. 2d 888; Butler v. Manhattan
Ry., (1893) 3 Misc. 453, 23 N. Y. S. 163, aff'd. 143 N. Y. 630, 37 N. E. 826; Bean v.
Green, (1878) 33 Ohio St. 444, 448.

[19] Fahey v. Clark, (1938) 125 Conn. 44, 3 A. 2d 313.

[20] Hollister and Smith v. Reznor, (1858) 9 Ohio St. 1, 9: "Where a witness is rejected
for *incompetency to testify in the case,* the court not having required the party producing the witness to state what he expected to prove by him, the bill of exceptions
need not set forth what the witness would prove or was expected to prove, in order
to show that the party producing the witness had been prejudiced. In other words,
where the witness offered is rejected as *incompetent to testify,* the court will hold
that the party offering the witness has been prejudiced by his exclusion, though the
facts he was expected to prove are not stated * * * the ground of exclusion being
one wholly irrespective of the *subject-matter* of his testimony."

Accord: Powell Brothers Truck Lines, Inc. v. Barnett, (1937) 194 Ark. 769, 109
S. W. 2d 673 (physician excluded); Zaremba v. Skurdialis, (1947) 395 Ill. 437, 70 N. E.
2d 617 (spouse excluded); Torrance v. Torrance, (1946) 147 Ohio St. 169, 70 N. E. 2d
365; Totten v. Estate of Miller, (1941) 139 Ohio St. 29, 37 N. E. 2d 961; Kirkpatrick
v. Milks, (1950) 257 Wis. 549, 44 N. W. 2d 574 (physician excluded); State v. Catellier,
(1947) 63 Wyo. 123, 178, 179 P. 2d 203 (physician excluded).

cf. State, *ex rel* Repp v. Cox, (1900) 155 Ind. 593, 596, 58 N. E. 849.

In Gulf, Mobile & N. R. R. v. Willis, (1934) 171 Miss. 732, 157 So. 899, 158 So. 551,
it was held that where the trial judge erroneously ruled that a dentist was a physician
within the meaning of the privilege statute and therefore an incompetent witness,
but the party calling the dentist neither interrogated him nor made an offer of proof
in the record, the error committed in excluding his testimony could not be noticed
on appeal.

disclosures then made by the plaintiff to such physician, the exclusion of the ultimate testimony was proper.[21]

Where, at the time the attending physician's deposition was offered in evidence by the defendant and was excluded by the court, there had been no waiver of the privilege, the subsequent introduction by the plaintiff of the depositions of two other physicians could not make the court's prior ruling erroneous. If the defendant desired to save any question as to the exclusion of the deposition, it was incumbent upon it to re-offer the same after the changed conditions.[22]

The rejection of evidence as a class may obviate the necessity of an offer to prove what a witness' response to a particular question would have been.[23] Where on cross-examination of the plaintiff's physician-witness, the court refused to allow counsel for the defense to ask him certain questions on the ground of privilege, it was not thereafter the duty of counsel to recall the witness upon the defendant's case and propound the identical questions which previously had been ruled out.[24]

88. Same: In Federal Courts

Rule 43(c) of the Federal Rules of Civil Procedure regulates offers of proof and prescribes methods for making a record of excluded evidence and the ruling thereon. The requirements of the rule are but a codification of prior and accepted practice.[1] The first portion of the rule applies to jury cases. If an objection to a question propounded to a witness is sustained by the court, the examining attorney is permitted to make a specific offer of what he

---

[21] Arizona Copper Co. v. Burciaga, (1918) 20 Ariz. 85, 89, 177 Pac. 29: "The trial court refused to hear the preliminary evidence, and thereby assumed that the said confidential relation of physician and patient existed; hence, the physician was disqualified to repeat the communication. The appellant does not assign as error the refusal of the trial court to hear such preliminary evidence, but assigns as error the order sustaining the objection made that the answer called for was privileged because the witness was then treating plaintiff and plaintiff's wife as their physician. The ruling was strictly correct in the circumstances then before the trial court."

[22] Travelers Ins. Co. v. Fletcher-American National Bank, (1926) 84 Ind. App. 563, 150 N. E. 825.

[23] Sprouse v. Magee, (1928) 46 Idaho 622, 269 Pac. 993.

[24] Albers v. Wilson, (1922) 201 App. Div. 775, 195 N. Y. S. 145.

[1] Downie v. Powers, (1951) 193 F. 2d 760, 768.

expects to prove by the answer of the witness.[2] As a precautionary measure against prejudicing the jury, the court may require the offer to be made out of the hearing of the jury. Furthermore, the court itself may add such other or further statement as clearly shows the character of the evidence, the form in which it was offered, the objection made, and the ruling thereon.[3] The same procedure may be followed in actions tried without a jury except that the court upon request shall take and report the evidence in full, unless it clearly appears that the evidence is not admissible on any ground or that the witness is privileged. The obvious purpose of Rule 43(c) is to allow the examining attorney, or the court, to make such a record that an appellate court can properly determine whether a ruling excluding evidence was erroneous and, if so, whether the error was prejudicial.

The making of a specific offer of proof is not, however, an indispensable condition for assignment of error in the exclusion of evidence.[4] An offer of proof as to excluded evidence is not essential if it is otherwise clear what the alleged error is.[5]

On the other hand, if the significance of the excluded evidence is not obvious, the offer of proof must be made in the record in order to preserve the question on appeal. Not having a record of the evidence offered but excluded, the appellate court could not

---

[2] The court, under proper circumstances, may curtail the proffer of excluded testimony, but it cannot ignore the spirit of the mandate of the rule and refuse to allow a party to make any offer at all for the record. Downie v. Powers, supra.

[3] This affords the trial court the opportunity to incorporate in the record a summary of the facts which made necessary its ruling; thus, the appellate court will have a better understanding of the question it may have to decide.

[4] Hoffman v. Palmer, (1942) 129 F. 2d 976, 994, aff'd. on other grounds, 318 U. S. 109, 87 Law. Ed. 645, 63 Su. Ct. 477, 144 A. L. R. 719; Iva Ikuko Toguri D'Aquino v. United States, (1951) 192 F. 2d 338, 374, cert. denied 343 U. S. 935, 96 Law. Ed. 1343, 72 Su. Ct. 772; Maguire v. Federal Crop Ins. Corp., (1950) 181 F. 2d 320; Meaney v. United States, (1940) 112 F. 2d 538, 130 A. L. R. 973.

See also 2 Barron and Holtzoff, Federal Practice and Procedure, § 969; 5 Moore's Federal Practice, § 43.11.

[5] Maguire v. Federal Crop Ins. Corp., infra note 4.

Where it is plain and certain what the witness' testimony would be, the making of an offer of proof could properly be regarded as a mere futility. Hawkins v. Missouri Pac. R. R., (1951) 188 F. 2d 348.

judge its competence.[6] In this connection, it must be remembered that under Rule 61 of the Federal Rules of Civil Procedure, error in the exclusion of evidence which does not prejudice the substantial rights of the parties must be disregarded. It is quite clear that any error in the exclusion of evidence which is not inconsistent with substantial justice and could not change the result of the trial will not be considered on appeal.[7] Therefore, to preserve the question for review an offer of proof must be made in the record when the materiality and competency of the evidence is not obvious, or where it does not appear what evidence the witness would have given had he been permitted to testify.[8]

Where the relationship of physician and patient has once obtained and the testimony of the physician is sought but excluded on the ground of privilege, the party seeking the testimony should make a tender of proof, out of the presence of the jury, so that the court may determine whether the proffered testimony is within or without the limitations of the privilege statute. If no offer is made, it will be assumed that the knowledge of the witness was based upon the relation of physician and patient.[9] Where the testimony of a physician was excluded but no offer of proof was made, it was held that what would have been his testimony was left to the realm of

---

[6] Hoffman v. Palmer, (1942) 129 F. 2d 976, 994, aff'd. on other grounds, 318 U. S. 109, 87 Law. Ed. 645, 63 Su. Ct. 477, 144 A. L. R. 719; Downie v. Powers, (1951) 193 F. 2d 760; Hawkins v. Missouri Pac. R. R., infra note 5; Patton v. Lewis, (1944) 146 F. 2d 544; Sorrels v. Alexander, (1944) 142 F. 2d 769.

[7] Hoffman v. Palmer, infra note 6, p. 116: "Mere 'technical errors' which do not affect the substantial rights of the parties are not sufficient to set aside a jury verdict in an appellate court. He who seeks to have a judgment set aside because of an erroneous ruling carries the burden of showing that prejudice resulted."

[8] Patton v. Lewis, (1944) 146 F. 2d 544.

Sorrels v. Alexander, (1944) 142 F. 2d 769, 770: "The ground of rejection was that the communication was privileged. We think this was clearly wrong, because this of itself is not enough. A reversal on this ground would be proper only if it is shown that the exclusion was harmful. * * * And because we do not know what evidence the witness would have given, there is a complete failure to show that the exclusion affected the substantial rights of the party in whose behalf it was offered. In such circumstances the error must be ignored."

See also Price v. United States, (1934) 68 F. 2d 133, 135, cert. denied 292 U. S. 632, 78 Law. Ed. 1063, 54 Su. Ct. 531.

[9] Stafford v. American Security & Trust Co., (1931) 60 App. D. C. 380, 55 F. 2d 542.

conjecture and could not serve as a basis for setting aside the verdict of the jury and granting a new trial.[10]

89. Who May Interpose Objection

The physician-patient privilege was enacted for the benefit of the patient only. It belongs to him, and he may claim or forego its protection.[1] If, therefore, the patient is present at the trial, the proper rule would seem to be that the privilege may be invoked only by him,[2] or by his attorney acting for him.[3] On the other hand, if the patient has no opportunity to claim his privilege and the evidence sought to be elicited comes within the purview of the statute, the better view is that it is absolutely incompetent *and may be objected to by anyone* unless the privilege has been waived by the patient, or is waived at the trial by a person lawfully authorized to act in his stead. Accordingly, if the patient be dead,[4] or is not a

---

[10] Tweith v. Duluth, M. & I. R. Ry., (1946) 66 F. Supp. 427.

[1] See § 13, herein.

The principle has been applied to other privileges. In Williamson v. Williamson, (1935) 183 Wash. 71, 48 P. 2d 588, 54 P. 2d 1215, the husband-wife privilege was not available to a mother-in-law in an action brought against her by her daughter-in-law for damages for alienation of her husband's affections.

See also Lindsey v. People, (1919) 66 Colo. 343, 181 Pac. 531.

[2] A few courts have permitted the physician-witness to claim the privilege notwithstanding the patient himself is in court. See § 16, herein.

[3] It is the customary practice to permit counsel for the patient to object to the disclosure of information protected by the statute; but, in a case involving the attorney-client privilege, it was held that the court, in its discretion, may require the client himself, if present, to claim it. McCooe v. Dighton, S. & S. St Ry., (1889) 173 Mass. 117, 53 N. E. 133. Holmes, J., (p. 118) "It is no part of the conduct of the case to object or consent to evidence which is excluded only because of a personal privilege. By accident, the privilege in this case belonged to the plaintiff, but it might as well have belonged to any one else, and clearly if it had belonged to a third person, it would not have rested with the plaintiff's lawyer to waive or assert it. We do not see that it matters that the privilege was the plaintiff's own. Inasmuch as to assert or waive it was not primarily a weapon for the trial, but a right standing on independent grounds, the court might in its discretion feel unwilling to assume that control of that weapon was intrusted to counsel in the case without an assurance to that effect from the party himself. * * * This being so, it was proper for the court to compel the plaintiff to take the full responsibility of the choice."

(1939) S. D. Code § 36.0102: * * * "The objection that the communication is privileged must be made by or in behalf of the person making the communication."

[4] In re Flint, (1893) 100 Cal. 391, 34 Pac. 863; Murphy v. Board of Police Pension

⟫→

party to the action or is not present to object,[5] *anyone* involved in the proceeding may object to the introduction of evidence which will disclose information within the protection of the patient's privilege. Moreover, the trial judge, *sua sponte,* may exclude such evidence,[6] and one legislature has made it his duty to do so.[7]

In the absence of a valid waiver of the privilege by the insured, the beneficiary of a policy of insurance may object to the disclosure of privileged information when it is sought to be elicited by the

←—

Fund, (1905) 2 Cal. App. 468, 83 Pac. 577; Brackney v. Fogle, (1901) 156 Ind. 535, 60 N. E. 303; Matter of Myer, (1906) 184 N. Y. 54, 76 N. E. 920, 6 Ann. Cas. 26; Davis v. Supreme Lodge, K. of H., (1900) 165 N. Y. 159, 58 N. E. 891; Westover v. Aetna Life Ins. Co., (1884) 99 N. Y. 56, 1 N. E. 104, approved in Matter of Warrington, (1951) 303 N. Y. 129, 100 N. E. 2d 170; Beil v. Supreme Lodge, K. of H., (1903) 80 App. Div. 609, 80 N. Y. S. 751; Edington v. Mutual Life Ins. Co., (1875) 5 Hun. (N. Y.) 1; New York Life Ins. Co. v. Hansen, (1941) 71 N. D. 383, 2 N. W. 2d 163; Parisky v. Pierstorff, (1939) 63 Ohio App. 503, 27 N. E. 2d 254; Maine v. Maryland Casualty Co., (1920) 172 Wis. 350, 178 N. W. 749, 15 A. L. R. 1536.

In Boyd v. Kilmer, (1926) 285 Pa. 533, 132 Atl. 709, relatives of the deceased client, who were not parties to the transaction in which the attorney acted, were not allowed to claim the privilege of the deceased client; that right being personal does not pass to a third party at the client's death. See also Dowie's Estate, (1890) 135 Pa. 210, 19 Atl. 936; 8 Wigmore, Evidence, §§ 2196, 2321.

[5] Darling v. Pacific Elec. Ry., (1925) 197 Cal. 702, 242 Pac. 703. (physician of absent witness refused to disclose nature of his patient's ailment which prevented his attendance in court); Fishleigh v. Detroit United Ry., (1919) 205 Mich. 145, 171 N. W. 549; Murray v. Physical Culture Hotel, Inc., (1939) 258 App. Div. 334, 16 N. Y. S. 2d 978, aff'd. 17 N. Y. S. 2d 862; Rodner v. Buchman, (1935) 246 App. Div. 777, 284 N. Y. S. 99; Weil v. Weil, (1912) 151 App. Div. 622, 136 N. Y. S. 190; Westphal v. State, (1948) 191 Misc. 688, 79 N. Y. S. 2d 634 (state claimed privilege of absent person mentally incompetent); Jones v. Jones, (1955) 208 Misc. 721, 144 N. Y. S. 2d 820. See also Bacon v. Frisbie, (1880) 80 N. Y. 394 (attorney-client privilege).

[6] Storrs v. Scougale, (1882) 48 Mich. 387, 12 N. W. 502. See also Griffiths v. Metropolitan Street Ry., (1902) 171 N. Y. 106, 63 N. E. 808; Matter of Hannah, (1887) 11 N. Y. State Rep. 807; Roth v. Equitable Life Assur. Soc., (1944) 186 Misc. 612, 50 N. Y. S. 2d 119, aff'd. 269 App. Div. 746, 55 N. Y. S. 2d 117.

[7] (1939) S. D. Code § 36.0103:

"It shall be the duty of the court, of its own motion and without waiting for objection, to advise a witness at the appropriate time of his right to refuse to answer any question requiring the disclosure of any privileged communication * * *. In all cases where it shall appear to the court that any person who is not present nor represented at the hearing should be protected in his right to have any communication made under the confidential relations provisions of section 36.0101 excluded, it shall be the duty of the court to make such objections and orders for such purpose as to the court may seem necessary."

insurer.[8] On the other hand, it has been held that an insurance company may claim the benefit of the statute against a plaintiff who had no legal right to waive the insured's privilege;[9] but there is some authority to the effect that an insurance company cannot invoke the privilege.[10]

A defendant cannot successfully object to plaintiff's calling as a witness a physician whom the defendant had employed to examine him.[11]

---

[8] Ranger v. Equitable Life Assur. Soc., (1952) 196 F. 2d 968; Eureka-Maryland Assur. Co. v. Gray, (1941) 74 App. D. C. 191, 121 F. 2d 104, cert. denied 314 U. S. 613, 86 Law. Ed. 494, 62 Su. Ct. 114; O'Brien v. General Acc., Fire & Life Assur. Co., (1930) 42 F. 2d 48; National Benevolent Soc. v. Barker, (1922) 155 Ark. 506, 244 S. W. 720; Metropolitan Life Ins. Co. v. Fitzgerald, (1919) 137 Ark. 366, 209 S. W. 77; National Annuity Ass'n. v. McCall, (1912) 103 Ark. 201, 146 S. W. 125, 48 L. R. A. (n. s.) 418; Penn Mutual Life Ins. Co. v. Wiler, (1884) 100 Ind. 92; Masonic Mutual Ben. Ass'n. v. Beck, (1881) 77 Ind. 203; Cross v. Equitable Life Assur. Soc., (1940) 228 Iowa 800, 293 N. W. 464; Pride v. Inter-State Business Men's Acc. Ass'n., (1928) 207 Iowa 167, 216 N. W. 62, 62 A. L. R. 31; Novak v. Chicago Fraternal Life Ass'n., (1932) 136 Kan. 609, 16 P. 2d 507; New York Life Ins. Co. v. Newman, (1945) 311 Mich. 368, 18 N. W. 2d 859; Krapp v. Metropolitan Life Ins. Co., (1906) 143 Mich. 369, 106 N. W. 1107; Briesenmeister v. Supreme Lodge, K. of P., (1890) 81 Mich. 525, 45 N. W. 977, 8 L. R. A. 682; United States Fidelity & Guar. Co. v. Hood, (1920) 124 Miss. 548, 87 So. 115, 15 A. L. R. 605; Tinsley v. Washington National Ins. Co., (1936) _____Mo. App._____, 97 S. W. 2d 874; Davis v. Supreme Lodge, K. of H., (1900) 165 N. Y. 159, 58 N. E. 891; Dilleber v. Home Life Ins. Co., (1877) 69 N. Y. 256; Edington v. Mutual Life Ins. Co., (1876) 67 N. Y. 185 (objection made by assignee of beneficiary); Roth v. Equitable Life Assur. Soc., (1945) 186 Misc. 403, 59 N. Y. S. 2d 707, aff'd. 270 App. Div. 923, 62 N. Y. S. 2d 612, appeal denied 296 N. Y. 1061, 69 N. E. 2d 565.

In Louisiana, the privilege does not apply in civil cases, but even if it did an objection by the beneficiary is of no avail. Rhodes v. Metropolitan Life Ins. Co., (1949) 172 F. 2d 183. For operation of statutory privilege in actions brought to recover proceeds of an insurance policy, see Nevada, Puerto Rico and New Zealand statutes, Appendix herein.

[9] Beil v. Supreme Lodge, K. of H., (1903) 80 App. Div. 609, 80 N. Y. S. 751; Maine v. Maryland Casualty Co., (1920) 172 Wis. 350, 178 N. W. 749, 15 A. L. R. 1536. The vigorous dissent of Judge Owen promptly led to an amendment of the privilege statute.

[10] Unionaid Life Ins. Co. v. Bank of Dover, (1936) 192 Ark. 123, 90 S. W. 2d 982; Hier v. Farmers Mutual Fire Ins. Co., (1937) 104 Mont. 471, 67 P. 2d 831, 110 A. L. R. 1051.

[11] Leard v. State, (1925) 30 Okla. Cr. 191, 235 Pac. 243; State, *ex rel* Berge v. Superior Court, (1929) 154 Wash. 144, 281 Pac. 335; Osborn v. Seattle, (1927) 142 Wash. 25, 252 Pac. 164.

Generally speaking, a physician does not have the right to claim the privilege of his patient.[12] Likewise, a person charged with a crime against another cannot, as a general rule, claim the privilege of his victim.[13] There is a conflict of opinion as to whether the State may invoke the privilege of the patient. Some courts hold it may;[14] others hold otherwise.[15] If the patient be an infant, or is incompetent, the objection may be made by his guardian or by a person acting in behalf of the patient.[16]

There is a multitude of cases where disputes have arisen between persons who claimed to have the right to waive the privilege of the deceased patient and those who claimed to have the right to insist upon its strict enforcement. In most of these cases, the primary issue concerned the mental competency of a deceased testator or grantor. Among those ranged on one side or the other in such controversies were heirs, executors, administrators, guardians, spouses, devisees, legatees, grantees, donees, next of kin, and even strangers. Each side strove either to introduce or exclude testimony of the deceased's physicians. Of course, much depended upon the court's construction of the particular statute with reference to the right of certain persons to waive the privilege.[17] However, the trend of modern decisions everywhere is to admit all relevant and material evidence whenever possible;[18] hence, it may fairly be said that

---

[12] § 16, herein.

[13] §§ 16, 70, herein.

[14] Westphal v. State, (1948) 191 Misc. 688, 79 N. Y. S. 2d 634; State v. Viola, (1947) .... Ohio App........., 82 N. E. 2d 306, appeal dismissed, 148 Ohio St. 716, 76 N. E. 2d 715, cert. denied, 334 U. S. 816, 96 Law. Ed. 1746, 68 Su. Ct. 1070. (It is not clear, however, whether the State or the Court invoked the privilege of the patient.)
    State v. Long, (1913) 257 Mo. 199, 165 S. W. 748. (question left undecided).
    See also § 16, herein.

[15] See § 16, herein.

[16] Sanne, a minor, by Dahlke, Gdn. v. Metropolitan Life Ins. Co., (1944) 218 Minn. 181, 15 N. W. 2d 524; Arnold v. Maryville, (1905) 110 Mo. App. 254, 85 S. W. 107; Griffiths v. Metropolitan Street Ry., (1902) 171 N. Y. 106, 63 N. E. 808; Jones v. Jones, (1955) 208 Misc. 721, 144 N. Y. S. 2d 820.

[17] See c. XVI, herein.

[18] Bruington v. Wagoner, (1917) 100 Kan. 10, 16, 164 Pac. 1057: "If we had a lawsuit here between heirs at law and it should present a situation where some of them, claiming as heirs at law, desired to waive the privilege, and some of them, likewise

>>>→

the right to waive will usually prevail over the right to object.[19]

90. Time for Objection

As a general rule, objection to the introduction of evidence pertaining to matters within the protection of the statutory privilege should be made at the time the evidence is offered. Failure to object to a question which elicits confidential information may result in a waiver of the privilege, and a consent to the disclosure may, sometimes, be implied.[1]

91. How Objection Made

Manifestly there is a distinction between the competency of evidence and the competency of a witness. A physician is not neces-

---

as heirs at law, objected to waiving it, the matter might present some difficulty, although this court is rather positively committed against any interpretation of rules of evidence which limits judicial inquiry in the ascertainment of truth."

[19] It would serve no useful purpose to cite the multitude of cases pro and con, since they have weight as controlling authority only when considered in connection with the particular facts out of which the controversies arose. However, the following selected cases may be helpful.

Calhoun v. Jacobs, (1944) 79 App. D. C. 29, 141 F. 2d 729, heirs v. grantee, a stranger; McCartney v. Holmquist, (1939) 70 App. D. C. 334, 106 F. 2d 855, 126 A. L. R. 375. legatee v. executor named in will but before probate thereof; Schornick v. Schornick, (1923) 25 Ariz. 563, 220 Pac. 397, 31 A. L. R. 159. heirs v. widow, but claiming as grantee; In re Flint, (1893) 100 Cal. 391, 34 Pac. 863, heir v. devisee; Stayner v. Nye, (1949) 227 Ind. 231, 85 N. E. 2d 496, heirs and personal representative v. grantee, a stranger; Gurley v. Park, (1893) 135 Ind. 440, 35 N. E. 279, nephew and niece v. daughter; Heuston v. Simpson, (1888) 115 Ind. 62, 17 N. E. 261, brother v. executor and devisees; Winters v. Winters, (1897) 102 Iowa 53, 71 N. W. 184, heirs v. devisee or legal representative; Gorman v. Hickey, (1937) 145 Kan. 54, 64 P. 2d 587, heirs v. executor who was personally interested; Rost v. Heyka, (1930) 130 Kan. 5, 285 Pac. 539, son v. brother and sisters; Chaffee v. Kaufman, (1923) 113 Kan. 254, 214 Pac. 618. grandchildren v. son and daughter, the executor, and a stranger legatee; Craig v. Craig, (1923) 112 Kan. 472, 212 Pac. 72. heirs v. strangers; Flack v. Brewster, (1920) 107 Kan. 63, 190 Pac. 616, heirs v. sister but defending as grantee; Bruington v. Wagoner, (1917) 100 Kan. 10, 164 Pac. 1057. children of deceased brother of grantor v. children of living sister but defending as grantees; Thompson v. Ish, (1889) 99 Mo. 160, 12 S. W. 510. son devisee v. heirs; Meyer v. Russell, (1926) 55 N. D. 546, 214 N. W. 857. heirs v. grantee; Grieve v. Howard, (1919) 54 Utah 225, 180 Pac. 423. special administrator v. heir defending as grantee; Will of King, (1947) 251 Wis. 269, 29 N. W. 2d 69. personal representative v. sole heir at law.

[1] See § 130, herein.

sarily a wholly incompetent witness, even though he be called to the stand by the patient's adversary. The privilege statute does not absolutely disqualify him to be a witness, but merely prohibits him from disclosing, without the consent of the holder of the privilege, certain information acquired by him in his professional character.[1] There is much to which an attending physician may testify without violating the statutory privilege.[2] The objection, therefore, should not be to the competency of the physician as a witness, but to a question which elicits from him information within the protection of the statute. Ordinarily, he can not with propriety be excluded as a witness, but he can be prevented from disclosing privileged matters.[3]

As a general rule, it is the duty of a party, when he objects to evidence, to state the grounds of his objection, so that the trial judge may understand the precise question or questions he is called upon to decide. It is also due to the party whose evidence is objected to, that the grounds of objection be specified so as to afford his counsel a fair opportunity to rephrase the question, or to ask preliminary or supplemental questions which will render the subject matter objected to competent, if possible, and thus have the case tried upon its merits.[4] When, therefore, the evidence sought to be elicited appears to be within the ban of the privilege statute, the objection must specifically be based upon that ground.[5] A mere general objection, or one that is based upon the broad grounds that the evidence sought is incompetent, irrelevant, and immaterial is not sufficient to raise the question of privilege.[6]

---

[1] § 13, herein.

[2] See c. X, herein.

[3] Of course, where by statute, *e. g.*, the dead man statute, a particular person is made incompetent to testify at all, the objection should be made to his competency as a witness as soon as the disqualification is revealed.

[4] See Busch, (1949) Law and Tactics in Jury Trials, §§ 482, 483.

[5] Kirkpatrick v. American Ry. Express Co., (1928) 177 Ark. 334, 6 S. W. 2d 524; Hopkins v. State, (1951) 212 Miss. 772, 55 So. 2d 467; Keeton v. State, (1936) 175 Miss. 631, 167 So. 68; State v. Armstrong, (1950) 232 N. C. 727, 62 S. E. 2d 50; Gallagher v. Portland Traction Co., (1947) 181 Ore. 385, 182 P. 2d 354.

[6] Hammel v. St. Louis, Iron Mt. & S. Ry., (1914) 113 Ark. 296, 298, 168 S. W. 144: "Practically the only question urged for reversal of the judgment is the action of the

≫→

Ordinarily, where evidence is received and a part of it is admissible and a part inadmissible, a general objection to its reception is not sufficient to save the question of the inadmissibility of the objectionable part. To save the objector's rights, he should clearly indicate the part of the evidence to which he objects and move its exclusion.[7] Hence, an objection which went to *all* of the physician's testimony when part of his answer did not disclose privileged matter, was properly overruled.[8] Where communications to a nurse are privileged if made when she is acting as the assistant or agent of the attending physician, a general objection to her testimony is not

← ⧉

court in admitting the evidence of the witness, Dr. H., over appellant's objection. It appears from the evidence of the witness that he acquired the information concerning appellant's condition while attending her in a professional capacity, and this information was evidently disclosed to him to enable him to prescribe as a physician, and it was therefore privileged. But the objection offered to the evidence was a general one, and the attention of the court was not called to the fact that the evidence was within the inhibition of the statute. * * * This evidence was not incompetent, nor was it irrelevant or immaterial, and a general objection to evidence only raises the question of competency or relevancy * * *. Appellant should have made specific objection that the witness was being interrogated in regard to a privileged communication, and, had this been done, the admission of the evidence would constitute error calling for a reversal of the case; but we think that a general objection to the admission of the evidence, as was made here, was insufficient to raise the question of the privileged character of the evidence. * * * The objection here made was a general one, and, while the evidence was privileged, it was both competent and relevant."

Accord: Kirkpatrick v. American Ry. Express Co., (1928) 177 Ark. 334, 6 S. W. 2d 524; State v. Carryer, (1915) _____ Mo. _____, 180 S. W. 850; Mulligan v. Sinski, (1913) 156 App. Div. 35, 140 N. Y. S. 835, aff'd. 214 N. Y. 678, 108 N. E. 1101; Enghlin v. Pittsburg County Ry., (1934) 169 Okla. 106, 36 P. 2d 32, 94 A. L. R. 1180.

Deutschmann v. Third Ave. R. R., (1903) 87 App. Div. 503, 511, 84 N. Y. S. 887: "The objection interposed to this question [eliciting privileged matter] was that it was incompetent, irrelevant, and immaterial. There was not a suggestion either to this question, or any of the questions which followed * * * to which the objection was interposed, that they were in violation of [the privilege statute], or that the examination in any wise violated the provisions of that section. Consequently this objection was waived, if it might have been insisted upon. An objection which specifies particular grounds is to be dealt with in respect of the grounds so stated. All others will be regarded as waived."

[7] Carson v. Metropolitan Life Ins. Co., (1951) 156 Ohio St. 104, 100 N. E. 2d 197, 28 A. L. R. 2d 344. See note (1952) 27 N. Y. U. L. Rev. 158.

[8] Pence v. Waugh, (1893) 135 Ind. 143, 34 N. E. 860; Sovereign Camp, W. of W. v. Farmer, (1917) 116 Miss. 626, 77 So. 655; Gallagher v. Portland Traction Co., (1947) 181 Ore. 385, 182 P. 2d 354.

sufficient; the objection should be made to *each* question calling for privileged information so that the court can determine whether or not the information was acquired by the nurse while assisting the physician.[9]

It has been held that the court, in its discretion, may, upon request, excuse the jury from the courtroom and permit the patient to claim his statutory privilege in the jury's absence; the theory being that a party should not be prejudiced by claiming a right which the law gives him.[10]

An objection to the competency of a physician-witness on the ground that the plaintiff had not waived her right to object, did not save for review the question whether the plaintiff had the power to waive the objection to competency.[11]

92. *Failure to Produce Evidence: In General*

The conduct of a party may be of the highest importance in determining whether the cause of action in a case in which he is the plaintiff, or the ground of defense if he is the defendant, is honest and just. Surely it is not unreasonable to expect that every litigant will bring to his support in presenting his case, the best and strongest evidence that is in his power[1] to produce. It is but natural that out of a desire to succeed he should do this. And so it has become a well-established rule of evidence that, without satisfactory explanation, the failure of a party to produce relevant evidence which is peculiarly within his possession or under his control, and which he would naturally be expected to produce if favorable to

---

[9] Meyer v. Russell, (1926) 55 N. D. 546, 214 N. W. 857.

[10] Johnson v. Kinney, (1942) 232 Iowa 1016, 7 N. W. 2d 188, 144 A. L. R. 997; followed in Howard v. Porter, (1949) 240 Iowa 153, 35 N. W. 2d 837. In Minnesota, the patient may be required to assert the privilege in the presence of the jury. Nelson v. Ackerman, (1957) 83 N. W. 2d 500. See McCooe v. Dighton, S. & S. St. Ry., (1899) 173 Mass. 117, 53 N. E. 133 (attorney-client privilege). See also Gulf Refining Co. v. Myrick, (1954) 220 Miss. 429, 71 So. 2d 217; Bauch v. Schultz, (1919) 109 Misc. 548, 180 N. Y. S. 188.

[11] Denny v. Robertson, (1944) 352 Mo. 609, 179 S. W. 2d 5.

[1] Lack of power to produce may be due to the person's absence from the jurisdiction, or to his illness, or to other circumstances.

him, gives rise to a legitimate inference that its production would have resulted unfavorably to him.[2]

Manifestly the rule does not require the production of the greatest amount of evidence, which it is within the power of the party to produce, as to any given fact. Concededly it is not necessary for a party to produce every available witness. All the law requires is sufficient proof, and a party is not bound to produce and examine all the witnesses who know anything of the matter in dispute, or, failing to do so, have the inference indulged against him that a witness, if produced, would not support his right.[3] And it does not necessarily follow that a party's failure to call a witness, or the exclusion of his testimony on the ground of privilege, amounts to a willful suppression of evidence.[4] On the other hand, where stronger evidence is available to a party and he chooses to rely upon evidence which is plainly inferior in probative value, he runs the risk of inviting distrust in his case,[5] and his failure to produce the better evidence will usually weigh heavily against him when the jury considers the case.[6] Furthermore, for lack of important evi-

---

[2] 10 R. C. L., Evidence, § 32.

2 Wigmore, Evidence, § 285: "The nonproduction of evidence that would naturally have been produced by an honest and therefore fearless claimant permits the inference that its *tenor is unfavorable to the party's cause.*"

Fulsom-Morris Coal & M. Co. v. Mitchell, (1913) 37 Okla. 575, 580, 132 Pac. 1103: "There is a rule of evidence that when a party has it in his possession or power to produce the best evidence of which the case in its nature is susceptible, and withholds it, the fair presumption is that the testimony is withheld from some sinister motive, and that its production would thwart his evil or fraudulent purpose."

For decisions showing applications of the rule, see notes: 5 A. L. R. 2d 893; 135 A. L. R. 1376; 131 A. L. R. 693; 116 A. L. R. 1170; 70 A. L. R. 1326; Ann. Cas. 1914 A 909.

[3] Bleecker v. Johnston, (1877) 69 N. Y. 309; Perlman v. Shanck, (1920) 192 App. Div. 179, 182 N. Y. S. 767; Baldwin v. Brooklyn Heights R. R., (1904) 99 App. Div. 496, 91 N. Y. S. 59; Fulsom-Morris Coal & M. Co. v. Mitchell, (1913) 37 Okla. 575, 132 Pac. 1103.

[4] Thomas v. Gates, (1899) 126 Cal. 1, 58 Pac. 315; Estate of Carpenter, (1892) 94 Cal. 406, 29 Pac. 1101; Wood v. Los Angeles Traction Co., (1905) 1 Cal. App. 474, 82 Pac. 547; William Laurie Co. v. McCullough, (1910) 174 Ind. 477, 90 N. E. 1014, Ann. Cas. 1913 A 49; New York Life Ins. Co. v. Newman, (1945) 311 Mich. 368, 18 N. W. 2d 859; Bleecker v. Johnston, (1877) 69 N. Y. 309; Caldwell v. Hoskins, (1920) 94 Ore. 567, 186 Pac. 50 (plaintiff failed to produce x-ray taken several months after injury).

[5] Clifton v. United States, (1846) 45 U. S. (IV How.) 242, 11 Law Ed. 957.

[6] Masonite Corp. v. Hill, (1934) 170 Miss. 158, 154 So. 295; Carney v. Krause, (1928)

≫→

dence due to the failure of the claimant to call his physician as a witness, the trial or appellate court may set aside a verdict in his favor,[7] or, in a personal injury case, reduce the amount of damages awarded by the jury.[8]

The failure of a party to produce available evidence, which under certain circumstances would be expected to be produced, creates an inference of fact, *not a presumption of law*.[9] The inference is merely persuasive, not conclusive.[10] It is much to be regretted, therefore, that, in a number of decisions,[11] courts have used expressions such as "creates the presumption," "it will be presumed," "it must be presumed," "the presumption will be indulged," "authorizes a strong presumption," the implication appearing to be that a presumption of law arises, rather than a *mere inference of fact*. In all probability, these courts intended no such meaning,[12] but had in mind a presumption of fact, which, of course,

---

......Ohio App.........., 6 Ohio Law Abst. 699; American Assur. Co. v. Early, (1912) 23 Ohio C. C. R. (n. s.) 418, aff'd 91 Ohio St. 367, 110 N. E. 1053; Katafiaz v. Toledo Cons. Elec. Co., (1902) 1 Ohio C. C. R. (n. s.) 129.

[7] Whitmore v. American Ry. Express Co., (1925) 219 Mo. App. 294, 269 S. W. 654; McClanahan v. St. Louis & San F. R. R., (1910) 147 Mo. App. 386, 126 S. W. 535; Vaughn v. Memorial Hospital, (1925) 100 W. Va. 290, 130 S. E. 481.

[8] Beard v. Williams, (1935) 172 Miss. 880, 161 So. 750; Willits v. Chicago, B. & Q. R. R., (1920) ...... Mo........, 221 S. W. 65.

[9] State v. Damon, (1943) 350 Mo. 949, 169 S. W. 2d 382; Perlman v. Schanck, (1920) 192 App. Div. 179, 182 N. Y. S. 767; Neale v. Nassau Elec. R. R., (1914) 161 App. Div. 95, 146 N. Y. S. 263; Kirkpatrick v. Allemannia Fire Ins. Co., (1905) 102 App. Div. 327, 92 N. Y. S. 466, aff'd 184 N. Y. 546, 76 N. E. 1098; Albert v. Philadelphia Rapid Transit Co., (1916) 252 Pa. 527, 97 Atl. 680; Green v. Brooks, (1906) 215 Pa. 492, 64 Atl. 672.

[10] Sorby v. Three Rivers Motors, (1955) 178 Pa. Super. 187, 114 A. 2d 347.

[11] *e.g.*, Clifton v. United States, (1846) 45 U. S. (IV How.) 242, 11 Law Ed. 957; Troutman v. Mutual Life Ins. Co., (1942) 125 F. 2d 769; Thomas v. Maryland Casualty Co., (1947) ......La. App.........., 32 So. 2d 472; Moore v. Natchitoches Coca-Cola B. Co., (1947) ......La. App.......... , 32 So. 2d 347; Guillory v. Union Sulphur Co., (1941) ...... La. App. ...... , 3 So. 2d 197; Robinson v. Haydel, (1936) 177 Miss. 233, 171 So. 7; Masonite Corp. v. Hill, (1934) 170 Miss. 158, 154 So. 295; Porter v. Chicago, B. & Q. R. R., (1930) 325 Mo. 381, 28 S. W. 2d 1035; Whitmore v. American Ry. Express Co., (1925) 219 Mo. App. 294, 269 S. W. 654; Vann v. Harden, (1948) 187 Va. 555, 47 S. E. 2d 314; Mohr v. Mohr, (1937) 119 W. Va. 253, 193 S. E. 121.

For possibility of error in the court's instructions to the jury, see § 101, herein.

[12] In Hall v. Vanderpool, (1893) 156 Pa. 152, 26 Atl. 1069, the trial judge used the word

is not a presumption at all, but a mere inference.[13] Failure to distinguish these terms[14] has led to much confusion in the application of the rule and has frequently resulted in the giving of erroneous instructions by the trial courts to juries.[15]

The inference resulting from a failure to produce evidence is not a substitute for substantive evidence.[16] Evidence of such conduct is persuasive rather than probative, and cannot be invoked as substantive proof of any facts essential to the case of one's adversary,[17] but only to corroborate the latter's proof when it constitutes a prima facie case.[18]

"presumption" in his instructions to the jury, but the Supreme Court held that it was used in the sense of an inference which the jury were at liberty to draw, and that the jury must have so understood.

[13] Ausmus v. People, (1910) 47 Colo. 167, 199, 107 Pac. 204, 19 Ann. Cas. 491.

[14] Wilkin, J., in Ensel v. Lumber Ins. Co., (1913) 88 Ohio St. 269, 282, 102 N. E. 955: "The error of counsel throughout this case, lies in a confusion of terms. They mistake inference for presumption—a slip too often unconsciously made by judges as well as lawyers. A presumption is a rule which the law makes upon a given state of facts; an inference is a conclusion which, by means of data founded upon common experience, natural reason draws from facts which are proven."

Gurley, Dist. J., in United States v. Segelnan, (1949) 86 F. Supp. 114, 120: "There is a decided difference in legal terminology between the meaning of the words 'presumption' and 'inference.' An 'inference' is nothing more than a permissible deduction from the evidence. A 'presumption' is compulsory and prima faciely establishes the fact to be true, or is compulsory, if not disproved. A presumption cannot be disregarded by a jury while an inference may or may not be depending on the deductions made by the jury from the evidence."

See also 20 Am. Jur., Evidence, § 162.

[15] Gatlin v. Allen, (1948) 203 Miss. 135, 33 So. 2d 304; Crapson v. United Chatauqua Co., (1931) ....Mo. App.........., 37 S. W. 2d 966; Perlman v. Shanck, (1920) 192 App. Div. 179, 182 N. Y. S. 767; Neale v. Nassau Elec. R. R., (1914) 161 App. Div. 95, 146 N. Y. S. 263; Mackovitch v. Becker, (1928) 93 Pa. Super. 514.

See also § 101, herein.

[16] Laffin v. Ryan, (1957) 4 A. D. 2d 21, 162 N. Y. S. 2d 730.

See note, 70 A. L. R. 1326.

[17] Schroeder v. Wells, (1925) ....Mo. App.........., 277 S. W. 578; Stocker v. Boston & M. R. R., (1930) 84 N. H. 377, 151 Atl. 457, 70 A. L. R. 1320; Laffin v. Ryan, (1957) 4 A. D. 2d 21, 162 N. Y. S. 2d 730; Milio v. Railway Motor Trucking Co., (1939) 257 App. Div. 640, 15 N. Y. S. 2d 73.

[18] Stocker v. Boston & M. R. R., (1930) 84 N. H. 377, 151 Atl. 457, 70 A. L. R. 1320; Perlman v. Shanck, (1920) 192 App. Div. 179, 182 N. Y. S. 767; Eldridge v. Terry & Tench Co., (1911) 145 App. Div. 560, 129 N. Y. S. 865.

It seems to be conceded everywhere that when the inference is allowable, counsel for the adverse party, in the course of his argument to the jury, is rightfully entitled to comment upon his opponent's failure to have produced the evidence which was peculiarly within his knowledge or control.[19]

With these general principles in mind, we may now consider their application in the jurisdictions where the physician-patient privilege statute is in force.

93. *Same: Effect of Privilege*

It is common knowledge that the vast majority of cases—perhaps ninety percent—in which the privilege is invoked are actions on policies of insurance—life, accident, and health; actions for damages for malpractice, or for personal injury, or for wrongful death; and testamentary actions. In addition to these are divorce cases, actions to obtain benefits under Workmen's Compensation Laws, lunacy inquisitions, and criminal proceedings where, usually, the charge is abortion, rape, seduction, or homicide. In most of these cases medical testimony is absolutely necessary to ascertain the truth. Certainly the surgeon who operated on the afflicted patient, the family physician who treated the testator, the hospital physician who attended the insured during his last illness, the physician who attended the injured claimant, and the nurse who assisted the medical man are, in all probability, the best informed and most reliable witnesses a party might produce to present to the jury the true facts concerning the condition of the patient. Who better than these can discover and explain the nature and extent of the patient's injury,[1] the character of his disease or physical impairment, his mental

---

[19] Cincinnati, H. & D. R. R. v. Gross, (1917) 186 Ind. 471, 114 N. E. 962; Huskey v. Metropolitan Life Ins Co., (1936) .... Mo. App. ......, 94 S. W. 2d 1075. See § 97, herein.

See also 88 C. J. S., Trial, § 184.

[1] McClanahan v. St. Louis & San Francisco R. R., (1910) 147 Mo. App. 386, 412, 126 S. W. 535: "Our examination of authority leads us to think that its great weight is to the effect that the failure of the plaintiff to produce these surgeons, who, more than anyone else, even the plaintiff herself, would have been qualified to testify as to the extent and nature of the injuries immediately following the accident, * * * is a circumstance that warrants us in entertaining serious doubt as to the good faith of the plaintiff."

capacity, or the cause of his death? Yet, incredible as it may seem, in many of these cases the surgeon, the attending or family physician, the nurse, or the hospital physician was not called as a witness by the party who had it in his power to produce and examine him; neither did he introduce in evidence the hospital record of the patient. Instead, the party relied upon the testimony of himself alone, or that of lay witnesses, or of a physician who had no personal knowledge of the patient's condition gained from treating him, but whose testimony as an expert was given in response to purely hypothetical questions.

In such cases, the question naturally arises: Does the failure of a party who has it in his power to call as a witness the attending physician, surgeon, nurse, or some other professional person who cared for or treated the patient, or to introduce in evidence the patient's hospital record or x-rays, create an inference that if the witness testified, or the hospital data were introduced, his testimony, or the facts disclosed by the hospital data, would be unfavorable and detrimental to his cause? The common sense view is that such inference is logical and just. It is expected generally that a party going into court to use the offices of the court in furtherance of his interests, is willing for the truth to prevail.

Admittedly there is a considerable conflict of authority on this question. In a number of jurisdictions, the courts have held that no unfavorable inference results; that to permit this would, in effect, nullify the physician-patient privilege statute.[2] In the great

---

[2] William Laurie Co. v. McCullough, (1910) 174 Ind. 477, 484, 90 N. E. 1014, Ann. Cas. 1913 A 49: "In electing not to call his physician as a witness, it is clear that a party may have motives and potent reasons in no way involving the suppression of evidence prejudicial to his interests in the case on trial. The law grants to the patient the unqualified right to exclude the testimony of his physician as to facts acquired in confidence, and the exercise of this privilege cannot be impaired by allowing opposing counsel in argument to impugn his motives or charge him with suppressing important and relevant evidence. The general rule, authorizing an inference from the withholding of important and material evidence upon the matter in issue, that such evidence if heard would be prejudicial to the cause of the party having it in his power to produce it, has no application to privileged communications which the law excludes on grounds of public policy." The court overruled Warsaw v. Fisher, (1899) 24 Ind. App. 46, 55 N. E. 42, on this point.

≫→

majority of cases, however, the courts have held that an unfavorable
inference may properly be drawn.[3]   In this respect the physician

←◀

In Lauer v. Banning, (1911) 152 Iowa 99, 131 N. W. 783, an action based on
alleged breach of promise of marriage, the court instructed the jury that no inference
could be drawn from plaintiff's failure to call her physician or her former lawyer.
(p. 103) "This instruction was correct. If one must, upon penalty of having a presumption raised against him, introduce his lawyer or physician, the statutes prohibiting
them from testifying are of no significance. Of course the ordinary rule is that if one
does not produce testimony within his control, or prevents the use of such testimony,
the presumption arises that such testimony, if produced, would be adverse to them.
But this rule does not apply to privileged communications for reasons too obvious to
mention."

Accord: Sherman v. Ross, (1936) 99 Colo. 354, 62 P. 2d 1151; Brackney v. Fogle,
(1901) 156 Ind. 535, 60 N. E. 303; Mortimer v. Daub, (1912) 52 Ind. App. 30, 98 N. E.
845; Rump v. Woods, (1912) 50 Ind. App. 347, 98 N. E. 369; Howard v. Porter, (1949)
240 Iowa 153, 35 N. W. 2d 837, but *cf.* Crago v. Cedar Rapids, (1904) 123 Iowa 48, 98
N. W. 354; Merrill v. St. Paul City Ry., (1927) 170 Minn. 332, 212 N. W. 533; Hobson
v. McLeod, (1933) 165 Miss. 853, 147 So. 778, but disapproved in Killings v. Metropolitan Life Ins. Co., (1940) 187 Miss. 265, 192 So. 577, 131 A. L. R. 684; Schroeder v. Wells,
(1925) _____Mo. App._____, 277 S. W. 578; Arnold v. Maryville, (1905) 110 Mo. App. 254,
85 S. W. 107; Meyer v. Russell, (1926) 55 N. D. 546, 214 N. W. 857, but *cf.* Blackstead
v. Kent, (1933) 63 N. D. 246, 247 N. W. 607.

See note, 131 A. L. R. 693.

[3] Representative decisions are: Brown v. Maryland Casualty Co., (1932) 55 F. 2d 159;
Peoria Life Ins. Co. v. Smith, (1931) 47 F. 2d 279; Bernhardt v. City and Suburban
Ry., (1920) 40 App. D. C. 265, 263 Fed. 1009; Crago v. Cedar Rapids, (1904) 123 Iowa
48, 98 N. W. 354; Hecke v. Henne, (1927) 238 Mich. 198, 213 N. W. 112; Griggs v.
Saginaw & Flint Ry., (1917) 196 Mich. 258, 162 N. W. 960; O'Connor v. Detroit, (1910)
160 Mich. 193, 125 N. W. 277; Vergin v. Saginaw, (1901) 125 Mich. 499, 84 N. W. 1075;
Cooley v. Foltz, (1891) 85 Mich. 47, 48 N. W. 176; Nelson v. Ackerman, (1957) _____
Minn._____, 83 N. W. 2d 500; Guin v. Mastrud, (1939) 206 Minn. 382, 288 N. W. 716;
Tri-State Transit Co. v. Mondy, (1943) 194 Miss. 714, 12 So. 2d 920; Killings v. Metro-
politan Life Ins. Co., (1940) 187 Miss. 265, 192 So. 577, 131 A. L. R. 684; Robinson v.
Haydel, (1936) 177 Miss. 233, 171 So. 7; Beard v. Williams, (1935) 172 Miss. 880, 161
So. 750; Brodsky v. Brodsky, (1950) _____Mo._____, 233 S. W. 2d 829; Hemminghaus v.
Ferguson, (1948) 358 Mo. 476, 215 S. W. 2d 481; McInnis v. St. Louis-Southern, Inc.,
(1937) 341 Mo. 677, 108 S. W. 2d 113; Porter v. Chicago, B. & Q. R. R., (1930) 325 Mo.
381, 28 S. W. 2d 1035; Evans v. Trenton, (1892) 112 Mo. 390, 20 S. W. 614; Foerstel v.
St. Louis Public Service Co., (1951) _____Mo. App._____, 241 S. W. 2d 792; Donet v.
Prudential Ins. Co., (1930) _____Mo. App._____, 23 S. W. 2d 1104; Whitmore v. Ameri-
can Ry. Express Co., (1925) 219 Mo. App. 294, 269 S. W. 654; McClanahan v. St. Louis
& San Francisco R. R., (1910) 147 Mo. App. 386, 126 S. W. 535; Sabowska v. Coney
Island & B. R. R., (1916) 174 App. Div. 913, 160 N. Y. S. 386; Minch v. New York &
Queen's County Ry., (1903) 80 App. Div. 324, 80 N. Y. S. 712; Kane v. Rochester Ry.,
(1902) 74 App. Div. 575, 77 N. Y. S. 776; Blackstead v. Kent, (1933) 63 N. D. 246, 247

≫→

stands like any other material witness who is available and can be produced by only one of the parties;[4] especially, as two judges have pointed out, since there is no prohibition in the statute as to the drawing of an adverse inference.[5]

Although an unfavorable inference more often is indulged against plaintiffs who ordinarily must bear the burden of persuasion, it may, under proper circumstances, be applied with equal force and effect against their adversaries. Where, in an action for damages for personal injury or in a proceeding to recover benefits under the Workmen's Compensation Law, a physician is employed by the defendant to examine the injured claimant for the purpose of ascertaining the nature and extent of his injury and, at the trial, the defendant fails to call the physician as a witness, the inference may properly be drawn that the physician's testimony would not be favorable to the defendant.[6] Ordinarily, under such circumstances,

---

← N. W. 607, but *cf*. Meyer v. Russell, (1926) 55 N. D. 546, 214 N. W. 857; Katafiaz v. Toledo Cons. Elec. Co., (1902) 1 Ohio C. C. R. (n. s.) 129, 14 Ohio C. C. Dec. 127; Ferne v. Chadderton, (1949) 363 Pa. 191, 6 A. 2d 104; Albert v. Philadelphia Rapid Transit Co., (1916) 252 Pa. 527, 97 Atl. 680; Marotto v. George D. Ellis & Sons, Inc., (1942) 149 Pa. Super. 221, 28 A. 2d 339; Hilton v. Edwards Memorial Church, (1944) 50 Pa. D. C. 341; Hoffman v. Hoffman, (1937) 31 Del. Co. (Pa.) 134.

The courts of West Virginia permit the inference, but the privilege there is applicable to justice of the peace practice only. Smith v. Smith, (1943) 125 W. Va. 489, 24 S. E. 2d 902; Mohr v. Mohr, (1937) 119 W. Va. 253, 193 S. E. 121; Vaughn v. Memorial Hospital, (1925) 100 W. Va. 290, 130 S. E. 481.

4 Robinson v. Haydel, (1936) 177 Miss. 233, 171 So. 7.

5 Ethridge, J., in Killings v. Metropolitan Life Ins. Co., (1940) 187 Miss. 265, 278, 192 So. 577, 131 A. L. R. 684; Hatch, J., in Deutschmann v. Third Ave. R. R., (1903) 87 App. Div. 503, 513, 84 N. Y. S. 887.

6 Anders v. Employers Liability Assur. Corp., (1951) _____ La. App. _____, 50 So. 2d 87; Johnson v. Demange-Godman Lumber Co., (1932) _____ La. App. _____, 141 So. 779; Wilkins v. Flint, (1901) 128 Mich. 262, 87 N. W. 195; Stacy v. Goff, (1954) 241 Minn. 301, 62 N. W. 2d 920; Shockman v. Union Transfer Co., (1945) 220 Minn. 334, 19 N. W. 2d 812; Gabelman v. Bolt, (1935) 336 Mo. 539, 80 S. W. 2d 171; Miller v. Collins, (1931) 328 Mo. 313, 40 S. W. 2d 1062; Doutt v. Watson, (1950) _____ Mo. App. _____, 231 S. W. 2d 230; Wilson v. J. G. Peppard Seed Co., (1922) _____ Mo. App. _____, 243 S. W. 390; Burke v. Shaw Transfer Co., (1922) 211 Mo. App. 353, 243 S. W. 449, aff'd 250 S. W. 384; Mosely v. Jones & L. Steel Co., (1944) 155 Pa. Super. 598, 39 A. 2d 161; Marshall v. Pittsburgh, (1935) 119 Pa. Super. 189, 180 Atl. 733. In People v. Fiori, (1908) 123 App. Div. 174, 108 N. Y. S. 416, defendant was convicted of murder. The state failed to call two physicians who had performed an autopsy on the victim and had testified

⟫→

no question of privilege is involved.[7]

94. Same: Inferior, Corroborative, or Cumulative Evidence

One of the recognized limitations upon the general rule is that no unfavorable inference is to be drawn from the non-production of evidence, unless such evidence, in respect to the fact to which it would have been relevant, would have been superior to the evidence which was adduced.[1] It is not the duty of a party in a civil action to call every person as a witness who may give material evidence in his favor, and the mere omission on his part to call a witness who has no other or better knowledge of the matter in dispute than those who are produced and give evidence, is not necessarily so suspicious as to warrant an inference that the testimony of the witness, had he been produced, would have been unfavorable to the party.[2] Where, after an accident, the plaintiff was visited by four physicians, one of whom was in the employ of the defendant and two of them were merely called in consultation once or twice by the attending physician who had made many visits upon the plaintiff, but, at the trial, the plaintiff called only her attending physician as a witness, no unfavorable inference could be drawn against her where there was nothing in the attending physician's testimony that would indicate that anything different or more satisfactory might have been obtained from any of the other physicians.[3]   In other

---

←

before the grand jury. The judgment was set aside on the ground that the trial court should have charged the jury, as requested by defendant, that that fact could be considered by the jury in determining whether the physicians would have testified favorably for the state had they been called to testify. See also People v. Raizen, (1925) 211 App. Div. 446, 208 N. Y. S. 185.

[7] See §§ 37, 38, 39, herein.

[1] Roehl v. Ralph, (1935) ......Mo. App........, 84 S. W. 2d 405; Oneill v. Bilotta, (1952) 18 N. J. Super. 82, 86 A. 2d 705, aff'd 10 N. J. 308, 91 A. 2d 231; Baldwin v. Brooklyn Heights R. R., (1904) 99 App. Div. 496, 91 N. Y. S. 59. See 2 Wigmore, Evidence, § 287.

[2] Bleecker v. Johnston, (1877) 69 N. Y. 309. See Perlman v. Shanck, (1920) 192 App. Div. 179, 182 N. Y. S. 767.

[3] Wood v. Los Angeles Traction Co., (1905) 1 Cal. App. 474, 82 Pac. 547.   See also Cherry-Burrell Co. v. Thatcher, (1940) 107 F. 2d 65; Russell v. St. Louis Public Service Co., (1952) ...... Mo........ , 251 S. W. 2d 595.

words, where it appears that the evidence which was not produced would have been relatively unimportant in the case, either as inferior to that already introduced, or else as merely corroborative of, or cumulative to, such evidence, then no unfavorable inference is warranted.[4] But it should be remembered that the line of demarcation between evidence that is cumulative and that which is not, is indefinite and shadowy at best. There is always the possibility that what appears to be cumulative evidence only, may be evidence which is far more probative than that already adduced, and a party may suffer the damaging effect of an adverse inference if he fails to produce it.

95. *Same: Evidence Equally Available to Both Parties*

Another and well-recognized limitation upon the general rule is that no unfavorable inference may be drawn on account of the nonproduction of a witness whose evidence is equally available to both parties.[1]

As pointed out earlier, when the inference is permitted, it is based not alone on the fact that a particular person is not produced

---

[4] Russell v. St. Louis Public Service Co., (1952) .... Mo......., 251 S. W. 2d 595; Jankowski v. Clausen, (1926) 167 Minn. 437, 209 N. W. 317; Pronk v. Brooklyn Heights R. R., (1902) 68 App. Div. 390, 74 N. Y. S. 375; Vann v. Harden, (1948) 187 Va. 555, 47 S. E. 2d 314. Di Gregorio v. United States, (1925) 7 F. 2d 295: "The rule has been much misunderstood, and is often misapplied. It does not obtain when the uncalled witness is purely cumulative, and when he was not in a better position to know the facts than those who were called. Any other rule would require a party to call all eyewitnesses at the risk of having it presumed that those not called would contradict those who were. The rule has no such purpose; it rests on the notion that the suppression of more cogent evidence than that produced is some indication that it would be unfavorable. Between witnesses having equal opportunity for observation it has never been applied." See also 10 R. C. L., Evidence, § 35; Ann. Cas. 1914 A 915.

[1] Atkinson v. United Ry., (1921) 286 Mo. 634, 228 S. W. 483; Cooper v. Metropolitan Life Ins. Co., (1936) .... Mo. App......., 94 S. W. 2d 1070; Huskey v. Metropolitan Life Ins. Co., (1936) ....Mo. App......., 94 S. W. 2d 1075; Waeckerley v. Colonial Baking Co., (1934) 228 Mo. App. 1185, 67 S. W. 2d 779; Carpenter v. Sun Indemnity Co., (1940) 138 Neb. 552, 293 N. W. 400; Mosely v. Reading Co., (1929) 295 Pa. 342, 145 Atl. 293; Sorby v. Three Rivers Motors, (1955) 178 Pa. Super. 187, 114 A. 2d 347; Smith v. Beard, (1941) 56 Wyo. 375, 110 P. 2d 260. See also People v. Raizen, (1925) 211 App. Div. 446, 208 N. Y. S. 185.

The rule applies with equal force to the nonproduction of other evidence such as hospital records and x-rays.

as a witness by a party, but on his nonproduction when it would be natural for the party to produce him if his testimony would have been favorable. To meet the requirement "when it would be natural for the party to produce the witness," it must be shown that the person was accessible and within the power of the party to produce.[2] Lack of power to produce may be due to the person's absence from the jurisdiction,[3] his illness, the cost involved in bringing him to court[4] or in taking his deposition, or to other circumstances beyond the control of the party.[5]

Perhaps the most comprehensive statements that explain the meaning of the terms "available," "availability," "accessible," as used in this connection, are set forth in the decisions of the courts of Missouri where the question has frequently been considered. In *Chavaries* v. *National Life & Accident Ins. Co.,*[6] Bennick, C., stated:

> Now the term "available," in the sense in which we are using it, does not mean merely available or accessible for the service of a subpoena, since any witness who can be found may be subpoenaed at the instance of either party to a cause. To the contrary, the question of whether a witness is "available" to one or the other of the contending parties depends upon such matters as the one party's superior means of knowledge of the existence and identity of the witness, the nature of the testimony that the witness would be expected to give in the light of his previous statements or declarations, if any, about the facts of the case, and the relationship borne by the witness to a particular party as the same would reasonably be expected to affect his personal interest in the outcome of the litigation, and make it natural that he would be expected to testify in favor of the one party and against the other. In other words, a witness may be said to have been peculiarly "available" to one party to an action, so that upon that

---

[2] Chicago, R. I. & Pac. Ry. v. King, (1946) 210 Ark. 872, 197 S. W. 2d 931.

[3] Baumhoer v. McLaughlin, (1947) _____Mo. App._____, 205 S. W. 2d 274; Smith v. Kansas City Public Service Co., (1933) 227 Mo. App. 675, 56 S. W. 2d 838.

[4] Stone v. Stone, (1943) 78 App. D. C. 5, 136 F. 2d 761.

[5] O'Neill v. Billotta, (1952) 18 N. J. Super. 82, 86 A. 2d 705, aff'd 10 N. J. 308, 91 A. 2d 231.

[6] (1937) _____Mo. App._____ , 110 S. W. 2d 790. The opinion was unanimously adopted by the court. See also Clayton v. St. Louis Public Service Co., (1955) _____Mo. App. _____, 276 S. W. 2d 621 (failure to produce physician's records).

party's failure to have produced him in court an inference will arise that his testimony would have been unfavorable, when, because of such party's opportunity for knowledge of or control over the witness, or the community of interest between the two, or the prior statements and declarations of the witness, it would be reasonably probable that the witness would have been called to the trial to testify for such party except for the fact that it was either known or feared that his testimony on the stand would have been damaging rather than favorable.[7]

A physician making a physical examination of a party pursuant to an order of the court becomes an officer of the court and he is, therefore, "available" to either party as a witness,[8] even though the appointment is made at the request of the adverse party.[9] In an action for annulment of marriage on the ground of fraud, plaintiff claimed that defendant had concealed from her the fact that he was suffering from syphilis. Prior to their marriage in Virginia, the

---

[7] Ordinarily an attending physician of the patient is not "equally available" to the adverse party as a witness in his behalf. Trzecki v. St. Louis Public Service Co., (1953) _____Mo._____, 258 S. W. 2d 676; Hemminghaus v. Ferguson, (1948) 358 Mo. 476, 215 S. W. 2d 481; McInnis v. St. Louis Southern, Inc., (1937) 341 Mo. 677, 108 S. W. 2d 113; Clayton v. St. Louis Public Service Co., (1955) _____Mo. App._____, 276 S. W. 2d 621; Fisher v. John Hancock Mut. Life Ins. Co., (1950) _____Mo. App._____, 229 S. W. 2d 246; Chavaries v. National Life & Acc. Ins. Co., (1937) _____Mo._____, 110 S. W. 2d 790; Waeckerley v. Colonial Baking Co., (1934) 228 Mo. App. 1185, 67 S. W. 2d 779; Donet v. Prudential Ins. Co., (1930) _____Mo. App._____, 23 S. W. 2d 1104.

[8] Pitcairn v. Perry, (1941) 122 F. 2d 881, cert. denied 314 U. S. 697, 86 Law. Ed. 557, 62 Su. Ct. 414.

[9] Atkinson v. United Ry., (1921) 286 Mo. 634, 228 S. W. 483; Hankins v. St. Louis-San Francisco Ry., (1930) _____ Mo. App._____, 31 S. W. 2d 596, 599: "When all that occurred is considered together, we cannot escape the conclusion that the purpose of counsel for plaintiff was to impress upon the jury that defendant had induced the court to appoint doctors to examine plaintiff and then did not use these doctors as witnesses and expected as a result that the jury would be impressed with the idea that the defendant was not fair in the conduct of its defense. These doctors, though appointed at the request of defendant, were, when appointed, officers of the court, and their testimony was as accessible to one side as the other, and neither the defendant nor the plaintiff were subject to criticism for not using them. If they would testify to facts that were favorable to plaintiff's case, he was free to avail himself of that testimony the same as the defendant, and any effort on the part of counsel for plaintiff to induce the jury to draw any unfavorable inference against the defendant because they did not use these doctors as witnesses after they had examined the plaintiff was manifestly erroneous."

parties were examined by a physician of the state Department of Health. Plaintiff claimed that he told her there was no reason why they should not marry; but she did not call him as a witness. The trial court refused to hold that plaintiff was deceived. Reversing the judgment, the appellate court held that it was not peculiarly within the power of the plaintiff to produce the physician as a witness; that he was equally available to the defendant and, therefore, no unfavorable inference could be drawn against her for failure to produce him.[10] In *Rothschild* v. *Barck,*[11] plaintiff sued to recover damages from the defendant surgeon for malpractice. Counsel for plaintiff sought to draw an unfavorable inference against defendant because of his failure to call certain hospital nurses as witnesses at the trial. It was held that the nurses were equally available to both parties; hence, no inference could be drawn against the defendant.

Some courts have held that where the plaintiff does not call his own physician as a witness and the defendant does not call him, no unfavorable inference can be drawn against the latter. One of the reasons assigned is that the physician is not "available" to the defendant since the physician is privileged, and the privilege is beyond the defendant's control. The prohibition of the statute would prevent the defendant from using his testimony.[12] Even though a party

---

[10] Stone v. Stone, (1943) 78 App. D. C. 5, 136 F. 2d 761.

[11] (1930) 324 Mo. 1121, 26 S. W. 2d 760.

In Raines v. Small, (1943) ....Mo. App........, 169 S. W. 2d 102, a personal injury case, plaintiff's physician testified in her behalf. The physician's nurse, who had assisted him in treating the plaintiff, was present in court throughout the trial, but neither party called her as a witness. Over objection of defendant, plaintiff's counsel was permitted to draw an unfavorable inference against defendant for his failure to call the nurse as a witness. The trial court granted a new trial. Affirming this ruling, it was held that the nurse was as available to plaintiff as a witness as she was to defendant; hence, no unfavorable inference could be drawn against defendant .

[12] Robinson v. Haydel, (1936) 177 Miss. 233, 171 So. 7; Hemminghaus v. Ferguson, (1948) 358 Mo. 476, 215 S. W. 2d 481; Clayton v. St. Louis Public Service Co., (1955) ....Mo. App. ...., 276 S. W. 2d 621; Waeckerley v. Colonial Baking Co., (1934) 228 Mo. App. 1185, 67 S. W. 2d 779; McClanahan v. St. Louis & San Francisco R. R., (1910) 147 Mo. App. 386, 126 S. W. 535; Eisenberg v. Irving Kemp, Inc., (1939) 256 App. Div. 698, 11 N. Y. S. 2d 449; Pronk v. Brooklyn Heights R. R., (1902) 68 App. Div. 390, 74 N. Y. S. 375. *Cf.* Wood v. Los Angeles Traction Co., (1905) 1 Cal. App. 474, 82 Pac. 547; Semmons v. National Travelers' Ben. Ass'n, (1917) 180 Iowa 666, 163 N. W. 338. See also 2 Wigmore, Evidence, § 286.

be conceded to have waived his rights under the privilege statute with respect to his physician as a witness at the trial, yet he cannot relieve himself of the unfavorable inference that may be drawn from his failure to call the physician by asserting that his adversary could call the witness—this because of the greater availability of the physician to the plaintiff, and the fact that the adverse party by calling the physician as a witness would be compelled to vouch for the physician's credibility and would also be deprived of the right of cross-examination.[13]

96. Same: Party May Explain Failure to Produce Evidence

It does not necessarily follow in every instance that the failure of a party to produce a particular witness is due to the fact that his

[13] Johns-Manville Products Co. v. Cather, (1950) 208 Miss. 268, 44 So. 2d 405; Trzecki v. St. Louis Public Service Co., (1953) ..... Mo. ..... , 258 S. W. 2d 676; McInnis v. St. Louis Southern, Inc., (1937) 341 Mo. 677, 108 S. W. 2d 113; Chavaries v. National Life & Acc. Ins. Co., (1937) ..... Mo. App. ... , 110 S. W. 2d 790; Donet v. Prudential Ins. Co., (1930) .....Mo. App. ..... , 23 S. W. 2d 1104.

Contra: Clary v. Breyer, (1943) 194 Miss. 612, 13 So. 2d 633; Waeckerley v. Colonial Baking Co., (1934) 228 Mo. App. 1185, 67 S. W. 2d 779 (it was held, however, no waiver had been made); Glossip v. Kelly, (1934) 228 Mo. App. 392, 67 S. W. 2d 513; Fulsom-Morris Coal & M. Co. v. Mitchell, (1913) 37 Okla. 575, 132 Pac. 1103. But an offer to waive the privilege is not effective if made at a point in the trial when little or no opportunity is afforded the adversary to produce the witness. In Clary v. Breyer, infra, (p. 622) it was said: "We therefore emphasize that there is no technical potency in a mere formal offer which of itself operates conclusively to shield plaintiff against adverse inferences or to impose upon the defendant procedural disadvantages. Both the sincerity of the tender and its legal efficacy must remain in direct ratio to the feasibility of compliance."

See also Gatlin v. Allen, (1948) 203 Miss. 135, 33 So. 2d 304.

However, in Glossip v. Kelly, infra, it was said (p. 399): "That defendant's counsel might have been required to have used unusual efforts to obtain the testimony of Dr. Gale [plaintiff's physician whom plaintiff had not called as a witness] does not in the least militate against the correctness of the court's rulings. Conditions frequently arise in the presentation of a lawsuit requiring quick and decisive action and unusual effort upon the part of a party litigant or his attorney."

In Clayton v. St. Louis Public Service Co., (1955) ..... Mo. App..... , 276 S. W. 2d 621, a personal injury case, plaintiff called her physician as a witness but he did not bring his records to court. Counsel for defendant, in his closing argument, commented on this fact but, on objection by plaintiff, the court ruled that defendant could have subpoenaed the records. Held: defendant did not have sufficient opportunity to do this. It was error for the court to nullify any unfavorable inference which defendant was entitled to draw.

testimony, if given, would be unfavorable. There may be good and sufficient reasons for not calling him even though his testimony might reasonably be expected to be favorable.[1] It is everywhere conceded that the party against whom an unfavorable inference may be indulged has the right to explain his inability to produce the evidence by showing circumstances which otherwise account for his failure.[2] It is proper, therefore, for either side to explain the absence of a witness the party would be expected to call when there is evidence on which to base the explanation.[3] In fairness to the party, there should be no restriction upon his right to rebut the inference which the jury might properly draw, except that the trial judge must be satisfied that his explanation furnishes a valid reason for his failure to produce the evidence.[4] Thus, a plaintiff cannot overcome the unfavorable inference resulting from his failure to call his physician as a witness by merely stating that the physician refused to appear in court, since the plaintiff could have coerced his appearance by the service of a subpoena.[5] In an action for annulment of marriage, there was no reason for penalizing the

---

[1] Poplet v. Surface Transportation Co., (1952) 109 N. Y. S. 2d 871, 879: "It could well be that he was not called as a witness, not because he would have given unfavorable testimony, but because he was an unreliable individual, possibly addicted to drink, perhaps a person with a record of criminal conviction, perhaps because he was known to possess a weak mind or memory, or because for a variety of reasons he might be expected to make an unfavorable impression upon a jury. It is the experience of trial lawyers generally that some witnesses having favorable testimony to give may nevertheless, for extraneous reasons, not safely be called."

     See also William Laurie Co. v. McCullough, (1910) 174 Ind. 477, 484, 90 N. E. 1014, Ann. Cas. 1913 A 49.

[2] Stone v. Stone, (1943) 78 App. D. C. 5, 136 F. 2d 761; Killings v. Metropolitan Life Ins. Co., (1940) 187 Miss. 265, 192 So. 577, 131 A. L. R. 684; Brungs v. St. Louis Public Service Co., (1950) ....Mo. App........, 230 S. W. 2d 181; Brotherton v. Barber Asphalt Paving Co., (1907) 117 App. Div. 791, 102 N. Y. S. 1089; Payne v. Gearhart, (1922) 15 Ohio App. 421; Toledo Ry. & Light Co. v. Poland, (1914) 7 Ohio App. 397, 27 Ohio C. C. (n. s.) 105 (whereabouts of nurse unknown).

[3] Baumhoer v. McLaughlin, (1947) ....Mo........, 205 S. W. 2d 274 (witness out of the jurisdiction).

     See Perlman v. Shanck, (1920) 192 App. Div. 179, 182 N. Y. S. 767.

[4] 2 Wigmore, Evidence, § 290(3).

[5] Bernhardt v. City & Suburban Ry., (1920) 49 App. D. C. 265, 263 Fed. 1009; Johns-Manville Products Co. v. Cather, (1950) 208 Miss. 268, 44 So. 2d 405. See also Minch v. New York & Queen's County Ry., (1903) 80 App. Div. 324, 80 N. Y. S. 712.

plaintiff for her failure to produce the physician who examined both parties before marriage, since the trial judge approved her petition to proceed in *forma pauperis* and she was unwilling to incur the expense of bringing the physician from another jurisdiction, especially when the case was uncontested and the allegations of fraud undisputed.[6]

Where the defendant's physician who examined the insured, when he applied for insurance, was not called as a witness by the defendant, the plaintiff could not draw an unfavorable inference therefrom, since the physician, when called to the stand by the plaintiff, explained that he was unable to recall the medical examination at all and it did not appear that there was any legally competent memorandum which he might use to aid him in testifying.[7]

In *Donet* v. *Prudential Ins. Co.*,[8] it was held that the plaintiff could not excuse his failure to call as witnesses the two physicians who had treated him at a hospital, by stating that he did not know them; it was incumbent upon him to seek out the physicians and produce them, or else suffer the consequences of an unfavorable inference.

Failure of a plaintiff in a personal injury action to call the physician who attended him, may be explained by showing facts from which it could be inferred that the physician was unfriendly to him and would not be fair to him.[9]

97. Same: The Right to Comment Upon Party's Failure to Produce Evidence

In jurisdictions where an unfavorable inference is allowable against a party for his failure to produce as a witness a physician who is more available to him than to his adversary, the latter may properly call attention to the fact and may comment upon it with a view of having the jury infer that the witness was not called because his testimony would not have been favorable to the party's

---

[6] Stone v. Stone, (1943) 78 App. D. C. 5, 136 F. 2d 761.

[7] McEwen v. New York Life Ins. Co., (1921) 187 Cal. 144, 201 Pac. 577.

[8] (1930) ......Mo. App. ...... , 23 S. W. 2d 1104.

[9] Bowles v. Wabash Ry., (1925) ......Mo. App....... , 271 S. W. 851.

cause.[1] Moreover, to deny the right to make such comment may constitute reversible error. The inference is of such strength and value that the denial of the right to comment thereon is held to constitute a denial of the right of argument to a jury.[2]

On the other hand, the rule appears to be general that no unfavorable comment can be made by counsel in his argument on account of the absence of a witness whose testimony is equally available[3] to both parties.[4] It is usually reversible error to permit an

---

[1] Bernhardt v. City & Suburban Ry., (1920) 49 App. D. C. 265, 263 Fed. 1009; Wilkins v. Flint, (1901) 128 Mich. 262, 87 N. W. 195; Shockman v. Union Transfer Co., (1945) 220 Minn. 334, 19 N. W. 2d 812; Guin v. Mastrud, (1939) 206 Minn. 382, 288 N. W. 716; Killings v. Metropolitan Life Ins. Co., (1940) 187 Miss. 265, 192 So. 577, 131 A. L. R. 684; Trzecki v. St. Louis Public Service Co., (1953) _____ Mo._____, 258 S. W. 2d 676; Eickmann v. St. Louis Public Service Co., (1953) 363 Mo. 651, 253 S. W. 2d 122; McInnis v. St. Louis-Southern, Inc., (1937) 341 Mo. 677, 108 S. W. 2d 113; State, *ex rel.* Gilday v. Trimble, (1931) 329 Mo. 198, 44 S. W. 2d 57; Atkinson v. United Railways, (1921) 286 Mo. 634, 228 S. W. 483; Clayton v. St. Louis Public Service Co., (1955) _____ Mo. App._____, 276 S. W. 2d 621; Chavaries v. National Life & Acc. Ins. Co., (1937) _____ Mo. App._____ , 110 S. W. 2d 790; Waeckerley v. Colonial Baking Co., (1934) 228 Mo. App. 1185, 67 S. W. 2d 779; Gilday v. Smith Bros., Inc., (1930) _____ Mo. App. _____ , 32 S. W. 2d 118; Donet v. Prudential Ins. Co., (1930) _____Mo. App._____ , 23 S. W. 2d 1104; Brotherton v. Barber Asphalt Paving Co., (1907) 117 App. Div. 791, 102 N. Y. S. 1089; Blackstead v. Kent, (1933) 63 N. D. 246, 247 N. W. 607; Albert v. Philadelphia Rapid Transit Co., (1916) 252 Pa. 527, 97 Atl. 680; Naus v. Chicago & M. Elec. Ry., (1924) 185 Wis. 178, 201 N. W. 281.

See also Nelson v. Ackerman, (1957) _____ Minn._____ , 83 N. W. 2d 500; Merrill v. St. Paul City Ry., (1927) 170 Minn. 332, 212 N. W. 533.

[2] McInnis v. St. Louis-Southern, Inc., (1937) 341 Mo. 677, 683, 108 S. W. 2d 113: "Plaintiff next contends that the evidence was sufficient to sustain the verdict of $10,000 and for that reason the error was not prejudicial. It is not a question of sufficiency of the evidence. It is a question of a litigant having been denied the right of argument to a jury. There is no way to determine from the record the effect of this ruling on the verdict. It is clear that defendant was entitled to make the argument and have the jury consider same in determining the question of damages. The error was prejudicial, and the judgment should be reversed."

See also Clayton v. St. Louis Public Service Co., (1955) _____Mo. App._____ , 276 S. W. 2d 621; Chavaries v. National Life & Acc. Ins. Co., (1937) _____ Mo. App._____ , 110 S. W. 2d 790; Smith v. Kansas City Public Service Co., (1933) 227 Mo. App. 675, 56 S. W. 2d 838; Brotherton v. Barber Asphalt Paving Co., (1907) 117 App. Div. 791, 102 N. Y. S. 1089.

[3] See § 95, herein, for meaning of "equally available."

[4] Rothschild v. Barck, (1930) 324 Mo. 1121, 26 S. W. 2d 760; Atkinson v. United Railway, (1921) 286 Mo. 634, 228 S. W. 483; Chavaries v. National Life & Acc. Ins. Co.,

⟫⟫→

argument of that character.[5]

In several jurisdictions where the courts have held that no unfavorable inference arises when a party exercises his statutory privilege by not calling his physician as a witness, counsel for the adverse party is not permitted to comment to the jury on such failure to produce the physician;[6] the theory being that to allow this would, in effect, put the patient at a disadvantage and utterly nullify the privilege.

98. Same: Effect of Improper Remarks or Argument of Counsel

Gratuitous statements of counsel, not warranted by the evidence, are generally frowned upon and regarded as improper by the courts for the obvious reason that the statements themselves, or the unfavorable inferences which naturally flow from them, might, and usually do, tend to distort the facts, mislead or improperly influence the jury, and interfere with the impartial and orderly function of the court; and in cases where such misconduct on the

---

(1937) .... Mo. App......., 110 S. W. 2d 790; Waeckerley v. Colonial Baking Co., (1934) 228 Mo. App. 1185, 67 S. W. 2d 779; Hankins v. St. Louis-San Francisco Ry., (1930) .... Mo. App......., 31 S. W. 2d 596.

Cf. Miller v. Collins, (1931) 328 Mo. 313, 40 S. W. 2d 1062; People v. Fiori, (1908) 123 App. Div. 174, 108 N. Y. S. 416.

[5] Atkinson v. United Ry., (1921) 286 Mo. 634, 228 S. W. 483; Raines v. Small, (1943) ....Mo. App......., 169 S. W. 2d 102; Murphy v. Tumbrink, (1930) ....Mo. App......., 25 S. W. 2d 133.

In Hankins v. St. Louis-San Francisco Ry., (1930) .... Mo. App......., 31 S. W. 2d 596, the court held that plaintiff's argument was unfair and prejudicial, yet it felt compelled to affirm the judgment since this was the second trial in which plaintiff recovered a verdict and the misconduct of his counsel probably had not affected the result.

See also Arnold v. Metropolitan Life Ins. Co., (1936) .... Mo. App......., 89 S. W. 2d 81. Effect of improper comment of counsel cured by court's prompt action in sustaining defendant's objection to it.

[6] William Laurie Co. v. McCullough, (1910) 174 Ind. 477, 90 N. E. 1014, Ann. Cas. 1913 A. 49, disapproving Warsaw v. Fisher, (1899) 24 Ind. App. 46, 55 N. E. 42; Brackney v. Fogle, (1901) 156 Ind. 535, 60 N. E. 303; Howard v. Porter, (1949) 240 Iowa 153, 35 N. W. 2d 837; Hobson v. McLeod, (1933) 165 Miss. 853, 147 So. 778, not followed in Killings v. Metropolitan Life Ins. Co., (1940) 187 Miss. 265, 192 So. 577, 131 A. L. R. 684; Meyer v. Russell, (1926) 55 N. D. 546, 214 N. W. 857. But cf. Blackstead v. Kent, (1933) 63 N. D. 246, 247 N. W. 607.

part of counsel has had that result, the courts have generally held it sufficient grounds for a reversal of the judgment.[1]

It is not every error committed by counsel in the stress of a hard fought trial or in the heat of an impassioned argument to the jury that will constitute reversible error, and a broad discretion must be allowed the trial judge in correcting such errors as may occur in the course of the trial. Counsel should be allowed all reasonable latitude in the argument of his case to the jury and be permitted to draw his own conclusions from the evidence or lack of evidence in some instances where the evidence is more available to one party than to the other. But this freedom of deduction and speech does not go to the extent of permitting counsel to draw deductions not based on the evidence, nor does it permit him to comment on the failure to call certain witnesses when these same witnesses were as accessible to one party as to the other. Tactics of this character are unfair and reprehensible and, unless restrained by the court, may, and usually do, constitute reversible error. Moreover, the action of the court in merely sustaining the objection of the complaining party and instructing the jury to disregard the offending remark or argument of counsel is not always sufficient to counteract its baleful influence upon the jury.[2]

Obviously, it is impossible to lay down an absolute rule which will govern all cases. Due to varying circumstances, it is conceivable that that which would constitute misconduct of counsel in one case, would fall far short of it in another. Presumably, the ultimate test must be: Was the remark or argument of counsel so utterly unfair and uncalled for, and so manifestly prejudicial to the complaining party as to deny him a fair trial and justify a reversal of the verdict? It need hardly be stated that as a general rule, misconduct of coun-

---

[1] Fidelity and Casualty Co. v. Niemann, (1931) 47 F. 2d 1056. See also note, 78 A. L. R. 766.

[2] Hankins v. St. Louis-San Francisco R. R., (1930) ....Mo. App........ , 31 S. W. 2d 596.

In Brown v. St. Paul City Ry., (1954) 241 Minn. 15, 62 N. W. 2d 688, 44 A. L. R. 2d 535, the court, on objection by defendant, had excluded a part of a hospital record relating patient's version of the manner of the accident. Plaintiff's counsel, however, in his argument to the jury, discussed the matters excluded. The court denied defendant's request that the jury be instructed to disregard the objectionable matters which plaintiff's counsel had discussed. Held: reversible error.

sel in this respect is not ground for a new trial or subject to review unless proper and timely objection is made by the opposing counsel.[3]

It is reversible error to permit plaintiff's counsel, in a personal injury case, to argue to the jury that plaintiff's physician was available to the defendant as a witness and would have been produced at the trial by the defendant had the physician's testimony been favorable to him.[4] And where the remarks of plaintiff's counsel were to the effect that the defendant had the absolute right to have a physical examination made of the plaintiff by physicians appointed by the court if the defendant so desired, it was held that the statement, being untrue, was highly prejudicial to the defendant and required a reversal of the judgment rendered for the plaintiff.[5]

---

[3] Southern Ry. v. Brown, (1906) 126 Ga. 1, 6, 54 S. E. 911: "When improper argument is made by counsel, counsel for the opposite party, in order to make the action of the judge in reference to the same the basis for a review, may object to the argument, and rest simply on the objection; and if the court fails to take any notice of the objection and allows the argument to proceed, this conduct may be reviewed; or he may, in addition to his objection, move for appropriate instructions to the jury, or for a reprimand or rebuke of counsel, in order that the jury may be impressed with the grave nature of the impropriety which has taken place; or, if the impropriety is of a very grave character, he may move for a mistrial, and upon the refusal of the court to do that which ought to have been done on the motion made, whatever its nature may be, the conduct of the judge will then be a subject for review by this court."

For cases pertaining to the subject, see Ann. Cas. 1916 A. 551. See also Raines v. Small, (1943) ......Mo. App......, 169 S. W. 2d 102; Murphy v. Tumbrink, (1930) ...... Mo. App......., 25 S. W. 2d 133, which involve the physician-patient relationship.

In Shields v. American Car & F. Co., (1927) ....Mo. App......., 293 S. W. 77, counsel for plaintiff, in his argument to the jury, made improper remarks about defendant's failure to call a named physician as a witness. Defendant's motion for a mistrial came too late. It should have been made when the remarks were uttered; not after the jury had retired to consider their verdict.

[4] Atkinson v. United Ry.,(1921) 286 Mo. 634, 228 S. W. 483; Evans v.Trenton, (1892) 112 Mo. 390, 20 S. W. 614; Fisher v. John Hancock Mut. Life Ins. Co., (1950) ...... Mo. App......., 229 S. W. 2d 246; Murphy v. Tumbrink, (1930) ....Mo. App......., 25 S. W. 2d 133; Hankins v. St. Louis-San Francisco Ry., (1930) ....Mo. App......., 31 S. W. 2d 596.

In Trzecki v. St. Louis Public Service Co., (1953) ....Mo. App......., 258 S. W. 2d 676 and in Raines v. Small, (1943) ....Mo. App......., 169 S. W. 2d 102, the trial court granted defendant's motion for a new trial on this ground. In each case the order was affirmed.

[5] Johnson v. Atchison, T. & St. Fe Ry., (1927) ....Mo. App......., 290 S. W. 462; Stuben-

>>>→

Counsel has no right under the guise of "argument" to make a witness of himself and inject into a case facts that are prejudicial to the adverse party. The *facts* of the case must go to the jury by way of the witness stand. In *Rice* v. *Hill,*[6] plaintiff's counsel, in his argument to the jury, said: "They had a doctor in court and they didn't call him to dispute Dr. Boord's testimony." There was nothing in the record showing that defendant's physician was in the courtroom; neither was he identified in any way, nor was it disclosed that he had examined the plaintiff. In the Supreme Court, the assignment of error based upon the trial court's refusal to declare a mistrial because of the remark of plaintiff's counsel was sustained. And where counsel for the plaintiff, who had failed to call the attending physician as a witness, told the jury what the physician had said about the nature of the plaintiff's injury and, notwithstanding the admonition of the court to desist, kept on arguing about matters not testified to at the trial, judgment for the plaintiff was reversed because of the misconduct of plaintiff's counsel.[7]

In a number of cases, however, the court, while conceding the remark or argument of counsel was clearly improper, nevertheless held that it was not so flagrant and manifestly harmful as to require reversal of the judgment;[8] especially where it appeared that the

---

←

haver v. Kansas City Ry., (1919) ..... Mo. App......., 213 S. W. 144; Bergfield v. Dunham, (1918) ....Mo. App. ....., 201 S. W. 640.

But plaintiff's counsel, in his argument, may question the timeliness and good faith of defendant's efforts to investigate the nature and extent of plaintiff's alleged injuries. Keehn v. D. R. F. Realty & Inv. Co., (1931) 328 Mo. 1031, 43 S. W. 2d 416.

[6] (1934) 315 Pa. 166, 172 Atl. 289.

See also 3 Am. Jur., *Appeal & Error,* § 1060.

[7] Evans v. Trenton, (1892) 112 Mo. 390, 20 S. W. 614.

See also Murphy v. Tumbrink, (1930) ..... Mo. App. ....., 25 S. W. 2d 133. In Larson v. Great Falls City Lines, (1947) 119 Mont. 593, 178 P. 2d 410, judgment for plaintiff was affirmed, since the trial court had admonished the jury that there was nothing in the evidence to support counsel's statements and the jury was expressly instructed to disregard them. See also Drotleff v. Renshaw, (1949) ..... Cal. App. ....., 202 P. 2d 847, aff'd. ..... Cal. ....., 208 P. 2d 969.

See note, L. R. A. 1918 D. 4.

[8] Chambers v. Tobin, (1954) 118 F. Supp. 555, rev'd. on other grounds, 204 F. 2d 732; State v. Cox, (1931) 329 Mo. 292, 46 S. W. 2d 849; Brungs v. St. Louis Public Service Co.,

⋙→

trial judge acted promptly on the objection of opposing counsel by admonishing or rebuking the offending counsel and instructing the jury to disregard his blameworthy statements.[9]

99. Comment Upon Exercise of the Privilege

There is a conflict of opinion as to whether it is proper for counsel to comment on a party's claim of a personal privilege with respect to the testimony of a particular witness. Generally speaking, the courts have held that it is improper for the adverse party to comment on the exercise of a privilege by a person to whom the law has granted this right.[1] With respect to the relationship of physician and patient, the great weight of authority supports the view that no unfavorable inference can be drawn against a party as the result of his exercise of the statutory privilege to exclude certain specific testimony of a physician, and no comment can be made thereon by the court, or by counsel for the opposite party in his argument to the jury.[2] To hold that, because the patient, or the

---

←—«««

(1950) _____Mo. App._____, 230 S. W. 2d 181; Arnold v. Metropolitan Life Ins. Co., (1936) _____ Mo. App. _____, 89 S. W. 2d 81; Monpleasure v. American Car & F. Co., (1927) _____ Mo. App._____, 293 S. W. 84; Waite v. Mosconi, (1948) 273 App. Div. 1040, 78 N. Y. S. 2d 615.

In Williams v. Spokane Falls & N. Ry., (1906) 42 Wash. 597, 84 Pac. 1129, plaintiff's counsel, in cross-examining one of plaintiff's physicians who had testified in behalf of defendant, purposely expanded his questions so as to include remarks which obviously were intended to convey to the jury the impression that the witness was guilty of indecent and unethical conduct in testifying for the defendant. The Supreme Court said that the cross-examination was very close to the line of error, but held that the plaintiff had the right to discredit the witness by showing interest or bias in the case, and that the trial judge had not abused his discretion in the matter.

[9] Drotleff v. Renshaw, (1949) _____ Cal. App._____, 202 P. 2d 847, aff'd. _____ Cal._____, 208 P. 2d 969; Larson v. Great Falls City Lines, (1947) 119 Mont. 593, 178 P. 2d 410.

[1] See note, 116 A. L. R. 1170.

[2] Brackney v. Fogle, (1901) 156 Ind. 535, 538, 60 N. E. 303: "Shall the efficacy of the statute be destroyed by indirection? To claim the protection of the statute is the legal right of the patient, or his representative, of no less inviolability than any other personal right, and it is wholly inconsistent with that right to say that its exercise in a judicial proceeding shall be allowed to prejudice the cause of him who claims it."

Sumpter v. National Grocery Co., (1938) 194 Wash, 598, 602, 78 P. 2d 1087, 116 A. L. R. 1166: "The statutory rule prescribed by the Legislature establishes a legal right to have certain specific testimony excluded, and it is implicit in the statute that

»»»→

holder of the privilege, does not waive or abandon the privilege, inferences adverse to his side of the controversy may be drawn by

---

← ⧏

such right may be exercised without making it the subject of unfavorable inference by the trier of facts. The exclusion of such evidence rests in a public policy and is for the general interest of the community. To hold that the exercise of the statutory privilege gives rise to adverse inferences by the jury would be to dissipate the protection which the statute provides; and to permit counsel to comment on the exercise of such privilege, would enable him to incite the jury to draw inferences adverse to the protection afforded by the statute."

Accord: Halsband v .Columbian National Life Ins. Co., (1933) 67 F. 2d 863, cert. denied 291 U. S. 681, 78 Law Ed. 1008, 54 Su. Ct. 531; Estate of Carpenter, (1892) 94 Cal. 406, 29 Pac. 1101; Metropolitan Life Ins. Co. v. Fidelity Trust Co., (1938) 214 Ind. 134, 14 N. E. 2d 911; William Laurie Co. v. McCullough, (1910) 174 Ind. 477, 90 N. E. 1014, Ann. Cas. 1913 A. 49, disapproving Warsaw v. Fisher, (1899) 24 Ind. App. 46, 55 N. E. 42; Howard v. Porter, (1949) 240 Iowa 153, 35 N. W. 2d 837; New York Life Ins. Co. v. Newman, (1945) 311 Mich. 368, 18 N. W. 2d 859; Sanne, a minor, by Dahlke, Gdn. v. Metropolitan Life Ins. Co., (1944) 218 Minn. 181, 15 N. W. 2d 524; New York Life Ins. Co. v. Hansen, (1941) 71 N. D. 383, 2 N. W. 2d 163; Meyer v. Russell, (1926) 55 N. D. 546, 214 N. W. 857; McLaughlin v. Massachusetts Indemnity Co., (1948) 85 Ohio App. 511, 84 N. E. 2d 114; Kelley v. Highfield, (1887) 15 Ore. 277, 14 Pac. 744; Kiehlhoefer v. Washington Water Power Co., (1908) 49 Wash. 646, 96 Pac. 220; Lane v. Spokane Falls & N. Ry., (1899) 21 Wash. 119, 57 Pac. 367, 46 L. R. A. 153. Undoubtedly the rule stems from a decision of the House of Lords in a case involving communications between attorney and client. Lord Chelmsford said: "The exclusion of such evidence is for the general interest of the community, and therefore to say that when a party refuses to permit professional confidence to be broken, everything must be taken most strongly against him, what is it but to deny him the protection which, for public purposes, the law affords him, and utterly to take away a privilege which can thus only be asserted to his prejudice." Wentworth v. Lloyd, [1864] 10 H. L. Cas. 589, 591.

Rule 39 of the Uniform Rules of Evidence (1953), provides: "Subject to paragraph (4), Rule 23, [relating to an accused's failure to testify] if a privilege is exercised not to testify or to prevent another from testifying, either in the action or with respect to particular matters, or to refuse to disclose or to prevent another from disclosing any matter, the judge and counsel may not comment thereon, no presumption shall arise with respect to the exercise of the privilege, and the trier of fact may not draw any adverse inference therefrom. In those jury cases wherein the right to exercise a privilege, as herein provided, may be misunderstood and unfavorable inferences drawn by the trier of the fact, or be impaired in the particular case, the court, at the request of the party exercising the privilege, may instruct the jury in support of such privilege."

It should, perhaps, be noticed that Rule 233 of the Model Code of Evidence (1942), which allowed the judge and counsel to comment on the exercise of the privilege, was not approved and adopted by the authors of the Uniform Rules of Evidence.

the jury, would be to fritter away the protection it was intended to afford.[3]

In a few cases, however, the courts have held that counsel may properly comment upon the exercise of a personal privilege, with the view of having the jury take this circumstance into consideration in making their decision.[4]

100. Challenging Party to Waive Privilege

In the few cases reported, it has been held that it is error to ask the patient, on cross-examination, if he will waive his statutory privilege and permit his physician to testify, since his refusal would tend to "put him on the spot," so to speak, and thereby, in a manner, force him to consent to the introduction in evidence of privileged matters which he has a perfect right to exclude.[1] Such manner of

---

[3] Pennsylvania R. R. v. Durkee, (1906) 147 Fed. 99, 8 Ann. Cas. 790.

[4] Peoria Life Ins. Co. v. Smith, (1931) 47 F. 2d 279 (physician-patient); Deutschmann v. Third Ave. R. R. (1903) 87 App. Div. 503, 84 N. Y. S. 887 (physician-patient). Two federal courts, sitting in New York, have refused to follow this decision. See Halsband v. Columbian National Life Ins. Co., (1933) 67 F. 2d 863, cert. denied 291 U. S. 681, 78 Law. Ed. 1008, 54 Su. Ct. 531; Pennsylvania R. R. v. Durkee, (1906) 147 Fed. 99, 8 Ann. Cas. 790. In Massachusetts, the courts have held that counsel may comment on a party's exercise of the attorney-client privilege. Phillips v. Chase, (1909) 201 Mass. 444, 450, 87 N. E. 755: "If evidence is material and competent except for a personal privilege of one of the parties to have it excluded under the law, his claim of privilege may be referred to in argument and considered by the jury, as indicating his opinion that the evidence, if received, would be prejudicial to him."

Holmes, J., in McCooe v. Dighton S. & S. St. R. R., (1899) 173 Mass. 117, 119, 53 N. E. 133: "In a civil case, if one of the parties insists upon his privilege to exclude testimony that would throw light upon the merits of the case and the truth of his testimony, we are of opinion that it is a proper subject for comment."

[1] In McConnell v. Osage, (1890) 80 Iowa 293, 45 N. W. 550, 8 L. R. A. 778, while the plaintiff was being cross-examined, she was asked: "Are you willing that the physicians who have treated you for the past ten or fifteen years may disclose to this jury any conversation you made to them, at times they treated you, in reference to your condition?" Objection to the question was overruled, and she answered that she was not. Reversing the judgment for defendant, Granger, J., (p. 303) said: "The statute gives the prohibition. It is a legal right, and a party should no more be required to state under oath that he did not want to surrender it than any other legal right he possessed. We think a fair trial requires that such a matter should not even be referred to; that a jury should not be impressed with a belief that there is even reluctance to giving such assent. The subject-matter of such a waiver has no place for reference in the taking of testimony except by the party permitted to make it. That

》→

cross-examination, if permitted, would practically destroy the protection which the law affords.[2] The same rule applies where the patient, or the holder of the privilege, is asked if he will waive the privilege so as to permit the introduction in evidence of the patient's hospital records.[3]

101. *Instructions to the Jury*

A wide disparity of opinion exists among the decisions which involve the propriety of giving or refusing instructions to the jury affirming or denying the jury's right to draw an unfavorable inference against a party because he fails to call a particular physician as a witness; or because, on the ground of privilege, he objects to the testimony of a physician when called by the adverse party, or to the introduction of a hospital record.

There is considerable authority for the view that it is improper for a court to instruct the jury that it may draw an unfavorable inference from the fact that a party has failed to produce evidence which is within the protection of the statutory privilege, or has invoked the privilege in order to exclude such evidence; the theory being that to permit such instruction would, in effect, nullify the privilege.[1] Moreover, it has been held that an instruction which,

---

prejudice resulted from the ruling in question is more than probable. After making oath that she would not consent to the testimony, the jury was left to assume something,—we know not what. It would naturally believe that, if assent had been given, testimony unfavorable to the plaintiff would have been the result. However, we need not speculate as to the probable consequences. It was celarly error."

Accord: Johnson v. Kinney, (1942) 232 Iowa 1016, 7 N. W. 2d 188, 144 A. L. R. 997; Donovan v. Donovan, (1941) 231 Iowa 14, 300 N. W. 656; Burgess v. Sims Drug Co., (1901) 114 Iowa 275, 86 N. W. 307, 54 L. R. A. 364; Arnold v. Maryville, (1905) 110 Mo. App. 254, 85 S. W. 107.

See also Brookhaven Lumber & Mfg. Co. v. Adams, (1923) 132 Miss. 689, 97 So. 484; Ross v. Great Northern Ry., (1907) 101 Minn. 122, 111 N. W. 951.

See note, 144 A. L. R. 1007.

[2] Andrews v. Washington National Ins. Co., (1936) ...... Mo. App......., 93 S. W. 2d 1045.

[3] McLaughlin v. Massachusetts Indemnity Ins. Co., (1948) 85 Ohio App. 511, 84 N. E. 2d 114; Andrews v. Washington National Ins. Co., (1936) ......Mo. App......., 93 S. W. 2d 1045.

[1] Sherman v. Ross, (1936) 99 Colo. 354, 359, 62 P. 2d 1151: "Tendered instruction No. 5 was to the effect that plaintiff having recently called a physician to examine him, and

even by indirection, leads to such an inference is improper.[2] In
some jurisdictions, the court may, in its discretion, explain to the
jury the nature and purpose of the privilege and give a specific
instruction to the effect that no adverse inference may be indulged
from the fact that a party failed to produce evidence of a privileged
character, or that he invoked the statutory privilege to exclude it.[3]

← ⫸
having failed to call such physician as a witness, the jury might infer that his testimony, if he had been called, would have been unfavorable to plaintiff. We have a
statute making communications between physician and patient privileged. The giving of instructions of this character would result in a prospective litigant either re-
fraining from seeking medical advice or, if he engaged in litigation thereafter, compel
him to surrender the privilege that the statute gives him or suffer the penalty of
having the jury assume that the doctor's testimony, if given, would be unfavorable to
him." The tendered instruction held properly refused.

    Accord: Pennsylvania R. R. v. Durkee, (1906) 147 Fed. 99, 8 Ann. Cas. 790; Cook
v. Los Angeles Ry., (1915) 169 Cal. 113, 145 Pac. 1013; Thomas v. Gates, (1899) 126
Cal. 1, 58 Pac. 315; Estate of Carpenter, (1892) 94 Cal. 406, 29 Pac. 1101; Brackney v.
Fogle, (1901) 156 Ind. 535, 60 N. E. 303; Merrill v. St. Paul City Ry., (1927) 170 Minn.
332, 212 N. W. 533; Arnold v. Maryville, (1905) 110 Mo. App. 254, 85 S. W. 107; Fulsom-
Morris Coal & M. Co. v. Mitchell, (1913) 37 Okla. 575, 132 Pac. 1103; Lane v. Spokane
Falls & N. Ry., (1899) 21 Wash. 119, 57 Pac. 367, 46 L. R. A. 153.

    See notes, 5 A. L. R. 2d 893; 131 A. L. R. 693.

    See also Rule 39 of the Uniform Rules of Evidence, § 99, herein, note 2.

[2] State Farm Mut. Automobile Ins. Co. v. Kramer, (1938) 105 Ind. App. 591, 14 N. E. 2d
741; Hobson v. McLeod, (1933) 165 Miss. 853, 147 So. 778. But *cf.* Killings v. Metropolitan Life Ins. Co., (1940) 187 Miss. 265, 192 So. 577, 131 A. L. R. 684.

[3] Pennsylvania R. R. v. Durkee, (1906) 147 Fed. 99, 8 Ann. Cas. 790; Lauer v. Banning,
(1911) 152 Iowa 99, 131 N. W. 783; Mortimer v. Daub, (1912) 52 Ind. App. 30, 98 N. E.
845; Rump v. Woods, (1912) 50 Ind. App. 347, 98 N. E. 369.

    See also Rule 39 of the Uniform Rules of Evidence, § 99, herein, note 2.

    In Sanne, a minor, by Dahlke, Gdn. v. Metropolitan Life Ins. Co., (1944) 218
Minn. 181, 15 N. W. 2d 524, the court instructed the jury that, as to privileged communications, certain evidence had been excluded. In explanation thereof, the court
said that the law prohibits the disclosure of confidential communications without the
consent of the patient or his representative; and the fact counsel for plaintiff objected
to that kind of evidence "should have no bearing as far as the decision of this lawsuit
is concerned. That evidence was excluded by authority of law * * * and it was the
duty of the guardian to look after the interests of his ward." The instruction was
held proper.

    Contrary to this view is Deutschmann v. Third Ave. R. R., (1903) 87 App. Div.
503, 84 N. Y. S. 887. Plaintiff requested the court to charge that: "Under the law,
communications from a patient to a physician are privileged and cannot be given in
testimony, except that the privilege be waived, and could have been waived in this
case by the plaintiff, but her refusal to waive it does not warrant the jury in indulging
⫸→

On the other hand, there is good authority for the view that it is proper to instruct the jury that it may draw an unfavorable inference under such circumstances.[4] However, the court should make it perfectly clear that the inference is optional, not compulsory,[5] and it must be very careful not to attribute any fixed degree of probative force to the inference when made.[6] It would seem, there-

←—◀

in any inference unfavorable to her or to her cause of action. She stood upon her legal rights, and because of doing so she cannot be prejudiced in the eyes of the jury. * * *" The court, however, (p. 513) said: "I will charge you upon that subject in this way. * * * The law itself does not prohibit any inference being drawn from that, and I think that, while you are not to raise any inference which is not justified under the evidence in the case, I shall decline to charge you that the law prevents you from drawing any inference whatsoever from the situation."

See § 99 herein, note 4 concerning this case.

[4] Griggs v. Saginaw & F. Ry., (1917) 196 Mich. 258, 162 N. W. 960; O'Connor v. Detroit, (1910) 160 Mich. 193, 125 N. W. 277; Vergin v. Saginaw, (1901) 125 Mich. 499, 84 N. W. 1075; Gulf Refining Co. v. Myrick, (1954) 220 Miss. 429, 71 So. 2d 217; Tri-State Transit Co. v. Mondy, (1943) 194 Miss. 714, 12 So. 2d 920; Killings v. Metropolitan Life Ins. Co., (1940) 187 Miss. 265, 192 So. 577, 131 A. L. R. 684; Robinson v. Haydel, (1936) 177 Miss. 233, 171 So. 7. *Cf.* Life & Casualty Ins. Co. v. Walters, (1937) 180 Miss. 384, 177 So. 47; Rondinella v. Metropolitan Life Ins. Co., (1904) 24 Pa. Super. 293; Sabowska v. Coney Island & B. R. R., (1916) 174 App. Div. 913, 160 N. Y. S. 386; People v. Fiori, (1908) 123 App. Div. 174, 108 N. Y. S. 416 (physicians not privileged, however); Kane v. Rochester Ry., (1902) 74 App. Div. 575, 77 N. Y. S. 776.

In Killings v. Metropolitan Life Ins. Co., infra, the court's instructions to the jury, approved by the Supreme Court, were: (p. 266) "The court instructs the jury for the defendant that the fact that the plaintiff has not introduced as a witness Dr. Waldrup will justify the jury in inferring that had Dr. Waldrup been introduced his testimony would not have been favorable to the plaintiff." * * * "The court instructs the jury for the defendant that under the law of Mississippi the defendant cannot offer as a witness any doctor to testify to anything learned by him of the plaintiff's physical condition while the relation of physician and patient existed between him and plaintiff."

In Clary v. Breyer, (1943) 194 Miss. 612, 13 So. 2d 633, the court held that the rule announced in Killings v. Metropolitan Life Ins. Co., infra, did not apply since the plaintiff had waived the privilege. The physician was available to the defendant as a witness and the court's charge that plaintiff's failure to call him gave rise to an unfavorable inference against her was error.

[5] § 92, herein. See also Alexander, Presumptions: Their Use and Abuse, (1945) 17 Miss. L. J. 1, 8-13.

[6] In Gatlin v. Allen, (1948) 203 Miss. 135, 33 So. 2d 304, defendant requested and was refused the following instruction: "The court instructs the jury for the defendant that under the law this defendant could not introduce Dr. S. to testify to the injury of the

⇉→

fore, that, in its instructions to the jury, the court should scrupulously avoid expressions such as "it is presumed," "creates a presumption," "authorizes a strong presumption," "you may presume," "the law presumes," and the like, even when used in the popular sense, since they carry unpredictable connotations to different minds, have a tendency to mislead the jury, and, under varying circumstances, may be considered by a reviewing court as a comment on the weight of the evidence.[7]

Since it is not practicable to formalize an instruction that would be proper in all cases, perhaps the most that can be said is that the better practice is to instruct the jury, in substance, that

---

plaintiff. The failure of the plaintiff to call Dr. S as a witness raises the presumption that if Dr. S were offered to testify by the plaintiff, that his testimony would be hurtful or harmful to the plaintiff's case." Affirming the judgment for plaintiff, Alexander, J., (p. 140) said, in part: "To state that a plaintiff's failure to call his physician 'raises the presumption' that the doctor's testimony would be harmful to plaintiff's case, is to stamp such circumstance with a judicial sanction and endow it with a legal status that raises it above its mere availability as factual material for logical reasoning."

Cross v. Passumpsic Fibre L. Co., (1916) 90 Vt. 397, 407, 98 Atl. 1010: "But we must be cautious in our use of language. A presumption and an inference are not the same thing. A 'presumption' is a deduction which the law requires a trier to make; an 'inference' is a deduction which the trier may or may not make according to his own conclusions. A presumption is mandatory; an inference, permissible."

[7] In Crapson v. United Chatauqua Co., (1931) ....Mo. App........, 37 S. W. 2d 966, defendant requested and was refused the following instruction: "On behalf of the defendant the court instructs the jury that the plaintiff admitted Dr. K treated her for the injury which she claims, and that from the failure of the plaintiff to call Dr. K as a witness in her behalf you may, in arriving at your verdict, presume that his evidence would not be favorable to her claim."

In affirming the judgment for plaintiff, the court said (p. 968): "Plaintiff's failure to call the physician, if available, who first attended her, would be a strong circumstance which would warrant an inference of fact that the evidence not so produced would fail to support the plaintiff. [citing cases] The foregoing authorities are relied upon by appellant as justification for the instruction requested. We think they are not in point. They do not authorize comment by the court upon the state of the evidence or an instruction upon a permissible inference of fact. This would, in a manner, be weighing the evidence which is within the exclusive province of the jury, and the court should not comment upon it."

In Smith v. Kansas City Public Service Co., (1933) 227 Mo. App. 675, 56 S. W. 2d 838, it was not error to refuse to instruct the jury "that the law presumes that the testimony of said doctors had they been presented and testified in this case, would have been unfavorable to plaintiff;" the instruction being a comment on the evidence.

See also State v. Damon, (1943) 350 Mo. 949, 169 S. W. 2d 382.

where a party fails to call a witness who is available and could aid his case, the jury are at liberty to take that fact into consideration and to weigh it along with all the other evidence when they come to decide the merits of the case.[8] How much weight should be given it is a legitimate matter for argument by counsel, and may depend upon many factors: the relationship of the witness, importance or non-importance of proposed testimony, extent of availability, validity of excuse for failure, or relevancy. For a trial judge to tell jurors how much import should be given the inference in comparison with other matters properly before them would be an infringement upon their right to weigh the evidence.[9]

It does not constitute error for the trial court to refuse an instruction requested by the defendant that the failure of the plaintiff to call a physician as a witness raises an inference that his testimony would be adverse to the plaintiff, when there is no showing that the witness is available,[10] or that he is not as accessible to the defendant as to the plaintiff.[11] Neither is it error to refuse to charge

---

[8] Hecke v. Henne, (1927) 238 Mich. 198, 213 N. W. 112; Vergin v. Saginaw, (1901) 125 Mich. 499, 84 N. W. 1075; Minch v. New York & Queen's County Ry., (1903) 80 App. Div. 324, 80 N. Y. S. 712; Ferne v. Chadderton, (1949) 363 Pa. 191, 6 A. 2d 104. Gaynor, J., in Wade v. Mount Vernon, (1909) 133 App. Div. 389, 390, 117 N. Y. S. 356: "The request to charge that the jury might infer that the testimony of the absent surgeon would have been unfavorable to the plaintiff was not strictly accurate and might have misled the jury. It was not for the court to rule as a matter of law that the jury might properly draw such an inference. On the contrary, it was at best for the jury to say whether on all the facts of the case they could and would do so. All that the court could properly charge was that they were at liberty to draw such an inference if, all considered, they thought it a fair inference. It was not for the court to say outright that the case was such that they could not draw it. That was for them to say." The court held, however, that the error was not so prejudicial as to warrant a reversal of the judgment. One judge dissented.

See also Laffin v. Ryan, (1957) 4 A. D. 2d 21, 162 N. Y. S. 2d 730.

[9] Edwards v. St. Louis & San Francisco R. R., (1912) 166 Mo. App. 428, 149 S. W. 321.

See also Bleecker v. Johnston, (1877) 69 N. Y. 309.

[10] Large v. Johnson, (1933) 124 Neb. 821, 248 N. W. 400.

[11] Carpenter v. Sun Indemnity Co., (1940) 138 Neb. 552, 293 N. W. 400; Large v. Johnson, (1933) 124 Neb. 821, 248 N. W. 400; Perlman v. Shanck, (1920) 192 App. Div. 179, 182 N. Y. S. 767.

The court may properly refuse to charge that an inference may be drawn against the defendant for failure to call the plaintiff's physicians as witnesses. Pronk v. Brooklyn Heights R. R., (1902) 68 App. Div. 390, 74 N. Y. S. 375. See also § 95, herein.

that plaintiff's failure to call a physician as a witness gives rise to an inference unfavorable to him, where there was no showing of any controverted question which the testimony of the physician might have aided in solving.[12] An instruction which permits an unfavorable inference to be drawn from a party's failure to call an available witness, is improper where the testimony, if given, would only be corroborative or cumulative.[13]

When the nonproduction of evidence by a party permits an unfavorable inference, it makes no difference whether the failure to produce is chargeable to the party himself or to his attorney, or both. Therefore, to instruct the jury that the inference was not to be drawn if the failure to produce was that of the party's attorney, is error.[14]

102. Exercise of Privilege: Application of Rule to Warranties in Insurance Policies

Under the Insurance Law of New York,[1] if, in an action involving a life, accident, or health insurance policy, a misrepresentation concerning his condition of health is proved by the insurer to have been made by the insured, and he or any other person having or claiming a right under such policy shall prevent full disclosure and proof of the nature of his malady or medical impairment, such misrepresentation shall be presumed to have been material.

In *Travelers Insurance Co.* v. *Pomerantz,*[2] the company sought to cancel a policy obtained by misrepresentation. Although the insured had denied that he had received medical attention within five years, the evidence showed that he had been treated by five

---

[12] Jankowski v. Clausen, (1926) 167 Minn. 437, 209 N. W. 317.

[13] Wood v. Los Angeles Traction Co., (1905) 1 Cal. App. 474, 82 Pac. 547; Pronk v. Brooklyn Heights R. R., (1902) 68 App. Div. 390, 74 N. Y. S. 375; Diffenbacher v. Lake Shore Coach Co., (1948) _____ Ohio App._____, 51 Ohio Law Abst. 481, 81 N. E. 2d 337; Adams v. Derian, (1934) 115 Pa. Super. 357, 175 Atl. 762.

See Perlman v. Shanck, (1920) 192 App. Div. 179, 182 N. Y. S. 767.

See also § 94, herein.

[14] O'Neill v. Billota, (1952) 18 N. J. Super, 82, 86 A. 2d 705, aff'd. 10 N. J. 308, 91 A. 2d 231 (physician-patient relationship not involved).

[1] N. Y. *Insurance Law*, § 149(4).

[2] (1924) 124 Misc. Rep. 250, 207 N. Y. S. 81.

physicians on twelve different occasions. When the company tried to show the nature of the insured's medical impairment by the testimony of the insured's physicians, the insured invoked the statutory privilege and their testimony was excluded. The company, therefore, was unable to prove that the medical attendances had been for any serious ailment. Thus, while it proved falsity, it could not prove that the false representation was material. The trial court dismissed the company's complaint. The judgment was affirmed by the Appellate Division,[3] but this, in turn, was reversed by the Court of Appeals on the ground that the company had established a *prima facie* case and was entitled to rescind the contract.[4]

The same rule applies in an action brought by the beneficiary to recover the proceeds of the policy, and it is immaterial that he has no power to waive the deceased's privilege.[5]

In an action on life insurance policies issued on the insured's representation that he had not consulted a physician, where the physicians' depositions in support of the company's motion for summary judgment showed that the insured had consulted the physicians and had submitted to examinations by them, but the nature of his ailment was not revealed because the plaintiff invoked the statutory privilege, summary judgment was properly granted.

---

[3] (1926) 218 App. Div. 431, 218 N. Y. S. 490, which held that no unfavorable inference could be drawn from the insured's invoking the statutory privilege.

[4] (1927) 246 N. Y. 63, 69, 158 N. E. 21: "It could not compel him to waive his privilege arising from his relation to his physicians and force them to disclose the diagnosis and the nature of the treatment. He may insist upon this privilege but he cannot be heard to claim that no *prima facie* case has been made out. He produced no witnesses and gave no evidence concerning vital facts which could be disclosed only by him. * * * To hold that the proof under such circumstances is less than *prima facie* would be to condone and encourage misrepresentations and to impose upon a litigant conditions impossible of fulfillment. Plaintiff proceeded as far as the law allows and far enough, in the absence of denial, to require a finding of material misrepresentation."

See also Peoria Life Ins. Co., (1931) 47 F. 2d 279; Metropolitan Life Ins. Co. v. Goldsmith, (1952) 201 Misc. 569, 112 N. Y. S. 2d 385; Empire City Savings Bank v. Ward, (1950) 101 N. Y. S. 2d 677, and note, (1951) 2 Syracuse L. Rev. 370. *Cf.* New York Life Ins. Co. v. Newman, (1945) 311 Mich. 368, 18 N. W. 2d 859.

[5] Roth v. Equitable Life Assur. Soc., (1945) 186 Misc. 403, 59 N. Y. S. 2d 707, aff'd. 270 App. Div. 923, 62 N. Y. S. 2d 612, appeal denied 296 N. Y. 1061, 69 N. E. 2d 565; Siebern v. Mutual Life Ins. Co., (1945) 269 App. Div. 846, 55 N. Y. S. 2d 603.

See also Polachek v. New York Life Ins. Co., (1934) 151 Misc. 172, 270 N. Y. S. 884, appeal denied, 267 N. Y. XXXIX.

By claiming the privilege, plaintiff thereby prevented full disclosure within the meaning of the New York statute creating a presumption that the misrepresentations were material.[6]

103. Admissibility of Evidence of Party's Refusal to Submit to Physical Examination

There are conflicting views upon the propriety and power of a court to require a party to an action, civil or criminal, to submit to a physical examination.[1] However, the general rule is that evidence is admissible in a civil action to show that a party to the action unreasonably refused to permit a physical examination or inspection of his person;[2] and this is true, with but few decisions to the contrary, even in jurisdictions which deny the power of a court to require such examination.[3]

In an action to recover damages for personal injury, it is proper for the defendant to inquire of the plaintiff, during cross-examination, as to whether he is willing to submit to a medical examination to ascertain the nature and extent of his injury.[4] The fact of his

[6] Engl v. Aetna Life Ins. Co., (1943) 139 F. 2d 469; Saunders v. United Mutual Life Ins. Co., (1957) 172 N. Y. S. 2d 443.

[1] See § 77, herein.

[2] See note, 175 A. L. R. 234.

[3] Austin & N. W. R. R. v. Cluck, (1903) 97 Tex. 172, 183, 77 S. W. 403, 64 L. R. A. 494, 1 Ann. Cas. 261: "The reason for refusing a physical examination of the plaintiff is not that the defendant is not entitled to have the benefit of the evidence, but because the court has no power to force the plaintiff to submit to such an examination. He has the right to submit or refuse, but in case he should refuse, the defendant is entitled to have that fact go to the jury to be considered by them in determining upon the credibility and sufficiency of the testimony upon which he seeks to recover. If the jury should believe that the refusal showed a purpose to conceal the truth, they might take that fact into account in weighing the evidence. If a satisfactory reason should be given for the refusal, and other evidence were sufficient, the refusal would not defeat a recovery."

Accord: Union Pac. R. R. v. Botsford, (1891) 141 U. S. 250, 35 Law. Ed. 734, 11 Su. Ct. 1000; Choy v. Otaguro, (1932) 32 Hawaii 543; Atchison, T. & S. F. Ry. v. Melson, (1913) 40 Okla. 1, 134 Pac. 388, Ann. Cas. 1915 D. 760; Chicago, R. I. & Pac. Ry. v. Hill, (1913) 36 Okla. 540, 129 Pac. 13, 43 L. R. A. (n. s.) 622.

[4] See cases in note 3, infra.

There is authority to the contrary. Cornell v. Great Northern Ry., (1920) 57 Mont. 117, 187 Pac. 902.

Mattice v. Klawans, (1924) 312 Ill. 299, 307, 143 N. E. 866: "The settled law of

refusal may be considered by the jury as bearing upon his good faith, and may justify an inference against him as in any other case of a party declining to produce the best evidence in his power.[5] It has been suggested that the court, upon request, may so instruct the jury.[6] When evidence of a party's refusal is admitted, obviously it becomes a proper subject of comment by counsel in his argument to the jury.[7]

104. *Admissibility of Privileged Matters*
for Purpose of Impeachment

The general rule is that, absent a waiver, evidence which would disclose confidential communications between physician and patient is no more admissible for the purpose of contradicting the testimony of the patient, or that of any witness who testifies in his

---

this State is that the plaintiff in an action of this kind [personal injury] cannot be required to submit to a physical examination as to his injuries, and it is but an evasion of that rule to permit the plaintiff to be required to state to the jury that he is not willing to submit to such an examination. To permit such a question to be asked in the presence of the jury practically compels him to submit to the examination because of the unfavorable effect likely to be produced upon the minds of the jury if he refuses."

[5] Union Pac. Ry. v. Botsford, (1891) 141 U. S. 250, 35 Law Ed. 734, 11 Su. Ct. 1000; Stack v. New York, N. Y. & H. R. R., (1900) 177 Mass. 155, 58 N. E. 686, 52 L. R. A. 328; Chicago, R. I. & Pac. Ry. v. Hill, (1913) 36 Okla. 540, 129 Pac. 13, 43 L. R. A. (n. s.) 622; Austin & N. W. R. R. v. Cluck, (1903) 97 Tex. 172, 77 S. W. 403, 64 L. R. A. 494, 1 Ann. Cas. 261.

[6] Cohen v. Philadelphia Rapid Transit Co., (1915) 250 Pa. 15, 95 Atl. 315, Ann. Cas. 1917 D 350.

Contra: Cornell v. Great Northern Ry., (1920) 57 Mont. 177, 187 Pac. 902.

[7] Choy v. Otaguro, (1932) 32 Hawaii 543; Stack v. New York, N. H. & H. R. R., (1900) 177 Mass. 155, 58 N. E. 686, 52 L. R. A. 328; Austin & N. W. R. R. v. Cluck, (1903) 97 Tex. 172, 77 S. W. 403, 64 L. R. A. 494, 1 Ann. Cas. 261.

In State v. Gatton, (1938) 60 Ohio App. 192, 20 N. E. 2d 265, defendant was charged with driving an automobile while intoxicated. After his arrest, request was made of him by a deputy sheriff that he submit to having either a blood test or a urinalysis made to determine the amount of alcohol in his system. Defendant refused to do either. At the trial, evidence showing the request was made and refused was admitted over defendant's objection; and in argument by the prosecutor the jury was urged to consider defendant's refusal as an inference of his guilt.

Held: the evidence was admissible and the argument permissible.

Contra: Duckworth v. State, (1957) _____ Okla. Cr. _____ , 309 P. 2d 1103. Accused refused to take an intoximeter test.

behalf, than for any other reason.[1] Such evidence is not made admissible because it will impeach[2] nor because it will operate to defeat falsehood.[3] The rule that evidence which is admissible for one purpose cannot be excluded simply because it is inadmissible for other purposes, does not apply, since the privilege statute prohibits its introduction for any purpose whatsoever.[4]

It will be remembered that not all information acquired by a physician is within the scope of the statutory privilege, but only that which was obtained during the relationship of physician and

---

[1] Arizona Copper Co. v. Garcia, (1923) 25 Ariz. 158, 214 Pac. 317. Plaintiff's brother testified that fragments of bone were removed from plaintiff's leg by a physician. Defendant offered to contradict that testimony by the testimony of the same physician, but was not permitted to do so.

Representative decisions which support the text are: Coca-Cola Bottling Co. v. Strather, (1936) 192 Ark. 999, 96 S. W. 2d 14; Missouri & N. Ark. R. R. v. Daniels, (1911) 98 Ark. 352, 136 S. W. 651; Holloway v. Kansas City (1914) 184 Mo. 19, 82 S. W. 89; Masson v. Metropolitan Life Ins. Co., (1931) 225 Mo. App. 925, 36 S. W. 2d 118; Noble v. Kansas City, (1902) 95 Mo. App. 167, 68 S. W. 969; McGinty v. Brotherhood of R. R. Trainmen, (1919) 169 Wis. 366, 172 N. W. 714.

In Cooley v. Davis, (1926) 221 Mo. App. 748, 286 S. W. 412, the physician's testimony was excluded not on the ground of privilege, but because it was directed to an immaterial fact.

In Heiman v. Market Street Ry., (1937) 21 Cal. App. 2d 311, 69 P. 2d 178, plaintiff's physician testified as to her injuries. Defendant was allowed to introduce in evidence plaintiff's hospital record signed by the physician which contradicted his testimony.

See also Ulm v. Moore-McCormick Lines, (1940) 115 F. 2d 492, 117 F. 2d 222, cert. denied 313 U. S. 567, 85 Law Ed. 1525, 61 Su. Ct. 941.

[2] Young v. McLaughlin, (1952) 126 Colo. 188, 247 P. 2d 813 (hospital record not admissible); Battis v. Chicago, R. I. & Pac. Ry., (1904) 124 Iowa 623, 100 N. W. 543. In Baker v. Industrial Comm'n., (1939) 135 Ohio St. 491, 21 N. E. 2d 593, the trial court permitted a question eliciting privileged information to be answered, but with an instruction to the jury that it could not be considered for any purpose except as tending to impeach the testimony of the plaintiff.

Held: error. It was not admissible for that or any other purpose.

[3] Donovan v. Donovan, (1941) 231 Iowa 14, 300 N. W. 656; Jacobs v. Cedar Rapids, (1917) 181 Iowa 407, 165 N. W. 891; Battis v. Chicago, R. I. & Pac. Ry., (1904) 124 Iowa 623, 100 N. W. 543; Finnegan v. Sioux City, (1900) 112 Iowa 232, 83 N. W. 907; McConnell v. Osage, (1890) 80 Iowa 293, 45 N. W. 550, 8 L. R. A. 778; Cohodes v. Menominee & M. L. & T. Co., (1912) 149 Wis. 308, 135 N. W. 879. Noelle v. Hoquiam Lumber & S. Co., (1907) 47 Wash. 519, 522, 92 Pac. 372: "The legislature made no exception to the rule of secrecy where it was necessary to contradict falsehood, but provided an exception only in case of consent of the patient."

See also Brammer v. Lappenbusch, (1934) 176 Wash. 625, 30 P. 2d 947.

[4] Rush v. Metropolitan Life Ins. Co., (1933) .... Mo. App......., 63 S. W. 2d 453.

patient,[5] and which was necessary to enable the physician to prescribe or act for the patient.[6] Hence, for the purpose of contradicting the testimony of the patient or any of his witnesses, the physician may be required to disclose any information he has acquired which is relevant and not within the ban of the statutory privilege.[7]

It need hardly be stated that if the patient waives his rights under the privilege, his physician may be required to disclose any relevant confidential information he may have acquired during his professional attendance. Although his testimony may contradict that of the patient and impeach the patient's credibility as a witness, it is nevertheless admissible.[8] Whether or not a waiver may be implied from the conduct of a party is a question not easily answered. There are widely disparate decisions on the subject.[9] However, the general rule is that where the patient voluntarily testifies in detail as to the nature and extent of his malady or injury and, in addition, discloses confidential communications between his physician and himself, he thereby abandons the protection of the privilege and surrenders his right to exclude the testimony of his physician on the same subject. Under such circumstances it is altogether fitting and just that the testimony of the physician be admitted for the purpose of impeaching the testimony and credibility of the patient or any of his witnesses, both professional and lay.[10]

---

[5] c. IX, herein.

[6] c. X, herein.

[7] State v. Lassieur, (1922) ....Mo........., 242 S. W. 900.

[8] McUne v. Fuqua, (1953) ....Wash........ , 253 P. 2d 632, 257 P. 2d 636.

[9] See c. XVIII, herein.

[10] Oliver v. Aylor, (1913) 173 Mo. App. 323, 328, 158 S. W. 733: "In our judgment, such waiver occurred by reason of the testimony of the plaintiff himself, and by the introduction of Dr. M as a witness in plaintiff's behalf. * * * In this, he opened wide the door, disclosing his version of what took place between himself and his physician and the condition of his injured hand. He had a right, under the statute, to have kept the information locked in the breast of himself and his physician; he had a right, also, to waive the privilege afforded by the statute and expose what could have been kept secret. Having elected on his part, voluntarily, to make such disclosure, it would, in our judgment, be unfair and contrary to all reason and justice to permit him to deny the defendant the right to show a different set of facts by the only other person who was in a position to know. * * * It will be noticed that the testimony offered

⫸→

105. Use of Memorandum or Record to Refresh Recollection of Medical Witness

Whenever, as the result of consent or waiver by the patient, or because the information sought to be elicited is not within the ban of the statutory privilege, a physician[1] is a competent witness, he, like any other witness, may make use of a memorandum, an office or hospital record, or other written aid to revive or refresh his memory. It would be asking too much to expect that he could keep every detail of his professional activities clear in his memory over an extended period of time. Called to testify as to the existence or nonexistence of a fact, the physician may be able to recall the fact by an effort of memory, and state the fact truthfully as of memory. On the other hand, he may not be able to recall the fact clearly; yet his memory may be stimulated and lighted up by the use of some memorandum or record. If then he is able to speak to the existence of the fact—independent of the memorandum or record—as of his own personal recollection, he is competent and will be permitted to testify. Ordinarily, the rule is that any memorandum or record, no matter when or by whom made or under what circumstances, is eligible for use as an aid to memory, if it reasonably appears that it does revive the present recollection of the witness.[2] In *People* v.

---

to be given by Dr. C does not open any new secret, or go into any other field with reference to what occurred or what did not occur from that which was disclosed by the plaintiff and Dr. M. The offer of Dr. C's testimony tended only to show a contradiction of a state of facts which had been gone into by the plaintiff and Dr. M. * * * There was reversible error in excluding the testimony of Dr. C."

[1] Or any other medical witness; *e. g.,* a nurse, interne, diagnostician, pathologist.

[2] *In re* Flint, (1893) 100 Cal. 391, 34 Pac. 863 (nurse's notes); Hall v. Sera, (1930) 112 Conn. 291, 152 Atl. 148; Smith Electric Co. v. Hinkley, (1929) 98 Fla. 132, 123 So. 564 (nurse's notes); Wright v. Upson, (1922) 303 Ill. 120, 135 N. E. 209 (nurse's notes); Willits v. Chicago, B. & Q. R. R., (1920) ....Mo........, 221 S. W. 65 (physician's notes); Whitely v. Stein, (1931) ....Mo. App........, 34 S. W. 2d 998 (hospital record); Fries v. Goldsby, (1956) 163 Neb. 424, 80 N. W. 2d 171 (chiropractor's records); State v. Fletcher, (1917) 90 N. J. L. 722, 101 Atl. 181 (physician's notes); State v. Shapiro, (1916) 89 N. J. L. 319, 98 Atl. 437 (nurse's chart); State v. Collins, (1881) 15 S. C. 373; Browning v. Hoffman, (1922) 90 W. Va. 568, 111 S. E. 492 (nurse's chart).

For discussions of the rule, see 3 Wigmore, Evidence, §§ 758-765; 5 Am. Jur., *Witnesses,* §§ 578-587; note, 125 A. L. R. 19.

Vann,[3] the defendant was convicted of raping a girl under 16 years of age. Called as a witness by the state, the physician, who had attended the mother at the birth of the child, was permitted to refresh his memory as to the date of the birth by an entry in his cash book, and to testify thereto.

As a general rule, the memorandum or record may not be used on direct examination as independent evidence of the facts recited therein, since it is the present recollection of the witness, not the memorandum or record, which is the evidence.[4] Ordinarily it is not necessary that the witness first exhaust his memory as to the details before making use of a memorandum or record to refresh his recollection.[5] The matter of refreshing a witness' memory rests very largely in the discretion of the trial judge and, if it does not appear he abused his discretion, his action will not justify a reversal of the judgment.[6]

Opposing counsel has the right to inspect the memorandum or record used by the witness to refresh his memory,[7] and may introduce it in evidence if it is to his advantage to do so.[8] It should be noted also that the use of a written aid to memory by the holder of a testimonial privilege may result in a waiver of its protection.[9]

---

[3] (1900) 129 Cal. 118, 61 Pac. 776. See also State v. Bowman, (1917) 272 Mo. 491, 199 S. W. 161; State v. Palmberg, (1906) 199 Mo. 233, 97 S. W. 566; State v. Hammond, (1915) 46 Utah 249, 148 Pac. 420.

[4] Baird v. Reilly, (1899) 92 Fed. 884 (hospital record); *In re* Flint, (1893) 100 Cal. 391, 34 Pac. 863 (nurse's bedside notes); Willitts v. Chicago, B. & Q. R. R., (1920) _____ Mo._____, 221 S. W. 65 (physician's notes); Russell v. Hudson River R. R., (1858) 17 N. Y. 134 (physician's notes); Armstrong v. Travelers Ins. Co., (1914) 4 Ohio App. 46, 22 Ohio C. C. R. (n. s.) 129 (autopsical report); People v. Matos, (1918) 26 P. R. R. 520 (autopsical report); Fries v. Goldsby, (1956) 163 Neb. 424, 80 N. W. 2d 171.

[5] Weis v. Weis, (1947) 147 Ohio St. 416, 72 N. E. 2d 245, 169 A. L. R. 668 (nurse's use of hospital chart).

[6] Winn v. Modern Woodmen O. A., (1911) 157 Mo. App. 1, 137 S. W. 292.

[7] Richardson v. Nassau Electric R. R., (1920) 190 App. Div. 529, 180 N. Y. S. 109 (notes used by plaintiff's medical expert); State v. Deslovers, (1917) 40 R. I. 89, 100 Atl. 64 (physician's autopsical notes). Cf. State v. Collins, (1881) 15 S. C. 373.

[8] Consult textual authorities cited in note 2, infra.

[9] Hill v. Hill, (1940) 106 Colo. 492, 107 P. 2d 597. The plaintiff used letters written by her to her lawyer to refresh her recollection and it was held that she thereby impliedly gave consent to their introduction in evidence and waived the privilege.

CHAPTER XVI

Waiver of the Privilege

106. Introductory

Practically all legal subjects, to a greater or less degree, are affected by the doctrine of waiver.[1] A general discussion of the doctrine is obviously outside the scope of this treatise; hence, it will be considered only as it affects the statutory rule of privilege concerning communications between physician and patient.

In the early years of the privilege, the legislatures apparently gave little or no consideration to the subject of waiver. Some of the statutes, by implication, permit the patient to consent to the disclosure of privileged matters, or expressly grant him the right to

---

[1] See general discussion of the doctrine, 56 Am. Jur., *Waiver*, §§ 1-24.

waive the rights conferred;[2] but no provision was made for waiver by other persons. Even today, in fourteen jurisdictions, the statute contains no provision whatever for waiver of the privilege;[3] moreover, some statutes are couched in the language of a prohibition, not in terms of privilege.[4] With this lamentable situation facing them, and, perhaps, because of the ever-increasing antipathy towards the privilege itself, a number of courts have resorted to liberal and, sometimes, dubious interpretations to get around the plain letter of the statute, thereby engrafting upon it waivers which the legislatures have not seen fit to expressly authorize.[5] But judicial decisions—and their number is legion—have not entirely solved the various problems of waiver, particularly since the force and effect of these have frequently been lessened by persuasive dissenting opinions.

To correct the palpable deficiencies in the statutes, a number of legislatures, in more recent years, have amended them by granting to designated classes and persons the right to waive, by fixing the time and prescribing the manner in which waivers may be made, and by specifying acts and conduct which constitute waiver of the privilege by the patient himself, or, if he be dead, by others purporting to act in his stead.[6]

---

[2] *e. g.,* Iowa, Mississippi, Nebraska, New York, Ohio, Wisconsin, Wyoming.
See Appendix, herein.

[3] Alaska, Idaho, Indiana, Missouri, Montana, North Carolina (the presiding judge may waive) ,Philippine Islands, Utah, Virgin Islands, Washington, West Virginia, New Zealand, Quebec, Victoria (Australia). See Appendix, herein.

[4] *e. g.,* Indiana, Kansas, Missouri, Oklahoma.
See Appendix, herein.

[5] Epstein v. Pennsylvania R. R., (1913) 250 Mo. 1, 21, 156 S. W. 699, 48 L. R. A. (n. s.) 394, Ann. Cas. 1915 A. 423: "It will not avail to say that we are bound to a hard-and-fast construction of our statute—that it is to us an iron-bound law of the Medes and Persians, eternally unchangeable—and that we cannot by construction engraft upon it a single abatement in jot or tittle, by invoking the doctrine of waiver, because, forsooth, there are no waivers or provisos therein expressly written. We have, as has every civilized court where the statute exists, already engrafted, by construction, waivers upon it, which are now so well-settled as not to admit of question or quibble."

[6] These will be discussed in appropriate sections which follow.

107. Proof of Waiver: In General

Waiver has been variously defined. Generally speaking, waiver is a voluntary relinquishment or renunciation of some right, a foregoing or giving up of some benefit or advantage, which, but for such waiver, a party would have enjoyed.[1] It may be proved by declarations, but an express statement of an intention to waive is not necessary.[2] It need not be in writing nor in any particular form.[3] Unquestionably, waiver may be *implied* as well as express[4] and be proved by acts and declarations manifesting an intent and purpose not to claim the supposed advantage; or by a course of acts and conduct, or by so neglecting and failing to act, as to induce the belief that it was the party's intention and purpose to waive.[5] Furthermore, if the party's conduct is such as to amount to waiver, it will

---

[1] Farlow v. Ellis, (1860) 15 Gray (Mass) 229. Andrews v. Washington National Ins. Co., (1936) _____Mo. App. _____, 93 S. W. 2d 1045, 1046: "According to the generally accepted definition, a waiver is the intentional relinquishment of a known right. It is a voluntary act, and implies an election by the party to dispense with something of value or to forego some advantage which he might at his option have demanded and insisted upon. To constitute a waiver of an existing right, benefit, or advantage, knowledge of its existence and an intention to relinquish it are essential."

[2] Eder v. Cashin, (1953) 281 App. Div. 456, 120 N. Y. S. 2d 165.

[3] Holcomb v. Harris, (1901) 166 N. Y. 257, 59 N. E. 820; Eder v. Cashin, (1953) 281 App. Div. 456, 120 N. Y. S. 2d 165.

[4] Buckminster's Estate v. Commissioner of Internal Revenue, (1944) 147 F. 2d 331; Munzer v. Swedish American Line, (1940) 35 F. Supp. 493; Lissak v. Crocker Estate Co., (1897) 119 Cal. 442, 51 Pac. 688; Moreno v. New Guadalupe Mining Co., (1918) 35 Cal. App. 744, 170 Pac. 1088; Burgess v. Sims Drug Co., (1901) 114 Iowa 275, 86 N. W. 307, 54 L. R. A. 364; Epstein v. Pennsylvania R. R., (1913) 250 Mo. 1, 156 S. W. 699, 48 L. R. A. (n. s.) 394, Ann. Cas. 1915 A. 423; Oliver v. Aylor, (1913) 173 Mo. App. 323, 158 S. W. 733; Holcomb v. Harris, (1901) 166 N. Y. 257, 59 N. E. 820; Speck v. International Ry., (1909) 133 App. Div. 802, 118 N. Y. S. 71; Pringle v. Burroughs, (1902) 70 App. Div. 12, 74 N. Y. S. 1055, aff'd. 100 App. Div. 366, 91 N. Y. S. 750, 185 N. Y. 375, 78 N. E. 150; Marx v. Manhattan Ry., (1890) 56 Hun 575, 10 N. Y. S. 159; McUne v. Fuqua, (1953) _____Wash._____, 253 P. 2d 632, 257 P. 2d 636. See also 8 Wigmore, Evidence, § 2388.

The Puerto Rico privilege statute provides that when the court finds as an inference from proper evidence that the consent mentioned in the statute has been given or implied, it may admit the evidence. It has been held that a patient's lack of understanding of his rights under the statutory privilege is a bar to any waiver. Coca-Cola Bottling Works v. Simpson, (1930) 158 Miss. 390, 130 So. 479, 72 A. L. R. 143.

[5] Farlow v. Ellis, (1860) 15 Gray (Mass.) 229.

be so held notwithstanding his express protest,[6] or mental reservation.[7] Ordinarily, to make out a case of implied waiver, there must be a distinct and unequivocal act indicating an intention to waive,[8] or else the acts or conduct relied on as constituting a waiver must involve some element of estoppel.[9]

It is plain that waiver should not be applied to every case mechanically and without reference to the facts, but with just discrimination and in view of the particular facts and circumstances of each case.[10] What will constitute a waiver of the privilege given to the patient is not always specified and must, therefore, be determined as a question of fact in each case from the acts and conduct of the patient, or of the holder of the privilege.[11] Usually the question of waiver is one for the court,[12] but where the facts upon which the alleged waiver is founded are in dispute, some courts have submitted the question to the jury.[13] The party who asserts that waiver

---

[6] Armstrong v. Topeka Ry., (1914) 93 Kan. 493, 144 Pac. 847.

In Marx v. Manhattan Ry., (1890) 56 Hun 575, 10 N. Y. S. 159, so far from a disclaimer of his privilege, the patient strenuously claimed it on the trial; but, contrary to his protest, the court raised a presumption of waiver.

[8] Wigmore, Evidence, § 2327: "A privileged person would seldom be found to waive, if his intention not to abandon could alone control the situation. There is always also the objective consideration that when his conduct touches a certain point of disclosure, fairness requires that his immunity shall cease, whether he intended that result or not. He cannot be allowed, after disclosing as much as he pleases, to withhold the remainder. He may elect to withhold or to disclose, but after a certain point, his election must remain final."

[7] Morris v. New York, Ontario & W. Ry., (1895) 148 N. Y. 88, 95, 42 N. E. 410: "When the plaintiff in this case called one of the physicians who disclosed the whole consultation, the law determined the legal effect of that act, irrespective of any mental reservation on her part."

[ə] Packard v. Coberly, (1928) 147 Wash. 345, 265 Pac. 1082. See also 56 Am. Jur., *Waiver*, § 17.

[ɔ] Fitzgerald v. Metropolitan Life Ins. Co., (1941) .... Mo. App. ...., 149 S. W. 2d 389.

[10] Epstein v. Pennsylvania R. R., (1913) 250 Mo. 1, 39, 156 S. W. 699, 48 L. R. A. (n. s.) 394, Ann. Cas. 1915 A. 423: "So used it is constantly applied in court as a most wholesome and useful device in reaching a just end."

[11] Rauh v. Deutscher Verein, (1898) 29 App. Div. 483, 51 N. Y. S. 985. Questions of this kind will be discussed in subsequent sections.

[12] Espenlaub v. State, (1936) 210 Ind. 687, 2 N. E. 2d 979; Burke v. Chicago & N. W. Ry., (1915) 131 Minn. 209, 154 N. W. 960.

[13] Metropolitan Life Ins. Co. v. Fitzgerald, (1919) 137 Ark. 366, 209 S. W. 77; Andrews

⤖

has taken place, has the burden of proof to show it.[14] But where the conduct of the holder of the privilege plainly shows a waiver of it, the adverse party is under no duty to declare that he intends to rely upon such waiver.[15]

It is generally conceded that the doctrine of waiver, as it affects the physician-patient privilege, does not conflict with any principle of public policy.[16]

108. Mode, Time, and Place of Waiver: The New York Statute

As a general rule, waiver, whether express or implied from conduct, may take place before or at the trial. In New York, prior to 1891, the privilege could be waived before trial.[1] Until then, the provisions relating to waiver were general and the only requirement was that it should be an express waiver, without regard to time or place. In 1891 and subsequent thereto, the legislature amended the statute. As it now stands, the privilege must be expressly waived upon the trial or examination, and must be made "in open court."[2] This requirement applies to the patient or, if he

---

←※

v. Washington National Ins. Co., (1936) ......Mo. App........, 93 S. W. 2d 1045.

See also 56 Am. Jur., *Waiver*, § 23.

14 Andrews v. Washington National Ins. Co., (1936) ......Mo. App........, 93 S. W. 2d 1045. See also 56 Am. Jur., *Waiver*, § 22.

15 Holcomb v. Harris, (1901) 166 N. Y. 257, 59 N. E. 820. *cf.,* Posner v. New York Life Ins. Co., (1940) 56 Ariz. 202, 106 P. 2d 488.

16 Adraveno v. Mutual Res. Fund Life Ass'n., (1888) 34 Fed. 870; Metropolitan Life Ins. Co. v. Brubaker, (1908) 78 Kan. 146, 96 Pac. 62, 18 L. R. A. (n. s.) 362, 16 Ann. Cas. 267; Grand Rapids & Ind. R. R. v. Martin, (1879) 41 Mich. 667, 3 N. W. 173; Epstein v. Pennsylvania R. R., (1913) 250 Mo. 1, 156 S. W. 699, 48 L. R. A. (n. s.) 394, Ann. Cas. 1915 A. 423; Keller v. Home Life Ins. Co., (1902) 95 Mo. App. 627, 69 S. W. 612; Matter of Elizabeth Cashman, (1939) 159 Misc. 881, 289 N. Y. S. 328, aff'd. 280 N. Y. 681, 21 N. E. 2d 193 (doctrine limited); New York Life Ins. Co. v. Snyder, (1927) 116 Ohio St. 693, 158 N. E. 176, 54 A. L. R. 406.

For interesting discussion of the privilege in Quebec, see Mutual Life Ins. Co. v. dame Jeannotte-Lamarche, [1935] Quebec Rep. 59 K. B. 510.

1 Foley v. Royal Arcanum, (1896) 151 N. Y. 196, 45 N. E. 456.

2 (1956) N. Y. *Civ. Prac. Act,* § 354. See Appendix, herein. The Minnesota statute, in actions to recover insurance benefits, is somewhat similar in this respect. See Appendix, herein.

be dead, to his personal representative who may act in his stead.[3]
Moreover, "a paper executed by a party prior to the trial providing
for such waiver shall be insufficient as such a waiver,"[4] except that
the attorneys for the respective parties, prior to trial, may stipulate
for such a waiver and this will be sufficient therefor.

The statute does not specify what shall constitute a waiver or
how it shall be manifested.[5] As interpreted by the courts, the phrase
"expressly waived" does not mean that the waiver must be formally
made, either orally or in writing, but the intent to waive must be
expressed either by word or act or omission to speak or act. In other
words, an express waiver of the privilege *may be implied* from the
conduct of the patient, or his personal representative, or from proceedings which he has taken or has allowed others to take.[6]

The examination of witnesses without the state upon a commission is a portion of the trial of the action; hence, the privilege
can be waived before a referee.[7] Where an application for discovery
before trial is denied on the ground of privilege, the court upon
the trial will be free to decide whether the proof offered by a party
constitutes a waiver and will allow reasonable time and opportunity
to the adverse party, in the event a waiver results, to subpoena and
examine the attending physician; also to produce the hospital

---

[3] Waiver by the personal representative is a limited one. See § 116, herein.

[4] See § 109, herein.

[5] Steinberg v. New York Life Ins. Co., (1933) 263 N. Y. 45, 188 N. E. 152, 90 A. L. R. 642.

[6] Cases of this kind will be discussed in appropriate sections of this chapter, but the
following are sufficient, for the present, to support the text: Apter v. Home Life Ins.
Co., (1935) 266 N. Y. 333, 194 N. E. 846, 98 A. L. R. 1281; Steinberg v. New York Life
Ins. Co., (1933) 263 N. Y. 45, 188 N. E. 152, 90 A. L. R. 642; Hethier v. Johns, (1922)
233 N. Y. 370, 135 N. E. 603; People v. Bloom, (1908) 193 N. Y. 1, 85 N. E. 824, 18 L. R.
A. (n. s.) 898, 15 Ann. Cas. 932; Capron v. Douglass, (1908) 193 N. Y. 11, 85 N. E. 827,
20 L. R. A. (n. s.) 1003; Holcomb v. Harris, (1901) 166 N. Y. 257, 59 N. E. 820; Morris
v. New York, Ontario & W. Ry., (1895) 148 N. Y. 88, 42 N. E. 410.

[7] Murray v. Physical Culture Hotel, Inc., (1939) 258 App. Div. 334, 16 N. Y. S. 2d 978,
aff'd. 17 N. Y. S. 2d 862; Fortang v. Alpert, (1939) 256 App. Div. 949, 10 N. Y. S. 2d
291; *In re* Ackerman's Estate, (1937) 163 Misc. 624, 298 N. Y. S. 38. See also Munzer v.
Swedish American Line, (1940) 35 F. Supp. 493; Scolavino v. State, (1946) 187 Misc.
253, 62 N. Y. S. 2d 17, 271 App. Div. 618, 67 N. Y. S. 2d 202, aff'd. 297 N. Y. 460, 74
N. E. 2d 174.

records of the patient as they may become material to the issue tendered.[8]

Where the patient, in an action to recover disability benefits, alleged in his complaint that he is afflicted with a heart ailment and that such allegation is the foundation of his causes of action, it is not a waiver of the privilege, since this can only be accomplished in open court on the trial, or by stipulation.[9]

109. *Anticipatory Waiver by Contract*

In numerous cases the courts have been called upon to determine the validity of an anticipatory waiver by contract, particularly the validity and effect of a statement or stipulation in a policy of life, accident, or health insurance, or in an application made therefor, waiving in advance all provisions of law prohibiting a physician, or nurse, who has attended the patient, from disclosing any knowledge or information acquired thereby.[1]

Practically all courts—except those of three jurisdictions which are affected by particular provisions of the statute on the subject—recognize that the waiver by an applicant for an insurance policy, either in his application or in the policy itself, of the disqualification of his physician or nurse to testify concerning confidential communications or information, is valid and binding upon the insured and those claiming an interest in the insurance contract.[2]

---

[8] Rubin v. Equitable Life Assur. Soc., (1945) 269 App. Div. 677, 53 N. Y. S. 2d 351; Lorde v. Guardian Life Ins. Co., (1937) 252 App. Div. 646, 300 N. Y. S. 721; Jaffe v. New York, (1949) 196 Misc. 710, 94 N. Y. S. 2d 60; LaPlante v. Garrett, (1953) 282 App. Div. 1096, 126 N. Y. S. 2d 470. Permission to appeal denied 130 N. Y. S. 2d 910.

[9] Rubin v. Equitable Life Assur. Soc., (1945) 269 App. Div. 677, 53 N. Y. S. 2d 351.

[1] The language of the statement or stipulation varies. For examples, see § 110, herein, notes 9, 10, 11, 12, 13, 14.

[2] Lutz v. New England Mutual Life Ins. Co., (1946) 161 F. 2d 833; New York Life Ins. Co. v. Taylor, (1945) 147 F. 2d 297, 79 App. D. C. 66, 158 F. 2d 328; Wirthlin v. Mutual Life Ins. Co., (1932) 56 F. 2d 137, 86 A. L. R. 138; Lincoln National Life Ins. Co. v. Hammer, (1930) 41 F. 2d 12; Adreveno v. Mutual Res. Fund. Life Ass'n., (1888) 34 Fed. 870; Adamos v. New York Life Ins. Co., (1937) 22 F. Supp. 162, aff'd. 94 F. 2d 943; Posner v. New York Life Ins. Co., (1940) 56 Ariz. 202, 106 P. 2d 488; Progressive Life Ins. Co. v. Hulbert, (1938) 196 Ark. 352, 118 S. W. 2d 268; Wooten v. Wooten, (1928) 176 Ark. 1174, 5 S. W. 2d 340; National Annuity Ass'n. v. McCall, (1912) 103 Ark. 201, 146 S. W. 125, 48 L. R. A. (n. s.) 418; Turner v. Redwood Mutual Life Ass'n.,

➢➢➢→

A waiver is not against public policy,[3] and its enforcement is not a violation of the terms or spirit of the privilege statute.[4] The pur-

---

(1936) 13 Cal. App. 2d 573, 57 P. 2d 222; Murphy v. Mutual Life Ins. Co., (1941) 62 Idaho 362, 112 P. 2d 993; Trull v. Modern Woodmen O. A., (1906) 12 Idaho 318, 85 Pac. 1081, 10 Ann. Cas. 53; Metropolitan Life Ins. Co. v. Willis, (1906) 37 Ind. App. 48, 76 N. E. 560; Miser v. Iowa State Trav. Men's Ass'n., (1937) 223 Iowa 662, 273 N. W. 155; Pride v. Inter-State Business Mens Acc. Ass'n., (1928) 207 Iowa 167, 216 N. W. 62, 62 A. L. R. 31; Metropolitan Life Ins. Co. v. Brubaker, (1908) 78 Kan. 146, 96 Pac. 62, 18 L. R. A. (n. s.) 362, 16 Ann. Cas. 267; New York Life Ins. Co. v. Burris, (1936) 174 Miss. 658, 165 So. 116; Sovereign Camp W. of W. v. Farmer, (1917) 116 Miss. 626, 77 So. 655; Cromeenes v. Sovereign Camp, W. of W., (1920) 205 Mo. App. 419, 224 S. W. 15; Hicks v. Metropolitan Life Ins. Co., (1916) 196 Mo. App. 162, 190 S. W. 661; Modern Woodmen O. A. v. Angle, (1907) 127 Mo. App. 94, 104 S. W. 297; Keller v. Home Life Ins. Co., (1902) 95 Mo. App. 627, 69 S. W. 612; Allen v. Massachusetts Mutual Life Ins. Co., (1948) 149 Neb. 233, 30 N. W. 2d 885; George v. Guarantee Mutual Life Co., (1944) 144 Neb. 285, 13 N. W. 2d 176; Willis v. Order of Railroad Telegraphers, (1941) 139 Neb. 46, 296 N. W. 443; Wolski v. National Life & Acc. Ins. Co., (1939) 135 Neb. 643, 283 N. W. 381; Falkinberg v. Prudential Ins. Co., (1937) 132 Neb. 831, 273 N. W. 478; Bryant v. Modern Woodmen O. A., (1910) 86 Neb. 372, 125 N. W. 621, 27 L. R. A. (n. s.) 326, 21 Ann. Cas. 365; Western Travelers' Acc. Ass'n. v. Munson, (1905) 73 Neb. 858, 103 N. W. 688, 1 L. R. A. (n. s.) 1068; Fuller v. Knights of Pythias, (1901) 129 N. C. 318, 40 So. 65; New York Life Ins. Co. v. Snyder, (1927) 116 Ohio St. 693, 158 N. E. 176, 54 A. L. R. 406; Templeton v. Mutual Life Ins. Co., (1936) 177 Okla. 94, 57 P. 2d 841; National Life & Acc. Ins. Co. v. Roberson, (1934) 169 Okla. 136, 36 P. 2d 479; Oklahoma Protective Ass'n. v. Montgomery, (1932) 160 Okla. 135, 16 P. 2d 135; Hassing v. Mutual Life Ins. Co., (1945) 108 Utah 198, 159 P. 2d 117.

    See note, 54 A. L. R. 412.

    Rule 37 of the Uniform Rules of Evidence (1953) provides: "A person who would otherwise have a privilege to refuse to disclose or to prevent another from disclosing a specified matter has no such privilege with respect to that matter if the judge finds that he or any other person while the holder of the privilege has (a) contracted with anyone not to claim the privilege, * * *."

    See 8 Wigmore, Evidence, § 2388(b).

    See also note, Waiver Clauses in Insurance Applications, (1937) 16 N. C. L. Rev. 53.

    The principle has also been applied to a contract of employment.

    In Fornea v. Goodyear Yellow Pine Co., (1938) 181 Miss. 50, 178 So. 914, a personal injury case, it appears that when the plaintiff entered the employ of the defendant, he executed a waiver of the benefits and protection of the privilege statute. It was held that the waiver was valid and that the attending physician of the plaintiff could testify, at the instance of the defendant, to the plaintiff's physical condition.

[3] See § 107, herein. However, as pointed out later, the courts of Michigan are opposed to this view.

[4] New York Life Ins. Co. v. Snyder, (1927) 116 Ohio St. 693, 702 158 N. E. 176, 54 A. L. R. 406: "To hold otherwise would be to open wide the doors of both fraud and suicide with respect to the procuring of life insurance policies, and it would jeopardize the soundness and safety of life insurance in general."

pose of the waiver is to remove the prohibition of the privilege statute and to permit the physician, or nurse, to testify. It places the medical witness on a parity with any other witness and makes him or her competent to testify.[5] Usually, the waiver is broad enough to exempt the insured's hospital record from the ban of the statute.[6] The benefits of the waiver are equally as available to the beneficiary as to the insurer.[7]

In two states, however, an anticipatory waiver of the privilege by the patient is invalid. As previously stated,[8] the New York statute requires that the waiver be made in open court on the trial of the action and it expressly states that a paper executed by a party prior to the trial providing for such waiver is insufficient as such a waiver. It is plain, therefore, that, in the courts of New York, a stipulation waiving the privilege made by the insured in an application for insurance, or contained in the policy itself, is void and of no effect.[9] In Michigan, the Supreme Court has held that the language of the privilege statute clearly expresses the legislative intent to prohibit, *as a matter of public policy,* anticipatory waivers which are to become operative after the death of the patient. An applicant for insurance, therefore, cannot lawfully waive in advance the benefits and protection of the statutory privilege.[10] In Minnesota, antic-

---

[5] Allen v. Massachusetts Mutual Life Ins. Co., (1848) 149 Neb. 233, 30 N. W. 2d 885.

[6] Murphy v. Mutual Life Ins. Co., (1941) 62 Idaho 362, 112 P. 2d 993; Russell v. Missouri Ins. Co., (1950) _____ Mo. App._____, 232 S. W. 2d 812; Mack v. Western & Southern Life Ins. Co., (1932) _____ Mo. App. _____, 53 S. W. 2d 1108. *Cf.* National Life & Acc. Ins. Co. v. Threlkeld, (1934) 189 Ark. 165, 70 S. W. 2d 851.

In Progressive Life Ins. Co. v. Hulbert, (1938) 196 Ark. 352, 118 S. W. 2d 268, the waiver specifically included hospital records.

[7] Trull v. Modern Woodmen O. A., (1906) 12 Idaho 318, 85 Pac. 1081, 10 Ann. Cas. 53; Miser v. Iowa State Trav. Men's Ass'n, (1937) 223 Iowa 662, 272 N. W. 155.

[8] § 108, herein.

[9] Supreme Lodge, K. of P. v. Meyer, (1904) 198 U. S. 508, 49 Law Ed. 1146, 25 Su. Ct. 754; Holden v. Metropolitan Life Ins. Co., (1900) 165 N. Y. 13, 58 N. E. 771.

[10] Gilchrist v. Mystic Workers of the World, (1915) 188 Mich. 466, 154 N. W. 575, Ann. Cas. 1918 C 757. A new trial was granted on other grounds and the question was again considered in Gilchrist v. Mystic Workers of the World, (1917) 196 Mich. 247, 163 N. W. 10. The court reaffirmed its earlier decision relative to the insured's waiver of the privilege. Some doubt was cast upon the Michigan law, as pronounced in the Gilchrist cases, by a decision of the federal Court of Appeals in Lawrence v.

⟫→

ipatory waivers by patients are not prohibited generally; however, the privilege statute expressly provides that *in an action to recover insurance benefits* no oral or written waiver of the privilege has any binding force or effect except that the same be made upon the trial where the evidence is offered or received.[11]

110. *Effect of Waiver in Insurance Contract*

Even though a waiver clause in a contract of insurance, or in the application therefor, is valid, there may still remain the question as to its meaning and effect. It stands to reason, of course, that if insurance companies desire to secure from their policy holders a waiver of so important a right as that granted by the privilege statute, it should be accomplished by a formal stipulation too plain and direct to be misunderstood.[1] Under well-known principles of law, any doubts or ambiguities emanating from the language upon which the asserted waiver is based must be resolved in favor of the insured or his beneficiary.[2] A stipulation in a policy, or in an application therefor, authorizing any physician or other person who has attended the insured to disclose to the insurance company any information thus acquired does not in any way refer to the statutory privilege since the statute relates only to the giving of testimony; therefore, the ban of the statute is not waived either directly or by implication.[3] And where one, in an application for insurance, has

---

Connecticut Mutual Life Ins. Co., (1937) 91 F. 2d 381. This doubt, however, appears to have been dispelled by the later decision of the Supreme Court of Michigan in Wohlfeil v. Bankers Life Co., (1941) 296 Mich. 310, 296 N. W. 269. See also Miller v. Pacific Mutual Life Ins. Co., (1953) 116 F. Supp. 365, aff'd 228 F. 2d 889, for a discussion of the Michigan cases.

[11] (1947) Minn. Stat. Ann. § 595.02. See Appendix, herein. See also Sorenson v. New York Life Ins. Co., (1935) 195 Minn. 298, 262 N. W. 868; Palmer v. Order of United Commercial Travelers, (1932) 187 Minn. 272, 245 N. W. 146.

[1] Masonic Mutual Ben. Ass'n v. Beck, (1881) 77 Ind. 203. See also note, 54 A. L. R. 412.

[2] Turner v. Redwood Mutual Life Ass'n, (1936) 13 Cal. App. 2d 573, 57 P. 2d 222; Noble v. United Ben. Life Ins. Co., (1941) 230 Iowa 471, 297 N. W. 881; Pride v. Inter-State Business Men's Acc. Ass'n, (1928) 207 Iowa 167, 216 N. W. 62, 62 A. L. R. 31; Geare v. United States Life Ins. Co., (1896) 66 Minn. 91, 68 N. W. 731.

[3] Noble v. United Ben. Life Ins. Co., (1941) 230 Iowa 471, 297 N. W. 881; Laury v. Northwestern Mutual Life Ins. Co., (1930) 180 Minn. 205, 214, 230 N. W. 648, 231

merely referred to a physician for the purpose of verifying his statements as to his condition of health, this cannot be construed as a waiver which will permit the insurer to examine the insured's physician in an action brought by the beneficiary of the policy.[4]

A provision in a policy of health and accident insurance requiring the insured, as a condition precedent to any liability of the insurer, to furnish it with a report in writing from the attending physician does not constitute a waiver of the privilege.[5] But where an industrial life insurance policy provided that "the company shall have the right at its option to make such investigation into matters upon which any claim may be based or the subject thereof as it may deem necessary in order to determine its liability," it was held that such provision constitutes a waiver by the insured of his rights under the statutory privilege.[6]

A clause in an industrial life insurance policy which provides that "proofs of death under this policy shall be made upon blanks to be furnished by the company and shall contain answers to each

---

N. W. 824: "The permission the insured gave in the application for physicians whom he had consulted to disclose facts to defendant should be construed to mean to disclose them if defendant sought to obtain such information prior to and as a basis upon which to accept the application and issue the policy."

See also Briesenmeister v. Supreme Lodge, K. of P., (1890) 81 Mich. 525, 45 N. W. 977, 8 L. R. A. 682; Moutzoukos v. Mutual Benefit, H. & Acc. Ass'n, (1927) 69 Utah 309, 254 Pac. 1005.

Contra: George v. Guarantee Mutual Life Ins. Co., (1944) 144 Neb. 285, 13 N. W. 2d 176; Oklahoma Protective Ass'n v. Montgomery, (1932) 160 Okla. 135, 16 P. 2d 135. See also Turner v. Redwood Mutual Life Ass'n, (1936) 13 Cal. App. 2d 573, 57 P. 2d 222.

[4] Masonic Mutual Ben. Ass'n v. Beck, (1881) 77 Ind. 203; Novak v. Chicago Fraternal Life Ass'n, (1932) 136 Kan. 609, 16 P. 2d 507; Edington v. Mutual Life Ins. Co., (1875) 5 Hun 1, rev'd on other grounds (1876) 67 N. Y. 185.

Robinson v. Supreme Commandery, (1902) 38 Misc. 97, 105, 77 N. Y. S. 111, 77 App. Div. 215, 79 N. Y. S. 13, aff'd (1904) 177 N. Y. 564, 69 N. E. 1130: "In this case the physician is named as one of whom the defendant might inquire as to the health of the applicant, before accepting the risk. Not availing itself of this offer it cannot claim to do so at the trial. If such were the correct construction, the applicant would have been innocently entrapped into the waiver of a privilege of whose existence he may have been ignorant." Of course, under the New York statute as amended, any waiver in an application for insurance is void. See § 109, herein.

[5] Provident Life & Acc. Ins. Co. v. Jemison, (1929) 153 Miss. 60, 120 So. 836.

[6] Wolski v. National Life & Acc. Ins. Co., (1939) 135 Neb. 643, 283 N. W. 381.

question propounded to" the physicians, was held to constitute a waiver of the privilege by the insured and renders the physician a competent witness as to confidential disclosures made to him by the insured.[7] In another case, however, it was held that such provision does not constitute a waiver since it discloses no intent to waive the privilege, for the insured might well have believed that the proofs of death would relate to nothing else than the fact of death.[8]

In a number of cases, the question has arisen as to whether an express stipulation for waiver applies not only to communications made to, or information acquired by, the physician *at the time of or prior to* its execution, but also to privileged matters knowledge of which was acquired by the physician *after* its execution. Most courts apparently have decided the question without giving much, if any, consideration to the exact wording of the clause or to the time when the communications were made or the information was obtained. It should be noted, however, that some of the clauses merely waive the benefits of the privilege without regard to the time when the physician acquired his knowledge of the patient's condition of health.[9] Others plainly authorize the physician to testify concerning the health and condition of the insured, past, present, or future.[10]

---

[7] *Ibid.* See also Western Travelers Acc. Ass'n v. Munson, (1905) 73 Neb. 858, 103 N. W. 688, 1 L. R. A. (n. s.) 1068.

[8] Frazier v.Metropolitan Life Ins. Co., (1911) 161 Mo. App. 709, 141 S. W. 936. See also Hicks v. Metropolitan Life Ins. Co., (1916) 196 Mo. App. 162, 190 S. W. 661.

[9] Clauses of this kind, with slight variations, generally provide:

> "I further waive for myself and beneficiaries the privileges and benefits of any and all laws which are now in force or may hereafter be enacted in regard to disqualifying any physician from testifying concerning any information obtained by him in a professional capacity."

See Adraveno v. Mutual Res. Fund Life Ass'n, (1880) 34 Fed. 870; Wooten v. Wooten, (1928) 176 Ark. 1174, 5 S. W. 2d 340; Trull v. Modern Woodmen O. A., (1906) 12 Idaho 318, 85 Pac. 1081, 10 Ann. Cas. 53; Miser v. Iowa State Traveling Men's Ass'n, (1937) 223 Iowa 662, 273 N. W. 155; Sovereign Camp, W. O. W. v. Farmer, (1917) 116 Miss. 626, 77 So. 655; Cromeenes v. Sovereign Camp, W. O. W., (1920) 205 Mo. App. 419, 224 S. W. 15; Keller v. Home Life Ins. Co., (1902) 95 Mo. App. 627, 69 S. W. 612; Bryant v. Modern Woodmen O. A., (1910) 86 Neb. 372, 125 N. W. 621, 27 L. R. A. (n. s.) 326, 21 Ann. Cas. 365.

[10] For example:

> "I expressly waive, to such extent as may be lawful, on behalf of myself

Some courts appear to construe the waiver clause with undue strictness. In *Geare* v. *United States Life Ins. Co.*,[11] the court held that the waiver applied only to the past, and did not include information thereafter acquired by the physician while attending the insured as a patient.[12] In *Pride* v. *Inter-State Business Men's Acc. Ass'n.*,[13] the court held that the waiver did not apply to the testimony of the physician to which objection was interposed, because the waiver was restricted to a physician who had been consulted previously, whereas the testimony offered was in reference to one who was consulted after the waiver. Relying largely upon this decision another court reached a similar conclusion although the lan-

---

and of any person who shall have or claim to have any interest in any policy issued hereunder, all provisions of law forbidding any physician or other person who has attended me or examined me, or who may hereafter attend or examine me, from disclosing any knowledge or information acquired thereby, and I expressly authorize such physician or person to make such disclosures."

See Lincoln National Life Ins. Co. v. Hammer, (1930) 41 F. 2d 12; New York Life Ins. Co. v. Renault, (1926) 11 F. 2d 281; Posner v. New York Life Ins. Co., (1940) 56 Ariz. 202, 106 P. 2d 488; Murphy v. Mutual Life Ins. Co., (1941) 62 Idaho 362, 112 P. 2d 993; Metropolitan Life Ins. Co. v. Willis, (1906) 37 Ind. App. 48, 76 N. E. 560; Metropolitan Life Ins. Co. v. Brubaker, (1908) 78 Kan. 146, 96 Pac. 62, 18 L. R. A. (n. s.) 362, 16 Ann. Cas. 267; Russell v. Missouri Ins. Co., (1950) _____ Mo. App._____, 232 S. W. 2d 812; Mack v. Western & Southern Life Ins. Co., (1932) _____ Mo. App. _____, 53 S. W. 2d 1108; Allen v. Massachusetts Mutual Life Ins. Co., (1948) 149 Neb. 233, 30 N. W. 2d 885; Falkinberg v. Prudential Ins. Co., (1937) 132 Neb. 831, 273 N. W. 478; Fuller v. Knights of Pythias, (1901) 129 N. C. 318, 40 So. 65; New York Life Ins. Co. v. Snyder, (1927) 116 Ohio St. 693, 158 N. E. 176, 54 A. L. R. 406; Templeton v. Mutual Life Ins. Co., (1936) 177 Okla. 94, 57 P. 2d 841; National Life & Acc. Ins. Co. v. Roberson, (1934) 169 Okla. 136, 36 P. 2d 479; Hassing v. Mutual Life Ins. Co., (1945) 108 Utah 198, 159 P. 2d 117. For other forms of waiver, see Willis v. Order of R. R. Telegraphers, (1941) 139 Neb. 46, 296 N. W. 443; Wilhelm v. Order of Columbian Knights, (1912) 149 Wis. 585, 136 N. W. 160.

11 (1896) 66 Minn. 91, 68 N. W. 731.

12 The insured's application for insurance contained, among others, the following question and answer:

"Does the person expressly waive all provisions of law forbidding any physician or surgeon who has attended him from disclosing the information which he thereby acquired? Answer: Yes."

13 (1928) 207 Iowa 167, 216 N. W. 62, 62 A. L. R. 31.

The question reads:

"In so far as you are permitted to do so under the laws of the state in which you now reside, for yourself and for your beneficiary, do you consent that any physician or surgeon who has been consulted by you may be examined, * * * ? "

guage of the waiver was materially different.[14]   In each of these
three cases, it might reasonably have been held that the waiver
included future as well as past communications or information,
since it is quite likely that the parties intended such an interpretation.

   There are several cases which cannot easily be classified, yet
merit some consideration. Where the application for life insurance
contains a waiver of the privilege against the insured's physician
testifying, even though the application becomes a part of the policy,
if valid, the application does not lose its quality as a waiver of the
privilege if the policy was invalid.[15] Such a waiver applies not only
to the policy itself, but to anything connected with a separate contract of reinstatement.[16] Where the insurer failed to attach the
application to the policy as required by statute, the insurer, in an
action on the policy, was not entitled to use the waiver of the statutory privilege in the application to support the admissibility of the
testimony of the physician who attended the insured.[17] If the insurer offers testimony of the attending physician of the deceased
insured and objection is made thereto by the claimant on the
ground of privilege, the insurer should make it clear to the court
that the insured, in his application, waived the privilege, if such
be the fact.[18] Furthermore, if counsel for the insurer did not rely
upon the waiver at the trial and no action was taken thereon by
the trial court, the insurer cannot raise the question on appeal.[19]
In National Life & Acc. Ins. Co. v. Threlkeld,[20] it was held that no

[14] Turner v. Redwood Mutual Life Ass'n, (1936) 13 Cal. App. 2d 573, 57 P. 2d 222.
The clause on which the insurer relied, reads:
   "I hereby authorize any doctor at any time to give said association any
   information he or she may have regarding me."
[15] Lutz v. New England Mutual Life Ins. Co., (1946) 161 F. 2d 833.
[16] Lincoln National Life Ins. Co. v. Hammer, (1930) 41 F. 2d 12.
[17] Campbell v. Monumental Life Ins. Co., (1940) __ __ Ohio App. ___ , 31 Ohio Law
Abst. 420, 34 N. E. 2d 268. Moreover, when the trial court improperly admitted in
evidence the application containing such waiver, the subsequent action of the beneficiary in thereafter offering it in evidence in her own behalf did not remove any
objection to the admissibility of the waiver which was a part of the application.
[18] Posner v. New York Life Ins. Co., (1940) 56 Ariz. 202, 106 P. 2d 488.
[19] See Connor, J., in Creech v. Sovereign Camp W. O. W., (1937) 211 N. C. 658, 191
S. E. 840.
[20] (1934) 189 Ark. 165, 70 S. W. 2d 851.

error was committed in excluding the testimony of two file clerks in hospitals wherein the insured was a patient. The waiver signed by the insured relative to the production of the testimony by physicians and nurses did not remove the incompetency of the two witnesses since they were neither physicians nor nurses and made no records of any kind in the case.

A waiver of the privilege is a waiver of the disqualification of the physician as to the whole transaction, and not as to a part of it.[21] The testimony of the physician cannot be confined to those ailments only which had been disclosed to him for the purpose of obtaining the policy.[22]

Where the applicant, of his own volition and at a time when he was not a patient, obtained the statement of the examining physician who, as the applicant well knew, had knowledge as to his former health and condition, and then joined with the physician in making material representations to the insurer, he waived the statutory privilege and the physician should have been permitted to testify to contradict the patient's statement that he had been treated for la grippe, whereas, in fact, he had been treated for a venereal disease.[23]

A waiver in the contract of insurance which authorizes the attending physician to testify in court upon the cause of death, does not make competent every statement which the physician may make on the subject, on the street, or even in the proofs of loss.[24]

111. *Who May Waive During Lifetime of Patient:*
Patient or His Attorney

As a general rule, the privilege may be waived by one having the right to claim it.[1] In some jurisdictions, the statute expressly empowers the patient to waive its protection; in others, it plainly

---

[21] Bryant v. Modern Woodmen O. A., (1910) 86 Neb. 372, 125 N. W. 621, 27 L. R. A. (n. s.) 326, 21 Ann. Cas. 365.

[22] Hassing v. Mutual Life Ins. Co., (1945) 108 Utah 198, 159 P. 2d 117.

[23] McGinty v. Brotherhood of R. R. Trainmen, (1917) 166 Wis. 83, 164 N. W. 249.

[24] (1912) American Assur. Co. v. Early, (1912) 23 Ohio C. C. R. (n. s.) 418, aff'd 91 Ohio St. 367, 110 N. E. 1053.

[1] Altus v. Martin, (1954) ....Okla........, 268 P. 2d 228.

contemplates that the patient may consent to his physician's testifying. Obviously, the lawmakers have seen no harm or injury to
the general public in leaving it optional with the patient as to
whether his physician should be permitted to testify as to what he
learned professionally, and consequently have confided to the patient the entire freedom to forego the benefits and protection of
the statute if he sees fit.[2] Even when the statute declares an attending physician incompetent as a witness and makes no provision
whatever for waiver of the protection it affords, the patient, nevertheless, may surrender his right to exclude the testimony of the
physician. The statute creates no absolute incompetency.[3]

The *raison d'etre* of the statute is the protection of the patient
from the betrayal of confidence. His communications are privileged, but the public has no concern in their suppression when the
patient himself has no such desire.[4] It is everywhere conceded,
therefore, that the patient may renounce and abandon the protection the statute would otherwise afford him.[5] Like other personal

[2] Schornick v. Schornick, (1923) 25 Ariz. 563, 220 Pac. 397, 31 A. L. R. 159.

A person mentally incompetent, for whom no committee or next friend has yet
been appointed, may not authorize an attorney to waive the privilege. The waiver
provisions of the New York statute derive from the voluntary act of the person affected, a volition such person is unable legally to exercise. Matter of Lanham, (1955)
1 Misc. 2d 264, 144 N. Y. S. 2d 401.

See also Taylor v. United States, (1955) 95 App. D. C. 373, 222 F. 2d 398.

[3] Penn Mutual Life Ins. Co. v. Wiler, (1884) 100 Ind. 92, 100: "Notwithstanding the
absolute prohibitory form of our present statute, we think it confers a privilege which
the patient, for whose benefit the provision is made, may claim or waive. It gives no
right to the physician to refuse to testify, and creates no absolute incompetency."

Statutes similar to that of Indiana making physicians "incompetent" to testify
are those of Kansas, Missouri, and Oklahoma. See Appendix, herein.

[4] See § 13, herein.

[5] Representative decisions in which the courts have decided the precise question or
have approved the doctrine by way of dicta, are: Calhoun v. Jacobs, (1944) 79 App. D.
C. 29, 141 F. 2d 729; Adraveno v. Mutual Res. Fund Ass'n, (1888) 34 Fed. 870; Schornick v. Schornick, (1923) 25 Ariz. 563, 220 Pac. 397, 31 A. L. R. 159; National Annuity
Ass'n v. McCall, (1912) 103 Ark. 201, 146 S. W. 125, 48 L. R. A. (n. s.) 418; San Francisco
v. Superior Court, (1951) 37 Cal. 2d 227, 231 P. 2d 26, 25 A. L. R. 2d 1418; Lissak v.
Crocker Estate Co., (1897) 119 Cal. 442, 51 Pac. 688; Moreno v. New Guadalupe Min.
Co., (1918) 35 Cal. App. 744, 170 Pac. 1088; Trull v. Modern Woodmen of America,
(1906) 12 Idaho 318, 85 Pac. 1081, 10 Ann. Cas. 53; William Laurie Co. v. McCullough,
(1910) 174 Ind. 477, 90 N. E. 1014, Ann. Cas. 1913 A 49; Morris v. Morris, (1889) 119
>>>→

privileges, even those protected by constitutional guarantee, the physician-patient privilege is one which the patient is at liberty to waive, and he would be deprived of a valuable right if he were prohibited from making a waiver.[6] Moreover, the attorney for the patient may waive the latter's privilege if the patient is present at the trial.[7]

Ind. 341, 21 N. E. 918; Penn Mutual Life Ins. Co. v. Wiler, (1884) 100 Ind. 92; Boyles v. Cora, (1942) 232 Iowa 822, 6 N. W. 2d 401; Pride v. Inter-State Business Men's Acc. Ass'n, (1928) 207 Iowa 167, 216 N. W. 62, 62 A. L. R. 31; Novak v. Chicago Fraternal Life Ass'n, (1932) 136 Kan. 609, 16 P. 2d 507; Flack v. Brewster, (1920) 107 Kan. 63, 190 Pac. 616; Armstrong v. Topeka Ry., (1914) 93 Kan. 493, 144 Pac. 847; New York Life Ins. Co. v. Newman, (1945) 311 Mich. 368, 18 N. W. 2d 859; Fraser v. Jennison, (1879) 42 Mich. 206, 3 N. W. 882; Olson v. Court of Honor, (1907) 100 Minn. 117, 110 N. W. 374, 8 L. R. A. (n. s.) 521, 10 Ann. Cas. 622; Sovereign Camp, W. of W. v. Farmer, (1917) 116 Miss. 626, 77 So. 655; Randolph v. Supreme Liberty Life Ins. Co., (1949) 359 Mo. 251, 221 S. W. 2d 155; Wells v. Jefferson, (1939) 345 Mo. 239, 132 S. W. 2d 1006; Epstein v. Pennsylvania R. R., (1913) 250 Mo. 1, 156 S. W. 699, 48 L. R. A. (n. s.) 394, Ann. Cas. 1915 A 423; Davenport v. Hannibal, (1891) 108 Mo. 471, 18 S. W. 1122; Thompson v. Ish, (1889) 99 Mo. 160, 12 S. W. 510; Keller v. Home Life Ins. Co., (1902) 95 Mo. App. 627, 69 S. W. 612; Hier v. Farmers Mutual Fire Ins. Co., (1937) 104 Mont. 471, 67 P. 2d 831, 110 A. L. R. 1051; Falkinberg v. Prudential Ins. Co., (1937) 132 Neb. 831, 273 N. W. 478; Friesen v. Reimer, (1933) 124 Neb. 620, 247 N. W. 561; Western Travelers Acc. Ass'n v. Munson, (1905) 73 Neb. 858, 103 N. W. 688, 1 L. R. A. (n. s.) 1068; McKinney v. Grand Street, etc., R. R., (1887) 104 N. Y. 352, 10 N. E. 544; Zimmer v. Third Ave. R. R., (1899) 36 App. Div. 265, 55 N. Y. S. 308; Weis v. Mount Sinai Hospital, (1955) 208 Misc. 1010, 147 N. Y. S. 2d 455; Yow v. Pittman, (1954) 241 N. C. 69, 84 S. E. 2d 297; Creech v. Sovereign Camp, W. of W., (1937) 211 N. C. 658, 191 S. E. 840; Thomas v. New York Life Ins. Co., (1935) 65 N. D. 625, 260 N. W. 605; Harpman v. Devine, (1937) 133 Ohio St. 1, 10 N. E. 2d 776, 114 A. L. R. 789; Industrial Comm'n v. Warnke, (1936) 131 Ohio St. 140, 2 N. E. 2d 248; Ausdenmoore v. Holzback, (1914) 89 Ohio St. 381, 106 N. E. 41; Jasper v. State, (1954) ⸺ Okla. Cr. ⸺, 269 P. 2d 375; Altus v. Martin, (1954) ⸺ Okla. ⸺, 268 P. 2d 228; Clawson v. Walgreen Drug Co., (1945) 108 Utah 577, 162 P. 2d 759; Grieve v. Howard, (1919) 54 Utah 225, 180 Pac. 423; McUne v. Fuqua, (1953) ⸺ Wash. ⸺, 253 P. 2d 632, 257 P. 2d 636; Noelle v. Hoquiam Lumber & S. Co., (1907) 47 Wash. 519, 92 Pac. 372; Mohr v. Mohr, (1937) 119 W. Va. 253, 193 S. E. 121; Estate of Gallun, (1934) 215 Wis. 314, 254 N. W. 542; Angerstein v. Milwaukee Monument Co., (1919) 169 Wis. 502, 173 N. W. 215; Markham v. Hipke, (1919) 169 Wis. 37, 171 N. W. 300; *In re* Will of Bruendl, (1899) 102 Wis. 45, 78 N. W. 169; Gagne v. Alliance Nationale, [1946] 13 I. L. R. (Quebec) 13. See also Mutual Life Ins. Co. v. dame Jeannotte-Lamarche, [1935] Quebec Rep. 59 K. B. 510.

6 Metropolitan Life Ins. Co. v. Brubaker, (1908) 78 Kan. 146, 96 Pac. 62, 18 L. R. A. (n. s.) 362, 16 Ann. Cas. 267; Grand Rapids & Ind. R. R. v. Martin, (1879) 41 Mich. 667, 3 N. W. 173.

7 Alberti v. New York, Lake Erie & W. R. R., (1889) 118 N. Y. 77, 23 N. E. 35, 6 L. R. A. 765.

An express waiver is not necessary; it may be implied from the acts and conduct of the patient.[8] Where an attending physician is requested by the testator, his patient, to witness his will and, in accordance with that request, does subscribe to the will as a witness, the patient thereby waives the restrictions on the competency of the physician as a witness prescribed by the statute and consents that such physician, in an action involving the validity of the will, may be called as a witness by either side and examined and cross-examined the same as any other subscribing witness.[9] The act of the patient in requesting his physician to become a witness to his will leaves no doubt as to his intention thereby to exempt him from the operation of the statute, and leave him free to perform the duties of the office assigned him, unrestrained by any objection which he had power to remove. It need hardly be stated, of course, that in becoming a subscribing witness, no professional skill is required or advice sought.[10] The physician acts as an individual, and he may testify to any matter, in relation to the execution and validity of the will, of which he acquired knowledge by virtue of his professional relationship, including the mental condition of the testator at the time of the testamentary act.[11]

In New York, a stipulation for waiver of the privilege signed by the patient before trial, is not sufficient. The statute requires that it be signed by the attorney for the patient. Geis v. Geis, (1906) 116 App. Div. 362, 101 N. Y. S. 845.

[8] See c. XVIII, herein.

[9] Storman v. Weiss, (1954) ....N. D........, 65 N. W. 2d 475; Weis v. Weis, (1945) 76 Ohio App. 483, 65 N. E. 2d 300, aff'd (1947) 147 Ohio St. 416, 72 N. E. 2d 245, 169 A. L. R. 668; Bahl v. Byal, (1914) 90 Ohio St. 129, 106 N. E. 766 (waiver apparently conceded; privilege not discussed); In re Bottger's Estate, (1942) 14 Wash. 2d 676, 129 P. 2d 518 (privilege not discussed); Points v. Nier, (1916) 91 Wash. 20, 157 Pac. 44, Ann. Cas. 1918 A 1046; Re Peterson's Estate, (1947) 250 Wis. 158, 26 N. W. 2d 553.

See 8 Wigmore, Evidence, § 2390(1).

The rule applies also where the physician acts as a witness to the patient's deed. Boyle v. Robinson, (1906) 129 Wis. 567, 109 N. W. 623.

[10] Matter of Freeman, (1887) 46 Hun (N. Y.) 458.

[11] See cases in note 9, infra.

The same principle has long been recognized in cases where, at the request of the testator, his attorney subscribed the will as a witness. i.e., Wilburn v. Williams, (1943) 193 Miss. 831, 11 So. 2d 306; Brown v. Brown, (1906) 77 Neb. 125, 108 N. W. 180; Matter of Coleman, (1888) 111 N. Y. 220, 19 N. E. 71; Knepper v. Knepper, (1921) 103 Ohio

Where the attending physician, who was a subscribing witness to the will, related upon direct examination the circumstances attending the execution of the will and gave his opinion that, at the time thereof, the testator appeared to be of sound mind, it was not a violation of the privilege statute to permit him, upon cross-examination, to be interrogated as to the character of the testator's affliction and to disclose that he suffered from a serious hemiplegy, a disease involving and affecting the brain.[12] However, the fact that the physician may be competent to testify to the will itself, does not make him competent to testify to the testator's mental competency at a later time when the testator executed a codicil, at which time the physician was not present.[13]

112. Same: Committee or Guardian of Patient Mentally Incompetent

If the patient is mentally incompetent, his committee, guardian, or any other person lawfully appointed to act for him, may waive the benefits of the statute where a disclosure of matters otherwise privileged is necessary to a proper determination of the controversy.[1] But, in a proceeding by a mother to have her daughter committed to a psychiatric school, the mother, as her daughter's

---

← ⚞

St. 529, 134 N. E. 476; McMaster v. Scriven, (1893) 85 Wis. 162, 55 N. W. 149. See 8 Wigmore, Evidence, § 2315; also note, 64 A. L. R. 184, 192.

In New York, the statutory requirement that the waiver be made in open court does not extend to a case where the attorney is a subscribing witness to the will. Matter of Cunnion, (1911) 201 N. Y. 123, 94 N. E. 648.

[12] Matter of Mullin's Estate, (1895) 110 Cal. 252, 42 Pac. 645.

[13] In re Estate of Nelson, (1901) 132 Cal. 182, 64 Pac. 294.

[1] Kendall v. Gore Properties, (1956) 236 F. 2d 673; Taylor v. United States, (1955) 95 App. D. C. 373, 222 F. 2d 398; Matter of Warrington, (1951) 303 N. Y. 129, 100 N. E. 2d 170; La Plante v. Garrett, (1953) 282 App. Div. 1096, 126 N. Y. S. 2d 470, appeal denied 130 N. Y. S. 2d 910; McGrath v. State, (1950) 200 Misc. 165, 104 N. Y. S. 2d 882; In re Handwerger, (1947) 79 N. Y. S. 2d 634.

The mere fact that the committee of the patient brings an action to recover damages for personal injury suffered by the patient does not, of itself, constitute a waiver. La Plante v. Garrett, infra. But cf. Van Heuverzwyn v. State, (1954)206 Misc. 896, 134 N. Y. S. 2d 922. The guardian of a minor, mentally incompetent, may waive the attorney-client privilege in order to permit the minor's former attorney to testify in his behalf. Yancy v. Erman, (1951) _____Ohio Com. Pleas_____, 99 N. E. 2d 524.

antagonist, may not waive the daughter's privilege with respect to the prognosis and recommendations of her personal physician.[2]

113. Same: Guardian, Parent, or Next Friend of Infant Patient

If the patient be a minor, his guardian, parent, or next friend may waive the statutory privilege; and this is true even though the action is one to which the minor is not a party.[1] In a prosecution for the rape of a minor, the grandmother, who stood in *loco parentis* to her, was allowed, over defendant's objection, to waive the child's privilege in order that the physician who attended her might testify as to the character of her injuries and to the further fact that she had contracted a venereal disease.[2] In another case,[3]

---

[2] *In re* Sippy, (1953) _____D. C. _____, 97 A. 2d 455.

[1] Corey v. Bolton, (1900) 31 Misc. 138, 63 N. Y. S. 915. The action was brought by the father, not in his son's right, but in his own, for the loss of the son's services and for the medical expenses resulting from an assault upon the son by the defendant. At the trial, the father waived the privilege on behalf of his son. The physician who attended the boy was then permitted to disclose, over defendant's objection, information which he acquired while treating the boy's injuries. Neither the son nor his mother, both in court, objected to the waiver.

Scott, J., dissented on the ground that the statute makes no provision for a waiver in behalf of an infant by a parent or guardian.

[2] Jenkins v. State, (1927) 146 Miss. 339, 343, 111 So. 433: "There are many cases in which the rights of minors in courts are to be enforced through suits brought in their behalf by their guardians or by those acting as next friend for them, and there must be in the very nature of the case in such cases, a power to consent to the admission of evidence, where it is competent and receivable in order to vindicate the rights of such child; and, where the evidence is favorable to the interest of the person in whose favor the privilege exists, and where the child and those acting for it and looking after its interest desire the use of such testimony, we see no objection to holding that the privilege can be waived. We think it was waived by the facts and circumstances existing in this record, although there was no expressed declaration to that effect by the child. It is not necessary now to determine what the effect of the admission would be if the evidence was hostile to the interest of the child, even though it was sought to be admitted by those acting for it."

[3] State v. Depoister, (1891) 21 Nev. 107, 25 Pac. 1000. One judge dissented on the ground that the parents had no power to waive the child's privilege. See also State v. Thomas, (1939) 1 Wash. 2d 298, 95 P. 2d 1036. The relation of physician and patient, however, did not exist.

In Yancy v. Erman, (1951) _____Ohio Com. Pleas_____, 99 N. E. 2d 524, the guardian of a minor was permitted to waive the attorney-client privilege.

the waiver was made by the child's mother and stepfather.

In an action by an infant against the state for personal injuries sustained by reason of the alleged negligence of the state, the guardian ad litem is the personal representative of the infant and has the power to waive the statutory privilege on his motion for discovery and inspection before trial.[4]

Unquestionably a guardian has no power to bind his ward by an act which is clearly inimical to the rights of the ward. The office of a guardian is one of trust. He is empowered to act for the ward in matters confided to him as guardian, in furtherance of his interests. Therefore, in an action upon a life insurance contract, the guardian cannot, by his own admissions in the proof of death furnished by him to the insurer, bind the ward as to the cause of the insured's death.[5]

114. Same: Husband or Wife of Patient

A husband or wife, as such, has no power to waive the privilege of his or her living spouse.[1] In a suit by an insurer to cancel a policy of disability insurance, statements of the insured's physician furnished by the insured's wife as part of the proofs of the insured's disability are not admissible as admissions on the part of her insured husband who was insane and incapable of authorizing her to furnish such statements.[2]

---

[4] Van Heuverzwyn v. State, (1954) 206 Misc. 896, 134 N. Y. S. 2d 922.

[5] Buffalo, Loan, Trust & Safe Deposit Co. v. Knights Templar and Masonic Mut. Aid Ass'n., (1891) 126 N. Y. 450, 457, 27 N. E. 942: "In procuring the physician's certificate, the guardian misapprehended his duty. It was an act tending to defeat the claim which he had undertaken to collect. The fact asserted in the certificate may have been the truth. But the guardian has no right to foreclose inquiry upon the subject, nor to prejudice the case by changing the burden of proof by an inconsiderate, unnecessary and prejudicial admission."

See also Corey v. Bolton, infra, note 1.

In Jenkins v. State, (1926) 146 Miss. 339, 111 So. 433, the question was mentioned but not decided.

[1] Cramer v. Hurt, (1899) 154 Mo. 112, 55 S. W. 258; cf. Demonbrun v. McHaffie, (1941) 348 Mo. 1120, 156 S. W. 2d 923, which regards the remarks of the court in Cramer v. Hurt on the issue of waiver, as dictum.

[2] Metropolitan Life Ins. Co. v. Ryan, (1943) 237 Mo. App. 464, 172 S. W. 2d 269.

115. Who May Waive After Death of Patient: Introductory

Before considering the particular classes of persons who may waive the privilege after the patient's death, assuming that it can be waived by someone, perhaps one should first inquire whether, as a matter of policy, anyone other than the patient should be given the right to waive his privilege. It is manifest that during the early years of the privilege there was a wide disparity of opinion on this important question.

As previously observed, some of the original statutes either expressly empowered the patient to waive the privilege or else it was plainly implied that he could do so.[1] Practically all of the statutes, however, were strangely silent as to the right or power of anyone else to waive such privilege for the patient, either during his lifetime or after his death. The courts had little difficulty in deciding that the patient himself could waive the benefits and protection of the statute, but they were not disposed at first to extend the right to others after the death of the patient.[2] A number of courts construed the statute strictly and held that there can be no waiver of the privilege after the death of the patient. The theory was that the privilege is a personal one and may be waived by the patient only; that death does not end the privilege; that the seal of secrecy must remain unbroken;[3] and that while it is not against public policy to permit the patient himself to waive the privilege without limitation, nevertheless, his memory should be protected against his heirs, personal representatives, and other persons pur-

---

[1] See § 106, herein.

[2] The discussion of this latter question presupposes, of course, that the patient died without having effectually waived the privilege.

[3] Westover v. Aetna Life Ins. Co., (1884) 99 N. Y. 56, 59, 1 N. E. 104: "The purpose of the laws would be thwarted, and the policy intended to be promoted thereby would be defeated, if death removed the seal of secrecy from the communications and disclosures which a patient should make to his physician. * * * After one has gone to his grave the living are not permitted to impair his fame and disgrace his memory by dragging to the light communications and disclosures made under the seal of the statutes."

McCaw v. Turner, (1921) 126 Miss. 260, 271, 88 So. 705: "The statute does not limit the privilege to the life of the patient, neither does it confer upon his heirs or devisees who may quarrel over his property the right to tarnish his reputation by causing his physician to disclose his infirmities."

porting to stand in his shoes and to represent his interest and estate.[4] In one state, the courts still adhere to this doctrine.[5]

This rule, however, was never widely approved and followed.[6] On the contrary, most of the courts held that the privilege might properly be waived after the death of the patient. It was said that when the patient dies and can no longer act for himself, or appoint others to act for him, the law steps in and names those who may act in his stead, by reason of the interest they have as heirs at law or by appointment as his personal representative.[7] Unquestionably this is the better view. Accumulated experience had exposed the unwisdom of the earlier rule and had demonstrated that far more harm than good resulted from its strict enforcement.[8] In due time, the legislatures of many states, observing the trend of judicial decisions and recognizing also the inadequacies of their own statutes, undertook, by amendment, to remedy them.

---

[4] *Re* Flint, (1893) 100 Cal. 391, 397, 34 Pac. 863: "To him [the patient], the considerations are even more weighty that the privilege remain inviolate after he has gone to his grave, for his good name is left behind deprived of his protecting care. His rights are not buried in the grave, and heirs and devisees quarreling among themselves over a division of his patrimony, in justice to his memory, should not be allowed to waive the privilege."

For other cases, see note, 31 A. L. R. 167.

[5] Auld v. Cathro, (1910) 20 N. D. 461, 128 N. W. 1025, 32 L. R. A. (n. s.) 71, Ann Cas. 1913 A 90.

[6] Indeed, some of the courts which originally followed this rule now permit waiver, due either to a statutory change or a change in judicial decision. Compare for instance, *Re* Will of Hunt, (1904) 122 Wis. 460, 100 N. W. 874, and Estate of Gallun, (1934) 215 Wis. 314, 254 N. W. 542. See also Grieve v. Howard, (1919) 54 Utah 225, 180 Pac. 423 (earlier rule abrogated).

[7] Schornick v. Schornick, (1923) 25 Ariz. 563, 220 Pac. 397, 31 A. L. R. 159. See also 8 Wigmore, Evidence, § 2193.

[8] Schornick v. Schornick, (1923) 25 Ariz. 563, 566, 220 Pac. 397, 31 A. L. R. 159: "If the right to waive the privilege dies with the patient, then whatever he may have communicated to his physician, or whatever the physician may have learned by observation or examination, although its disclosure would save his estate or preserve his good name, is doomed to eternal oblivion."

See also Olson v. Court of Honor, (1907) 100 Minn. 117, 123, 110 N. W. 374, 8 L. R. A. (n. s.) 521, 10 Ann. Cas. 622.

The strong dissent of Owen, J., in Maine v. Maryland Casualty Co., (1920) 172 Wis. 350, 178 N. W. 749, 15 A. L. R. 1536, caused the legislature to promptly amend its statute by permitting waiver after death of the patient.

It is quite apparent that the weight of authority, under the existing statutes of most of the states,[9] is committed to the proposition that the right to waive is not limited to the patient himself, but after his death extends to those who may properly be regarded as standing in his place or representing him; and this is true even in the case of statutory provisions which are written in terms of competency, not in terms of privilege.[10]

116. Same: Personal Representative

It is now almost universally conceded that the personal representative[1] of the deceased patient may waive the privilege. Or-

---

[9] While there is a similarity in the statutory provisions in some of the states, yet in other states the provisions are quite different. This accounts in part for the fact that there is still a conflict of opinion as to the persons by whom, and the circumstances under which, the waiver may be made.

[10] Among the cases supporting the modern liberal rule are: Thompson v. Smith, (1939) 70 App. D. C. 65, 103 F. 2d 936, 123 A. L. R. 76; Hyatt v. Wroten, (1931) 184 Ark. 847, 43 S. W. 2d 726; Schirmer v. Baldwin, (1930) 182 Ark. 581, 32 S. W. 2d 162; National Annuity Ass'n. v. McCall, (1912) 103 Ark. 201, 146 S. W. 125, 48 L. R. A. (n. s.) 418; Marker v. McCue, (1931) 50 Idaho 462, 297 Pac. 401; Stayner v. Nye, (1949) 227 Ind. 231, 85 N. E. 2d 496; Penn Mutual Life Ins. Co. v. Wiler, (1884) 100 Ind. 92; Winters v. Winters, (1897) 102 Iowa 53, 71 N. W. 184; Denning v. Butcher, (1894) 91 Iowa 425, 59 N. W. 69; Gorman v. Hickey, (1937) 145 Kan. 54, 64 P. 2d 587; Re Koenig's Estate, (1956) 247 Minn. 580, 78 N. W. 2d 364; Estate of Cunningham, (1944) 219 Minn. 80, 17 N. W. 2d 85; Olson v. Court of Honor, (1907) 100 Minn. 117, 110 N. W. 374, 8 L. R. A. (n. s.) 521, 10 Ann. Cas. 622; Spurr v. Spurr, (1920) 285 Mo. 163, 226 S. W. 35; Thompson v. Ish, (1889) 99 Mo. 160, 12 S. W. 510; Groll v. Tower, (1884) 85 Mo. 249; Baker v. Mardis, (1928) 221 Mo. App. 1185, 1 S. W. 2d 223; Re Ackerman's Estate, (1937) 163 Misc. 624, 298 N. Y. S. 38; Estate of Gray, (1911) 88 Neb. 835, 130 N. W. 746, 33 L. R. A. (n. s.) 319, Ann. Cas. 1912 B. 1037; Grieve v. Howard, (1919) 54 Utah 225, 180 Pac. 423; Re Thomas' Estate, (1931) 165 Wash. 42, 4 P. 2d 837, 7 P. 2d 1119; Estate of Gallun, (1934) 215 Wis. 314, 254 N. W. 542.

For other cases, see note, 31 A. L. R. 167; 126 A. L. R. 380.

Sprouse v. Magee, (1928) 46 Idaho 622, 631, 269 Pac. 993: "Many decisions upholding the right of waiver after death of the patient have reached their conclusion partly if not entirely upon the ground that such valuable evidence as is generally furnished by such disclosure, in some instances indispensable, could not have been intended to be forever hidden, or that such a statute, tending to the suppression of the truth, should be strictly limited in its application."

[1] "Representative" is often used loosely by the courts in this connection and does not carry the technical meaning of that word, but includes the personal representative of the deceased and also his heirs, next of kin, or even the beneficiary under a policy of life insurance. However, for the purposes of this section, it will be assumed that the

»»→

dinarily, an executor or administrator represents the deceased. In most controversies he acts in his stead, as in prosecuting or defending claims for or against the estate, and as a proponent of the will. The privilege belongs to the patient and he may waive it if he sees fit, and what he may do in his lifetime, the personal representative may also do after his death.[2] This is the common sense view.[3] As pointed out earlier, comparative recent amendments to

←—

primary and ordinary meaning of the words "representative," or "legal representative," or "personal representative," when there is nothing in the text to control their meaning, is "executors and administrators," they being the representatives designated by the deceased in his will, or appointed by the court.

In Polachek v. New York Life Ins. Co., (1933) 147 Misc. 16, 263 N. Y. S. 230, aff'd. 240 App. Div. 1028, 268 N. Y. S. 995, it was held that the words "personal representative," as used in the New York privilege statute, apply only to executors and administrators.

[2] Schornick v. Schornick, (1923) 25 Ariz. 563, 220 Pac. 397, 31 A. L. R. 159; Marker v. McCue, (1931) 50 Idaho 462, 297 Pac. 401; Long v. Garey Investment Co., (1906) ...... Iowa ......, 110 N. W. 26; Denning v. Butcher, (1894) 91 Iowa 425, 59 N. W. 69; Re Koenig's Estate, (1956) 247 Minn. 580, 78 N. W. 2d 364; Estate of Cunningham, (1944) 219 Minn. 80, 17 N. W. 2d 85; Hier v. Farmers Mutual Fire Ins. Co., (1937) 104 Mont. 471, 67 P. 2d 831, 110 A. L. R. 1051; Parker v. Parker, (1907) 78 Neb. 535, 111 N. W. 119; Matter of Ericson, (1951) 200 Misc. 1005, 106 N. Y. S. 2d 203.

See 8 Wigmore, Evidence, § 2391.

See also note, 31 A. L. R. 167; 126 A. L. R. 380.

Contra: Auld v. Cathro, (1910) 20 N. D. 461, 128 N. W. 1025, 32 L. R. A. (n. s.) 71, Ann Cas. 1913 A 90. See also National Mutual Life Ass'n v. Godrich, [1909] 10 Comm. L. R. 1 (Australia) (question mentioned but not decided). In a number of jurisdictions the precise question does not appear to have been decided; in others, it has been referred to in dicta or left undecided. In Flack v. Brewster, (1920) 107 Kan. 63, 190 Pac. 616, the question concerned the right of the heirs to waive the privilege, but the court indicated that it can be waived as well by the personal representative and those interested in the preservation of the patient's estate. To a similar effect is Fish v. Poorman, (1911) 85 Kan. 237, 116 Pac. 898. In Smith v. Davis, (1949) 168 Kan. 210, 212 P. 2d 322, a will contest, the questions whether the executor may waive the privilege and whether such waiver, if permitted, is effective where a privileged communication is objected to by the heirs at law, were left undecided.

[3] See opinion of Start, C. J., in Olson v. Court of Honor, (1907) 100 Minn. 117, 110 N. W. 374, 8 L. R. A. (n. s.) 521, 10 Ann. Cas. 622.

8 Wigmore, Evidence, § 2391: "The *personal representative* of the deceased may waive the privilege. One who is entrusted with the management of the deceased's property may surely be trusted to protect the memory and reputation of the deceased, in so far as it is liable to injury by the disclosure of his physical condition when alive. It is incongruous to hold that the person who manages the litigation of the deceased's

»——→

the statutes in a number of states account for the modification or abandonment of a contrary rule previously announced by the courts in such states.[4] In one state, at least, the change was made by judicial decision.[5]

Notwithstanding the fact that the right of the personal representative to waive the privilege is generally countenanced, it does not necessarily follow that it can be exercised in all cases and under all circumstances. There are exceptions to the general rule, and these may be attributed not only to the specific language of some of the statutory provisions governing the right of waiver,[6] but also to certain limitations and conditions engrafted upon the rule by the courts in a few of the jurisdictions. Perhaps it is proper here to discuss some of these.

In the District of Columbia, only the "legal representative" may waive the privilege,[7] and until he is actually appointed as such by the proper court, no authority exists to waive it.[8] The waiver need not be express, but may be implied, and it is implied when the legal representative introduces testimony concerning the

---

property-interests has no power to waive rules of Evidence for the purpose of advancing those interests."

Of course, the courts have authority to prevent disclosures which would tend to blacken the memory of the deceased patient. Winters v. Winters, (1897) 102 Iowa 53, 71 N. W. 184; Estate of Gray (1911) 88 Neb. 835, 130 N. W. 746, 33 L. R. A. (n. s.) 319, Ann. Cas. 1912 B. 1037. See also New York statute. Appendix, herein.

[4] *e. g.*, the statutes of California, Mississippi, New York, Ohio and Wisconsin.

[5] The rule announced in Estate of Van Alstine, (1903) 26 Utah 193, 72 Pac. 942, was abrogated in Grieve v. Howard, (1919) 54 Utah 225, 180 Pac. 423.

[6] See statutes of California, Canal Zone, District of Columbia, Guam, Michigan, Minnesota, Mississippi, Nebraska, Nevada, New York, Ohio, and Wisconsin. Appendix, herein.

[7] Thompson v. Smith, (1939) 70 App. D. C. 65, 103 F. 2d 936, 123 A. L. R. 76; Carmody v. Capital Traction Co., (1915) 43 App. D. C. 245, Ann. Cas. 1916 D. 706. However, in Calhoun v. Jacobs, (1944) 79 App. D. C. 29, 141 F. 2d 729, the grantor's heirs, in an action to set aside a conveyance to a stranger, were permitted to waive the privilege over the latter's objection, there being no controversy between the heirs and no executor had been appointed.

[8] Calhoun v. Jacobs, (1944) 79 App. D. C. 729, 141 F. 2d 729; McCartney v. Holmquist, (1939) 70 App. D. C. 334, 106 F. 2d 855, 126 A. L. R. 375; Labofish v. Berman, (1932) 60 App. D. C. 397, 55 F. 2d 1022; Hutchins v. Hutchins, (1919) 48 App. D. C. 495; *Re* Cottrill's Estate, (1941) 39 F. Supp. 689.

deceased patient's condition of health which was in issue at the trial.[9]

In Indiana, the statute is written in terms of competency, not privilege, and makes no provision for waiver after the death of the patient. However, in will contests, the executor or administrator of the estate of the deceased patient may waive the privilege where he is seeking to maintain the patient's will or to conserve the interests of his estate.[10] But an administrator cannot waive the privilege for the sole purpose of resisting an application to remove him.[11] In an action to set aside the probate of a prior will and to probate a subsequent one, the executor of the first will was not allowed to waive the privilege in order that he might introduce the testimony of the attending physician showing the mental capacity of the testatrix when she made the second will.[12] The right to waive has also been extended to actions to set aside a deed of the deceased patient, where the heirs and personal representatives joined in waiving the privilege in order that they might introduce testimony of the attending physician as to the patient's physical and mental condition at the time the transaction was consummated.[13] The waiver may be express, or it may be implied from the conduct of the legal representative in standing by and permitting privileged testimony to be given without objection.[14]

---

[9] Buckminster's Estate v. Commissioner of Internal Revenue, (1944) 147 F. 2d 331.

[10] Morris v. Morris, (1889) 119 Ind. 341, 21 N. E. 918; Sager v. Moltz, (1923) 80 Ind. App. 122, 139 N. E. 687; Studabaker v. Faylor, (1912) 52 Ind. App. 171, 98 N. E. 318.

In Gurley v. Park, (1893) 135 Ind. 440, 35 N. E. 279, there was no legal representative of the deceased patient and the court refused to allow her nephew and niece to waive the privilege. See also Towles v. McCurdy, (1904) 163 Ind. 12, 71 N. E. 129; Brackney v. Fogle, (1901) 156 Ind. 535, 60 N. E. 303. For application of the attorney-client privilege, see Kern v. Kern, (1900) 154 Ind. 29, 55 N. E. 1004.

[11] Scott v. Smith, (1908) 171 Ind. 453, 85 N. E. 774.

[12] Heaston v. Krieg, (1906) 167 Ind. 101, 77 N. E. 805. It should be noted, perhaps, that the executor's wife was a legatee under the first will. In Stayner v. Nye, (1949) 227 Ind. 231, 85 N. E. 2d 496, the court said: (p. 240) "The case of Heaston v. Krieg * * * must be regarded as an anomalous exception to the general rule, and the authority thereof strictly limited to the peculiar facts of that case."

[13] Stayner v. Nye, (1947) 227 Ind. 231, 85 N. E. 2d 496; Studabaker v. Faylor, (1912) 52 Ind. App. 171, 98 N. E. 318.

[14] Studabaker v. Faylor, (1912) 52 Ind. App. 171, 98 N. E. 318. The Indiana cases are discussed in (1948) 23 Ind. L. J. 295.

In Michigan, it has long been the rule that, in will contests, the legal representative may waive the privilege.[15] However, his right to waive is not confined to testamentary proceedings, and may be exercised in other classes of actions.[16]

In Mississippi, the courts consistently held that the ban of the statute survives the death of the patient and could not be waived by the patient's personal representatives or his heirs.[17] However, the statute has since been amended and they now have the power to waive.

In New York, problems concerning waiver of the privilege, after the death of the patient, have plagued the courts for many years and still do. The statute has been amended on numerous occasions and much of the mass of litigation involving the privilege in this state can be attributed to this fact. In its original form, the statute contained no provision for waiver of the privilege; therefore, after the death of the patient, no person, not even his legal representative, could waive it.[18] In 1891, the statute was amended[19] so as to permit the physician to disclose any information acquired by him while attending the deceased patient "except communications and such facts as would tend to disgrace the memory of the patient" where the provisions of the statute had been expressly waived[20] at the trial by the personal representative of

---

[15] Fraser v. Jennison, (1879) 42 Mich. 206, 3 N. W. 882.

    The words "legal representative" do not include the mother of the deceased patient who is his next of kin. *Re* Mansbach's Estate, (1907) 150 Mich. 348, 114 N. W. 65.

[16] Harvey v. Silber, (1942) 300 Mich. 510, 2 N. W. 2d 483.

[17] Watkins v. Watkins, (1926) 142 Miss. 210, 106 So. 753; McCaw v. Turner, (1921) 126 Miss. 260, 88 So. 705.

[18] Loder v. Whelpley, (1888) 111 N. Y. 239, 18 N. E. 874; Westover v. Aetna Life Ins. Co., (1884) 99 N. Y. 56, 1 N. E. 104.

[19] (1891) N. Y. Laws, c. 381.

[20] Eder v. Cashin, (1953) 281 App. Div. 456, 460, 120 N. Y. S. 2d 165: "It will be noted that this section [354 Civ. Prac. Act] uses the phrase 'expressly waived.' * * * The waiver need not be in writing and it is not necessary that there be an express statement of an intention to waive. The common sense view would seem to be that a waiver by a personal representative need not be expressed in writing, or in any particular form, but may appear from the proof offered by such representative and the issues tendered." See also Holcomb v. Harris, (1901) 166 N. Y. 257, 59 N. E. 820.

such deceased patient.[21] Later, the legislature extended the right of waiver to the surviving spouse and other designated persons in actions where the validity of the patient's will is in question.[22] As used in the statute, the words "personal representatives" apply only to executors and administrators,[22a] and do not include the beneficiary of a life insurance policy.[23] However, they do include an executrix who, pursuant to the Decedent Estate Law, brings an action for damages for the wrongful death of the patient.[24] It is not necessary to a waiver of the statute that all parties entitled to waive the privilege should join therein, but either or any may do so.[25]

It should be noted that the power of the personal representative of the deceased patient is not as broad as that of the patient himself.[26] In fact, until 1955, it was greatly limited. Prior thereto,

---

[21] Executors named in the will may waive the privilege although the will be not yet probated. Greff v. Havens, (1946) 186 Misc. 914, 66 N. Y. S. 2d 124.

Contra: Humphreys v. Board of Education, (1957) 5 M. 2d 594, 160 N. Y. S. 2d 64.

[22] (1893) N. Y. Laws, c. 295.

The attending physician or nurse may disclose information acquired professionally when it is sought "in any litigation wherein the interests of the personal representative of such deceased patient are deemed by the trial judge to be adverse to those of the estate of the deceased patient, by any party in interest, or if the validity of the last will and testament of such deceased patient is in question, by the executor or executors named in the will, or the surviving husband, widow or any heir-at-law or any of the next of kin, of such deceased, or any other party in interest."

Except in situations mentioned in the statute, only the personal representative may waive the privilege. Matter of Presender, (1954) 285 App. Div. 109, 135 N. Y. S. 2d 418. See also Matter of Meyer, (1954) 206 Misc. 368, 132 N. Y. S. 2d 825.

Of course under the amendment of 1955, such confidential communications as would tend to disgrace the memory of the patient and such facts as would tend to disgrace his memory, cannot be disclosed in any case.

[22a] Sulz v. Mutual Reserve Fund Life Ass'n., (1895) 145 N. Y. 563, 574, 40 N. E. 242, 245, 28 L. R. A. 379; Polachek v. New York Life Ins. Co., (1933) 147 Misc. 16, 263 N. Y. S. 230, aff'd. 240 App. Div. 1028, 268 N. Y. S. 995; Humphreys v. Board of Education, (1957) 5 M. 2d 594, 160 N. Y. S. 2d 64.

[23] Entian v. Provident Mutual Life Ins. Co., (1935) 155 Misc. 227, 279 N. Y. S. 580.

[24] Eder v. Cashin, (1953) 281 App. Div. 456, 120 N. Y. S. 2d 165. Although merely a nominal party, and perhaps in the strict sense of the term not the personal representative of the decedent, she may waive the privilege.

[25] *Re* Hopkins' Will, (1902) 73 App. Div. 559, 77 N. Y. S. 178, reversed on other grounds 172 N. Y. 360, 65 N. E. 173. See also Matter of Mele, (1916) 94 Misc. 555, 157 N. Y. S. 669.

[26] Matter of Elizabeth Cashman, (1936) 159 Misc. 881, 289 N. Y. S. 328, aff'd. (1939)

》》→

the personal representative was forbidden to disclose "confidential communications, and such facts as would tend to disgrace the memory of the patient." For some time the question as to what the legislature meant by "confidential communications" remained an open one. In *Matter of Elizabeth Cashman*[27] it was considered, but no precise rule was given. The question again came before the Court of Appeals in *Matter of Coddington*.[28] This decision, which practically nullified the provision for waiver, held that, except such facts as could be observed by a layman, *all* information which the physician obtained in the course of attending the patient must be regarded and treated as "confidential."[29] This highly restrictive interpretation was promptly disapproved by many members of the bar[30] and shortly thereafter the statute was amended.[31] It now provides that a proper waiver being made, a physician may testify to any matter concerning a deceased patient except facts and confidential communications as would tend to disgrace the memory of the patient. In view of the amendment, the rule in *Matter of Coddington* has been abrogated and physicians and nurses, where there is a valid waiver of the privilege, may now testify as to what had

---

280 N. Y. 681, 21 N. E. 2d 193; Mulligan v. Sinski, (1913) 156 App. Div. 35, 140 N. Y. S. 835, aff'd. (1915) 214 N. Y. 678, 108 N. E. 1101; Eder v. Cashin, (1953) 281 App. Div. 456, 120 N. Y. S. 2d 165; Murray v. Physical Culture Hotel, Inc., (1939) 258 App. Div. 334, 16 N. Y. S. 2d 978, aff'd. 17 N. Y. S. 2d 862; Killip v. Rochester General Hospital, (1955) 1 Misc. 2d 349, 146 N. Y. S. 2d 164.

27 (1936) 159 Misc. 881, 289 N. Y. S. 328, (1937) 250 App. Div. 871, 297 N. Y. S. 150. (1937) 280 N. Y. 681, 21 N. E. 2d 193. Neither the Appellate Division nor the Court of Appeals wrote an opinion in affirming the decision of the Surrogate. See 8 Wigmore, Evidence, § 2391, note 1, for criticism of this decision.

28 (1954) 307 N. Y. 181, 120 N. E. 2d 777.

For a discussion of the Cashman and Coddington Cases, see notes in (1954) 40 Corn. L. Q. 148; (1955) 24 Fordham L. Rev. 493; (1955) 68 Harv. L. Rev. 725; (1954) 29 N. Y. U. L. Rev. 1722.

29 The opinion of Justice Van Voorhis, dissenting, is well worth reading.

30 Justice Conway, speaking for the majority of the court in the Coddington Case, intimated that the rule announced might, in certain cases, operate quite harshly, but that the remedy would be with the Legislature and not with the Court of Appeals.

31 N. Y. Laws of 1955, c. 466. For the history and purpose of this amendment, see Bulletin #7, pp. 431-433 of the Committee on State Legislation of the Association of the Bar of the City of New York (April 21, 1955); Year Book, (1955) of the Association of the Bar of the City of New York, p. 333.

formerly been barred as confidential communications provided only that they are not such as tend to disgrace the memory of the deceased patient.[32]

There still remains the question: What sort of facts and confidential communications would tend to disgrace the memory of the deceased? The answer is not an easy one. It would be difficult, indeed, to lay down a precise rule which will apply to any and all situations. An executor cannot waive the privilege so as to permit the attending physician to testify that the patient was an alcoholic and suffered from delirium tremens since such evidence would certainly disgrace his memory.[33] But testimony disclosing that the deceased had suffered from tuberculosis,[34] or that he died as the result of a mouth infection following the extraction of a tooth does not tend to disgrace his memory.[35] And one judge has held that disclosing the fact that the patient suffered from arteriosclerosis does not tend to disgrace his memory.[36] There is a lack of harmony among the courts as to whether evidence pertaining to the patient's act of self-destruction tends to disgrace his memory. Three courts have admitted such evidence;[37] one has not.[38]

---

[32] Matter of Boyle (1955) 208 Misc. 942, 145 N. Y. S. 2d 386.

[33] Mulligan v. Sinski, (1913) 156 App. Div. 35, 140 N. Y. S. 835, aff'd. 214 N. Y. 678, 108 N. E. 1101.

[34] Murray v. Physical Culture Hotel, Inc., (1939) 258 App. Div. 334, 16 N. Y. S. 2d 978, aff'd 17 N. Y. S. 2d 862.

[35] Waldron v. State, (1948) 193 Misc. 113, 82 N. Y. S. 2d 822.

[36] Van Voorhis, J., dissenting, in Matter of Coddington, (1954) 307 N. Y. 181, 120 N. E. 2d 777.

[37] Stiles v. Clifton Springs Sanitarium Co., (1947) 74 F. Supp. 907. The executrix of the deceased patient may waive the privilege in order to prove by medical witnesses that the deceased was suffering from a mental disorder when he committed suicide. Such evidence explains an otherwise reprehensible act.

Killip v. Rochester General Hospital, (1955) 1 Misc. 2d 349, 146 N. Y. S. 2d 164. Motion by administrator of estate of deceased patient to examine hospital records showing that he jumped from window of hospital while temporarily insane, granted.

Bolts v. Union Central Life Ins. Co., (1940) 20 N. Y. S. 2d 675, 677: "Unless the circumstances leading to suicide are in themselves immoral or disgraceful, the mere act of self-destruction, of itself, does not necessarily tend to disgrace the memory of the decedent."

[38] Eder v. Cashin, (1953) 281 App. Div. 456, 120 N. Y. S. 2d 165. See also Meyer v. Supreme Lodge, K. of P., (1904) 178 N. Y. 63, 70 N. E. 111, 198 U. S. 508, 49 Law Ed. 1146, 25 Su. Ct. 754, 64 L. R. A. 839, to the effect that suicide is a disgraceful act.

In Ohio, prior to the revision of the statute in 1953, the courts had consistently held that the personal representative of the deceased patient could not waive the privilege so as to permit the attending physician to testify.[39] Now he may do so.[40]

In Wisconsin, the courts, for many years, held that after the death of the patient, neither the personal representative nor anyone else could waive the privilege.[41] In 1927, the statute was amended and now provides that, in case of the patient's death or disability, "his personal representative or other person authorized to sue for personal injury" may waive the privilege.[42] In a tax case, the court expressed some doubt whether the personal representative could waive the privilege in any action other than for damages for personal injury,[43] but later, in a case involving almost identical facts, held that the words "personal representatives" means the executor or administrator of the deceased, and allowed the executors to waive the privilege.[44] In an action for the probate of the will of the deceased patient, the father, who was the sole heir at law of the deceased, could not waive the privilege over the objection of the proponents, since he was not the personal representative and therefore had no authority under the statute to waive its provisions.[45]

---

[39] McKee v. New Idea, Inc., (1942) ....Ohio App........, 36 Ohio Law Abst. 563, 44 N. E. 2d 697; Colwell v. Dwyer, (1940) ....Ohio App........, 33 Ohio Law Abst. 455, 35 N. E. 2d 789; Parisky v. Pierstorff, (1939) 63 Ohio App. 503, 27 N. E. 2d 254. The same rule applied with respect to the attorney-client privilege. Swetland v. Miles, (1920) 101 Ohio St. 501, 130 N. E. 22. It should, perhaps, be mentioned that in one case, because the action was brought under the liberal provisions of the Workmen's Compensation Law, waiver was permitted. Industrial Comm'n. v. Warnke, (1936) 131 Ohio St. 140, 2 N. E. 2d 248.

[40] (1953) Ohio Rev. Code § 2317.02.

[41] Borosich v. Metropolitan Life Ins. Co., (1926) 191 Wis. 239, 210 N. W. 829; Maine v. Maryland Casualty Co., (1920) 172 Wis. 350, 178 N. W. 749, 15 A. L. R. 1536; Casson v. Schoenfeld, (1918) 166 Wis. 401, 166 N. W. 23, L. R. A. 1918 C. 162.

[42] It also authorizes the beneficiary of an insurance policy to waive the privilege. See Appendix, herein.

[43] Will of Harnischfeger, (1932) 208 Wis. 317, 242 N. W. 153, 243 N. W. 453.

[44] Estate of Gallun, (1934) 215 Wis. 314, 254 N. W. 542.

[45] Will of King, (1947) 251 Wis. 269, 29 N. W. 2d 69.

117. Same: Heir, Devisee, Legatee, Donee and Next of Kin

In a few jurisdictions, the statute expressly designates the person or persons who may waive the privilege after the death of the patient; in others, the question has been resolved by the courts. In Mississippi, the statute provides that the privilege of the deceased patient may be waived by his personal representative "or legal heirs in case there be no personal representative."[1] In several jurisdictions, the statute grants to the heirs, or to certain ones, the right to waive, but it is a limited one.[2] As shown earlier, some of the statutes grant the right to the personal representative only.[3]

In some jurisdictions where the statute makes no provision whatever for waiver after the death of the patient, the courts, by judicial construction,[4] have usually permitted an heir[5] to waive the privilege. Generally speaking, the reasons justifying a waiver by the personal representative justify also a waiver by the heirs.[6] The general rule is, therefore, that, except where the statute expressly limits the authority to waive to the personal representative or to other designated persons, the heirs of the patient, or his next of kin, devisees, legatees, and donees may waive the protection of

---

[1] (1950) Miss. Code. Ann. § 1697. Appendix, herein.

The waiver clause was added in 1944. Prior thereto, neither the personal representative nor the heirs could waive the privilege. Watkins v. Watkins, (1926) 142 Miss. 210, 106 So. 753; McCaw v. Turner, (1921) 126 Miss. 260, 88 So. 705.

[2] California, Canal Zone, Guam, Michigan, Nevada, New York. Appendix, herein.

[3] § 116, herein.

[4] Gorman v. Hickey, (1937) 145 Kan. 54, 62, 64 P. 2d 587: "It must be kept in mind that it is only by judicial expansion of the terms of our statute that the privilege of the patient is accorded either to his heirs or to his personal representative; and it would close an important avenue for the judicial ascertainment of the truth to push that statutory privilege so far as to exclude the physician's testimony when the executor objects to its admission, although the heirs, his nearest blood kindred, were ready to waive it."

[5] Generally speaking, the word "heir," as used by most of the courts in this connection, is not restricted to its ordinary technical meaning but is used in its broadest sense and includes those who, because of their relationship, stand for the deceased patient in protecting and conserving his property and interests or claim rights to his estate through devise, bequest, or inheritance.

[6] Schornick v. Schornick, (1944) 25 Ariz. 563, 220 Pac. 397, 31 A. L. R. 159; 8 Wigmore, Evidence, § 2391.

the statute as to the privileged nature of information obtained by
the attending physician of the patient, or, as to that which is set
forth in a hospital record.[7]

There are a few decisions to the effect that, in will contests,
the right to waive can be exercised only by the heir who seeks to
uphold the will, not by one who seeks to strike it down.[8] The distinction is not sound[9] and the majority of the courts which have

---

[7] Representative cases supporting this general proposition are: Schornick v. Schornick, (1944) 25 Ariz. 563, 220 Pac. 397, 31 A. L. R. 159; Hyatt v. Wroten, (1931) 184 Ark.
847, 43 S. W. 2d 726; Schirmer v. Baldwin, (1930) 182 Ark. 581, 32 S. W. 2d 162; Shapter's Estate, (1906) 35 Colo. 578, 85 Pac. 688, 6 L. R. A. (n. s.) 575; Sprouse v. Magee,
(1928) 46 Idaho 622, 269 Pac. 993; Stayner v. Nye, (1949) 227 Ind. 231, 85 N. E. 2d 496;
Swain's Estate, (1919) 189 Iowa 28, 174 N. W. 493; Barry v. Walker, (1911) 152 Iowa
154, 128 N. W. 386; Altig v. Altig, (1908) 137 Iowa 420, 114 N. W. 1056; Winters v.
Winters, (1897) 102 Iowa 53, 71 N. W. 184; Gorman v. Hickey, (1937) 145 Kan. 54, 64 P.
2d 587; Flack v. Brewster, (1920) 107 Kan. 63, 190 Pac. 616; Bruington v. Wagoner,
(1917) 100 Kan. 10, 164 Pac. 1057; Fish v. Poorman, (1911) 85 Kan. 237, 116 Pac. 898;
Oldenberg v. Leiberg, (1913) 177 Mich. 150, 142 N. W. 1076; Re Koenig's Estate, (1956)
247 Minn. 580, 78 N. W. 2d 364 (hospital record); Spurr v. Spurr, (1920) 285 Mo. 163,
226 S. W. 35; Thompson v. Ish, (1889) 99 Mo. 160, 12 S. W. 510; Baker v. Mardis,
(1928) 221 Mo. App. 1185, 1 S. W. 2d 223; Estate of Gray, (1911) 88 Neb. 835, 130 N. W.
746, 33 L. R. A. (n. s.) 319, Ann. Cas. 1912 B. 1037; Porter's Estate, (1953) 208 Okla.
475, 257 P. 2d 517; Thomas's Estate, (1931) 165 Wash. 42, 4 P. 2d 837, 7 P. 2d 1119;
Gagne v. Alliance Nationale, [1946] 13 I. L. R. 13 (Quebec).

For additional cases, see note, 31 A. L. R. 167; 126 A. L. R. 380.

Contra: Auld v. Cathro, (1910) 20 N. D. 461, 128 N. W. 1025, 32 L. R. A. (n. s.)
71, Ann. Cas. 1913 A. 90; See also Will of King, (1947) 251 Wis. 269, 29 N. W. 2d 69;
Will of Hunt, (1904) 122 Wis. 460, 100 N. W. 874. The recent amendment to the Ohio
statute authorizes the spouse, executor or administrator to waive the privilege. The
rule that heirs, as such, cannot waive, remains unchanged.

[8] Towles v. McCurdy, (1904) 163 Ind. 12, 15, 71 N. E. 129: "For obvious reasons, when
the controversy is among heirs and devisees, the set of such heirs or devisees who
strive to overthrow the will cannot, for their own benefit, and against the wishes of
the other set, who desire to sustain it, waive the objection to evidence otherwise
incompetent, to the detriment of the interests of those who seek to establish the will."
Pence v. Myers, (1913) 180 Ind. 282, 101 N. E. 716.

[9] Re Koenig's Estate, (1956) 247 Minn. 580, 587, 78 N. W. 2d 364, 368: "Is there any
sound reason why the heirs who are contesting the validity of the will may not do so?
It should be kept in mind that the subject of inquiry is whether the instrument under
consideration is the decedent's will at all. If the testator lacked mental capacity to
make a will, the instrument is not a will at all. Nor is the person nominated as executor a legal representative. In such case the position of the heirs who claim the testator
lacked mental capacity is no more adverse to the estate than the position of the one
who asserts mental capacity. The whole purpose of the inquiry is to determine what
》》→

considered the question hold that either the contestants or the proponents may waive the privilege of the patient-testator.[10] Obviously there need not be unanimity among the heirs or others entitled to effect a waiver of the privilege, but all or any may exercise the right to waive it.[11] The heirs or donees of a common ancestor may waive the privilege even though the latter do not claim as heirs.[12]

The waiver need not be express, but may be implied where the heir fails to object to the introduction of privileged matter when it is first offered,[13] or when he himself introduces in evidence the physician's testimony or other privileged information.[14]

is the truth of the matter with respect to the mental competency of the testator." The proponent of the will was the executrix named therein who was also a residuary legatee.

For another criticism of the restrictive rule, see Winters v. Winters, (1897) 102 Iowa 53, 58, 71 N. W. 184.

[10] Shapter's Estate, (1906) 35 Colo. 578, 85 Pac. 688, 6 L. R. A. (n. s.) 575; Swain's Estate, (1919) 189 Iowa 28, 174 N. W. 493; Barry v. Walker, (1911) 152 Iowa 154, 128 N. W. 386; Winters v. Winters, (1897) 102 Iowa 53, 71 N. W. 184; Gorman v. Hickey, (1937) 145 Kan. 54, 64 P. 2d 587; Oldenberg v. Leiberg, (1913) 177 Mich. 150, 142 N. W. 1076 (by statute); Spurr v. Spurr, (1920) 285 Mo. 163, 226 S. W. 35; Thompson v. Ish, (1889) 99 Mo. 160, 12 S. W. 510; Estate of Gray, (1911) 88 Neb. 835, 130 N. W. 746, 33 L. R. A. (n. s.) 319, Ann. Cas. 1912 B. 1037.

In a will contest in New York, an heir or next of kin contesting the will may waive the privilege but not as to facts or communications such as tend to disgrace the memory of the patient. Matter of Elizabeth Cashman, (1936) 159 Misc. 881, 289 N. Y. S. 328, aff'd. (1939) 280 N. Y. 861, 21 N. E. 2d 193; Lippe v. Brandner, (1907) 120 App. Div. 230, 105 N. Y. S. 225.

See discussion of New York cases, § 116, herein.

In South Dakota, the privilege does not apply in will contests, hence either side may introduce the testimony of the attending physician. Golder's Estate, (1916) 37 S. D. 397, 158 N. W. 735.

[11] Gorman v. Hickey, (1937) 145 Kan. 54, 64 P. 2d 587; Lippe v. Brandner, (1907) 120 App. Div. 230, 105 N. Y. S. 225; Matter of Hopkins, (1902) 73 App. Div. 559, 77 N. Y. S. 178, reversed on other grounds 172 N. Y. 360, 65 N. E. 173; Matter of Murphy, (1895) 85 Hun. 575, 33 N. Y. S. 198. *Re* Koenig's Estate, (1956) 247 Minn. 580, 587, 78 N. W. 2d 364, 369: "While the question probably is not before us here, it should be the rule also that there need not be unanimity among the heirs before there can be a waiver."

[12] Rost v. Heyka, (1930) 130 Kan. 5, 285 Pac. 539.

[13] Studabaker v. Faylor, (1912) 52 Ind. App. 171, 98 N. E. 318.

See § 130, herein.

[14] Hyatt v. Wroten, (1931) 184 Ark. 847, 43 S. W. 2d 726; Schirmer v. Baldwin, (1930)

Furthermore, where the heir is not permitted to waive the privilege, he may nevertheless, by voluntarily introducing the testimony of the patient's physician, be estopped from claiming the protection of the statutory privilege when the adverse party offers the testimony of another physician who also attended the patient.[15]

In an action brought by the heir to set aside a conveyance made by the deceased grantor-patient on the ground of the latter's mental incompetency, the heir may waive the privilege over objection by the grantee.[16]

118. Same: Spouse

In several jurisdictions, the surviving spouse of the deceased patient is expressly authorized by the statute to waive the privilege. In Ohio,[1] the right is unlimited; in other jurisdictions, it is expressly restricted to specified classes of actions or proceedings.[2]

Where the statute is silent as to the right or power of anyone to waive the privilege after the death of the patient, the courts gen-

←※

182 Ark. 581, 32 S. W. 2d 162; Sager v. Moltz, (1923) 80 Ind. App. 122, 139 N. E. 687 (devisees); Chaffee v. Kaufman, (1923) 113 Kan. 254, 214 Pac. 618; Flack v. Brewster, (1920) 107 Kan. 63, 190 Pac. 616; Monroe's Will, (1946) 270 App. Div. 1039, 63 N. Y. S. 2d 141 (next of kin); Pringle v. Burroughs, (1902) 70 App. Div. 12, 74 N. Y. S. 1055, aff'd. 185 N. Y. 375, 78 N. E. 150; Porter's Estate, (1953) 208 Okla. 475, 257 P. 2d 517; Thomas's Estate, (1931) 165 Wash. 42, 4 P. 2d 837, 7 P. 2d 1119.

15 Estate of Visaxis, (1928) 95 Cal. App. 617, 273 Pac. 165; Weis v. Weis, (1947) 147 Ohio St. 416, 72 N. E. 2d 245, 169 A. L. R. 668.

16 Calhoun v. Jacobs, (1944) 79 App. D. C. 29, 141 F. 2d 729 (heirs v. stranger); Schornick v. Schornick, (1923) 25 Ariz. 563, 220 Pac. 397, 31 A. L. R. 159 (son of deceased v. widow of deceased); Stayner v. Nye, (1949) 227 Ind. 231, 85 N. E. 2d 496 (heirs and administrator v. stranger); Studabaker v. Faylor, (1912) 52 Ind. App. 171, 98 N. E. 318 (heirs v. stranger); Fish v. Poorman, (1911) 85 Kan. 237, 116 Pac. 898 (heirs v. stranger).

In Flack v. Brewster, (1920) 107 Kan. 63, 190 Pac. 616 and in Bruington v. Wagoner, (1917) 100 Kan. 10, 164 Pac. 1057, the controversy was between heirs of the grantor, but in each case the defendants defended *as grantees,* not as heirs; hence, they stood in the attitude of a stranger to the estate and could not waive the privilege.

Cf. Rost v. Heyka, (1930) 130 Kan. 5, 285 Pac. 539.

1 (1953) Ohio Rev. Code § 2317.02. See Appendix, herein. Prior to the amendment of 1953, the widow, in an action brought under the Workmen's Compensation Law, could waive the privilege of her deceased husband. Industrial Commission v. Warnke, (1936) 131 Ohio St. 140, 2 N. E. 2d 248.

2 e. g., California (wrongful death); Guam (wrongful death); Canal Zone (wrongful death); Nevada (wrongful death); New York (will contests). See Appendix, herein.

erally permit the spouse of the deceased patient to waive the privilege, particularly where the spouse is attempting to enforce his or her rights in the estate of the deceased.[3] In an action brought by the widow to recover damages for the wrongful death of her husband, the court assumed without argument that in such action she was the representative of the deceased and had the right to waive his privilege.[4] In New York, the statute expressly provides that when the validity of the patient's will is in question the surviving spouse may waive the privilege.[5]

The waiver need not be express, but may be implied, and generally will be implied where the surviving spouse introduces in

---

[3] Boyles v. Cora, (1942) 232 Iowa 822, 846, 6 N. W. 2d 401: "If executors, heirs, legatees and devisees in will contests may waive the privilege of the statute to protect their rights under the will of the testator, or in his property, and if administrators and heirs may waive the privilege in suits to set aside conveyances in order to protect their property rights, we know of no sound reason why a surviving spouse may not waive the privilege in an action to set aside an alleged wrongful deed of a deceased spouse, in order to protect the dower or distributive share in the property so disposed of. The rights of the widow in the estate of her deceased husband are fixed by statute, by the same authority which specifies the rights of heirs. These rights of appellee are on a plane as high as those of an heir, and of similar character, and are as much entitled to protection. The widow is as certainly entitled to waive the privilege of the statute as in an heir, or a devisee having no relationship to the testator, or as an executor or administrator, who may have no real interest in the estate." In discussing the right of the executor, administrator, or heir to waive the privilege, the courts, by way of dicta, have frequently treated the surviving spouse as a personal representative of the deceased and have generally approved his or her right to waive the privilege of the deceased spouse. See cases cited in §§ 116, 117, herein.

[4] Groll v. Tower, (1884) 85 Mo. 249. *Accord:* Denny v. Robertson, (1944) 352 Mo. 609, 179 S. W. 2d 5.

Contra: Mageau v. Great Northern Ry., (1908) 103 Minn. 290, 115 N. W. 651, 15 L. R. A. (n. s.) 511, 14 Ann. Cas. 551, where it was held that the spouse has no power to waive, this being a right which only the personal representative may exercise.

Moreover, it has been held that, in a proceeding under the Workmens' Compensation Act, the widow of the deceased employee-patient cannot waive the latter's privilege. Bassil v. Ford Motor Co., (1936) 278 Mich. 173, 270 N. W. 258, 107 A. L. R. 1491. The Supreme Court of Ohio has held otherwise. See note 1, infra. Whether the defendant, on trial for the murder of his wife, could waive her privilege, was not decided in State v. DeZeler, (1950) 230 Minn. 39, 41 N. W. 2d 313, 15 A. L. R. 2d 1137, since the record failed to disclose that the defendant had been prejudiced.

[5] (1955) N. Y. Civ. Prac. Act § 354. See Appendix, herein. It is not necessary to a waiver that the executor, heir, and spouse should join therein, but either or any may do so. Hopkin's Will, (1902) 73 App. Div. 559, 77 N. Y. S. 178, rev'd. on other grounds 172 N. Y. 360, 65 N. E. 173. See also § 117, note 11.

evidence the testimony of the attending physician or other privileged information.[6]

119. Same: Party in Interest: The New York Rule

In New York, there are two situations in which the privilege provided by section 352 of the Civil Practice Act may be waived by a "party in interest" so as to permit physicians and nurses to disclose information as to the mental or physical condition of the patient who is deceased, which they acquired while attending him, except, of course, such confidential communications and such facts as would tend to disgrace the memory of the patient.[1]

Section 354 of the Civil Practice Act provides that the provisions of section 352 may be waived by "any party in interest" in any litigation wherein the interests of the personal representative of the deceased patient are deemed by the trial judge to be adverse to those of the estate of the deceased patient. However, no such waiver by a party in interest may be made unless (a) there has been an appointment of a personal representative of the deceased, (b) the matter has been brought to trial and a determination made by the trial court of such adverse interest, or (c) upon the appointment of a personal representative, a stipulation is made prior to the trial consenting to such waiver, signed by counsel for the litigants.[2]

---

[6] Moreno v. New Guadalupe Mining Co., (1918) 35 Cal. App. 744, 170 Pac. 1088; Stayton v. Stayton, (1938) 148 Kan. 172, 81 P. 2d 1; Doty v. Crystal Ice & Fuel Co., (1925) 118 Kan. 323, 235 Pac. 96; Denny v. Robertson, (1944) 352 Mo. 609, 179 S. W. 2d 5.

But where the widow testified only to the general condition of her husband and did not disclose any communication between her husband and his physician, no waiver resulted.

Gillen v. Industrial Comm'n., (1938) 59 Ohio App. 241, 17 N. E. 2d 663.

[1] For discussion of this limitation, see § 116, herein.

[2] Kinbacher v. Schneider, (1949) 194 Misc. 969, 89 N. Y. S. 2d 350. The plaintiff, mother of the deceased, brought an action against the defendant, deceased's husband, to set aside two deeds to real property. In aid of this action, plaintiff moved for an order requiring certain officials of two hospitals to produce all records for the purpose of inspection, pertaining to the admission and diagnosis of the deceased grantor. The deceased left no will, or assets other than the subject of this action. No administrator of the estate of the deceased had been appointed. Plaintiff contended she was a party in interest and as such had the right to waive the deceased's privilege.

Plaintiff's motion was denied.

See also Matter of Ericson, (1951) 200 Misc. 1005, 106 N. Y. S. 2d 203.

Section 354 also provides that if the validity of the will of the deceased patient is in question, the privilege may be waived by certain designated persons, or by "any other party in interest." It has been held that one who is not a relative or beneficiary under the will in question, but is the sole beneficiary under a former will, may not waive the privilege since he is not a party in interest.[3] This seems to be an unreasonable interpretation of the statute and places an unwarranted restriction upon the phrase "or any other party in interest." Other courts have held that the phrase was clearly intended to include *all* persons interested in the estate, whether relatives or not.[4] A nephew of the deceased, who is also named as a residuary legatee is a party in interest and, in a will contest, may waive the privilege of the deceased testator.[5] It will be observed that the language of the statute designating those who may waive the privilege is in the disjunctive and not conjunctive form. It does not require that *all* parties must waive the privilege.[6]

120. *Same: Beneficiary of Insurance Policy*

In three jurisdictions, the statute expressly empowers the beneficiary, in an action to recover the proceeds of an insurance policy, to waive the privilege of the deceased insured.[1] In other

---

[3] *Re* Faiher's Will, (1933) 239 App. Div. 246, 248, 268 N. Y. S. 120: "It is our view that the contestant, not being a relative, and sustaining no trust relation to the deceased that would call upon her to guard the privacy of the testator, did not have such an interest as would authorize her to waive the privacy provided for in section 352 of the Civil Practice Act; and the surrogate committed no error in excluding the testimony of the physician upon the waiver of the contestant."

[4] Matter of Murphy's Will, (1895) 85 Hun. 575, 33 N. Y. S. 198; Matter of Ackerman's Estate, (1937) 163 Misc. 624, 298 N. Y. S. 38; Matter of Mele's Estate, (1916) 94 Misc. 555, 157 N. Y. S. 669.

See also Matter of Boyle, (1955) 208 Misc. 942, 145 N. Y. S. 2d 386

In Matter of Cleveland's Will, (1948) 273 App. Div. 623, 78 N. Y. S. 2d 897, the court confined the rule of the Faiher Case "strictly to the facts thereof."

[5] Matter of Cleveland's Will, (1948) 273 App. Div. 623, 78 N. Y. S. 2d 897.

[6] *Ibid.* See also Matter of Monroe's Will, (1946) 270 App. Div. 1039, 63 N. Y. S. 2d 141.

[1] Minnesota, Puerto Rico, and Wisconsin.

See Appendix, herein.

See also Rule 27(4) of the Uniform Rules of Evidence (1953) and Rule 223(3) of the Model Code of Evidence (1942).

jurisdictions, the question whether or not the beneficiary may waive the insured's privilege is one of statutory construction upon which there is a disparity of opinion, depending upon the wording of the particular statute and the different attitudes of the courts towards the purpose and policy of the privilege in general.

The view taken by the majority of the courts which have considered the question, is that the privilege of the insured may be waived by the beneficiary in an action on the policy or the certificate of insurance.[2] In such case, the beneficiary may be said to represent the insured patient for such purpose. In other jurisdictions, however, the courts, due largely to the restrictive language of the statute involved, have not permitted the beneficiary to waive the deceased's privilege. In New York, the statute does not designate a beneficiary of insurance as one entitled to waive the privilege; therefore, the courts refuse to extend the right to him.[3] In Ohio, it has been held that the beneficiary cannot waive the privi-

---

[2] National Annuity Ass'n. v. McCall, (1912) 103 Ark. 201, 146 S. W. 125, 48 L. R. A. (n. s.) 418. See also Aetna Life Ins. Co. v. McAdoo, (1939) 106 F. 2d 618, construing Arkansas statute.

Penn Mutual Life Ins. Co. v. Wiler, (1884) 100 Ind. 92; Luce v. Service Life Ins. Co., (1939) 227 Iowa 532, 288 N. W. 681; Johnson v. Fidelity & Cas. Co., (1915) 184 Mich. 406, 151 N. W. 593, L. R. A. 1916 A. 475; Olson v. Court of Honor, (1907) 100 Minn. 117, 110 N. W. 374, 8 L. R. A. (n. s.) 521, 10 Ann. Cas. 622; Bouligny v. Metropolitan Life Ins. Co., (1942) _____ Mo. App. _____ , 160 S. W. 2d 474; Willis v. Order of Railroad Telegraphers, (1941) 139 Neb. 46, 296 N. W. 443; Sovereign Camp W. O. W. v. Grandon, (1902) 64 Neb. 39, 89 N. W. 448.

See also O'Brien v. General Acc., Fire, & Life Assur. Co., (1930) 42 F. 2d 48, construing Nebraska statute.

United States National Life & Cas. Co. v. Heard, (1931) 148 Okla. 274, 298 Pac. 619; National Life & Acc. Ins. Co. v. Bell, (1930) 144 Okla. 236, 291 Pac. 106.

In Kirsch v. Federal Life Ins. Co., (1939) 149 Kan. 309, 87 P. 2d 591, the beneficiary was permitted to introduce the testimony of the deceased's physician since no heir-at-law or personal representative objected.

[3] Saad v. New York Life Ins. Co., (1922) 201 App. Div. 544, 194 N. Y. S. 445, aff'd. 235 N. Y. 550, 139 N. E. 730; Roth v. Equitable Life Assur. Soc., (1945) 186 Misc. 403, 59 N. Y. S. 2d 707, aff'd. 270 App. Div. 923, 62 N. Y. S. 2d 612, appeal denied 296 N. Y. 1061, 69 N. E. 2d 565; Polachek v. New York Life Ins. Co., (1934) 147 Misc. 16, 263 N. Y. S. 230, aff'd. 240 App. Div. 1028, 268 N. Y. S. 995; Beil v. Supreme Lodge, K. of H., (1903) 80 App. Div. 609, 80 N. Y. S. 751; Entian v. Provident Mutual Life Ins. Co., (1935) 155 Misc. 227, 279 N. Y. S. 580. Cf. Engl v. Aetna Life Ins. Co., (1943) 139 F. 2d 469. See also note, (1949) 1 Syracuse L. Rev. 101.

lege,[4] and the recent amendment of the statute,[5] does not seem to change the rule, unless the beneficiary be also the surviving spouse, or the executor or administrator of the estate of the deceased insured. In *Shuman* v. *Supreme Lodge, K. of H.*,[6] the plaintiff was once the beneficiary in his father's policy of insurance. Shortly before his death, the insured changed the beneficiary and named his brother. Plaintiff claimed that when this change was made, his father was mentally incompetent. At the trial, the plaintiff, over objection by the insured's brother, was permitted to introduce as a witness the deceased's physician to show the mental incapability of the insured. This was reversible error since the plaintiff had no right to waive the deceased's privilege.

Where waiver by the beneficiary is permitted, it need not be express but may be implied from his acts or conduct.[7] As pointed out earlier, it has been held that to make out a case of implied waiver there must be a clear, unequivocal and decisive act showing such purpose, or acts amounting to an estoppel.[8]

Where a written waiver by a beneficiary is limited to a specific period of time, it can have no application to the offered tes-

---

[4] Russell v. Penn Mutual Life Ins. Co., (1941) 70 Ohio App. 113, 41 N. E. 2d 251; Thompson v. National Life & Acc. Ins. Co., (1941) 68 Ohio App. 439, 37 N. E. 2d 621.

[5] (1953) Ohio Rev. Code § 2317.02. See Appendix, herein. Prior to the revision of the Wisconsin statute, the beneficiary of an insurance policy could not waive the insured's privilege. Borosich v. Metropolitan Life Ins. Co., (1926) 191 Wis. 239, 210 N. W. 829; Maine v. Maryland Cas. Co., (1920) 172 Wis. 350, 178 N. W. 749, 15 A. L. R. 1536. Undoubtedly, the strong dissent of Owen, J., in this case brought about the amendment which now permits the beneficiary to waive the privilege. See Appendix, herein.

[6] (1900) 110 Iowa 480, 81 N. W. 717. Both claimants of the fund were blood relatives of the deceased, but neither of them asserted rights in that capacity; rather, each claimed to be an appointee of the deceased.

[7] O'Brien v. General Acc., Fire & Life Assur. Co., (1930) 42 F. 2d 48; National Annuity Ass'n. v. McCall, (1912) 103 Ark. 201, 146 S. W. 125, 48 L. R. A. (n. s.) 418; Toler v. Atlantic Life Ins. Co., (1952) ___ Mo. App. ___ , 248 S. W. 2d 53; Bouligny v. Metropolitan Life Ins. Co., (1942) ___ Mo. App. ___ . 160 S. W. 2d 474; Willis v. Order of Railroad Telegraphers, (1941) 139 Neb. 46, 296 N. W. 443; Sovereign Camp, W. O. W. v. Grandon, (1902) 64 Neb. 39, 89 N. W. 448; United States National Life & Cas. Co. v. Heard, (1931) 148 Okla. 274, 298 Pac. 619.

See also the Nevada statute. Appendix, herein.

[8] Fitzgerald v. Metropolitan Life Ins. Co., (1941) ___ Mo. App. ___ , 149 S. W. 2d 389; Andrews v. Washington National Life Ins. Co., (1936) ___ Mo. App. ___ , 93 S. W. 2d 1045.

timony of a physician whose information was acquired during a period outside the scope of such waiver.[9]

When, in an application for life insurance, the insured waives the benefits and protection of the physician-patient privilege statute, the waiver is equally as available to the beneficiary of the policy as to the insurer.[10]

---

[9] Scott v. Metropolitan Life Ins. Co., (1941) 140 Neb. 581, 300 N. W. 835.

[10] Trull v. Modern Woodmen, O. A., (1906) 12 Idaho 318, 85 Pac. 1081, 10 Ann. Cas. 53; Miser v. Iowa State Traveling Mens Ass'n., (1937) 223 Iowa 662, 273 N. W. 155.

CHAPTER XVII

Waiver Resulting From Commencement of Certain Actions and Proceedings

121. Actions for Damages for Personal Injury

The voluntary bringing of a lawsuit by a person seeking the recovery of damages for personal injury should constitute a waiver of the physician-patient privilege.[1] Having initiated litigation which necessarily involves the disclosure of his alleged injury and impaired physical condition, the claimant should not be permitted to maintain a barrier of secrecy against an opponent's inquiry as to the true nature and extent thereof.[2] A patient may enforce secrecy

---

[1] 8 Wigmore, Evidence, § 2389: "In the first place, the *bringing of an action* in which an essential part of the issue is the existence of physical ailment should be a *waiver* of the privilege for all communications concerning that ailment. The whole reason for the privilege is the patient's supposed unwillingness that the ailment should be disclosed to the world at large; hence the bringing of a suit in which the very declaration, and much more the proof, discloses the ailment to the world at large, is of itself an indication that the supposed repugnancy to disclosure does not exist. If the privilege means anything at all in its origin, it means this as a sequel."

See also McCormick, Evidence, § 106.

[2] Vanderbilt, (1949) Minimum Standards of Judicial Administration, p. 578: "In personal injury claims particularly is the privilege ridiculously incongruous; for the plaintiff comes into court alleging a specific injury and then refuses to let the court listen to testimony concerning that injury."

if he chooses, but once he makes public his physical condition by pleadings and by evidence in court in order to serve his own pecuniary ends, any good and sufficient reason for shutting out the testimony of the medical men who attended him no longer obtains.[3]

In a few jurisdictions, the statute provides, in substance, that where a person brings suit to recover damages for personal injury, such action will be deemed to constitute a consent by the person bringing such suit that any physician who has prescribed for or treated him shall testify.[4]

In the absence of such a provision, however, the courts, which have considered the question, universally hold that a person does not waive the privilege by the mere filing of an action for damages for personal injury.[5]

---

[3] The jury is certainly entitled to know whether the plaintiff's physical condition (such as halting gait, paralysis, loss of voice, blindness) for which he claims damages from the defendant resulted from his injury, or was caused by the ravages of some insidious disease from which he has long suffered. The amount of truth that has been concealed by the statutory rule is unquestionably extensive. The law reports contain many cases where the plaintiff, by invoking the privilege, has successfully suppressed reliable medical testimony and hospital records tending to show that the afflictions of which he complained were the natural consequences of a previous disease or ailment such as syphilis, gonorrhea, pernicious anemia, tuberculosis, cancer, or some other destructive malady.

[4] California, Canal Zone, Guam, Hawaii, Nevada.

Appendix, herein.

For construction of the California statute, see San Francisco v. Superior Court, (1951) 37 Cal. 2d 227, 231 P. 2d 26, 25 A. L. R. 2d 1418; Ballard v. Pacific Greyhound Lines, (1946) 28 Cal. 2d 357, 170 P. 2d 465; Phillips v. Powell, (1930) 210 Cal. 39, 290 Pac. 441; Moreno v. New Guadalupe Mining Co., (1917) 35 Cal. App. 744, 170 Pac. 1088.

In Michigan, the statute provides that if the plaintiff calls as a witness a physician who treated him for his injury, he waives the privilege as to any and all other physicians who may have treated him for the same injury. See Mulvena v. Alexander, (1936) 278 Mich. 265, 270 N. W. 291; La Count v. Von Platen-Fox Co., (1928) 243 Mich. 250, 220 N. W. 697.

In Pennsylvania, the privilege does not extend to actions for personal injury.

Rule 27(4) of the Uniform Rules of Evidence (1953) and Rule 223(3) of the Model Code of Evidence (1942) deny the application of the privilege to such cases.

[5] Federal Mining & Smelting Co. v. Dalo, (1918) 252 Fed. 356; Union Pac. R. R. v. Thomas, (1907) 152 Fed. 365; Kansas City Southern Ry. v. Miller, (1915) 117 Ark. 396, 175 S. W. 1164; Polin v. St. Paul Union Depot Co., (1924) 159 Minn. 410, 199 N. W. 87; Marfia v. Great Northern Ry., (1914) 124 Minn. 466, 145 N. W. 385; Hemminghaus

⋙→

122. *Actions for Damages for Malpractice*

The general rule is that where a patient sues his physician for malpractice, he impliedly waives the benefits and protection of the statutory privilege and consents to the physician testifying to all matters connected with his treatment of the patient's malady or injury.[1] This is the common sense view. If a patient makes public in a court of justice confidential matters pertaining to his malady or injury for the purpose of obtaining a judgment for damages against his physician, he cannot shut out the testimony of the physician himself or that of any other medical man who was present at the time covered by the testimony. By his voluntary act, the patient breaks down the barriers, and the professional duty of secrecy ceases. Any other rule would deprive the physician of his principal, if not only, means of defense and render him practically

v. Ferguson, (1948) 385 Mo. 476, 215 S. W. 2d 481; Jones v. Brooklyn, Bath & W. E. R. R., (1888) 3 N. Y. S. 253, aff'd. 121 N. Y. 683, 24 N. E. 1098; Butler v. Manhattan Ry., (1893) 3 Misc. 453, 23 N. Y. S. 163, aff'd. 143 N. Y. 630, 37 N. E. 826; La Plante v. Garrett, (1953) 282 App. Div. 1096, 126 N. Y. S. 2d 470. But *cf.* Van Heuverzwyn v. State, (1954) 206 Misc. 896, 134 N. Y. S. 2d 922.

Woodson, J., in Smart v. Kansas City, (1907) 208 Mo. 162, 185, 105 S. W. 709, 14 L. R. A. (n. s.) 565, 13 Ann. Cas. 932: "If this statute is waived by the mere filing of the suit, then the patient cannot avail himself or herself of its provisions, and the disqualification of the physician and surgeon is removed, and they are thereby authorized to disclose all information acquired by them in the examination and treatment of their patients. If no suit is brought by the patient, there could be no occasion for the physician or surgeon disclosing the confidential communications; but the instant one is brought and trial had, and that being the only possible occasion upon which the patient could avail himself of the statutory privilege, he is met with the proposition of implied waiver, and, as an inevitable result, the statutory privilege could not be invoked in that case, nor in any other. In other words, as long as suit is not instituted, the physician is disqualified by the statute, and in that case there is no express or implied waiver, but under that condition he could not testify because there is no case pending in which to testify; but if suit is instituted, that fact waives the statutory privilege, and he becomes a competent witness and is authorized to disclose all confidential communications. Such reasoning leads to an absurdity, and totally emasculates the statute."

Randa v. Bear, (1957) ___Wash.___, 312 P. 2d 640, 645: "The majority rule, however, has been that the bringing of an action in which an essential issue is the existence of a physical ailment does not constitute a waiver."

See also Kassow v. Robertson, (1957) ___Ohio Com. Pleas___, 143 N. E. 2d 926.

[1] To avoid repetition, questions pertaining to waiver in this class of actions are discussed in § 73, herein.

helpless to refute the charges of his patient, however false or unfair they might be.[2]

123. *Action for Damages for Death of Patient*

In a few states, the statute expressly provides that when any
person designated therein brings an action to recover damages on
account of the death of a patient, such person thereby consents to
the introduction in evidence of the testimony of any physician who
attended said deceased.[1] In the absence of such a provision, the
mere bringing of such an action does not constitute a waiver of the
privilege.[2]

124. *Actions for Compensation Under Workmen's Compensation Acts*

Generally speaking, the making and prosecuting of a claim for
compensation under a Workmen's Compensation Law does not, of
itself, constitute a waiver of the privilege.[1] In some states, however, the Workmen's Compensation Law expressly provides that
the privilege cannot be availed of in such proceedings.[2]

125. *Actions to Recover Proceeds of Insurance Policies*

In the absence of a provision in the statute to the contrary, the
mere bringing of an action to recover the proceeds of an insurance

---

[2] Rule 27(4) of the Uniform Rules of Evidence (1953) and Rule 223(3) of the Model
Code of Evidence (1942) deny the application of the privilege to such actions.

[1] California, Canal Zone, Guam, Nevada.

     See also Nebraska statute, Appendix, herein.

     Rule 27(4) of the Uniform Rules of Evidence (1953) and Rule 223(3) of the Model
Code of Evidence (1942) deny the application of the privilege to such actions.

[2] Jaffe v. New York, (1949) 196 Misc. 710, 94 N. Y. S. 2d 60.

[1] It has been held, however, that when a claim is not alone filed but is prosecuted, the
privilege is waived since the valid prosecution thereof necessarily involves the giving
of testimony on behalf of the claimant, with respect to the injuries alleged to have
been caused by the accident. Matter of Maryland Casualty Co., (1948) 274 App. Div.
211, 80 N. Y. S. 2d 181.

     See also La Count v. Von Platen-Fox Co., (1928) 243 Mich. 250, 220 N. W. 697.

[2] For application of the statute in Workmen's Compensation cases, see § 76, herein.

policy, does not, as a general rule, constitute a waiver of the insured's privilege.[1] Where, however, to maintain successfully an action upon a medical service contract it was obviously necessary for the patient, seeking to recover its benefits, to disclose in detail the treatment and diagnosis of her alleged ailment, it was held that the patient, by filing suit upon such contract, waived the statutory privilege and that the trial court erred in denying the insurer an opportunity to present medical evidence in its attempt to show that the patient's ailment came within the exclusionary provisions of the contract.[2]

In one state, the statute expressly provides that the bringing of an action upon an insurance contract by any person designated in the statute, shall constitute a consent by such person to the testimony of any physician who attended the deceased patient.[3]

---

[1] Maryland Casualty Co. v. Maloney, (1915) 119 Ark. 434, 178 S. W. 387, L. R. A. 1915 A 519; Foman v. Liberty Life Ins. Co., (1932) 227 Mo. App. 70, 51 S. W. 2d 212.

Contra: Weitzman v. Equitable Life Assur. Soc., (1941) 26 N. Y. S. 2d 643.

[2] Randa v. Bear, (1957) .... Wash. ...., 312 P. 2d 640, 645, 646: "In the present case, it is obvious that the use of the physician-patient privilege deprived the court of all opportunity to ascertain the material facts necessary to its determination of the principal issue raised by the pleadings, to-wit, whether or not respondent's claim in fact fell within the exclusionary provisions of the medical service contract. When respondent filed her cross-complaint against appellant, she knew that she had the burden of proving that the services in question were rendered by the hospital, that they were necessary, and that the amount charged for them was reasonable. Respondent further knew that, in order to prove these matters, she would have to testify regarding them herself and probably introduce corroborating testimony of her doctors. In so doing, she undoubtedly intended to waive the physician-patient privilege, and consequently appellant would have been able to introduce the evidence described in its various offers of proof. The court would thus have been able to render a decision after a full presentation of the material facts by both parties instead of upon one-sided, self-serving testimony of respondent. * * * We hold that respondent, by bringing a suit upon the medical service contract to which she was a party, and thus placing in issue her physical condition and the ailment for which she was treated, waived the privilege afforded her by the statute."

[3] Nevada. See Appendix, herein.

Whether this consent can be availed of by the claimant only, or by the insurance company as well: *quaere.*

CHAPTER XVIII

Waiver by Conduct

126. Application of Doctrine of Waiver to Conduct of Holder of Privilege: In General

No question in the entire field of litigation involving the physician-patient privilege statute has received as much consideration by the courts as that which is the subject of this chapter, nor has there been a greater disparity in their decisions. In actions for damages for personal injury, for the death of the patient, and for malpractice; in suits brought to recover the proceeds of life, accident, or health insurance; in actions to recover benefits due under Workmen's Compensation Acts; in will contests, actions for divorce, and in some criminal prosecutions, the claim has frequently been made that the patient, or the holder of the privilege, has expressly waived the protection of the statute by his conduct in voluntarily disclosing confidential information pertaining to the patient's physical or mental condition or the cause of death, or by permitting the same to be made public at the instance of the adverse party. In determining these questions, much will depend upon the nature and extent of the disclosure, the circumstances under which it was made, the person by whom it was made, and, of course, the attitude of the court as between a liberal or strict construction of the statute. In some instances, the courts, in construing the statute, seem to have lost sight of the plain purpose and intent of the statute and, unmindful of the doctrine of waiver, have arbitrarily shut out material and relevant evidence which, in all fairness, ought to have been admitted.

The policy of the statute, which we have hitherto discussed,[1] is to shield the relationship of physician and patient, and to protect those who are required to consult physicians from the disclosure of intimate secrets and confidential information which might humiliate and embarrass the patient in his lifetime and disgrace his memory when dead. The secret, whatever it be, is locked in the breast of the patient, or of the holder of the privilege, and he is given the key: no one but he can remove the prohibition of the statute. The common sense view, therefore, would seem to be that if he voluntarily removes the barrier of secrecy and permits confidential matters to be made public, the statutory privilege is waived.[2]

Whether the waiver is by the affirmative action of the patient, or of the holder of the privilege, in calling forth the privileged testimony or evidence, or by his negative action in not preventing the other party from introducing it, the logical effect is to deprive

---

[1] § 9, herein.

[2] See Wigmore, Evidence, §§ 2388-2391.

the statute of all further protection since there is nothing left to protect against. After the publication of the privileged matter, no further injury can be inflicted upon the rights and interests which the statute was intended to protect, and there is no further need for its enforcement.

In nearly every personal injury case, one of the questions which the jury must necessarily decide is whether the plaintiff's injuries for which he seeks damages, were sustained as a result of the accident, or existed to some extent prior thereto. The plaintiff voluntarily opens up that issue when he testifies to the nature and extent of his alleged injuries and produces his medical evidence. By so uncovering ailments and infirmities in court, does he not break the seal of secrecy and absolve the physician from the obligation of silence?[3] Is it to be tolerated that, to mulct another in damages, the plaintiff may inflame a jury with a false and exaggerated description of his injury, and yet a physician who attended him is not to be allowed to prevent a miscarriage of justice by a truthful statement of the case? Unquestionably the patient may keep the door of the sickroom closed, but should he be allowed to open it so as to give a distorted and imperfect view of what is taking place there, and then close it tight when the actual facts are about to be disclosed?[4]

It is our considered opinion that a person is entitled to have his malady, physical imperfection, or injury protected from public curiosity but if he goes into a court of justice and bases his action upon the existence, or non-existence, of some disability, physical or mental, and testifies in detail thereto, or introduces the testimony of a physician upon the subject, he is no longer entitled to claim a privilege for his condition, past or present, and the statute does not contemplate protecting him in such case. Having once consented to the publication of that which he could have kept secret, the patient ought never again be permitted to insist upon

---

[3] Rule 27(4) of the Uniform Rules of Evidence (1953) and Rule 223(3) of the Model Code of Evidence (1942) deny the statutory privilege in such actions.

[4] See dissenting opinion of Mr. Justice Hughes in Arizona & New Mexico Ry. v. Clark, (1915) 235 U. S. 669, 680, 59 Law Ed. 415, 35 Su. Ct. 210, L. R. A. 1916 C 834.

the silence which the statute was designed to afford.[5] The same reasoning applies, where, if the patient be dead, the evidence is introduced by one who is entitled to invoke the privilege of the deceased patient.

There is, however, an irreconcilable conflict in the decisions of the courts on this subject, due in part to the variety of circumstances under which the claim of waiver has been made. It is fitting and proper, therefore, that these be discussed separately.

127. Patient's Disclosure or Consent to Publication Out of Court

However incongruous it may seem, the general rule is that the publication out of court of the patient's injury, ailment, or physical imperfection, by himself or by another with his consent, does not constitute a waiver of the statutory privilege and will not deprive him of the right to invoke its protection when the same

[5] Representative cases, from some of which the author has borrowed freely in presenting the views set forth in the text, are: Schlarb v. Henderson, (1936) 211 Ind. 1, 4 N. E. 2d 205; Pittsburgh, Cincinnati, C. & St. L. Ry. v. O'Conner, (1909) 171 Ind. 686, 85 N. E. 969; Lane v. Boicourt, (1891) 128 Ind. 420, 27 N. E. 1111; Woods v. Lisbon, (1911) 150 Iowa 433, 130 N. W. 372; Demonbrun v. McHaffie, (1941) 348 Mo. 1120, 156 S. W. 2d 923; State v. Long, (1913) 257 Mo. 199, 165 S. W. 748; Epstein v. Pennsylvania R. R., (1913) 250 Mo. 1, 156 S. W. 699, 48 L. R. A. (n. s.) 394, Ann. Cas. 1915 A 423; Elliott v. Kansas City, (1906) 198 Mo. 593, 96 S. W. 1023, 6 L. R. A. (n. s.) 1082, 8 Ann. Cas. 653; Jennings v. National Life & Acc. Ins. Co., (1931) 226 Mo. App. 777, 46 S. W. 2d 226; Oliver v. Aylor, (1913) 173 Mo. App. 323, 158 S. W. 733; Webb v. Metropolitan Street Ry., (1901) 89 Mo. App. 604; Ansnes v. Loyal Protective Ins. Co., (1937) 133 Neb. 665, 276 N. W. 397; Steinberg v. New York Life Ins. Co., (1933) 263 N. Y. 45, 188 N. E. 152, 90 A. L. R. 642; People v. Bloom, (1908) 193 N. Y. 1, 85 N. E. 824, 18 L. R. A. (n. s.) 898, 15 Ann. Cas. 932; Capron v. Douglass, (1908) 193 N. Y. 11, 85 N. E. 827, 20 L. R. A. (n. s.) 1003; Morris v. New York, Ontario & W. Ry., (1895) 148 N. Y. 88, 42 N. E. 410; McKinney v. Grand Street, etc. R. R., (1888) 104 N. Y. 352, 10 N. E. 544; Schlotterer v. Brooklyn & N. Y. Ferry Co., (1903) 89 App. Div. 508, 85 N. Y. S. 847; Rauh v. Deutscher Verein, (1898) 29 App. Div. 483, 51 N. Y. S. 985; Treanor v. Manhattan Ry., (1891) 16 N. Y. S. 536; Marx v. Manhattan Ry., (1890) 56 Hun 575, 10 N. Y. S. 159; Chicago, Rock Island & Pac. R. R. v. Hughes, (1917) 64 Okla. 74, 166 Pac. 411; Roeser v. Pease, (1913) 37 Okla. 222, 131 Pac. 534; Forrest v. Portland Ry., Light & P. Co., (1913) 61 Ore. 240, 129 Pac. 1048; McUne v. Fuqua, (1953) ___Wash.___, 253 P. 2d 632, 257 P. 2d 636; Cretney v. Woodmen Accident Co., (1928) 196 Wis. 29, 219 N. W. 448, 62 A. L. R. 675.

information is elicited from him or others in a court of law where his physical condition is an issue at the trial.[1]

In a personal injury case, the defendant called as a witness the plaintiff's attending physician. It was shown that he had photographed the plaintiff because of the peculiar nature of the malady from which he suffered; that subsequently he published an article concerning the plaintiff in a medical journal and exhibited him on several occasions to members of the medical profession. Upon this showing, the court, over objection of the plaintiff, permitted the witness to testify to what the plaintiff had told him about his malady. This was reversible error since there was no waiver "upon the trial" as required by the statute.[2]

In *State* v. *Miller*,[3] the defendant was charged with a sex offense. The state called as a witness his attending physician who testified that the defendant was afflicted with a venereal disease, a fact, which, according to the testimony of several witnesses, the defendant himself had disclosed to others near the time of the alleged offense. Reversing the judgment of conviction, the Supreme Court held that the proof offered was not sufficient to establish a waiver of the statutory privilege.[4]

---

[1] The principle has also been applied to other statutory privileges. In Allen v. Allen, (1933) ....Mo. App........., 60 S. W. 2d 709, a divorce action, plaintiff offered to testify to confidential communications between himself and his wife. He claimed she had waived the husband-wife privilege because she, on several occasions, had related the same things to her relatives and friends. Held: no waiver.

In Matter of Eno, (1921) 196 App. Div. 131, 187 N. Y. S. 765, the testator showed the draft copies of his will to a third person after making certain memoranda and alterations thereon. It was held that he did not thereby waive the ban of secrecy and authorize his attorney to testify in reference thereto.

[2] Scher v. Metropolitan Street Ry., (1902) 71 App. Div. 28, 75 N. Y. S. 625. The decision is questionable. The statute should not apply in such a case. There is no secret to protect, and no further reason to enforce the statute since its purpose has already been defeated.

See Rule 37 of the Uniform Rules of Evidence (1953) and Rule 231(b) of the Model Code of Evidence (1942).

[3] (1919) 105 Wash. 475, 178 Pac. 459.

[4] Parker, J., said in part: (p. 479) "These alleged disclosures rested entirely upon the testimony of other witnesses, and not upon anything that appellant or his counsel said or did at the time of trial. Even the testimony of these witnesses tends to show that

⟫→

On the other hand, the testimony of a physician as to the paternity of a child was held competent since the patient herself had made public statements concerning the matter.[5] And where the insured made claim for the benefits of a health insurance policy and voluntarily sent to the insurer his physician's report on the condition of the insured's gall bladder, he waived the right to object to the physician's testimony on that subject.[6]

Where a motorist freely permitted the taking of a sample of his blood to test it for alcoholic content, knowing the purpose of such taking, he waived the statutory privilege which would otherwise have prevented the physician from revealing the information so acquired by him.[7]

---

appellant, in making his admissions to them, denied having the disease at the time of the alleged commission of the offense. However that may be, we think a patient's consent to his physician's testifying cannot be shown solely by the testimony of witnesses concerning the patient's previous admissions or disclosures. No decision has come to our attention holding that such is the law. It seems to us that the consent must be evidenced to the trial court by some word or act of the patient at the time of the trial, so that the trial court can conclusively know, without depending on the veracity of third persons as witnesses, that the patient has waived the privilege accorded him by the statute."

It is respectfully submitted that this decision practically nullifies the doctrine of implied waiver where the circumstances upon which it is based occur outside of court.

See dictum in Burgess v. Sims Drug Co., (1901) 114 Iowa 275, 282, 86 N. W. 307, 54 L. R. A. 364.

See also dictum in Briesenmeister v. Supreme Lodge, K. of P., (1890) 81 Mich, 525, 535, 45 N. W. 977, 8 L. R. A. 682.

[5] Matter of Strong's Estate, (1938) 168 Misc. 716, 6 N. Y. S. 2d 300, aff'd. 256 App. Div. 971, 11 N. Y. S. 2d 225.

See also Metropolitan Life Ins. Co. v. Brubaker, (1908) 78 Kan. 146, 96 Pac. 62, 18 L. R. A. (n. s.) 362, 16 Ann. Cas. 267.

[6] Bolton v. Inter-Ocean Life & Cas. Co., (1915) 187 Mo. App. 167, 172 S. W. 1187. See comment on this point in Hicks v. Metropolitan Life Ins. Co., (1916) 196 Mo. App. 162, 174, 190 S. W. 661.

But where the insured, in his application for insurance, stated that a physician had treated him for grippe, the insurer, in an action on the policy, cannot call such physician to show that he had treated the insured for heart trouble. Jones v. Preferred Bankers Life Assur. Co., (1899) 120 Mich. 211, 79 N. W. 204.

Contra: McGinty v. Brotherhood of Railway Trainmen, (1917) 166 Wis. 83, 164 N. W. 249.

[7] Schwartz v. Schneuriger, (1955) 269 Wis. 535, 69 N. W. 2d 756.

128. Disclosure in Pleadings, or in Opening Statement of Counsel

A general statement of the patient's injury or physical condition, and the claimed consequences of same, when contained in a pleading or affidavit filed in a lawsuit, will not likely be held sufficient to constitute a waiver of the statutory privilege. Manifestly, the determination of the question must rest in the sound discretion of the trial court and will depend very largely upon the extent to which the patient, or his representative, has entered into the details of the patient's injury, or condition, or has revealed other confidential matters within the protection of the statute. It would seem impracticable to state a precise rule which would be applicable to all situations.

If the patient, in his pleadings, refers to certain verbal communications between himself and his physician, he thereby gives consent to the physician's testifying to knowledge gained by such communications, but such reference does not open the door to the physician to testify also as to his knowledge acquired by personal examination of the patient.[1] And where, before trial, the representative of the deceased patient, in support of a preliminary motion, had filed an affidavit of the attending physician in which he made certain statements regarding his treatment of the patient, the affidavit could not be received in evidence in lieu of testimony and as substantive proof, since the statutory privilege had not been waived by the filing thereof.[2]

In an action brought by the plaintiff to recover the benefits of a health insurance policy, no waiver resulted from the fact that the petition disclosed confidential information concerning the plaintiff's physical condition, where it was signed by plaintiff's attorney and was unverified; moreover, it did not appear that the plaintiff

---

[1] Inspiration Consolidated Copper Co. v. Mendez, (1917) 19 Ariz. 151, 166 Pac. 278, 1183, aff'd 250 U. S. 400, 63 Law. Ed. 1058, 39 Su. Ct. 553. See also Arizona & New Mexico Ry. v. Clark, (1915) 235 U. S. 669, 59 Law. Ed. 415, 35 Su. Ct. 210, L. R. A. 1915 C 834.

[2] Polish Roman Catholic Union v. Palen, (1942) 302 Mich. 557, 5 N. W. 2d 463. See also Jones v. Jones, (1955) 208 Misc. 721, 144 N. Y. S. 2d 820; Baxter v. Baxter, (1957) 169 N. Y. S. 2d 871.

ever saw the petition or was familiar with its contents prior to the trial.[3]

Where in an action brought by a physician to recover compensation for services rendered to the defendant and his deceased daughter, the defendant sought and obtained a bill of particulars concerning the illness and treatment of the defendant and his daughter, the defendant was held to have waived the privilege since he himself had caused the information to be made public by his pleadings.[4] But interposing a general denial to a physician's complaint for the value of services rendered to the defendant does not constitute a waiver of the privilege.[5]

In New York, where the privilege is not lost unless it be expressly waived by the holder thereof in open court at the trial of the action, allegations contained in a pleading or affidavit concerning matters of a confidential nature do not constitute a waiver of the privilege.[6]

It is true that counsel may make a statement during a trial, either as an opening statement or during the progress of the trial, which will bind his client, provided it be made in such manner and under such circumstances as to warrant the court in giving it that effect. However, there seems to be no authority for the proposition that an opening statement by counsel as to what the testimony will show has the effect of waiving the privileged character of information obtained by a physician from his patient where no

---

[3] Massachusetts Bonding & Ins. Co. v. Jones, (1939) 185 Okla. 551, 94 P. 2d 885.

[4] Fortang v. Alpert, (1939) 256 App. Div. 949, 10 N. Y. S. 2d 291. Lane v. Boicourt, (1891) 128 Ind. 420, 424, 27 N. E. 1111: "What is made public by pleadings and by evidence in a court of justice can by no possibility be privileged to benefit the party who thus gives it such wide publicity."

[5] Van Allen v. Gordon, (1894) 83 Hun. 379, 31 N. Y. S. 907.

[6] Rubin v. Equitable Life Assur. Soc., (1945) 269 App. Div. 677, 53 N. Y. S. 2d 351; Vilardi v. Vilardi, (1951) 200 Misc. 1043, 107 N. Y. S. 2d 342; Baxter v. Baxter, (1957) 169 N. Y. S. 2d 871.

Contra: Dollard v. Dollard, (1939) 257 App. Div. 836, 12 N. Y. S. 2d 897. Plaintiff by the allegations in her reply and moving affidavit waived the protection of the statute. It should be noted that the court cited three cases, in each of which, however, the waiver was made in open court at the trial.

testimony whatsoever as to the privileged matter has been introduced by the party asserting and claiming the privilege.[7]

129. Disclosure During Taking of Deposition

Waiver of the privilege may result from the voluntary divulgement of privileged matters by the patient, or his representative,
during the taking of a deposition, or in answers to interrogatories.
Where, prior to the trial, the patient's oral examination as a party
was taken, in which she gave in evidence the medical treatment she
received from her physician, it was held that having voluntarily
broken the seal of secrecy, she could not thereafter recall the privilege; hence, it was error to exclude the testimony of the physician
when called as a witness by the defendant.[1] And where the patient,
in her answers to interrogatories, voluntarily revealed that she had
been confined in a hospital for the insane, she waived the protection of the privilege so far as it concerned communications with
physicians regarding her mental condition.[2]

---

[7] Vermillion v. Prudential Ins. Co., (1936) 230 Mo. App. 993, 1004, 93 S. W. 2d 45:
"We do not see how it can be said in this case that plaintiff voluntarily and intentionally relinquished the right to claim the privilege of excluding the hospital records on
the ground that they contained confidential communications between patient and
doctor, merely because of a statement made by her counsel as to the condition of
health of the insured, which was not followed up by any evidence on the part of
plaintiff or any witnesses called by her."

[1] Blish v. Greer, (1918) 74 Ind. App. 469, 120 N. E. 606. In Green v. Nirenberg Sons,
Inc., (1938) 166 Misc. 652, 3 N. Y. S. 2d 81, plaintiff's intestate, shortly before her death,
had her own deposition taken for the purpose of perpetuating her testimony for trial.
By doing this she herself removed the ban of secrecy as to her physical condition and
thereby waived the privilege, thus making available to the defendant for inspection
the records of the hospital relating to her condition during her stay there.

In Matter of Loewenthal's Petition, (1956) 101 Ohio App. 355, 134 N. E. 2d 158,
plaintiff, in a personal injury action, for the purpose of perpetuating his testimony,
gave his deposition on direct examination. Thereafter, defendant subpoenaed the
petitioner, who was plaintiff's physician, for the purpose of interrogating him by
way of deposition regarding plaintiff's injuries. On objection by plaintiff's counsel,
the petitioner refused to testify and was held in contempt. On appeal it was held that
plaintiff by testifying in his own behalf had waived the privilege and that the physician must, therefore, testify by way of deposition. The court, however, limited its
decision to the precise question involved and declined to decide what effect such
waiver might have upon the trial proceedings.

[2] Munzer v. Swedish American Line, (1940) 35 F. Supp. 493.

Where a plaintiff, in a personal injury action, takes the deposition of his own physician but does not introduce the same in evidence at the trial, he will be deemed to have waived the privilege and the defendant may himself introduce the deposition of the physician as evidence in his behalf.[3] But where the defendant took the depositions of two physicians who had attended the deceased, and thereafter, for the purpose of breaking the force of their testimony, the plaintiff took their depositions and filed them in court but did not use them, no waiver resulted and the defendant, therefore, could not introduce in evidence the testimony of the plaintiff's physicians.[4]

The requirement of the New York statute that a waiver of the privilege must be made in open court at the trial of the action or by stipulation of counsel for the respective parties, is fully met by the signing of various papers for the commission.[5] The examination of witnesses without the jurisdiction upon a commission is considered a portion of the trial of the action for the purpose of meeting said requirement.[6]

Where a letter written by the insured's physician was admissible in evidence, the taking of the depositions of two other attending physicians so as to be prepared to meet statements contained in the letter, was not a waiver of the privilege so as to admit the deposition of the physician who wrote the letter.[7]

---

[3] Clifford v. Denver & Rio Grande R. R. (1907) 188 N. Y. 349, 80 N. E. 1094. The same principle has been applied where the attorney-client privilege was involved. Watson v. Watson, (1919) 104 Kan. 578, 180 Pac. 242, 182 Pac. 643.

Likewise, the incompetency of a witness under the dead man statute was waived by the adverse party's taking his deposition, whether it was filed in court or not. Baker v. Baker, (1952) 363 Mo. 318, 251 S. W. 2d 31, 33 A. L. R. 2d 1431. See also McClenahan v. Keyes, (1922) 188 Cal. 574, 206 Pac. 454. Plaintiff was a physician.

[4] Aetna Life Ins. Co. v. Deming, (1889) 123 Ind. 384, 24 N. E. 86, 24 N. E. 375. Why was it not claimed that privilege was waived by plaintiff's failure to object to the physician's testifying in the first instance? See § 130, herein.

[5] Clifford v. Denver & Rio Grande R. R., (1907) 188 N. Y. 349, 80 N. E. 1094.

[6] Murray v. Physical Culture Hotel, Inc., (1939) 258 App. Div. 334, 16 N. Y. S. 2d 978, 17 N. Y. S. 2d 862.

[7] Travelers Ins. Co. v. Fletcher American National Bank, (1926) 84 Ind. App. 563, 150 N. E. 825.

130. Failure to Object to Introduction of Evidence Disclosing Privileged Matters

The physician-patient privilege statute does not create a right effective without claim or assertion. Like other statutes protecting confidential relationships, it is a mere testimonial privilege that has no effective existence or potency unless properly invoked when the privilege matter is first presented.[1] When, therefore, a question is put to the patient or to a physician necessarily calling for testimony which is within the protection of the statute, or when an attempt is made to introduce in evidence the patient's hospital chart or any other confidential record or document within the ban of the statute, and a fair opportunity is given the patient, or any person entitled to assert and claim the privilege, to interpose an objection, he must make it then, or lose his right to object afterwards during the trial.[2] This is a simple and forthright rule easily

---

[1] Hoyt v. Hoyt, (1889) 112 N. Y. 493, 513, 20 N. E. 402. Peterson, The Patient-Physician Privilege in Missouri, (1952) 20 Kan. L. Rev. 122, 127: "Since the privilege deals with an evidentiary matter it would seem obvious that a waiver could be had simply by failure of the party who would otherwise have been entitled to assert the privilege to object thereto."

See Rule 27(2) of the Uniform Rules of Evidence. (1953)

Appendix, herein.

[2] Kirkpatrick v. American Ry. Express Co., (1928) 177 Ark. 334, 6 S. W. 2d 524; San Francisco v. Superior Court, (1951) 37 Cal. 2d 227, 231 P. 2d 26, 25 A. L. R. 2d 1418; Lissak v. Crocker Estate Co., (1897) 119 Cal. 442, 51 Pac. 688; Wolf v. People, (1947) 117 Colo. 279, 187 P. 2d 926; Metropolitan Life Ins. Co. v. Kaufman, (1939) 104 Colo. 13, 87 P. 2d 758; Studabaker v. Faylor, (1912) 52 Ind. App. 171, 98 N. E. 318; State v. Koenig, (1949) 240 Iowa 592, 36 N. W. 2d 765; Burgess v. Sims Drug Co., (1901) 114 Iowa 275, 86 N. W. 307, 54 L. R. A. 364; Armstrong v. Topeka Ry., (1914) 93 Kan. 493, 144 Pac. 847; Lincoln v. Detroit, (1894) 101 Mich. 245, 59 N. W. 617; Briesenmeister v. Supreme Lodge K. of P., (1890) 81 Mich. 525, 45 N. W. 977, 8. L. R. A. 682; Burke v. Chicago & N. W. Ry., (1915) 131 Minn. 209, 154 N. W. 960; Epstein v. Pennsylvania R. R., (1913) 250 Mo. 1, 156 S. W. 699, 48 L. R. A. (n. s.) 394; Ann. Cas. 1915 A. 423; Elliott v. Kansas City, (1906) 198 Mo. 593, 96 S. W. 1023, 6 L. R. A. (n. s.) 1082, 8 Ann. Cas. 653; State v. Powell, (1919) _____ Mo. _____, 217 S. W. 35; Marx v. Parks, (1931) _____ Mo. App. _____, 39 S. W. 2d 570; Ryan v. Metropolitan Life Ins. Co., (1930) _____ Mo. App. _____, 30 S. W. 2d 190; May v. Northern Pac. Ry., (1905) 32 Mont. 522, 81 Pac. 328, 70 L. R. A. 111, 4 Ann. Cas. 605; Capron v. Douglass, (1908) 193 N. Y. 11, 85 N. E. 827, 20 L. R. A. (n. s.) 1003; People v. Bloom, (1908) 193 N. Y. 1, 85 N. E. 824, 18 L. R. A. (n. s.) 898, 15 Ann. Cas. 932; Hoyt v. Hoyt, (1889) 112 N. Y. 493, 20 N. E. 402; Miller v. New York, (1955) 286 App. Div. 1033, 145 N. Y. S. 2d 295; Strader v. Collins, (1952) 280

≫→

followed and easy of application.[3]

By failing to object to the question, the party will be deemed to have waived the privilege and his consent to the disclosure will be implied.[4] It is too late to object if the question has already been answered; and a motion to strike out the answer will not lie.[5] Accordingly, silence on the part of the patient, or one entitled to assert the privilege, during testimony disclosing a privileged com-

---

App. Div. 582, 116 N. Y. S. 2d 318; Matter of Gannon's Will, (1893) 2 Misc. 829, 21 N. Y. S. 960, aff'd. 139 N. Y. 654, 35 N. E. 207; Williams v. Spokane Falls & N. Ry., (1906) 42 Wash 597, 84 Pac. 1129; French v. Fidelity & Casualty Co., (1908) 135 Wis. 259, 115 N. W. 869, 17 L. R. A. (n. s.) 1011.

See also Scolavino v. State, (1946) 187 Misc. 253, 62 N. Y. S. 2d 17, 271 App. Div. 618, 67 N. Y. S. 2d 202, aff'd. 297 N. Y. 460, 74 N. E. 2d 174.

It has been held that the principle has no application where the party merely failed to object either through inadvertence or indifference. Maryland Casualty Co. v. Maloney, (1915) 119 Ark. 434, 178 S. W. 387, L. R. A. 1915 A. 519.

For application of the rule when the evidence is elicited *on cross-examination,* see § 139, herein.

The Puerto Rico statute provides that a court may admit privileged matters when timely objection has not been made thereto. See Appendix, herein.

See also Kansas statute. Appendix, herein.

The rule may be applied to other types of privileged communications.

See Steen v. First National Bank, (1924) 298 Fed. 36.

3 Burke v. Chicago & N. W. Ry., (1915) 131 Minn. 209, 154 N. W. 960.

4 Lissack v. Crocker Estate Co., (1897) 119 Cal. 442, 51 Pac. 688; Wolf v. People, (1947) 117 Colo. 279, 187 P. 2d 926; State v. Koenig, (1949) 240 Iowa 592, 36 N. W. 2d 765; Armstrong v. Topeka Ry., (1914) 93 Kan. 493, 144 Pac. 847; Briesenmeister v. Supreme Lodge, K. of P., (1890) 81 Mich. 525, 45 N. W. 977, 8 L. R. A. 682; Epstein v. Pennsylvania R. R., (1913) 250 Mo. 1, 156 S. W. 699, 48 L. R. A. (n. s.) 394, Ann. Cas. 1915 A. 423; Elliott v. Kansas City, (1906) 198 Mo. 593, 96 S. W. 1023, 6 L. R. A. (n. s.) 1082, 8 Ann. Cas. 653; State v. Powell, (1919) _____Mo._____, 217 S. W. 35; People v. Runion, (1958) 3 N. Y. 2d 637, 148 N. E. 2d 165; Deutschmann v. Third Ave. R. R., (1903) 87 App. Div. 503, 84 N. Y. S. 887; Williams v. Spokane Falls & N. Ry., (1906) 42 Wash. 597, 84 Pac. 1129.

The objection must be based specifically on the ground of privilege; not on the ground that the evidence offered is incompetent, irrelevant and immaterial.

State v. Carryer, (1915) _____ Mo._____, 180 S. W. 850; Enghlin v. Pittsburg County Ry., (1934) 169 Okla. 106, 36 P. 2d 32, 94 A. L. R. 1180.

See also § 91, herein.

5 Lissack v. Crocker Estate Co., (1897) 119 Cal. 442, 51 Pac. 688; Wheelock v. Godfrey, (1893) 100 Cal. 578, 35 Pac. 317; Briesenmeister v. Supreme Lodge, K. of P., (1890) 81 Mich. 525, 45 N. W. 977, 8 L. R. A. 682; Hoyt v. Hoyt, (1889) 112 N. Y. 493, 20 N. E. 402; *Cf.* State v. Stafford, (1909) 145 Iowa 285, 123 N. W. 167.

munication or any substantial part of it, will operate as a waiver of the privilege. A party cannot be allowed to sit by and gamble upon the outcome of an action by willingly admitting incompetent evidence in the hope of an advantage to himself, and afterwards, when he finds that the gamble has been injurious to his case, claim that there was error in its admission and then ask to have it stricken out.[6] When, however, the answer is not responsive to the question and could not reasonably be anticipated, a motion to strike it out is proper.[7]

Where, upon a trial, an objection to the testimony of physicians, on the ground of privilege, has once been distinctly raised and overruled, it need not be repeated to the same class of evidence; and an omission to repeat the objection is not a waiver.[8]

As a general rule, a question as to the admissibility and competency of evidence cannot be raised for the first time in a reviewing court.[9] An appellate court will not consider a question of privilege which was not raised by timely objection in the trial court. The parties must stand or fall upon the case as made in that court. An appellate court is not a forum in which to make a new case.[10]

6 Briesenmeister v. Supreme Lodge, K. of P., (1890) 81 Mich. 525, 534, 45 N. W. 977, 8 L. R. A. 682: "It is a personal privilege, and the party entitled to the protection which the statute gives cannot stand by without objection, and experiment upon the result of permitting the testimony to remain in the case if it is favorable to him, or moving to strike it out if it is unfavorable."

Accord: Lissack v. Crocker Estate Co., (1897) 119 Cal. 442, 51 Pac. 688; Hoyt v. Hoyt, (1889) 112 N. Y. 493, 20 N. E. 402; *Re* Gannon's Will, (1893) 2 Misc. 329, 21 N. Y. S. 960, aff'd. 139 N. Y. 654, 35 N. E. 207.

7 Pence v. Waugh, (1893) 135 Ind. 143, 149, 34 N. E. 860: "Objections, in practice, are usually addressed to the questions, and it is not a favorable practice to permit counsel to delay until it may be learned if answers are injurious before objecting. The character of the answer is always indicated by the question asked, and opportunity is given for objection before answer. If the answer is not what might have been anticipated from the question, then it is not properly responsive, and the rights of the adverse party are not lost by delay in objecting, for he may then move to strike out the answer."

See also State v. Stafford, (1909) 145 Iowa 285, 123 N. W. 167.

8 Dilleber v. Home Life Ins. Co., (1877) 69 N. Y. 256. This is the customary practice. See Brady v. Stafford, (1926) 115 Ohio State 67, 152 N. E. 188.

9 State, *ex rel* Walker v. Clark, (1944) 144 Ohio St. 305, 58 N. E. 2d 773.

10 Estate of Huston, (1912) 163 Cal. 166, 124 Pac. 852; Mutual Life Ins. Co. v. Good,

Where an attempt is made to introduce in evidence privileged matters during the taking of the deposition of a witness, objection thereto should be made at that time. The statute contemplates that, in the absence of consent or a valid waiver of the privilege, the confidential information should be shut off at the source.[11]

Where, in a personal injury case, the court appointed two physicians to examine the plaintiff, one of whom had been his personal physician, but the plaintiff made no objection to his appointment, it was too late to make an objection on account of his alleged incompetency when the physician was called to testify. By submitting to the examination, the plaintiff waived his right to exclude the physician's testimony.[12]

131. Disclosure by Physician Called as Witness by Holder of Privilege

It is generally conceded that the calling of an attending physician as a witness by the patient, is an express waiver of the seal of secrecy imposed by the statute, if the witness undertakes to relate the nature or treatment of the patient's ailment, injury, or mental condition.[1] The adverse party, therefore, may examine the witness

---

(1913) 25 Colo. App. 204, 136 Pac. 821; State v. Carryer, (1915) ....Mo........, 180 S. W. 850; Martin v. Metropolitan Life Ins. Co., (1943) ....Mo. App........, 174 S. W. 2d 222; State v. Fouquette, (1950) 67 Nev. 505, 536, 221 P. 2d 404; Edington v. Mutual Life Ins. Co., (1875) 5 Hun. (N. Y.) 1, rev'd. on other grounds 67 N. Y. 185; *Re* Gannon's Will, (1893) 2 Misc. 329, 21 N. Y. S. 960, aff'd. 139 N. Y. 654, 35 N. E. 207.

See also § 143, herein.

McLaughlin v. Massachusetts Indemnity Co., (1948) 85 Ohio App. 511, 84 N. E. 2d 114. Rule approved but the court found that the objection had substantially been made.

There is some authority for the view that a violation of the statute may constitute reversible error notwithstanding the evidence was received without objection at the trial. Taylor v. United States, (1954) 95 App. D. C. 373, 222 F. 2d 398; Price v. Standard Life & Acc. Ins. Co., (1903) 90 Minn. 264, 95 N. W. 1118.

[11] Kirkpatrick v. American Ry. Express Co., (1928) 177 Ark. 334, 6 S. W. 2d 524.

See also §§ 79, 82, herein.

[12] Powell Bros. Truck Lines, Inc. v. Barnett, (1937) 194 Ark. 769, 109 S. W. 2d 673.

[1] Hyatt v. Wroten, (1931) 184 Ark. 847, 43 S. W. 2d 726; Travelers Bldg. & Loan Ass'n. v. Hawkins, (1931) 182 Ark. 1148, 34 S. W. 2d 474; Missouri & N. Ark. R. R. v. Daniels, (1911) 98 Ark. 352, 136 S. W. 651; Matter of Daniels, (1903) 140 Cal. 335, 73 Pac. 1053;

fully and at length as to all relevant matters learned by him in
attending the patient professionally, including the records upon
which he has chosen to base his testimony,[2] and, ordinarily, the
interrogation of the witness is not limited to the particular time,
occasion, ailment, or injury to which he testified upon direct examination.[3]

Schlarb v. Henderson, (1936) 211 Ind. 1, 4 N. E. 2d 205; Pittsburgh, C. C. & St. Louis
R. R. v. O'Connor, (1909) 171 Ind. 686, 85 N. E. 969; Epstein v. Pennsylvania R. R.,
(1913) 250 Mo. 1, 156 S. W. 699, 48 L. R. A. (n. s.) 394, Ann. Cas. 1915 A. 423; Mellor
v. Missouri Pac. Ry., (1890) 105 Mo. 455, 14 S. W. 758, 16 S. W. 849, 10 L. R. A. 36;
Carrington v. St. Louis, (1886) 89 Mo. 208, 1 S. W. 240; Webb. v. Metropolitan Street
Ry., (1901) 89 Mo. App. 604; Sovereign Camp, W. O. W. v. Grandon, (1902) 64 Neb.
39, 89 N. W. 448; Steinberg v. New York Life Ins. Co., (1933) 263 N. Y. 45, 188 N. E.
152, 90 A. L. R. 642; Clifford v. Denver & Rio Grande R. R., (1907) 188 N. Y. 349, 80
N. E. 1094; Morris v. New York, Ontario & W. Ry., (1895) 148 N. Y. 88, 42 N. E. 410;
McUne v Fuqua, _____Wash._____, 253 P. 2d 632, 257 P. 2d 636; Mohr v. Mohr, (1937)
119 W. Va. 253, 193 S. E. 121.

See Rule 27(7) Uniform Rules of Evidence (1953); Rule 223(1) Model Code of
Evidence (1942)

In some jurisdictions, the statute so provides.

e. g. Colorado, Hawaii, and Nebraska. See Appendix, herein.

See also 8 Wigmore, Evidence, § 2390(2).

[2] Maas v. Midway Chevrolet Co., (1945) 219 Minn. 461, 18 N. W. 2d 233, 158 A. L. R.
215; Kemp v. Metropolitan Street Ry., (1904) 94 App. Div. 322, 88 N. Y. S. 1.

[3] Patrick v. Smith Baking Co., (1942) 64 Idaho 190, 129 P. 2d 651; Ellis v. Baird, (1903)
31 Ind. App. 295, 67 N. E. 960; Maas v. Midway Chevrolet Co., (1945) 219 Minn. 461,
18 N. W. 2d 233, 158 A. L. R. 215; Demonbrun v. McHaffie, (1941) 348 Mo. 1120, 156
S. W. 2d 923; Wells v. Jefferson, (1939) 345 Mo. 239, 132 S. W. 2d 1006; Albers v. Wilson, (1922) 201 App. Div. 775, 195 N. Y. S. 145; Patnode v. Foote, (1912) 153 App. Div.
494, 138 N. Y. S. 221; Seaman v. Mott, (1908) 127 App. Div. 18, 110 N. Y. S. 1040; Marquardt v. Brooklyn Heights R. R., (1908) 126 App. Div. 272, 110 N. Y. S. 657; Powers
v. Metropolitan Street Ry., (1905) 105 App. Div. 358, 94 N. Y. S. 184; Kemp v. Metropolitan Street Ry., (1904) 94 App. Div. 322, 88 N. Y. S. 1; Lawson v. Morning Journal
Ass'n., (1898) 32 App. Div. 71, 52 N. Y. S. 484; Lampel v. Goldstein, (1917) 167 N. Y. S.
576; McDonnell v. Monteith, (1930) 59 N. D. 750, 231 N. W. 854; Williams v. State,
(1951) _____Okla. Cr._____, 226 P. 2d 989; Chicago, Rock Island & Pac. R. R. v. Hughes,
(1917) 64 Okla. 74, 166 Pac. 411.

In Seaman v. Mott, infra, Jenks, J. said: (p. 21) "When the patient called the
physician to give evidence as to his injury, pain and suffering attributed to this accident, the patient could not exclude, as privileged, the questions by the defendant as
to professional treatment prior to this accident, for such questions might have shown
the prior existence of such physical conditions, at least to a degree."

In a few cases, the cross-examination seems to have been limited strictly to matters testified to by the physician on direct examination. Dotton v. Albion, (1885) 57

Where the representative of a deceased patient calls the attending physician as a witness, he waives the privilege and the witness, at the instance of the adverse party, may testify to all information pertaining to the patient's condition which he acquired while attending him professionally.[4]

Where, in a personal injury case, the plaintiff called his physician as a witness and asked a hypothetical question setting forth certain injuries, but no question was asked regarding plaintiff's injuries, there was no waiver of the privilege and the witness, over objection, was not allowed to testify to plaintiff's condition and the probable duration thereof.[5]

Although a patient waives the privilege by permitting his physician to testify at the instance of the adverse party,[6] he has the right to discredit the witness by showing interest or bias in the case, and legitimate cross-examination is perfectly proper for that purpose.[7]

The holder of the privilege does not waive its benefits by obtaining permission of the court to interrogate the patient's physician who is called as a witness by the adverse party, where the sole purpose of such examination is to show that the relationship of

---

Mich. 575, 24 N. W. 786; Sovereign Camp, W. O. W. v. Grandon, (1902) 64 Neb. 39, 89 N. W. 448; State v. Litteral, (1947) 227 N. C. 527, 43 S. E. 2d 84.

[4] Hyatt v. Wroten, (1931) 184 Ark. 847, 43 S. W. 2d 726; Wheelock v. Godfrey, (1893) 100 Cal. 578, 35 Pac. 317; Sager v. Motz, (1923) 80 Ind. App. 122, 139 N. E. 687; Thompson v. Ish, (1889) 99 Mo. 160, 12 S. W. 510; Holcomb v. Harris, (1901) 166 N. Y. 257, 59 N. E. 220; Kemp v. Metropolitan Street Ry., (1904) 94 App. Div. 322, 88 N. Y. S. 1; United States National Life & Cas. Co. v. Heard, (1931) 148 Okla. 274, 298 Pac. 619.

The statutes of Colorado, Hawaii and Nebraska so provide.

See Appendix, herein.

In Sovereign Camp, W. O. W. v. Grandon, (1902) 64 Neb. 39, 89 N. W. 448, defendant called the deceased's physician as a witness but he was not allowed to disclose deceased's condition. On cross-examination, plaintiff had exhibited a written statement signed by the witness to the effect that the deceased was not dangerously sick until the night before he died. It was held that plaintiff opened up the question of the deceased's condition and thereby waived the privilege; that the court erred in refusing to allow defendant to further examine the physician as to the condition of the deceased at the time referred to in his written statement.

[5] Nelson v. Johnson, (1925) 41 Idaho 697, 243 Pac. 647.

[6] See § 130, herein.

[7] Williams v. Spokane Falls & N. Ry., (1906) 42 Wash. 597, 84 Pac. 1129.

physician and patient existed and thus lay the foundation for an objection based on the statutory prohibition of the physician's testimony.[8]

Since the adverse party has the absolute right to cross-examine, in a direct and specific manner, the physician-witness called by the patient, a denial of this right was held to constitute prejudicial error which was not cured by the fact that the evidence sought to be elicited was subsequently allowed to come before the jury.[9] But there is sound authority to the contrary.[10]

Cross-examination by the plaintiff, under the Federal Rules of Civil Procedure, of plaintiff's attending physicians while they were defendants in a personal injury action brought against them and a hospital, did not constitute waiver of the privilege when such physicians were subsequently called as expert witnesses by the defendant hospital after they had been eliminated as parties.[11]

Where, in an action for separation, the wife introduced the testimony of her brother that one of the psychiatrists whom she had consulted at her husband's suggestion, had told the brother that she was mentally ill and in need of medical treatment, she waived the privilege and it was error to exclude the testimony of the psychiatrists, called as witnesses by the husband, as to their findings concerning her mental condition.[12]

---

[8] Hicks v. Metropolitan Life Ins. Co., (1916) 196 Mo. App. 162, 190 S. W. 661. See also Nugent v. Cudahy Packing Co., (1905) 126 Iowa 517, 102 S. W. 442.

[9] Powers v. Metropolitan Street Ry., (1905) 105 App. Div. 358, 94 N. Y. S. 184.

[10] Matter of Daniels, (1903) 140 Cal. 335, 73 Pac. 1053; Patrick v. Smith Baking Co., (1942) 64 Idaho 190, 129 P. 2d 651; Radermacher v. Radermacher, (1938) 59 Idaho 716, 87 P. 2d 461. See also Lauer v. Banning, (1908) 140 Iowa 319, 118 N. W. 446; Canning v. Chicago & Milwaukee Ry., (1916) 163 Wis. 448, 157 N. W. 532.

In Stalker v. Breeze, (1917) 186 Ind. 221, 114 N. E. 968, the decedent's clinical record, kept by hospital nurses, was improperly admitted in evidence. However, the adverse party called as a witness one of the nurses who made a portion of the record and examined her in regard thereto. It was held that the error was rendered harmless by the party asking his own witness, one of the nurses, to testify as to part of the contents of the same record.

[11] Von Eye v. Hammes, (1956) 147 F. Supp. 174.

[12] Davis v. Davis, (1955) 1 App. Div. 2d 675, 146 N. Y. S. 2d 630.

132. Patient Offering Himself as Witness: Statutory Provisions

In a number of jurisdictions, the statute specifically provides that if a patient offers himself as a witness, he waives the protection which the privilege would otherwise afford. There is, however, a lack of uniformity in the language of such provision, and, as a consequence thereof, there is a corresponding lack of uniformity among the decisions interpreting and applying it.[1] Much depends upon the circumstances of the particular case and, of course, upon the attitude of the court towards the privilege in general, *viz.,* whether it will construe the statute strictly or whether it will give it a liberal interpretation.

In Arizona, the patient may testify to his injuries and the treatment thereof without waiving the privilege, but if he testifies to communications between himself and his physician that is to be deemed a consent to the examination of the physician. The word "communications" does not include information obtained by a physical examination of the patient.[2] New Mexico has a similar statute.

In Colorado and in Oklahoma,[3] if a person offer himself or a

---

[1] See Appendix, herein, for statutes mentioned in this section.

See also note, 114 A. L. R 798.

[2] Arizona & New Mexico Ry. v. Clark, (1915) 235 U. S. 669, 59 Law Ed. 415, 35 Su. Ct. 210, L. R. A. 1915 C. 834; Southwest Metals Co. v. Gomez, (1925) 4 F. 2d 215, 39 A. L. R. 1416; Phelps Dodge Corp. v. Guerrero, (1921) 273 Fed. 415; Arizona Copper Co. v. Garcia, (1923) 25 Ariz. 158, 214 Pac. 317; Arizona Eastern R. R. v. Mathews, (1919) 20 Ariz. 282, 180 Pac. 159, 7 A. L. R. 1149; Inspiration Consolidated Copper Co. v. Mendez, (1917) 19 Ariz. 151, 166 Pac. 278, 1183.

[3] The construction of this provision by the courts of Oklahoma is similar to that of the courts of Arizona. Where the patient, when testifying, makes no reference to any "communications" between himself and his physician, no waiver results.

Hudson v. Blanchard, (1956) ____Okla. ____, 294 P. 2d 554, 560: "Consideration of our own statute * * * impels the conclusion that waiver (of the privilege accorded by statute) is not accomplished by a party taking the witness stand and testifying to the facts of an injury. Unless the waiver of privilege provided by the statute be held to go only to 'communications,' with the attending physician, it becomes obvious the statute is meaningless and a nullity. The reason is readily apparent. An injured party who takes the witness stand and testifies to the facts of an injury (for which compensation is sought) immediately is held to have waived the statutory privilege. This then permits the physician to testify directly, not only as to verbal communications

》》》→

physician as a witness, that shall be deemed a consent to the examination of the witness with respect to matters within the scope of the privilege.

In Hawaii,[4] consent shall be deemed to have been given to any physician in all cases in which a party to an action shall offer himself or any physician as a witness to testify to the physical condition of such party. In Nebraska,[5] if a party to any action shall offer evidence with reference to his physical or mental condition, or the alleged cause thereof, or if the personal representative of a deceased person shall offer such evidence as to such deceased person, the privilege shall be deemed to have been waived as to any physician who has attended the party, or the deceased person.

In North Dakota, if a person testifies as a witness as to any subject which comes within the protection of the statute, he shall be deemed to have consented to the examination of a physician on the same subject. In Ohio,[6] Oregon,[7] South Dakota, and Wyom-

---

←※

with the patient, but also as to knowledge gained by physical examination. The statute obviously was not conceived with any such result in mind."

Granting there are varying facts and circumstances, this decision, on principle, seems to be at odds with some of the earlier decisions construing this provision of the statute. See Strebeck v. Eagle Picher Mining & S. Co., (1953) ＿＿＿Okla.＿＿＿ , 259 P. 2d 536 (waiver resulted); Williams v. State, (1951) ＿＿ Okla. Cr.＿＿＿ , 226 P. 8d 989 (waiver resulted); Terrell v. First National Bank & T. Co., (1950) 204 Okla. 24, 226 P. 2d 431 (waiver resulted); Hudman v. State, (1949) 89 Okla. Cr. 160, 205 P. 2d 1175 (waiver resulted); Massachusetts Bonding & Ins. Co. v. Jones, (1939) 185 Okla. 551, 94 P. 2d 885 (no waiver); Lazzell v. Harvey, (1935) 174 Okla. 86, 49 P. 2d 519 (waiver resulted); Chicago, Rock Island & Pac. Ry. v. Shelton, (1929) 135 Okla. 53, 273 Pac. 988 (no waiver); American Bankers Ins. Co. v. Hopkins, (1917) 67 Okla. 150, 169 Pac. 489 (no waiver); Chicago, Rock Island & Pac. Ry. v. Hughes, (1917) 64 Okla. 74, 166 Pac. 411 (waiver resulted); Tulsa v. Wicker, (1914) 42 Okla. 539, 141 Pac. 963 (waiver resulted); Fulsom-Morris Coal & Mining Co. v. Mitchell, (1913) 37 Okla. 575, 132 Pac. 1103 (waiver resulted); Roeser v. Pease, (1913) 37 Okla. 222, 131 Pac. 534 (waiver resulted).

[4] The statute also provides that in a personal injury case any physician may testify.

[5] See O'Brien v. General Acc., Fire & Life Assur. Corp., (1930) 42 F. 2d 48; Ansnes v. Loyal Protective Ins. Co., (1937) 133 Neb. 665, 276 N. W. 397; Friesen v. Reimer, (1933) 124 Neb. 620, 247 N. W. 561.

[6] The Supreme Court has unduly restricted the waiver clause. See Baker v. Industrial Comm'n., (1939) 135 Ohio St. 491, 21 N. E. 2d 593; Harpman v. Devine, (1937) 133 Ohio St. 1, 10 N. E. 2d 776, 114 A. L. R. 789; Ausdenmoore v. Holzback, (1914) 89 Ohio St. 381, 106 N. E. 41. But *cf.* Spitzer v. Stillings, (1924) 109 Ohio St. 297, 142 N. E. 365

≫→

ing, if the patient voluntarily testifies, the physician may be compelled to testify on the same subject.

In Puerto Rico, consent to the giving of testimony occurs when the person who made the privileged communication testifies to same, and the person to whom it was made may be examined fully as to such communication.

133. Patient Testifying Generally

There is substantial authority for the view that a person does not, by voluntarily testifying on direct examination as to his injury or ailment, without unduly going into details or referring to communications to or by his physician, waive the protection of the statutory privilege. The statute, it is said, does not contemplate that waiver follows from the mere fact that the patient himself testifies to his physical condition.[1] In doing so he need not disclose communications between himself and his physician, and if he does not, the communications are still privileged.[2] Obviously, no

---

←—⫸

and King v. Barrett, (1860) 11 Ohio St. 261, which involve the same waiver clause with respect to the attorney-client privilege.

The word "testifies" is not limited to the trial in court; hence, a patient voluntarily testifying for his own benefit by way of deposition, waives the privilege. Matter of Loewenthal's Petition, (1956) 101 Ohio App. 355, 134 N. E. 2d 158.

[7] Forrest v. Portland Ry., Light & P. Co., (1913) 64 Ore. 240, 244, 129 Pac. 1048: "The subject under consideration as stated in the complaint and about which the plaintiff spoke herself as a witness was her physical condition, including a displacement of her uterus and injuries to her nervous system. When she testified on that subject, under the provisions of [the privilege statute] she consented to the examination of her physician or surgeon on the same subject."

[1] Armstrong v. Topeka Ry., (1914) 93 Kan. 493, 506, 144 Pac. 847.

[2] Arizona & New Mexico Ry. v. Clark, (1915) 235 U. S. 669, 59 Law Ed. 415, 35 Su. Ct. 210, L. R. A. 1915 C. 834; Phelps Dodge Corp. v. Guerrero, (1921) 273 Fed. 415; Federal Mining & S. Co. v. Dalo, (1918) 252 Fed. 356; Union Pac. Ry. v. Thomas, (1907) 152 Fed. 365; Arizona Eastern R. R. v. Mathews, (1919) 20 Ariz. 282, 180 Pac. 159, 7 A. L. R. 1149; Southern Indiana Gas. & E. Co. v. Vaughn, (1928) 88 Ind. App. 561, 163 N. E. 107; Pearson v. Butts, (1938) 224 Iowa 376, 276 N. W. 65; Walmer-Roberts v. Hennessey, (1921) 191 Iowa 86, 181 N. W. 798; McConnell v. Osage, (1890) 80 Iowa 293, 45 N. W. 550, 8 L. R. A. 778; Doll v. Scandrett, (1937) 201 Minn. 316, 276 N. W. 281; Polin v. St. Paul Union Depot Co., (1924) 159 Minn. 410, 199 N. W. 87; Marfia v. Great Northern Ry., (1914) 124 Minn. 466, 145 N. W. 385; McAllister v. St. Paul City Ry., (1908) 105 Minn. 1, 116 N. W. 917; Smart v. Kansas City, (1907) 208 Mo. 162, 105 S. W. 709, 14

⫸→

precise rule can be laid down as to just how far the patient may go in describing his injury or ailment without surrendering the privilege which entitles him to exclude the testimony of a physician who attended him, or the records of a hospital in which he was cared for.[3] This is a decision which ordinarily rests in the wise discretion of the trial judge.

In some cases, the courts seem to have been quite lenient with the patient, or his representative, and have held that no waiver results even though some evidence was offered by him concerning the treatment rendered by the physician or portions of the latter's conversation with the patient.[4]

L. R. A. (n. s.) 565, 13 Ann. Cas. 932; Cable v. Johnson, (1933) _____Mo. App._____, 63 S. W. 2d 433; May v. Northern Pac. Ry., (1905) 32 Mont. 522, 539, 81 Pac. 328, 70 L. R. A. 111, 4 Ann. Cas. 605: "But so far as our investigation discloses, no court of last resort has ever held that the mere fact that the patient testifies generally concerning his condition constitutes a waiver of the privilege granted by the statute." Jones v. Brooklyn, Bath & W. E. R. R., (1888) 3 N. Y. S. 253, aff'd. 121 N. Y. 683, 24 N. E. 1098; Dunkle v. McAllister, (1902) 70 App. Div. 273, 74 N. Y. S. 902; Fox v. Union Turnpike Co., (1901) 59 App. Div. 363, 69 N. Y. S. 551; Bauch v. Schultz, (1919) 109 Misc. 548, 180 N. Y. S. 188; Harpman v. Devine, (1937) 133 Ohio St. 1, 10 N. E. 2d 776, 114 A. L. R. 789; Ausdenmoore v. Holzback, (1914) 89 Ohio St. 381, 106 N. E. 41; Gillen v. Industrial Comm'n., (1938) 59 Ohio App. 241, 17 N. E. 2d 663 (testimony of widow of deceased patient); Hudson v. Blanchard, (1956) _____Okla._____, 294 P. 2d 554; Chicago, Rock Island & Pac. Ry. v. Shelton, (1929) 135 Okla. 53, 273 Pac. 988; Brennan v. Manufacturers Life Ins. Co., (1919) 11 Puerto Rico Fed. 203; Clawson v. Walgreen Drug Co., (1945) 108 Utah 577, 162 P. 2d 759; Brammer v. Lappenbusch, (1934) 176 Wash. 625, 30 P. 2d 947; Noelle v. Hoquiam Lumber & S. Co., (1907) 47 Wash. 519, 521, 92 Pac. 372: "No case has been called to our attention which holds that a person may not describe his injuries as he sees and feels them, without a reference to what his attending physician or surgeon may have told him, and that an adverse party may then call such physician and prove by him that the patient is mistaken or has testified untruthfully." But *cf.* Randa v. Bear, (1957) _____Wash._____, 312 P. 2d 640. Cohodes v. Menominee & M. Light & Traction Co., (1912) 149 Wis. 308, 135 N. W. 879; Green v. Nebagamain, (1902) 113 Wis. 508, 89 N. W. 833.

See opinion of Thurman, J., in Dahlquist v. Denver & Rio Grande R. R., (1918) 52 Utah 438, 174 Pac. 833.

See also note, 114 A. L. R. 798.

[3] Fox v. Union Turnpike Co., (1901) 59 App. Div. 363, 69 N. Y. S. 551. Rauh v. Deutscher Verein, (1898) 29 App. Div. 483, 486, 51 N. Y. S. 985: "What will constitute a waiver of this privilege given to the patient is not prescribed, and must be determined as a question of fact in each particular case from the acts of the plaintiff [patient] during the conduct of the trial."

[4] General Acc., Fire & Life Assur. Corp. v. Savage, (1929) 35 F. 2d 587; Southwest Metals

134. Holder of Privilege Introducing Evidence Disclosing in Detail Nature and Extent of Patient's Injury, Malady, or Disability

The general rule is that where the patient, for the purposes of gain or advantage, introduces evidence, or, without objection, permits the introduction of evidence, which discloses the details of his injury, malady, or disability, he removes the barrier of the statutory privilege and opens the door to a full judicial inquiry into the entire subject so brought into the case.[1]

Manifestly, if the patient himself breaks the seal of secrecy and voluntarily gives publicity to the whole matter, he plainly abandons the protection of the statute which would otherwise be available to him; and this is true whether the publicity is given by the testimony of the patient himself, or by the testimony of his physician, or by the testimony of his other witnesses. The adverse party, therefore, may call as a witness any physician who has attended the patient and he may testify concerning the injury, ailment, or disability of which the patient complains. It is both logical and just that when the patient voluntarily makes public the details of his affliction, or gives his version of what the physician

---

Co. v. Gomez, (1925) 4 F. 2d 215, 39 A. L. R. 1416; Phelps Dodge Corp. v. Guerrero, (1921) 273 Fed. 415; Kansas City Southern Ry. v. Miller, (1915) 117 Ark. 396, 175 S. W. 1164; Brayman v. Russell & Pugh Lumber Co., (1917) 31 Idaho 140, 169 Pac. 932; Indianapolis & M. Rapid Transit Co. v. Hall, (1905) 165 Ind. 557, 76 N. E. 242; Williams v. Johnson, (1887) 112 Ind. 273, 13 N. E. 872; Slater v. Sorge, (1911) 166 Mich. 173, 131 N. W. 565; Ostrowski v. Mockbridge, (1954) 242 Minn. 265, 65 N. W. 2d 185, 47 A. L. R. 2d 733; Polin v. St. Paul Union Depot Co., (1924) 159 Minn. 410, 199 N. W. 87; Struble v. DeWitt, (1911) 89 Neb. 726, 132 N. W. 124; Dunkle v. McAllister, (1902) 70 App. Div. 273, 74 N. Y. S. 902; Fox v. Union Turnpike, (1901) 59 App. Div. 363, 69 N. Y. S. 551; Hudson v. Blanchard, (1956) .... Okla.........., 294 P. 2d 554; Wesseler v. Great Northern Ry., (1916) 90 Wash. 234, 155 Pac. 1063, 157 Pac. 461.

For application of the principle to the attorney-client privilege, see note 51 A. L. R. 2d 521.

[1] Professor Chafee expressed some doubt as to the effectiveness of the rule. "But even this rule about waiver does not promote truth-telling any too well. The patient may tell some rather big lies about his health without 'going into details,' and the courts are by no means clear in defining the point where details begin."

Privileged Communications: Is Justice Served or Obstructed by Closing the Doctor's Mouth on the Witness Stand?, (1943) 52 Yale L. J. 607, 610.

Some of the cases cited in note 4, § 133, herein, are good examples.

said or did, he should not be permitted to insist that the protection and benefits of the statute continue to exist as to his physician. When he chooses to make public that which could have been kept secret, the privilege no longer exists and the physician may testify on the same subject.[2] The adverse party may also introduce in

[2] Representative decisions are: Schlarb v. Henderson, (1936) 211 Ind. 1, 4 N. E. 2d 205; Lane v. Boicourt, (1891) 128 Ind. 420, 423, 27 N. E. 1111; "When the obligation to silence is broken, it is broken for the defendant as well as for the plaintiff. As to all witnesses of the transaction, it is fully opened to investigation, if opened at all, by the party having a right to keep it closed. * * * A patient may enforce secrecy if he chooses; but where he himself removes the obligation he cannot avail himself of the statute to exclude witnesses to the occurrence."

Woods v. Lisbon, (1911) 150 Iowa 433, 130 N. W. 372; Armstrong v. Topeka Ry., (1914) 93 Kan. 493, 144 Pac. 847; Mulvena v. Alexander, (1936) 278 Mich. 265, 270 N. W. 291; La Count v. Von Platen-Fox Co., (1928) 243 Mich. 250, 220 N. W. 697; Wells v. Jefferson, (1939) 345 Mo. 239, 132 S. W. 2d 1006; Epstein v. Pennsylvania R. R., (1913) 250 Mo. 1, 156 S. W. 699, 48 L. R. A. (n. s.) 394, Ann. Cas. 1915 A. 423; Foerstel v. St. Louis Public Service Co., (1951) _____ Mo. App._____ , 241 S. W. 2d 792; Priebe v. Crandall, (1916) _____Mo. App._____ , 187 S. W. 605; McPherson v. Harvey, (1916) _____Mo. App._____ , 183 S. W. 653, 654: "In her own testimony, as well as in that of her physician and surgeon, plaintiff went into the subject of her malady, exposing everything and concealing nothing, except the highly important fact, if it be a fact, that the malady was not caused by the injury, but was one of long standing and had been accurately diagnosed, but unsuccessfully treated, by a physician for almost two years."

Michaels v. Harvey, (1915) _____ Mo. App._____, 179 S. W. 735; Oliver v. Aylor, (1913) 173 Mo. App. 323, 158 S. W. 733; O'Brien v. Western Implement Mfg. Co., (1909) 141 Mo. App. 331, 125 S. W. 805; Apter v. Home Life Ins. Co., (1935) 266 N. Y. 333, 194 N. E. 846, 98 A. L. R. 1281; Steinberg v. New York Life Ins. Co., (1933) 263 N. Y. 45, 188 N. E. 152, 90 A. L. R. 642; Hethier v. Johns, (1922) 233 N. Y. 370, 135 N. E. 603; Capron v. Douglass, (1908) 193 N. Y. 11, 85 N. E. 827, 20 L. R. A. (n. s.) 1003; Clifford v. Denver & Rio Grande R. R., (1907) 188 N. Y. 349, 80 N. E. 1094; Davis v. Davis, (1955) 1 App. Div. 2d 675, 146 N. Y. S. 2d 630; Fennelly v. Schenectady Ry., (1922) 201 App. Div. 211, 193 N. Y. S. 641; Dewey v. Cohoes & L. Bridge Co., (1915) 170 App. Div. 117, 155 N. Y. S. 887; Terier v. Dare, (1911) 146 App. Div. 375, 131 N. Y. S. 51; Powers v. Metropolitan Street Ry., (1905) 105 App. Div. 358, 94 N. Y. S. 184; Green v. Nirenberg Sons, Inc., (1938) 166 Misc. 652, 3 N. Y. S. 2d 81.

Matter of Loewenthal's Petition, (1956) 101 Ohio App. 355, 134 N. E. 2d 158; Strebeck v. Eagle Picher Mining & S. Co., (1953) _____Okla._____ , 259 P. 8d 536; Tulsa v. Wicker, (1914) 42 Okla. 539, 141 Pac. 963; Fulsom-Morris Coal & Mining Co. v. Mitchell, (1913) 37 Okla. 575, 132 Pac. 1103; Roeser v. Pease, (1913) 37 Okla. 222, 131 Pac. 534; Forrest v. Portland Ry., Light & P. Co., (1913) 64 Ore. 240, 129 Pac. 1048; Randa v. Bear, (1957) _____Wash._____, 312 P. 2d 640; McUne v. Fuqua, (1953) _____Wash._____ , 253 P. 2d 632, 257 P. 2d 636; State v. Wilson, (1935) 182 Wash. 319, 47 P. 2d 21.

Contra: Nolan v. Glynn, (1913) 163 Iowa 146, 142 N. W. 1029, Ann. Cas. 1916 C.

>>>→

evidence relevant portions of the patient's hospital record not otherwise inadmissible.[3]

If the patient be dead and the holder of the privilege brings or defends an action which puts in issue the physical or mental condition of the deceased patient and introduces evidence disclosing in detail his condition, the privilege is waived and any physician who attended him may testify thereto at the instance of the adverse party.[4] The patient's hospital record may also be received in evidence.[5]

Where the patient voluntarily testifies that he now suffers, or at an earlier time suffered, from a specified disability, disease, or mental disorder, he waives the privilege and any physician who, at the time mentioned or at a different time, has treated him for the alleged condition may testify, at the instance of the adverse party, to any information he may have acquired while attending the patient, and may relate the true nature, origin, and duration thereof notwithstanding his testimony may contradict that of the patient.[6]

559; Cable v. Johnson, (1933) ....Mo. App........, 63 S. W. 2d 433. The doctrine of waiver seems unduly limited in these two cases.

See also note, 114 A. L. R. 798.

Of course, if the patient testifies to a physicial condition which is plainly observable by anyone, there would probably be no waiver with respect to privileged matters not otherwise disclosed by him.

For statutory provisions relating to waiver, see § 132, herein.

[3] Munzer v. Swedish American Line, (1940) 35 F. Supp. 493; Maas v. Midway Chevrolet Co., (1945) 219 Minn. 461, 18 N. W. 2d 233, 158 A. L. R. 215; Galli v. Wells, (1922) 209 Mo. App. 460, 239 S. W. 894; Weis v. Weis, (1947) 147 Ohio St. 416, 72 N. E. 2d 245, 169 A. L. R. 668.

[4] National Annuity Ass'n. v. McCall, (1912) 103 Ark. 201, 146 S. W. 125, 48 L. R. A. (n. s.) 418; Estate of Visaxis, (1928) 95 Cal. App. 617, 273 Pac. 165; Moreno v. New Guadalupe Mining Co., (1918) 35 Cal. App. 744, 170 Pac. 1088; Doty v. Crystal Ice & Fuel Co., (1925) 118 Kan. 323, 235 Pac. 96; Denny v. Robertson, (1944) 352 Mo. 609, 179 S. W. 2d 5; Holcomb v. Harris, (1901) 166 N. Y. 257, 59 N. E. 820; Eder v. Cashin, (1953) 281 App. Div. 456, 120 N. Y. S. 2d 165; Weis v. Weis, (1947) 147 Ohio St. 416, 72 N. E. 2d 245, 169 A. L. R. 668; Porter's Estate, (1953) 208 Okla. 475, 257 P. 2d 517.

[5] Buckminster's Estate v. Commissioner of Internal Revenue, (1944) 147 F. 2d 331; Green v. Nirenberg Sons, Inc., (1938) 166 Misc. 652, 3 N. Y. S. 2d 81.

See also Feldman v. Connecticut Mutual Life Ins. Co., (1944) 142 F. 2d 628.

[6] Munzer v. Swedish American Line, (1940) 35 F. Supp. 493; State v. Cochran, (1947)

135. Holder of Privilege Introducing Evidence Relating to Examination, Communications, and Treatment

If the patient, as a part of his case, *voluntarily* testifies concerning what was said or done by his physician in the treatment of his injury or malady, he waives the privilege and exempts the evidence of the physician relative to such matters from the operation of the statute. By causing the communications between himself and his physician to be recited in public, he has deprived them of their confidential character. The adverse party, therefore, may call the physician as a witness and ask him to give his version

←≪

356 Mo. 778, 203 S. W. 2d 707; State v. Sapp, (1947) 356 Mo. 705, 203 S. W. 2d 425; Weissman v. Wells, (1924) 306 Mo. 82, 267 S. W. 400; State v. Long, (1913) 257 Mo. 199, 165 S. W. 748; Jennings v. National Life & Acc. Ins. Co., (1931) 226 Mo. App. 777, 46 S. W. 2d 226; Oliver v. Aylor, (1913) 173 Mo. App. 323, 158 S. W. 733; Webb. v. Metropolitan Street Ry., (1901) 89 Mo. App. 604; Friesen v. Reimer, (1933) 124 Neb. 620, 247 N. W. 561; Apter v. Home Life Ins. Co., (1935) 266 N. Y. 333, 194 N. E. 846, 98 A. L. R. 1281; Steinberg v. New York Life Ins. Co., (1933) 263 N. Y. 45, 188 N. E. 152, 90 A. L. R. 642; Seaman v. Mott, (1908) 127 App. Div. 18, 110 N. Y. S. 1040; Marquardt v. Brooklyn Heights R. R., (1908) 126 App. Div. 272, 110 N. Y. S. 657; Lampel v. Goldstein, (1917) 167 N. Y. S. 576; Baker v. Industrial Comm'n., (1939) 135 Ohio St. 491, 21 N. E. 2d 593. Physician allowed to testify to patient's disease but not to verbal communications between himself and patient since patient did not voluntarily testify in respect to any such communications.

Bowers v. Industrial Comm'n., (1939) _____ Ohio App._____ , 30 Ohio Law Abst. 353; Metropolitan Life Ins. Co. v. McKim, (1935) 54 Ohio App. 66, 6 N. E. 2d 9; Williams v. State, (1951) _____ Okla. Cr. _____ , 226 P. 2d 989; Terrell v. First National Bank & Trust Co., (1950) 204 Okla. 24, 226 P. 2d 431; Hudman v. State, (1949) 89 Okla. Cr. 160, 205 P. 2d 1175; Chicago, Rock Island & Pac. R. R. v. Hughes, (1917) 64 Okla. 74, 166 Pac. 411; Forrest v. Portland Ry., Light & P. Co., (1913) 64 Ore. 240, 129 Pac. 1048.

In a personal injury case, plaintiff voluntarily introduced evidence to the effect that he was not afflicted with syphilis. Defendant was permitted to call as a witness a physician who attended plaintiff to show that a Wasserman test indicated he did have the disease. Northern Indiana Public Service Co. v. McClure, (1940) 108 Ind. App. 253, 24 N. E. 2d 788. In Livingston v. Omaha & Council Bluffs St. Ry., (1919) 104 Neb. 118, 175 N. W. 662, plaintiff, in her direct examination, testified that she had never had any venereal disease and had not taken treatment for any ailment of that sort. Defendant called as witnesses two physicians who testified they had examined or treated her before the accident but they were not permitted to disclose the nature of her malady or the treatment rendered. In Donovan v. Donovan, (1941) 231 Iowa 14, 300 N. W. 656, a divorce case, plaintiff testified she suffered a nervous breakdown and consulted a physician in the spring of 1940. The court rejected defendant's offer to prove by her physician that he had examined her in the fall of 1940 and discovered she had a social disease.

of what was actually said on the occasions related by the patient.[1] Moreover, it has been held that the physician may be interrogated as to relevant matters other than those brought out in the patient's testimony.[2]

---

[1] Union Pac. R. R. v. Thomas, (1907) 152 Fed. 365; Chambers v. Tobin, (1954) 118 F. Supp. 555, rev'd on other grounds 204 F. 2d 732; General Acc., Fire & Life Assur. Corp. v. Savage, (1929) 35 F. 2d 587, 592; Missouri & N. Ark. R. R. v. Daniels, (1911) 98 Ark. 352, 136 S. W. 651; Reed v. Rex Fuel Co., (1913) 160 Iowa 510, 141 N. W. 1056; State v. Bennett, (1908) 137 Iowa 427, 110 N. W. 150; Coca-Cola Bottling Works v. Simpson, (1930) 158 Miss. 390, 130 So. 479, 72 A. L. R. 143; Wells v. Jefferson, (1939) 345 Mo. 239, 132 S. W. 2d 1006; Blankenbaker v. St. Louis & San Francisco R. R., (1916) _____ Mo._____, 187 S. W. 840; State v. Long, (1913) 257 Mo. 199, 165 S. W. 748; Epstein v. Pennsylvania R. R., (1913) 250 Mo. 1, 156 S. W. 699, 48 L. R. A. (n. s.) 394, Ann. Cas. 1915 A. 423; Holloway v. Kansas City, (1904) 184 Mo. 19, 82 S. W. 89; Jennings v. National Life & Acc. Ins. Co., (1931) 226 Mo. App. 777, 46 S. W. 2d 226 (plaintiff also introduced written reports made by his physician); Highfil v. Missouri Pac. Ry., (1902) 93 Mo. App. 219; Webb v. Metropolitan Street Ry., (1901) 89 Mo. App. 604; Culver v. Union Pac. R. R., (1924) 112 Neb. 441, 199 N. W. 794; Hethier v. Johns, (1922) 233 N. Y. 370, 135 N. E. 603; McKenney v. American Locomotive Co., (1914) 164 App. Div. 625, 149 N. Y. S. 826; Rauh v. Deutscher Verein, (1898) 29 App. Div. 483, 51 N. Y. S. 985; Marx v. Manhattan Ry., (1890) 56 Hun. 575, 10 N. Y. S. 159; Forrest v. Portland Ry., Light & P. Co., (1913) 64 Ore. 240, 129 Pac. 1048; Brennan v. Manufacturers' Life Ins. Co., (1919) 11 Puerto Rico Fed. 203; Clawson v. Walgreen Drug Co., (1947) 108 Utah 577, 162 P. 2d 759; Moutzoukos v. Mutual Benefit, Health & Acc. Ass'n., (1927) 69 Utah 309, 254 Pac. 1005; Dahlquist v. Denver & Rio Grande R. R., (1918) 52 Utah 438, 174 Pac. 833; Canning v. Chicago & Milwaukee E. Ry., (1916) 163 Wis. 448, 157 N. W. 532.

Dolan v. United Casualty Co., (1940) 259 App. Div. 784, 18 N. Y. S. 2d 387: "Even assuming, without deciding, that the plaintiff is correct in her contention that the physician could have been prevented from disclosing information which he acquired while attending the plaintiff in a professional capacity, he could at least have denied that he told plaintiff what she says he told her." Counsel offering the physician's testimony should be careful to do so in a proper manner. See Indianapolis & M. Rapid Transit Co. v. Hall, (1905) 165 Ind. 557, 76 N. E. 242; Williams v. Johnson, (1887) 112 Ind. 273, 13 N. E. 872.

In Buckminster's Estate v. Commissioner of Internal Revenue, (1944) 147 F. 2d 331, the privileged evidence was introduced by the representative of the deceased patient. See also O'Brien v. General Acc., Fir & Life Assur. Corp., (1930) 42 F. 2d 48. It should be remembered, however, that some courts hold that where the disclosure is slight only, no waiver results. See § 133, herein.

As to privileged matters brought out in cross-examination, see § 139, herein.

[2] Missouri Pac. Transportation Co. v. Moody, (1939) 199 Ark. 483, 134 S. W. 2d 868; Demonbrun v. McHaffie, (1941) 348 Mo. 1120, 156 S. W. 2d 923.

Contra: Donovan v. Donovan, (1941) 231 Iowa 14, 300 N. W. 656; Burns v. Waterloo, (1919) 187 Iowa 922, 173 N. W. 16, 174 N. W. 644; Nolan v. Glynn, (1918) 163

⟫→

If the patient testifies to, or introduces evidence by other witnesses relating to, an examination or treatment by the physician, this opens up the subject and the physician may testify to his version of the matter and may be used to contradict the patient or his witnesses.[3] In some cases, the physician has been allowed to testify beyond the specific treatments or examinations testified to by the patient, if his testimony concerns the same injury or malady.[4]

←≪

Iowa 146, 142 N. W. 1029, Ann. Cas. 1916 C. 559. See also Struble v. DeWitt, (1911) 89 Neb. 726, 132 N. W. 124. Whether proffered evidence relates to same subject is left to discretion of trial judge.

[3] Lane v. Boicourt, (1891) 128 Ind. 420, 27 N. E. 1111; Blish v. Greer, (1918) 74 Ind. App. 469, 120 N. E. 606; Burns v. Waterloo, (1919) 187 Iowa 922, 173 N. W. 16, 174 N. W. 644; Epstein v. Pennsylvania R. R., (1913) 250 Mo. 1, 156 S. W. 699, 48 L. R. A. (n. s.) 394, Ann. Cas. 1915 A 423; Priebe v. Crandall, (1916) ....Mo. App........, 187 S. W. 605; Oliver v. Aylor, (1913) 173 Mo. App. 323, 158 S. W. 733; Highfil v. Missouri Pac. Ry., (1902) 93 Mo. App. 219; Hethier v. Johns, (1922) 233 N. Y. 370, 135 N. E. 603; Kraus v. Sobel, (1922) 203 App. Div. 582, 196 N. Y. S. 845; McKenney v. American Locomotive Co., (1914) 164 App. Div. 625, 149 N. Y. S. 826; Rauh v. Deutscher Verein, (1898) 29 App. Div. 483, 51 N. Y. S. 985; Meshel v. Crotona Park Sanitarium, Inc., (1935) 154 Misc. 221, 276 N. Y. S. 989; Marx v. Manhattan Ry., (1890) 56 Hun 575, 10 N. Y. S. 159; Brennan v. Manufacturers' Life Ins. Co., (1919) 11 Puerto Rico Fed. 203; Tulsa v. Wicker, (1914) 42 Okla. 539, 141 Pac. 963; Clawson v. Walgreen Drug Co., (1945) 108 Utah 577, 162 P. 2d 759; Randa v. Bear, (1957) ....Wash........, 312 P. 2d 640.

Struble v. DeWitt, (1911) 89 Neb. 726, 732, 132 N. W. 124: "A considerable latitude must be allowed a trial judge in such matters." It has been held that waiver results where the patient, or his representative, calls *lay witnesses* to testify to communications between the physician and the patient, or to the treatment rendered. O'Brien v. General Acc., Fire & Life Assur. Corp., (1930) 42 F. 2d 48; Estate of Visaxis, (1928) 95 Cal. App. 617, 273 Pac. 165; Moreno v. New Guadalupe Mining Co., (1918) 35 Cal. App. 744, 170 Pac. 1088; Lane v. Boicourt, (1891) 128 Ind. 420, 27 N. E. 1111; Burns v. Waterloo, (1919) 187 Iowa 922, 173 N. W. 16, 174 N. W. 644; Woods v. Lisbon, (1911) 150 Iowa 433, 130 N. W. 372; Davis v. Davis, (1955) 1 App. Div. 2d 675, 146 N. Y. S. 2d 630.

Contra: Arizona Copper Co. v. Garcia, (1923) 25 Ariz. 158, 214 Pac. 317; Nordyke & Marmon Co. v. Whitehead, (1914) 183 Ind. 7, 106 N. E. 867; Indianapolis & Martinsville Rapid Transit Co. v. Hall, (1905) 165 Ind. 557, 76 N. E. 242 (question not properly presented to trial court); American Bankers Ins. Co. v. Hopkins (1917) 67 Okla. 150, 169 Pac. 489.

[4] Becknell v. Hosier, (1893) 10 Ind. App. 5, 37 N. E. 580; Woods v. Lisbon, (1911) 150 Iowa 433, 130 N. W. 372; Demonbrun v. McHaffie, (1941) 348 Mo. 1120, 156 S. W. 2d 923; Wells v. Jefferson, (1939) 345 Mo. 239, 132 S. W. 2d 1006; Weissman v. Wells, (1924) 306 Mo. 82, 267 S. W. 400; Ansnes v. Loyal Protective Ins. Co., (1937) 133 Neb. 665, 276 N. W. 397; Friesen v. Reimer, (1933) 124 Neb. 620, 247 N. W. 561; Powers

≫→

The theory is that the waiver is entire and cannot be severed. The privilege cannot be waived in part and enforced in part. The common sense view is that the patient cannot remove the seal of secrecy from so much of the privileged matters as make for his advantage, and insist that it shall not be removed by so much as makes to the advantage of his adversary. It is not permissible, therefore, for the patient to select out certain communications or portions of the treatment, or certain visits and examinations and, by detailing them, limit his adversary's evidence to those particular matters or occurrences.[5]

136. Patient Testifying to Previous Good Health

Where a person bases his action in a court of justice upon an alleged physical disability resulting from an accident or other occurrence for which he claims another is responsible, and voluntarily testifies, or offers the testimony of others, to the effect that his physical condition before the accident or occurrence was good, in order to establish the necessary issue of proximate cause, he should have no right by claim of privilege to protect his testimony or that of his witnesses from the truth by excluding the testimony of the physician who knows that his physical condition prior to the accident or occurrence was not good and was not as represented by

v. Metropolitan Street Ry., (1905) 105 App. Div. 358, 94 N. Y. S. 184; Terrell v. First National Bank & Trust Co., (1950) 204 Okla. 24, 226 P. 2d 431; Lazzell v. Harvey, (1935) 174 Okla. 86, 49 P. 2d 519; Chicago, Rock Island & Pac. R. R. v. Hughes, (1917) 64 Okla. 74, 166 Pac. 411; Dahlquist v. Denver & Rio Grande R. R., (1918) 52 Utah 438, 174 Pac. 833.

Contra: Nolan v. Glynn, (1913) 163 Iowa 146, 142 N. W. 1029, Ann. Cas. 1916 C. 559.

5 Becknell v. Hosier, (1893) 10 Ind. App. 5, 37 N. E. 580; Coca-Cola Bottling Works v. Simpson, (1930) 158 Miss. 390, 130 So. 479, 72 A. L. R. 148; Demonbrun v. McHaffie, (1941) 348 Mo. 1120, 156 S. W. 2d 923; Wells v. Jefferson, (1939) 345 Mo. 239, 132 S. W. 2d 1006; State v. Long, (1913) 257 Mo. 199, 165 S. W. 748; Holloway v. Kansas City, (1904) 184 Mo. 19, 82 S. W. 89; Culver v. Union Pac. R. R., (1924) 112 Neb. 441, 199 N. W. 794; Bryant v. Modern Woodmen of America, (1910) 86 Neb. 372, 125 N. W. 621, 27 L. R. A. (n. s.) 326, 21 Ann. Cas. 365; Powers v. Metropolitan Street Ry., (1905) 105 App. Div. 358, 94 N. Y. S. 184; Rauh v. Deutscher Verein, (1898) 29 App. Div. 483, 51 N. Y. S. 985; Williams v. State, (1951) ____Okla. Cr.____, 226 P. 2d 989; Chicago, Rock Island & Pac. R. R. v. Hughes, (1917) 64 Okla. 74, 166 Pac. 411; Dahlquist v. Denver & Rio Grande R. R., (1918) 52 Utah 438, 174 Pac. 833.

him or his witnesses. Having voluntarily introduced such evidence to advance his own cause, the plaintiff has made his previous condition of health an issue in the case, and the defendant ought to have the right to call the plaintiff's physician as a witness to testify on the same subject. The plaintiff himself has plainly opened up that issue and by so doing, he, in effect, represents that the ailments and disabilities which he or his witnesses describe as a basis for recovery of damages did not exist prior to the accident or occurrence which gave rise to the claimed liability. In all fairness, therefore, the plaintiff should be deemed to have waived the statutory privilege as to any medical testimony, or as to any hospital record, which tends to contradict or impeach the testimony he has introduced on this subject. There is good authority for this view, but there are decisions to the contrary.

In a personal injury case, the plaintiff testified that before the accident, but not afterwards, his health was good and that he had not consulted a physician "for years." After a verdict for the plaintiff, the defendant discovered a physician who had treated the plaintiff twenty times before the accident for various ailments. Defendant's motion for a new trial was granted but only upon the issue of damages, and he was permitted to call the physician to disprove the evidence offered by plaintiff as to his condition of health before the accident.[1] In *Lazzell v. Harvey*,[2] plaintiff testified that before the accident his health was good and described the kind of work he was able to perform. He also said he had a good voice and sang in a quartet, but since his injury he had lost his voice and could scarcely talk above a whisper. The trial court properly held that he had waived the privilege and defendant could call two physicians who had treated plaintiff to show that his chief trouble was syphilis. In an action upon an insurance policy, plaintiff claimed

---

[1] McUne v. Fuqua, (1953) ....Wash........., 253 P. 2d 632, 257 P. 2d 636. For similar facts and rulings, see McPherson v. Harvey, (1912) .... Mo. App........., 183 S. W. 653; Roeser v. Pease, (1913) 37 Okla. 222, 131 Pac. 534.

See also Polcsa v. East River Management Corp., (1957) 160 N. Y. S. 2d 658; Hudson v. Blanchard, (1956) ....Okla........., 294 P. 2d 554.

[2] (1935) 174 Okla. 86, 49 P. 2d 519. See also Weissman v. Wells, (1924) 306 Mo. 82, 267 S. W. 400.

to have ruptured himself while unloading timber. He testified that before the occurrence he was physically fit. Defendant claimed that the plaintiff was afflicted with a double hernia before the occurrence mentioned, and was permitted to call as a witness a physician who examined the plaintiff at the instance of another company, to show that the plaintiff was not physically fit prior to the occurrence.[3] In an action on an insurance policy, the plaintiff-beneficiary claimed that the insured's death was accidental. Defendant claimed it was suicide. Doubtless anticipating this defense, the plaintiff, as a part of her case, offered lay testimony to prove that, before his death, the insured was in sound condition, mentally and physically. Plaintiff herself testified and quoted the insured's physician to that effect. Under the Nebraska statute, the physician who attended the insured was permitted to testify at the instance of defendant that the insured was impotent.[4]

On the other hand, some courts have held that where a claimant testifies that his health was good prior to the accident, the door is not thereby opened for testimony by his physician on any or all diseases which the claimant may have had; that the word "health" is too general to remove the ban of secrecy imposed by the statute.[5] In *Harpman* v. *Devine*,[6] a personal injury case, the plaintiff testified that before the accident his health had been good but thereafter he had suffered from a variety of specified ailments and disabilities; however, he made no reference to any communications between himself and his physician. The defendant claimed that the plain-

---

[3] Moutzoukos v. Mutual Benefit, Health & Acc. Ass'n., (1927) 69 Utah 309, 254 Pac. 1005.

In Chicago, Rock Island & Pac. R. R. v. Hughes, (1917) 64 Okla. 74, 166 Pac. 411, plaintiff testified that before the accident he was in good health and had never suffered similar injuries. He claimed he received a rupture of the right groin for which he was treated by two physicians. Defendant called one of them as its witness and he was permitted to testify that plaintiff had told him that several years before he was injured while riding a horse, and that a rupture had resulted at that time.

[4] O'Brien v. General Acc., Fire & Assur. Corp., (1930) 42 F. 2d 48.

[5] Baker v. Industrial Comm'n., (1939) 135 Ohio St. 491, 21 N. E. 2d 593. The court concedes that if the patient testifies about one particular injury or disease, the physician may also testify on that one subject. But he can testify to no other.

[6] (1937) 133 Ohio St. 1, 10 N. E. 2d 776, 114 A. L. R. 789.

The dissenting opinion of Zimmerman, J., concurred in by Weygandt, Ch.J., is very convincing. One judge did not participate.

tiff's complaints were the usual consequences of pernicious anemia from which plaintiff had suffered prior to the accident. To prove this, defendant offered the testimony of a physician who had treated plaintiff before the accident. Plaintiff's objection on the ground of privilege was sustained, the privilege not having been waived.[7]

In a personal injury action, the plaintiff testified that prior to the accident in which she suffered injury her health had been good and that she had been able to do heavy work indoors and outdoors. Her testimony, if true, showed her to be a remarkably robust and vigorous woman, save for a few minor ailments she suffered during that period. The defendant claimed that her testimony was false and offered that of a physician who had attended her on numerous occasions prior to her injury. It was held that she had not waived the privilege and that the physician could not testify to information acquired by him during his professional attendance upon her.[8]

---

[7] Myers, J., (p. 6): "Defendant maintains that when plaintiff, in his direct examination which was voluntary, testified that his health before the time of the accident was good, he thereby testified on a 'subject' under the statute in such a manner as to permit the defendant to introduce testimony respecting his health during that period, including the communications, advice and treatment of plaintiff by Dr. F. It is asserted that when plaintiff testified that his health was good he thereby 'opened the door' and waived the privilege accorded him by the statute. It is claimed that health is a subject that is not only a general term but necessarily includes communications and advice especially in the case at bar. While there is much force in such an argument, such an interpretation would render the statute useless and ineffective in every case where the plaintiff or patient has testified generally respecting his health."

Comments on this decision have not been favorable. Professor Chafee, in (1939) 52 Yale L. J. 607, 610, says: "The absurdity of this solicitude for the patient's privacy is illustrated by Harpman v. Devine."

(1938) 51 Harv. L. Rev. 931: "The decision reflects a surprising judicial sympathy toward the much criticized physician-patient privilege. The offered testimony of Dr. F. might well have been held to be 'on the same subject' as the plaintiff's testimony concerning his antecedent physical condition * * *."

William L. Hart (later a member of the Ohio Supreme Court), Review of Ohio Case Law for 1937, (1938) 10 Ohio Op. 164, 176: "The application of the rule adopted by the court will tend to bring the administration of the law into disrepute, and will support the charge that the law often fails to serve the ends of justice."

See also (1937) U. Cin. L. Rev. 544; (1937) 4 Ohio St. L. J. 103.

[8] McConnell v. Osage, (1890) 80 Iowa 293, 45 N. W. 550, 8 L. R. A. 778.

Where the plaintiff testified to her good health and general condition prior to the injury for which she sought damages and her physician testified that after the accident he examined her and found she had womb trouble, the defendant was not permitted to prove by two physicians who had treated her two years before that she was suffering from the same condition at that time.[9]

In *Walmer-Roberts* v. *Hennessey*,[10] the plaintiff testified she was well and strong before the accident, but thereafter suffered ailments some of which existed at the time of trial. The defendant called as a witness a physician who examined her after the accident, but he was not allowed to state whether or not he found any evidence of injury at all.

In an action brought by the beneficiary to recover the proceeds of an insurance policy, it appeared that the insured, in her application, warranted she was in good health. The defendant called as a witness a physician who had attended the insured prior to the date of the policy. He was permitted to testify that she was not in good health at that time, but was not allowed to state the nature of the disease from which she then suffered.[11]

137. Proof of Loss or Death: Physician's Certificate of Death

The general rule is that the furnishing by the beneficiary to the insurer of a physician's certificate of death as part of the proof

---

[9] Missouri & N. Ark. R. R. v. Daniels, (1911) 98 Ark. 352, 136 S. W. 651. It does not appear that the court seriously considered the question of a general waiver resulting from her representations as to her previous good health, but based its decision on the ground that the calling of one physician is not a waiver as to others.

See also Hirschberg v. Southern Pac. Co., (1919) 180 Cal. 774, 183 Pac. 141; Dotton v. Albion, (1885) 57 Mich. 575, 24 N. W. 786.

[10] (1921) 191 Iowa 86, 181 N. W. 798.

[11] Prudential Ins. Co. v. Lear, (1908) 31 App. D. C. 184. The acceptance of an insurance policy containing a condition that the insured is in sound health does not operate as a waiver of the privilege and does not authorize the decedent's attending physician to testify at the instance of the company, to what he learned about the deceased through his diagnosis of her. Humble v. John Hancock Mut. Life Ins. Co., (1931) 28 Ohio N. P. (n. s.) 481, aff'd _____ Ohio App._____, 31 N. E. 2d 887.

Contra: Wills v. National Life & Acc. Ins. Co., (1928) 28 Ohio App. 497, 162 N. W. 822 (dictum).

of death, does not constitute a waiver of the physician-patient privilege, and, in an action on the policy, the physician may not, without the consent of the holder of the privilege, testify concerning confidential information acquired while attending the deceased in his professional capacity.[1] Nevertheless, the certificate itself may, under proper circumstances, be introduced in evidence by the insurer as an admission against interest by the beneficiary,[2] subject, however, to contradiction or explanation.

Where the beneficiary, in furnishing the insurer a proof of death, expressly assents to the introduction in evidence of the insured's hospital or medical records, or to the testimony or the written statement of the insured's physician, the privilege, of course, is

---

[1] Ranger, Inc. v. Equitable Life Assur. Soc., (1952) 196 F. 2d 968; Fidelity & Casualty Co. v. Meyer, (1912) 106 Ark. 91, 152 S. W. 995, 44 L. R. A. (n. s.) 493; Polish Roman Catholic Union v. Palen, (1942) 302 Mich. 557, 5 N. W. 2d 463; Repala v. John Hancock Mut. Life Ins. Co., (1924) 229 Mich. 463, 201 N. W. 465; Gilchrist v. Mystic Workers of the World, (1915) 188 Mich. 466, 154 N. W. 575, Ann. Cas. 1918 C. 757; Krapp v. Metropolitan Life Ins. Co., (1906) 143 Mich. 369, 106 N. W. 1107; Fitzgerald v. Metropolitan Life Ins. Co., (1941) __ Mo. App. ___, 149 S. W. 2d 389; Masson v. Metropolitan Life Ins. Co., (1931) 225 Mo. App. 925, 36 S. W. 2d 118; Hicks v. Metropolitan Life Ins. Co., (1916) 196 Mo. App. 162, 190 S. W. 661; Frazier v. Metropolitan Life Ins. Co., (1911) 161 Mo. App. 709, 141 S. W. 936; Scott v. Metropolitan Life Ins. Co., (1941) 140 Neb. 581, 300 N. W. 835; Redmond v. Industrial Benefit Ass'n., (1896) 78 Hun. 104, 28 N. Y. S. 1075, aff'd. 150 N. Y. 167, 44 N. E. 769; Acee v. Metropolitan Life Ins. Co., (1927) 219 App. Div. 246, 219 N. Y. S. 152; Polachek v. New York Life Ins. Co., (1934) 147 Misc. 16, 263 N. Y. S. 230, aff'd. 240 App. Div. 1028, 268 N. Y. S. 995; Becker v. Metropolitan Life Ins. Co., (1904) 43 Misc. 99, 87 N. Y. S. 980, judgment rev'd on grounds that facts sought to be elicited were not within scope of privilege, 99 App. Div. 5, 90 N. Y. S. 1007; American Assur. Co. v. Early, (1912) 23 Ohio C. C. (n. s.) 418, aff'd. 91 Ohio St. 367, 110 N. E. 1053; Eklund v. Metropolitan Life Ins. Co., (1936) 89 Utah 273, 57 P. 2d 362. See 8 Wigmore, Evidence, § 2390 (4). See also notes, 17 A. L. R. 359; 42 A. L. R. 1455; 96 A. L. R. 341.

But *cf.* Sommer v. Guardian Life Ins. Co., (1937) 253 App. Div. 763, 300 N. Y. S. 938; National Benevolent Soc. v. Russell, (1935) 173 Okla. 331, 48 P. 2d 1047.

See also §§ 67, 68, 69, herein.

[2] Martin v. Metropolitan Life Ins. Co., (1943) __ Mo. App. ___, 174 S. W. 2d 222, 225; "The rule excluding communications between physician and patient may not be invoked as against a statement made by a physician in proofs of death. This is so because such a statement is admitted in evidence as an admission of the beneficiary, not as testimony of the physician."

See also §§ 68, 69, herein.

waived and the insurer is entitled to introduce such evidence at the trial.[3]

Where, in an action to recover the proceeds of the policy, the beneficiary, or the holder of the privilege, himself introduces in evidence the proofs of death which include the certificate of death made and signed by the attending physician, the better rule seems to be that the privilege is thereby waived and the adverse party may call such physician to testify as to all matters referred to in said certificate,[4] or he may introduce in evidence the hospital record of the deceased patient.[5] There is, however, ample authority to the contrary.[6]

---

[3] Progressive Life Ins. Co. v. Hulbert, (1938) 196 Ark. 352, 118 S. W. 2d 268; Luce v. Service Life Ins. Co., (1939) 227 Iowa 532, 288 N. W. 681; Scott v. Metropolitan Life Ins. Co., (1941) 140 Neb. 581, 300 N. W. 835 (waiver limited in time by its terms to a period of three years prior to its date); Willis v. Order of Railroad Telegraphers, (1941) 139 Neb. 46, 296 N. W. 443; Winiarski v. John Hancock Mut. Life Ins. Co., (1934) 241 App. Div. 284, 270 N. Y. S. 562.

See also §§ 67, 68, 69, herein.

In Michigan, such waiver clause is invalid. Wohlfeil v. Bankers Life Co., (1941) 296 Mich. 310, 296 N. W. 269.

In National Life & Acc. Ins. Co. v. Bell, (1930) 144 Okla. 236, 291 Pac. 106, the beneficiary was allowed to withdraw the waiver before acted upon. See also Frazier v. Metropolitan Life Ins. Co., (1911) 161 Mo. App. 709, 141 S. W. 936.

For anticipatory waiver by insured, see § 109, herein; for effect thereof, see § 110, herein.

[4] Schirmer v. Baldwin, (1930) 182 Ark. 581, 32 S. W. 2d 162 (will contest; certificate of physician introduced in evidence by contestants); Bouligny v. Metropolitan Life Ins. Co., (1942) __ Mo. App. __ , 160 S. W. 2d 474; National Benevolent Soc. v. Russell, (1935) 173 Okla. 331, 48 P. 2d 1047.

See also Matter of Monroe's Will, (1946) 270 App. Div. 1039, 63 N. Y. S. 2d 141; Becker v. Metropolitan Life Ins. Co., (1904) 99 App. Div. 5, 90 N. Y. S. 1007; McGinty v. Brotherhood of Railway Trainmen, (1917) 166 Wis. 83, 164 N. W. 249.

[5] Bouligny v. Metropolitan Life Ins. Co. (1942) __ Mo. App. __ , 160 S. W. 2d 474.

[6] State Mutual Life Assur. Co. v. Wittenberg, (1957) 239 F. 2d 87; Ranger v. Equitable Life Assur. Soc., (1952) 196 F. 2d 968; Miller v. Pacific Mutual Life Ins. Co., (1953) 116 F. Supp. 365, aff'd. 228 F. 2d 889; Fidelity & Casualty Co. v. Meyer, (1912) 106 Ark. 91, 152 S. W. 995, 44 L. R. A. (n. s.) 493; Scott v. Metropolitan Life Ins. Co., (1941) 140 Neb. 581, 300 N. W. 835; Acee v. Metropolitan Life Ins. Co., (1927) 219 App. Div. 246, 219 N. Y. S. 152; Eklund v. Metropolitan Life Ins. Co., (1936) 89 Utah 273, 57 P. 2d 362.

See also American Assur. Co. v. Early, (1912) 23 Ohio C. C. (n. s.) 418, aff'd. 91 Ohio St. 367, 110 N. E. 1053.

138. Holder of Privilege Authorizing Physician or Hospital to Disclose Confidential Information

Occasionally a claimant seeking the benefits believed to be due him under a health or accident insurance policy, or a beneficiary claiming the proceeds of a life insurance policy, to facilitate a settlement of his claim, will authorize a physician to disclose information to the insurer regarding the nature of the insured's disease or ailment, or will instruct a hospital to permit the insurer to inspect its records relating to the nature and treatment of the insured's malady or the cause of his death.[1] There is a conflict of opinion as to whether such conduct on the part of the claimant constitutes a waiver of the privilege and permits the insurer, in an action on the policy, to introduce in evidence the testimony of the attending physician or the records of the hospital pertaining to the insured's condition or the cause of his death.

Ordinarily, such authorization merely releases the physician or hospital from the ethical duty of secrecy and permits each to disclose to the insurer the information requested, but it does not remove the ban of the statute prohibiting the physician from testifying in court,[2] nor does it permit the introduction in evidence of privileged matters contained in the hospital's records.[3]

---

[1] Some insurance companies require this as a part of the obligation to furnish proof of death. See Ferguson v. Quaker City Life Ins. Co., (1957)_____D. C._____, 129 A. 2d 189; Metropolitan Life Ins. Co. v. Kendall, (1955) 225 Ark. 731, 284 S. W. 2d 863.

[2] Metropolitan Life Ins. Co. v. Kendall, (1955) 225 Ark. 731, 284 S. W. 2d 863; Moutzoukos v. Mutual Benefit, Health & Acc. Ass'n., (1927) 69 Utah 309, 321, 254 Pac. 1005: "The plaintiff's willingness to allow any physician that had ever treated him to give information within his knowledge as to plaintiff's past or present physical condition should not be construed as a consent that said physicians might testify to such information against the plaintiff in an action to recover on the policy."

In Michigan, an authorization of this kind, even if intended as a waiver, would be invalid as such. Ranger, Inc. v. Equitable Life Ins. Soc., (1952) 196 F. 2d 968.

[3] Aetna Life Ins. Co. v. McAdoo, (1939) 106 F. 2d 618; Metropolitan Life Ins. Co. v. Kendall, (1955) 225 Ark. 731, 284 S. W. 2d 863. In Fitzgerald v. Metropolitan Ins. Co., (1941)_____Mo. App._____, 149 S. W. 2d 389, the beneficiary authorized any physician consulted by the insured or any hospital in which he had been treated to permit a representative of the insurer to make or obtain a copy or abstract of any records concerning the insured. No copy or abstract was ever taken or made. At the trial, the hospital records were excluded when offered by defendant. Held: such

Some courts, however, regard such authorization as an absolute waiver and abandonment of the privilege and hold that it makes competent the testimony of the physician and the records of the hospital.[4] However, to constitute a waiver there must be a clear, unequivocal and decisive act showing such purpose, or acts amounting to an estoppel,[5] and the contents thereof must be known and understood by the person making it.[6] It has been held that once the

---

←〟

authorization did not operate as a waiver of the privilege and a consent to their introduction in evidence.

In Ost v. Ulring, (1940) 207 Minn. 500, 292 N. W. 207, an action for damages for wrongful death, the defendant sought to introduce in evidence the records of a hospital in which the deceased had been a patient. They were excluded on objection by plaintiff, the administratrix of the estate of the deceased. It appeared that she, as the beneficiary of two policies of insurance on the life of the deceased, in making proof of death, had written a letter to the hospital authorizing it to exhibit its records to the insurer. It was held that she did not thereby waive the right and privilege she had as representative of the next of kin to object to the introduction of the records in the trial of the action for wrongful death.

[4] Toler v. Atlanta Life Ins. Co., (1952) ......Mo. App......., 248 S. W. 2d 53; Willis v. Order of Railroad Telegraphers, (1941) 139 Neb. 46, 296 N. W. 443.

[5] Fitzgerald v. Metropolitan Life Ins. Co., (1941) ...... Mo. App......., 149 S. W. 2d 389.

Ferguson v. Quaker City Life Ins. Co., (1957) ......D. C. ...... , 129 A. 2d 189, 192: "The appellant as beneficiary signed a form, admittedly as part of her obligation to furnish proof of death, authorizing the release of information from the medical records in question to any insurance company for 'insurance purposes only.' * * * The record shows that appellant did not waive the instant privilege at the trial. Can she be deemed to have waived it beforehand by signing a form with the sole purpose of proving the death of the insured? The form, * * * contained no waiver of the physician-patient privilege in express terms. And the intent, with reasonable knowledge of all the facts and rights involved, to forego the statutory advantage she held, cannot be made out because appellant is shown to have signed a form which she thought necessary to prove the death of the insured. 'Waiver is not a trick to catch one napping.' Therefore the hospital records were not admissable in this case as to the reason for the insured's hospitalizations."

[6] Andrews v. Washington National Ins. Co., (1936) ...... Mo. App......., 93 S. W. 2d 1045. Illiterate beneficiary, not knowing its contents, signed the authorization under the impression induced by insurer's agent that it was a mere formality but necessary for her to obtain the proceeds of the policy. The question whether or not she waived the privilege was submitted to the jury which returned a verdict in her favor.

waiver has been made, it cannot be withdrawn after it has been acted upon.[7]

139. Cross-examination: Involuntary Disclosure

It is well-established that testimony elicited by cross-examination of a patient as to privileged communications or information is not voluntary and therefore does not constitute a waiver of the physician-patient privilege.[1] It would seem, however, that since it

---

[7] Graham v. Guarantee Trust Life Ins. Co., (1954) ____Mo. App.____, 267 S. W. 2d 692. In his proof of loss, plaintiff undertook to answer questions as to the nature of his ailment but he did not answer questions relating to specified diseases which he might have had before. However, he wrote: "Get statement from Hospital." The insurer examined the hospital records and rejected plaintiff's claim. After suit was brought, defendant sought depositions at the hospital to preserve the evidence then available but plaintiff instructed the hospital to keep the information secret. Held: plaintiff having waived the privilege by consenting to defendant's inspection of the records, could not withdraw the waiver after it had been acted upon.

[1] Union Pac. R. R. v. Thomas, (1907) 152 Fed. 365; Coca Cola Bottling Co. v. Strather, (1936) 192 Ark. 999, 96 S. W. 2d 14; Missouri & N. A. R. R. v. Daniels, (1911) 98 Ark. 352, 136 S. W. 651; Hirschberg v. Southern Pac. Co., (1919) 180 Cal. 774, 183 Pac. 141; Citizens Street R. R. v. Shepherd, (1902) 30 Ind. App. 193, 65 N. E. 765; Cowan v. Allamakee County Benevolent Soc., (1943) 232 Iowa 1387, 8 N. W. 2d 433; Johnson v. Kinney, (1942) 232 Iowa 1016, 7 N. W. 2d 188, 144 A. L. R. 997; Donovan v. Donovan, (1941) 231 Iowa 14, 300 N. W. 656; Walmer-Roberts v. Hennessey, (1921) 191 Iowa 86, 181 N. W. 798; Arnold v. Fort Dodge, Des Moines & S. R. R., (1919) 186 Iowa 538, 173 N. W. 252; Jacobs v. Cedar Rapids, (1917) 181 Iowa 407, 164 N. W. 891; Lauer v. Banning, (1911) 152 Iowa 99, 131 N. W. 783; Burgess v. Sims Drug Co., (1901) 114 Iowa 275, 86 N. W. 307, 54 L. R. A. 364; Lammiman v. Detroit Citizens St. Ry., (1897) 112 Mich. 602, 71 N. W. 153; Briggs v. Chicago Great Western Ry., (1957) 248 Minn. 418, 80 N. W. 2d 625; Hilary v. Minneapolis St. Ry., (1908) 104 Minn. 432, 116 N. W. 933; Coca Cola Bottling Works v. Simpson, (1930) 158 Miss. 390, 130 So. 479, 72 A. L. R. 143; Hemminghaus v. Ferguson, (1948) 358 Mo. 476, 215 S. W. 2d 481; Holloway v. Kansas City, (1904) 184 Mo. 19, 82 S. W. 89; Gilpin v. Aetna Life Ins. Co., (1939) 234 Mo. App. 566, 132 S. W. 2d 686; Rush v. Metropolitan Life Ins. Co., (1933) ____Mo. App.____, 63 S. W. 2d 453; Cable v. Johnson, (1933) ____ Mo. App.____, 63 S. W. 2d 433; Monpleasure v. American Car & Foundry Co., (1927) ____Mo. App.____, 293 S. W. 84; Vermillion v. Prudential Life Ins. Co., (1936) 230 Mo. App. 993, 93 S. W. 2d 45; May v. Northern Pac. Ry., (1905) 32 Mont. 522, 81 Pac. 328, 70 L. R. A. 111, 4 Ann. Cas. 605; Larson v. State, (1912) 92 Neb. 24, 137 N. W. 894; Hughes v. Kackas, (1957) 3 A. D. 2d 402, 161 N. Y. S. 2d 541; Murphy v. New York, N. H. & H. R. R., (1916) 171 App. Div. 599, 157 N. Y. S. 962; Butler v. Manhattan Ry., (1893) 3 Misc. 453, 23 N. Y. S. 163, aff'd. 143 N. Y. 630, 37 N. E. 826; Vilardi v. Vilardi, (1951) 200 Misc. 1043, 107 N. Y. S. 2d 342; Gunn v. Robinson,

⇛→

is plainly within the power of the holder of the privilege to exclude the evidence, his failure to make timely objection thereto when the evidence is sought to be elicited, should be a complete waiver.[2] Whether the waiver is by the affirmative action of the patient in calling forth the privileged testimony, or by his negative action in not preventing the other party from calling it forth, the logical result is the same; the secret is out. Furthermore, by failing to avail himself of the protection which the statute affords, his testimony should no longer be regarded as involuntary and there is some authority to this effect.[3] Other courts, however, when this point

---

←≪

(1918) 103 Misc. 547, 171 N. Y. S. 692, rev'd. on other grounds 188 App. Div. 948, 176 N. Y. S. 901; Baker v. Industrial Comm'n., (1939) 135 Ohio St. 491, 21 N. E. 2d 593; Harpman v. Devine, (1937) 133 Ohio St. 1, 10 N. E. 2d 776, 114 A. L. R. 789; Massachusetts Bonding & Ins. Co. v. Jones, (1939) 185 Okla. 551, 94 P. 2d 885; Chicago, R. I. & Pac. Ry. v. Shelton, (1929) 135 Okla. 53, 273 Pac. 988; Randa v. Bear, (1957) ...... Wash. ......, 312 P. 2d 640; Packard v. Coberly, (1928) 147 Wash. 345, 265 Pac. 1082.

See 8 Wigmore, Evidence, § 2270.

The question whether counsel can elicit privileged matters on cross-examination and then claim it as a waiver, was mentioned but not decided in Edwards v. St. Louis and San Francisco R. R. (1912) 166 Mo. App. 428, 149 S. W. 321 and in Rauh v. Deutscher Verein, (1898) 29 App. Div. 483, 51 N. Y. S. 985.

The rule has also been applied where, on cross-examination, the privileged matter was elicited from the representative of the deceased patient. See Cowan v. Allamakee County Benevolent Soc., infra; Rush v. Metropolitan Life Ins. Co., infra.

The rule is the same with respect to privileged matter elicited from the patient by deposition, since it is taken under the rules applicable to cross-examination. Heminghaus v. Ferguson, infra.

See also Hughes v. Kackas, (1957) 3 A. D. 2d 402, 161 N. Y. S. 2d 541.

2 McCormick, Evidence, § 106. See also People v. Runion, (1958) 3 N. Y. 2d 637, 148 N. E. 2d 167.

3 Munzer v. Swedish American Line, (1940) 35 F. Supp. 493 (patient's answers to defendant's interrogatories, without objection, held a waiver of privilege); People v. Runion, (1958) 3 N. Y. 2d 637, 148 N. E. 2d 165; Miller v. New York, (1955) 286 App. Div. 1033, 145 N. Y. S. 2d 295; Vukovic v. Walnut Grove Country Club, (1953) ...... Ohio App......., 124 N. E. 2d 463. See also Armstrong v. Topeka Ry., (1914) 93 Kan. 493, 144 Pac. 847.

In Metropolitan Life Ins. Co. v. McKim, (1935) 54 Ohio App. 66, 6 N. E. 2d 9, the court seems to hold that plaintiff's disclosure of his condition on cross-examination was voluntary.

For effect of failure to object to disclosure of privileged matters, see § 130, herein.

has been urged, have declined to so hold.[4]

Of course, if the patient, or his representative, makes proper objection when the evidence is sought to be elicited, but the court does not uphold his claim of privilege, his answers would not be voluntary and no waiver would result therefrom.[5] And if the patient, his representative, or his physician, on cross-examination, is compelled to disclose privileged information, his subsequent explanation thereof or redirect examination should not be deemed a waiver of the privilege.[6] As we have pointed out earlier, the patient,

---

[4] Burgess v. Sims Drug Co., (1901) 114 Iowa 275, 280, 86 N. W. 307, 54 L. R. A. 364: "No doubt, under this privilege, the client or patient may refuse to answer on cross-examination when asked with reference to the privileged communication. But we are not willing to hold that the failure to insist on this privilege makes the testimony which he may give on cross-examination voluntary, in such sense as to constitute a waiver of his privilege with reference to the communication to his attorney or physician. * * * In the case before us it is evident that any objection of the witness on cross-examination to testify as to the communications might well have been prejudicial, and therefore that the answer of the witness with reference thereto cannot be treated as a waiver of the privilege, for it is essentially not voluntary. If counsel saw fit, on cross-examination to inquire into the matter, he must be bound by the answer, and cannot afterwards claim that the witness, by answering without objection, voluntarily waived the privilege."

Accord: Holloway v. Kansas City, (1904) 184 Mo. 19, 82 S. W. 89; Cable v. Johnson, (1933) ___ Mo. App. ___, 63 S. W. 2d 433; Monpleasure v. American Car & Foundry Co., (1927) ___Mo. App.___, 293 S. W. 84; Larson v. State, (1912) 92 Neb. 24, 137 N. W. 894; Hughes v. Kackas, (1957) 3 A. D. 2d 402, 161 N. Y. S. 2d 541; Vilardi v. Vilardi, (1951) 200 Misc. 1043, 107 N. Y. S. 2d 342 (good presentation of this point of view).

[5] Citizens Street R. R. v. Shepherd, (1902) 30 Ind. App. 193, 65 N. E. 765; Cowan v. Allamakee County Benevolent Soc., (1943) 232 Iowa 1387, 8 N. W. 2d 433; Gilpin v. Aetna Life Ins. Co., (1939) 234 Mo. App. 566, 132 S. W. 2d 686; Murphy v. New York, N. H. & H. R. R., (1916) 171 App. Div. 599, 157 N. Y. S. 962.

See also Vukovic v. Walnut Grove Country Club, (1953) ___Ohio App.___, 124 N. E. 2d 463. (facts not clear).

But the patient may not answer particular questions which he thinks will be advantageous to him and decline to answer others. He cannot play fast and loose with his privilege. Armstrong v. Topeka Ry. (1914) 93 Kan. 493, 144 Pac. 847.

[6] Gilpin v. Aetna Life Ins. Co., (1939) 234 Mo. App. 566, 132 S. W. 2d 686; Gunn v. Robinson, (1918) 103 Misc. 547, 171 N. Y. S. 692, rev'd. on other grounds 188 App. Div. 948, 176 N. Y. S. 901.

See also Tinsley v. Washington National Ins. Co., (1936) ___ Mo. App.___, 97 S. W. 2d 874; Leeds v. Prudential Ins. Co., (1935) 128 Neb. 395, 258 N. W. 672, 96 A. L. R. 1414 (cross-examination of third person, present at professional conference,

⟫→

or the holder of the privilege, may not be asked on cross-examination if he will waive the privilege.[7]

Where, in a personal injury action, three physicians and a hospital were joined as defendants, the fact that plaintiff cross-examined the physicians while they were defendants did not constitute waiver of the privilege when such physicians were subsequently called to testify as experts in behalf of the hospital after they had been eliminated as parties.[8]

140. Waiver of Privilege as to One Physician as a Waiver as to Other Physicians

There is a notable conflict of opinion on the question whether a waiver of the privilege as to one physician will have the effect to waive the privilege as to another physician.[1] In several jurisdictions, the legislatures themselves have resolved the problem by including an express provision in the statute to the effect that if two or more physicians are, or have been, in attendance upon the patient for the same injury or ailment, the patient, or the holder of the privilege, by calling any one of them to testify concerning said con-

---

does not waive privilege as to the physician).

In Hamel v. Southern Ry., (1917) 113 Miss. 344, 74 So. 276, defendant claimed that plaintiff waived the privilege because she introduced a physician of the deceased in rebuttal. The contention was unsound for the reason that the introduction of his testimony in rebuttal could in no way cure the error that had been committed in the first instance when defendant introduced the testimony of the deceased's physician at a time when plaintiff had introduced no attending physician's testimony as to the cause of her husband's death. However, if the holder of the privilege goes outside the usual limits of rebuttal and seeks to introduce new and independent evidence of a privileged character, the privilege is waived as to the subject matter of such evidence. Sovereign Camp W. O. W. v. Grandon, (1902) 64 Neb. 39, 89 N. W. 448. See also Patnode v. Foote, (1912) 153 App. Div. 494, 138 N. Y. S. 221. But cf. General Accident, Fire & Life Assur. Co. v. Savage, (1929) 35 F. 2d 587, where the cross-examiner expressly stated this was being done without intending to waive the protection of the privilege.

[7] § 100, herein.

[8] Von Eye v. Hammes et al., (1956) 147 F. Supp. 174.

[1] See cases collected in notes, 98 A. L. R. 1248; 90 A. L. R. 646; 62 A. L. R. 680.
See also 8 Wigmore, Evidence, § 2390 (3); McCormick, Evidence, § 106.

dition, shall be deemed to have waived the privilege attaching to the other physicians.[2]

Absent such a provision, many courts have held that a waiver of the privilege by the patient as to one or more of his physicians does not necessarily operate to effect a waiver of the privilege as to any other physician who may have examined or treated him, where such examinations or treatments by the several physicians were made at different times, and not together in consultation or as an unitary affair; moreover, the rule has also been applied in actions where, the patient having died, the testimony of one or more of his attending physicians was first introduced by the legal representative of the patient.[3] The theory of the rule is that, by virtue of the stat-

---

[2] *e. g.*, Arkansas, Hawaii, Michigan, Nebraska. See Appendix, herein.

The amendment of the Arkansas statute in 1937 was passed as an emergency measure, "it being ascertained by the General Assembly that grave injustices are being done and suffered by the litigants throughout the state on account of the law as it now stands, permitting evidence to be introduced by one side in trials with no opportunity upon the part of the opposing side to controvert such testimony * * *." Sec. 3 of Acts 1937, No. 251.

The Arkansas statute extends the privilege to nurses as well as to physicians. In Albritton v. C. M. Ferguson & Son, (1938) 197 Ark. 436, 122 S. W. 2d 620, plaintiffs called the patient's physician to testify. Defendant called a nurse and, over objection by plaintiffs, she was permitted to testify. Plaintiff's theory was that although they put on a physician, defendant could not offer a nurse, or if they put on a nurse defendant could not have offered a physician. Held: such interpretation of the statute is too technical. Plaintiffs having waived the privilege as to the physician, waived it as to all nurses or physicians.

See also State v. Burchett, (1957)_____ Mo._____, 302 S. W. 2d 9.

[3] The following cases support the text, but it should be noticed that, in a few jurisdictions, some of the early decisions, due to a change in the attitude of the courts towards the privilege in general, have since been modified or overruled; others have been nullified by subsequent amendments of the statute. Metropolitan Street Ry. v. Jacobi, (1901) 112 Fed. 924 (decision under New York statute); National Benevolent Soc. v. Barker, (1922) 155 Ark. 506, 244 S. W. 720; Missouri & N. Ark. R. R. v. Daniels, (1911) 98 Ark. 352, 136 S. W. 651. (The rule announced in these Arkansas cases has been nullified by statute). Hirschberg v. Southern Pac. Co., (1919) 180 Cal. 774, 183 Pac. 141 (modified by statute); Mays v. New Amsterdam Casualty Co., (1913) 40 App. D. C. 249, cert. denied 238 U. S. 624, 59 Law Ed. 1494, 35 Su. Ct. 662, 46 L. R. A. (n. s.) 1108; Baltimore & Ohio R. R. v. Morgan, (1910) 35 App. D. C. 195; Harrington v. Hadden, (1949) 69 Idaho 22, 202 P. 2d 236; Jones v. Caldwell, (1911) 20 Idaho 5, 116 Pac. 110, 48 L. R. A. (n. s.) 119; Acme-Evans Co. v. Schnepf, (1938) 214 Ind. 394, 403, 14 N. E. 2d 561: "This court has expressed, in the strongest terms,

⇛→

its disapproval of permitting a physician, over the objection of the patient, to testify to facts learned in the sickroom, even where other physicians have testified for the patient." Aspy v. Botkins, (1903) 160 Ind. 170, 66 N. E. 462; Springer v. Byram, (1894) 137 Ind. 15, 36 N. E. 361, 23 L. R. A. 244 (dictum); Penn Mutual Life Ins. Co. v. Wiler, (1884) 100 Ind. 92; Travelers Ins. Co. v. Fletcher American National Bank, (1926) 84 Ind. App. 563, 150 N. E. 825; Citizens Street R. R. v. Shepherd, (1902) 30 Ind. App. 193, 65 N. E. 765; Johnson v. Kinney, (1942) 232 Iowa 1016, 7 N. W. 2d 188, 144 A. L. R. 997; Pearson v. Butts, (1938) 224 Iowa 376, 276 N. W. 65; Jacobs v. Cedar Rapids, (1917) 181 Iowa 407, 164 N. W. 891; Baxter v. Cedar Rapids, (1897) 103 Iowa 599, 72 N. W. 790; Slater v. Sorge, (1911) 166 Mich. 173, 131 N. W. 565; Dotton v. Albion, (1885) 57 Mich. 575, 24 N. W. 786 (The rule of these Michigan cases has been nullified by statute); Ostrowski v. Mockbridge, (1954) 242 Minn. 265, 65 N. W. 2d 185, 47 A. L. R. 2d 733; Ost v. Ulring, (1940) 207 Minn. 500, 292 N. W. 207; Marfia v. Great Northern Ry., (1914) 124 Minn. 466, 145 N. W. 385; New Orleans & N. R. R. v. Jackson (1926) 145 Miss. 702, 110 So. 586 (rule does not deprive a party of a substantial right); Brookhaven Lumber & Mfg. Co. v. Adams, (1923) 132 Miss. 689, 97 So. 484; United States Fidelity & G. Co. v. Hood, (1920) 124 Miss. 548, 87 So. 115, 15 A. L. R. 605; Newton Oil Mill v. Spencer, (1917) 116 Miss. 568, 77 So. 605; Hamel v. Southern Ry., (1917) 113 Miss. 344, 74 So. 276 (plaintiff, in rebuttal, introduced testimony of a physician of the deceased to offset testimony of a physician which had erroneously been admitted in evidence. Held: no waiver resulted since the testimony in rebuttal did not cure the error that had been committed in the first instance. Illinois Central R. R. v. Messina, (1916) 111 Miss. 884, 72 So. 779 (strong dissent by Stevens, J.): Smart v. Kansas City, (1907) 208 Mo. 162, 105 S. W. 709, 14 L. R. A. (n. s.) 565, 13 Ann. Cas. 932 (see partial dissent of Lamm, J.); Mellor v. Missouri Pac. Ry., (1890) 105 Mo. 455, 461, 14 S. W. 758, 16 S. W. 849, 10 L. R. A. 36: "Plaintiff by calling Dr. G. to testify in his behalf, merely waived his incompetency for the purposes of the case, but cannot thereby be justly deemed to have assented to the examination of every other witness pronounced incompetent by the statute, who might possess confidential knowledge on the same general subject."

Cable v. Johnson (1933) ...... Mo. App....... , 63 S. W. 2d 433 (defendant not permitted to introduce testimony of a physician who had treated plaintiff five or six years before the accident and for an entirely different ailment); Hartley v. Calbreath, (1907) 127 Mo. App. 559, 106 S. W. 570. (Except perhaps the Cable case, the rule announced in these Missouri cases has since been nullified by the Supreme Court.) Tracey v. Metropolitan Street Ry., (1900) 49 App. Div. 197, 63 N. Y. S. 242, aff'd. 168 N. Y. 653, 61 N. E. 1135 (question not properly presented for review); Barker v. Cunard Steamship Co. (1895) 91 Hun. 495, 36 N. Y. S. 256, aff'd. 157 N. Y. 693, 51 N. E. 1089; Jones v. Brooklyn, Bath & W. E. R. R. (1888) 3 N. Y. S. 253, aff'd. 121 N. Y. 683, 24 N. E. 1098 (plaintiff's physician, called as witness by defendant, testified without objection by plaintiff. Held: no waiver by plaintiff as to other physicians who attended him); Record v. Saratoga Springs, (1887) 46 Hun. 448, aff'd. 120 N. Y. 646, 24 N. E. 1102; Hope v. Troy & L. R. R., (1886) 40 Hun. 438, aff'd., two judges dissenting, 110 N. Y. 643, 17 N. E. 873; Milligan v. Clayville Knitting Co., (1910) 137 App. Div. 383, 121 N. Y. S. 763; Duggan v. Phelps, (1903) 82 App. Div.

ute, the patient alone is given the right to remove the ban of secrecy. He may be willing to waive the objection to the incompetency as to a particular physician whom he calls as a witness, and yet be unwilling to forego the protection of the statute as to another physician or other physicians who examined or treated him at a different time for the same condition. In other words, the rule is based upon the proposition that the statute permits the patient, or his representative, to use the testimony of one or more of the patient's physicians if he thinks the evidence will benefit his case, and to object and exclude that of other attending physicians whose testimony might contradict or depreciate that given by the medical witness or witnesses carefully selected by him.[4]

Comfortably authoritative, however, is the rule that where the subject matter of the privileged communication or information is made an issue in the case, civil or criminal, and the party making it an issue voluntarily divulges the matter by introducing the testimony of one or more of the patient's physicians, the ban of secrecy is lifted and the way is opened for the other side to go into the question in the same manner. To any open-minded person, it must appear illogical and unfair to permit patients, their heirs or personal representatives, to make public confidential matters by the

---

←

509, 18 N. Y. S. 916; Hennessy v. Kelly, (1900) 55 App. Div. 449, 66 N. Y. S. 871; Gunn v. Robinson, (1918) 103 Misc. 547, 171 N. Y. S. 692, rev'd. on other grounds 188 App. Div. 948, 176 N. Y. S. 901. (The rule announced in these New York cases has since been repudiated by the Court of Appeals.) Malone v. Industrial Comm'n., (1940)   Com. Pleas   , 32 Ohio Law Abst. 231, aff'd. (1942) 140 Ohio St. 292, 43 N. E. 2d 266; Russell v. Penn Mutual Life Ins. Co. (1941) 70 Ohio App. 113, 41 N. E. 2d 251; Lamarand v. National Life & Acc. Ins. Co., (1937) 58 Ohio App. 415, 16 N. E. 2d 701 (failure of plaintiff to object to testimony of one physician called as witness by defendant does not waive privilege so as to permit defendant to call another physician to testify on the same subject); United States National Life & Cas. Co. v. Heard, (1931) 148 Okla. 274, 298 Pac. 619; Chicago, Rock Island & Pac. Ry. v. Shelton, (1929) 135 Okla. 53, 273 Pac. 988; Romanat v. White Star Bus Line, Inc., (1932) 43 P. R. 901.

4 Whether or not giving this effect to the statute tends to advance the cause of justice seems to have received little, of any, consideration. See Missouri & N. Ark. R. R. v. Daniels, (1911) 98 Ark. 352, 136 S. W. 651 (later nullified by statute); Record v. Saratoga Springs, (1887) 46 Hun. 448, aff'd. 120 N. Y. 646, 24 N. E. 1102 (overruled by later decisions).

testimony of physicians who are favorable to their interests and then claim the protection of the privilege by closing the mouths of other physicians similarly situated whose testimony might not be as advantageous to their interests. When consent is given for the disclosure by one physician, the reason for the statute no longer exists. The secret is out.[5] When a waiver is once made it is general and not special, and its effect should not be limited to a particular purpose or to a particular person.[6]

It is respectfully submitted that in the interests of truth and fair play, the more sensible rule is that when the patient, or his representative, voluntarily makes public the nature and extent of the patient's ailment, physical or mental, by the testimony of one or more of the attending physicians, he relinquishes the benefits of the statutory privilege, and opens the door to a full judicial inquiry into the subject matter; and the adverse party has the right to refute this testimony by the same kind and character of evidence, *viz.*, expert or professional testimony of the very physicians who saw, examined and, perhaps, treated the patient's ailment or injury at or about the same time. This, we believe, is the better rule, and the present trend of judicial opinion is in this direction.[7] There is no

[5] Epstein v. Pennsylvania R. R. (1913) 250 Mo. 1, 34, 156 S. W. 699, 48 L. R. A. (n. s.) 394, Ann. Cas. 1915 A. 423: "In our view whenever these consultations, and these secrets of the sick-chamber are publicly upon the trial held up to view by the plaintiff himself, by his own voluntary testimony (as in the instant case), or by his offering one, out of two or more of his own physicians, or by his failure and neglect to interpose a timely objection when his physicians are offered by the adverse side, then the bar of the privilege no longer exists. The reason for the rule has thus utterly failed, why should the rule then not also fail?"

[6] Metropolitan Life Ins. Co. v. Kaufman, (1938) 104 Colo. 13, 87 P. 2d 758; Cretney v. Woodmen Accident Co., (1928) 196 Wis. 29, 36, 219 N. W. 448, 62 A. L. R. 675: "When consent is given for the disclosure by one physician, the reason for the statute no longer exists, and the waiver is a waiver of the whole privilege and not a consent to the introduction of designated witnesses."

[7] State v. Long, (1914) 257 Mo. 199, 221, 165 S. W. 748: "If a patient is suffering from a given malady, and is treated by several physicians near the same time, for the same trouble or malady, then if she and one of her physicians with her consent, make public the character of her trouble, she has waived the right to longer keep the exact character of that trouble further secret, and the other physicians are competent to testify as to what this malady or trouble was in reality. Any other rule would be but to permit a patient in a court of justice to play fast and loose."

>>>→

reason why this rule should not be equally applicable to the statements of physicians which are contained in hospital records.[8]

Prior to the decision in *Capron* v. *Douglass,*[9] numerous cases
had been decided by the courts of New York in which it was held
that a waiver of the privilege as to one physician was not a waiver
as to others.[10] Since that decision, however, the courts have uniformly held that the patient, or his representative, by calling a
physician to testify as to the patient's condition, physical or mental,
not only waives the privilege as to that physician but also as to other

---

Oliver v. Aylor, (1913) 173 Mo. App. 323, 329, 158 S. W. 733: "The defendant
offered to show by Dr. C. a state of facts directly contradicting the testimony of both
the plaintiff and Dr. M. * * * Such testimony could be excluded only on the theory
that under the law of this State the plaintiff has a right * * * to detail in his own
language, and introduce as a witness a physician of his own choosing to testify, as to
the treatment and condition of his injury, thereby waiving the statute as to one
of his physicians as to what occurred during the course of treatment, and then successfully object to the testimony of his other physician when defendant seeks by introducing that physician as a witness to contradict plaintiff's statement of the treatment and condition. * * * It will be noticed that the testimony offered to be given
by Dr. C. does not open any new secret or go into any other field with reference to
what occurred or what did not occur from that which was disclosed by the plaintiff
and Dr. M. The offer of Dr. C's testimony tended only to show a contradiction of
a state of facts which had been gone into by the plaintiff and Dr. M." It was reversible error to exclude the testimony of Dr. C.

Accord: Metropolitan Life Ins. Co. v. Kaufman, (1939) 104 Colo. 13, 87 P. 2d
758 (time element is not a controlling factor); Stayton v. Stayton, (1938) 148 Kan.
172, 81 P. 2d 1; Chaffee v. Kaufman, (1923) 113 Kan. 254, 214 Pac. 618; Mulvena v.
Alexander, (1936) 278 Mich. 265, 270 N. W. 291 (by statute); La Count v. Von Platen-
Fox Co., (1928) 243 Mich. 250, 220 N. W. 697 (by statute); State v. Burchett, (1957)
_____ Mo._____ , 302 S. W. 2d 9; Ansnes v. Loyal Protective Ins. Co., (1937) 133 Neb.
665, 276 N. W. 397 (by statute); Friesen v. Reimer, (1933) 124 Neb. 620, 247 N. W.
561 (by statute); Hudman v. State, (1949) 89 Okla. Cr. 160, 205 P. 2d 1175, but *cf.*
Oklahoma cases cited in note 3, infra.; Dahlquist v. Denver & Rio Grande R. R.,
(1918) 52 Utah 438, 174 Pac. 833, but *cf.* General Accident, Fire & Life Assur. Corp.
v. Savage, (1929) 35 F. 2d 587, construing Utah statute; *Re* Quick's Estate, (1931) 161
Wash. 537, 297 Pac. 198; Cretney v. Woodmen Accident Co., (1928) 196 Wis. 29, 219
N. W. 448, 62 A. L. R. 675.

8 Bouligny v. Metropolitan Life Ins. Co., (1942) _____ Mo. App. _____ , 160 S. W. 2d 474.
9 (1908) 193 N. Y. 11, 85 N. E. 827, 20 L. R. A. (n. s.) 1003. The surgeons acted in
concert. As far as the courts of New York are concerned, this decision has finally
laid to rest any idea that a patient is at liberty to play fast and loose with the
physician-patient privilege.
10 See New York cases cited in note 3, infra.

physicians who examined or treated him at or about the same time for the same malady or injury.[11] The courts of Missouri have also repudiated their earlier rule,[12] and now hold that a waiver of privilege established through the testimony of one physician extends to all who have attended the patient for substantially the same ailment, physical or mental, notwithstanding their examinations and treatments may have been made at different times and places.[13]

---

[11] Fennelly v. Schenectady Ry., (1922) 201 App. Div. 211, 193 N. Y. S. 641; Dewey v. Cohoes & L. Bridge Co., (1915) 170 App. Div. 117, 155 N. Y. S. 887. In Strader v. Collins, (1952) 280 App. Div. 582, 116 N. Y. S. 2d 318, plaintiff did not object to the testimony of one of his physicians whom defendant called as a witness. Defendant then called another physician, but, on objection by plaintiff, his testimony was excluded. Held: reversible error. The privilege once waived is waived for all time; furthermore, the waiver is not confined to the particular physician who testifies, "but extends to any other doctor who has examined the plaintiff concerning the particular ailment involved."

The time element is not necessarily a controlling factor. In Steinberg v. New York Life Ins. Co., (1933) 263 N. Y. 45, 188 N. E. 152, 90 A. L. R. 642, an action to recover disability benefits, plaintiff called as a witness a physician who had examined him *for the first time* on the day of the trial. He testified that the insured was then suffering from a moderately advanced case of tuberculosis and that the disease had probably existed since January 1, 1932, seven months before the trial. Defendant called as witnesses two physicians who testified that prior to December, 1928, plaintiff consulted them, but they were not permitted to disclose the malady from which he was at that time suffering. Held: reversible error. Hubbs, J. (p. 52): "It is urged by respondent that even if it was proper to permit testimony to be given by the doctors called by the defendant as to respondent's physical condition during the seven months preceding the trial referred to in the testimony given by the doctor called by respondent, it would not have been proper to allow testimony by them as to his condition over three years before that time when the applications for insurance were signed. Such contention overlooks or ignores the purpose of the statute. There would be no more humiliation, mortification or disgrace in having the fact disclosed that he was suffering from pulmonary tuberculosis over three years and seven months before the trial than in the fact that he had the disease seven months before the trial. If his condition could not be shown as it existed three years before, could it be shown as it existed three months or three weeks before? The disease is a progressive one. Respondent may or may not have suffered from it at the time he signed the applications for insurance. That was the issue in the case, and in fairness to the appellant, it was entitled to have received the testimony of doctors who examined him before the application was signed." See also Apter v. Home Life Ins. Co., (1935) 266 N. Y. 333, 194 N. E. 846, 98 A. L. R. 1281.

[12] See Missouri cases cited in note 3, infra.

According to the weight of authority, where two or more physicians attend the patient on the same occasion or, as an unitary affair, examine or treat him, or participate in the same surgical operation, and the circumstances are such that the patient has a right to insist that the knowledge gained by them shall not be disclosed, the patient, or his representative, by calling one of them to testify in his behalf at a trial in which the patient's condition is in dispute, thereby waives the right to insist upon secrecy and the other physician or physicians may, therefore, be called to testify and be examined fully by the adverse party. The holder of the privilege cannot sever it, waiving it in part and retaining it in part. If he waives it at all, it then ceases to exist, not partially, but entirely.[14] A small

---

[13] State v. Burchett, (1957) ..... Mo. ......, 302 S. W. 2d 9; State v. Cochran, (1947) **356** Mo. 778, 203 S. W. 2d 707; State v. Sapp, (1947) 356 Mo. 705, 203 S. W. 2d 425; **Wells v.** Jefferson, (1939) 345 Mo. 239, 132 S. W. 2d 1006; Weissman v. Wells, (1924) **306 Mo.** 82, 267 S. W. 400; State v. Long, (1913) 257 Mo. 199, 165 S. W. 748; Epstein v. Pennsylvania R. R. (1913) 250 Mo. 1, 156 S. W. 699, 48 L. R. A. (n. s.) 394, Ann. Cas. 1915 A. 423; Foerstel v. St. Louis Public Service Co., (1951) ..... Mo. App. ....., 241 S. W. 2d 792; Bouligny v. Metropolitan Life Ins. Co., (1942) ..... Mo. App. ....., **160** S. W. 2d 474; Priebe v. Crandall, (1916) ..... Mo. App. ....., 187 S. W. 605; McPherson v. Harvey, (1916) ..... Mo. App. ....., 183 S. W. 653; Michaels v. Harvey, (1915) ..... Mo. App. ..... , 179 S. W. 735; Oliver v. Aylor, (1913) 173 Mo. App. 323, 158 S. W. 733; O'Brien v. Western Implement Mfg. Co., (1909) 141 Mo. App. 331, 125 S. W. 805. In Hemminghaus v. Ferguson, (1948) 358 Mo. 476, 215 S. W. 2d 481, a personal injury case, three physicians testified for plaintiff and said that the injury to his brain brought on a nervous condition. It was held, however, that plaintiff's introduction of this evidence did not constitute waiver of the privilege as to a physician who had treated plaintiff for dropsy eight years before and there was no showing that plaintiff's dropsical condition had any connection with the nervous condition such as was claimed to have been produced by the injury sustained by plaintiff.

[14] Missouri & N. Ark. R. R. v. Daniels, (1911) 98 Ark. 352, 136 S. W. 651 (the statute now provides for such waiver); Schlarb v. Henderson, (1936) 211 Ind. 1, 4 N. E. 2d 205 (distinguishing the rule applicable where the physicians act separately); Lane v. Boicourt, (1891) 128 Ind. 420, 27 N. E. 1111 (well-reasoned decision); Northern Indiana Public Service Co. v. McClure, (1940) 108 Ind. App. 253, 24 N. E. 2d 788; Woods v. Lisbon, (1911) 150 Iowa 433, 130 N. W. 372; Armstrong v. Topeka Ry., (1914) 93 Kan. 493, 144 Pac. 847; Leifson v. Henning, (1941) 210 Minn. 311, 298 N. W. 41; Doll v. Scandrett, (1937) 201 Minn. 316, 276 N. W. 281 (three judges dissented); Denny v. Robertson, (1944) 352 Mo. 609, 179 S. W. 2d 5; Epstein v. Pennsylvania R. R., (1913) 250 Mo. 1, 156 S. W. 699, 48 L. R. A. (n. s.) 394, Ann. Cas. 1915 A. 423; Capron v. Douglass, (1908) 193 N. Y. 11, 85 N. E. 827, 20 L. R. A. (n. s.) 1003; Morris v. New York, Ontario & W. Ry., (1895) 148 N. Y. 88, 42 N. E. 410; Ortner v. Darien, ➤➤➤

minority is opposed to this view.[15]

141. Waiver of Privilege at One Trial as a Waiver at a Subsequent Trial

Whether the statutory privilege, once waived, can be invoked upon a subsequent trial, is a question upon which there is a conflict of authority. The better rule appears to be that the privilege, when once waived by the holder thereof on the trial of an action, cannot successfully be claimed by him in a subsequent trial of the same

---

←≪

(1911) 146 App. Div. 884, 130 N. Y. S. 1123; Speck v. International Ry., (1909) 133 App. Div. 802, 118 N. Y. S. 71; Romanat v. White Star Bus Line, Inc., (1932) 43 P. R. 901; McUne v. Fuqua, (1953) _____Wash._____, 253 P. 2d 632, 257 P. 2d 636. O'Brien, J., in Morris v. New York, Ontario & W. Ry., infra, p. 92: "In this case it was the privilege of the plaintiff to insist that both physicians should remain silent as to all information they obtained at the consultation, but she waived this privilege when she called Dr. Payne as a witness and required him to disclose it. The plaintiff could not sever her privilege and waive it in part and retain it in part. If she waived it at all it then ceased to exist, not partially, but entirely. The testimony of Dr. Payne having been given in her behalf, every reason for excluding that of his associate ceased. The whole question turns upon the legal consequences of the plaintiff's act in calling one of the physicians as a witness. She then completely uncovered and made public what before was private and confidential. It amounted to a consent on her part that all who were present at the interview might speak freely as to what took place. The seal of confidence was removed entirely, not merely broken in two parts and one part removed and the other retained."

The rule is especially applicable in actions for damages for malpractice. See Lane v. Boicourt, infra; Becknell v. Hosier, (1893) 10 Ind. App. 5, 37 N. E. 580; Capron v. Douglass, infra. See also § 73, 122, herein.

15 Jones v. Caldwell, (1911) 20 Idaho 5, 17, 116 Pac. 110, 48 L. R. A. (n. s.) 119: "It is also very clear that our statute forbids and prohibits the examination of a physician without the consent of the patient, and this privilege extends to the *individual witness,* and not to the *consultation* or *transaction* in which he was a physician. In other words, each individual physician is a witness within the meaning of the statute, rather than a number of physicians who may be present, or participate in a consultation, being treated as one witness, as appears to be done by Prof. Wigmore."

Accord: Travelers Ins. Co. v. Fletcher American National Bank, (1925) 84 Ind. App. 563, 150 N. E. 825, but *cf.* Schlarb v. Henderson, infra, note 14; Davis v. Elzey, (1921) 126 Miss. 789, 88 So. 630, rev'd on other grounds 89 So. 666; United States Fidelity & G. Co. v. Hood, (1921) 124 Miss. 548, 87 So. 115, 15 A. L. R. 605. See also Tweith v. Duluth, Missabe, & I. R. Ry., (1946) 66 F. Supp. 427, construing Minnesota statute and distinguishing Doll v. Scandrett, infra., since the plaintiff here did not call his own physician as *his* witness but called him as an *adverse* witness.

cause. The waiver remains in full force and effect until the final determination of the litigation.[1] Moreover, the rule has been applied in a situation where the subsequent action was an entirely different one, but the holder of the privilege was the same in each case. In an action for damages for personal injury, the defendant called as witnesses four physicians who had treated the plaintiff and they testified, without objection by the plaintiff, that he was suffering from paralysis caused by syphilis. Later, the State prosecuted him for perjury. At this trial, the State called these four physicians as witnesses. Over objection by the accused on the ground of privilege, the physicians were permitted to testify to his condition, the court holding that by waiving the privilege at the trial of the civil action, the accused had thereby waived his right to object to their testimony at the trial of the criminal action.[2] In an action by an insurance company to rescind and cancel its policy, it was held that the beneficiary could not object to the examination of certain medical witnesses before trial since she, as administratrix of the insured, in a separate action brought by her against another insurance com-

---

[1] Metropolitan Life Ins. Co. v. Kaufman, (1939) 104 Colo. 13, 87 P. 2d 758 (three separate actions were brought by plaintiff against defendant involving substantially the same issues. One had been tried, the others were still pending. At the first trial, plaintiff waived the privilege. Held: the waiver extends to the two remaining cases.) Pittsburg, Cincinnati, C. & St. L. Ry. v. O'Connor, (1909) 171 Ind. 686, 85 N. E. 969; Studabaker v. Faylor, (1912) 52 Ind. App. 171, 98 N. E. 318; State v. Long, (1914) 257 Mo. 199, 165 S. W. 748; Elliott v. Kansas City, (1906) 198 Mo. 593, 96 S. W. 1023, 6 L. R. A. (n. s.) 1082, 8 Ann. Cas. 653; Ryan v. Metropolitan Life Ins. Co., (1930) _____ Mo. App._____, 30 S. W. 2d 190; McKinney v. Grand Street, etc. R. R., (1887) 104 N. Y. 352, 10 N. E. 544; Schlotterer v. Brooklyn & N. Y. Ferry Co., (1903) 89 App. Div. 508, 85 N. Y. S. 847.

Contra: Grattan v. Metropolitan Life Ins. Co., (1883) 92 N. Y. 274. This case appears to have been ignored rather than directly overruled in the later cases. Moreover, the facts as to the alleged waiver were somewhat vague.

The rule has also been applied to other testimonial privileges. See Deacon v. Bryans, (1931) 212 Cal. 87, 298 Pac. 30 (dead man's statute); Green v. Crapo, (1902) 181 Mass. 55, 62 N. E. 956 (attorney-client); Billingsley v. Gulick, (1932) 256 Mich. 606, 240 N. W. 46, 79 A. L. R. 166 (dead man's statute); Niederlehner v. Weatherly, (1946) 78 Ohio App. 263, 69 N. E. 2d 787, appeal dismissed 146 Ohio St. 697, 67 N. E. 2d 713 (dead man's statute).

For other cases pro and con, see note, 79 A. L. R. 173.

[2] People v. Bloom, (1908) 193 N. Y. 1, 85 N. E. 824, 18 L. R. A. (n. s.) 898, 15 Ann. Cas. 932.

pany, had waived the benefits of the statute and that such waiver operated also as a waiver of the privilege in the action to rescind.[3]

Two sound reasons support and justify the rule: *first,* the purpose of the statute, *viz.,* to protect medical confidences from public disclosure has been voluntarily defeated by the party for whose benefit the privilege was created; therefore, since the reason for the privilege has ceased to exist, the privilege also ceases to exist;[4] *second,* the privilege should not remain under such circumstances for the mere sake of giving the holder thereof an additional weapon to use or not as he chooses.[5] A party should not be permitted to take inconsistent positions in the trial of a case.[6] When he voluntarily discloses, or permits others to disclose, privileged matters which he hopes will advance his cause, he should not, when he finds such disclosures were detrimental, be permitted to shift his position and arbitrarily prevent the disclosure of the same matters at a later trial.[7]

---

[3] General American Life Ins. Co. v. Ettinger, (1943) 266 App. Div. 876, 42 N. Y. S. 2d 836. A similar decision was rendered in Ryan v. Metropolitan Life Ins. Co., (1930) ......Mo. App......., 30 S. W. 2d 190. Of course, where the testimony of the insured's attending physician was not privileged in the first trial or proceeding, the fact that the physician was allowed to testify at such trial without objection was not a waiver of the privilege and did not prevent it being invoked in a later trial at which time the same physician's testimony was within the protection of the privilege. Metropolitan Life Ins. Co. v. Ryan, (1943) 237 Mo. App. 464, 172 S. W. 2d 269.

[4] Elliott v. Kansas City, (1906) 198 Mo. 593, 96 S. W. 1023, 6 L. R. A. (n. s.) 1082, 8 Ann. Cas. 653; McKinney v. Grand Street, etc. R. R., (1887) 104 N. Y. 352, 10 N. E. 544.

[5] Studabaker v. Faylor, (1912) 52 Ind. App. 171, 172, 98 N. E. 318: "This privilege may be waived, and when the matters have been once published to the world, no reason remains to hold the privilege in force. The statute was not enacted to enable persons to avoid liability or to win a suit by making it difficult to obtain evidence, but was made in order to allow them to prevent certain private affairs from becoming public property."

See also McKinney v. Grand Street, etc. R. R., (1887) 104 N. Y. 352, 10 N. E. 544.

[6] Billingsley v. Gulick, (1932) 256 Mich. 606, 240 N. W. 46, 79 A. L. R. 166 (involving dead man's statute).

[7] In Deacon v. Bryans, (1931) 212 Cal. 87, 93, 298 Pac. 30, involving waiver of the dead man's statute, it was held that a waiver of objection to incompetency made at one stage of the taking of testimony is a waiver during the whole progress of that proceeding. "A disqualification having once been waived, remains waived in all subsequent proceedings including those taken at a subsequent trial. The reason for

》》》→

It is immaterial whether the privilege was waived at the first trial by the voluntary act of the patient himself, or of his representative, in calling forth the privileged testimony,[8] or by his failure to object when it was offered by the opposite party.[9] The effect is the same. Having released and made public the secrets at the first trial, he has removed them for all purposes of the litigation from the operation of the statute.

---

the rule apparently is that a litigant cannot be permitted to speculate as to what his examination of a witness may bring forth. Having made his selection of one of two courses which he may pursue, he has no right, after he discovers that the course selected is not to his advantage, and after he has put the opposite party to the expense, and has consumed the time of the courts in a trial of the case in accordance with the course selected, to change his position and make another and different selection. Such a course would be unfair both to the opposite party and to the court and should not be countenanced in a court of justice."

[8] Pittsburg, Cincinnati, C. & St. L. Ry. v. O'Connor, (1909) 171 Ind. 686, 85 N. E. 969; McKinney v. Grand Street, etc. R. R., (1887) 104 N. Y. 352, 10 N. E. 544. See also Niederlehner v. Weatherly, (1946) 78 Ohio App. 263, 69 N. E. 2d 787, appeal dismissed 146 Ohio St. 697, 67 N. E. 2d 713 (involving dead man's statute).

[9] People v. Bloom, (1908) 193 N. Y. 1, 85 N. E. 824, 18 L. R. A. (n. s.)898, 15 Ann. Cas. 932: "The defendant did not cause or procure the evidence of the physicians to be admitted when the civil action was tried, but he made no attempt to prevent its admission, although it was within his power to keep it out, or to avail himself of the privilege conferred by statute. He did not waive by acting, but by failing to act. * * * The section no longer applies when the information that the statute would have kept secret if the patient had so elected has been made known in a judicial proceeding with his consent. After intentionally permitting its publication to the world by the physician, himself, upon one trial, it would seem almost grotesque to sustain an objection made upon a later trial that the evidence is privileged from disclosure because it might tend to humiliate or disgrace. There can be no disclosure of that which is already known, for when a secret is out it is out for all time and cannot be caught again like a bird and put back in a cage. The disgrace and humiliation were caused by the first trial, not by the second. The legislature did not intend to continue the privilege when there was no reason for its continuance and it would simply be an obstruction to public justice."

Accord: Metropolitan Life Ins. Co. v. Kaufman, (1939) 104 Colo. 13, 87 P. 2d 758; Studabaker v. Faylor, (1912) 52 Ind. App. 171, 98 N. E. 318; Armstrong v. Topeka Ry., (1914) 93 Kan. 493, 144 Pac. 847; Elliott v. Kansas City, (1906) 198 Mo. 593, 96 S. W. 1023, 6 L. R. A. (n. s.) 1082, 8 Ann. Cas. 653; Ryan v. Metropolitan Life Ins. Co., (1930) ......Mo. App......., 30 S. W. 2d 190; Schlotterer v. Brooklyn & N. Y. Ferry Co., (1903) 89 App. Div. 508, 85 N. Y. S. 847.

In a few jurisdictions, however, the courts have held that a waiver of the privilege at the first trial of a case does not extend to a subsequent trial of the same case, and does not preclude the right to prevent the introduction of substantially the same evidence at a later trial.[10] Some of these courts regard the privilege as one which includes both the security against publication, and the right to control the introduction of evidence of confidential information or knowledge coming to or possessed by the patient's physician; furthermore, they hold that the latter right exists notwithstanding the former has ceased to be of any benefit.[11] Such views seem to disre-

---

[10] Arizona Eastern R. R. v. Mathews, (1919) 20 Ariz. 282, 180 Pac. 159, 7 A. L. R. 1149; Maryland Casualty Co. v. Maloney, (1915) 119 Ark. 434, 178 S. W. 387, L. R. A. 1915 A. 519 (the qualifications and limitations suggested by the court render the rule doubtful); Lauer v. Banning, (1911) 152 Iowa 99, 131 N. W. 783; Burgess v. Sims Drug Co., (1901) 114 Iowa 275, 86 N. W. 307, 54 L. R. A. 364; Gratten v. Metropolitan Life Ins. Co., (1883) 92 N. Y. 274 (see note 1, infra.); Polish Roman Catholic Union v. Polin, (1942) 302 Mich. 557, 5 N. W. 2d 463 (before trial, defendant, in support of a preliminary motion, had filed affidavit of physician revealing privileged matters); Briesenmeister v. Supreme Lodge, K. of P., (1890) 81 Mich. 525, 45 N. W. 977, 8 L. R. A. 682; Herpolsheimer v. Citizens Ins. Co., (1907) 79 Neb. 685, 113 N. W. 152 (attorney-client privilege); Goodyear Tire & Rubber Co. v. Motz, (1935) _____ Ohio App. _____, 19 Ohio Law Abst. 14.

In their attempt to justify their rule, some of the courts stress the fact that the evidence introduced at the first trial was offered by the opposite party, not by the patient himself, or by his representative. The point is without merit, since the holder of the privilege had the power to exclude it. Perhaps it should be noted also that some of the cases are not convincing authority in view of the contrary decisions in the same state involving other testimonial privileges. *e. g.,* Billingsley v. Gulick, (1932) 256 Mich. 606, 240 N. W. 46, 79 A. L. R. 166; Niederlehner v. Weatherly, (1946) 78 Ohio App. 263, 69 N. E. 2d 787, appeal dismissed 146 Ohio St. 697, 67 N. E. 2d 713.

[11] Briesenmeister v. Supreme Lodge, K. of P., (1890) 81 Mich. 525, 535, 45 N. W. 977, 8 L. R. A. 682: "The privilege conferred is that the physician shall not disclose or testify to those matters which the statute inhibits without the consent of the party to whom the privilege is extended, and this objection may be interposed whenever and as often as the party's rights may be affected by proffered testimony, if the objection be timely made. In a new trial the testimony is placed before a new jury, and I think the Gratten Case lays down the better rule."

See also Maryland Casualty Co. v. Maloney, (1915) 119 Ark. 434, 178 S. W. 387, L. R. A. 1915 A. 519; Burgess v. Sims Drug Co., (1901) 114 Iowa 275, 86 N. W. 307, 54 L. R. A. 364; Pondrom v. Gray, (1926) _____Tex. Civ. App. _____ , 289 S. W. 79 (attorney-client privilege). The reasons given in the Briesenmeister Case practically

≫→

gard utterly the only justification the privilege has and tend to transform it into a handy and effective device for winning questionable lawsuits. It seems hardly credible that any legislature ever intended that the privilege could be used for such purpose.[12]

In a personal injury case, it was held that a waiver at the first trial, resulting from the plaintiff's physician having testified to privileged matters at the instance of the defendant without objection by the plaintiff, could not be considered, where, in the second trial, the defendant did not raise the question at any time until the argument upon a motion for a new trial.[13]

142. Withdrawal of Privilege at Same Trial

As a general rule, when a waiver of the privilege has once been acted upon during the same trial at which the privilege was waived, it may not thereafter be withdrawn.[1] The reason is obvious. Once evidence has been introduced concerning confidential information

---

nullify the doctrine of implied waiver; moreover, the Grattan Case has since been repudiated by the courts of New York.

[12] McKinney v. Grand Street, etc. R. R., (1887) 104 N. Y. 352, 355, 10 N. E. 544; "The patient cannot use this privilege both as a sword and a shield, to waive when it enures to her advantage, and wield when it does not."

[13] Ballard v. Yellow Cab Co., (1944) 20 Wash. 2d 67, 145 P. 2d 1019.

[1] Representative cases are: Young v. Terminal Railroad Ass'n., (1947) 70 F. Supp. 106 (under Missouri statute); Lissack v. Crocker Estate Co., (1897) 119 Cal. 442, 51 Pac. 688; Stalker v. Breeze, (1917) 186 Ind. 221, 114 N. E. 968; Pittsburg, Cincinnati, C. & St. L. Ry. v. O'Connor, (1908) 171 Ind. 686, 85 N. E. 969; Armstrong v. Topeka Ry., (1914) 93 Kan. 493, 144 Pac. 847; Briesenmeister v. Supreme Lodge, K. of P., (1890) 81 Mich. 525, 45 N. W. 977, 8 L. R. A. 682; Demonbrun v. McHaffie, (1941) 348 Mo. 1120, 156 S. W. 2d 923; State v. Long, (1914) 257 Mo. 199, 165 S. W. 748; Epstein v. Pennsylvania R. R. (1913) 250 Mo. 1, 156 S. W. 699, 48 L. R. A. (n. s.) 394, Ann. Cas. 1915 A. 423; Apter v. Home Life Ins. Co., (1935) 266 N. Y. 333, 194 N. E. 846, 98 A. L. R. 1281; Capron v. Douglass, (1908) 193 N. Y. 11, 85 N. E. 827, 20 L. R. A. (n. s.) 1003; Hoyt v. Hoyt, (1889) 112 N. Y. 493, 20 N. E. 402; Strader v. Collins, (1952) 280 App. Div. 582, 116 N. Y. S. 2d 318; Patnode v. Foote, (1912) 153 App. Div. 494, 138 N. Y. S. 221; Marquardt v. Brooklyn Heights R. R., (1908) 126 App. Div. 272, 110 N. Y. S. 657; Powers v. Metropolitan Street Ry., (1905) 105 App. Div. 358, 94 N. Y. S. 184; Strong's Estate, (1938) 168 Misc. 716, 6 N. Y. S. 2d 300, aff'd. 256 App. Div. 971, 11 N. Y. S. 2d 225. See note, 158 A. L. R. 219.

(1939) S. D. Code, § 36.0102 provides: " * * * If a person once waives such privilege, as to any particular communication, he cannot thereafter claim it."

See § 140 as to whether a waiver as to one physician is a waiver as to others.

in consequence of the waiver, the information is no longer secret and its confidentiality cannot be restored again by the withdrawal of the waiver. The purpose of the statute has been defeated; therefore, the privilege no longer exists.

As we have pointed out earlier, where the holder of the privilege himself calls an attending physician to testify to the condition of the patient, he waives the privilege and may not thereafter withdraw the waiver.[2] And, generally speaking, the same result will follow where the patient himself opens wide the door of the sickroom, revealing everything, concealing nothing.[3] Furthermore, where the holder of the privilege permits the attending physician to testify at the instance of the adverse party without making objection thereto, the privilege is waived and may not later be recalled. There are bounds to the enforcement of the privilege which will not be disregarded when one who, being entitled to its benefits, has waived or failed to avail himself of them.[4] The rule is not limited to privileged testimony but applies to privileged records as well.[5] When the plaintiff, in a personal injury action, broke the seal of

---

[2] § 131, herein.

[3] §§ 134, 135, herein.

[4] § 130, herein.

[5] Maas v. Midway Chevrolet Co., (1945) 219 Minn. 461, 464, 18 N. W. 2d 233, 158 A. L. R. 215: "After having once knowingly waived the privilege as to a certain physician, the waiver cannot be withdrawn during the course of the trial, and it naturally follows that such physician is subject to cross-examination on all phases of his testimony, including the records upon which he has chosen to base his testimony." In Young v. Terminal Railroad Ass'n., (1947) 70 F. Supp. 106, a personal injury action, plaintiff admitted, on cross-examination, he had been rejected by the armed services and he was asked if defendant could procure the record of his physical examination. Plaintiff consented. When the record was obtained from his Selective Service file and was offered by defendant, plaintiff objected thereto on the ground of privilege. The court excluded it. Held: error. "Once a waiver of the privilege has been executed it cannot be recalled and plaintiff's objection when the medical report was offered was ineffectual to countermand his own prior waiver."

See also Stalker v. Breeze, (1917) 186 Ind. 221, 114 N. E. 968. In Graham v. Guarantee Trust Life Ins. Co., (1954)_____Mo. App._____, 267 S. W. 2d 692, plaintiff, *before trial*, waived the privilege as to his hospital record. Held: the waiver could not be withdrawn after defendant acted upon it before the trial.

secrecy between herself and her physician by having her own deposition taken before trial, she could not afterward recall such waiver.[6]

There is authority, however, for the proposition that a waiver of the privilege may be withdrawn at any time before it has been acted upon during the same trial at which the privilege was waived.[7]

Where before, or at the trial, the waiver was given without sufficient understanding of the legal effect of such action,[8] or was induced by fraud or misrepresentation,[9] the courts, in some instances, have permitted the patient, or his representative, to "withdraw" or "recall" the waiver, regardless of whether it had been acted upon or not. The words "withdraw" or "recall" are somewhat misleading since the real reason for sustaining the privilege is that there was no valid waiver in the first place. In several instances the courts have held that the holder of the privilege should be given ample opportunity to consult with his attorney in order that he may

---

[6] Blish v. Greer, (1918) 74 Ind. App. 469, 120 N. E. 606. See also Scolavino v. State, (1946) 187 Misc. 253, 62 N. Y. S. 2d 17, 271 App. Div. 618, 67 N. Y. S. 2d 202, aff'd. 297 N. Y. 460, 74 N. E. 2d 174. See also § 129, herein.

[7] Donovan v. Donovan, (1941) 231 Iowa 14, 300 N. W. 656. In this divorce suit, plaintiff testified on cross-examination that she did not have a venereal disease and when she was asked whether she would permit her physician to take the witness stand and testify to her condition she answered in the affirmative. Before the physician was called as a witness, plaintiff, on advice of counsel, asked leave to withdraw her waiver and she was permitted to do so. The Supreme Court held that "under the circumstances" she had the right to withdraw her waiver of privilege. Just what these circumstances were is not explained but it may be inferred that the court based its ruling on the fact that the withdrawal of the waiver took place before any advantage had accrued to either litigant on account thereof.

It has also been held that where the waiver occurs prior to the trial, it can be withdrawn at any time before it is acted upon where neither of the parties has altered his position by reason of the waiver. National Life & Acc. Ins. Co. v. Bell, (1930) 144 Okla. 236, 291 Pac. 106. See also Herpolsheimer v. Citizens Ins. Co., (1907) 79 Neb. 685, 113 N. W. 152 (attorney-client privilege).

[8] Metropolitan Life Ins. Co. v. Fitzgerald (1919) 137 Ark. 366, 209 S. W. 77; Donovan v. Donovan, (1941) 231 Iowa 14, 300 N. W. 656; Ross v. Great Northern Ry., (1907) 101 Minn. 122, 111 N. W. 951; Coca Cola Bottling Works v. Simpson, (1930) 158 Miss. 390, 130 So. 479, 72 A. L. R. 143; Andrews v. Washington National Ins. Co., (1936) ⸺ Mo. App. ⸺, 93 S. W. 2d 1045.

[9] Kloppenberg v. Minneapolis, St. Paul & S. Ste. M. Ry., (1913) 123 Minn. 173, 143 N. W. 322; Andrews v. Washington National Ins. Co., (1936) ⸺ Mo. App. ⸺, 93 S. W. 2d 1045.

have full knowledge of his legal rights before electing whether he will forego the protection of the privilege.[10] Where the facts pertaining to the alleged waiver are in dispute, the court should, perhaps, submit the question to the jury as to whether or not the patient, or his representative, actually has waived the privilege.[11]

143. *Waiver Must Be Claimed in Trial Court*

As a general rule, whether or not a waiver of the privilege has been made by, or has resulted from the conduct of, a party, is a question that must be raised and fought out in the trial court. An appellate court will not consider a question pertaining to waiver which was not plainly presented to the trial court. Having tried the case on one theory, the unsuccessful party cannot shift his ground and, for the first time, base his case in the appellate court on a new and different theory. It would be most unfair to reverse the trial court upon a question not presented to it.[1]

---

[10] Donovan v. Donovan, (1941) 231 Iowa 14, 300 N. W. 656; Ross v. Great Northern Ry., (1907) 101 Minn. 122, 111 N. W. 951. Coca Cola Bottling Works v. Simpson, (1930) 158 Miss. 390, 396, 130 So. 479, 72 A. L. R. 148: "Appellant's contention is that when the privilege is once waived by the patient, the waiver cannot be revoked. That is probably true as a general rule, but a patient's informal expression of willingness that his physician should testify, made on the witness stand before consulting his counsel, is not a waiver of the privilege."

See note, 72 A. L. R. 148.

[11] Metropolitan Life Ins. Co. v. Fitzgerald (1919) 137 Ark. 366, 209 S. W. 77; Andrews v. Washington National Ins. Co., (1936) ____ Mo. App.____, 93 S. W. 2d 1045.

[1] Travelers Ins. Co. v. Fletcher American National Bank, (1926) 84 Ind. App. 563, 150 N. E. 825; Burns v. Waterloo, (1919) 187 Iowa 922, 173 N. W. 16, 174 N. W. 644; Bouligny v. Metropolitan Life Ins. Co., (1942)____Mo. App.____, 160 S. W. 2d 474; Tinsley v. Washington National Ins. Co., (1936) ____ Mo. App.____, 97 S. W. 2d 874; Edwards v. St. Louis and San Francisco R. R., (1912) 166 Mo. App. 428, 149 S. W. 321; Creech v. Sovereign Camp. W. O. W., (1937) 211 N. C. 658, 191 S. E. 840.

APPENDIX

ALASKA

Alaska Comp. Laws § 58-6-6 (1949)

A physician or surgeon shall not, against the objection of his patient, be examined in a civil action or proceeding as to any information acquired in attending the patient which was necessary to enable him to prescribe or act for the patient.

Note: this appears in the Code of Civil Procedure.

Alaska Comp. Laws § 66-13-52 (1949)

* * * The admissibility of evidence and the competency and privileges of witnesses shall be governed, except otherwise provided by law, by the principles of the common law as they may be interpreted by the courts of the United States in the light of reason and experience.

Note: this appears in the Code of Criminal Procedure.

ARIZONA

Ariz. Rev. Stat. Ann. § 12-2235 (1956)

In a civil action a physician or surgeon shall not, without the consent of his patient, be examined as to any communication made by his patient with reference to any physical or supposed physical disease or any knowledge obtained by personal examination of the patient.

Ariz. Rev. Stat. Ann. § 12-2236 (1956)

A person who offers himself as a witness and voluntarily testifies with reference to the communications referred to in § 12-2234 and 12-2235 thereby consents to the examination of such attorney, physician or surgeon.

Note: § 12-2234 concerns the attorney-client privilege. The above sections appear in Tit. 12, Courts and Civil Proceedings.

Ariz. Rev. Stat. Ann. § 13-1801 (1956)

The laws for determining competency of witnesses in civil actions are

447

also applicable to criminal actions and proceedings, except as otherwise provided by this chapter.

Ariz. Rev. Stat. Ann. § 13-1802 (1956)
A person shall not be examined as a witness in the following cases:
* * *
(5) A physician or surgeon, without consent of his patient, as to any information acquired in attending the patient which was necessary to enable him to prescribe or act for the patient.
Note: the last two sections appear in the Criminal Code.

ARKANSAS
Ark. Stat. Ann. § 28-607 (1947)
Hereafter no person authorized to practice physic or surgery and no trained nurses shall be compelled to disclose any information which he may have acquired from his patient while attending in a professional character and which information was necessary to enable him to prescribe as a physician or do any act for him as a surgeon or trained nurse. Provided, if two or more physicians or nurses are, or have been in attendance on the patient for the same ailment, the patient by waiving the privilege attaching to any of said physicians or nurses, by calling said physician or nurse to testify concerning said ailment, shall be deemed to have waived the privilege attaching to the other physicians or nurses. Note: this appears in the Code of Practice in Civil Actions.

Ark. Stat. Ann. § 43-2004 (1947)
The provisions of the Code of Practice in Civil Actions shall apply to and govern the summoning and coercing the attendance of witnesses, and compelling them to testify in all prosecutions, criminal or penal actions or proceedings, . . .
Note: this appears in the Code of Criminal Procedure.

CALIFORNIA
Cal. Code Civ. Proc. § 1881 (1953)
There are particular relations in which it is the policy of the law to encourage confidence and to preserve it inviolate; therefore, a person cannot be examined as a witness in the following cases:
* * *

4. [*Physician and patient*] A licensed physician or surgeon cannot, without the consent of his patient, be examined in a civil action, as to any information acquired in attending the patient, which was necessary to enable him to prescribe or act for the patient; provided, however, that either before or after probate, upon the contest of any will executed, or claimed to have been executed, by such patient, or after the death of such patient, in any action involving the validity of any instrument executed, or claimed to have been executed, by him, conveying or transferring any real or personal property, such physician or surgeon may testify to the mental condition of said patient and in so testifying may disclose information acquired by him concerning said deceased which was necessary to enable him to prescribe or act for such deceased; provided further, that after the death of the patient, the executor of his will, or the administrator of this [sic] estate, or the surviving spouse of the deceased, or if there be no surviving spouse, the children of the deceased personally, or, if minors, by their guardian, may give such consent, in any action or proceeding brought to recover damages on account of the death of the patient; provided further, that where any person brings an action to recover damages for personal injuries, such action shall be deemed to constitute a consent by the person bringing such action that any physician who has prescribed for or treated said person and whose testimony is material in said action shall testify; and provided further, that the bringing of an action, to recover for the death of a patient, by the executor of his will, or by the administrator of his estate, or by the surviving spouse of the deceased, or if there be no surviving spouse, by the children personally, or, if minors, by their guardian, shall constitute a consent by such executor, administrator, surviving spouse, or children or guardian, to the testimony of any physician who attended said deceased.

Cal. Penal Code § 1321 (1949)
The rules for determining the competency of witnesses in civil actions are applicable also to criminal actions and proceedings, except as otherwise provided in this code.

CANAL ZONE
Canal Zone Code, T. 4, § 1904 (1934)
* * *

(4) A licensed physician or surgeon cannot, without the consent of his patient, be examined in a civil action as to any information acquired in

attending the patient, which was necessary to enable him to prescribe or act for the patient: *Provided, however,* That after the death of the patient, the executor of his will, or the administrator of his estate, or the surviving spouse of the deceased, or, if there be no surviving spouse, the children of the deceased personally, or, if minors, by their guardian, may give such consent, in any action or proceeding brought to recover damages on account of the death of the patient: *Provided further,* That where any person brings an action to recover damages for personal injuries, such action shall be deemed to constitute a consent by the person bringing such action that any physician who has prescribed for or treated said person and whose testimony is material in said action shall testify: *And provided further,* That the bringing of an action to recover for the death of a patient, by the executor of his will, or by the administrator of his estate, or by the surviving spouse of the deceased, or if there be no surviving spouse, by the children personally, or, if minors, by their guardian, shall constitute a consent by such executor, administrator, surviving spouse, or children or guardian, to the testimony of any physician who attended said deceased.

Canal Zone Code, T. 6, § 671 (1934)
The rules for determining the competency of witnesses in civil actions are applicable also to criminal actions and proceedings except as otherwise provided in the title.
Note: this section appears in the Code of Criminal Procedure.

COLORADO

Colo. Rev. Stat. § 153-1-7 (1953)
There are particular relations in which it is the policy of the law to encourage confidence and to preserve it inviolate; therefore, a person shall not be examined as a witness in the following cases:
* * *

(4) A physician or surgeon duly authorized to practice his profession under the laws of this state, or any other state, shall not be examined without the consent of his patient, as to any information acquired in attending the patient, which was necessary to enable him to prescribe or act for the patient; provided, this section shall not apply to a physician or surgeon who is sued by or on behalf of a patient or by or on behalf of the heirs, executors or administrators of a patient on any cause of action arising out of or connected with the physician's care or treat-

ment of such patient, or to physicians or surgeons who were in consultation with the physician or surgeon so sued on the case out of which said suit arises.

Colo. Rev. Stat. § 153-1-8 (1953)

If a person offer himself as a witness, that is to be deemed a consent to the examination; also the offer of a wife, husband, attorney, clergyman, physician, surgeon or certified public accountant as a witness, shall be deemed a consent to the examination, within the meaning of subsections (1), (2), (3), (4) and (6) of section 153-1-7.

Note: the above sections appear in the chapter on Witnesses.

Colo. Rev. Stat. § 39-7-13 (1953)

All trials for criminal offenses shall be conducted according to the course of the common law, except when this chapter points out a different mode, and the rules of evidence also of the common law, unless changed by this chapter, shall be binding on all courts and juries in criminal cases. * * *

Note: this appears in the chapter on Criminal Proceedings.

DISTRICT OF COLUMBIA

D. C. Code § 14-308 (Supp. 1956)

In the courts of the District of Columbia no physician or surgeon shall be permitted, without the consent of the person afflicted, or of his legal representative, to disclose any information, confidential in its nature, which he shall have acquired in attending a patient in a professional capacity and which was necessary to enable him to act in that capacity, whether such information shall have been obtained from the patient or from his family or from the person or persons in charge of him: *Provided,* That this section shall not apply to evidence in criminal cases where the accused is charged with causing the death of, or inflicting injuries upon a human being, and the disclosure shall be required in the interests of public justice: *Provided further,* That this section shall not apply to evidence relating to the mental competency or sanity of an accused in criminal trials where the accused raises the defense of insanity, or in the pretrial or posttrial proceedings involving any criminal case where a question arises concerning the mental condition of an accused or convicted person.

TERRITORY OF GUAM
Guam Code Civ. Proc. § 1881 (1953)

There are particular relations in which it is the policy of the law to encourage confidence and to preserve it inviolate; therefore, a person cannot be examined as a witness in the following cases:

* * *

(4) A licensed physician or surgeon cannot without the consent of his patient, be examined in a civil action as to any information acquired in attending the patient, which was necessary to enable him to prescribe or act for the patient: *Provided, however,* that either before or after probate, upon the contest of any will executed, or claimed to have been executed, by such patient, or after the death of such patient, in any action involving the validity of any instrument executed, or claimed to have been executed, by him, conveying or transferring any real or personal property, such physician or surgeon may testify to the mental condition of said patient and in so testifying may disclose information acquired by him concerning said deceased which was necessary to enable him to prescribe or act for such deceased: *Provided further,* that after the death of the patient, the executor of his will, or the administrator of his estate, or the surviving spouse of the deceased, or, if there be no surviving spouse, the children of the deceased personally, or if minors, by their guardian, may give such consent, in any action or proceeding brought to recover damages on account of the death of the patient: *Provided further,* that where any person brings an action to recover damages for personal injuries, such action shall be deemed to constitute a consent by the person bringing such action that any physician who has prescribed for or treated said person and whose testimony is material in said action shall testify; *And provided further,* that the bringing of an action, to recover for the death of a patient, by the executor of his will, or by the administrator of his estate, or by the surviving spouse of the deceased, or if there be no surviving spouse, by the children personally, or, if minors, by their guardian, shall constitute a consent by such executor, administrator, surviving spouse, or children or guardian, to the testimony of any physician who attended said deceased.

Guam Code of Criminal Procedure § 1321 (1953)

The rules for determining the competency of witnesses in civil actions are applicable also to criminal actions and proceedings, except as otherwise provided in this code.

HAWAII

Hawaii Rev. Laws § 222-20 (1955)

* * * No physician or surgeon shall, without the consent of the patient, divulge in any civil suit, action or proceeding, unless the sanity of the patient be the matter in dispute, any information which he may have acquired in attending the patient, and which was necessary to enable him to prescribe or act for the patient; provided, that such consent shall be deemed to have been given to any physician or surgeon in every civil suit, action or proceeding which has been brought by any person for damages on account of personal injuries and in all cases in which a party to a suit, action or proceeding offers himself or any physician or surgeon or any person as a witness to testify to the physical condition of such party.

IDAHO

Idaho Code Ann. § 9-203 (1948)

There are particular relations in which it is the policy of the law to encourage confidence and to preserve it inviolate; therefore, a person can not be examined as a witness in the following cases:

* * *

(4) A physician or surgeon can not, without the consent of his patient, be examined in a civil action as to any information acquired in attending the patient which was necessary to enable him to prescribe or act for the patient.

Idaho Code Ann. § 19-2110 (1948)

The rules of evidence in civil actions are applicable also to criminal actions, except as otherwise provided in this code.

Note: this section appears in the Code of Criminal Procedure.

INDIANA

Ind. Stat. Ann. § 2-1714 (1946 Replacement)

The following persons shall not be competent witnesses:

* * *

Fourth. Physicians, as to matter communicated to them, as such, by patients, in the course of their professional business, or advice given in such cases.

Ind. Stat. Ann. § 9-1602 (1956 Replacement)
The rules of evidence prescribed in civil cases and concerning the
competency of witnesses shall govern in criminal cases, except as otherwise provided in this act.
Note: this section appears in the Code of Criminal Procedure.

IOWA
Iowa Code Ann. § 622.10 (1950)
No practicing attorney, counselor, physician, surgeon, or the stenographer or confidential clerk of any such person, who obtains such
information by reason of his employment, minister of the gospel or
priest of any denomination shall be allowed, in giving testimony, to
disclose any confidential communication properly entrusted to him in
his professional capacity, and necessary and proper to enable him to
discharge the functions of his office according to the usual course of
practice or discipline. Such prohibition shall not apply to cases where
the party in whose favor the same is made waives the rights conferred.

Iowa Code Ann. § 782.1 (1950)
The rules of evidence prescribed in civil procedure shall apply to
criminal proceedings as far as applicable and not inconsistent with the
provisions of this chapter.
Note. this section appears in the Code of Criminal Procedure.

KANSAS
Kan. Gen. Stat. Ann. § 60-2805 (1949)
The following persons shall be incompetent to testify:
* * *

Sixth. A physician or surgeon concerning any communication made to
him by his patient with reference to any physical or supposed physical
disease, defect, or injury, or the time, manner or circumstances under
which the ailment was incurred, or concerning any knowledge obtained by a personal examination of any such patient, without the consent of the patient.
But if a person without objection on his part testifies concerning any
such communication, the * * * physician communicated with may
also be required to testify on the same subject as though consent had
been given within the meaning of the last three subdivisions.
Note: the above appears in the Code of Civil Procedure.

Kan. Gen. Stat. Ann. § 62-1413 (1949)
The provisions of law in civil cases relative to compelling the attendance and testimony of witnesses, their examination * * * shall extend to criminal cases so far as they are in their nature applicable thereto, subject to the provisions contained in any statute.
Note: this section appears in the Code of Criminal Procedure.

KENTUCKY

Ky. Rev. Stat. § 213.200 (1955)
For the purpose of this chapter, the confidential relations and communications between physician and patient are placed upon the same basis as those provided by law between attorney and client, and nothing in this chapter shall be construed to require any such privileged communication to be disclosed.
Note: this section appears in chapter 213 relating to Births and Deaths.

Ky. Rev. Stat. § 319.110 (1955)
For the purpose of this chapter, the confidential relations and communications between certified clinical psychologist and client are placed upon the same basis as those provided by law between attorney and client, and nothing in this chapter shall be construed to require any such privileged communication to be disclosed.
Note: this section appears in chapter 319 relating to Clinical Psychologists.

LOUISIANA

La. Rev. Stat. Ann. § 15:476 (1951)
No physician is permitted, whether during or after the termination of his employment as such, unless with his patient's express consent, to disclose any communication made to him as such physician by or on behalf of his patient, or the result of any investigation made into the patient's physical or mental condition, or any opinion based upon such investigation, or any information that he may have gotten by reason of his being such physician; provided, that the provisions of this article shall not apply to any physician, who, under the appointment of the court, and not by a selection of the patient, has made investigation into the patient's physical or mental condition; provided, further, that any physician may be cross-examined upon the correctness of any certificate issued by him.

Note: this section appears in the Code of Criminal Procedure. There is no privilege in a *civil action*.

La. Rev. Stat. Ann. § 15:478 (1951)

The right to exclude the testimony, as provided in the three articles last preceding, is purely personal, and can be set up only by the person in whose favor the right exists. If the right is waived, the legal adviser, the physician and the clergyman, as the case may be, may be examined and cross-examined to the same extent as any other witness.

MICHIGAN

Mich. Stat. Ann. § 27.911 (1938)

No person duly authorized to practice medicine or surgery shall be allowed to disclose any information which he may have acquired in attending any patient in his professional character, and which information was necessary to enable him to prescribe for such patient as a physician, or to do any act for him as a surgeon: *Provided, however,* That in case such patient shall bring an action against any defendant to recover for any personal injuries, or for any malpractice, if such plaintiff shall produce any physician as a witness in his own behalf, who has treated him for such injury, or for any disease or condition, with reference to which such malpractice is alleged, he shall be deemed to have waived the privilege hereinbefore provided for, as to any or all other physicians, who may have treated him for such injuries, disease or condition: *Provided further,* That after the decease of such patient, in a contest upon the question of admitting the will of such patient to probate, the heirs at law of such patient, whether proponents or contestants of his will, shall be deemed to be personal representatives of such deceased patient for the purpose of waiving the privilege hereinbefore created.

Mich. Stat. Ann. § 28.945(1) (Revised Vol. 1954)

* * * Any communications between attorneys and their clients, between clergymen and the members of their respective churches, and between physicians and their patients are hereby declared to be privileged and confidential when such communications were necessary to enable such attorneys, clergymen, or physicians to serve as such attorney, clergyman, or physician.

Note: this section appears in the Code of Criminal Procedure and concerns the grand jury and inquiry about crime before trial.

Mich. Stat. Ann. § 28.1045 (Revised Vol. 1954)
The rules of evidence in civil actions, in so far as the same are applicable, shall govern in all criminal and quasi criminal proceedings except as otherwise provided by law.
Note: this section appears in the Code of Criminal Procedure.

MINNESOTA
Minn. Stat. Ann. § 595.02 (1947)
Every person of sufficient understanding, including a party, may testify in any action or proceeding, civil or criminal, in court or before any person who has authority to receive evidence, except as follows:
* * *
(4) A licensed physician or surgeon shall not, without the consent of his patient, be allowed to disclose any information or any opinion based thereon which he acquired in attending the patient in a professional capacity, and which was necessary to enable him to act in that capacity; after the decease of such patient, in an action to recover insurance benefits, where the insurance has been in existence two years or more, the beneficiaries shall be deemed to be the personal representatives of such deceased person for the purpose of waiving the privilege hereinbefore created, and no oral or written waiver of the privilege hereinbefore created shall have any binding force or effect except that the same be made upon the trial or examination where the evidence is offered or received.

MISSISSIPPI
Miss. Code Ann. § 1697 (1956 Recomp. Vol. II)
All communications made to a physician or surgeon by a patient under his charge or by one seeking professional advice, are hereby declared to be privileged, and such physician or surgeon shall not be required to disclose the same in any legal proceeding, except at the instance of the patient or in case of the death of the patient, by his personal representative or legal heirs in case there is no personal representative.

MISSOURI
Mo. Rev. Stat. Ann. § 491.060 (Vernon 1952)
The following persons shall be incompetent to testify:
* * *

(5) A physician or surgeon, concerning any information which he may have acquired from any patient while attending him in a professional character, and which information was necessary to enable him to prescribe for such patient as a physician, or do any act for him as a surgeon.

MONTANA
Mont. Rev. Codes Ann. § 93-701-4 (1947)
There are particular relations in which it is the policy of the law to encourage confidence and to preserve it inviolate; therefore, a person cannot be examined as a witness in the following cases:
* * *

(4) A licensed physician or surgeon cannot, without the consent of his patient, be examined in a civil action as to any information acquired in attending the patient, which was necessary to enable him to prescribe or act for the patient.
Note: this section appears in the Code of Civil Procedure.

Mont. Rev. Codes Ann. § 94-7209 (1947)
The rules of evidence in civil actions are applicable also to criminal actions, except as otherwise provided in this code.
Note: this section appears in the Code of Criminal Procedure.

NEBRASKA
Neb. Rev. Stat. § 25-1206 (Reissue of 1956)
No practicing attorney, counselor, physician, surgeon, minister of the gospel or priest of any denomination, shall be allowed in giving testimony to disclose any confidential communication, properly entrusted to him in his professional capacity, and necessary and proper to enable him to discharge the functions of his office according to the usual course of practice or discipline.

Neb. Rev. Stat. § 25-1207 (Reissue of 1956)
The prohibitions of the preceding sections do not apply to cases where the party in whose favor the respective provisions are enacted, waives

the rights thereby conferred; and if a party to any action now pending, or hereafter brought, shall offer evidence with reference to his physical or mental condition, or the alleged cause thereof, or if the personal representative of a deceased person in any such action shall offer such evidence as to such deceased person, the right conferred by section 25-1206 shall be deemed to have been waived as to any physician or surgeon who shall have attended said party or said deceased person.

NEVADA

Nev. Comp. Laws Ann. § 8974 (Supp. 1943-1949)

A licensed physician or surgeon shall not, without the consent of his patient, be examined as a witness as to any information acquired in attending the patient, which was necessary to enable him to prescribe or act for the patient; provided, however, in any suit or prosecution against a physician or surgeon for malpractice, the defendant may call any other physician or surgeon as witnesses on behalf of defendant, without the consent of such patient or party suing or prosecuting; provided, further, that either before or after probate, upon the contest of any will executed, or claimed to have been executed, by such patient, or after the death of such patient, in any action involving the validity of any instrument executed, or claimed to have been executed, by him, conveying or transferring any real or personal property, such physician or surgeon may testify to the mental condition of said patient and in so testifying may disclose information acquired by him concerning said deceased which was necessary to enable him to prescribe or act for such deceased; provided further, that after the death of the patient, the executor of his will, or the administrator of his estate, or the surviving spouse of the deceased, or if there be no surviving spouse, the children of the deceased personally, or, if minors, by their guardian, may give such consent, in any action or proceeding brought to recover damages on account of the death of the patient; provided further, that where any person brings an action to recover damages for personal injuries, such action shall be deemed to constitute a consent by the person bringing such action that any physician who has prescribed for or treated said person and whose testimony is material in said action shall testify; and provided further, that the bringing of an action, to recover for the death of a patient, by the executor of his will, or by the administrator of his estate, or by the surviving spouse of the deceased, or if there be no surviving spouse, by the children personally, or, if minors, by their guardian, shall constitute a consent by such executor, administrator, surviving spouse, or children or guardian, to the testimony of any physician who attended said deceased; and provided further, that, if the patient be dead and during his lifetime had not given such consent, the bringing of an action by a beneficiary, assignee or payee or by the legal representative of the insured, to recover on any life, health or accident insurance policy, shall constitute a consent by such beneficiary, assignee, payee or legal representative to the testimony of any physician who attended said deceased.

Note: this section appears in the Civil Practice Act.

Nev. Comp. Laws Ann. § 11249 (1929)

The rules for determining the competency of witnesses in civil actions are applicable also to criminal actions and proceedings, except as otherwise provided for in this act. * * *.

Nev. Comp. Laws Ann. § 11251 (1929)

The rules of evidence in civil actions shall be applicable also to criminal actions, except as otherwise provided in this act.

Note: the last two sections appear in the Code of Criminal Procedure.

NEW MEXICO
N. M. Stat. Ann. § 20-1-12 (1953)

* * *

(d) A person duly authorized to practice physic or surgery, or a professional or registered nurse, cannot be examined without the consent of his patient as to any communication made by his patient with reference to any real or supposed venereal or loathesome disease or any knowledge concerning such disease obtained by personal examination of such patient; nor shall any doctor or nurse employed by a workmen's compensation claimant be examined relating to a workmen's compensation claim without the consent of his patient as to any communication made by his patient with reference to any physical or supposed physical disease or injury or any knowledge obtained by personal examination of such patient except in instances where the doctor has examined or treated the patient at the expense of the employer, and such payment is consented to by the patient.

* * *

(f) If a person offer himself as a witness and voluntarily testify with reference to the communications specified in this act [section], that is to be deemed a consent to the examination of the person to whom the communications were made as above provided.

NEW YORK

N. Y. Civ. Prac. Act § 352 (Gilbert—Bliss Supp. 1957)

A person duly authorized to practice physic or surgery, or dentistry, or a registered professional or licensed practical nurse, shall not be allowed to disclose any information which he acquired in attending a patient in a professional capacity, and which was necessary to enable him to act in that capacity, unless, in cases where the disclosure of the information so acquired by a dentist is necessary for identification purposes, in which case the dentist may be required to testify solely with respect thereto, or unless, where the patient is a child under the age of sixteen, the information so acquired indicates that the patient has been the victim or subject of a crime, in which case the physician, dentist or nurse may be required to testify fully in relation thereto upon any examination, trial or other proceeding in which the commission of such crime is a subject of inquiry.

* * *

N. Y. Civ. Prac. Act § 354 (Gilbert—Bliss Supp. 1957)

The last three sections apply to any examination of a person as a witness unless the provisions thereof are expressly waived upon the trial or examination by the person confessing, the patient or the client. But a physician or surgeon or a registered professional or licensed practical nurse, upon a trial or examination, may disclose any information as to the mental or physical condition of a patient who is deceased, which he acquired in attending such patient professionally, except such confidential communications as would tend to disgrace the memory of the patient and such facts as would tend to disgrace his memory, when the provisions of section three hundred and fifty-two have been expressly waived on such trial or examination by the personal representatives of the deceased patient, or in any litigation wherein the interests of the personal representative of such deceased patient are deemed by the trial judge to be adverse to those of the estate of the deceased patient, by any party in interest, or if the validity of the last will and testament of such deceased patient is in question, by the executor or executors named in said will, or the surviving husband, widow or any heir-at-law or any of the next of kin, of such deceased, or any other party in interest. * * * The waivers herein provided for must be made in open court, on the trial of the action or proceeding, and a paper executed by a party prior to the trial providing for such waiver shall be insufficient as such a waiver. But the attorneys for the respective parties, prior to the trial, may stipulate for such waiver, and the same shall be sufficient therefor.

Note: the omitted portion of this section concerns disclosures which may properly be made by an attorney or his employees in testamentary proceedings.

NEW ZEALAND
Cons. Stat. of New Zealand, Evidence Act, Sec. 8 (1908)
* * *

(2) A physician or surgeon shall not, without the consent of his patient, divulge in any civil proceeding (unless the sanity of the patient is the matter in dispute) any communication made to him in his professional character by such patient, and necessary to enable him to prescribe or act for such patient.

(3) Nothing in this section shall protect any communication made for any criminal purpose, or prejudice the right to give in evidence any statement or representation at any time made to or by a physician or surgeon in or about the effecting by any person of an insurance on the life of himself or any other person.

NORTH CAROLINA
N. C. Gen. Stat. Ann. § 8-53 (Recomp. 1953)

No person, duly authorized to practice physic or surgery, shall be required to disclose any information which he may have acquired in attending a patient in a professional character, and which information was necessary to enable him to prescribe for such patient as a physician, or to do any act for him as a surgeon: Provided, that the presiding judge of a superior court may compel such disclosure, if in his opinion the same is necessary to a proper administration of justice.

NORTH DAKOTA
N. D. Rev. Code § 31-0106 (1943)

A person cannot be examined as a witness in the following cases:
* * *

(3.) A physician or surgeon, without the consent of his patient, cannot be examined as to any information acquired in attending the patient which was necessary to enable him to prescribe or act for the patient.

N. D. Rev. Code § 31-0107 (1943)
If a person testifies as a witness as to any subject which comes within the protection of any of the provisions of the first three subsections of 31-0106, he shall be deemed to have consented to the examination of an attorney, clergyman, priest, physician, or surgeon on the same subject matter.

OHIO
Ohio Rev. Code § 2317.02 (Baldwin Cum. Issue 1956)
The following persons shall not testify in certain respects:
(A) An attorney, concerning a communication made to him by his client in that relation or his advice to his client; or a physician, concerning a communication made to him by his patient in that relation, or his advice to his patient; but the attorney or physician may testify by express consent of the client or patient, or if the client or patient be deceased, by the express consent of the surviving spouse or the executor or administrator of the estate of such deceased client or patient; and if the client or patient voluntarily testifies, the attorney or physician may be compelled to testify on the same subject;
* * *

Ohio Rev. Code § 2945.41 (Baldwin 1953)
The rules of evidence in civil causes, where applicable, govern in all criminal cases.
Note: this section appears in the Code of Criminal Procedure.

OKLAHOMA
Okla. Stat. Ann. tit. 12 § 385 (Supp. 1956)
The following persons shall be incompetent to testify:
* * *

(6). A physician or surgeon concerning any communication made to him by his patient with reference to any physical or supposed physical disease, or any knowledge obtained by a personal examination of any such patient: Provided, that if a person offer himself as a witness, that is to be deemed a consent to the examination; also if an attorney,

clergyman or priest, physician or surgeon on the same subject, within the meaning of the last three subdivisions of this section.
Note: this appears in the Code of Civil Procedure.

Okla. Stat. Ann. tit. 22 § 702 (Supp. 1956)
Except as otherwise provided in this and the following chapter, the rules of evidence in civil cases are applicable also in criminal cases:
* * *
Note: this appears in the Code of Criminal Procedure.

OREGON
Ore. Rev. Stat. § 44.040 (Repl. Part 1955)
(1) There are particular relations in which it is the policy of the law to encourage confidence, and to preserve it inviolate; therefore a person cannot be examined as a witness in the following cases:
* * *
(d) A regular physician or surgeon shall not, without the consent of his patient, be examined in a civil action, suit or proceeding, as to any information acquired in attending the patient, which was necessary to enable him to prescribe or act for the patient.
(2) If a party to the action, suit or proceeding offers himself as a witness, it is deemed a consent to the examination also of a wife, husband, attorney, clergyman, physician or surgeon on the same subject.

Ore. Rev. Stat. § 136.510 (1955)
The law of evidence in civil actions is also the law of evidence in criminal actions and proceedings, except as otherwise specially provided in the statutes relating to crimes and criminal procedure.
Note: this section appears in the Code of Criminal Procedure.

PENNSYLVANIA
Pa. Stat. Ann. tit. 28 § 328 (1930)
No person authorized to practice physics or surgery shall be allowed, in any civil case, to disclose any information which he acquired in attending the patient in a professional capacity, and which was necessary to enable him to act in that capacity, which shall tend to blacken the character of the patient, without the consent of said patient, except in civil cases, brought by such patient, for damages on account of personal injuries.

PHILIPPINE ISLANDS

Philippine Islands Code Civ. Proc. § 383 (1925)

The following persons can not be witnesses:

* * *

(8) No person duly authorized to practice medicine, surgery or obstetrics shall be compelled, without the consent of the patient, in any civil case to disclose any information which he may have acquired in attending such patient in a professional capacity, which information was necessary to enable him to act in that capacity and which shall tend to blacken the character of the patient.

Note: The laws of the Philippine Islands are now in the process of revision and recodification.

PUERTO RICO

P. R. Laws Ann. tit. 32, § 1734 (1956)

A person can not be examined as a witness in the following cases:

* * *

(4.) A physician or surgeon or the assistant of either of them can not, without the consent of the patients, be examined in a civil action as to any information acquired in attending the patient, which was necessary to enable the physician or surgeon to prescribe or act for the patient; but this subdivision does not apply in an action between a physician or surgeon and his patients in which the treatment of the patient by the physician or surgeon is in issue; *And provided,* That a physician or surgeon is competent to testify as to the cause of the death of any person.

P. R. Laws Ann. tit. 32, § 1735 (1956)

Consent to the giving of such testimony as is mentioned in section 1734 of this title is conclusively implied in the following cases:

1. When the person who made any communication mentioned in that section testifies, without objection on his part, as to such communication or any part thereof, the person to whom such communication was made may be examined fully, in the same action or proceeding, as to such communication.

* * *

4. In an action brought by the beneficiary to recover on a policy of life insurance, taken out by the person whose life was insured, a physician or surgeon may, with the consent of the beneficiary, testify as to any

information acquired by him in attending the deceased, but must not be compelled to so testify.

Nothing in this section contained affects the right of the court to admit any of the testimony mentioned in section 1734 of this title, when no objection is seasonably interposed thereto, or when the court finds, as an inference from proper evidence, that the consent mentioned in that section has been given or implied.

Note: these sections appear in the Code of Civil Procedure.

QUEBEC

Rev. Stat. c. 264 § 60 (2) (1941)

No physician may be compelled to declare what has been revealed to him in his professional character.

SOUTH DAKOTA

S. D. Code § 36.0101 (1939)

No person offered or called as a witness in any action or special proceeding in any court or before any officer or person having authority to examine witnesses or hear evidence shall be excluded or excused from testifying by reason of * * * , or because any communication inquired about was confidentially made to the witness, except as hereinafter provided:

* * *

(3) A physician or surgeon, or other regular practitioner of the healing art, cannot, without the consent of his patient, be examined in a civil action as to any information acquired in attending the patient which was necessary to enable him to prescribe or act for the patient;

S. D. Code § 36.0102 (1939)

If a person offer himself as a witness he thereby waives any privilege he might otherwise claim, which would prevent the examination of his attorney, spiritual adviser, or healing practitioner on the same subject within the meaning of subdivisions (2), (3), and (4) of section 36.0101. If a person once waives such privilege, as to any particular communication, he cannot thereafter claim it.

S. D. Code § 36.0103 (1939)

It shall be the duty of the court, of its own motion and without waiting for objection, to advise a witness at the appropriate time of his right to refuse to answer any question requiring the disclosure of any privileged communication * * *.

In all cases where it shall appear to the court that any person who is not present nor represented at the hearing should be protected in his right to have any communication made under the confidential relations provisions of section 36.0101 excluded, it shall be the duty of the court to make such objections and orders for such purpose as to the court may seem necessary.

S. D. Code § 34.3631 (1939)

The rules of evidence in civil cases are applicable also to criminal cases, except as otherwise provided in this title.

Note: this section appears in the Code of Criminal Procedure.

UTAH

Utah Code Ann. § 78-24-8 (1953)

There are particular relations in which it is the policy of the law to encourage confidence and to preserve it inviolate. Therefore, a person cannot be examined as a witness in the following cases:
* * *

(4) A physician or surgeon cannot, without the consent of his patient, be examined, in a civil action, as to any information acquired in attending the patient which was necessary to enable him to prescribe or act for the patient.

Note: this appears in the Code of Civil Procedure.

Utah Code Ann. § 77-44-1 (1953)

The rules for determining the competency of witnesses in civil actions shall be applicable also to criminal actions and proceedings, except as otherwise provided in this Code.

Utah Code Ann. § 77-44-2 (1953)

The rules of evidence in civil actions shall be applicable also to criminal actions, except as otherwise provided in this Code.

Note: the last two sections appear in the Code of Criminal Procedure.

VICTORIA (AUSTRALIA)

Vol. II Gen. Public Acts of Victoria, Evidence Act, Sec. 28 (1929)

* * * No physician or surgeon shall without the consent of his patient

divulge in any civil suit, action or proceeding (unless the sanity of the patient is the matter in dispute) any information which he has acquired in attending the patient and which was necessary to enable him to prescribe or act for the patient.

VIRGIN ISLANDS

Virgin Islands Code § 855 (1957)

(1) As used in this section, (a) "patient" means a person who, for the sole purpose of securing preventive, palliative, or curative treatment, or a diagnosis preliminary to such treatment, of his physical or mental condition, consults a physician, or submits to an examination by a physician; (b) "physician" means a person authorized or reasonably believed by the patient to be authorized, to practice medicine in the state or jurisdiction in which the consultation or examination takes place; (c) "holder of the privilege" means the patient while alive and not under guardianship or the guardian of the person of an incompetent patient, or the personal representative of a deceased patient; (d) "confidential communication between physician and patient" means such information transmitted between physician and patient, including information obtained by an examination of the patient, as is transmitted in confidence and by a means which, so far as the patient is aware, discloses the information to no third persons other than those reasonably necessary for the transmission of the information or the accomplishment of the purpose for which it is transmitted.

(2) Except as provided by paragraphs (3), (4), (5) and (6) of this section, a person, whether or not a party, has a privilege in a civil action or in a prosecution for a misdemeanor to refuse to disclose, and to prevent a witness from disclosing, a communication, if he claims the privilege and the judge finds that (a) the communication was a confidential communication between patient and physician, and (b) the patient or the physician reasonably believed the communication to be necessary or helpful to enable the physician to make a diagnosis of the condition of the patient or to prescribe or render treatment therefor, and (c) the witness (i) is the holder of the privilege or (ii) at the time of the communication was the physician or a person to whom disclosure was made because reasonably necessary for the transmission of the communication or for the accomplishment of the purpose for which it was transmitted or (iii) is any other person who obtained knowledge or possession of the communication as the result of an intentional breach of the physician's

duty of nondisclosure by the physician or his agent or servant and (d) the claimant is the holder of the privilege or a person authorized to claim the privilege for him.

(3) There is no privilege under this section as to any relevant communication between the patient and his physician (a) upon an issue of the patient's condition in an action to commit him or otherwise place him under the control of another or others because of alleged mental incompetence, or in an action in which the patient seeks to establish his competence or in an action to recover damages on account of conduct of the patient which constitutes a criminal offence other than a misdemeanor, or (b) upon an issue as to the validity of a document as a will of the patient, or (c) upon an issue between parties claiming by testate or intestate succession from a deceased patient.

(4) There is no privilege under this section in an action in which the condition of the patient is an element or factor of the claim or defense of the patient or of any party claiming through or under the patient or claiming as a beneficiary of the patient through a contract to which the patient is or was a party.

(5) There is no privilege under this section as to information which the physician or the patient is required to report to a public official or as to information required to be recorded in a public office, unless the statute requiring the report or record specifically provides that the information shall not be disclosed.

(6) No person has a privilege under this section if the judge finds that sufficient evidence, aside from the communication, has been introduced to warrant a finding that the services of the physician were sought or obtained to enable or aid anyone to commit or to plan to commit a crime or a tort, or to escape detection or apprehension after the commission of a crime or a tort.

(7) A privilege under this section as to a communication is terminated if the judge finds that any person while a holder of the privilege has caused the physician or any agent or servant of the physician to testify in any action to any matter of which the physician or his agent or servant gained knowledge through the communication.

Note: This section is based on Rule 27 of the Uniform Rules of Evidence.

WASHINGTON
Wash. Rev. Code § 5.60.060 (1951)
The following persons shall not be examined as witnesses:
* * *
(4) A regular physician or surgeon shall not, without the consent of his patient, be examined in a civil action as to any information acquired in attending such patient, which was necessary to enable him to prescribe or act for the patient.

Wash. Rev. Code § 10.52.020 (1951)
Witnesses competent to testify in civil cases shall be competent in criminal prosecutions, but regular physicians or surgeons, clergymen or priests, shall be protected from testifying as to confessions, or information received from any defendant, by virtue of their profession and character; * * *.

Wash. Rev. Code § 10.58.010 (1951)
The rules of evidence in civil actions, so far as practicable, shall be applied to criminal prosecutions.
Note: the last two sections appear in the Code of Criminal Procedure.

WEST VIRGINIA
W. Va. Code § 4992 (1955)
The following persons are incompetent to testify, as hereinafter provided, and not otherwise:
* * *
(e) A physician or surgeon, without his patient's consent, concerning any communication made to him by his patient, which was necessary to enable him to prescribe and treat the case.
Note: this appears in the chapter relating to Justices and Constables. No statute exists in this state governing testimony of physicians in courts of record.

WISCONSIN
Wis. Stat. § 325.21 (1953)
No physician or surgeon shall be permitted to disclose any information he may have acquired in attending any patient in a professional character, necessary to enable him professionally to serve such patient, except only (1) in trials for homicide when the disclosure relates di-

rectly to the fact or immediate circumstances of the homicide, (2) in all lunacy inquiries, (3) in actions, civil or criminal, against the physician for malpractice, (4) with the express consent of the patient, or in case of his death or disability, of his personal representative or other person authorized to sue for personal injury or of the beneficiary of an insurance policy on his life, health, or physical condition.

WYOMING

Wyo. Comp. Stat. Ann. § 3-2602 (1945)

The following persons shall not testify in certain respects:

(1.) An attorney, concerning a communication made to him by his client in that relation, or his advice to his client; or a physician, concerning a communication made to him by his patient in that relation, or his advice to his patient; but the attorney or physician may testify by express consent of the client or patient; and if the client or patient voluntarily testify, the attorney or physician may be compelled to testify, on the same subject.

THE UNIFORM RULES OF EVIDENCE (1953)

[Rule 27. *Physician-Patient Privilege*

(1) As used in this rule, (a) "patient" means a person who, for the sole purpose of securing preventive, palliative, or curative treatment, or a diagnosis preliminary to such treatment, of his physical or mental condition, consults a physician, or submits to an examination by a physician; (b) "physician" means a person authorized or reasonably believed by the patient to be authorized, to practice medicine in the state or jurisdiction in which the consultation or examination takes place; (c) "holder of the privilege" means the patient while alive and not under guardianship or the guardian of the person of an incompetent patient or the personal representative of a deceased patient; (d) "confidential communication between physician and patient" means such information transmitted between physician and patient, including information obtained by an examination of the patient, as is transmitted in confidence and by a means which, so far as the patient is aware, discloses the information to no third persons other than those reasonably necessary for the transmission of the information or the accomplishment of the purpose for which it is transmitted.

(2) Except as provided by paragraphs (3), (4), (5) and (6) of this rule, a person, whether or not a party, has a privilege in a civil action or in a prosecution for a misdemeanor to refuse to disclose, and to prevent a witness from disclosing, a communication, if he claims the privilege and the judge finds that (a) the communication was a confidential communication between patient and physician, and (b) the patient or the physician reasonably believed the communication to be necessary or helpful to enable the physician to make a diagnosis of the condition of the patient or to prescribe or render treatment therefor, and (c) the witness (i) is the holder of the privilege or (ii) at the time of the communication was the physician or a person to whom disclosure was made because reasonably necessary for the transmission of the communication or for the accomplishment of the purpose for which it was transmitted or (iii) is any other person who obtained knowledge or possession of the communication as the result of an intentional breach of the

physician's duty of nondisclosure by the physician or his agent or servant and (d) the claimant is the holder of the privilege or a person authorized to claim the privilege for him.

(3) There is no privilege under this rule as to any relevant communication between the patient and his physician (a) upon an issue of the patient's condition in an action to commit him or otherwise place him under the control of another or others because of alleged mental incompetence, or in an action in which the patient seeks to establish his competence or in an action to recover damages on account of conduct of the patient which constitutes a criminal offence other than a misdemeanor, or (b) upon an issue as to the validity of a document as a will of the patient, or (c) upon an issue between parties claiming by testate or intestate succession from a deceased patient.

(4) There is no privilege under this rule in an action in which the condition of the patient is an element or factor of the claim or defense of the patient or of any party claiming through or under the patient or claiming as a beneficiary of the patient through a contract to which the patient is or was a party.

(5) There is no privilege under this rule as to information which the physician or the patient is required to report to a public official or as to information required to be recorded in a public office, unless the statute requiring the report or record specifically provides that the information shall not be disclosed.

(6) No person has a privilege under this rule if the judge finds that sufficient evidence, aside from the communication has been introduced to warrant a finding that the services of the physician were sought or obtained to enable or aid anyone to commit or to plan to commit a crime or a tort, or to escape detection or apprehension after the commission of a crime or a tort.

(7) A privilege under this rule as to a communication is terminated if the judge finds that any person while a holder of the privilege has caused the physician or any agent or servant of the physician to testify in any action to any matter of which the physician or his agent or servant gained knowledge through the communication.]

Rule 37. *Waiver of Privilege by Contract or Previous Disclosure*

A person who would otherwise have a privilege to refuse to disclose or to prevent another from disclosing a specified matter has no such privilege with respect to that matter if the judge finds that he or any other person while the holder of the privilege has (a) contracted with anyone not to claim the privilege or, (b) without coercion and with knowledge of his privilege, made disclosure of any part of the matter or consented to such a disclosure made by anyone.

Rule 38. Admissibility of Disclosure Wrongfully Compelled

Evidence of a statement or other disclosure is inadmissible against the holder of the privilege if the judge finds that he had and claimed a privilege to refuse to make the disclosure but was nevertheless required to make it.

Rule 39. Reference to Exercise of Privileges

Subject to paragraph (4), Rule 23, [Privilege of Accused] if a privilege is exercised not to testify or to prevent another from testifying, either in the action or with respect to particular matters, or to refuse to disclose or to prevent another from disclosing any matter, the judge and counsel may not comment thereon, no presumption shall arise with respect to the exercise of the privilege, and the trier of fact may not draw and adverse inference therefrom. In those jury cases wherein the right to exercise a privilege, as herein provided, may be misunderstood and unfavorable inferences drawn by the trier of the fact, or be impaired in the particular case, the court, at the request of the party exercising the privilege, may instruct the jury in support of such privilege.

Rule 40. Effect of Error in Overruling Claim of Privilege

A party may predicate error on a ruling disallowing a claim of privilege only if he is the holder of the privilege.

TABLE OF CASES

References are to pages

N

X-Y-Z

INDEX

(Numbers following entries refer to sections.)